Fodor's 98

The South

The complete guide, thoroughly up-to-date

Packed with details that will make your trip

The must-see sights, off and on the beaten path

What to see, what to skip

Mix-and-match vacation itineraries

City strolls, countryside adventures, beach excursions

Smart lodging and dining options

Transportation tips, distances and directions

Key contacts, savvy travel tips

When to go, what to pack

Clear, accurate, easy-to-use maps

Fodor's Travel Publications, Inc.
New York • Toronto • London • Sydney • Auckland
www.fodors.com/

Fodor's The South

EDITORS: Linda Cabasin, Audra Epstein, David Low

Area Editors: Gene Bourg, Charlotte Durham, Lynn Grisard Fullman, Jane Garvey, Honey Naylor, Mary Sue Lawrence, Lisa Towle

Editorial Contributors: Robert Andrews, David Brown, Heidi Sarna, Helayne Schiff, M. T. Schwartzman (Gold Guide editor), Dinah A. Spritzer

Editorial Production: Janet Foley

Maps: David Lindroth, *cartographer*; Steven K. Amsterdam, *map editor*

Design: Fabrizio La Rocca, *creative director*; Guido Caroti, *associate art director*; Jolie Novak, *photo editor*

Production/Manufacturing: Rebecca Zeiler

Cover Photograph: Everett Johnson/Southern Stock

Copyright

ISBN 0–679–03535–4

Special Sales

Fodor's Travel Publications are available at special discounts for bulk purchases for sales promotions or premiums. Special editions, including personalized covers, excerpts of existing guides, and corporate imprints, can be created in large quantities for special needs. For more information, contact your local bookseller or write to Special Markets, Fodor's Travel Publications, 201 East 50th Street, New York, NY 10022. Inquiries from Canada should be directed to your local Canadian bookseller or sent to Random House of Canada, Ltd., Marketing Department, 1265 Aerowood Drive, Mississauga, Ontario L4W 1B9. Inquiries from the United Kingdom should be sent to Fodor's Travel Publications, 20 Vauxhall Bridge Road, London SW1V 2SA, England.

PRINTED IN THE UNITED STATES OF AMERICA

10 9 8 7 6 5 4 3 2 1

CONTENTS

ON THE ROAD WITH FODOR'S

WE'RE ALWAYS THRILLED to get letters from readers, especially one like this:

It took us an hour to decide what book to buy and we now know we picked the best one. Your book was wonderful, easy to follow, very accurate, and good on pointing out eating places, informal as well as formal. When we saw other people using your book, we would look at each other and smile.

Our editors and writers are deeply committed to making every Fodor's guide "the best one"—not only accurate but always charming, brimming with sound recommendations and solid ideas, right on the mark in describing restaurants and hotels, and full of fascinating facts that make you view what you've traveled to see in a rich new light.

About Our Writers

Our success in achieving our goals—and in helping to make your trip the best of all possible vacations—is a credit to the hard work of our extraordinary writers.

Born to a Creole–Acadian mother with an affinity for cooking, **Gene Bourg** maintains an acute interest in the unique cuisines of New Orleans. "Eating Out" columnist for the *Times-Picayune* from 1985 to 1994, he is currently a freelance food writer and host of *News You Can Eat*, a weekly program on New Orleans radio station WBYU. He adds his insight to our New Orleans dining reviews.

Charlotte Durham, who updated the Tennessee and Mississippi chapters, has lived in East, Middle, and West Tennessee and vacations annually on the Mississippi Gulf Coast. She has written, edited, and assigned stories for Memphis newspapers since 1975. She spends her free time traveling the back roads of the Mid-South, sampling the region's restaurants and shops. Someday, she hopes to retire to Chattanooga and start putting her large cookbook collection to good use.

Lynn Grisard Fullman, updater of the Alabama chapter, is a Birmingham-based freelance writer whose travel features have won numerous awards. The author of four books, she has also contributed to other Fodor's titles, including the Alabama chapter of *The South's Best Bed & Breakfasts.* She's a member of the Society of American Travel Writers and the International Food, Wine, and Travel Writers Association.

Since 1992, Georgia updater **Jane Garvey** has been chasing the ideal food-and-wine match for readers of the *Atlanta Journal-Constitution,* for whom she writes a column on the subject. She also writes for a number of local magazines. She has coauthored a residents' guide to Atlanta, a city in which she has nibbled and sipped for more than 25 years. A former magazine editor and college professor, she now enjoys travel, reading, and writing about Georgia history, hiking, white-water rafting, and a host of other salubrious pursuits.

Mary Sue Lawrence, who added fresh insights to the South Carolina chapter, is a freelance writer and editor whose features on travel, entertainment, health, and business have appeared in national and British magazines. A Charlestonian, she lives on the nearby Isle of Palms. She has also contributed to *Fodor's The South's Best Bed & Breakfasts.*

"Southern Superlatives" and the Louisiana chapter were written by gregarious **Honey Naylor,** a Louisiana native whose checkered past includes her own piano/accordion radio show at age 15, a stint teaching ballroom dancing, and an array of entertainment jobs (acting, dancing, and playing in a piano bar). This longtime resident of New York began her writing career 10 years ago after returning to live in New Orleans. She just couldn't keep her observations bottled up, so we gave her an outlet back then and have been thoroughly entertained by her lively writing ever since.

Born in North Carolina to a family whose roots in the Tar Heel state go back generations, **Lisa Towle** considers herself a child of the South. Her formative years were spent in North Carolina, Florida, and Georgia. As an adult it seemed circumstances conspired to keep her in far-flung (read: cold) locales and away from the land of the sun and ACC basketball. Like a good homing pigeon, though, she found her way back to North Carolina, where she now works as a writer, contributing to a number of publications.

New This Year

Lisa Towle has added several sections to the North Carolina chapter, including Greensboro and High Point, two of the growing Triad cities (Winston-Salem is the third). These cities have historic attractions as well as being business centers. Cherokee, the mountain town near the North Carolina entrance to Great Smoky Mountains National Park, receives expanded coverage, too. In Louisiana, New Orleans includes a section for Anne Rice's many fans, describing sights associated with the author and her books. Mary Sue Lawrence broadened the dining selections for Charleston to reflect the latest trends and added material on Greenville and Pendleton in the lovely Upcountry of western South Carolina. You'll also see good walks and drives for major cities such as Atlanta, Savannah, New Orleans, Memphis, Nashville, Chattanooga, and Charleston. Finally, a new Pleasures and Pastimes section orients you to some of the South's special highlights.

And this year, Fodor's joins Rand McNally, the world's largest commercial mapmaker, to bring you a detailed color map of the South. Just detach it along the perforation and drop it in your tote bag.

We're also proud to announce that the American Society of Travel Agents has endorsed Fodor's as its guidebook of choice. ASTA is the world's largest and most influential travel trade association, operating in more than 170 countries, with 27,000 members pledged to adhere to a strict code of ethics reflecting the Society's motto, "Integrity in Travel." ASTA shares Fodor's devotion to providing smart, honest travel information and advice to travelers, and we've long recommended that our readers consult ASTA member agents for the experience and professionalism they bring to the table.

On the Web, check out Fodor's site (www.fodors.com/) for information on major destinations around the world and travel-savvy interactive features. The Web site also lists the 85-plus radio stations nationwide that carry the Fodor's Travel Show, a live call-in program that airs every weekend. Tune in to hear guests discuss their wonderful adventures—or call in to get answers for your most pressing travel questions.

How to Use This Book

Organization

Up front is the **Gold Guide,** an easy-to-use section divided alphabetically by topic. Under each listing you'll find tips and information that will help you accomplish what you need to in the South. You'll also find addresses and telephone numbers of organizations and companies that offer destination-related services and detailed information and publications.

The first chapter in the guide, Destination: The South, helps get you in the mood for your trip. New and Noteworthy cues you in on trends and happenings, What's Where gets you oriented, Pleasures and Pastimes describes the activities and sights that really make the South unique, Great Itineraries presents some special-interest trip ideas, Fodor's Choice showcases our top picks, and Festivals and Seasonal Events alerts you to special events you'll want to seek out.

Chapters in *The South '98* are arranged in alphabetical order. Each chapter is divided by geographical area; within each area, towns are covered in logical geographical order, and attractive stretches of road and minor points of interest between them are indicated by the designation *En Route.* And within town sections, all restaurants and lodgings are grouped together.

To help you decide what to visit in the time you have, all chapters begin with recommended itineraries; you can mix and match those from several chapters to create a complete vacation. The A-to-Z section that ends all chapters covers getting there and getting around. It also provides helpful contacts and resources.

Icons and Symbols

★	Our special recommendations
✕	Restaurant
🏠	Lodging establishment
✕🏠	Lodging establishment whose

✕⊞	Lodging establishment whose restaurant warrants a special trip
⚠	Campground
Ⓒ	Good for kids (rubber duckie)
☞	Sends you to another section of the guide for more information
✉	Address
☎	Telephone number
☉	Opening and closing times
🎫	Admission prices (those we give apply to adults; substantially reduced fees are almost always available for children, students, and senior citizens)

Numbers in white and black circles that appear on the maps, in the margins, and within the tours correspond to one another.

Dining and Lodging

The restaurants and lodgings we list are the cream of the crop in each price range. Price charts appear in the Pleasures and Pastimes section that follows each chapter introduction.

Hotel Facilities

We always list the facilities that are available—but we don't specify whether they cost extra: When pricing accommodations, always ask what's included. In addition, assume that all rooms have private baths unless otherwise noted.

Restaurant Reservations and Dress Codes

Reservations are always a good idea; we note only when they're essential or when they are not accepted. Book as far ahead as you can, and reconfirm when you get to town. Unless otherwise noted, the restaurants listed are open daily for lunch and dinner. We mention dress only when men are required to wear a jacket or a jacket and tie. Look for an overview of local habits in the Pleasures and Pastimes section that follows each chapter introduction.

Credit Cards

The following abbreviations are used: **AE**, American Express; **D**, Discover; **DC**, Diners Club; **MC**, MasterCard; and **V**, Visa.

Please Write to Us

You can use this book in the confidence that all prices and opening times are based on information supplied to us at press time; Fodor's cannot accept responsibility for any errors. Time inevitably brings changes, so always confirm information when it matters—especially if you're making a detour to visit a specific place. In addition, when making reservations be sure to mention if you have a disability or are traveling with children, if you prefer a private bath or a certain type of bed, or if you have specific dietary needs or other concerns.

Were the restaurants we recommended as described? Did our hotel picks exceed your expectations? Did you find a museum we recommended a waste of time? If you have complaints, we'll look into them and revise our entries when the facts warrant it. If you've discovered a special place that we haven't included, we'll pass the information along to our correspondents and have them check it out. So send us your feedback, positive *and* negative: e-mail us at editors@fodors.com (specifying the name of the book on the subject line) or write the South editor at Fodor's, 201 East 50th Street, New York, New York 10022. Have a wonderful trip!

Karen Cure
Editorial Director

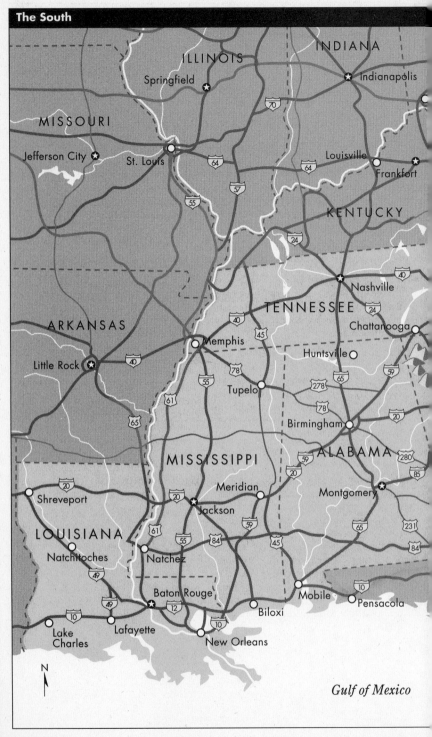

Gulf of Mexico

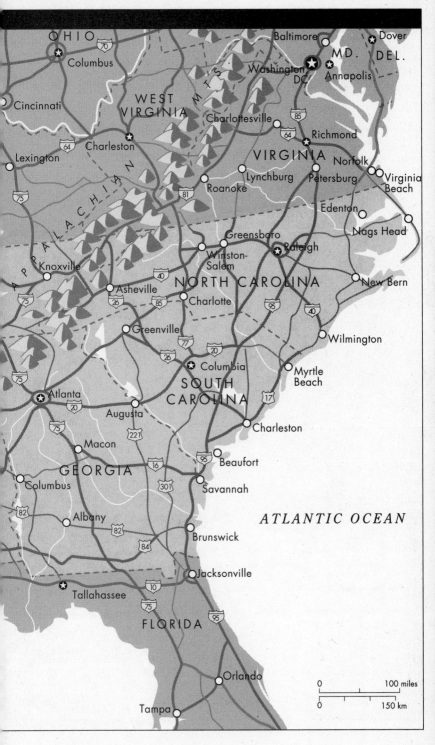

The United States

CANADA

Vancouver
Victoria
BRITISH COLUMBIA
Calgary
ALBERTA
SASKATCHEWAN
MANITOBA
Regina
Winnipeg
Trans-Canada Hwy.
Seattle
Olympia
WASHINGTON
Columbia R.
Spokane
Portland
Salem
OREGON
Great Falls
MONTANA
Helena
Missouri R.
Billings
NORTH DAKOTA
Fargo
Bismarck
SOUTH DAKOTA
Pierre
Missouri R.
IDAHO
Boise
Snake R.
WYOMING
NEBRASKA
Lincoln
Carson City
Sacramento
San Francisco
NEVADA
Fresno
Salt Lake City
UTAH
Cheyenne
Denver
Colorado Springs
COLORADO
KANSAS
Las Vegas
CALIFORNIA
Colorado R.
Santa Barbara
Los Angeles
San Diego
Flagstaff
ARIZONA
Phoenix
Tucson
Santa Fe
Albuquerque
NEW MEXICO
El Paso
OKLAHOMA
Oklahoma City
Amarillo
PACIFIC OCEAN
BAJA CALIFORNIA
SONORA
Dallas
Rio Grande
TEXAS
Austin
San Antonio
CHIHUAHUA

RUSSIA
ARCTIC OCEAN
Bering Strait
Nome
Bering Sea
ALASKA
Fairbanks
CANADA
Anchorage
ALEUTIAN ISLANDS
Juneau
PACIFIC OCEAN
MEXICO
COAHUILA
NUEVO LEON
TAMAULIPAS

0   400 miles
0   400 km
N

Honolulu
Oahu
Maui
HAWAII
Hawaii
PACIFIC OCEAN

SMART TRAVEL TIPS A TO Z

Basic Information on Traveling in the South, Savvy Tips to Make Your Trip a Breeze, and Companies and Organizations to Contact

A

AIR TRAVEL

MAJOR AIRLINE OR LOW-COST CARRIER?

Most people choose a flight based on price. Yet there are other issues to consider. Major airlines offer the greatest number of departures; smaller airlines—including regional, low-cost, and no-frill airlines—usually have a more limited number of flights daily. Major airlines have frequent-flyer partners, which allow you to credit mileage earned on one airline to your account with another. Low-cost airlines offer a definite price advantage and fewer restrictions, such as advance-purchase requirements. Safety-wise, low-cost carriers as a group have a good history, but **check the safety record before booking** any low-cost carrier; call the Federal Aviation Administration's Consumer Hotline (☞ Airline Complaints, *below*).

➤ MAJOR AIRLINES: **Air Canada** (☎ 800/776–3000). **American** (☎ 800/433–7300). **America West** (☎ 800/235–9292). **Continental** (☎ 800/525–0280). **Delta** (☎ 800/221–1212). **Northwest Airlines** (☎ 800/225–2525). **TWA** (☎ 800/221–2000). **United** (☎ 800/241–6522). **US Airways** (☎ 800/428–4322).

For further information on airports and airlines serving the South, see individual state chapters.

➤ SMALLER AIRLINES: **Air South** (☎ 800/247–7688). **American Eagle** (☎ 800/433–7300). **Atlantic Southeast** (☎ 800/221–1212). **Comair** (☎ 800/221–1212). **Kiwi** (☎ 800/538–5494). **Markair** (☎ 800/521–9854). **Midway** (☎ 888/226–4392). **Midwest Express** (☎ 800/452–2022). **Northwest Airlink** (☎ 800/225–2525). **ValuJet** (☎ 800/825–8538).

➤ FROM THE U.K.: **American** (☎ 0345/789789), **British Airways** (☎ 0345/222111), and **Delta** (☎ 0800/414767) have direct service to a number of cities in the South.

GET THE LOWEST FARE

The least-expensive airfares to the South are priced for round-trip travel. Major airlines usually require that you **book in advance and buy the ticket within 24 hours,** and you may have to **stay over a Saturday night.** It's smart to **call a number of airlines, and when you are quoted a good price, book it on the spot**—the same fare may not be available on the same flight the next day. Airlines generally allow you to change your return date for a fee of $25–$50. If you don't use your ticket you can apply the cost toward the purchase of a new ticket, again for a small charge. However, most low-fare tickets are nonrefundable. To get the lowest airfare, **check different routings.** If your destination or home city has more than one gateway, compare prices to and from different airports. Also price off-peak flights, which may be significantly less expensive.

To save money on flights from the United Kingdom and back, **look into an APEX or Super-PEX ticket.** APEX tickets must be booked in advance and have certain restrictions. Super-PEX tickets can be purchased at the airport on the day of departure— subject to availability.

DON'T STOP UNLESS YOU MUST

When you book, **look for nonstop flights** and remember that "direct" **flights stop at least once.** Try to **avoid connecting flights,** which require a change of plane. Two airlines may jointly operate a connecting flight, so ask if your airline operates every segment—you may find that your preferred carrier flies you only part of the way.

USE AN AGENT

Travel agents, especially those who specialize in finding the lowest fares (☞ Discounts & Deals, *below*), can be especially helpful when booking a plane ticket. When you're quoted a price, **ask your agent if the price is likely to get any lower.** Good agents know the seasonal fluctuations of airfares and can usually anticipate a sale or fare war. However, waiting can be risky: The fare could go *up* as seats become scarce, and you may wait so long that your preferred flight sells out. A wait-and-see strategy works best if your plans are flexible, but if you must arrive and depart on certain dates, don't delay.

Airlines routinely overbook planes, knowing that not everyone with a ticket will show up, but sometimes everyone does. When that happens, airlines ask for volunteers to give up their seats. In return these volunteers usually get a certificate for a free flight and are rebooked on the next flight out. If there are not enough volunteers the airline must choose who will be denied boarding. The first to get bumped are passengers who checked in late and those flying on discounted tickets, **so get to the gate and check in as early as possible,** especially during peak periods.

Always **bring a photo ID to the airport.** You may be asked to show it before you are allowed to check in.

ENJOY THE FLIGHT

For better service, **fly smaller or regional carriers,** which often have higher passenger-satisfaction ratings. Sometimes you'll find leather seats, more legroom, and better food.

For more legroom, **request an emergency-aisle seat**; don't, however, sit in the row in front of the emergency aisle or in front of a bulkhead, where seats may not recline.

If you don't like airline food, **ask for special meals when booking.** These can be vegetarian, low-cholesterol, or kosher, for example.

COMPLAIN IF NECESSARY

If your baggage goes astray or your flight goes awry, complain right away. Most carriers require that you file a claim immediately.

➤ AIRLINE COMPLAINTS: U.S. Department of Transportation **Aviation Consumer Protection Division** (✉ C-75, Room 4107, Washington, DC 20590, ☎ 202/366–2220). **Federal Aviation Administration (FAA) Consumer Hotline** (☎ 800/322–7873).

AIRPORTS

➤ AIRPORT INFORMATION: For information on airports serving the South, see individual state chapters.

B

BOAT TRAVEL

➤ STEAMBOATS: **Delta Queen Steamboat Co.** (✉ Robin St. Wharf, New Orleans, LA 70130, ☎ 504/586–0631 or 800/543–1949) has paddlewheel steamers that travel the rivers of the South.

BUS TRAVEL

➤ BUS LINES: **Greyhound** (☎ 800/231–2222) operates passenger buses connecting the South's towns and cities.

C

CAMERAS, CAMCORDERS, & COMPUTERS

Always **keep your film, tape, or computer disks out of the sun.** Carry an extra supply of batteries, and **be prepared to turn on your camera, camcorder, or laptop** to prove to security personnel that the device is real. Always **ask for hand inspection of film,** which becomes clouded after successive exposure to airport x-ray machines, and **keep videotapes and computer disks away from metal detectors.**

➤ PHOTO HELP: **Kodak Information Center** (☎ 800/242–2424). *Kodak Guide to Shooting Great Travel Pictures,* available in bookstores or from Fodor's Travel Publications (☎ 800/533–6478); $16.50 plus $4 shipping.

CAR RENTAL

Rates in Atlanta, Georgia, begin at $40 a day and $150 a week for an economy car with air-conditioning, an automatic transmission, and unlimited mileage. This does not include tax on car rentals, which is 5%. Rates in Raleigh and Durham in North Carolina begin at $35 a day and $123 a week. This does not include tax on car rentals, which is 8%. These rates are typical of those found in larger cities in the South.

➤ MAJOR AGENCIES: **Alamo** (☎ 800/327-9633; 0800/272-2000 in the U.K.). **Avis** (☎ 800/331-1212; 800/879-2847 in Canada). **Budget** (☎ 800/527-0700; 0800/181181 in the U.K.). **Dollar** (☎ 800/800-4000; 0990/565656 in the U.K., where it is known as Eurodollar). **Hertz** (☎ 800/654-3131; 800/263-0600 in Canada; 0345/555888 in the U.K.). **National InterRent** (☎ 800/227-7368; 0345/222525 in the U.K., where it is known as Europcar InterRent).

CUT COSTS

To get the best deal, **book through a travel agent who is willing to shop around.** When pricing cars, **ask about the location of the rental lot.** Some off-airport locations offer lower rates, and their lots are only minutes from the terminal via complimentary shuttle. You also may want to **price local car-rental companies,** whose rates may be lower still, although their service and maintenance may not be as good as those of a name-brand agency. Remember to ask about required deposits, cancellation penalties, and drop-off charges if you're planning to pick up the car in one city and leave it in another.

Also **ask your travel agent about a company's customer-service record.** How has it responded to late plane arrivals and vehicle mishaps? Are there often lines at the rental counter, and, if you're traveling during a holiday period, does a confirmed reservation guarantee you a car?

NEED INSURANCE?

When driving a rented car you are generally responsible for any damage to or loss of the vehicle. You also are liable for any property damage or personal injury that you may cause while driving. Before you rent, **see what coverage you already have** under the terms of your personal auto-insurance policy and credit cards.

For about $14 a day, rental companies sell protection, known as a collision- or loss-damage waiver (CDW or LDW) that eliminates your liability for damage to the car; it's always optional and should never be automatically added to your bill.

In most states you don't need CDW if you have personal auto insurance or

other liability insurance. However, **make sure you have enough coverage to pay for the car.** If you do not have auto insurance or an umbrella policy that covers damage to third parties, purchasing CDW or LDW is highly recommended.

BEWARE SURCHARGES

Before you pick up a car in one city and leave it in another, **ask about drop-off charges or one-way service fees,** which can be substantial. Note, too, that some rental agencies charge extra if you return the car before the time specified on your contract. To avoid a hefty refueling fee, **fill the tank just before you turn in the car,** but be aware that gas stations near the rental outlet may overcharge.

MEET THE REQUIREMENTS

In the United States you must be 21 to rent a car, and rates may be higher if you're under 25. You'll pay extra for child seats (about $3 per day), which are compulsory for children under five, and for additional drivers (about $2 per day). Residents of the United Kingdom will need a reservation voucher, a passport, a U.K. driver's license, and a travel policy that covers each driver, in order to pick up a car.

CHILDREN & TRAVEL

CHILDREN IN THE SOUTH

Be sure to plan ahead and **involve your youngsters** as you outline your trip. When packing, include things to keep them busy en route. On sightseeing days try to schedule activities of special interest to your children. If you are renting a car don't forget to **arrange for a car seat** when you reserve. Most hotels in the South allow children under a certain age to stay in their parents' room at no extra charge, but others charge them as extra adults; be sure to **ask about the cutoff age for children's discounts.**

FLYING

As a general rule, infants under two not occupying a seat fly free. If your children are two or older **ask about children's airfares.**

In general the adult baggage allowance applies to children paying half or more of the adult fare.

According to the FAA it's a good idea to use safety seats aloft for children weighing less than 40 pounds. Airlines, however, can set their own policies: U.S. carriers allow FAA-approved models but usually require that you buy a ticket, even if your child would otherwise ride free, since the seats must be strapped into regular seats. Airline rules vary regarding their use, so it's important to **check your airline's policy about using safety seats during takeoff and landing.** Safety seats cannot obstruct any of the other passengers in the row, so get an appropriate seat assignment as early as possible.

When making your reservation, **request children's meals or a free-standing bassinet** if you need them; the latter are available only to those seated at the bulkhead, where there's enough legroom. Remember, however, that bulkhead seats may not have their own overhead bins, and there's no storage space in front of you—a major inconvenience.

GROUP TRAVEL

If you're planning to take your kids on a tour, look for companies that specialize in family travel.

➤ FAMILY-FRIENDLY TOUR OPERATORS: **Families Welcome!** (✉ 92 N. Main St., Ashland, OR 97520, ☎ 541/482–6121 or 800/326–0724, FAX 541/482–0660).

CONSUMER PROTECTION

Whenever possible, **pay with a major credit card** so you can cancel payment if there's a problem, provided that you can provide documentation. This is a good practice whether you're buying travel arrangements before your trip or shopping at your destination.

If you're doing business with a particular company for the first time, **contact your local Better Business Bureau and the attorney general's offices** in your state and the company's home state, as well. Have any complaints been filed?

Finally, if you're buying a package or tour, always **consider travel insurance** that includes default coverage (☞ Insurance, *below*).

➤ LOCAL BBBs: **Council of Better Business Bureaus** (✉ 4200 Wilson Blvd., Suite 800, Arlington, VA 22203, ☎ 703/276–0100, FAX 703/525–8277).

CUSTOMS & DUTIES

ENTERING THE U.S.

Visitors age 21 and over may import the following into the United States: 200 cigarettes or 50 cigars or 2 kilograms of tobacco, 1 liter of alcohol, and gifts worth $100. Prohibited items include meat products, seeds, plants, and fruits.

ENTERING CANADA

If you've been out of Canada for at least seven days you may bring in C$500 worth of goods duty-free. If you've been away for fewer than seven days but more than 48 hours, the duty-free allowance drops to C$200; if your trip lasts 24–48 hours, the allowance is C$50. You may not pool allowances with family members. Goods claimed under the C$500 exemption may follow you by mail; those claimed under the lesser exemptions must accompany you.

Alcohol and tobacco products may be included in the seven-day and 48-hour exemptions but not in the 24-hour exemption. If you meet the age requirements of the province or territory through which you reenter Canada you may bring in, duty-free, 1.14 liters (40 imperial ounces) of wine or liquor *or* 24 12-ounce cans or bottles of beer or ale. If you are 16 or older you may bring in, duty-free, 200 cigarettes and 50 cigars; these items must accompany you.

You may send an unlimited number of gifts worth up to C$60 each duty-free to Canada. Label the package UNSOLICITED GIFT—VALUE UNDER $60. Alcohol and tobacco are excluded.

➤ INFORMATION: **Revenue Canada** (✉ 2265 St. Laurent Blvd. S, Ottawa, Ontario K1G 4K3, ☎ 613/993–0534; 800/461–9999 in Canada).

ENTERING THE U.K.

From countries outside the European Union, including the United States, you may import, duty-free, 200 cigarettes or 50 cigars; 1 liter of spirits or 2 liters of fortified or sparkling wine or liqueurs; 2 liters of still table wine; 60 milliliters of perfume; 250 milliliters of toilet water; plus £136 worth of other goods, including gifts and souvenirs.

➤ INFORMATION: **HM Customs and Excise** (⊠ Dorset House, Stamford St., London SE1 9NG, ☎ 0171/202–4227).

D
DISABILITIES & ACCESSIBILITY

TIPS & HINTS

When discussing accessibility with an operator or reservationist, **ask hard questions.** Are there any stairs, inside *or* out? Are there grab bars next to the toilet *and* in the shower/tub? How wide is the doorway to the room? To the bathroom? For the most extensive facilities meeting the latest legal specifications, **opt for newer accommodations,** which are more likely to have been designed with access in mind. Older buildings or ships may offer more limited facilities. Be sure to **discuss your needs before booking.**

➤ COMPLAINTS: **Disability Rights Section** (⊠ U.S. Dept. of Justice, Box 66738, Washington, DC 20035-6738, ☎ 202/514–0301 or 800/514–0301, FAX 202/307–1198, TTY 202/514–0383 or 800/514–0383) for general complaints. **Aviation Consumer Protection Division** (☞ Air Travel, *above*) for airline-related problems. **Civil Rights Office** (⊠ U.S. Dept. of Transportation, Departmental Office of Civil Rights, S-30, 400 7th St. SW, Room 10215, Washington, DC 20590, ☎ 202/366–4648) for problems with surface transportation.

TRAVEL AGENCIES & TOUR OPERATORS

The Americans with Disabilities Act requires that travel firms serve the needs of all travelers. That said, you should note that some agencies and operators specialize in making travel arrangements for individuals and groups with disabilities.

➤ TRAVELERS WITH MOBILITY PROBLEMS: **Access Adventures** (⊠ 206 Chestnut Ridge Rd., Rochester, NY 14624, ☎ 716/889–9096), run by a former physical-rehabilitation counselor. **Hinsdale Travel Service** (⊠ 201 E. Ogden Ave., Suite 100, Hinsdale, IL 60521, ☎ 630/325–1335), a travel agency that benefits from the advice of wheelchair traveler Janice Perkins. **Wheelchair Journeys** (⊠ 16979 Redmond Way, Redmond, WA 98052, ☎ 206/885–2210 or 800/313–4751), for general travel arrangements.

➤ TRAVELERS WITH DEVELOPMENTAL DISABILITIES: **New Directions** (⊠ 5276 Hollister Ave., Suite 207, Santa Barbara, CA 93111, ☎ 805/967–2841, FAX 805/964–7344). **Sprout** (⊠ 893 Amsterdam Ave., New York, NY 10025, ☎ 212/222–9575 or 888/222–9575, FAX 212/222–9768).

DISCOUNTS & DEALS

Be a smart shopper and **compare all your options before making a choice.** A plane ticket bought with a promotional coupon may not be cheaper than the least expensive fare from a discount ticket agency. For high-price travel purchases, such as packages or tours, keep in mind that what you get is just as important as what you save. Just because something is cheap doesn't mean it's a bargain.

LOOK IN YOUR WALLET

When you use your credit card to make travel purchases you may get free travel-accident insurance, collision-damage insurance, and medical or legal assistance, depending on the card and the bank that issued it. American Express, MasterCard, and Visa provide one or more of these services, so **get a copy of your credit card's travel-benefits policy.** If you are a member of the American Automobile Association (AAA) or an oil-company-sponsored road-assistance plan, always **ask hotel or car-rental reservationists about auto-club discounts.** Some clubs offer additional discounts on tours, cruises, or admission to attractions. And don't forget that auto-club membership entitles you to free maps and trip-planning services.

DIAL FOR DOLLARS

To save money, **look into "1-800" discount reservations services,** which use their buying power to get a better price on hotels, airline tickets, even car rentals. When booking a room, always **call the hotel's local toll-free number** (if one is available) rather than the central reservations number—you'll often get a better price. Always ask about special packages or corporate rates.

➤ AIRLINE TICKETS: ☎ 800/FLY–4–LESS. ☎ 800/FLY–ASAP.

SAVE ON COMBOS

Packages and guided tours can both save you money, but don't confuse the two. When you buy a package your travel remains independent, just as though you had planned and booked the trip yourself. Fly-drive packages, which combine airfare and car rental, are often a good deal.

JOIN A CLUB?

Many companies sell discounts in the form of travel clubs and coupon books, but these cost money. You must use participating advertisers to get a deal, and only after you recoup the initial membership cost or book price do you begin to save. If you plan to use the club or coupons frequently you may save considerably. Before signing up, find out what discounts you get for free.

➤ DISCOUNT CLUBS: **Entertainment Travel Editions** (✉ 2125 Butterfield Rd., Troy, MI 48084, ☎ 800/445–4137); $23–$48, depending on destination. **Great American Traveler** (✉ Box 27965, Salt Lake City, UT 84127, ☎ 800/548–2812); $49.95 per year. **Moment's Notice Discount Travel Club** (✉ 7301 New Utrecht Ave., Brooklyn, NY 11204, ☎ 718/234–6295); $25 per year, single or family. **Privilege Card International** (✉ 237 E. Front St., Youngstown, OH 44503, ☎ 330/746–5211 or 800/236–9732); $74.95 per year. **Sears's Mature Outlook** (✉ Box 9390, Des Moines, IA 50306, ☎ 800/336–6330); $14.95 per year. **Travelers Advantage** (✉ CUC Travel Service, 3033 S. Parker Rd., Suite 1000, Aurora, CO 80014, ☎ 800/548–1116 or 800/648–4037); $49 per year, single or family. **Worldwide Discount Travel Club** (✉ 1674 Meridian Ave., Miami Beach, FL 33139, ☎ 305/534–2082); $50 per year family, $40 single.

DRIVING

State lawmakers now set speed limits, even for federal interstate highways. Limits vary from state-to-state and from rural to urban areas, so **check posted speeds frequently.** See the individual state chapters in this book for interstate speed limits.

➤ AUTO CLUBS: In the United States, **American Automobile Association** (☎ 800/564–6222). In Canada, **Canadian Automobile Association** (☎ 613/226–7631). In the United Kingdom, **Automobile Association** (AA, ☎ 0990/500–600), **Royal Automobile Club** (RAC, ☎ 0990/722–722 membership, 0345/121–345 insurance).

E
EMERGENCIES

In many areas of the South, **dial 911 for police, fire, and ambulance.** See the individual state chapters in this guide for more information.

G
GAY & LESBIAN TRAVEL

➤ GAY- & LESBIAN-FRIENDLY TRAVEL AGENCIES: **Advance Damron** (✉ 1 Greenway Plaza, Suite 800, Houston, TX 77046, ☎ 713/850–1140 or 800/695–0880, ℻ 713/888–1010). **Club Travel** (✉ 8739 Santa Monica Blvd., West Hollywood, CA 90069, ☎ 310/358–2200 or 800/429–8747, ℻ 310/358–2222). **Islanders/Kennedy Travel** (✉ 183 W. 10th St., New York, NY 10014, ☎ 212/242–3222 or 800/988–1181, ℻ 212/929–8530). **Now Voyager** (✉ 4406 18th St., San Francisco, CA 94114, ☎ 415/626–1169 or 800/255–6951, ℻ 415/626–8626). **Yellowbrick Road** (✉ 1500 W. Balmoral Ave., Chicago, IL 60640, ☎ 773/561–1800 or 800/642–2488, ℻ 773/561–4497). **Skylink Women's Travel** (✉ 3577 Moorland Ave., Santa Rosa, CA 95407, ☎ 707/585–8355 or 800/225–5759, ℻ 707/584–5637), serving lesbian travelers.

I
INSURANCE

Travel insurance is the best way to **protect yourself against financial loss.** The most useful policies are trip-cancellation-and-interruption, default, medical, and comprehensive insurance.

Without insurance you will lose all or most of your money if you cancel your trip, regardless of the reason. It's essential that you **buy trip-cancellation-and-interruption insurance,** particularly if your airline ticket, cruise, or package tour is nonrefundable and cannot be changed. When considering how much coverage you need, look for a policy that will cover

THE GOLD GUIDE / SMART TRAVEL TIPS

the cost of your trip plus the nondiscounted price of a one-way airline ticket, should you need to return home early. Also **consider default or bankruptcy insurance,** which protects you against a supplier's failure to deliver.

Citizens of the United Kingdom can buy an annual travel-insurance policy valid for most vacations during the year in which it's purchased. If you are pregnant or have a preexisting medical condition, make sure you're covered. According to the Association of British Insurers, a trade association representing 450 insurance companies, it's wise to buy extra medical coverage when you visit the United States.

If you have purchased an expensive vacation, comprehensive insurance is a must. **Look for comprehensive policies that include trip-delay insurance,** which will protect you in the event that weather problems cause you to miss your flight, tour, or cruise. A few insurers sell waivers for preexisting medical conditions. Companies that offer both features include Access America, Carefree Travel, Travel Insured International, and Travel Guard (☞ *below*).

Always **buy travel insurance directly from the insurance company**; if you buy it from a travel agency or tour operator that goes out of business you probably will not be covered for the agency or operator's default—a major risk. Before you make any purchase, **review your existing health and home-owner's policies** to find out whether they cover expenses incurred while traveling.

➤ TRAVEL INSURERS: In the United States, **Access America** (✉ 6600 W. Broad St., Richmond, VA 23230, ☎ 804/285–3300 or 800/284–8300), **Carefree Travel Insurance** (✉ Box 9366, 100 Garden City Plaza, Garden City, NY 11530, ☎ 516/294–0220 or 800/323–3149), **Near Travel Services** (✉ Box 1339, Calumet City, IL 60409, ☎ 708/868–6700 or 800/654–6700), **Travel Guard International** (✉ 1145 Clark St., Stevens Point, WI 54481, ☎ 715/345–0505 or 800/826–1300), **Travel Insured International** (✉ Box 280568, East Hartford, CT 06128-0568, ☎ 860/528–7663 or 800/243–3174), **Travelex Insurance Services** (✉ 11717

Burt St., Suite 202, Omaha, NE 68154-1500, ☎ 402/445–8637 or 800/228–9792, FAX 800/867–9531), **Wallach & Company** (✉ 107 W. Federal St., Box 480, Middleburg, VA 20118, ☎ 540/687–3166 or 800/237–6615). In Canada, **Mutual of Omaha** (✉ Travel Division, 500 University Ave., Toronto, Ontario M5G 1V8, ☎ 416/598–4083; 800/268–8825 in Canada). In the United Kingdom, **Association of British Insurers** (✉ 51 Gresham St., London EC2V 7HQ, ☎ 0171/600–3333).

L

LODGING

APARTMENT & VILLA RENTALS

If you want a home base that's roomy enough for a family and comes with cooking facilities, **consider a furnished rental.** These can save you money, however some rentals are luxury properties, economical only when your party is large. Home-exchange directories list rentals (often second homes owned by prospective house swappers), and some services search for a house or apartment for you (even a castle if that's your fancy) and handle the paperwork. Some send an illustrated catalog; others send photographs only of specific properties, sometimes at a charge. Up-front registration fees may apply.

➤ RENTAL AGENTS: **Property Rentals International** (✉ 1008 Mansfield Crossing Rd., Richmond, VA 23236, ☎ 804/378–6054 or 800/220–3332, FAX 804/379–2073). **Rent-a-Home International** (✉ 7200 34th Ave. NW, Seattle, WA 98117, ☎ 206/789–9377 or 800/488–7368, FAX 206/789–9379). **Hideaways International** (✉ 767 Islington St., Portsmouth, NH 03801, ☎ 603/430–4433 or 800/843–4433, FAX 603/430–4444) is a travel club whose members arrange rentals among themselves; yearly membership is $99.

HOME EXCHANGES

If you would like to exchange your home for someone else's, **join a home-exchange organization,** which will send you its updated listings of available exchanges for a year and will include your own listing in at least one of them. Making the arrangements is up to you.

➤ EXCHANGE CLUBS: **HomeLink International** (✉ Box 650, Key West, FL 33041, ☎ 305/294–7766 or 800/638–3841, FAX 305/294–1148) charges $83 per year.

M
MONEY

ATMS

Before leaving home, **make sure that your credit cards have been programmed for ATM use.**

➤ ATM LOCATIONS: **Cirrus** (☎ 800/424–7787). **Plus** (☎ 800/843–7587).

N
NATIONAL PARKS

You may be able to **save money on park entrance fees** by getting a discount pass. The Golden Eagle Pass ($50) gets you and your companions free admission to all parks for one year (camping and parking are extra). Both the Golden Age Passport, for U.S. citizens or permanent residents age 62 and older, and the Golden Access Passport, for travelers with disabilities, entitle holders to free entry to all national parks plus 50% off fees for the use of many park facilities and services. Both passports are free; you must show proof of age and U.S. citizenship or permanent residency (such as a U.S. passport, driver's license, or birth certificate) or proof of disability. All three passes are available at all national park entrances. Golden Eagle and Golden Access passes are also available by mail.

➤ PASSES BY MAIL: **National Park Service** (✉ Dept. of the Interior, Washington, DC 20240).

P
PACKING FOR THE SOUTH

Much of the South has hot, humid summers and sunny, mild winters. For colder months, pack a lightweight coat, slacks, and sweaters; you'll need heavier clothing in the more northerly states, where cold, damp weather prevails and snow is not unusual. Keeping summer's humidity in mind, **pack absorbent natural fabrics that breathe**; bring an umbrella, but leave the plastic raincoat at home. You'll want a jacket or sweater for summer evenings and for too-cool air-conditioning. And **don't forget insect repellent.**

Bring an extra pair of eyeglasses or contact lenses in your carry-on luggage, and if you have a health problem, **pack enough medication** to last the entire trip. It's important that you **don't put prescription drugs or valuables in luggage to be checked**: it might go astray. Travelers who suffer allergies might experience some additional discomfort during spring or fall, when regional pollens could trigger unexpected reactions.

LUGGAGE

In general you are entitled to check two bags on flights within the United States. A third piece may be brought on board, but it must fit easily under the seat in front of you or in the overhead compartment.

Airline liability for baggage is limited to $1,250 per person on flights within the United States. On international flights it amounts to $9.07 per pound or $20 per kilogram for checked baggage (roughly $640 per 70-pound bag) and $400 per passenger for unchecked baggage. Insurance for losses exceeding these amounts can be bought from the airline at check-in for about $10 per $1,000 of coverage; note that this coverage excludes a rather extensive list of items, which is shown on your airline ticket.

Before departure, **itemize your bags' contents** and their worth, and label the bags with your name, address, and phone number. (If you use your home address, cover it so that potential thieves can't see it readily.) Inside each bag, **pack a copy of your itinerary.** At check-in, **make sure that each bag is correctly tagged** with the destination airport's three-letter code. If your bags arrive damaged or fail to arrive at all, file a written report with the airline before leaving the airport.

PASSPORTS & VISAS

CANADIANS

A passport is not required to enter the United States.

U.K. CITIZENS

British citizens need a valid passport to enter the United States. If you are staying for fewer than 90 days on vacation, with a return or onward ticket, you probably will not need a visa. However, you will need to fill out the Visa Waiver Form, 1-94W, supplied by the airline.

➤ INFORMATION: **London Passport Office** (☎ 0990/21010) for fees and documentation requirements and to request an emergency passport. **U.S. Embassy Visa Information Line** (☎ 01891/200–290) for U.S. visa information; calls cost 49p per minute or 39p per minute cheap rate. **U.S. Embassy Visa Branch** (✉ 5 Upper Grosvenor St., London W1A 2JB) for U.S. visa information; send a self-addressed, stamped envelope. Write the **U.S. Consulate General** (✉ Queen's House, Queen St., Belfast BTI 6EO) if you live in Northern Ireland.

S
SENIOR-CITIZEN TRAVEL

To qualify for age-related discounts, **mention your senior-citizen status up front** when booking hotel reservations (not when checking out) and before you're seated in restaurants (not when paying the bill). Note that discounts may be limited to certain menus, days, or hours. When renting a car, **ask about promotional car-rental discounts,** which can be cheaper than senior-citizen rates.

➤ EDUCATIONAL TRAVEL PROGRAMS: **Elderhostel** (✉ 75 Federal St., 3rd floor, Boston, MA 02110, ☎ 617/426–8056).

STUDENTS

➤ STUDENT IDS & SERVICES: **Council on International Educational Exchange** (✉ CIEE, 205 E. 42nd St., 14th floor, New York, NY 10017, ☎ 212/822–2600 or 888/268–6245, ℻ 212/822–2699), for mail orders only, in the United States. **Travel Cuts** (✉ 187 College St., Toronto, Ontario M5T 1P7, ☎ 416/979–2406 or 800/667–2887) in Canada.

➤ HOSTELING: **Hostelling International—American Youth Hostels** (✉ 733 15th St. NW, Suite 840, Washington, DC 20005, ☎ 202/783–6161, ℻ 202/783–6171). **Hostelling International—Canada** (✉ 400-205 Catherine St., Ottawa, Ontario K2P 1C3, ☎ 613/237–7884, ℻ 613/237–7868). **Youth Hostel Association of**

England and Wales (✉ Trevelyan House, 8 St. Stephen's Hill, St. Albans, Hertfordshire AL1 2DY, ☎ 01727/855215 or 01727/845047, ℻ 01727/844126). Membership in the United States, $25; in Canada, C$26.75; in the United Kingdom, £9.30.

➤ STUDENT TOURS: **Contiki Holidays** (✉ 300 Plaza Alicante, Suite 900, Garden Grove, CA 92840, ☎ 714/740–0808 or 800/266–8454, ℻ 714/740–2034).

T
TELEPHONES

CALLING HOME

AT&T, MCI, and Sprint long-distance services make calling home relatively convenient and let you avoid hotel surcharges. Typically you dial an 800 number in the United States.

➤ TO OBTAIN ACCESS CODES: **AT&T USADirect** (☎ 800/874–4000). **MCI Call USA** (☎ 800/444–4444). **Sprint Express** (☎ 800/793–1153).

TOUR OPERATORS

Buying a prepackaged tour or independent vacation can make your trip to the South less expensive and more hassle-free. Because everything is prearranged you'll spend less time planning.

Operators that handle several hundred thousand travelers per year can use their purchasing power to give you a good price. Their high volume may also indicate financial stability. But some small companies provide more personalized service; because they tend to specialize, they may also be more knowledgeable about a given area.

A GOOD DEAL?

The more your package or tour includes, the better you can predict the ultimate cost of your vacation. Make sure you know exactly what is covered, and **beware of hidden costs.** Are taxes, tips, and service charges included? Transfers and baggage handling? Entertainment and excursions? These can add up.

If the package or tour you are considering is priced lower than in your wildest dreams, **be skeptical.** Also, **make sure your travel agent knows the accommodations** and other services. Ask about the hotel's location, room size, beds, and whether it has a pool, room service, or programs for children, if you care about these. Has your agent been there in person or sent others you can contact?

BUYER BEWARE

Each year consumers are stranded or lose their money when tour operators—even very large ones with excellent reputations—go out of business. So **check out the operator.** Find out how long the company has been in business, and ask several agents about its reputation. **Don't book unless the firm has a consumer-protection program.**

Members of the National Tour Association and United States Tour Operators Association are required to set aside funds to cover your payments and travel arrangements in case the company defaults. Nonmembers may carry insurance instead. Look for the details, and for the name of an underwriter with a solid reputation, in the operator's brochure. Note: When it comes to tour operators, **don't trust escrow accounts.** Although the Department of Transportation watches over charter-flight operators, no regulatory body prevents tour operators from raiding the till. You may want to protect yourself by buying travel insurance that includes a tour-operator default provision. For more information, *see* Consumer Protection, *above.*

It's also a good idea to choose a company that participates in the American Society of Travel Agents' Tour Operator Program (TOP). This gives you a forum if there are any disputes between you and your tour operator; ASTA will act as mediator.

➤ TOUR-OPERATOR RECOMMENDATIONS: **National Tour Association** (⊠ NTA, 546 E. Main St., Lexington, KY 40508, ☎ 606/226–4444 or 800/755–8687). **United States Tour Operators Association** (⊠ USTOA, 342 Madison Ave., Suite 1522, New York, NY 10173, ☎ 212/599–6599, FAX 212/599–6744). **American Society of Travel Agents** (☞ *below*).

USING AN AGENT

Travel agents are excellent resources. In fact, large operators accept book-

ings made only through travel agents. But it's a good idea to **collect brochures from several agencies,** because some agents' suggestions may be influenced by relationships with tour and package firms that reward them for volume sales. If you have a special interest, **find an agent with expertise in that area**; ASTA (☞ Travel Agencies, *below*) has a database of specialists worldwide. Do some homework on your own, too: Local tourism boards can provide information about lesser-known and small-niche operators, some of which may sell only direct.

SINGLE TRAVELERS

Prices for packages and tours are usually quoted per person, based on two sharing a room. If traveling solo, you may be required to pay the full double-occupancy rate. Some operators eliminate this surcharge if you agree to be matched with a roommate of the same sex, even if one is not found by departure time.

GROUP TOURS

Among companies that sell tours to the South, the following are nationally known, have a proven reputation, and offer plenty of options. The classifications used below represent different price categories, and you'll probably encounter these terms when talking to a travel agent or tour operator. The key difference is usually in accommodations, which run from budget to better, and better-yet to best.

➤ DELUXE: **Globus** (⊠ 5301 S. Federal Circle, Littleton, CO 80123-2980, ☎ 303/797–2800 or 800/221–0090, FAX 303/347–2080). **Maupintour** (⊠ 1515 St. Andrews Dr., Lawrence, KS 66047, ☎ 913/843–1211 or 800/255–4266, FAX 913/843–8351). **Tauck Tours** (⊠ Box 5027, 276 Post Rd. W, Westport, CT 06881-5027, ☎ 203/226–6911 or 800/468–2825, FAX 203/221–6828).

➤ FIRST CLASS: **Brendan Tours** (⊠ 15137 Califa St., Van Nuys, CA 91411, ☎ 818/785–9696 or 800/421–8446, FAX 818/902–9876). **Collette Tours** (⊠ 162 Middle St., Pawtucket, RI 02860, ☎ 401/728–3805 or 800/832–4656, FAX 401/728–1380). **Gadabout Tours** (⊠ 700 E. Tahquitz Canyon Way, Palm

Springs, CA 92262, ☎ 619/325–5556 or 800/952–5068). **Mayflower Tours** (✉ Box 490, 1225 Warren Ave., Downers Grove, IL 60515, ☎ 630/960–3793 or 800/323–7604, FAX 630/960–3575).

➤ BUDGET: **Cosmos** (☞ Globus, *above*).

PACKAGES

Like group tours, independent vacation packages are available from major tour operators and airlines. The companies listed below offer vacation packages in a broad price range.

➤ AIR/HOTEL: **American Airlines Fly AAway Vacations** (☎ 800/321–2121). **Continental Vacations** (☎ 800/634–5555). **Delta Dream Vacations** (☎ 800/872–7786). **SuperCities** (✉ 139 Main St., Cambridge, MA 02142, ☎ 617/621–0099 or 800/333–1234). **United Vacations** (☎ 800/328–6877). **US Airways Vacations** (☎ 800/455–0123).

➤ CUSTOM PACKAGES: **Amtrak's Great American Vacations** (☎ 800/321–8684).

THEME TRIPS

For additional operators and trips, see the individual state chapters.

➤ BICYCLING: **Backroads** (✉ 801 Cedar St., Berkeley, CA 94710-1800, ☎ 510/527–1555 or 800/462–2848, FAX 510-527–1444).

➤ LEARNING: **Smithsonian Study Tours and Seminars** (✉ 1100 Jefferson Dr. SW, Room 3045, MRC 702, Washington, DC 20560, ☎ 202/357–4700, FAX 202/633–9250).

➤ SPAS: **Spa-Finders** (✉ 91 5th Ave., #301, New York, NY 10003-3039, ☎ 212/924–6800 or 800/255–7727).

A good travel agent puts your needs first. Look for an agency that has been in business at least five years, emphasizes customer service, and has someone on staff who specializes in your destination. In addition, **make sure the agency belongs to the American Society of Travel Agents** (ASTA). If your travel agency is also acting as your tour operator, *see* Tour Operators, *above*.

➤ LOCAL AGENT REFERRALS: **American Society of Travel Agents** (ASTA, ☎ 800/ 965–2782 24-hr hot line, FAX 703/684–8319). **Alliance of Canadian Travel Associations** (✉ 1729 Bank St., Suite 201, Ottawa, Ontario K1V 7Z5, ☎ 613/521–0474, FAX 613/521–0805). In Great Britain, **Association of British Travel Agents** (✉ 55–57 Newman St., London W1P 4AH, ☎ 0171/637–2444, FAX 0171/637–0713).

Travel catalogs specialize in useful items, such as compact alarm clocks and travel irons, that can **save space when packing.**

➤ MAIL-ORDER CATALOGS: **Magellan's** (☎ 800/962–4943, FAX 805/568–5406). **Orvis Travel** (☎ 800/541–3541, FAX 540/343–7053). **TravelSmith** (☎ 800/950–1600, FAX 800/950–1656).

U

The U.S. government can be an excellent source of inexpensive travel information. When planning your trip, **find out what government materials are available.**

➤ ADVISORIES: **U.S. Department of State** (✉ Overseas Citizens Services Office, Room 4811 N.S., Washington, DC 20520); enclose a self-addressed, stamped envelope. **Interactive hot line** (☎ 202/647–5225, FAX 202/647–3000). **Computer bulletin board** (☎ 301/946–4400).

➤ PAMPHLETS: **Consumer Information Center** (✉ Consumer Information Catalogue, Pueblo, CO 81009, ☎ 719/948–3334) for a free catalog that includes travel titles.

V

For general information and brochures before you go, contact the state tourism bureaus below.

➤ STATE TOURISM BUREAUS: **Alabama Bureau of Tourism and Travel** (✉ 401 Adams Ave., Montgomery, AL 36104, ☎ 334/242–4169 or 800/252–2262, FAX 334/242–4554). **Georgia Department of Industry, Trade and Tourism** (✉ Box 1776, Atlanta, GA 30301, ☎ 404/656–3590; 800/847–4842 for brochures; FAX 404/651–9063). **Louisiana Office** of Tourism (✉ Box 94291, Baton Rouge, LA 70804-9291, ☎ 504/342-8119; 800/334-8626 for brochures; FAX 504/342-8390). **Mississippi Division of Tourism** (✉ Box 1705, Ocean Springs, MS 39566, ☎ 601/359-3297; 800/927-6378 for brochures; FAX 601/359-5757). **North Carolina Department of Commerce, Travel and Tourism Division** (✉ 301 N. Wilmington St., Raleigh, NC 27601, ☎ 919/733-4171; 800/847-4862 for brochures; FAX 919/733-8582). **South Carolina Division of Tourism** (✉ 1205 Pendleton St., Columbia, SC 29201, ☎ 803/734-0122; 800/872-3505 for brochures; FAX 803/734-0138). **Tennessee Department of Tourist Development** (✉ 320 6th Ave. N, Rachel Jackson Bldg., 5th floor, Nashville, TN 37243, ☎ 615/741-2159; 800/836-6200 for brochures; FAX 615/741-7225).

W

WHEN TO GO

Spring is probably the most attractive season in this part of the United States. Throughout the region, cherry blossoms are followed by azaleas, dogwood, and camellias from April into May, and by apple blossoms in May. Summer can be hot and humid in many areas, but temperatures will be cooler along the coasts or in the mountains. Folk, craft, art, and music festivals tend to take place in summer, as do sports events. State and local fairs are held mainly in August and September, though there are a few in early July and into October. Fall can be a delight, with spectacular foliage, particularly in the mountains. The region is large and conditions vary; see the individual state chapters for more information.

CLIMATE

In winter, temperatures generally average in the low 40s inland, in the 60s by the shore. Summer temperatures, modified by mountains in some areas, by water in others, range from the high 70s to the mid-80s, now and then the low 90s.

➤ FORECASTS: **Weather Channel Connection** (☎ 900/932-8437), 95¢ per minute from a Touch-Tone phone.

The following are average daily maximum and minimum temperatures for key Southern cities.

Climate in the South

BIRMINGHAM, ALABAMA

Jan.	56F	13C	May	82F	28C	Sept.	86F	30C
	35	2		58	14		63	17
Feb.	58F	14C	June	89F	32C	Oct.	77F	25C
	37	3		66	19		51	11
Mar.	65F	18C	July	90F	32C	Nov.	64F	18C
	42	6		69	21		40	4
Apr.	74F	23C	Aug.	90F	32C	Dec.	56F	13C
	50	10		65	20		35	2

ATLANTA, GEORGIA

Jan.	52F	11C	May	79F	26C	Sept.	83F	28C
	36	2		61	16		65	18
Feb.	54F	12C	June	86F	30C	Oct.	72F	22C
	38	3		67	19		54	12
Mar.	63F	17C	July	88F	31C	Nov.	61F	16C
	43	6		70	21		43	6
Apr.	72F	22C	Aug.	86F	30C	Dec.	52F	11C
	52	11		70	21		38	3

NEW ORLEANS, LOUISIANA

Jan.	63F	17C	May	83F	28C	Sept.	86F	30C
	47	8		68	20		74	23
Feb.	65F	18C	June	88F	31C	Oct.	79F	26C
	50	10		74	23		65	18
Mar.	72F	22C	July	90F	32C	Nov.	70F	21C
	56	13		76	24		56	13
Apr.	77F	25C	Aug.	90F	32C	Dec.	65F	18C
	61	16		76	24		49	9

JACKSON, MISSISSIPPI

Jan.	59F	15C	May	85F	29C	Sept.	88F	31C
	38	3		63	17		65	18
Feb.	63F	17C	June	92F	33C	Oct.	81F	27C
	41	5		70	21		54	12
Mar.	68F	20C	July	94F	34C	Nov.	67F	19C
	47	8		72	22		43	6
Apr.	76F	24C	Aug.	94F	34C	Dec.	61F	16C
	54	12		70	21		40	4

RALEIGH, NORTH CAROLINA

Jan.	50F	10C	May	78F	26C	Sept.	81F	27C
	29	− 2		55	13		60	16
Feb.	52F	11C	June	85F	29C	Oct.	71F	22C
	30	− 1		62	17		47	8
Mar.	61F	16C	July	88F	31C	Nov.	61F	16C
	37	3		67	19		38	3
Apr.	72F	22C	Aug.	87F	31C	Dec.	52F	11C
	46	8		66	18		52	11

CHARLESTON, SOUTH CAROLINA

Jan.	59F	15C	May	81F	27C	Sept.	84F	29C
	41	6		64	18		69	21
Feb.	60F	16C	June	86F	30C	Oct.	76F	24C
	43	7		71	22		59	15
Mar.	66F	19C	July	88F	31C	Nov.	67F	19C
	49	9		74	23		49	9
Apr.	73F	23C	Aug.	88F	31C	Dec.	59F	11C
	56	13		73	23		42	6

NASHVILLE, TENNESSEE

Jan.	46F	8C	May	79F	26C	Sept.	83F	28C
	28	− 2		57	14		61	16
Feb.	51F	11C	June	87F	31C	Oct.	72F	22C
	30	− 1		65	18		48	9
Mar.	60F	16C	July	90F	32C	Nov.	59F	15C
	38	3		69	21		32	3
Apr.	71F	22C	Aug.	89F	32C	Dec.	50F	10C
	48	9		68	20		31	− 1

1 Destination: The South

SOUTHERN SUPERLATIVES

IF YOU HEAR a Southern farmhand threaten to cut off one of his arms and eat it, don't scream and call for help. That's just his way of saying that he's ravenous—or, as he is also likely to put it, "so hungry my stomach thinks my throat's been cut." A Southern man is not just tired or ill-used. He feels "like I've been rode hard and put up wet" (the reference being to letting a hard-ridden horse unlather before stabling it). A Southern woman in the midst of a tizzy is "running around setting my hair on fire." And if things don't work out right, she may "have to go to bed with a cold rag on my head"; in an extreme case, she may "go completely to pieces."

A proclivity to exaggerate is at the very core of every Southerner's soul, and he or she will take any opportunity to exercise it—for all Southerners simply *love* to talk. A Southerner setting out to make a transaction, whether it's buying a Coke or a condo, is viscerally aware that in the South the first order of business is almost never business. It's "visiting"—passing the time of day.

Out of these two tendencies—to talk and to talk big—has sprung the age-old Southern tradition of spinning colorfully embroidered stories, which in turn has spawned some great American storytellers. The original version of Thomas Wolfe's novel *Of Time and the River* was about the length of 12 average novels, or twice the length of *War and Peace.* Simply unable to stem the flow of words, he stopped writing only after his editor told him that the novel was finished. Thomas Wolfe was a Southerner, a native of Asheville, North Carolina, which means that he was born with a bad case of logorrhea.

Other notable Southern storytellers are Mississippi's two Pulitzer Prize winners, Tennessee Williams and Eudora Welty, and its Nobel Prize winner, William Faulkner. All three wrote of eccentric, complex, and occasionally bizarre characters caught up in byzantine plots, as did Savannah-born Flannery O'Connor, author of *Wise Blood.*

Faulkner wrote his first novel in an apartment overlooking Pirates Alley in New Orleans—a city that gave the world Truman Capote and Lillian Hellman, and which Tennessee Williams called "my spiritual home." A Pulitzer was awarded posthumously to New Orleanian John Kennedy Toole, who wrote the wildly funny *A Confederacy of Dunces.* Frances Parkinson Keyes bought a historic home in the French Quarter of New Orleans, where she wrote *Dinner at Antoine's* and *Steamboat Gothic.* The brilliant Walker Percy, a native of Birmingham, Alabama, won the National Book Award for his first novel, *The Moviegoer,* and continued to turn out literary gems from his home in Covington, Louisiana.

In Flat Rock, North Carolina, the home of Pulitzer Prize–winning poet and biographer Carl Sandburg is a National Historic Site. Pat Conroy, who wrote *Prince of Tides,* lived in Atlanta for many years. Margaret Mitchell, also an Atlanta resident, wrote only one book in her life, but that book was *Gone With the Wind*—the best-selling novel of all time.

For other Southerners, the words soar off the page and into the air. The South gave birth to the blues, to jazz, and to songwriters and singers of every stripe. The King—Elvis—grew up in Tupelo, Mississippi, and launched his astonishing career in a Memphis recording studio. Each year millions of Presley fans make the pilgrimage to Graceland, his showy home and final resting place in Memphis. Florence, Alabama, gave us W. C. Handy, who first played his "St. Louis Blues" in a Memphis saloon, and Savannah produced Johnny Mercer, a songwriter of considerable notes. The versatile Wynton Marsalis, the late Louis Armstrong, and the lively Pete Fountain are among the scores of great jazzmen from New Orleans, where jazz itself was born. Husky-voiced jazz and blues singer Nina Simone grew up in western North Carolina. Another great vocalist, Leontyne Price of Laurel, Mississippi, sang the role of Bess on Broadway in *Porgy and Bess* before giving voice to opera on a grand scale.

Opera lovers the world over flock to the annual Spoleto Festival USA in Charleston, which also features theater, ballet, and jazz. In the spring, musicians from as far away as Australia and Finland turn up for the Jazz and Heritage Festival in New Orleans, a city that is not exactly jazzless the rest of the year. Out in the bayous of South Louisiana, contagious Cajun music has virtually the whole world two-stepping; and up in the Blue Ridge Mountains of North Carolina, the hills sing with bluegrass music. Tennessee has produced more country-music songwriters, singers, and musicians than you can shake a mike at, and Nashville, the "Country Music Capital of the World," is the foot-stomping ground of the Grand Ole Opry.

"Dixie," incidentally, penned in 1859 by Yankee Dan Emmett, was a marching song originally played by bands of both the North and the South as they paraded into the Recent Unpleasantness—a period of time known to everyone but Southerners as the Civil War.

THE CIVIL WAR, with a few exceptions, notably Gettysburg, was fought on Southern soil. South Carolina, inflamed by the rhetoric of firebrand John C. Calhoun, was the first state to secede, causing a Union loyalist to snap, "South Carolina is too small for a republic and too big for a lunatic asylum." But the first shots rang out over Charleston Harbor, and the bloody war began. Virtually every Southern city, country crossroads, and sleepy creek was touched by the war, and even now the memories linger, preserved for all time in yet more colorful stories, passed along from generation to generation in the rooms of antebellum mansions throughout the South.

Today, south of the Mason-Dixon Line (surveyed in the 1700s by British astronomers Charles Mason and Jeremiah Dixon to settle a territorial dispute between Pennsylvania and Maryland), there are almost as many Civil War commemorative plaques as there are black-eyed peas. A slew of the South's most famous sights were once the scenes of fierce battles. Glitzy, modern Atlanta literally grew up out of the ashes Sherman left behind. Lookout Mountain, Tennessee, with its stunning view, was a

vantage point that both sides fought for keenly, and down in Mississippi, Vicksburg held Grant off for 47 days and nights before surrendering. New Orleans fell not long after Farragut shouted, "Damn the torpedoes! Full speed ahead!"

The region is also fertile territory for aficionados of earlier American history. Fort Moultrie, South Carolina, is the site of the fledgling nation's first decisive victory over the British during the Revolutionary War.

Natchitoches, Louisiana, was the first permanent settlement in the territory comprising the Louisiana Purchase, and the town has a small but beautifully restored historic district. (Holding title to the "oldest" or "first in this country" is dear to the hearts of tradition-cherishing Southerners.) New Orleans's French Quarter, famed for Bourbon Street jazz haunts and exquisite Creole cuisine, is the original colony founded by French Creoles, and there are important historic districts in Winston-Salem, Savannah, Charleston, and Mobile.

But the South is much more than time-honored historic sites. It is a vast sports arena for snow-skiers and water-skiers, scuba divers and horseback riders, spelunkers and kayakers, shrimpers and saltwater anglers, hikers, bikers, tennis buffs, golfers, and beachcombers.

Lush carpets of white sand roll down the Atlantic Coast and sweep along the Gulf of Mexico. Seekers of sun and fun head for such resorts as Sea Island, Georgia, and, in the Carolinas, Cape Hatteras, Hilton Head Island, and Myrtle Beach. Alabama barely sticks its big toe in the Gulf, but Mobile Bay's swank resorts and colorful artists' colonies are among the state's most popular attractions. Twenty-six miles of sun-kissed beaches stretch along the Mississippi coast, dotted with resorts such as Pascagoula, Pass Christian, and Biloxi.

If beaches bore you, there are plenty of hills to head for. The breathtakingly beautiful Blue Ridge Mountains roll through the Carolinas and northern Georgia, and the Great Smokies soar over the North Carolina–Tennessee border. Playgrounds abound in "them thar hills," such as Gatlinburg, Tennessee, and Blowing Rock, North Carolina.

One last note before you go: If you expect to hear the Hollywood version of a Southern accent, you're likely to be surprised. About the only generalization that can be made is that the Southern voice is gentle and soft—except at football games and hog-calling contests. You *will* hear drawls and "y'alls." ("Y'all," incidentally, is a contraction of "you all." It's the equivalent of "you guys," something you will almost never hear a Southerner say.) In South Louisiana, the language isn't even English—it's Cajun French. And in New Orleans you'll hear an accent that is soft, slightly slurred, but decidedly Brooklynese.

The truth is, the voices of the South are as rich and varied as the land itself. In its shops, restaurants, and homes you can be sure you'll hear those melodic Southern voices say, "Y'all come back."

And that's not just whistling Dixie.

— Honey Naylor

NEW AND NOTEWORTHY

Alabama

If you're visiting Birmingham in 1998, consider a visit to the **McWane Center,** a hands-on science museum opening in the spring. You may also want to check out **VisionLand,** a 75-acre amusement park due to open in nearby Bessemer. Plans include a theme park with mechanical rides, a water park, and a family amusement center with indoor games.

In Huntsville, the **Alabama Constitution Village** will add the Early Southern Life Center, a hands-on history experience, during the second half of 1998. You'll be able to interact with Alabama's past rather than simply look at artifacts. The **Huntsville Museum of Art** will move into a larger structure, doubling its exhibit space and adding a café.

Georgia

In Atlanta, **Centennial Olympic Park** and **Turner Field,** the new home of the Atlanta Braves, are two legacies of the Centennial Olympic Games. On the culinary front, acclaimed chef Guenter Seeger left The Dining Room at the Ritz-Carlton, Buckhead.

He was preparing to open his own restaurant, **Seeger's,** in Buckhead at press time. Macon's recently opened **Georgia Music Hall of Fame** celebrates the state's contributions to the world of music; honors go out to musicians of all genres, including Ray Charles, R.E.M., and Robert Shaw. In Pooler, the **Mighty Eighth Air Force Museum** commemorates the Savannah-formed World War II squadron.

Savannah continues to attract visitors who have read the best-selling *Midnight in the Garden of Good and Evil* and want to explore the city for themselves. The upcoming movie version of this tale of an antiques dealer accused of murder is fueling interest in the city. From July 2 to 6, Savannah will welcome **America's Sail '98,** a gathering of Tall Ships from around the world. A Parade of Sail will take place in Savannah Harbor, followed by festivities during which some ships will be open to the public. The Tall Ship handicapped race begins on July 6 and finishes on Long Island, New York, on July 10.

Louisiana

As tourism grows, the New Orleans **hotel boom** continues. Construction on the Hotel du Parc, a 123-room boutique hotel in the Central Business District, was slated for completion by the end of 1997. In sports news, the city may be home to an **ice hockey** team in time for the 1998–99 season. The team would belong to the East Coast Hockey League. The AAA New Orleans Zephyrs now play ball at the new 10,000-seat **Zephyr Field** in Jefferson Parish.

Fans of vampire-chronicler **Anne Rice** are always thirsty for news. Rice's family company, Kith and Kin, operates Rice-rich tours of New Orleans' Garden District. The company recently joined with a California vineyard to produce Rice's new vintage wine, a blood-red Cuvée Lestat. Look for her new restaurant in '98—Café Lestat, of course.

Mississippi

In Clarksdale, the **Delta Blues Museum** has completed the first phase of its two-phase renovation plan. While phase one focused on restoration of the building into which the museum will move, phase two will strengthen its music archives.

Gambling continues to be a popular sport in Mississippi. New casinos are surfacing all over the state, particularly in Tunica County, in the northwest corner of the state; Biloxi, on the Gulf of Mexico; and Greenville, on the Mississippi.

North Carolina

The Crystal Coast, consisting of the **Outer Banks** south of Ocracoke, is recognized as one of the best ocean diving destinations on the East Coast. Interest in diving the numerous wrecks in the nearby Gulf Stream waters was intensified in 1997 by the discovery of the site of what is believed to be the 19th-century wreck of *Queen Anne's Revenge,* the flagship of the pirate Blackbeard's fleet, just off Beaufort Inlet. Excavations and archiving will continue through 1998.

In Durham the **North Carolina Museum of Life and Science** plans to open the Bio-Quest development during 1998. Billed as the nation's first interactive Butterfly House and Insectarium, the three-story-high glass structure will contain luxuriant flowering plants and 1,000 exotic butterflies in free flight.

South Carolina

On a practical note, in September 1998 the **area code** for the Charleston area will change from 803 to 843.

In September 1998, **Around Alone,** the single-handed yacht race around the world (formerly the BOC Challenge) begins in Charleston, as it did in 1994. New Charleston-area **accommodations** will include the Wentworth Mansion, a B&B in an 1886 brick home, and the Inn at Wild Dunes, part of the Wild Dunes resort on the Isle of Palms; these weren't available for inspection at press time. In **restaurant news,** Charleston chef Louis Osteen (formerly of Louis's Charleston Grill) was set to open Louis's Restaurant at 200 Meeting Street. Talented chef Bob Waggoner of Nashville has taken over the Charleston Grill. North Charleston will open the **Carolina Ice Palace,** a twin-rink family entertainment complex with a virtual reality arcade.

A major airport expansion will be completed in **Columbia,** the state capital, early in the year. The latest attraction in Myrtle Beach is **Ripley's Aquarium,** with touch tanks for kids and an underwater tunnel exhibit that's longer than a football field. In North Myrtle Beach, the **House of Blues** joins the area's entertainment venues, showcasing blues, rock, jazz, and country music. The **Fantasy Harbor** complex in Myrtle Beach has a new theater, the All-American Music Theatre.

Tennessee

In Memphis, the **Memphis Music Hall of Fame** has migrated from the Old Daisy Theater to a new home on 2nd Street. The **Sun Studio Beale Street** museum fills the vacancy in the Old Daisy Theater with exhibits that trace the history of Beale Street. By late 1997, the Memphis Area Transit Authority plans to finish an extension of its **trolley line,** providing better access to area attractions. Renovation of **Central Station,** a Memphis landmark, will resurrect the old Amtrak facility as a shopping and dining area. Also under construction is **Peabody Place,** a retail and restaurant center spread out in several historic buildings at the foot of the Peabody Hotel. The construction of **Coolidge Park** in Chattanooga began in 1997. The park will include a historic carousel, a dining pavilion, and waterfront walkways.

WHAT'S WHERE

Alabama

From sites where Native Americans lived for 8,000 years before the arrival of European settlers, to forts occupied during French colonial settlement in the 1700s and the American Revolution in the 1800s, to antebellum mansions that survived the Civil War, Alabama is a state loaded with history. It also brims with natural beauty—wooded hills and vast caves in the northeast, expansive lakes and broad rivers in the interior, and snow-white beaches along the Gulf Coast—within an easy drive of thriving cities such as Birmingham, Montgomery, and Mobile.

Georgia

Georgia is notable for its contrasting landscapes and varied cities and towns, each reflecting its own special Southern charm. The northern part of the state has the Appalachian Mountains and their waterfalls; Dahlonega, the site of the nation's first gold rush; and Alpine Helen, a re-created Bavarian village in the Blue Ridge Mountains. Also in the north is Atlanta, a fast-growing city that serves as a banking center; and Macon, an antebellum town with thousands of cherry trees. If you drive some five hours southeast from Atlanta, you'll reach Savannah, which has the nation's largest historic district, filled with restored colonial and 19th-century buildings. From Savannah, the state's 100-mi Atlantic coast runs south to the Florida border. Along this stretch is a string of lush, subtropical barrier islands, the Golden Isles, which include the elegant seaside communities of Jekyll, Sea, and St. Simons islands. Farther south is Cumberland Island National Seashore, a sanctuary of marshes, beaches, forests, lakes, and ponds. Southern Georgia consists of black, gator-infested swampland, including the mysterious rivers and lakes of the Okefenokee.

Louisiana

Louisiana is a state divided, both physically and philosophically, around midstate in Alexandria. North Louisiana, with its rolling hills and piney woods, is strongly Southern in flavor and appeal, while flatter, marshy South Louisiana is considered Cajun Country, with sharp differences in food, music, and even language. Riverboats ply the mighty Mississippi and antebellum homes line the wayside in both regions, but it's New Orleans, home of the famous Mardi Gras festivities, great music, and fine restaurants, that garners the lion's share of attention, drawing most visitors to South Louisiana.

Mississippi

Filled with Civil War battlegrounds and slightly partisan tales of ancestors who fought valiantly for the Confederacy, Mississippi has some of the best-preserved examples of antebellum architecture in the South. The Natchez Trace, a beautiful string of magnolias and hilltop vistas, cuts across the heart of Dixie, passing through Tupelo (Elvis Presley's birthplace), Jackson (the capital), and antebellum Natchez. The mighty Mississippi provides the natural western border of the state, winding slowly through the Delta past the port towns of Greenville and Vicksburg. The Gulf Coast offers sun, sand, fishing, and general lazing, while in the north of the state Oxford, a sophisti-

cated courthouse town, still vibrates with the words of William Faulkner, Eudora Welty, and Tennessee Williams.

North Carolina

Historic sights and natural wonders abound in North Carolina, from Old Salem, where the 1700s spring to life in modern-day Winston-Salem, to the Great Smoky and Blue Ridge mountains, where waterfalls cascade over high cliffs into gorges thick with evergreens. On the Cape Hatteras and Cape Lookout national seashores, tides wash over the wooden skeletons of ancient shipwrecks and lighthouses stand as they have for 200 years. Here, too, you'll find sophisticated cities such as Charlotte and Raleigh, world-class golf in the Pinehurst Sandhills, and fields of tobacco in the rich farmland of the gently rolling Piedmont.

South Carolina

South Carolina's scenic Lowcountry shoreline is punctuated by the lively port city of Charleston, decked out with fine museums (several in restored antebellum homes) and anchored by the recreational resorts of Myrtle Beach and Hilton Head at either end of the coast. The state capital, Columbia, is set in the fertile interior, and the Blue Ridge Mountains form the western border of the state. Also to the west are the rolling fields of Thoroughbred Country, noted for top racehorses and sprawling mansions, and Upcountry, at the state's northwestern tip, with incredible mountain scenery and white-water rafting.

Tennessee

Among Tennessee's dominating characteristics is its geography. Bordered by the Great Smoky Mountains on the east and the Mississippi River on the west, the state offers breathtaking scenery. Carved by rivers and mountains into three vertical regions, the state spans more than 500 mi east–west, but only about 115 mi north–south. Here are forests, fields, and streams for the nature lover, outlet malls for the die-hard shopper, and an array of amusements for the whole family. Memphis and Nashville are musts for music lovers, and Chattanooga has attractions that range from an aquarium to nearby Chickamauga/Chattanooga National Military Park.

PLEASURES AND PASTIMES

Dining

Southern dining comes in a variety of flavors: You can choose down-home cookin' like Mama used to make, with plenty of country ham, corn bread, and fried catfish, or you can savor the refined creations of brash young chefs who use fresh local ingredients in inventive new ways. You'll find both styles of cooking in Atlanta and many other Southern cities. In Louisiana, try Creole food, with its French influences, and hearty, heavily seasoned Cajun dishes. South Carolina's Lowcountry cooking highlights such specialties as she-crab soup, stuffed oysters, and pecan pie. And don't forget to sample the local barbecue, with seasonings that vary from state to state, or the fine fresh fish and seafood available at casual waterfront eateries or elegant dining rooms all along the coast. Your culinary explorations won't end with Southern cuisines, though. The increasing sophistication of the South has spurred the growth of restaurants that offer everything from good French and Italian fare to Thai and Tex-Mex.

History

On and off the beaten path, the South is rich in history. The lives of Native Americans, the area's first inhabitants, can be studied in such sites as Moundville Archaeological Park in Alabama and the Museum of the Cherokee Indian in Cherokee, North Carolina. You'll find evidence of early French settlers in New Orleans and Mobile, and Old Salem in Winston-Salem re-creates the world of Moravian immigrants. Colonial history comes alive at Revolutionary War sites, whether at Kings Mountain National Military Park in Upcountry South Carolina or at Guilford Courthouse National Military Park near Greensboro, North Carolina. Throughout the South you can visit plantation houses or walk through historic districts in cities like Savannah that stand as testimony to the antebellum era. The Civil War is commemorated on the great battlefields of Chickamauga, Shiloh, Vicksburg, and many others, but studying a Civil War monument in a town square can also take you to the heart of that wrenching conflict. In a later era, the South was the birthplace of the civil rights movement, and its landmarks and memorials stand proudly across the region, from the Ebenezer Baptist Church in Atlanta to the Civil Rights Memorial in Montgomery.

Music

Many people would say that the South is inseparable from music, and no visit here would be complete without taking in some performances and exploring the area's music museums. New Orleans, the birthplace of jazz, has plenty of choices, and in South Louisiana you can dance to the beat of Cajun music. The Mississippi Delta and Memphis gave birth to the blues, and on Beale Street and at museums or shrines such as Elvis's Graceland you can trace the fortunes of the blues and rock and roll. Nashville, with the Grand Ole Opry, is the place for country music, but there's plenty of blues and rock, too. For fine bluegrass, you can head to the mountains of western North Carolina. But whether you're in Atlanta or Asheville, clubs and an abundance of musical festivals celebrate a full range of sounds. Classical music isn't neglected, either: Spoleto Festival USA in Charleston is just one showcase, and many cities have fine orchestras and chamber groups.

Outdoor Activities and Sports

Name your sport, and you'll discover superb places to pursue it throughout the South. This is a golfer's paradise, from the courses of the Robert Trent Jones Golf Trail in Alabama to the resorts of North Carolina's Pinehills. Boaters can explore the lakes of South Carolina's Heartland or travel the Intracoastal Waterway, and rivers provide thrilling white-water rafting and excellent flatwater canoeing in every state. All this water holds challenges for anglers, whether in fresh water or out on the ocean. The region's mountains, from the Blue Ridge to the Great Smokies, have well-marked hiking trails, including the Appalachian Trail, to help you get away from it all. And if beaches are your passion, take your pick: the white sands of the Gulf Coast, the windswept shores of Cape Hatteras National Seashore in North Carolina, the bustling resorts at Myrtle Beach in South Carolina, or Georgia's lush barrier islands, known as the Golden Isles.

GREAT ITINERARIES

The following recommended itineraries, arranged by both theme and area, are offered as a guide to planning individual travel.

Prominent Sites of African-American History

Alabama Tour

Alabama's historic civil rights sites provide a close look at the long struggle for racial equality, culminating in the changes undergone during the 1960s.

Duration: Five to seven days.

One day: In Mobile, see the antebellum State Street A.M.E. (African Methodist Episcopal) Zion Church and the St. Louis Street Missionary Baptist Church, one of four black congregations established in Alabama prior to 1865. Check out the black heritage display at Ft. Condé and the National African-American Archives and Museum.

Two or three days: Travel to Montgomery and visit the Civil Rights Memorial and Dexter Avenue King Memorial Baptist Church, considered by many the birthplace of the civil rights movement. Then move on to Selma and see the Edmund Pettus Bridge, famous during the 1960s for clashes between civil rights marchers and police. Near the bridge, don't miss the National Voting Rights Museum. Make an excursion east from Montgomery to the Tuskegee Institute National Historic Site, which consists of Booker T. Washington's home, The Oaks; the George Washington Carver Museum; and Tuskegee University.

One or two days: From Montgomery, go north to Birmingham and visit its Civil Rights District, the centerpiece of which is the Birmingham Civil Rights Institute. A few blocks south is the Alabama Jazz Hall of Fame, where jazz greats with Alabama ties are spotlighted. Among those honored is Erskine Hawkins, who wrote "Tuxedo Junction." Next, take in the Alabama Sports Hall of Fame; it pays tribute to many of the state's great African-American athletes.

One day: Travel north to Decatur and visit the Old Courthouse, noted for the 1933 retrial of the Scottsboro Boys. Northwest is Florence, site of the W. C. Handy Home and Museum.

Information: ☞ Chapter 2.

Tennessee/Mississippi Tour

For a glimpse of African-American life in the Deep South, visit the cotton country of the Mississippi Delta.

Duration: Four or five days.

One day: Begin in Memphis with a stop at the National Civil Rights Museum, on the site of Martin Luther King Jr.'s 1968 assassination. After this, you can walk through the shops and blues clubs in the Beale Street Historic District. About 45 mi northeast is Henning, hometown of the late Alex Haley and setting for his novel *Roots*.

One or two days: Next stop is Jackson, to get an overview of the civil-rights movement's history in Mississippi. See the Old Capitol Historical Museum and Eudora Welty Library, which houses a number of exhibits on writers from the South.

Two days: Head to Oxford and the Ole Miss campus where an African-American was first graduated in 1963; see the Center for the Study of Southern Culture, which focuses on Southern music and folklore. Then go 62 mi southwest to Clarksdale and tour the Delta Blues Museum, which honors famous blues musicians.

Information: ☞ Chapters 5 and 8.

Lowcountry Tour

Blacks and whites in South Carolina's Lowcountry have always lived side by side, though, as evidenced by the 1739 Stono Plantation Rebellion and the 1822 Denmark Vesey plot to take over Charleston, not always peaceably. This natural distrust also motivated blacks to develop a lilting dialect called Gullah to communicate exclusively with one another. Historic sites in the Lowcountry recall this unique black experience.

Duration: Two days.

One day: In Charleston, begin with a walking tour of Cabbage Row, home of DuBose Heyward and setting for his novel *Porgy*. Then see the Emmanuel A.M.E. Church—the place of worship of the South's oldest A.M.E. congregation. Also here is the Old Exchange and Provost

Dungeon, site of the city's busiest slave market. The Avery Research Center in the historic district has an archives and museum that document the heritage of Low-country blacks.

One day: Travel on to the Beaufort area, where you'll see the Penn Center Historic District and York W. Bailey Cultural Museum on St. Helena Island. This community center consists of 17 buildings on the campus of a school that was established in 1862 for freed slaves. Also in Beaufort County is Daufuskie Island, until recently inhabited exclusively by descendants of slaves.

Information: ☞ Chapter 7.

Prominent Civil War Sites

The Southeastern Tour

South Carolina seceded from the Union on December 20, 1860, and the first shot of the war was fired the following April. The following itineraries take in the major sites and sights in South Carolina, Georgia, and Alabama.

Duration: Seven to nine days.

One day: Begin in Charleston, South Carolina, and visit the Fort Sumter National Monument. On April 12, 1861, Confederate General P. G. T. Beauregard ordered the first shot fired, and the bloody four-year struggle began.

Two or three days: Drive the 300 mi south to Atlanta, Georgia. See the Eternal Flame of the Confederacy and visit the Cyclorama, depicting the 1864 Battle of Atlanta. Finally, explore 3,200-acre Stone Mountain Park, where there's a Confederate Memorial carved into the mountain—the world's largest monument.

Two days: From Atlanta, drive 160 mi southwest to Montgomery, Alabama, the Cradle of the Confederacy. Visit the State Capitol, which was the first capitol of the Confederacy, and the First White House of the Confederacy, which was occupied by President Jefferson Davis and his family.

Two or three days: From Montgomery head southwest toward Mobile. Next stop is Fort Morgan, about 20 mi from Gulf Shores. A museum in Fort Morgan describes the dramatic 1864 Battle of Mobile Bay, dur-ing which Admiral David Farragut shouted, "Damn the torpedoes! Full speed ahead!"

Information: ☞ Chapters 2, 3, and 7.

The South Central Tour

The long, colorful trek through Mississippi, Louisiana, and Tennessee offers Civil War–history buffs a wealth of well-preserved battle sites.

Duration: Eight to 10 days.

Two or three days: From Mobile, head west toward New Orleans (146 mi). Overlooking the Gulf of Mexico between Gulf-port and Biloxi, Mississippi, is Beauvoir, the home of Confederate president Jefferson Davis. At the Louisiana–Mississippi border, turn off to Baton Rouge (bypassing New Orleans, which fell to the Union in 1862) and then north to the Port Hudson State Commemorative Area, a 650-acre area on the site where, in 1863, 6,800 Confederates held off 30,000 to 40,000 Federals from May 23 till July 9. Continue north to Vicksburg, the Mississippi River city that withstood Grant's siege for 47 days and nights before falling. Here, visit the Vicksburg National Military Park.

Three days: From Vicksburg, Mississippi, make the 242-mi trip to Jackson; then head north to Memphis. Another 100 mi east of there is Shiloh National Military Park and Cemetery, commemorating those who died in the April 1862 battle, one of the bloodiest of the Civil War.

Three to four days: Head south to Chattanooga. See the Battles for Chattanooga Museum, touted as the world's largest battlefield display of its kind, and visit the eight locations of the Chickamauga-Chattanooga National Military Park, whose headquarters is 10 mi south of the city. This is one of the nation's largest and oldest national military parks.

Information: ☞ Chapters 4, 5, and 8.

FODOR'S CHOICE

No two people will agree on what makes a perfect vacation, but it's fun and helpful to know what others think. We hope you'll have a chance to experience some of Fodor's Choices yourself in the South.

For detailed information about each entry, refer to the appropriate chapter.

Special Moments

★ **Birmingham Civil Rights Institute, Alabama.** Observing the multimedia exhibits covering the movement from the 1920s to today, you can't help but reflect on the civil rights struggle through the years.

★ **Okefenokee National Wildlife Refuge, southeast Georgia.** Savor nature at its most primeval as alligators and frogs bellow their respective mating calls in spring.

★ **The King Center, Atlanta, Georgia.** Memories of the civil rights movement in the 1950s and 1960s come alive as you view the eternal flame burning at Martin Luther King Jr.'s tomb in front of the downtown center.

★ **Historic District, Savannah, Georgia.** Architecture buffs will have a field day strolling by the hundreds of restored buildings within a 2½-mi-square area.

★ **Pirate's Alley, New Orleans, Louisiana.** Romance comes alive in this section of town, redolent of Old New Orleans, especially when viewed through the early-morning mists.

★ **French Quarter, New Orleans, Louisiana.** From the deck of a riverboat, colors and shapes draw the eye to this section of the shoreline.

★ **Elvis's birthplace, Tupelo, Mississippi.** You'll understand how meager and humble were the beginnings of the King of Rock and Roll when you step into this tiny, two-room cabin.

★ **Plantation dinner, Monmouth, Mississippi.** Diners step back 150 years in time to experience the graciousness and grandeur of a formal soiree at this beautiful plantation in Natchez.

★ **Old Salem, Winston-Salem, North Carolina.** A 1700s village of brick-and-wood structures peopled by tradesmen and gentlewomen in period costume provides a slice of living history.

★ **Cape Hatteras National Seashore, North Carolina.** Stretching from Oregon Inlet to Ocracoke Island, this scenic coastline is dotted with beach communities, historic lifesaving stations, wildlife refuges, and beaches cluttered only by wild sea oats.

★ **Cypress Gardens, South Carolina.** A boat tour among the spring blossoms reflecting in the black waters of the gardens is a visual dazzler.

★ **Viewing the Great Smokies from Lookout Tower at Clingmans Dome, East Tennessee.** Here you'll see forested mountains capped by a gray haze of clouds as the early-morning mists melt into midday. The drive up is more difficult in the morning mists, but those mists impart the true Smokies feel.

Dining

★ **Roussos Restaurant, Mobile, Alabama.** The crab claws, baked oysters, and seafood gumbo draw a crowd of locals here. $$

★ **Voyagers, Orange Beach, Alabama.** The airy, two-level dining room of the Perdido Beach Resort is one of the most elegant restaurants on Alabama's Gulf Coast. $$

★ **Silvertron Cafe, Birmingham, Alabama.** Tin ceilings, fresh flowers, and historic photographs of Birmingham create a down-to-earth atmosphere for traditional, but expertly prepared, poultry, fish, and pasta dishes. $–$$

★ **Elizabeth on 37th, Savannah, Georgia.** In an elegant turn-of-the-century mansion in the city's Victorian district, the emphasis is on seafood enhanced by delicate sauces. $$$$

★ **Bacchanalia, Atlanta, Georgia.** Mediterranean cuisine with Asia influences is served in the intimate dining room of a former residence. $$$

★ **Ciboulette, Atlanta, Georgia.** Hot smoked salmon, herb-crusted rack of lamb, and game dishes are inventively prepared at this popular French bistro. $$$

★ **Mrs. Wilkes Dining Room, Savannah, Georgia.** Expect long lines waiting to devour the reasonably priced, well-prepared Southern food, served family-style at big tables. $

★ **Brigtsen's, New Orleans, Louisiana.** Cajun and Creole culinary styles are blended to produce some of the best South Louisiana dishes you'll find anywhere. $$$

★ **Lafitte's Landing, Donaldsonville, Louisiana.** Celebrity chef John Folse (of

PBS fame) serves his regional fare in this charming Acadian cottage. $$$

⭐ **Joe's "Dreyfus Store," Livonia, Louisiana.** The old general store is still outfitted with polished-wood cabinets and other period memorabilia, an interesting, relaxed setting for the South Louisiana cuisine featured here. $$

⭐ **Prudhomme's Cajun Café, Carencro, Louisiana.** This rustic Acadian cottage is center stage for the marvelous Cajun cuisine of Enola Prudhomme, sister of celeb Paul Prudhomme, and a master chef and cookbook author in her own right. $$

⭐ **City Grocery Store, Oxford, Mississippi.** Spic-and-span decor, attentive service, and inventive Southern cuisine are your reward for visiting this favorite. $$$–$$$$

⭐ **Nick's, Jackson, Mississippi.** As any local who comes here to dine on the tasty seafood will tell you, no visit to Jackson is complete without a meal here. $$$

⭐ **Gabrielle's at Richmond Hill, Asheville, North Carolina.** The fabulous dinners at this Victorian inn are not to be missed—held by some to be the most imaginative (wild boar sausage and grilled antelope medallions) and delicious food in the state. $$$$

⭐ **Lamplighter, Charlotte, North Carolina.** Fine gourmet cuisine served in the softly lit interior of an old Dilworth home is the hallmark of this favorite. $$$$

⭐ **WickedSmile, Raleigh, North Carolina.** Regulars at this chic, revamped 1920s warehouse refer to the French- and Italian-influenced American cuisine (tomato consommé with vegetable ravioli and fresh basil) as "art on a plate." $$$

⭐ **Magnolias, Charleston, South Carolina.** Lots of Lowcountry dishes and a magnolia theme infuse this refurbished warehouse with Southern charm. $$–$$$

⭐ **Collectors Cafe, Myrtle Beach, South Carolina.** This pleasantly arty spot includes a gallery, so you can shop after you try the barbecue duck or veal-stuffed ravioli. $$

⭐ **Chez Philippe, Memphis, Tennessee.** The ornate, art deco setting is incredible, and the food never fails to measure up to the surroundings. $$$$

⭐ **Burning Bush Restaurant, Gatlinburg, Tennessee.** The atmosphere is colonial, the menu Continental at this pleaser. $$–$$$

⭐ **212 Market, Chattanooga, Tennessee.** Light, healthy cuisine—poached salmon in ginger-lime sauce or vegetable terrine—served in a colorful, contemporary setting draws a crowd here. $$–$$$

Lodging

⭐ **Perdido Beach Resort, Orange Beach, Alabama.** Fantastic views, a splendid beach location, and lovely Mediterranean style set this one apart. $$$$

⭐ **The Tutwiler, Birmingham, Alabama.** Marble floors, chandeliers, and period reproduction furnishings are fitting touches in this elegant National Historic Landmark. $$$$

⭐ **Malaga Inn, Mobile, Alabama.** Two antiques-furnished town houses built by a wealthy landowner in 1862 house this romantic retreat, and the intimate restaurant in the former carriage house is an added bonus. $–$$

⭐ **Cloister Hotel, Sea Island, Georgia.** This famed resort with spacious rooms in a Spanish Mediterranean building has a superb spa and outdoor activities galore—golf, tennis, swimming, skeet shooting, sailing, biking, and fishing. $$$$

⭐ **Kehoe House, Savannah, Georgia.** Elegance, refinement, and Victorian opulence make a stay at this bed-and-breakfast inn a grand experience in every way. $$$$

⭐ **Mulberry Inn, Savannah, Georgia.** This traditional dependable lodging features a number of artistic treasures in its public rooms, including valuable Chinese vases and 18th-century oil paintings. $$$$

⭐ **Ritz-Carlton, Buckhead, Atlanta, Georgia.** The Ritz's signature 18th- and 19th-century furnishings grace this discreetly elegant gem close to Lenox Mall and Phipps Plaza shopping. $$$$

⭐ **Windsor Court Hotel, New Orleans, Louisiana.** The elegant, luxurious Windsor is built around a $7 million private collection of English art. $$$$

⭐ **Loyd Hall Plantation, Cheneyville, Louisiana.** A quiet country retreat features surprisingly upscale accommodations furnished in grand 19th-century Louisiana antiques. $$

★ **Marriott's Residence Inn, Baton Rouge, Louisiana.** All suites, affordable rates, and a great location make this one a favorite. $$

★ **Cedar Grove, Vicksburg, Mississippi.** Civil War cannonballs are still visible in the walls of this enormous 1840s mansion set near the river in Vicksburg. $$$$

★ **Millsaps-Buie House, Jackson, Mississippi.** This 1888 Queen Anne Victorian, complete with turret and columned porch, is a lovely bed-and-breakfast furnished with antiques. $$$–$$$$

★ **Fearrington House, Chapel Hill, North Carolina.** This French-style country inn was once a working farm and looks like an English country village. You'll get top-notch service in a genteel atmosphere. $$$$

★ **Grove Park Inn, Asheville, North Carolina.** The city's premier resort, Grove Park Inn has Arts and Crafts furnishings. It has been the haunt of guests like Thomas Edison and F. Scott Fitzgerald since its opening in 1913. $$$$

★ **First Colony Inn, Nags Head, North Carolina.** Four-poster beds, English antiques, and whirlpool tubs lend an air of romance to this inn by the ocean, reminiscent of the beach hotels of years past. $$$–$$$$

★ **Charleston Place, Charleston, South Carolina.** The upscale address for Charleston, this full-service hotel is conveniently located in the historic district. $$$$

★ **John Rutledge House Inn, Charleston, South Carolina.** One of the newer inns in Charleston, the elegant John Rutledge House is impeccably furnished and maintained. $$$$

★ **Kingston Plantation, Myrtle Beach, South Carolina.** This self-contained resort, loaded with facilities such as a full-service spa and a marina, has a great location on a broad beach well removed from the bustle of the pavilion area. $$$$

★ **Westin Resort, Hilton Head Island, South Carolina.** Top of the line for Hilton Head, the Westin concentrates on luxury and service. $$$$

★ **Buckhorn Inn, Gatlinburg, Tennessee.** This unassuming country inn set on 40 secluded acres has been a celebrity hideaway for decades. $$$$

★ **Opryland Hotel, Nashville, Tennessee.** Of the multitudes close to Opryland, this resort hotel is top flight. $$$$

★ **Peabody Hotel, Memphis, Tennessee.** Legendary in the Delta, this grande dame was the locale for movie scenes in *The Firm.* Observing the Peabody ducks on parade is a unique part of the experience here. $$$$

Nightlife

★ **Blind Willie's, Atlanta, Georgia.** This is one of the country's best blues venues. Only first-rate, nationally famous musicians get the nod.

★ **Dancing at Mulate's, Breaux Bridge, Louisiana.** Devote at least one night to the foot-stompin' fun at Mulate's.

★ **New Orleans funk at Tipitina's, New Orleans, Louisiana.** This music blends R&B and Afro-Caribbean rhythms to create a sound entirely unique to New Orleans. This is the music the locals prefer.

★ **Traditional jazz at Preservation Hall, New Orleans, Louisiana.** When most people think of the New Orleans sound, traditional jazz comes to mind, and there's no better showcase than Preservation Hall.

★ **The blues on Beale Street, Memphis, Tennessee.** Whether you're at B. B. King's Blues Club or the Rum Boogie, savor the atmosphere of this legendary street.

FESTIVALS AND SEASONAL EVENTS

Starting with Mardi Gras in New Orleans and ending with Christmas in Natchez, Mississippi, the Southern states hold a wide variety of festivals and special events throughout the year. Call local or state visitor information offices for further information.

WINTER

➤ DECEMBER: **Christmas** is celebrated all over the South, with events in almost every city. Highlights include Creole Christmas in the French Quarter of New Orleans and Old Salem Christmas, which re-creates a Moravian Christmas in Winston-Salem, North Carolina. Tennessee holiday events of note are Christmas in the City in Knoxville, Smoky Mountain Christmas in Gatlinburg, and Nashville's Trees of Christmas. **New Year's** events include the Peach Bowl, played in Atlanta; the Liberty Bowl, played in Memphis; and the First Night Charlotte festival, held on the Town Square in Charlotte, North Carolina.

➤ JANUARY: The year begins with two major college **football competitions,** the Senior Bowl in Mobile, Alabama, and the Sugar Bowl, played in New Orleans. In South Carolina, Orangeburg invites the country's finest coon dogs to compete in the **Grand American Coon Hunt.** Regional **runners**

race in the Savannah Marathon and Half Marathon in Savannah, Georgia, and the Charlotte Observer Marathon and Runner's Expo in Charlotte, North Carolina. **Martin Luther King Jr. Week** is celebrated in Atlanta. The **New Orleans Classical Music Festival** takes place late in the month.

➤ FEBRUARY: The big event of the month is **Mardi Gras** in New Orleans—the South's biggest parade and party; the week is also celebrated in Mobile and Gulf Shores, Alabama, and Biloxi and Natchez, Mississippi. **Black History Month** is observed throughout the South, with special events at Tuskegee University in Tuskegee, Alabama, and the W. C. Handy home in Florence, Alabama. In North Carolina, Asheville welcomes visitors to its annual **Winterfest Arts and Crafts Show.** Wilmington stages the **North Carolina Jazz Festival**. In Jackson, Mississippi, the **Dixie National Livestock Show** runs most of the month in conjunction with the **Dixie National Rodeo** and the **Dixie National Western Festival.**

SPRING

➤ MARCH: The Old South comes alive: **Antebellum mansion and garden tours** are given in Natchez, Port Gibson, Vicksburg, and Columbus, Mississippi, and in Charleston and

Beaufort, South Carolina. A **Revolutionary War battle** is reenacted on the anniversary of the Battle of Guilford Courthouse in Greensboro, North Carolina. The Grand Village of the Natchez Indians in Mississippi hosts the **Natchez Pow-Wow. Spring is celebrated** with a Cherry Blossom Festival in Macon, Georgia; the Spring Flower Show in Montgomery, Alabama; Springfest on Hilton Head Island, South Carolina; and the Great Smoky Arts and Crafts Community Spring Show in Gatlinburg, Tennessee. **St. Patrick's Day** in Savannah is one of the nation's largest celebrations of the day. In Louisiana, Ville Platte hosts the **Boggy Bayou Festival.** New Orleans celebrates its **Tennessee Williams/New Orleans Literary Festival.**

➤ APRIL: In Alabama, a **Civil War reenactment** draws thousands to Selma in late April. Eufaula, Alabama, stages its annual **Pilgrimage and Antiques Show. Spring festivals** abound, including Dogwood Festivals in Atlanta, Georgia, Fayetteville, North Carolina, and Knoxville, Tennessee. Also consider the Okefenokee Spring Fling in Waycross, Georgia; the Strawberry Festival in Ponchatoula, Louisiana; and the Spring Wildflower Pilgrimage in Gatlinburg, Tennessee. **Fish and shellfish lovers** should take note of the World Catfish Festival in Belzoni, Mississippi; the World's Biggest Fish Fry in Paris, Tennessee; and the Louisiana Crawfish Festival in St.

Bernard, Louisiana. **Music festivals** include the New Orleans Jazz and Heritage Festival and, in Wilkesboro, North Carolina, the Merle Watson Memorial Festival, featuring Doc Watson's renowned bluegrass picking.

➤ MAY: Festivals take to the air this month with the **Alabama Jubilee Hot Air Balloon Classic** in Decatur. The annual **Hang Gliding Spectacular** is in Nags Head, North Carolina. **Memphis in May** is a monthlong salute to the city that includes the world championship **Barbecue Cooking Contest. Spoleto Festival USA,** in Charleston, South Carolina, is one of the world's biggest arts festivals; **Piccolo Spoleto,** running concurrently, showcases local and regional talent. Mississippi hosts **two music festivals,** the Atwood Music Festival in Monticello and the Jimmie Rodgers Country Music Festival in Meridian. In South Carolina, Beaufort's **Gullah Festival** highlights the fine arts, customs, language, and dress of Lowcountry African-Americans.

SUMMER

➤ JUNE: June is **food month** in Louisiana, with the Okra Festival in Kenner, the Jambalaya Festival in Gonzales, the Great French Market Tomato Festival in New Orleans, the Louisiana Blueberry Festival in Mansfield, the Feliciana Peach Festival in Clinton,

and the famed Louisiana Catfish Festival in Des Allemands. Alabama hosts the **Gehart Chamber Music Festival** in Guntersville and June Jam— featuring the music group Alabama—in Fort Payne, as well as a **Seafood Festival** in Bayou la Batre, south of Mobile. Georgiana, Alabama, pays tribute to country music's legendary **Hank Williams Sr.** on the first Saturday in June. Mississippi hosts Biloxi's colorful **Black Heritage and Culture Juneteenth Celebration.** Monticello's **Pioneer Pilgrimage of Lawrence County** celebrates Southern pioneer life in Mississippi. Summer gets underway at the **Sun Fun Festival** on Myrtle Beach's Grand Strand on the South Carolina coast. The **Summer Lights Music City Festival** is held in Nashville during the first weekend in June, while the second week in June brings the **International Country Music Fan Fair.** The **Carnival Music Festival** is held in Memphis.

➤ JULY: **Independence Day** celebrations are annual traditions around the South, including in Atlanta, Savannah, and Columbus, Georgia, and in Greenville, South Carolina, which hosts **Freedom Weekend Aloft,** the second-largest balloon rally in the country. **Deep Sea Fishing Rodeos** take place at both Dauphin Island, Alabama, and Gulfport, Mississippi; the latter is one of the largest fishing contests in the South. **Cajun Bastille Day** is celebrated in Baton Rouge for three days. Both Franklinton, Louisiana, and Mize, Mississippi, host **Water-**

melon Festivals. In North Carolina, clog and figure dancing are part of the **Shindig-on-the-Green** in Asheville. The annual **Highland Games & Gathering of the Scottish Clans** is held on Grandfather Mountain near Linville, North Carolina.

➤ AUGUST: Memphis, Tennessee, is home to the biggest event this month, **Elvis International Tribute Week.** Smaller happenings around the South include the **Roscoe Turner Hot Air Balloon Race** in Corinth, Mississippi. North Carolina holds an **Apple Festival** in Hendersonville. The **Louisiana Shrimp and Petroleum Festival** is in Morgan City. August **music festivals** include a Beach Music Festival in Jekyll Island, Georgia, and the annual Mountain Dance and Folk Festival in Asheville, North Carolina. For four days in mid-August, the **Highway 127 Corridor Sale** (☎ 800/327–3945) lures shoppers along 450 mi of road, including sections in Tennessee and Alabama, to a mammoth outdoor sale and community festivals.

AUTUMN

➤ SEPTEMBER: Truly a **festival month,** September welcomes local events throughout the South. In **Alabama,** Greensboro stages the Alabama Catfish Festival and Gulf Shores hosts the annual Orange Beach Fishing Rodeo, while Tuscumbia holds Harvest Jam at the Alabama Music Hall of

Fame. In **Georgia,** Atlanta's Fine Arts and Crafts Festival is held in Piedmont Park, and the Hot Air Balloon Festival floats over Helen. In **Louisiana,** some of the best festivals are the Zydeco Music Festival in Plaisance, the Frog Festival in Rayne, Festival Acadiens in Lafayette, and the Louisiana Sugar Cane Festival in New Iberia. In **Mississippi,** Columbus has the Possum Town Pig Fest, Indianola the Indian Bayou Arts and Crafts Festival, Biloxi the Seafood Festival, and Greenville the Delta Blues Festival. The annual **Woolly Worm Festival** takes place in Banner Elk, North Carolina. Nashville hosts the **Tennessee State Fair.**

➤ OCTOBER: Autumn brings more **celebrations of food,** including Alabama's National Shrimp Festival in Gulf Shores, the National Peanut Festival in Dothan, and the Chitlin' Jamboree in Clio. The **National Pecan Festival** is held in Albany, Georgia. The **Pig Jig** in Vienna, Georgia, celebrates the glories of authentic Southern barbecue. A barbecue and parade of pigs guarantee fun at the **Lexington Barbecue Festival** in North Carolina. Allart, Tennessee, hosts the two-day **Great Pumpkin Festival,** with contests, crafts, and gospel singing. **Oktoberfest** is celebrated in Helen, Georgia, in Myrtle Beach and Walhalla, South Carolina, and in Memphis and Clarkville, Tennessee. The "Ghost Capital of the World"—Georgetown, South Carolina—stages a **Ghost Tour.** In Mississippi, the **Scottish Highland Games** are held in Biloxi. Natchez, Mississippi, stages the **Fall Pilgrimage,** highlighted by the prestigious Antiques Forum. In Canton, Mississippi, the **Canton Flea Market** features antiques and objets d'art on the Courthouse Square. During the last week of the month, Oneonta, Alabama, holds its annual **Covered Bridge Festival.**

➤ NOVEMBER: **Thanksgiving** celebrations take place all over: The Creek Indian Thanksgiving Day Homecoming and Pow-Wow is held in Poarch, Alabama, and the Richland Pumpkin Festival is held in Richland, Mississippi. **Christmas preparations** include Mistletoe Markets in Albany, Georgia, and Jackson, Mississippi, and the start of Christmas at Roseland in Shreveport, Louisiana. Autumn **food festivals** include the Taste of Montgomery in Montgomery, Alabama, and the Pecan Festivals in Theodore, Alabama, and Colfax, Louisiana. The Catfish Festival takes place in Society Hill, South Carolina, and the Chitlin' Strut in Salley, South Carolina.

2 Alabama

From the Civil War to civil rights, Alabama has experienced the upheavals in Southern society. Steeped in history, rich in culture and tradition, and possessing a wealth of natural beauty from forested mountains to lovely Gulf beaches, the Cotton State provides myriad opportunities to enjoy life in the heart of Dixie.

LABAMA IS A STATE OF SURPRISES. Visitors marvel at its physical beauty: the rocky, wooded hills and vast caves of the northeast; the expansive lakes and broad rivers of the interior; and the snow-white beaches of the Gulf Coast. The traveler who ventures off the interstates will find something unexpected at almost every turn—a cascading waterfall or showy stand of wildflowers, an archaeological excavation or colonial fort, perhaps one of Alabama's 14 covered bridges.

Updated by
Lynn Grisard
Fullman

Alabama has had its share of accomplished sons and daughters. William Christopher Handy, son of a Methodist minister descended from slaves, was born at Florence in 1873. A teacher, bandleader, and author, the Father of the Blues is best remembered for such songs as "Memphis Blues" and "St. Louis Blues." In nearby Tuscumbia, the tiny frame cottage where Helen Keller overcame the loss of hearing and sight sits as a monument to her inspirational life. Farther south, Tuskegee Institute, founded in 1881 by the distinguished black educator Booker T. Washington, was where the young botanist George Washington Carver headed the agricultural department and did his seminal work in plant derivatives and crop diversification.

History and Southern tradition are around every bend of the road, whether you follow the path of Civil War soldiers or that of civil rights marchers. Many sections of the state have preserved the elegant antebellum homes so typical of the 19th century, yet the cities have an eye on the future. At Huntsville's high-tech Space and Rocket Center, the Saturn rocket was designed. The state's largest city, Birmingham, is a major medical center. The new and progressive blend nicely with the old and historic—Montgomery's modern state government buildings stand just one block from the First White House of the Confederacy.

Pleasures and Pastimes

Beaches
Some people find it difficult to believe that a state filled with mountains also has beaches. Yet those who discover the coast will find pure white sand, a family atmosphere, outstanding seafood restaurants, amusement parks, and golf courses. In Bon Secour National Wildlife Refuge, you can hike in an undisturbed pocket of coastline. Fishing boats, which are especially abundant in Orange Beach, are available for half- or full-day charters. Whether you visit Alabama's beaches to take in the sun or to fish and hike, you won't be disappointed.

Dining
From the tons of fresh seafood served along the coast to the traditional Southern dishes and vegetables found inland, there's something for every taste in Alabama. An abundance of catfish farms throughout the state provide fresh delicacies to be served with a hearty helping of hush puppies. The state is rich in long-standing favorites such as barbecue and grits (and everyone knows who has the best barbecue in town, though opinions may vary), but you can also find sophisticated chefs working their magic at some of the best restaurants in the South.

CATEGORY	COST*
$$$$	over $35
$$$	$25–$35
$$	$10–$25
$	under $10

*per person for a three-course meal, excluding drinks, service, and 8% tax

Alabama

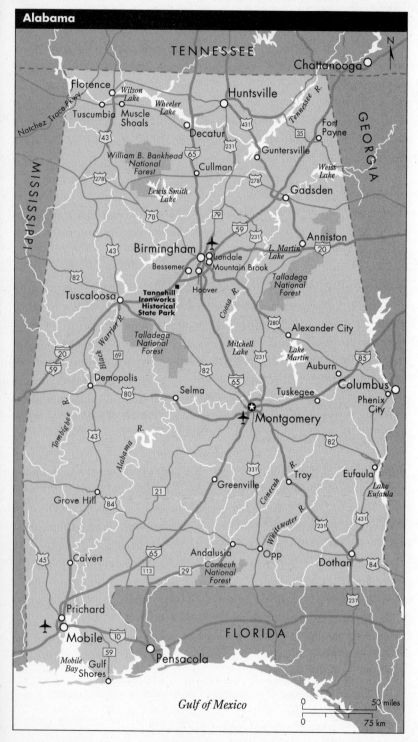

TENNESSEE

Chattanooga

Florence
Wilson Lake
Tuscumbia
Muscle Shoals
Wheeler Lake
Huntsville
Natchez Trace Pkwy.
43
Decatur
435
35
Fort Payne
231
65
Guntersville
GEORGIA
William B. Bankhead National Forest
Cullman
278
278
Weiss Lake
278
Lewis Smith Lake
Gadsden
70
79
43
59
Anniston
231
20
Birmingham
Irondale
L. Martin Lake
82
Bessemer
Mountain Brook
Talladega National Forest
Tuscaloosa
Tannehill Ironworks Historical State Park
Hoover
Coosa R.
280
Alexander City
20
Talladega National Forest
69
Mitchell Lake
231
85
Lake Martin
Auburn
59
Black Warrior R.
82
65
Demopolis
Selma
Tuskegee
Columbus
80
43
Montgomery
Phenix City
Tombigbee R.
Alabama R.
82
21
Greenville
331
Troy
Eufaula
Lake Eufaula
Grove Hill
84
Conecuh R.
231
45
Calvert
65
Andalusia
Opp
Whitewater R.
431
Dothan
113
29
Conecuh National Forest
84
231
Prichard
Mobile
10
FLORIDA
59
Mobile Bay
Gulf Shores
Pensacola

Gulf of Mexico

0   50 miles
0   75 km

N
MISSISSIPPI

Lodging

Lodging around Alabama falls into several categories. There's a growing trend toward country inns and B&Bs in many of the rural northern counties, while the cities are a pleasant blend of remodeled older hotels and modern business complexes. Along the coast, full-service resorts with their own golf courses provide a relaxing stay with a spectacular view of the Gulf of Mexico.

CATEGORY	COST*
$$$$	over $90
$$$	$70–$90
$$	$50–$70
$	under $50

*All prices are for a standard double room, excluding 4%–5% tax (depending on the county).

Spring Pilgrimage

Each spring a number of Alabama towns, among them Selma and Eufala, hold "pilgrimages"—tours of historic homes (including many private residences not otherwise open to the public), mansions, plantations, churches, gardens, and even cemeteries. Hosts and hostesses in period costume greet visitors and tell tales of life in bygone days. It's a lovely time to visit, with the gardens decked out in dogwood, azalea, and magnolia. Candlelight tours add a romantic touch.

Exploring Alabama

With the Appalachian Mountains stretching into the center of the state, Alabama has two very different types of terrain. The northern part of the state is quite mountainous, the southern part fairly flat and covered with extensive pine forests. Each, however, is filled with outdoor recreational opportunities, historic sites, and plenty of chances to sample a touch of Southern tradition and culture. The small towns and back roads of Alabama are often a throwback to earlier, less hectic times, when people knew their neighbors.

Great Itineraries

You could easily spend a month touring the state, but three to five days in each area of the state can provide a good sampling of Alabama life. If you have 10 days, you can cross from the mountains to the shore.

IF YOU HAVE 3 DAYS

You'll find historic sites mixed in with plenty of Southern culture on a short visit to Montgomery and Birmingham. In ⊞ **Montgomery,** you can stand on the steps of the State Capitol where Jefferson Davis took the oath of office as president of the Confederacy and look out at the Dexter Avenue King Memorial Baptist Church where Dr. Martin Luther King Jr. preached a hundred years later. Country music fans can trace the life of Hank Williams Sr. from his boyhood home in **Georgiana,** 60 mi south of Montgomery, to his final resting place at Montgomery's Oakwood Cemetery. Ninety minutes north via I-65 is the state's largest city, ⊞ **Birmingham.** Here you will find diverse sites including the Birmingham Civil Rights Institute, Birmingham Museum of Art, Birmingham Zoo, and the Alabama Sports Hall of Fame. Outside the city, Tannehill Ironworks Historical State Park is laced with hiking trails and steeped in Civil War history.

IF YOU HAVE 5 DAYS

You can spend two days seeing the sights of ⊞ **Birmingham,** then take a trip along the Tennessee River basin. You could begin along Alabama's portion of the Natchez Trace near the Mississippi border, then stop at ⊞ **The Shoals** (the quad-cities of Tuscumbia, Sheffield, Muscle Shoals, and Florence) to visit Helen Keller's birthplace at Ivy Green, the Alabama Music Hall of Fame, and the W. C. Handy Home. Moving eastward, plan a day at ▣ **Huntsville**'s U.S. Space and Rocket Center and Alabama Constitution Village. For your final day, venture farther eastward; stay near beautiful Lake Guntersville State Park in ▣ **Guntersville** or in peaceful ▣ **Mentone,** near the Georgia border.

IF YOU HAVE 5 DAYS

Another five-day option is to explore Alabama's **Gulf Coast,** where you'll have to resist the temptation to do more than sun yourself and sample seafood. Either Gulf Shores or Orange Beach is good for overnights on your first three days. You can have fun at Waterville, USA (a water park) or hike in Bon Secour National Wildlife Refuge. Another day's option is to explore Gulf State Park; you can fish there, too. You can charter a deep-sea fishing boat for a day, or just a sailboat. If shopping appeals, head for the Riviera Centre, just north of Foley. On your fourth day (if you're willing to leave the beach), drive 50 mi north to ▣ **Mobile,** exploring Fort Morgan en route. In Mobile, Fort Condé, the USS *Alabama,* and the Oakleigh Garden Historic District will occupy you, but save at least half a day for the spectacular Bellingrath Gardens and Home in nearby **Theodore.**

IF YOU HAVE 10 DAYS

In 10 days you can travel across Alabama from The Shoals to the seashore. Begin in the northwest in ▣ **The Shoals,** visiting the homes of Helen Keller and W. C. Handy. Spend the next day in ▣ **Decatur,** exploring the town's historic districts and Point Mallard Park or Wheeler Wildlife Refuge. On your third day, visit ▣ **Huntsville**'s U.S. Space and Rocket Center and Alabama Constitution Village. Spend day four relaxing at Lake Guntersville State Park, overnighting in ▣ **Guntersville.** The next day, wind your way south to Childersburg and DeSoto Caverns Park before heading to ▣ **Birmingham.** Spend day six exploring the city; the following morning, proceed southwest to ▣ **Tuscaloosa,** where you can visit the the Paul W. "Bear" Bryant Museum and the Warner Collection. At nearby Moundville Archaeological Park, native life has been preserved. On day eight, drive south into what was plantation country, stopping to see the old homes in **Demopolis** before proceeding to ▣ **Selma,** with its Civil War and civil rights heritage. On day nine, start early as you head for I–65 South and **Mobile.** You can tour historic Ft. Condé or the battleship USS *Alabama.* You may want to visit Bellingrath Gardens and Home in **Theodore** or drive south to the beaches of the **Gulf Coast.**

When to Tour Alabama

Although the state is a year-round haven, be advised that sometimes the summer heat and humidity can be a bit overpowering, especially for those not used to it. The summer is, however, prime time for the white-sand beaches and superb deep-sea fishing. The offshore breezes along the Gulf coast help keep you comfortable.

Spring, when the azaleas are in full bloom, is perhaps the most beautiful time of all, and late spring is perfect for the wildflowers of northern Alabama along the Tennessee River basin and atop Lookout Mountain near Mentone. Fall visitors will find almost summerlike conditions along the coast until November. It may be a little cool at night, but the warm sunny days are ideal for strolling along the sand dunes.

Winters, although not severe, do get a touch cold at times, but normally the temperatures moderate quickly. Golf is played year-round, but wintertime golfers and bird-watchers might need a sweater or jacket to ward off the chill.

BIRMINGHAM AND NORTH ALABAMA

Huntsville, The Shoals, Tuscaloosa

From the Tennessee border south to Birmingham and Tuscaloosa, you'll find rolling hills, recreational paradises, natural beauty, and history all competing for your attention.

Numbers in the margin correspond to points of interest on the Birmingham and North Alabama maps.

Birmingham

90 mi north of Montgomery.

Birmingham, set in a valley below the foothills of the Appalachians, first blossomed around the coal mines and the iron industry in the late 1800s. Its rapid growth earned it a nickname: the Magic City. Today the largest employer here is the University of Alabama at Birmingham, with a fast-growing medical center. The city was a center for civil rights activity; Dr. Martin Luther King Jr. was put in jail here for fighting racial inequality. A new city emerged after this turmoil, and in 1992 the city dedicated the Birmingham Civil Rights Institute. Today Birmingham is a glimmering, hospitable, thriving metropolis that has some appealing historic areas and a number of museums.

★ ❶ Alabama has long been noted for its excellence in sports, and the **Alabama Sports Hall of Fame Museum,** adjacent to the Civic Center, displays memorabilia of such Alabama heroes as coach Bear Bryant, Jesse Owens, Willie Mays, Billy Williams, and Hank Aaron. ⊠ *22nd St. N and Civic Center Blvd.,* ☎ *205/323–6665.* ⊠ *$5.* ⊙ *Mon.–Sat. 9–5, Sun. 1–5.*

❷ The **Birmingham Museum of Art** has one of the world's largest collections of Wedgwood, the largest collection of contemporary Chinese paintings outside the People's Republic of China, and some extraordinary examples of western American art, plus Italian Renaissance and pre-Columbian art. ⊠ *2000 8th Ave. N,* ☎ *205/254–2565.* ⊠ *Free.* ⊙ *Tues.–Sat. 10–5, Sun. noon–5.*

❸ The **16th Street Baptist Church** was the site of one of the saddest and most memorable occurrences of the civil rights movement. On the morning of September 15, 1963, a bomb exploded, killing four young black girls who were attending Sunday school in the basement. A plaque erected to their memory bears this legend: May Men Learn to Replace Bitterness and Violence with Love and Understanding. The bombing is the subject of *4 Little Girls,* Spike Lee's 1997 film. ⊠ *6th Ave. N and 16th St. N,* ☎ *205/251–9402.* ⊠ *$1 for tour.* ⊙ *Tues.–Fri. 10–4 (but it's best to call in advance), Sat. by appointment.*

★ ❹ The **Birmingham Civil Rights Institute** traces the civil rights movement from the 1920s through the present day, showing the changes from the segregated city of the past via exhibits, multimedia presentations, music, and storytelling. ⊠ *6th Ave. and 16th St. N,* ☎ *205/328–9696.* ⊠ *$3.* ⊙ *Tues.–Sat. 10–5, Sun. 1–5.*

The **Jazz Hall of Fame,** two blocks from the Civil Rights Institute, has photos and memorabilia of the state's jazz greats, including Erskine Hawkins, Cleveland Eaton, and Frank Adams. ⊠ *4th Ave. and 17th St. N,* ☎ *205/254–2720.* ⊠ *Free.* ⊙ *Tues.–Sat. 10–5, Sun. 1–5.*

❺ **Sloss Furnaces,** a National Historic Landmark, is a massive ironworks that between 1882 and 1971 produced pig iron from ore dug from the

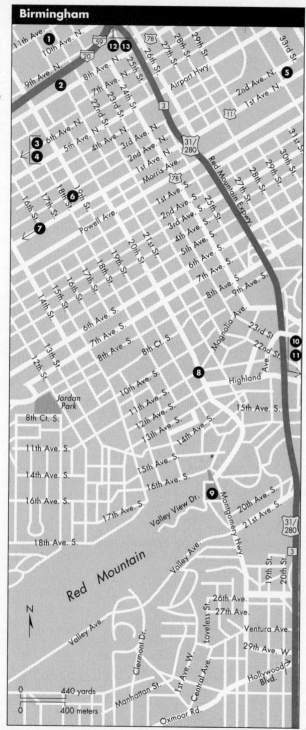

Birmingham

hills surrounding Birmingham. Retired blast-furnace workers sometimes conduct tours of the plant. At other times tours are self-guided. ⊠ *1st Ave. N and 32nd St.,* ☎ *205/324–1911.* ☎ *Free.* ☉ *Tues.–Sat. 10– 4, Sun. noon–4.*

☺ ❻ The **McWane Center,** opening spring 1998, is a hands-on science learning center with an IMAX theater for large-screen movies. It's meant for kids but adults will love it as well. ⊠ *216 19th St. N,* ☎ *205/558– 2000. Hrs and admission not set at press time.*

❼ **Arlington** is Birmingham's only remaining antebellum mansion. (The city really didn't develop until many years after the Civil War.) It was used as a headquarters by Union General James H. Wilson in March 1865, as he and his troops swept south through Alabama to Selma, destroying iron furnaces along the way. Today the classic Greek Revival structure houses Civil War memorabilia and some prime examples of 19th-century furniture. ⊠ *331 Cotton Ave. SW,* ☎ *205/ 780–5656.* ☎ *$3.* ☉ *Tues.–Sat. 10–4, Sun. 1–4.*

❽ The revitalized **Five Points South** area (⊠ Around 20th St., Magnolia Ave., and 11th Ave. S, just south of downtown) has quaint shops and a nice variety of restaurants. This historic neighborhood was originally one of Birmingham's first streetcar suburbs. Named for the landmark circle where five streets converge, Five Points South has a mix of architecture, including Spanish Baroque (as in the Highlands United Methodist Church, ⊠ 1045 20th St. S) and Art Deco.

❾ **Vulcan Park,** on top of Red Mountain, provides a panoramic view of Birmingham and a close-up encounter with the statue of Vulcan. The base of this now-rusting monument, which is the world's tallest cast-iron statue, is actually an enclosed observation deck. There's also a circular stairway inside for the hardy, or an elevator for those wishing to go up and down the easy way. Bring a picnic lunch to enjoy under the shade trees afterward. ⊠ *Valley Ave. at U.S. 31S,* ☎ *205/328–6198.* ☎ *$1.* ☉ *Daily 8 AM–10:30 PM.*

★ ❿ The wooded **Birmingham Zoo** is home to some 800 exotic and endangered animals representing 202 species from around the world. Don't miss the white rhinoceroses, elephants, gorillas, giraffes, and llamas in outdoor exhibits; reptiles, tropical birds, and snow leopards are indoors. ⊠ *2630 Cahaba Rd.,* ☎ *205/879–0409.* ☎ *$5.* ☉ *Daily 9–5, with extended summer hrs.*

⓫ Under a great glass dome at the **Botanical and Japanese Gardens,** waterfalls cascade into pools with plants of every shade of green and flowers of every color imaginable. Outside, a quiet Japanese garden has small bridges over bubbling brooks and an authentic teahouse. Wear your best walking shoes: The gardens are as extensive as they are beautiful. The gardens are adjacent to the Birmingham Zoo. ⊠ *2612 Lane Park Rd.,* ☎ *205/879–1227.* ☎ *Free.* ☉ *Daily sunrise–sunset.*

⓬ The **Southern Museum of Flight,** near the airport, has the Alabama Aviation Hall of Fame, the first Delta Airlines plane, and World War II training planes. In addition to housing artifacts, this museum specializes in painstakingly renovating old aircraft. ⊠ *4343 73rd St. N,* ☎ *205/833–8226.* ☎ *$3.* ☉ *Tues.–Sat. 9:30–4:30, Sun. 1–4:30.*

⓭ At the **Ruffner Mountain Nature Center,** cutaway sections of the mountain ridge are labeled to explain the area's geologic history. There are also well-marked nature trails, a wildflower garden, and bird observation stations. ⊠ *1214 81st St. S (about 8 mi east of downtown via 1st Ave. N exit from I–59),* ☎ *205/833–8112.* ☎ *Free.* ☉ *Tues.–Sat. 9–5, Sun. 1–5.*

OFF THE
BEATEN PATH

TANNEHILL IRONWORKS HISTORICAL STATE PARK – Built around reconstructed ironworks and blast furnaces that produced munitions for the
Confederacy, the park has a museum, crafts demonstrations, a pioneer
farm, a country store, and a train ride. There are also hiking trails, fishing opportunities, and a campground. The log-walled Furnace Master's
Restaurant specializes in home cooking, with hot, fresh biscuits a morning favorite. ✉ *Bucksville exit off I–59 (about 30 mi west of Birmingham),* ☎ *205/477–5711.* ✉ *$2.* ☉ *Daily 7 AM–sunset.*

Dining and Lodging

$$$$ ✕ **Arman's At ParkLane.** Housed in a former brick grocery store in
  ★   Birmingham's elite English Village neighborhood, Arman's has Euro-
         pean decor and an elegant but not pretentious atmosphere. Among the
         contemporary Italian foods are specialties such as wood oven–roasted
         fillet of red snapper and salmon grilled with honey and balsamic vine-
         gar. ✉ *2117 Cahaba Rd.,* ☎ *205/871–5551. Reservations essential.
         AE, DC, MC, V. Closed Sun. No lunch.*

$$$–$$$$ ✕ **Jimmy's at Brookwood.** At this space age–looking eatery, you'll find
  ★   everything from fried green tomatoes to seared Thai shrimp and mus-
         tard-crusted New York strip steak. A specialty is Baby Blue salad with
         spicy pecans, blue cheese, and honey and balsamic vinegar dressing.
         Don't miss the desserts and an outstanding Sunday brunch. ✉ *509
         Brookwood Blvd.,* ☎ *205/868–9180. AE, DC, MC, V. No dinner Sun.*

$$$ ✕ **Highlands: A Bar and Grill.** Owner-chef Frank Stitt continues to
  ★   achieve national acclaim with innovative Southern cooking influenced
         by country French cuisine. The dining room, reminiscent of a French
         bistro, has vintage posters and buttercup yellow walls. The menu
         changes daily but may include pork rillettes with foie gras and spicy
         coleslaw; braised duck with Tennessee whiskey, apples, and savoy cab-
         bage; and roast Carolina quail and pork tenderloin with creamy grits,
         blackstrap molasses, and mustard greens. ✉ *2011 11th Ave. S,* ☎ *205/
         939–1400. Reservations essential. AE, MC, V. Closed Sun.–Mon. No
         lunch.*

$$$ ✕ **Meadowlark Farms.** Owners Nick and Raphael Cairns have trans-
         formed this former farmhouse in suburban Alabaster, 20 minutes from
         downtown, into a European-style country inn. The intimate dining rooms
         gleam with fine china, silver, crystal, antiques, and fine art reproduc-
         tions. Specialties include chateaubriand, rack of lamb, duck with
         brandy fruit sauce, and stuffed red snapper. ✉ *I–65 to Exit 242, then
         south on U.S. 31 to County Rd. 66/Industrial Rd., Alabaster,* ☎ *205/
         663–3141. Reservations essential. D, MC, V. No lunch.*

$$ ✕ **Fish Market Restaurant.** All kinds of fresh fish are served here, from
         West Indies salad (with lump crabmeat) to seafood gumbo, grilled snap-
         per to blackened redfish, fried scallops to raw oysters. Chef George
         Sarris is at his best with the Greek-style fish dishes. The decor is restau-
         rant nautical: fishnets, lobster traps, and carved fish. The restaurant
         also functions as a fish market. ✉ *611 21st St. S,* ☎ *205/322–3330.
         Reservations not accepted. AE, D, MC, V. Closed Sun.*

$$ ✕ **Michael's Sirloin Room.** One of the most popular steak houses in
  ★   Birmingham doubles as a sports bar, with photos of all the local greats
         from Bear Bryant to Willie Mays on the Wall of Fame, and the televi-
         sion always tuned to the sport of the day. The specialty is a hearty cut
         of prime steer butt, usually at least two inches thick, charbroiled for
         a smoky taste. Other dishes are served, including veal, lamb, and pork
         cooked Greek style: heavy on the oregano and garlic. ✉ *431 20th St.
         S,* ☎ *205/322–0419. AE, D, DC, MC, V. Closed Sun.*

$-$$ ✕ **Nabeel's Cafe.** To dine at Nabeel's is to escape to Europe, to treat yourself to something not typically found in Birmingham. Greek-born John Krontiras, his Italian-born wife, Ottavia, and their son, Anthony, serve foods prepared with some artistry, whether it's an eggplant casserole, spinach-and-feta croissant, or spinach pie. Expect lots of Greek items at modest prices. ✉ *1706 Oxmoor Rd.,* ☎ *205/879–9292. AE, MC, V. Closed Sun.*

$-$$ ✕ **Silvertron Café.** Since 1986 owner Alan Potts has been creating
★ outstanding dishes with ingredients including chicken, pasta, black Angus beef, and orange roughy. A specialty is the chicken salad, made from baked chicken breast and topped with almonds. This casual eatery has walls covered with photos of early Birmingham, fresh flowers on the tables, and ever-efficient service. Save room for a Bailey's brownie but ask for two spoons: Only the brave can eat this one alone. ✉ *3813 Clairmont Ave.,* ☎ *205/591–3707. AE, MC, V.*

$ ✕ **Irondale Café.** This homey little restaurant was the inspiration for Fannie Flagg's Whistlestop Cafe in *Fried Green Tomatoes at the Whistlestop Cafe.* And yes, fried green tomatoes are available, as well as a dozen other fresh vegetables, at least six entrées, and an array of desserts—all served cafeteria-style. Mary Jo and Bill McMichael have redecorated the place to include one room replicating the original '30s café; a '50s- and '60s-style room; and a contemporary dining room. ✉ *1906 1st Ave. N, Irondale (7 mi east of Birmingham),* ☎ *205/956–5258. D, MC, V. Closed Sat. No dinner Sun.–Mon.*

$ ✕ **Max's.** This is the place for home-cooked foods like your mama used to make—chicken and dressing, meat loaf and mashed potatoes, and 25 kinds of pies, including banana cream. Take time to enjoy framed photos of the area and its people in early years. ✉ *2720 Pelham Pkwy.,* ☎ *205/664–0034. AE, D, MC, V. No dinner Sun.*

$$$$ 🛏 **Pickwick Hotel.** Part of the Five Points South area, the eight-story
★ Pickwick was built in 1931 as an office building and converted in 1986 to a bed-and-breakfast hotel. Rooms have been decorated art-deco style, with pink walls, green carpets, and elegant period furnishings. Suites have kitchenettes, wet bars, and dining tables. High tea is served Monday through Thursday from 3 to 5, and there's a cappuccino bar. ✉ *1023 20th St. S, 35205,* ☎ *205/933–9555 or 800/255–7304,* 🖷 *205/933–6918. 35 rooms, 28 suites. Breakfast room. AE, DC, MC, V.*

$$$$ 🛏 **Sheraton Birmingham Hotel.** This deluxe hotel, with a curved glass and concrete facade, is connected by a skywalk to the Birmingham Jefferson Civic Center. A 16-story atrium overlooks public areas. Geared to business travelers, the spacious contemporary rooms are decorated in bright colors and have such extras as irons, coffeemakers, and large desks. ✉ *2101 Civic Center Blvd., 35203,* ☎ *205/324–5000,* 🖷 *205/307–3045. 770 rooms, 51 suites. Restaurant, café, 2 lounges, indoor pool, sauna, health club, business services. AE, D, DC, MC, V.*

$$$$ 🛏 **Sheraton Perimeter Park South.** On the southern edge of Birmingham, this hotel overlooks the Colonnade shopping center with its restaurants and specialty shops. Filled with traditional furniture including armoires and sofas, guest rooms have rich maroon, blue, and green color schemes; desks, data ports, and voice mail appeal to the business traveler. ✉ *8 Perimeter Dr., 35243,* ☎ *205/967–2700 or 800/567–6647,* 🖷 *205/972–8603. 205 rooms, 2 suites. Restaurant, café, 2 lounges, pool, business services. AE, D, DC, MC, V.*

$$$$ 🛏 **The Tutwiler.** A National Historic Landmark, the Tutwiler was built
★ in 1913 as luxury apartments and converted into a hotel in 1986. The lobby is elegant, with marble floors, chandeliers, brass banisters, antiques, and lots of flowers. Rooms have period reproductions, includ-

ing armoires and high-back chairs, plus velour love seats. This one is pure class. ⊠ *Park Place at 21st St. N, 35203,* ☎ *205/322–2100 or 800/845–1787,* ℻ *205/325–1183. 96 rooms, 52 suites. Restaurant, pub. AE, D, DC, MC, V.*

$$$$ 🛏 **Wynfrey Hotel.** The posh Wynfrey rises 15 stories above the Riverchase Galleria (☞ Shopping, *below*) mall. An Italian marble floor, Chippendale furniture, an Oriental rug, fresh flowers, and a brass escalator set a formal tone in the lobby. Rooms are furnished in English and French traditional styles but don't measure up to the elegance of the lobby. The top three floors have two bi-level suites each. ⊠ *U.S. 31, 1000 Riverchase Galleria, Hoover 35244,* ☎ *205/987–1600 or 800/476–7006,* ℻ *205/988–4597. 310 rooms, 19 suites. Restaurant, café, 2 lounges, pool, health club. AE, DC, MC, V.*

$$$ 🛏 **Radisson Hotel.** This 14-story hotel is near the University Medical Center and Five Points South. The lobby has a piano lounge, crystal chandeliers, and a marble floor. Rooms are contemporary, in mauve and peach tones. ⊠ *808 20th St. S, 35205,* ☎ *205/933–9000 or 800/333–3333,* ℻ *205/933–0920. 287 rooms, 11 suites. Restaurant, lobby lounge, pool, sauna, steam room. AE, D, DC, MC, V.*

$$–$$$ 🛏 **Courtyard by Marriott.** Business travelers and families alike appreciate this appealing alternative to hotels. Rooms, done in mauve and blue tones, have pine furniture; oversize desks and irons are standard. There are also beautifully landscaped grounds and attractive public areas. ⊠ *500 Shades Creek Pkwy., 35209,* ☎ *205/879–0400 or 800/321–2211,* ℻ *205/879–6324. 126 rooms, 14 suites. Restaurant, pool, hot tub, exercise room. AE, D, DC, MC, V.*

$$ 🛏 **Holiday Inn Downtown (Historic Redmont Hotel).** The city's oldest hotel, dating from 1925, has modern conveniences as well as an Art Deco lobby and lounge that retain a sense of the past. The two-room suites, with parlors and large baths, are very popular. At press time, room renovations were planned. This downtown property is one block from the financial district and four blocks from I–59. For a fee, guests can use the YMCA nearby. ⊠ *2101 5th Ave. N, 35203,* ☎ *205/324–2101,* ℻ *205/324–0610. 112 rooms, 8 suites. Restaurant, lounge, airport shuttle. AE, D, DC, MC, V.*

$$ 🛏 **Ramada Inn Airport.** Three minutes from the airport, this 12-story hotel is a typical Ramada, except for the eye-catching winding staircase in the chandeliered lobby. ⊠ *5216 Airport Hwy., 35212,* ☎ *205/591–7900 or 800/767–2426,* ℻ *205/592–6476. 186 rooms, 7 suites. Restaurant, lounge, pool, exercise room, meeting rooms. AE, D, DC, MC, V.*

Nightlife and the Arts

For an up-to-date listing of happenings in the arts, get the current issue of *Birmingham* magazine on the newsstand. For ticket information, contact the Greater Birmingham Convention and Visitors Bureau (☎ 205/458–8000 or 800/458–8085).

NIGHTLIFE

The Comedy Club (⊠ 1818 Data Dr., ☎ 205/444–0008) showcases nationally known and up-and-coming comedians nightly except Monday. **Park Place Lounge** (⊠ Sheraton Perimeter, U.S. 280 at I–459, ☎ 205/972–8606 or 205/967–2700) spins dance tunes nightly.

Music lovers frequent the **22nd Street Jazz Café and Brewery** (⊠ 710 22nd St. S, ☎ 205/252–0407).

THE ARTS

The **State of Alabama Ballet** (☎ 205/252–2475) performs periodically at the Civic Center from September through March.

Opera Birmingham (✉ Commerce Center, Suite 1114, 2027 1st Ave. N, ☎ 205/322–6737), under the direction of Metropolitan Opera baritone Vernon Hartman, presents two or three major productions each season, September–May.

The **Birmingham Jefferson Civic Center** (✉ Between 9th and 11th Aves. N, 19th and 21st Sts., ☎ 205/458–8400)—a four-block complex with an exhibition hall, a theater, a concert hall, and the Coliseum—hosts touring Broadway companies, major rock concerts, and exhibitions. The **Terrific New Theatre** (✉ 2821 2nd Ave. S, ☎ 205/328–0868) hosts touring drama groups. **Town and Gown Theatre** (☎ 205/934–5088), a semiprofessional community theater based on the University of Alabama at Birmingham campus (but not a college theater group), puts on five musical and dramatic works from September through May. The **Birmingham Children's Theater** (☎ 205/458–8181), the nation's largest professional children's theatrical group, performs for children from September through May at the Civic Center.

Rock concerts are held at the Civic Center (☎ 205/458–8400), the Sloss Furnaces's covered amphitheater (✉ 1st Ave. N and 32nd St., ☎ 205/324–1911), and the Oak Mountain Amphitheater in Pelham (✉ U.S. 119 off I–65, ☎ 205/978–5088 or 205/985–9797). Organ shows on a "mighty Wurlitzer" accompany silent pictures at the **Alabama Theatre** (✉ 1817 3rd Ave. N, ☎ 205/252–2262).

For a month or more each spring, Birmingham celebrates the ballet, opera, painting, sculpture, literature, symphony, and other art forms at its **Festival of the Arts** (☎ 205/252–7652). Performances and exhibits are staged at various locations throughout the city, though the Civic Center is usually the hub. In June the city hosts an arts celebration, **City Stages** (☎ 205/715–6700, ext. 8200), in downtown Linn Park.

Outdoor Activities and Sports

BASEBALL

The **Birmingham Barons,** a Chicago White Sox affiliate in the Southern League, play at Hoover Metropolitan Stadium (☎ 205/988–3200) in Hoover, southeast of Birmingham on AL 150.

CANOEING

North of Birmingham in Blount County, **Morgan Outfitters** (☎ 800/788–7070) offers canoeing and white-water rafting on the Black Warrior River. South of Birmingham, beginning and intermediate canoeing can be found on the Cahaba River, especially near Montevallo; call **Limestone Park Canoe Rental** (☎ 205/926–9672) or **Bulldog Bend Canoeing Park** (☎ 205/926–7382) about rentals. **Over the Mountain Outfitters** (☎ 205/969–0766) rents canoes and, like many area outfitters, sells copies of John Foshee's excellent *Canoeing in Alabama* (University of Alabama Press).

FISHING

Excellent crappie or bass fishing can be found about 30 mi east of Birmingham at **Logan Martin Lake** (✉ Take I–20 East and look for numerous markers, ☎ 205/831–6860). There's fine fishing for crappie or bass at the lakes in **Oak Mountain State Park** in Pelham (✉ 15 mi south on I–65, Exit 246, Cahaba Valley Rd., ☎ 205/620–2520).

GOLF

In the Birmingham area, the Robert Trent Jones Golf Trail continues with **Oxmoor Valley** (✉ 100 Sun Belt Pkwy., ☎ 205/942–1177), where golfers can choose among three courses. **Oak Mountain State Park** (☎ 205/620–2522; ☞ Fishing, *above*), just south of Birmingham, is both scenic and challenging. A good local course is **Hawkins Park** (⊠ 8920 Roebuck Blvd., ☎ 205/836–7318).

HIKING AND JOGGING

Oak Mountain State Park (☞ Fishing, *above*), south of Birmingham in Pelham, is laced with trails for hiking or jogging. Joggers favor the quiet streets in and around the city's **Five Points South.**

TENNIS

Birmingham's **Park and Recreation Board** (☎ 205/254–2391) maintains a number of public courts.

Shopping

ANTIQUES

The Garage (⊠ 2304 10th Terr. S, ☎ 205/254–9018) specializes in architectural and stone items.

SHOPPING DISTRICTS AND MALLS

Mountain Brook Village (⊠ Cahaba Rd.), a small shopping area tucked away in the hollows of Birmingham's ritziest neighborhood, has a number of specialty shops, including **Pappagallo.**

Riverchase Galleria (⊠ Intersection of I–459 and U.S. 31, ☎ 205/985–3039) is one of the largest shopping malls in the Southeast. The bi-level mall has a huge food court and more than 200 stores, including **Macy's, Rich's, JCPenney, McRae's, Sears,** and **Parisian** department stores, plus such clothiers as **Banana Republic.**

Brookwood Village (⊠ 623 Brookwood Village, between U.S. 280 and U.S. 31 S, ☎ 205/871–0406) is anchored by **Rich's** and **McRae's** and has 75 specialty stores, including some with upscale merchandise. There's also a food court.

OFF THE BEATEN PATH

ONEONTA – This rural community 35 mi north of Birmingham on Route 75 has three spectacular old wooden covered bridges. They're especially picturesque when the fall foliage brings the Blount County countryside into play as a backdrop. In late October Oneonta hosts its annual Covered Bridge Festival—four days of fun, entertainment, arts and crafts, and special tours to see the bridges and colorful leaves. For information, contact the Blount County–Oneonta Chamber of Commerce (⊠ 227 2nd Ave. E, Oneonta 35121, ☎ 205/274–2153).

Cullman

50 mi north of Birmingham on I–65.

Beside an unusual collection of miniature buildings, this town in the heart of an agricultural area has the Cullman County Museum (⊠ 211 2nd Ave. N, ☎ 205/739–1258) and is near a number of parks.

 At **Ave Maria Grotto,** you'll see nearly 150 miniature churches, buildings, and shrines, painstakingly created in imitation of originals found in the United States and Europe by a Benedictine monk over the course of 50 years. Brother Joseph had never been to most of these places, but through books and pictures the monk created amazingly accurate copies of such structures as the Vatican in Rome and Notre-Dame in Paris. Only a few feet in height, these buildings were constructed from materials ranging from semiprecious stones to soup cans and building blocks. They are set in a landscaped garden. ⊠ *1600 St. Bernard Dr. SE,* ☎ *205/734–4110.* ⊡ *$4.50.* ☉ *Daily 7 AM–sunset.*

North Alabama

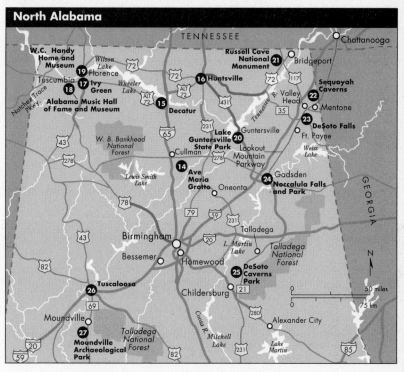

Dining

$–$$ ✕ **All Steak.** This locally owned restaurant has kept diners happy for more than 60 years. The menu includes steaks, chicken, fish, fresh vegetables, and home-cooked cakes and pies. Tasty orange rolls are their trademark. ⊠ *414 2nd Ave. SW,* ☎ *205/734–4322. No credit cards.*

Decatur

⓯ *30 mi north of Cullman on I–65 and U.S. 31, 80 mi north of Birmingham.*

Some of Decatur's appeal comes from two historic districts that hold the state's largest concentration of Victorian homes; the **Decatur Convention and Visitors Bureau** (☎ 205/350–2028) can provide information about these and about local festivals. The town is on Wheeler Lake, formed by a TVA dam downstream, and has become a center for recreation in the mountain lakes region.

The **Old Decatur Courthouse** (⊠ Corner of Ferry and Cain Sts.) was the site of the 1933 retrial of the Scottsboro Boys, nine young black men. The case won international attention and led to the Supreme Court ruling that a jury of one's peers meant that blacks could not be excluded from serving as jurors.

Point Mallard Park is a 750-acre spread with a swimming pool, wave pool, and water slide, mid-May–Labor Day, plus the South's only open-air ice rink from mid-November–mid-March, campgrounds, an 18-hole championship golf course, miniature golf, a duck pond, and a 4-mi hiking and biking trail. ⊠ *1800 Point Mallard Dr.,* ☎ *205/350–3000 or 800/669–9283.* 🔄 *$10.* ☙ *Park year-round, activities daily 10–6 (until 9 Mon., Tues., Thurs. in season).*

★ **Wheeler National Wildlife Refuge** is a haven for more than 300 species of waterfowl and other birds. You can sit in a building overlooking the lake and watch thousands of ducks and geese; special one-way glass and spotting scopes allow viewing without disturbing the birds. This is a wintering waterfowl refuge, so don't expect to see many ducks in summer. In winter, late afternoons are the best viewing time. Shaded walking trails provide a pleasant stroll through the natural beauty. The visitor center has outstanding displays. ⊠ *AL 67, 2 mi west of I–65,* ☎ *205/350–6639.* ⊠ *Free.* ☉ *Daily dawn–dusk.*

Dining and Lodging

$$–$$$ ✕ **Simp McGhee's.** Named after the riverboat captain who was a close
★   friend of Kate Lackner, a turn-of-the-century madam, this fish restaurant, one of Alabama's best, is in an early 1900s general-store building. The large pub-style bar is original, the high ceiling is pressed tin, and the old red-oak floor is stained dark. The downstairs dining room has a casual, publike atmosphere; upstairs is more formal, with white linen tablecloths and candlelight. Although steak and chicken dishes appear on the menu, most folks come for fish. The fillet gumbo is popular, but the house specialty is the pontchartrain: fresh fish of the day topped with shrimp and crabmeat, in a butter and wine sauce, all served on a bed of wild rice. ⊠ *725 Bank St.,* ☎ *205/353–6284. AE, D, DC, MC, V. Closed Sun.*

$ ✕ **Shelley's Iron Gate.** For noontime dining in turn-of-the-century Victorian atmosphere, Shelley's is the place to go in Decatur. Specializing in gigantic salad dishes, this old house-turned-restaurant provides a meal laced with character as well as outstanding flavor. ⊠ *402 Johnson St.,* ☎ *205/350–6795. AE, MC, V. No dinner Sun.–Tues.*

$$ 🛏 **Holiday Inn Hotel and Suites.** Remodeled in 1997, this five-story, concrete-stucco chain hotel has a huge indoor recreation area, the Holidome, with games, an exercise room, and a pool. Accommodations are divided into three areas: the high-rise tower, with some rooms overlooking the Tennessee River; the Holidome, whose rooms face the indoor pool; and motel-style rooms with their own entrances. All the rooms have either king-size or double beds. Two-room suites have dining room and kitchenette facilities, and two televisions. ⊠ *1106 6th Ave., 35601,* ☎ *205/355–3150 or 800/553–3150,* 🖷 *205/350–5262. 181 rooms, 24 suites. Restaurant, bar, indoor pool, outdoor pool, hot tub, exercise room, airport shuttle. AE, D, DC, MC, V.*

Huntsville

⑯ *90 mi north of Birmingham via I–65.*

The largest town in North Alabama, Huntsville is best known for the center that helped produce a rocket that took astronauts to the moon. Yet the "Rocket City" has a clutch of other attractions, including golf courses as well as historic homes and museums.

★ At the **U.S. Space and Rocket Center,** a NASA research facility, you can learn the fascinating story of space exploration and experience some of the training that real astronauts must undergo. The center offers a bus tour of the NASA labs and shuttle test sites, hands-on exhibits in the museum, an Omnimax theater with films photographed in space, and an outdoor park filled with spacecraft, including a full-size model of a space shuttle. ⊠ *1 Tranquility Base,* ☎ *205/837–3400 or 800/ 637–7223.* ⊠ *$14; includes museum, film, NASA tour.* ☉ *Memorial Day–Labor Day, daily 9–6; Labor Day–Memorial Day, daily 9–5.*

★ **Alabama Constitution Village** is the site of Alabama's Constitutional Convention of 1819. Authentic demonstrations of skills such as woodworking, printing, cooking, and weaving are performed by craftsmen in period dress. ⊠ *109 Gates Ave.,* ☎ *205/535–6565 or 800/678– 1819.* ⊠ *$6.* ☉ *Feb.–Dec., Mon.–Sat. 9–5.*

The **Historic Huntsville Depot,** built in 1860, offers a glimpse of railroad life in the mid-19th century. For an extra fee you can take a 30-minute trolley ride around town. ⊠ *320 Church St.,* ☎ *205/539–1860.* ⊠ *$6.* ☉ *Mar.–Dec., Mon.–Sat. 9–5.*

Dining and Lodging

$$ ✕ **Cafe Berlin.** Paintings and photographs of European café scenes adorn the walls, and crisp tablecloths and taped music ensure that the German theme is not forgotten. The menu is lighter than most Teutonic-style restaurants, and while schnitzel and wurst are prepared a number of ways, you can also order fish, chicken, and steak dishes, and enormous salads. The Black Forest Gâteau is a favorite dessert. ⊠ *505 Airport Rd.,* ☎ *205/880–9920. AE, D, MC, V.*

$–$$ ✕ **Greenbrier Restaurant.** This rustic eatery in Madison was built by
★ hand in 1952 by the owner, Jack Webb. Many modern conveniences have been added, but the original hand-hewn decor makes eating at the Greenbrier fun. Good catfish, barbecue, ribs, and chicken have kept it a local favorite. The chicken is served with a special white barbecue sauce. Add generous portions, tasty coleslaw, and hot hush puppies, and you'll know why people drive long distances to eat here. ⊠ *27028 Old Hwy. 20, Madison (8 mi west of Huntsville, 2 mi off I–565),* ☎ *205/351–1800. No credit cards.*

$$$ ⊞ **Huntsville Hilton.** Claiming the prize location in town, the Hilton is within walking distance of the historic district and museums, and many rooms overlook either Big Spring Park and Lake or the Von Braun Civic Center. The lobby has an upscale, classical ambience created by Oriental rugs, antique chairs and tables, and a grand piano, which provides entertainment most evenings. The spacious rooms have irons, hair dryers, and coffeemakers. ⊠ *401 Williams Ave., 35801,* ☎ *205/533– 1400 or 800/544–3197,* ᴲᴬˣ *205/534–7787. 268 rooms, 9 suites. Restaurant, bar, pool, hot tub, exercise room, comedy club. AE, D, DC, MC, V.*

Outdoor Activities and Sports

The three golf courses at **Hampton Cove** (⊠ 450 Old Hwy. 431S, Owens Cross Roads, ☎ 205/551–1818), part of the Robert Trent Jones Golf Trail, are 12 mi from Huntsville.

The Shoals

70 mi west of Huntsville.

The adjoining quad-cities of Tuscumbia, Florence, Sheffield, and Muscle Shoals are known throughout Alabama simply as The Shoals. Spreading out on both sides of the Tennessee River basin, The Shoals is an attractive area rich in culture and history. Nearby Wilson Dam, begun in 1918 as a power supply center for munitions plants in World War I, later became the cornerstone of the Tennessee Valley Authority (TVA). This government agency, created in 1933, is involved with the integrated development of the region; its dams and reservoirs have greatly affected the economics of the area, providing both business and recreational opportunities.

★ **Ivy Green** is the childhood home of Helen Keller. At the carriage house, behind the simple white frame main house, Annie Sullivan taught young Helen the meaning of language. This inspirational story, *The Miracle Worker,* is performed on the grounds Friday and Saturday nights from mid-June to mid-July. ⊠ *300 W. North Commons, Tuscumbia,* ☎ *205/383–4066.* ⊠ *$3; The Miracle Worker $5–$8.* ☉ *Mon.–Sat. 8:30–4, Sun. 1–4.*

★ ⑱ At the **Alabama Music Hall of Fame and Museum,** you can wander through the history of Alabama's musical heritage—seeing the original contracts of Elvis Presley's deal with Sun Records, the actual touring bus of the country-music band Alabama, and exhibits on the likes of Hank Williams, Lionel Richie, and Nat "King" Cole. The second weekend of September brings the annual **Harvest Jam** festival, which draws performers and fans from across the country. ⊠ *U.S. 72 W, Tuscumbia,* ☎ *205/381–4417 or 800/239–2643.* ⊠ *$6.* ☉ *Mon.–Sat. 9–5, Sun. 1–5.*

⑲ The **W. C. Handy Home and Museum** is the birthplace of the internationally acclaimed Father of the Blues. Handy (1873–1958), a mainly self-taught songwriter and band leader, was one of the first to write down the blues. The cabin has been furnished with items typical of the period when he grew up. In the museum, a treasure trove of his memorabilia has been preserved. Here you'll see his piano and famous golden trumpet, and testimonials to his genius by such contemporaries as George Gershwin and Louis Armstrong. The annual **W. C. Handy Music Festival** (☎ 205/766–7642), held during the first full week in August, draws thousands. ⊠ *620 W. College St., Florence,* ☎ *205/760–6434.* ⊠ *$2.* ☉ *Tues.–Sat. 10–4.*

Dining and Lodging

$$ ✕ **Dale's Restaurant.** Dine in comfort as red-jacketed waiters serve flame-
★ grilled steaks seasoned with Dale's famous marinade. A healthy variety of chicken and seafood dishes rounds out the menu. ⊠ *1001 Mitchell Blvd., Florence,* ☎ *205/766–4961. AE, DC, MC, V. Closed Sun. No lunch.*

$$ ✕ **Renaissance Grille.** In this casual restaurant atop the Renaissance Tower overlooking the Tennessee River basin, you can choose from fine steaks or seafood as you watch the sun set from a vantage point 350 ft above the river. ⊠ *One Hightower Pl., Florence,* ☎ *205/718–0092. AE, D, DC, MC, V.*

$–$$ ✕ **Louisiana, the Restaurant.** You'll find a large selection of specialties with influence from New Orleans's French Quarter. Seafood items, including shrimp and crawfish, may be fried, served in cream sauce, or wrapped in crepes. There are also grilled steaks and chicken. ⊠ *406 N. Montgomery Ave., Sheffield,* ☎ *205/386–0801. AE, D, DC, MC, V. Closed Sun.–Mon.*

$$ ✕▥ **Joe Wheeler State Park Lodge.** At the center of a 3,400-acre state park, this three-story fieldstone-and-redwood lodge slopes down a hill, giving every room a view of Wheeler Lake. All rooms have balconies; suites have living rooms and tiny kitchenettes. Recreational opportunities abound: Boats are available for trips on the lake; countless hiking trails lead to secluded spots and picnic areas throughout the park; and redwood walkways run from the guest rooms down to the pool area. Nearby are small, rustic log cabins, which are no-frills but comfortable. ⊠ *U.S. 72, near Rogersville (between Decatur and Florence), Drawer K, Rogersville 35652,* ☎ *205/247–5461 or 800/544–5639,* ℻ *205/247–5471. 69 rooms, 6 suites, 24 cabins. Restaurant, pool, 18-hole golf course, 4 tennis courts. AE, MC, V.*

$$ ☆ **Holiday Inn–The Shoals.** Serving both Florence and Sheffield, this motel has a courteous staff and spacious rooms that have traditional furniture, hair dryers, and computer jacks. There's live entertainment Friday and Saturday. ⊠ *4900 Hatch Blvd., Sheffield 35660,* ☎ *205/ 381–4710,* FAX *205/381–4710, ext. 403. 201 rooms, 3 suites. Restaurant, lounge, pool, hot tub, exercise room. AE, D, MC, V.*

$ ☷ **Best Western Executive Inn, Florence.** All the commercial accommodations in Florence are basic motel style, and this renovated two-story redbrick building near the center of town, built in the 1960s as a Holiday Inn, is the best of them. The Olympic-size pool is a pleasant extra. ⊠ *504 S. Court St., 35630,* ☎ *205/766–2331 or 800/248– 5336,* FAX *205/766–3567. 119 rooms, 1 suite. Restaurant, bar, pool. AE, D, DC, MC, V.*

$ ☷ **Key West Inn.** For those seeking a clean, comfortable motel at budget prices, this is the place. It's not loaded with amenities, but the comfortable atmosphere provides a pleasurable night's stay. ⊠ *1800 U.S. 72, Tuscumbia 35674,* ☎ *205/383–0700. 41 rooms. D, MC, V.*

Guntersville

40 mi southeast of Huntsville via U.S. 431.

20 The town of Guntersville, a Tennessee Valley Authority port, draws visitors because of the lake and a number of parks. **Lake Guntersville State Park** lies along the southern bank of the Tennessee River just east of Guntersville and in the shadow of Sand Mountain. The natural beauty combines with a wealth of outdoor recreational opportunities, such as golf, hiking, camping, and world-class bass fishing, to make the park one of Alabama's most popular destinations. ⊠ *7966 AL 227,* ☎ *205/ 571–5444.* ☷ *Free.*

Dining and Lodging

$$ ✕☷ **Lake Guntersville State Park Lodge.** Visitors are drawn to the lodge by its natural surroundings; the lodge itself is a fairly standard motel-type accommodation with simple furnishings. Rooms on the bluff side have balconies with great views of lake and forest. There are also lakefront two-bedroom cottages, which are as modern and plain as the lodge rooms but have a sitting room and a kitchen. The A-frame chalets have living rooms and two bedrooms. The **Chandelier Dining Room** overlooks the gigantic man-made lake and offers thick steaks, and chicken and seafood dishes. Try the seafood divan, a casserole of shrimp, crabmeat, mushrooms, and broccoli. Fried mushrooms and fried zucchini are tasty starters, and for dessert the hot fudge cake is a notch above the rest. ⊠ *1155 Lodge Dr., 35976,* ☎ *205/571–5448 or 800/ 548–4553. 94 rooms, 6 suites, 20 chalets, 15 cottages. Restaurant, coffee shop, pool, 18-hole golf course, 2 tennis courts. AE, MC, V.*

Bridgeport

65 mi east of Huntsville via U.S. 72.

21 Four miles outside Bridgeport is a cave with evidence of prehistoric settlement in the area. **Russell Cave National Monument,** an archaeological site, was occupied by the Native Americans' prehistoric ancestors 8,000 years before the arrival of European settlers. You can tour the cave shelter—the entrance to more than 7 mi of cavernous passages— and view museum exhibits of prehistoric artifacts and a Native American burial ground. There are also tool and cooking demonstrations, a slide program, a nature trail, a garden, a hiking trail, and picnic grounds. ⊠ *3729 AL 98,* ☎ *205/495–2672.* ☷ *Free.* ☼ *Daily 9–5.*

Valley Head

25 mi southeast of Bridgeport on AL 117 to AL 11, 115 mi northeast of Birmingham via I–59.

Near the Georgia state line, this small town is a pleasant hideaway.

㉒ A half-mile guided tour through the **Sequoyah Caverns** in Sand Mountain brings visitors past rock formations mirrored in lakes. In the 1930s, dances were held in the largest room, now called the Ballroom. Outside, there's a picnic area, a small zoo, hiking trails, and a campground with a swimming pool and playground. ⊠ *Rte. 1,* ☎ *205/635–0024 or 800/843–5098.* ⌨ *$7.* ☉ *Mar.–Nov., daily 8:30–5; Dec.–Feb., weekends 8:30–5. Campgrounds open year-round.*

Mentone

2 mi east of Valley Head on AL 117, 117 mi northeast of Birmingham via I–59.

Mentone, whose name means "musical valley spring," has narrow, twisting streets filled with shops, restaurants, and craft places, many in historic buildings. Bed-and-breakfasts flourish in this quiet retreat.

Dining and Lodging

$ × **Log Cabin Deli.** This early 1800s original pine-log cabin was once
★ used as a Native American fur-trading post. Dine on the open front porch, the screened back porch, or in the main dining room, with its great rock fireplace. The hand-cut cedar tables and rough wooden floors complete the rustic effect. Everything here is home-cooked, and the deli has become famous for its soups, hefty sandwiches (just try to finish the cabin roast beef special), country ham, and Southern-style vegetables. ⊠ *AL 117,* ☎ *205/634–4560. No credit cards. Closed Mon.*

$$ ⌂ **Mentone Inn.** Lookout Mountain forms the backdrop for this early 1900s country inn whose flagstone paths, lined with flowers and evergreens, lead to the entrance. A stone foundation supports screened or glassed-in porches, which have rocking chairs. The living room has pine paneling, comfortable beige furniture, a grandfather clock, and a stone fireplace. Bedrooms are furnished with 1920s pieces and multicolored matching bedspreads and curtains; most have art deco night tables. A full breakfast is included in the rate. ⊠ *AL 117, Box 290, Mentone 35984,* ☎ *205/634–4836 or 800/455–7470. 12 rooms. Outdoor hot tub. AE, MC, V.*

Fort Payne

15 mi south of Mentone via I–59, 100 mi northeast of Birmingham.

Fort Payne, known as the "sock capital of the world" because of the huge number of socks produced here, offers a pleasantly slow-paced lifestyle. It's near a lovely state park, and you can also visit the **Depot Museum** (⊠ 105 5th St. NE, ☎ 205/845–5714), with artifacts from local history, and the **Alabama Museum** (⊠ 101 Glenn Blvd. SW, ☎ 205/845–1646), dedicated to the music group Alabama.

㉓ **DeSoto Falls,** a 100-ft waterfall, is one of the loveliest attractions in the 5,000-acre **DeSoto State Resort Park.** Unsupervised swimming is allowed in DeSoto Lake, and the park has a supervised pool, picnic area, and campgrounds as well. **Little River Canyon,** one of the deepest canyons east of the Rocky Mountains, is just outside the park's boundary. The scenery is breathtaking at this 600-ft-deep and 16-mi-wide canyon. ⊠ *DeSoto State Resort Park, County Rd. 89,* ☎ *205/845–*

0051 or 800/252–7275. ✉ *Free; picnicking 50¢.* ☉ *Daily 7 AM–dusk.*

Gadsden

35 mi south of Fort Payne via I–59, 80 mi northeast of Birmingham.

At the southern end of Lookout Mountain, Gadsden has an impressive waterfall. Lookout Mountain Parkway, a scenic 100-mi drive that ends in Chattanooga, also begins here (☎ 205/549–0351 for information). In mid-May the town hosts **Riverfest** (☎ 205/547–9181 for information), a three-day, family-oriented event with good music and several blocks of food and arts and crafts. You can ride the Coosa River on the *Alabama Princess* riverboat, too.

㉔ **Noccalula Falls and Park** is a 100-acre woodland area with a 90-ft waterfall, miniature golf, train rides, a small zoo, a botanic garden, a covered bridge, and a 1776 pioneer homestead—four log cabins were moved here from the backwoods of Tennessee. There are also campgrounds and picnic areas. ✉ *1500 Noccalula Rd.,* ☎ *205/549–4663.* ✉ *Homestead and garden $1.50; train ride $1.* ☉ *Daily 9–sunset.*

Talladega

40 mi south of Gadsden on AL 21.

Talladega's attractions are diverse: You can visit a racing hall of fame, hike or drive in a national forest, or tour the town's Silk Stocking historic district. Near the Talladega Superspeedway, the **International Motorsports Hall of Fame** (✉ 3198 Speedway Blvd., ☎ 205/362–5002) has more than 100 racing vehicles and memorabilia.

Considered by many to be the state's best hiking experience, the trails of a nearby unit of the **Talladega National Forest** (☎ 205/362–2909 for district ranger) wind through the southernmost extension of the Appalachian Mountains. You'll discover hardwood trees, lakes, scenic overlooks, and mountain streams.

Outdoor Activities and Sports

The **Talladega Superspeedway** (✉ 3366 Speedway Blvd., ☎ 205/362–2261) hosts two major NASCAR races each year.

Childersburg

72 mi southwest of Gadsden via U.S. 411/231, 40 mi southeast of Birmingham via U.S. 280.

Years before frontier settlers arrived here in the early 19th century, the area was a sacred Native American capital called Coosa. The town has evolved into a lumber and farming community, but visitors know it best for its caverns.

㉕ **DeSoto Caverns Park** is the site of a 2,000-year-old Native American burial ground. These vast onyx caves were rediscovered in 1540 by Hernando DeSoto and later served as a Confederate gunpowder mining center and a Prohibition speakeasy. Curious formations of stalagmites and stalactites allow the imagination free rein. Part of your cave tour includes a sound, laser, light, and water show in the largest cave, which is more than 12 stories high. A campground and picnic grove, gemstone mining, a water-fight maze, and other activities provide plenty of diversions. ✉ *5181 DeSoto Caverns Pkwy.,* ☎ *205/378–7252 or 800/933–2283.* ✉ *$10.25; FunPac ticket (includes tour, maze, and gemstone mining) $13.75.* ☉ *Mon.–Sat. 9–5, Sun. 12:30–5.*

Tuscaloosa

26 *50 mi west of Birmingham via I–20/59.*

Thanks to the teams of the University of Alabama, this city's leading export may well be football, but its wealth of cultural offerings cannot be overlooked. History and architecture aficionados can take a tour with the **Tuscaloosa County Preservation Society**, at the Battle-Friedman House (☎ 205/758–2238 or 205/758–6138); music lovers can stop in to hear the estimable **Tuscaloosa Symphony Orchestra** (☎ 205/752–5515); and crafts collectors can enjoy October's outstanding **Kentuck Festival of the Arts** (☎ 205/758–1257) in nearby Northport, a town that has attracted many artists. Further information on the area can be obtained from the **Tuscaloosa Convention and Visitors Bureau** (✉ 1305 Greensboro Ave., ☎ 205/391–9200 or 800/538–8696), open weekdays 8–5.

The **Paul W. "Bear" Bryant Museum** follows the University of Alabama's 100-year tradition of football preeminence. The museum has many of Coach Bryant's personal belongings, as well as those of others who have laid the foundation for the University of Alabama football program. ✉ *300 Paul W. Bryant Dr.,* ☎ *205/348–4668.* 💲 *$2.* ☉ *Daily 9–4.*

★ The **Warner Collection,** displayed in two locations and comprising several hundred paintings as well as dozens of artifacts and sculptures, is quite possibly the nation's largest private collection of American painting. The Asian-style, beautifully landscaped **Gulf States Paper Corporation Headquarters** houses a range of art, including works by the Wyeths, Albert Bierstadt, Frederic Remington, Thomas Cole, and George Catlin. A short drive away is the even more impressive collection in the exquisitely furnished **Mildred Warner House,** a log cabin built in 1822 (with an 1835 brick addition). William Aiken Walker's revealing Southern folk paintings, which depict 19th-century African-American life, are enough to make a visit worthwhile. There are works by such painters as Mary Cassatt, Winslow Homer, John Singer Sargent, Childe Hassam, Georgia O'Keeffe, and James A. M. Whistler. *Gulf States Paper Corporation:* ✉ *1400 River Rd. NE,* ☎ *205/553–6200.* 💲 *Free.* ☉ *Sat. 10–5, Sun. 1–5; tours weekdays at 5:30 and 6:30. Mildred Warner House:* ✉ *1925 8th St.,* ☎ *205/345–4062.* 💲 *Free.* ☉ *Tours on the hr Sat. 10–5, Sun. 1–5.*

Dining

$$ ✕ **The Globe.** Ten minutes from downtown Tuscaloosa, across the Black Warrior River, you'll find the town of Northport and the big barnlike structure that once housed a dry goods store. Two actors have turned it into an adventurous dining establishment. Named after Shakespeare's first theater, the restaurant has a long English tavern–style bar in one of the two dining rooms; giant line drawings of scenes from Shakespeare's plays adorn the walls. But the international menu is the true star, including such entrées as pan-sautéed orange roughy, vegetarian quesadillas, Thai emerald curry, and broiled tilapia. The only thing that's typically Southern is the friendly service. ✉ *430 Main Ave., Northport,* ☎ *205/391–0949. Reservations not accepted. AE, D, MC, V.*

Moundville

14 mi south of Tuscaloosa on U.S. 69.

27 Near Moundville is a site that illuminates the lives of the area's prehistoric residents. **Moundville Archaeological Park** contains a number of artifacts found nearby that can be traced to the prehistoric forefathers of local Seminole, Creek, and Cherokee Native Americans. On the grounds are 20 earthen temple mounds (the largest of which supports a reconstructed Native American temple), an archaeological museum, a reconstructed native village, a nature trail leading to the Black Warrior River, picnic areas, and a campground. ⊠ *AL 69S,* ☎ *205/371–2572.* 🖭 *$4.* ⊙ *Museum daily 9–5, park daily 8–8.*

Birmingham and North Alabama A to Z

Arriving and Departing

BY BUS

Birmingham's **Greyhound Lines** (☎ 800/231–2222) terminal is on 17th Avenue North and Park Place. Greyhound also serves Huntsville, Decatur, and Florence.

BY CAR

I–59 goes northeast from Birmingham to Chattanooga, southwest to Tuscaloosa, and on into Mississippi. I–20 runs east to Anniston and Atlanta. I–65 goes north to Decatur and Nashville and south to Montgomery and Mobile. U.S. 72 and Alt. U.S. 72 run east–west across the northern part of the state and connect Florence, Tuscumbia, Decatur, and Huntsville.

BY PLANE

Birmingham International Airport (☎ 205/595–0533) is less than 3 mi from central downtown and is served by American, ComAir, Continental, Delta/Swissair, Northwest/KLM, Southwest, TW Express, United, US Airways/British Airways, and US Airways Express. Taxis are readily available; the fare to most hotels is about $10 for one passenger, $5 for each additional passenger. Many hotels provide limousine service from the airport by prior arrangement. If you're traveling by car, follow the clearly marked signs downtown.

Huntsville International Airport (☎ 205/772–9395), at Exit 7 off I–565, is served by American, Delta, Northwest, and US Airways. **Muscle Shoals Airport** (☎ 205/381–2869) is served by Northwest.

BY TRAIN

The only **Amtrak** station (☎ 205/324–3033 or 800/872–7245) in North and Central Alabama is on Morris Avenue, in downtown Birmingham. Trains run daily.

Getting Around

A car is a necessity in this region, where sights, accommodations, and restaurants are spread throughout the cities and towns.

BY BUS

The **Metro Area Express** (MAX) (☎ 205/521–0101) serves Birmingham. Buses require exact change—$1 fare, 25¢ transfer—and only run weekdays, typically 6–6.

BY TAXI

Birmingham's **Yellow Cab** (☎ 205/252–1131) charges $2.95 for the first mile, $1.20 for each additional mile.

Contacts and Resources

EMERGENCIES

Ambulance (☎ 911). **Police** (☎ 911). **University Hospital** (⊠ 1900 5th Ave. S, ☎ 205/934–5105) has the all-night emergency room closest to downtown Birmingham.

GUIDED TOURS

The **Greater Birmingham Convention and Visitors Bureau** (☞ Visitor Information, *below*) has free brochures for self-guided tours of the downtown and Five Points South areas.

PHARMACY

Revco (✉ 48 Green Springs Hwy. in Red Mountain Plaza, ☎ 205/942–1629) is open 24 hours.

RADIO STATIONS

AM: WERC 960, talk; WDJC 1260, Christian. **FM:** WBHM 90.3, public; WVSU 91.1, jazz; WZRR 99.5, classic rock; WHMA 100.5, country; WZZK 104.7, country; WODL 106.9, oldies.

VISITOR INFORMATION

Greater Birmingham Convention and Visitors Bureau (✉ 2200 9th Ave. N, 35203, ☎ 205/458–8000 or 800/458–8085). **Cullman Area Chamber of Commerce** (✉ 211 2nd Ave. NE, 35055, ☎ 205/734–0454). **Decatur Convention and Visitors Bureau** (✉ 719 6th Ave. SE, 35602, ☎ 205/350–2028 or 800/524–6181). **Huntsville/Madison County Convention and Visitors Bureau** (✉ 700 Monroe St., Huntsville 35801, ☎ 205/533–5273 or 800/772–2348). **Tuscaloosa Convention and Visitors Bureau** (✉ 1305 Greensboro Ave., 35401, ☎ 205/391–9200 or 800/538–8696).

MONTGOMERY AND CENTRAL ALABAMA

Selma, Demopolis, Tuskegee

The flatlands of Alabama's central section provide the stage for the story of the Civil War, the civil rights movement, and life on Southern plantations of another century. Montgomery is a good base for exploring the Old South plantations, historic sites, and big fishing lakes of this region.

Numbers in the margin correspond to points of interest on the Downtown Montgomery and Central and South Alabama maps.

Montgomery

From the days when the Civil War was the national preoccupation to another era when civil rights dominated the headlines, Montgomery has been in the forefront of Southern life. As you stand on the spot where Jefferson Davis took the oath of office as president of the Confederacy, you can gaze upon the Dexter Avenue King Memorial Baptist Church where Dr. Martin Luther King Jr. preached his message of freedom. A century apart in time and worlds apart in symbolism, the two landmarks are a mere block apart geographically.

Today Montgomery is the epitome of a progressive Southern business city. New hotels and restaurants spring up frequently, along with skyscraper office complexes. Still, many historic homes and buildings remain. Alabama's capital city is rich in its past and strives to become richer in its future.

★ ㉘ The **State Capitol** was built in 1851 and briefly (for a few months in 1861) served as the first capitol for the Confederate States of America. On the front portico, a bronze star marks the spot where Jefferson Davis stood to take the oath of office as president of the Confederacy. There is an amazing piece of interior design: The stairway curling up the sides of the circular hallway is freestanding, without visible support. The state's rich history has been caught by an artist's brush in great, colorful murals. In the large House chamber and smaller Senate chamber, there are gigantic brick fireplaces. ✉ *600 Dexter Ave., at Bainbridge St.,* ☎ *334/242–3935.* ☉ *Mon.–Sat. 9–4.*

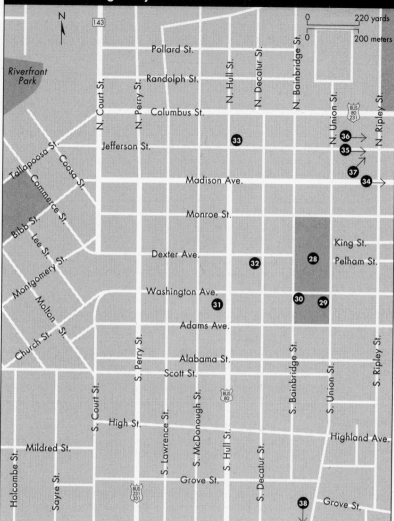

Downtown Montgomery

㉙ Built in 1840, the **First White House of the Confederacy** was occupied by Jefferson Davis and his family while the Confederacy was being organized. Today it contains many of their possessions, plus other artifacts of the Civil War period. The house is across the street from the State Capitol. ✉ *644 Washington Ave.,* ☎ *334/242–1861.* ☞ *Free.* ⊙ *Tours weekdays 8–4:30, weekends 9–4.*

㉚ The **Alabama Department of Archives and History** houses the first state-funded archives in the United States as well as galleries with artifacts documenting the state's past, with an emphasis on 19th-century Alabama. ✉ *624 Washington Ave.,* ☎ *334/242–4363.* ☞ *Free.* ⊙ *Weekdays 8–5, Sat. 9–5. Reference room closed Tues.*

★ **㉛** On the grounds of the Southern Poverty Law Center, the **Civil Rights Memorial** has water flowing over a table that bears the names of about 40 people who gave their lives for racial equality. On a wall behind this, over which water also flows, is a biblical quote used in a speech by Dr. Martin Luther King Jr.: "Until justice rolls down like waters and righteousness like a mighty stream." The sculptor, Maya Lin, created the Vietnam Veterans Memorial in Washington, D.C. ✉ *400 Washington Ave.* ☞ *Free.* ⊙ *24 hrs.*

㉜ The **Dexter Avenue King Memorial Baptist Church** is where Dr. Martin Luther King Jr. began his career as a minister in 1955. From the church he directed the Montgomery bus boycott, which began after Rosa Parks was arrested for refusing to give up her seat to white people. The church's sanctuary and the basement Sunday-school rooms are open to visitors. A mural covering one basement wall depicts people and events associated with Dr. King and the civil rights movement. ✉ *454 Dexter Ave.,* ☎ *334/263–3970.* ☞ *Free.* ⊙ *Tours Mon.–Thurs. at 10 and 2, Fri. at 10.*

㉝ **Old Alabama Town,** about six blocks northwest of the capitol between Madison Avenue and Columbus Street, consists of 40 newly restored houses, barns, stores, and other structures from between 1818 and the turn of the century. The **Loeb Reception Center** has a self-guided cassette walking tour that covers the 10 house museums clustered in the "Living Block." Volunteers give tours of the **Ordeman-Shaw House** (✉ 230 N. Hull St), an Italianate town house with restored outbuildings and gardens. The "Working Block," just off Columbus Street on the district's north side, includes a gristmill, blacksmith shop, the **Cotton Gin and Cotton Museum,** the **Haigler Plantation Office,** and the **Rose-Morris Craft Center.** ✉ *Loeb Reception Center, 301 Columbus St.,* ☎ *334/240–4500.* ☞ *Cassette tour $7.* ⊙ *Mon.–Sat. 9–3, Sun. 1–3.*

㉞ Alabama's oldest fine arts museum, the **Montgomery Museum of Fine Arts** has an impressive facility within the same park that houses the Alabama Shakespeare Festival Theatre. Highlights are works by Southern artists; ARTWORKS, a hands-on gallery for children and adults; a permanent gallery exhibiting the Blount, Inc. Corporate Collection of American Art; and a gift shop, auditorium, and print gallery, as well as galleries for changing exhibitions. You can dine in the Terrace Cafe. ✉ *1 Museum Dr.,* ☎ *334/244–5700.* ☞ *Free.* ⊙ *Tues.–Wed. and Fri.–Sat. 10–5, Thurs. 10–9, Sun. noon–5.*

㉟ The 40-acre **Montgomery Zoo** is home to 800 animals from five continents. Dining, a gift shop, and a train ride are offered as well. Extensive renovations enable visitors to view the animals in what appear to be their natural habitats. Don't miss the bald eagles, black bears, and monkey island. ✉ *2301 Coliseum Pkwy.,* ☎ *334/240–4900.* ☞ *$4.50.* ⊙ *Daily 9–5.*

36 The **Hank Williams Memorial** tombstone marks the burial place of one of Alabama's own, country-music singer and songwriter Hank Williams; after his untimely death at age 29 on New Year's Day 1953, he was brought here for one of the city's grandest funerals. It was held at City Hall, with top country stars delivering eulogies and singing sad songs. The memorial depicts him, along with sheet music from his most popular songs, including "Your Cheatin' Heart." ⊠ *Oakwood Cemetery Annex, 1305 Upper Wetumpka Rd.,* ☎ *334/264–4938.*

37 **Jasmine Hill Gardens and Outdoor Museum,** atop a wooded hill, are 17 acres of beautiful gardens with replicas of Greek sculptures and of the ruins of the Temple of Hera. The visitor center is an exact replica of the original temple facade as it once stood intact on Mount Olympus. ⊠ *3001 Jasmine Hill Rd.,* ☎ *334/567–6463 or 334/263–1440.* ⊡ *$5.* ⊙ *Mar.–Nov., Tues.–Sun. 9–5.*

38 The **F. Scott and Zelda Fitzgerald Museum** displays belongings of this colorful couple in their former home. Zelda Fitzgerald grew up in the area, and some of her artwork hangs at Montgomery's Museum of Fine Arts. Her husband, F. Scott, is famous for *The Great Gatsby, Tender is the Night,* and numerous short stories. A 25-minute video on their life in Montgomery is shown. ⊠ *919 Felder Ave.,* ☎ *334/264–4222.* ⊡ *Free.* ⊙ *Wed.–Fri. 10–2, weekends 1–5, and by appointment.*

Dining and Lodging

$$$ ✕ **Vintage Year.** Chef Judy Martin's menu features snapper, tuna, shrimp, salmon, and other fish prepared in the style of the new American cuisine, with all ingredients as fresh as possible, including an assortment of fresh herbs. Lamb shank and duck are also popular items. The decor is elegant, and the neighborhood bar is a favorite meeting place. ⊠ *405 Cloverdale Rd.,* ☎ *334/264–8463. Reservations essential. AE, DC, MC, V. Closed Sun.–Mon. No lunch.*

$$ ✕ **Jubilee Seafood Company.** In a very pleasant small café, Bud Skinner cooks some of the finest and freshest seafood dishes in town, including snapper prepared in a variety of ways (including Greek-style—sautéed in olive oil and spices and topped with roasted almonds), soft-shell crabs, crab claws, and other delicacies. For a real treat, try the barbecued shrimp, which are marinated in a secret red sauce, wrapped in bacon, and charbroiled. Bud also has a tasty West Indies salad with marinated crab. ⊠ *1057 Woodley Rd., Cloverdale Plaza,* ☎ *334/262–6224. Reservations not accepted. AE, DC, MC, V. Closed Sun.–Mon. No lunch.*

$$ ✕ **Sahara Restaurant.** Joe and Mike Deep's Sahara, in Cloverdale, is one of Montgomery's traditional Southern restaurants. Linen tablecloths and uniformed servers add to the charm. Fresh snapper, grouper, and scampi are broiled to taste, and succulent steaks are grilled over coals. The seafood gumbo is a specialty. ⊠ *511 E. Edgemont Ave.,* ☎ *334/ 262–1215. AE, D, DC, MC, V. Closed Sun.*

$$ ✕ **Wesley's in Old Cloverdale.** This is one of Montgomery's many popular restaurant and nightspot combinations. Start with a plate piled high with spicy nachos, then enjoy an Italian, seafood, or Cajun entrée. On the lighter side, try a specialty pizza or calzone baked in a wood-burning oven. There's a popular champagne brunch on Sunday. Entertainment begins about 9 Wednesday through Saturday nights. ⊠ *1061 Woodley Rd.,* ☎ *334/834–2500. Reservations essential weekends. AE, DC, MC, V.*

$ ✕ **Chris' Hot Dog Stand.** A Montgomery tradition for over 75 years, ★ this eatery has booths and an old-fashioned lunch counter with stools. Mr. Chris's famous sauce combines chili peppers, onions, and a variety of herbs that give his hot dogs a one-of-a-kind flavor. For a treat, try the hot dog with "kitchen chili," a heavy, hot chili of beans and onions that you eat with a knife and fork. ✉ *138 Dexter Ave.,* ☏ *334/ 265–6850. Reservations not accepted. No credit cards. Closed Sun.*

$ ✕ **Corsino's.** Serving Montgomery since 1954, family-run Corsino's is
★ one of the city's most popular restaurants. The noontime crowd gathers daily from state government offices and downtown businesses to enjoy some of the South's finest pasta dishes. You can also choose a savory, foot-long Italian sandwich served on hot, homemade Italian bread, or a hand-tossed New York–style pizza. The restaurant isn't fancy, just comfortable and friendly. ✉ *911 S. Court St.,* ☏ *334/263– 9752. Reservations not accepted. No credit cards. Closed weekends.*

$ ✕ **Country's Barbecue.** Outstanding barbecue is the trademark of Country's; you can watch the smoke and smell the pork that's cooking ever so slowly as you drive past. A good assortment of chicken and side dishes are also available. ✉ *2740 E. South Blvd.,* ☏ *334/284– 1411. Reservations not accepted. AE, MC, V.*

$ ✕ **Farmer's Market Cafeteria.** In a downtown industrial-style metal building, the cafeteria is about as plain as restaurants get, except for the photos on the walls reminding diners of past sports heroes. Fried chicken, catfish, country-style smothered steak, and fresh vegetables are served. The hearty breakfast with smoked bacon and homemade biscuits is a local tradition. ✉ *315 N. McDonough St.,* ☏ *334/262–9163. Reservations not accepted. No credit cards. Closed weekends. No dinner.*

$ ✕ **Martin's Restaurant.** Martin's is plain but comfortable. Here you'll find generous helpings of home-cooked fresh vegetables, Southern fried chicken, and delicious panfried catfish fresh from Alabama ponds. The corn-bread muffins literally melt in your mouth. ✉ *1796 Carter Hill Rd.,* ☏ *334/265–1767. No credit cards. Closed Sat.*

$ ✕ **Sassafras Tearoom.** You can buy the table you eat off and enjoy a
★ superb meal in the Victorian atmosphere of this century-old shop-cum-eatery in the Cottage Hill district. Operated by retired colonel Jim Wallace and his wife, Mary, the restaurant draws professionals and antiques hunters alike. Sassafras tea, either hot or cold, accompanies crunchy chicken salad, buttermilk pie, and other home-cooked delectables. ✉ *532 Clay St.,* ☏ *334/265–7277. AE, D, DC, MC, V.*

$$$$ ▥ **Embassy Suites Hotel.** This downtown all-suite high-rise hotel be-
★ tween the Civic Center and the old railroad station epitomizes Montgomery's new image. A spectacular atrium lobby makes you think you're walking through a tropical rain forest. Glass elevators give you a bird's-eye view. Included are a full cooked-to-order breakfast and a two-hour manager's reception each evening. ✉ *300 Tallapoosa St., 36104,* ☏ *334/269–5055,* FAX *334/269–0360. 237 suites. Restaurant, lounge, indoor pool, hot tub, exercise room, sauna, steam room, business services, meeting rooms. AE, D, DC, MC, V.*

$$$–$$$$ ▥ **Holiday Inn Hotel and Suites Historic Downtown.** Extensive renovations have given the former Madison Hotel a whole new look. In keeping with the New Orleans theme, wrought iron is abundant throughout the lobby. Elvis Presley once slept here, but you're more likely to run into legislators and businesspeople than rock stars. The Civic Center is two blocks away. ✉ *120 Madison Ave., 36104,* ☏ *334/ 264–2231,* FAX *334/263–3179. 153 rooms, 19 suites. 2 restaurants, 2 lounges, pool, meeting rooms. AE, D, DC, MC, V.*

$$$–$$$$ ▥ **Marriott Courtyard.** This handsome, contemporary low-rise motor inn with a sunny gardenlike courtyard offers amenities popular with business travelers—spacious rooms, king-size beds, oversize work desks, excellent lighting, and hot water dispensers for in-room coffee. ✉ *5555 Carmichael Rd., near I–85 Exit 6, 36117,* ☏ *334/272–5533,*

FAX *334/279–0853. 134 rooms, 12 suites. Restaurant, lounge, pool, hot tub, exercise room, meeting rooms. AE, D, DC, MC, V.*

$$ 🖭 **La Quinta Motor Inn.** The lobby of this chain property is decorated in muted tones, with a terra-cotta-tiled floor and silk flowers. Rooms are contemporary, in light earth tones. ⊠ *1280 Eastern Bypass, 36117-2231,* ☎ *334/271–1620,* FAX *334/244–7919. 130 rooms. Pool. AE, D, DC, MC, V.*

$$ 🖭 **Red Bluff Cottage.** In the heart of downtown and overlooking the
★ Alabama River, this cottage is bright and cheerful. Rooms are filled with antiques, some of them dating to the 18th century, collected by the Reverend Mark Waldo, who served an Episcopal parish in this city for many years, and his wife, Anne. The music room/library contains a harpsichord, a piano, and lots of books. Full breakfast is served. ⊠ *551 Clay St., Box 1026, 36101,* ☎ *334/264–0056,* FAX *334/263–3054. 4 rooms. Library. AE, D, MC, V.*

$–$$ 🖭 **Best Western–Montgomery Lodge.** This two-story hotel 3 mi from the airport has a lobby bookcase stocked for guests' use. Rooms have been redecorated in royal blue or cranberry; most have recliners, and three have king-size water beds. All have coffeemakers. ⊠ *977 W. South Blvd., 36105,* ☎ *334/288–5740 or 800/528–1234,* FAX *334/286–0042. 100 rooms, 1 suite. Restaurant, lounge, pool, meeting rooms. AE, D, DC, MC, V.*

Nightlife and the Arts

NIGHTLIFE

Crockmier's Restaurant (⊠ 5620 Calmar Dr., ☎ 334/277–1840) offers live music Wednesday, Friday, Saturday, and Sunday. **Wesley's in Old Cloverdale** (☞ Dining and Lodging, *above*) offers a variety of live music from blues to acoustic acts Wednesday through Saturday nights.

THE ARTS

The **Montgomery Symphony Orchestra** (☎ 334/240–4004) performs at the **Davis Theatre for the Performing Arts** (⊠ 251 Montgomery St., ☎ 334/241–9567). Other arts-related events are held at the 1,200-plus-seat auditorium as well.

Shakespearean plays, modern drama, and musicals are performed on two stages at the **Alabama Shakespeare Festival Theatre** (⊠ Wynton Blount Cultural Park, 1 Festival Dr., ☎ 334/271–5353 or 880/841–4273) on the east side of Montgomery. Drama authorities have called it the finest facility of its kind in the world. The season runs from October through August; tickets cost $15–$25.

Traveling theater groups play at the large auditorium at Montgomery's **Civic Center** (⊠ 300 Bibb St., ☎ 334/241–2100). At the campus theater of **Auburn University at Montgomery** (⊠ 7300 University Dr., ☎ 334/244–3632), student actors perform drama and comedy.

Outdoor Activities and Sports

DOG RACING

Greyhound races are held at **Victoryland,** about 20 mi east of Montgomery, just off I–85N in Shorter (☎ 334/269–6087 or 800/688–2946). There's racing and pari-mutuel betting every night but Sunday, and several matinees during the week. No one under 19 is admitted.

GOLF

Montgomery is home to **Lagoon Park** (⊠ 2855 Lagoon Park Dr., ☎ 334/271–7000), a very flat course with plenty of water hazards and trees, consistently rated by *Golf Digest* as one of the top 50 public courses in the United States. **River Run** (⊠ AL 5, ☎ 334/271–2811) has a pro shop and putting greens. **Kolomi** (⊠ 800 Dozier Rd., Mt. Meigs, ☎ 334/279–6686) is adjacent to the Tallaposa River.

MINIATURE GOLF

Mountasia Fantasy Golf (⊠ 5761 Atlanta Hwy., ☎ 334/277–4653) takes golfers on a safari through and around a man-made mountain, complete with large model elephants and other animals, and a cave.

TENNIS

Montgomery's **Lagoon Park** (⊠ 2855 Lagoon Park Dr., ☎ 334/271–7001) has 17 lighted courts and is open daily.

Shopping

ANTIQUES

Herron House (⊠ 422 Herron St., ☎ 334/265–2063) has Montgomery's largest stock of porcelain, glass, and silver, plus 18th- and 19th-century furniture. **Bodiford's Antique Mall** (⊠ 919 Hampton St., ☎ 334/265–4220) is a collection of 16 small stores gathered under one big roof.

MALLS

In addition to its anchor stores—**Sears, Parisian, McRae's,** and **Gayfer's**—**Eastdale Mall** (⊠ On the Eastern Bypass and Atlanta Hwy., ☎ 334/277–7359) has a variety of specialty stores, record and book stores, restaurants, eight movie theaters, and an ice-skating rink. **Montgomery Mall** (⊠ 2925–A Montgomery Mall at South Blvd. and McGehee Ave., ☎ 334/281–0242) is anchored by **JCPenney, Parisian,** and **Gayfer's** and has a food court.

Selma

39 *45 mi west of Montgomery via U.S. 80.*

Selma has played major roles in both Civil War and civil rights history. With the Confederacy's second-largest arson and foundry, Selma was a target of Union attack in 1865. Almost 100 years after that fighting—which was Alabama's only major inland Civil War battle—Selma came again to the forefront on March 21, 1965, as the stage of "Bloody Sunday." Dr. Martin Luther King Jr. led a group of civil rights demonstrators on a 50-mi march from downtown Selma's Edmund Pettus Bridge to Montgomery. The journey resulted ultimately in the passing of the nation's Voting Rights Act. The path of that walk is one of six All-American Roads in the nation.

Controversy may have sealed Selma's place in history, but the town has a wealth of sites worth visiting. These include **Old Town,** the largest historic district in the state with more than 1,200 buildings, including the Greek Revival Sturdivant Hall, and **Martin Luther King Jr. Street,** a historic walking tour; the Chamber of Commerce (☎ 334/875–7241) has tapes for self-guided tours of these. The **National Voting Rights Museum and Institute** (⊠ 1012 Water St., ☎ 334/418–0800) offers a record of the important role of voting rights in the civil rights struggle.

Each year in late March, a **Historic Selma Pilgrimage** (☎ 800/457–3562) takes visitors through several antebellum homes. In late April one of the largest annual **Civil War reenactments** (☎ 334/875–7241 or 800/457–3562) in the nation draws thousands to the site of the Battle of Selma, on the Alabama River. Year-round you can stop by the **Visitor Information Center** for advice on what to see in the area. ⊠ 2207 *Broad St.,* ☎ 334/875–7485. ☉ *Daily 8–8.*

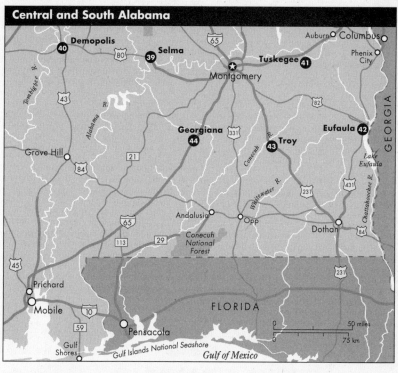

Central and South Alabama

Demopolis

40 *40 mi west of Selma via U.S. 80.*

Demopolis takes great pride in its rich Southern heritage. Take time to ride past antebellum homes and 18th-century buildings in the historic downtown area. The 10,000-acre **Demopolis Lake** offers fishing, boating, swimming, picnicking, and campgrounds. For details, contact the **Demopolis Area Chamber of Commerce** (⊠ 102 E. Washington St., ☎ 334/289–0270), open weekdays 8:30–5, or the **Information Center** (☎ 334/289–5772) at the Best Western Hotel on U.S. 80, open evenings and weekends.

Gaineswood, built between 1843 and 1861, has been called one of the finest Greek Revival mansions in the South. The house has been extensively restored, down to reproductions of the original French wallpapers. It contains the original furnishings, such as carved four-posters and a flutina—a one-of-a-kind musical instrument invented by the original owner (who also designed Gaineswood itself). Interior architectural elements include elaborate columns and pilasters; friezes and medallions of wood, plaster, cast iron, and leather; and ceiling-dome skylights. ⊠ 805 Whitfield St. E, ☎ 334/289–4846. ⊡ $5. ☉ Mon.–Sat. 9–5, Sun. 1–5.

Bluff Hall was built in 1832 as a Federal-style house and remodeled in the Greek Revival style several years later. It stands on a chalky cliff above the Tombigbee River and features a columned front portico, a huge double parlor with Corinthian columns, and Empire and Victorian furnishings donated by friends and descendants of the original owner. Also on display is a collection of period clothing. ⊠ 405 N. Commissioners Ave., ☎ 334/289–1666. ⊡ $5. ☉ Jan.–Feb., Tues.–Sat. 10–4, Sun. 2–4; Mar.–Dec., Tues.–Sat. 10–5, Sun. 2–5.

Tuskegee

❹❶ *35 mi east of Montgomery via U.S. 80.*

In addition to being the home of the historic Tuskegee Institute, Tuskegee has some antebellum houses and is near Tuskegee National Forest (☎ 334/727–2652), with fishing and hiking opportunities.

The **Tuskegee Institute National Historic Site** includes the school founded by educator Booker T. Washington in 1881, one of America's first black universities; the institute's Victorian buildings, many designed and constructed by students; a replica of the childhood home of Booker T. Washington; and his actual redbrick Victorian home, **The Oaks.** The **George Washington Carver Museum** on the campus includes Carver's original laboratory and a historical study of the Tuskegee Institute. An agricultural chemist, Carver helped improve agricultural practices and also discovered hundreds of uses for the peanut, sweet potato, and soybean. A walking tour of the Historic Campus district originates at the Carver Museum. ✉ *U.S. 29S,* ☎ *334/727–3200.* ☞ *Free.* ☉ *Daily 9–5.*

Eufaula

❹❷ *90 mi east of Montgomery on U.S. 82.*

Eufaula is a town rich in Southern tradition and antebellum homes; it's also near a national wildlife refuge and has great fishing opportunities. Some homes built between 1834 and 1911 hold open house during the **Eufaula Spring Pilgrimage** (☎ 334/687–3793) in early April.

Open year-round, the **Shorter Mansion,** a white-columned house museum built in 1884, is a fine example of neoclassical architecture and a showplace of the Seth Lore National Historic District. ✉ *340 N. Eufaula Ave.,* ☎ *334/687–3793.* ☞ *$3.* ☉ *Mon.–Sat. 9–4, Sun. 1–4.*

Fendall Hall, one of the great 19th century Italianate-style houses surviving in Alabama, has deep overhanging eaves, a hip roof topped with a cupola, and a long, wraparound porch. ✉ *917 W. Barbour St.,* ☎ *334/687–8469.* ☞ *$4.* ☉ *Mon., Thurs., Sat. 10–4.*

Outdoor Activities and Sports
Lake Eufaula is one of the best bass lakes in the country, with 8-to-10-pound largemouth bass caught with regularity.

Lakepoint State Park Resort (✉ U.S. 431 N, ☎ 334/687–6676) north of town has six lighted tennis courts and a golf course.

Troy

❹❸ *50 mi south of Montgomery on U.S. 231.*

This town is home to Troy State University and a fine pioneer museum. The **Pike Pioneer Museum** complex has more than 10,000 artifacts of the pioneer period—clothing, furniture, farm implements—plus spinning and weaving demonstrations. Don't miss the turn-of-the-century shops, schoolhouse, log house, well-stocked general store, and 1883 steam logging locomotive. Special events—such as fall and spring Pioneer Days, and the Jean Lake Art Show—take place throughout the year. Folklife artisans appear the first Saturday of the month, April to December. A picnic area is adjacent to the amphitheater. ✉ *248 U.S. 231N,* ☎ *334/566–3597.* ☞ *$3.* ☉ *Mon.–Sat. 9–5, Sun. 1–5.*

Georgiana

44 *60 mi south of Montgomery on I–65.*

The small, rural community of Georgiana was the birthplace of one of country music's greatest performers—Hank Williams Sr. (1923–1953).

★ The City of Georgiana has established the **Hank Williams Sr. Boyhood Home and Museum,** and fans from around the world have donated Hank Williams memorabilia to fill the house to the brim. Rockers line the large wraparound porch, so you can relax as you listen to the songs of this country-music legend. Many of Williams's personal items are on display, along with an excellent collection of photographs. On the first Saturday in June, Georgiana comes alive for **Hank Williams Sr. Day,** as fans and performers pay tribute to their idol. The music goes on long into the night. ⊠ *127 Rose St.,* ☎ *334/376–2396.* ☞ *$3.* ☉ *Tues.–Sat. 10–5, Sun. 1–5.*

Montgomery and Central Alabama A to Z

Arriving and Departing

BY BUS

Greyhound Lines (⊠ 950 W. South Blvd., Montgomery, ☎ 334/286–0658 or 800/231–2222).

BY CAR

I–65 runs north to Birmingham and south to Mobile. I–85 begins in Montgomery and runs northeast to Atlanta. U.S. 80 runs west past the airport to Selma.

BY PLANE

Dannelly Field (☎ 334/281–5040) is 7 mi southwest of downtown Montgomery. It is served by Atlantic Southeast, Delta, Northwest Airlink, and US Airways.

Taxis are readily available and relatively inexpensive at the airport. Many hotels provide transportation from the airport by prior arrangement. To get to the airport by **car** from downtown, take Exit 167 off I–65 to U.S. 80W and go 3 mi to airport entrance. To reach downtown from the airport, turn north onto I–65, follow signs to I–85, and take the first exit, Court Street.

BY TRAIN

The nearest **Amtrak** service to Montgomery and Central Alabama is in Birmingham (☎ 800/872–7245). Montgomery has a **Thruway Intermodal Transit Terminal** (⊠ 335 Coosa St., ☎ 800/872–7245 for information) offering bus service to Amtrak stations in Birmingham and Mobile.

Getting Around

BY BUS

Montgomery buses (☎ 334/262–7321) run from 5 AM to 9:30 PM, although some routes may vary. Exact change is required: $1.50 fare, 15¢ transfer.

BY CAR

U.S. 80 cuts east–west across the state, connecting Demopolis, Selma, Montgomery, and Tuskegee. U.S. 82 runs east–west through Montgomery and Eufaula.

BY TAXI

Taxis in Montgomery charge $1.50 for the first ⅒ mi, $1.10 for each additional mile. Try **Yellow Cab** (☎ 334/262–5225).

Contacts and Resources

EMERGENCIES

Ambulance (☎ 911). **Police** (☎ 911). For medical emergencies, contact the **Montgomery Baptist Medical Center** (✉ 2105 E. South Blvd., ☎ 334/288–2100).

GOLF

Several sections of Alabama's **Robert Trent Jones Golf Trail** are in this region: the **Grand National** course at Auburn/Opelika, **Highland Oaks** at Dothan, and **Cambrian Ridge** at Greenville (considered by many golfers to be the most spectacular on the trail). The three sites offer seven courses: Some are long, some are short, but all are challenging and scenic. For reservations and information about any Trail courses, call 800/949–4444. Greens fees with cart run $54–$64.

GUIDED TOURS

Gray Line (✉ 335 Coosa St., ☎ 334/365–6443) has van and bus tours of area sights. The **Montgomery Visitors Center** (☞ Visitor Information, *below*) sells a cassette driving tour of the downtown area for $9 (tape and book) or $2 (book only); they also show a free eight-minute video that will help you organize your own tour.

PHARMACY

Harco Drugs (✉ Capitol Plaza Shopping Center, South Bypass, Montgomery, ☎ 334/281–1312) is open weekdays 8 AM–midnight, weekends 8 AM–10 PM.

RADIO STATIONS

AM: WACV 1170, talk; WXVI 1600, jazz. **FM:** WBAM 98.9, country; WZHT 105.7, soul.

VISITOR INFORMATION

Montgomery Visitors Center (✉ 401 Madison Ave., ☎ 334/262–0013). **Eufaula/Barbour County Chamber of Commerce** (✉ 102 N. Orange Ave., Eufaula 36027, ☎ 334/687–5283 or 800/524–7529).

MOBILE AND THE GULF COAST

Mobile, one of the oldest cities in Alabama, is perhaps the most graceful. The city has profuse plantings of azaleas—a feature highlighted each spring with the Azalea Trail Festival. Nearby is Bellingrath Gardens, one of the most spectacular public gardens in the country, especially in spring, when more than 250,000 plants are indeed resplendent.

Mardi Gras began in Mobile, long before New Orleans ever celebrated Fat Tuesday, and today the city celebrates the pre-Lenten season, usually in February, with parades and merrymaking day and night. March is the time of the Historic Mobile Homes Tour, when 19th-century Federal-style town houses, Creole cottages, and antebellum plantation homes are opened to visitors for daytime and candlelight tours.

The area of the Gulf Coast around Gulf Shores, to the south of Mobile, encompasses about 50 mi of pure white-sand beach, including a former peninsula called Pleasure Island and Dauphin Island to the west. Though hotels and condominiums take up a good deal of the beachfront, some of it remains public. Here you'll find small-town Southern beach life, with excellent deep-sea fishing as well as freshwater fishing in the bays and bayous, water sports of all types, and world-class golf.

Those with more time might explore the eastern shore of Mobile Bay—Spanish Fort, Daphne, and Fairhope—where, sometime between June and September, locals and tourists eagerly await the mythical phenomenon, "Jubilee." Supposedly, fish, crabs, and shrimp venture into shallow water at this time, become dazed and disoriented, and fall prey to fisherfolk in great quantities. The Eastern Shore revels in the laid-back atmosphere of yesteryear: live oaks laced with Spanish moss; sprawling clapboard houses with wide porches overlooking the lazy, dark water of the bay; and interesting watering holes where local artists and writers meet informally. At Point Clear, south of Fairhope, is the Victorian-style Marriott's Grand Hotel, host since the mid-19th century to the vacationing wealthy.

Numbers in the margin correspond to numbers on the Mobile and the Gulf Coast map.

Mobile

㊺ *170 mi southwest of Montgomery on I–65.*

Ft. Condé was the name the French gave the site known today as Mobile, in 1711; around it blossomed the first white settlement in what is now Alabama. For eight years it was the capital of the French colonial empire, and it remained under French control until 1763, long after the capital had moved to New Orleans. This French connection survives in the area's strong Creole-flavor cuisine, which rivals New Orleans's in fieriness.

Mobile, a busy international port, is noted for its tree-lined boulevards fanning out from Bienville Square. This lovely park at the center of the city is shaded by moss-draped live oaks and has an ornate cast-iron fountain in the center. Bands play here during weekday lunch hours for office workers and visitors who eat their lunches in the square. In the revitalized downtown, many businesses are conducted from buildings that predate the Civil War.

In the center of town, **Ft. Condé** survives as a reminder of the city's beginnings, thanks to a restoration that preserved it when its remains were discovered—150 years after the fort was destroyed—during construction of the I–10 interchange (an I–10 tunnel now runs under the fort). A reconstructed portion of the 1724–35 French fort houses the **visitor center** for the city, as well as a museum and several re-created rooms. Costumed guides interpret and enlighten. ⊠ *150 S. Royal St.,* ☎ *334/434–7304.* ⊑ *Free.* ⊙ *Daily 8–5.*

The **Oakleigh Garden Historic District** begins a block north of Ft. Condé; signs lead to **Oakleigh,** an imposing Greek Revival mansion with a stairway circling under ancient live oaks to a small portico. The high-ceiling half-timber house was built between 1833 and 1838 and is typical of the most expensive dwellings of its day. Fine period furniture, portraits, silver, jewelry, kitchen implements, toys, and more are displayed. Next door is the **Cox-Deasy House,** another antebellum home that is not quite as old as Oakleigh (1850) and by no means as grand. A raised cottage, the Cox-Deasy House was not meant to be a showplace for the planter society, but rather a warm, comfortable home. ⊠ *350 Oakleigh Pl.,* ☎ *334/432–1281.* ⊑ *$5 for both homes.* ⊙ *Mon.–Sat. 10–4. Guided tours every ½ hr, last tour begins at 3:30.*

Several of Mobile's churches figure prominently in the area's rich African-American history: The **State Street A.M.E. Zion Church** (⊠ 502 State St., ☎ 334/432–3965) is one of the oldest and most striking African-American Methodist churches in town. The **St. Louis Street Missionary Baptist Church** (⊠ 108 N. Dearborn St., ☎ 334/438–3823) hosted the conference that established Selma University.

The **National African-American Archives and Museum** holds portraits and biographies of well-known African-Americans. There is also a col-

Mobile and the Gulf Coast

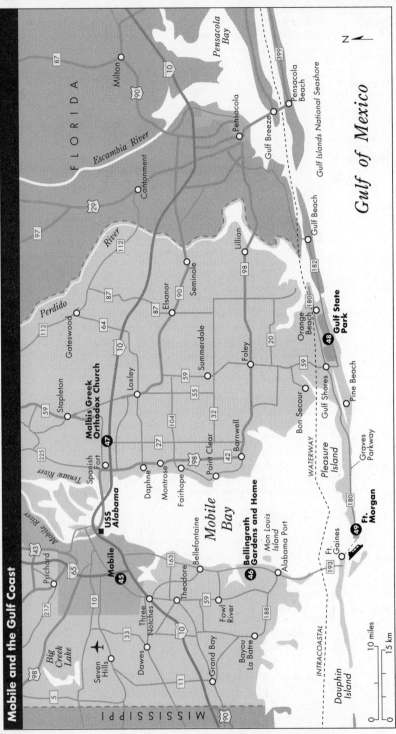

lection of carvings, artifacts, documents, and books. ⊠ *564 Dr. Martin Luther King Jr. Ave.,* ☎ *334/433–8511.* 🎫 *$1.* ⊙ *Weekdays 8:30–5, weekends by appointment.*

The **USS Alabama** is anchored in Mobile Bay just east of downtown Mobile off I–10. Public subscription saved the mighty gray battleship from being scrapped ignominiously after her heroic World War II service, which ranged from Scapa Flow to the South Pacific. A tour of the ship gives a fascinating look into the life of a 2,500-member crew. Anchored next to the battleship is the submarine **USS** *Drum,* another active battle weapon during World War II, also open to visitors. Other exhibits in the 100-acre **Battleship Park** include a B-52 bomber called *Calamity Jane* and a P-51 Mustang fighter plane. ⊠ *2703 Battleship Pkwy. (U.S. 90),* ☎ *334/433–2703 or 800/426–4929.* 🎫 *$8; parking $2.* ⊙ *Daily 8 AM–sunset.*

Dining and Lodging

$$$ ✕ **La Louisiana.** This antiques-filled old house on the city outskirts is a delightful setting for fresh seafood prepared with a touch of French Creole. Shrimp dishes are heavy with cream sauces unless you order them lightly fried. The seafood gumbo is made the Mobile way: heavy on shrimp, oysters, and okra. ⊠ *2400 Airport Blvd.,* ☎ *334/476–8130. Reservations essential. Jacket and tie. AE, D, DC, MC, V.*

$$ ✕ **Pillars.** As you sit amid fine antiques from the 18th and 19th centuries in a huge old mansion with wide porches overlooking live oaks, it is easy to imagine yourself in another time, listening to the latest news from the battlefront at Vicksburg or Shiloh. The beautifully cooked snapper with a white-wine-and-cream sauce is delicious. Rack of lamb is cooked over a charcoal grill. ⊠ *1757 Government St.,* ☎ *334/478–6341. AE, D, DC, MC, V. Closed Sun. No lunch.*

$$ ✕ **Roussos Restaurant.** A local favorite, with a nautical look created
★   by lots of fishnets and scenes of ships at sea, Roussos is known for its crab claws, fried in a light batter and served with a catsup-horseradish sauce. Diners can have their seafood fried, broiled, or served Greek-style (the blend of spices and oils helps bring out the fresh flavor). The appetizers are big favorites too—especially the Roussos baked oysters and Mr. George's seafood gumbo. ⊠ *166 S. Royal St.,* ☎ *334/433–3322. AE, D, DC, MC, V.*

$$$$ ✕🏠 **Adam's Mark Mobile.** This 28-story waterfront hotel is connected to the Mobile Convention Center by a covered skywalk. The large guest rooms have floor-to-ceiling windows with views of downtown Mobile or Mobile Bay, and a separate dressing area with a full-length mirror. The lobby and restaurants have oak paneling and are done in shades of rose and soft jade. The **Riverview Cafe and Grill** specializes in Gulf Coast seafood; there's lighter fare and live entertainment six nights a week in the **Tiffany Rose Restaurant.** ⊠ *64 S. Water St., 36602,* ☎ *334/438–4000,* 🅵🅰🆇 *334/415–3060. 375 rooms, 12 suites. 2 restaurants, bar, pool, hot tub, sauna, exercise room, meeting rooms. AE, D, DC, MC, V.*

$$$$ 🏠 **Portman House Inn.** In the heart of Mobile's historic district, the
★   Mediterranean Revival–style Portman House Inn, built in 1922, has heavy moldings and trims, leaded- and stained-glass windows, working fireplaces, wood floors with area rugs, and a relaxed ambience. A former carriage house at the rear of the property has two apartment-style units. Rooms are large and well-appointed with feather beds, coffeemakers, sunrooms or terraces, and private baths with whirlpool tubs. ⊠ *1615 Government St., 36604,* ☎ *334/471–1703 or 800/471–*

1701, FAX 334/471–1718. 8 rooms. Kitchenettes, business services. AE, D, DC, MC, V.

$$$–$$$$ 🖫 **Radisson Admiral Semmes Hotel.** This restored historic hotel in the
   ★   historic district is a favorite with local politicians. It's also popular with
party goers, particularly during Mardi Gras, because of its excellent
location directly on the parade route. Rooms are furnished in Queen
Anne and Chippendale styles. ✉ *251 Government St., 36602, ☎ 334/
432–8000, FAX 334/405–5942. 147 rooms, 22 suites. Restaurant,
lounge, pool, business services. AE, D, DC, MC, V.*

$–$$ 🖫 **Malaga Inn.** A delightful, romantic getaway place, the Malaga com-
   ★   prises two town houses built by a wealthy landowner in 1862. The lobby
is furnished with 19th-century antiques and opens onto a landscaped
central courtyard with a fountain. The rooms are large, airy, and furnished with massive antiques. Ask for the front suite, with 14-ft ceilings and crimson velveteen wallpaper. ✉ *359 Church St., 36602, ☎
FAX 334/438–4701, ☎ 800/235–1586. 39 rooms. Restaurant, lounge,
pool. AE, D, MC, V.*

Nightlife and the Arts

Much of Mobile's nightlife centers around downtown's former commercial district, **Dauphin Street,** which today is filled with restaurants,
nightspots, and a microbrewery.

The **Joe Jefferson Players** (☎ 334/471–1534), a well-established amateur group, performs plays and musicals at the Joe Jefferson Playhouse
(✉ 11 S. Carlen St.). The 1927 **Saenger Theater** (☎ 334/433–2787)
hosts orchestras and touring companies. The **Mobile Civic Center** (✉
401 Civic Center Dr., ☎ 334/434–7381) presents theater groups, orchestras, and a variety of concerts. The Playhouse in the Park's **Pixie
Players** (☎ 334/344–1537) is a children's theatrical group.

Outdoor Activities and Sports

DOG RACING

At the **Mobile Greyhound Park** (✉ Off I–10W, about 10 mi from Mobile, ☎ 334/653–5000), there's pari-mutuel betting and a restaurant
overlooking the finish line. The track offers simulcasts.

GOLF

Magnolia Grove (✉ 7000 Lamplighter Dr., ☎ 334/645–0075 or 800/
949–4444) is the southernmost offering of Alabama's **Robert Trent
Jones Golf Trail.** The facility has 54 holes of championship golf: two
par 72 courses and an 18-hole par three course that is anything but
easy. **Azalea City Golf Club** (✉ 1000 Gaillard Dr., ☎ 334/342–4221)
is operated by the city of Mobile. Other interesting area courses include **TimberCreek** (✉ 9650 TimberCreek Blvd., ☎ 334/621–9900)
in Daphne. **Rock Creek** (✉ 140 Clubhouse Dr., ☎ 334/928–4223) is
in Fairhope, on the eastern shore of Mobile Bay.

NATURE-WATCHING

Wildland Expeditions, led by Captain Gene Burrell on the *Gator Bait,*
explores the Mobile-Tensaw Delta on two-hour trips that leave from
Chickasaw (just north of Mobile). You'll get close-up views of plants
and animals, especially alligators during the warm weather months.
☎ *334/460–8206. ⏹ $20. No trips Mon.*

Shopping

Most shopping in Mobile is in malls and shopping centers in the suburban areas. Stores are generally open Monday–Saturday 10–9, Sunday 1–6. Sales tax is 9%.

ANTIQUES

Antiques buffs love Mobile because it offers over 25 individual shops and three malls that specialize in antiques. **Red Barn Antique Mall** (⊠ 418 Dauphin Island Pkwy., ☎ 334/473–9227) has at least 15 shops with a variety of antiques from glassware and books to furniture. **Al Atchison Antiques** (⊠ 554 Government St., ☎ 334/438–9421), one of the largest antiques dealers in the South, is packed with antique brass beds and other American and European furniture.

MALLS

The **Bel Air Mall** (⊠ 1 block east of I–65 Beltline off Airport Blvd., ☎ 334/478–1893) has 175 stores under one roof, including **JCPenney, Parisian, Target, Dillard's,** and **Sears. Springdale Mall-Plaza** (⊠ Airport Blvd. and I–65, ☎ 334/479–9871), anchored by **Gayfer's, McRae's,** and **Montgomery Ward,** has more than 100 stores.

SOUVENIRS

Tanner Mercantile (⊠ 2101 Airport Blvd., ☎ 334/476–5282), operated by Joel and Catherine Tanner, specializes in Mobile souvenirs and gourmet coffees, including their trademark blend, Café Pecan Mobile. A deli here serves homemade foods. **Museum Gift Shoppe** (⊠ 355 Government St., ☎ 334/694–0069) is a good place to pick up general souvenirs, books, and local art items.

Theodore

20 mi south of Mobile.

★ ④⑥ One of the most popular gardens in the South is near the town of Theodore. **Bellingrath Gardens and Home** is the site of magnificent azalea gardens, part of 65 acres of gardens set amid a 905-acre semitropical landscape. Show time for the azaleas is spring, when some 250,000 plantings of 200 different species are ablaze with color. But Bellingrath is a year-round wonder: In summer, 2,500 rosebushes are in bloom; in autumn, 60,000 chrysanthemum plants; in winter, fields of poinsettias. Countless other species and varieties of flowering plants spring up along a river, a stream, and a lake populated by ducks and swans. Guides are on hand to assist or explain, but a free map lets you plan your own strolls along flagstone paths and across charming bridges. The gardens are also a sanctuary to more than 200 species of birds; in April and October, large numbers of migratory birds drop by.

Coca-Cola bottling pioneer Walter D. Bellingrath began the nucleus of the gardens in 1917, when he and his wife bought a large tract of land as a fishing camp. Their travels, however, prompted them to create, instead, a garden rivaling some they had seen in Europe, and before long they opened it to the public. Today the brick home they built is open to visitors and has one of the finest collections of antiques in the Southeast. On display, too, is the world's largest collection of Boehm porcelain birds. One-hour **boat cruises** on the Fowl River leave from the dock next to the Bellingrath Home at regular intervals. ⊠ *12401 Bellingrath Rd.,* ☎ *334/973–2217 or 800/247–8420.* 🖾 *Gardens $7; gardens and home $13.95; value pack (gardens, home, and cruise) $18.95.* ☉ *Gardens daily 8 AM–sunset, home opens daily at 9 with closings varying by season.*

Malbis

10 mi east of Mobile on U.S. 90 via I–10.

㊼ Malbis is the outgrowth of a development begun in 1906 by a Greek immigrant and former monk who bought tracts of land and established a cannery, bakery, farm, and power plant; today it includes portions of a residential golf community, TimberCreek. The **Malbis Greek Orthodox Church** is a replica of a beautiful Byzantine church in Athens, Greece. It was built in 1965 as a memorial to the faith of Jason Malbis, founder of the community. The marble for the interior was imported from the same quarries that provided stone for the Parthenon, and a master painter was brought over from Greece to paint murals on the walls and the 75-ft dome of the rotunda. The stained-glass windows are stunning. ⊠ *County Rte. 27,* ☎ *334/626–3050.* ⊡ *Free.* ☉ *Tours daily 9–noon and 2–5.*

Point Clear

This bend in the road is a leading resort destination on the eastern shore of Mobile Bay because of the incomparable Grand Hotel.

Lodging

$$$$ ☆ 🏨 **Marriott's Grand Hotel.** Nestled amid 550 acres of beautifully landscaped grounds on Mobile Bay, the "Grand" has been a cherished tradition since 1847. Extensively refurbished by Marriott, it is one of the South's premier resorts. Its two-story cypress-paneled and -beamed lobby evokes an aura of traditional elegance. Spacious rooms and cottages are also traditionally furnished. ⊠ *U.S. Scenic 98, 36564,* ☎ *334/928–9201 or 800/544–9933,* ℻ *334/928–6271. 227 units, 23 suites. 3 restaurants, coffee shop, lounge, pool, hot tub, sauna, 2 18-hole golf courses, 8 tennis courts, horseback riding, beach, boating, fishing, bicycles, children's programs, playground. AE, D, DC, MC, V.*

The Gulf Coast

50 mi south of Mobile via U.S. 90E and AL 59.

With sugary white sand and gentle warm water, the beach along this coastal paradise known as Pleasure Island is by far its greatest attraction. The cooling offshore breezes provide a nice respite from the normal hot, humid temperatures found around Alabama in the summer. While the Gulf Shores beach area has plenty of concessions and is usually crowded, those seeking isolated beach walks need only venture a couple of miles west. To the east of Gulf Shores is Orange Beach, a heavily developed coastal strip between the Gulf of Mexico and Perdido Bay, with its peaceful inlets and lagoons.

☆ **㊽** **Gulf State Park** (⊠ 20115 AL 135, Gulf Shores, ☎ 334/948–7275, 800/544–4853, or 800/252–7275) covers more than 6,000 acres of Pleasure Island. Along with 2½ mi of pure white beaches and glimmering dunes, the park has two freshwater lakes with canoeing and fishing, plus biking, hiking, and jogging trails through pine forests. Near the large beach pavilion, a concrete fishing pier juts about 800 ft into the Gulf. There is also a gulf-front resort lodge and convention center, 468 campsites, and 21 cottages, plus tennis courts and a golf course.

The 6,200 acres of the **Bon Secour National Wildlife Refuge** (⊠ AL 180 W, ☎ 334/540–7720) are home to native and migratory birds and a number of endangered species, including the loggerhead sea turtle. You can hike or swim at some of the five units of the refuge.

🐤 **Waterville USA,** set on 17 acres, has a wave pool with 3-ft waves, seven exciting water slides, and a lazy river ride around the park. For younger children there are gentler rides in a supervised play area. There is also a 36-hole miniature golf course and a video-game arcade. ✉ *906 Gulf Shores Pkwy. (AL 59), Gulf Shores,* 🕾 *334/948–2106.* 🎫 *$16.* ☉ *Memorial Day–Labor Day.*

49 **Ft. Morgan** was built in the early 1800s to guard the entrance to Mobile Bay. The fort saw fiery action during the Battle of Mobile Bay in 1864: Confederate torpedoes sank the ironclad *Tecumseh,* after Union Admiral David Farragut gave his famous command "Damn the torpedoes! Full speed ahead!" The original outer walls still stand; inside, a museum chronicles the fort's history and displays artifacts from Indian days through World War II, with an emphasis on the Civil War. ✉ *51 Hwy. 180W, Mobile Point,* 🕾 *334/540–7125.* 🎫 *$2.* ☉ *Weekdays 8–5, weekends 9–5.*

Dining and Lodging

$$ ✕ **Bayside Grill.** For fine dining overlooking the back bays that channel to the Gulf, you can't beat this choice. You can order your fresh seafood dishes with a variety of excellent sauces or have them plain. Vegetables are especially well prepared. ✉ *Canal Rd., Orange Beach,* 🕾 *334/981–4899. AE, D, DC, MC, V.*

$$ ✕ **Voyagers.** Roses and art-deco touches set the tone for this airy, el-
★ egant dining room. Two-level seating allows beach or poolside views from every table. Some favorites are trout with roasted pecans in Creole meunière sauce and soft-shell crab topped with Creole sauce Choron. Follow up with fried-apple beignet with French vanilla sauce or crepe soufflé praline. Service is deft, and there's an extensive wine selection. ✉ *Perdido Beach Resort, 27200 Perdido Beach Blvd., Orange Beach,* 🕾 *334/981–9811. Reservations essential. AE, D, DC, MC, V.*

$–$$ ✕ **King Neptune's Seafood Restaurant.** A combination of outstand-
★ ing steamed seafood choices and casual, family-style dining make King Neptune's one of Gulf Shores' most enjoyable restaurants. Specialties include royal red shrimp, blue crabs, and po'boys. ✉ *AL 59S, Gulf Shores,* 🕾 *334/968–5464. Reservations not accepted. AE, MC, V.*

$ ✕ **Hazel's Family Restaurant.** This plain family-style restaurant with
★ a full menu serves a good, hearty breakfast (the biscuits are famous), soup-and-salad lunches, and buffet dinners with such seafood dishes as flounder Florentine. There's also a self-service bar serving soft ice cream. ✉ *Gulf View Square Shopping Center, AL 182, Orange Beach,* 🕾 *334/981–4628. Reservations not accepted. AE, D, DC, MC, V.*

$$$$ 🏨 **Perdido Beach Resort.** The eight- and nine-story towers of the re-
★ sort are Mediterranean stucco and red tile. The lobby is tiled in terracotta and decorated with mosaics by Venetian artists and a brass sculpture of gulls in flight. Rooms are furnished in comfortable Mediterranean style, and all have a beach view and balcony. The location and scenic views here are outstanding. ✉ *27200 Perdido Beach Blvd., Box 400, Orange Beach 36561,* 🕾 *334/981–9811 or 800/634–8001,* 🖷 *334/981–5670. 333 rooms, 12 suites. Restaurant, café, piano bar, indoor-outdoor pool, 2 hot tubs, 2 saunas, 4 tennis courts, exercise room, video games. AE, DC, MC, V.*

$$$–$$$$ 🏨 **Gulf Shores Plantation.** This 320-acre family resort, 12 mi west of
★ Gulf Shores, faces the Gulf and has condominiums with fully equipped kitchens in high-rises overlooking the beach. Abundant recreational activities are available. The peace and quiet of this pristine stretch of beach make up for the resort's somewhat remote location. In 1996 Kiva Dunes Golf Course, adjacent to the resort, was rated the second best

new public course in America by *Golf Digest.* ✉ *AL 180W, Box 1299, Gulf Shores 36547,* ☎ *334/540–5000 or 800/554–0344,* FAX *334/540–6050. 400 units. Café, pizzeria, lounge, indoor and outdoor pools, 18-hole golf course, 8 tennis courts, gift shop. AE, MC, V.*

$$$–$$$$ 🏨 **Lighthouse.** This complex of five two- to four-story buildings, surrounded by brightly colored exotic flowers, is set on a 680-ft private beach. The waterfront rooms have private balconies, and some units have kitchens. All have contemporary furnishings. ✉ *455 E. Beach Blvd., Box 233, Gulf Shores 36547,* ☎ *334/948–6188. 200 rooms. 3 pools. AE, D, DC, MC, V.*

$$$–$$$$ 🏨 **Quality Inn Beachside.** This spacious hotel is made up of one three-story and one six-story building. The modern guest rooms are decorated in pastels and have private balconies and coffeemakers; most face the Gulf; half have kitchens. In the art deco–style atrium lobby, with glass-brick walls, is a 70-ft swimming pool and a waterfall. Glass-walled elevators rise six stories. ✉ *931 W. Gulf Beach Blvd. (AL 182), Drawer 1013, Gulf Shores 36547,* ☎ *334/948–6874 or 800/844–6913,* FAX *334/948–5232. 158 rooms. Restaurant, food court, lounge, indoor pool, outdoor pool, hot tub. AE, D, DC, MC, V.*

$$–$$$ 🏨 **Original Romar House.** This unassuming beach cottage is filled with surprises—from the Caribbean-style upstairs sitting area to the Purple Parrot Bar to the luxurious art deco–style guest rooms. A full breakfast is included in the rate. ✉ *23500 Perdido Beach Blvd., Orange Beach 36561,* ☎ *334/981–6156 or 800/487–6627,* FAX *334/974–1163. 6 rooms. Bar, hot tub, bicycles. AE, MC, V.*

Nightlife and the Arts

On the Alabama–Florida line is the **Flora-Bama Lounge** (✉ Beach Rd., Pensacola, FL, ☎ 334/980–5118 or 334/980–5119), with live entertainment nightly. It's the place where country singer Jimmy Buffett got his start.

Shirley & Wayne's (✉ 25125 Beach Blvd., Orange Beach, ☎ 334/981–4818) has live entertainment most Monday through Saturday nights while you dine and/or dance.

Outdoor Activities and Sports

BIKING

Gulf State Park (✉ 20115 AL 135, ☎ 334/948–7275) in Gulf Shores has biking trails through pine forests and rents bicycles. **Island Recreation Services** (✉ 360 E. Beach Blvd., ☎ 334/948–7334) in Gulf Shores rents bikes and water-sports equipment.

FISHING

Freshwater and saltwater fishing in the Gulf area are excellent. **Gulf State Park** (✉ 20115 AL 135, ☎ 334/948–7275) in Gulf Shores has fishing from an 825-ft pier and rents flat-bottom boats for lake fishing. **Deep-sea fishing** from charter boats is very popular; in Gulf Shores, you can sign on board the *Moreno Queen* (☎ 334/981–3474 or 800/317–4850) or one of many other charter boats for a full- or half-day fishing expedition, and neighboring Orange Beach has 40 boats to choose from. For a brochure on Orange Beach's offerings, call 800/745–7263. Catches from these deep-sea expeditions include king mackerel, amberjack, tuna, white marlin, blue marlin, grouper, bonito, sailfish, and red snapper.

GOLF

In recent years, coastal Alabama has developed into one of the nicest golfing destinations in the Southeast. More courses are opening, and the names of their architects read like a *Who's Who* of the golfing world—Robert Trent Jones Sr., Arnold Palmer, and Jerry Pate, to name just a few. With winter temperatures averaging in the 60° range and pleasant breezes, the area has become a true year-round-fun spot. Prices for all the courses range from about $28 to $40 for greens fees and a cart.

The spectacular **Kiva Dunes** course at Gulf Shores Plantation Resort (⊠ 12 mi west of Gulf Shores on AL 180, ☎ 334/540–7000 or 800/554–0344), designed by Jerry Pate, combines oceanfront dunes golf with Scottish-style links golf. The **Craft Farms** complex (⊠ AL 59 just north of Gulf Shores, ☎ 334/968–7500) has 27 holes on the Arnold Palmer–designed course at **Cotton Creek** and another 18 on the **Woodlands course** designed by Larry Nelson. About 12 mi north of Gulf Shores in Foley, the **Dunes at Glenlakes** (⊠ 9530 Clubhouse Dr., ☎ 334/943–8000), a course designed by Bruce Devlin, has 18 challenging holes and plays over 7,000 yards. The course at **Gulf State Park** (⊠ 20115 AL 135, ☎ 334/948–7275) in Gulf Shores isn't quite as new and challenging as others in the area, but it is one of the most scenic and best maintained courses along the coast.

HORSEBACK RIDING

Country Trail Rides (☎ 334/943–7694 for reservations) offers guided group trail rides for $20 per person; they're located between Gulf Shores and Foley.

SAILING AND WATER SPORTS

Sailboats that can be rented with captain include the *T. J. Spithre,* a 53-ft catamaran (☎ 334/981–9706 for Island Sailing Center), and the *Daedalus* (☎ 334/986–7018) in Gulf Shores.

Fun Marina (☎ 334/981–8587) in Orange Beach offers parasailing and rents Jet Skis, pontoon boats, and 16-ft bay-fishing boats. In Gulf Shores, **Island Recreation Services** (⊠ 360 E. Beach Blvd., ☎ 334/948–7334) rents boogie boards, body boards, surfboards, and sailboats.

Shopping

Riviera Centre, a handsome complex of outlet stores 8 mi north of Gulf Shores, offers savings of up to 75% off regular retail prices. Stores include **Danskin, Calvin Klein, Liz Claiborne, American Tourister, Polo/Ralph Lauren, Manhattan, Bass Shoes, Pfaltzgraff,** and other top names. ⊠ *AL 59S, Foley,* ☎ *334/943–8888 or 800/523–6873.* ☉ *Mon.–Sat. 9–9, Sun. 10–6. Hrs vary Jan.–Feb.*

Mobile and the Gulf Coast A to Z

Arriving and Departing

BY BUS

Greyhound (☎ 800/231–2222) has stations in Mobile (⊠ 2545 Government Blvd., ☎ 334/478–6089) and in Pensacola, Florida (⊠ 505 W. Burgess Rd., ☎ 904/476–4800).

BY CAR

I–10 travels east from Mobile into Florida through Pensacola, west into Mississippi. I–65 slices Alabama in half vertically, passing through Birmingham and Montgomery and ending at Mobile. Gulf Shores is connected with Mobile via I–10 and AL 59; AL 180 and 182 are the main beach routes.

BY PLANE

The **Mobile Regional Airport at Bates Field** (☎ 334/633–0313), about 5 mi west of the city, is served by Delta, Northwest Airlink, and Continental Express. **Pensacola Regional Airport** (☎ 904/435–1746), some 40 mi east of Gulf Shores in Florida, is served by Continental, Delta, Northwest, and US Airways.

BY TRAIN
Amtrak (☎ 800/872–7245) service on the *Sunset Limited* links Mobile with both the East and West coasts. Westbound trains run Monday, Wednesday, and Saturday; eastbound trains run Sunday, Tuesday, and Thursday.

Getting Around
The most practical way to get around this area is by car.

Contacts and Resources

EMERGENCIES
Ambulance (☎ 911). **Police** (☎ 911). The **University of South Alabama Hospital** (✉ 2451 Fillingim St., ☎ 334/471–7000) in Mobile offers all-night medical care at its emergency room.

GUIDED TOURS
Gray Line Tours (☎ 334/432–2229 or 800/338–5597), in Mobile, has one- to 3½-hour trolley or motorcoach tours, departing from Ft. Condé daily, to Mobile's historic points of interest, as well as to Bellingrath Gardens and the USS *Alabama*.

Memorable Mobile Tours, Inc. (☎ 334/344–8687 or 800/441–1146) conducts customized guided tours of Mobile and Eastern Shore area attractions.

RADIO STATIONS
In Mobile, **AM:** WGOK 900, gospel and jazz; WKSJ 1270, country. **FM:** WGCX 92.1, classic rock; WABB 97.5, contemporary rock; WWRO 100.7, oldies; WDWG 104.1, country.

VISITOR INFORMATION
Write the **Mobile Convention & Visitors Corporation** (✉ Box 204, Mobile 36601, ☎ 334/415–2000 or 800/566–2453). You can visit **Ft. Condé** (✉ 150 S. Royal St., ☎ 334/434–7304), which has the official welcome center for Mobile. **Alabama Gulf Coast Area Convention and Visitors Bureau** (✉ 26650 Perdido Beach Blvd., Orange Beach 36561, ☎ 334/968–7511 or 800/745–7263).

ALABAMA A TO Z

Arriving and Departing

By Car
Surrounded by Mississippi, Georgia, Tennessee, Florida, and the Gulf of Mexico, Alabama is accessible by a number of interstates. I–10 cuts across the southern tip of the state, providing direct route from Mississippi on the west and the Florida Panhandle on the east. From Atlanta, I–85 takes you to the southern part of the state; I–20 takes you to Birmingham and points in North Alabama. The main north–south routes are I–65 coming down from Nashville and I–59 from the Chattanooga area. U.S. 80 cuts east–west across the state, connecting Demopolis, Selma, Montgomery, and Tuskegee. U.S. 82 runs northwest to southeast from Tuscaloosa through Montgomery and Eufaula.

Some sample mileages are: Birmingham to Huntsville, 95 mi; Birmingham to Mobile, 253 mi; Birmingham to Montgomery, 90 mi; Birmingham to Gulf Shores, 274 mi; Birmingham to Tuscaloosa, 57 mi.

By Plane
Major airports are **Birmingham International Airport** (☎ 205/595–0533), Montgomery's **Dannelly Field** (☎ 334/281–5040), **Huntsville Inter-**

national Airport (☎ 205/772–9395), and **Mobile Municipal Airport** (☎ 334/633–0313). Many visitors to the Gulf Coast find it convenient to fly into the **Pensacola Regional Airport** (☎ 904/435–1746) in Pensacola, Florida.

By Train
Amtrak (☎ 800/872–7245) has daily service to Birmingham. Service into Mobile is on Sunday, Tuesday, and Thursday. East–west routes are serviced by Amtrak's *Sunset Limited* across the southern part of the state; north–south travelers board *The Crescent* from New York and Washington, or New Orleans.

Getting Around

By Bus
Greyhound (☎ 800/231–2222) has service to the major cities—Birmingham, Huntsville, Mobile, and Montgomery—with intermediate stops at many of Alabama's smaller cities. Check for scheduled stops.

By Car
In Alabama, you can turn right during a red light unless otherwise noted by street signs. The speed limit on interstate highways is 70 mph.

By Train
Montgomery has a Thruway Intermodal Transit Terminal (✉ 335 Coosa St., ☎ 800/872–7245 for information) offering bus service to Amtrak service in Birmingham and Mobile.

Contacts and Resources

B&B Reservation Agencies
Alabama has no central telephone number for bed-and-breakfasts. Use a B&B brochure available from the Alabama Bureau of Tourism and Travel (☞ Visitor Information, *below*) to make reservations at individual B&Bs.

Emergencies
In towns and cities, dial **911** for police, fire, and ambulance assistance.

Outdoor Activities and Sports
FISHING
Neither residents nor nonresidents 16 or over may fish in Alabama without a valid fishing license; for information, call 334/242–3826.

GOLF
Some of Alabama's most scenic and challenging courses are part of the **Robert Trent Jones Golf Trail,** 18 courses spread out among seven locations around the state, providing 324 holes of challenging golf. Call a toll-free number (☎ 800/949–4444) for reservations and information about any of the locations.

There's good golf in Alabama's **state parks** (☎ 800/252–7275). Greens fees with cart range from $30 to $40.

State Parks
Alabama's 24 state parks include a wide variety of recreational activities and lodging accommodations. Visitors have the choice of resort lodges, hotels, campgrounds, chalets, and cabins, both modern and rustic. Several parks have marinas, golf courses, and tennis facilities. Contact **Alabama State Parks** (✉ 64 N. Union St., Folsom Administrative Bldg., Suite 547, Montgomery 36130, ☎ 800/252–7275) for reservations or information on Alabama's state parks.

Visitor Information

Alabama Bureau of Tourism and Travel (✉ 401 Adams Ave., Montgomery 36104, ☎ 334/242–4169 or 800/252–2262). **Welcome centers:** I–59 near Valley Head, I–59 at Cuba, I–65 at Elkmont, I–10 north of Seminole, I–10 at Grand Bay, I–20 east of Heflin, I–85 at Lanett, U.S. 231 south of Dothan.

Call the Alabama Bureau of Tourism and Travel (☎ 800/252–2262) for a free copy of **"Alabama's Black Heritage,"** a 56-page guide devoted to African-American culture that includes hundreds of sites from churches and old homes to monuments, museums, and galleries.

3 Georgia

Georgia, the Empire State of the South, is the largest state east of the Mississippi River in terms of geography. Its varied terrain ranges from the foothills of the Appalachian Mountains in the north, to the great coastal plain running from the state's center toward the shore, to the beaches of the Golden Isles and the delicate ecology of the Okefenokee in the southeast. From progressive Atlanta to antebellum Macon and colonial Savannah, each of Georgia's cities and towns has its own special charm.

Updated by
Jane F. Garvey

EORGIA IS LIKE A CLEVERLY MADE PATCHWORK quilt. Its landscape encompasses the hazy blue foothills of the Appalachian Mountains in the north, the coastal plain connecting the heartland to the unspoiled beaches of the Atlantic, and the mysterious black-water swamps of the state's southern portion. Most visitors travel its interstate highways (I–75, I–85, I–95, and I–16), but the adventurous traveler who decides to explore the state's byways will be rewarded with pristine vistas and detours through charming towns.

Within the landscape lies a rich diversity of unusual flora, including mountain laurel, rhododendron, azaleas, and camellias. Famous Spanish moss drapes live oak trees in the southern and coastal areas, and flat fields of white puffy cotton line the horizon through the middle of the state. Known for its peaches, Georgia is also proud of its apples, and the fruit trees' soft blooms create splendid sights in spring. Hiking in the north Georgia mountains could reveal its wealth of deer charging through the forest. Along the coast, alligators, egrets, and herons take the visitor in stride.

As varied as its landscape, Georgia's citizens reflect the diversity of early settlers, native peoples, and new arrivals. In the 18th century, not only English and Scottish immigrants but also Jewish settlers, both Sephardic and Ashkenazic, and German religious refugees (the Salzburgers) arrived to take up positions of importance and prominence in the Georgia colony. Africans and native peoples—chiefly Cherokee and Creek—added their cultural spice to the mix, creating a state that is richer in ethnic character than is often recognized. Irish immigrants arriving throughout the 19th century and Greeks, Middle Easterners, and Asians in the late 19th and early 20th centuries contributed to the state's diversity. Georgians speak with accents that vary from the classic, slightly nasal mountain "twang" to the distinctive, soft coastal lilt of upper-crust Savannahians.

Georgia's towns each define in their own way that famous "Southern charm" of fable and film. Bustling Atlanta, the state capitol since the Civil War ended in 1865, has been compared with Margaret Mitchell's heroine, Scarlett O'Hara, the classic Steel Magnolia, gentle in form but brash and tough in substance. Colonial Savannah, with the nation's largest historic district, lures visitors to its 21 cobblestone squares, giant parterre gardens, waterfront gift shops, jazz bars, and parks draped in Spanish moss. Dahlonega, site of the nation's first gold rush in 1828, is a typical example of the small Georgia town with its central square dominated by a county courthouse. Macon, full of flowering Japanese cherry trees and images of both the antebellum and Victorian South, celebrates its heritage as home to poet and flutist Sidney Lanier. A few small towns are named for glittering foreign capitals that they resemble not in the slightest: Vienna (pronounced vi-en-ah); Madrid (may-drid); Rome, Athens, Cairo (cay-row), and so forth.

Georgia's 100-mi coast runs from the mouth of the Savannah River south to the mouth of the St. Marys River. The seaside resort communities blend Southern elegance with a casual sensibility. St. Simons Island, about 70 mi south of Savannah, attracts a laid-back crowd of anglers, beachgoers, golfers, and tennis players. On nearby Jekyll Island, the lavish lifestyle of America's early 19th-century rich and famous is still evident in their stately Victorian "cottages." Cumberland Island's protected forests and miles of sandy coastline, the isolated solitude of Little St. Simons Island, and the dark waters of the Okefenokee are favorite haunts of nature lovers.

Other historical riches include thousand-year-old Native American homesites and burial mounds, antebellum mansions, war heroes' memorials, and intriguing monuments built by eccentric folk artists and obsessive gardeners. Georgia's large number of state parks have superb facilities for white-water rafting, canoeing, fishing, golf, and tennis, plus nature trails through mountain forests delicately laced with wild rhododendron, dogwoods, and azaleas.

Pleasures and Pastimes

Leisure time can be spent white-water rafting on the Chattooga River in northeast Georgia, dining on delicacies from Southeast Asia or the substantial Southern fare of traditional country cuisine, or attending concerts ranging from classical to popular to country-and-western to blues and jazz. The history enthusiast eager to savor the details of 19th-century Southern life will find more than a fair share of battlefields to explore, including the dark woods and open fields of Chicamauga, historic antebellum towns such as Madison and Washington, and unusual historic sites such as New Echota, the lost capital of the Cherokee Nation. For the sports enthusiast, there's fishing, golf and tennis, sailing and rowing, and a World Champion baseball team, the Atlanta Braves.

Dining

Dining in Georgia has its ups and downs. Areas that have attracted substantial tourism boast fairly respectable to downright outstanding restaurants. Others lag far behind, their best offerings the chain restaurants that lack all pretense to culinary creativity or service, or the local barbecue joint. When dining in a small town, inquire of the local fire department; firefighters often know which are the best restaurants in town.

Atlanta sets the positive pace, of course, with cutting-edge culinary experiences by outstanding chefs. Dress in Atlanta—and elsewhere in the state—is casual unless otherwise noted. On the byways of Georgia, barbecue stands and restaurants still cook the whole pig, serving customers its meat pulled off the bone for sandwiches or its tender ribs, both bathed in tangy sauce. Brunswick stew, a hunter's stew, is the standard accompaniment. Some of these places are full-fledged restaurants; others have no place to sit at all. If you're off the beaten path, these establishments offer your best chance for decent food.

CATEGORY	COST*
$$$$	over $50
$$$	$35–$50
$$	$25–$35
$	under $25

per person for a three-course meal, excluding drinks, service, and 6% tax

Historic Sites

Historic sites make a trip to Georgia worth special planning. From the moment visitors enter the state along the interstate highways, brown markers with white lettering alert them to the locations of the state's principal historical sights along those routes. Georgia's towns constitute a special glimpse into the past. Savannah, founded in 1733, can be viewed from carriage or bus via specialty tours, by private car, or on foot; it's an excellent walking city. Macon, founded in 1823, showcases a wealth of fine antebellum and Victorian mansions that may be viewed by private car or on specialty tours. Augusta, founded in 1736, has a fine Riverwalk, a restored downtown, and the 19th- and 20th-century houses of Olde Town and Summerville.

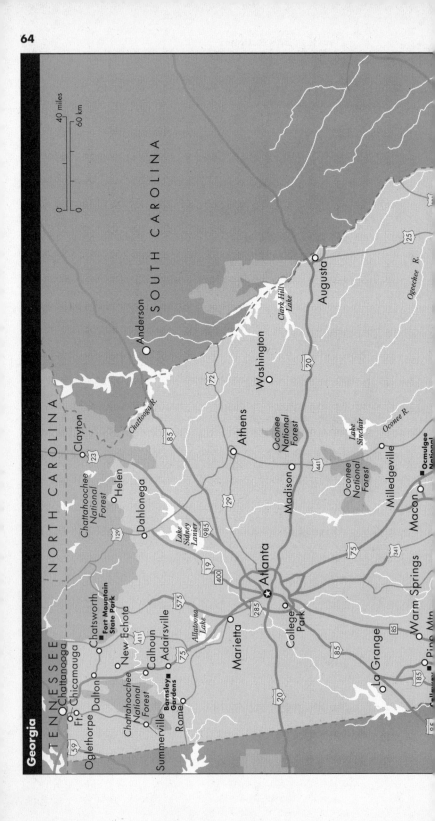

Georgia

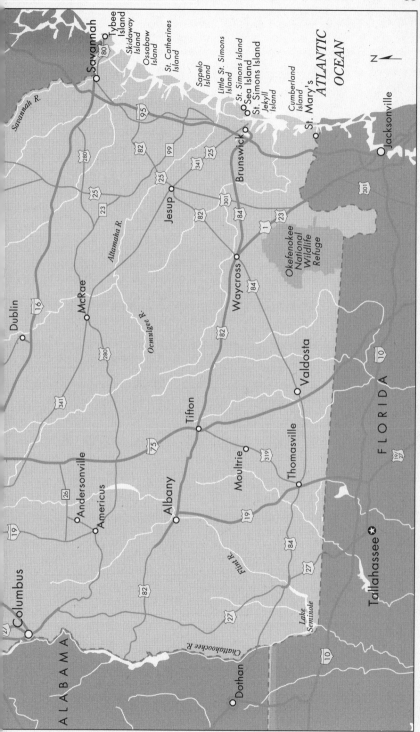

Lodging

Most important national and some international hotel and motel chains have establishments in Georgia. Atlanta, for instance, is now headquarters for Holiday Inn Worldwide. But within the past decade, bed-and-breakfast inns have arisen throughout the state, some providing exquisite lodging, others doing a perfunctory job. In addition, campsites are marked along the interstate highways, and the state has a fine network of parks, some of which offer campsites and overnight facilities. Always telephone ahead to bed-and-breakfast inns and campsites for reservations, as these are very popular accommodations.

CATEGORY	ATLANTA*	OTHER AREAS*
$$$$	over $160	over $100
$$$	$115–$160	$75–$100
$$	$80–$115	$50–$75
$	under $80	under $50

*All prices are for a standard double room, excluding 13% tax and service.

Nightlife

No night in Georgia need ever be boring. Clubs, music venues, theater, film, symphony, and comedy revues all make nightlife hum. For one thing, Georgia is a music hotbed. Blues and jazz, country-and-western and gospel, and rock and roll are all part of this region's—and Georgia's—homegrown musical tradition. Local composers and performers who made their marks on the national music scene include Savannah's Johnny Mercer, Macon's Otis Redding and the Allman Brothers, and Augusta's James Brown, the godfather of soul. Macon's Little Richard and Albany's Ray Charles still perform. Local groups that have gained national and international fame include R.E.M. and the B-52's from Athens, Indigo Girls from Decatur, and Black Crowes from Marietta. In country-and-western music, Travis Tritt started out in Marietta and Trisha Yearwood in Monticello. To hear rising new stars, call local radio stations for information about venues.

In the classical department, opera diva Jessye Norman is from Augusta, and violinist Robert McDuffie is from Macon. The state abounds in symphony orchestras, chamber groups, and classical and jazz ensembles, many of which perform on college campuses. For details, contact a local college campus or consult the local newspaper.

Theater is vital not only in Atlanta, but also throughout the state, home to thespians Joanne Woodward (Thomasville), Julia and Eric Roberts (Smyrna), Holly Hunter (Conyers), Melvin Douglas (Macon), Pernell Roberts (Waycross), and playwright Alfred Uhry (Atlanta). If you can catch a performance of *Swamp Gravy,* performed by residents of Colquitt, Georgia, or *Reach of Song,* based on the poetry of mountain poet Byron Herbert Reece, you'll enjoy traditional local subject matter and music.

Exploring Georgia

Georgia has several distinct touring areas. The Foothills of the Appalachian mountains run from west to east in north Georgia, making this a popular destination for tourists especially in spring and fall. Camping, white-water rafting, hiking, antiques hunting, and enjoying the many seasonal festivals keep visitors busy year-round. Atlanta alone warrants serious exploration. The coast offers other opportunities, especially for the history aficionado. From Savannah, Georgia's oldest city, to Augusta, its third oldest, Colonial and Civil War history literally awaits at every turn. It's in east Georgia where you'll see most of the columned antebellum homes visitors have come to expect. The barrier islands have fine beaches in summertime, as well as opportunities for enjoying nature-focused expeditions. The best spot for would-be naturalists, of course, is the Okefenokee Natural Wildlife Refuge.

Great Itineraries

IF YOU HAVE 3 DAYS

Explore the coast to get a true taste of what early Georgia was all about. Spend a day and night in ⬚ **Augusta,** being sure to visit Meadow Garden, home of George Walton, youngest signer (age 26) of the Declaration of Independence. The Morris Museum of Southern Art is a showcase of Southern art, ranging from luminous 19th-century landscapes to folk art and the challenging abstracts of Augusta native Jasper Johns. Give the remaining two days over to an exploration of ⬚ **Savannah**; stay at a bed-and-breakfast inn (be sure to have reservations, especially for weekends) and view any of the fine restored homes the city offers. Spend some time along **Riverfront Plaza,** enjoying the waterfront, dining in restaurants, and just plain kicking back. Other must-see sights include the 1815 **Isaiah Davenport House** and the **Colonial Park Cemetery,** the final resting place for some of America's founders. Spring and fall are the best times to visit both these cities, but in spring, you may be able to catch a tour of Savannah's glorious private gardens.

IF YOU HAVE 7 DAYS

Add a trip to ⬚ **Atlanta** to the itinerary described in If You Have 3 Days (☞ *above*). History enthusiasts will want to visit the **Atlanta History Center** and its gardens, viewing its exhibits that focus on the history of the city and touring its two house museums. A fine little exhibition, the **African American Panoramic Experience,** chronicles the history of black people in America. The **Atlanta Cyclorama** showcases a huge painting of the 1864 Battle of Atlanta. The **Chattahoochee National Recreational Area** is a great spot for joggers, walkers, hikers, and nature lovers. At **Stone Mountain Park,** you can see the Confederate Memorial (the world's largest sculpture), two Civil War museums, and the Road to Tara Museum. Atlanta is famous for its springtime, and no doubt this is a glorious time to visit. But fall is exquisite, too, as the hardwoods change color, beginning about early October.

IF YOU HAVE 10 DAYS

Follow the itinerary suggested in If You Have 7 Days (☞ *above*). Then take a run up to the north Georgia mountains, visiting **Clayton,** with its many art and antiques shops; to ⬚ **Dahlonega,** where you can relive your dreams of panning gold in "them thar hills"; or to **Chicamauga,** site of one of the Civil War's most important conflicts. The north Georgia mountains are glorious from spring through fall. Or turn south and visit the heart of the state, taking in ⬚ **Macon,** with its antebellum and Victorian homes and museums. Spring in middle Georgia is splendid with azaleas and other flowers in full bloom. Many garden and historic home tours are scheduled at this time.

When to Tour Georgia

Spring is probably the best time to visit, although autumn, especially beginning in early October, is another glorious season.

ATLANTA

Founded in 1837 as the end of the Western & Atlantic railroad line and thus named Terminus, Atlanta today is a transportation hub, not just for the country but for the world: Hartsfield Atlanta International Airport is the nation's third busiest in daily passenger flights. Direct flights to Europe, South America, and Asia have made Atlanta easily accessible to the more than 1,000 international businesses that operate here, and the nearly 50 countries that have representation in the city through consulates, trade offices, and chambers of commerce. The city has emerged as a banking center, and is the world headquarters for such Fortune 500 companies as CNN, Coca-Cola, Delta Air Lines, Holiday Inn Worldwide, and United Parcel Service.

Atlanta's character has evolved from a mix of peoples: Transplanted Northerners and those from elsewhere account for 50% of the population and have undeniably affected the mood and character of the city. Irish immigrants had a major role in the city's early history, along with Germans and Austrians; the Hungarian-born Rich brothers founded Atlanta's principal department store. And the immigrants keep coming. In the past two decades, Atlanta has seen spirited growth in its Asian and Latin-American communities. Now owners of profitable businesses, Atlanta's Asian-American and Latino citizens can point with pride to their economic and civic accomplishments. Their restaurants, shops, and institutions have become part of the city's texture.

For more than three decades, Atlanta has been linked to the civil rights movement. Among the many accomplishments of Atlanta's African-American community is the Nobel Peace Prize that Martin Luther King Jr. won in 1964. Dr. King's widow, Coretta Scott King, continues to operate the King Center, which she founded after her husband's assassination in 1968. In 1972 Andrew Young was elected the first black congressman from the South since Reconstruction. After serving as ambassador to the United Nations during President Jimmy Carter's administration, Young was elected mayor of Atlanta. He is now a consultant with an international firm.

The traditional South, which in a romantic version consists of lacy moss dangling from tree limbs, thick sugary Southern drawls, a leisurely pace, and luxurious antebellum mansions, is rarely found here. Even before the Civil War, the columned house was a rarity. The frenetic pace of building that characterized the period after the Civil War seems to continue unabated. Still viewed by die-hard Southerners as the heart of the Old Confederacy, Atlanta has become the best example of the New South, a fast-paced modern city proud of its heritage.

In the past two decades, Atlanta has experienced unprecedented growth. A good measure of that is its ever-changing downtown skyline, along with skyscrapers constructed in the Midtown, Buckhead, and outer perimeter (set by I–285) business districts. Since the late 1970s, dozens of architecturally dazzling skyscrapers designed by such luminaries as Philip Johnson, I. M. Pei, and Marcel Breuer have reshaped the city's profile. Residents, however, are less likely to measure the city's growth by skyscrapers than by increasing traffic jams, crowds, higher prices, and the ever-burgeoning subdivisions that continue to push urban sprawl farther and farther into surrounding rural areas. Although the Chamber of Commerce advertises Atlanta as a 20-county metropolitan area, the core of Atlanta revolves around five counties. The City of Atlanta is primarily in Fulton and DeKalb counties, with the southern part and the airport in Clayton County. Outside I–285, Cobb and Gwinnett counties on the northwest and northeast corners of the city are experiencing much of Atlanta's population increase.

Atlanta's lack of a grid system in most parts of the city will confuse some drivers. Some streets change their name along the same stretch of road, including the city's most famous thoroughfare, Peachtree Street, which follows a mountain ridge from downtown to suburban Norcross outside of north I–285; it becomes Peachtree Road after it crosses I–85 and then splits into Peachtree Industrial Boulevard beyond the Buckhead neighborhood and the original Peachtree Road, which heads into Chamblee. Adding to the confusion, 60 other streets in the metropolitan area use the word Peachtree in their names. Before setting out anywhere, get the complete street address of your destination, including landmarks, cross streets, or other guideposts, as street numbers and even street signs often are difficult to find.

Downtown

Downtown Atlanta clusters around the hub known as Five Points. Here is the MARTA station that intersects north–south and east–west lines. On the surface, Five Points is formed by the intersection of Peachtree Street with Marietta, Broad, and Forsyth streets.

Numbers in the text correspond to numbers in the margin and on the Downtown Atlanta map.

A Good Walk

Start your walk in the Martin Luther King Jr. National Historic District, where you may get a sense of what the civil rights movement and its principal leader were all about. Here, first visit the **Martin Luther King Jr. Birth Home** ① on Auburn Avenue, and, on the next block west, the **Martin Luther King Jr. Center for Nonviolent Social Change** ②, where Dr. King is entombed. Next stop at the nearby **Ebenezer Baptist Church** ③, where Dr. King preached along with his grandfather, father, and brother. Proceed a few blocks west near the I–75/85 overpass to enjoy the **John Wesley Dobbs Plaza** ④, a good place to take a breather. The **Odd Fellows Building** ⑤ on the other side of Auburn Avenue just after you walk under the expressway is a handsome structure, not to be missed. At this point, go south on Bell Street and walk one block to Edgewood Avenue to visit the **Sweet Auburn Curb Market** ⑥. Walk one block west on Edgewood Avenue, and you'll reach the **Baptist Student Center** ⑦, a fine example of Victorian architecture. Returning north to Auburn Avenue, you'll see the **Atlanta Daily World Building** ⑧, and next to it the **African-American Panoramic Experience (APEX)** ⑨.

Continue down Auburn Avenue just a few steps, and step inside the lobby of the **Atlanta Life Insurance Company** ⑩ to view its fabulous art collection; then proceed across the street to make a stop at the **Auburn Avenue Research Library on African-American Culture and History** ⑪. Next, walk west on Auburn until you reach Peachtree Center Avenue; turn left and walk one block south to Edgewood Avenue. Then turn right along a triangle-shape wedge of land (Hurt Plaza), where you'll see the **Hurt Building** ⑫, a rare Atlanta example of Chicago-style architecture. Follow Edgewood Avenue west a few paces to Pryor Street, where you can take a break at **Woodruff Park** ⑬.

At this point, the walk branches in three directions, which are most efficiently managed by taking MARTA trains to get quickly from one spot to the next. The valiant will, of course, prefer to continue on foot.

Proceed north on Peachtree Street from Woodruff Park, and note Atlanta's **Flatiron Building** ⑭ on the west side of Peachtree and the **Candler Building** ⑮ on the east side of the street. Nearby on Peachtree Street at John Wesley Dobbs Avenue is the modern **Georgia-Pacific Building** ⑯, and across from it are **Margaret Mitchell Park** ⑰ and **the Atlanta-Fulton Public Library** ⑱. Continuing north up Peachtree Street, note the modern **Ritz-Carlton, Atlanta** ⑲ hotel, the **One Ninety One Peachtree Tower** ⑳, and **Peachtree Center** ㉑, which includes the small but worthwhile **Atlanta International Museum of Art and Design** ㉒, then go east on Baker Street and walk one block to Courtland Street; turn north

70

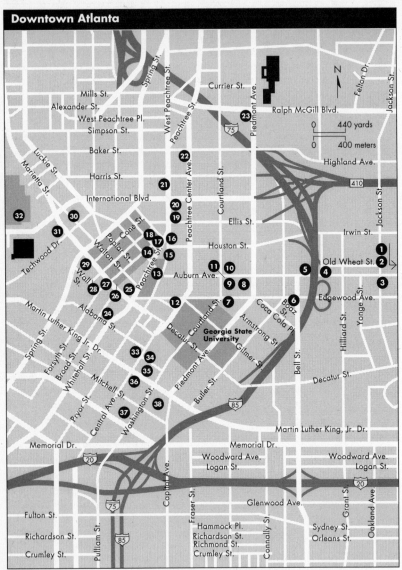

Atlanta Neighborhoods

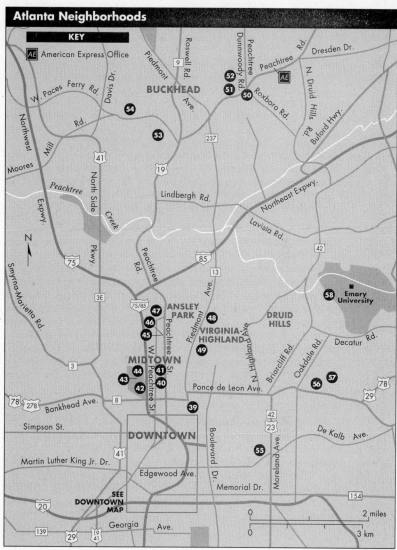

KEY

AE American Express Office

BUCKHEAD

ANSLEY PARK

VIRGINIA-HIGHLAND

MIDTOWN

DRUID HILLS

DOWNTOWN

Emory University

SEE DOWNTOWN MAP

0   2 miles

0   3 km

Georgia State
Capitol, **38**

Georgian Terrace, **41**

High Museum of
Art, **46**

Hurt Building, **12**

John Wesley Dobbs
Plaza, **4**

Lenox Square, **50**

Margaret Mitchell
Park, **17**

Martin Luther King
Jr. Birth Home, **1**

Martin Luther King
Jr. Center for
Nonviolent Social
Change, **2**

Michael C. Carlos
Museum, **58**

NationsBank
Building, **26**

NationsBankPlaza
Tower, **42**

Odd Fellows
Building, **5**

One Atlantic Center, **43**

One Ninety One
Peachtree Tower, **20**

Peachtree Center, **21**

Phipps Plaza, **52**

Piedmont Park, **49**

Rhodes Memorial
Hall, **47**

Ritz-Carlton,
Atlanta, **19**

Ritz-Carlton,
Buckhead, **51**

SciTrek, **39**

Shrine of the
Immaculate
Conception, **36**

Statue of Henry
Grady, **27**

Sweet Auburn Curb
Market, **6**

Underground
Atlanta, **33**

William-Oliver
Building, **25**

Woodruff Arts
Center, **45**

Woodruff Park, **13**

World of Coca-Cola, **35**

on Courtland until you reach Ralph McGill Boulevard. Here you'll find an open-air folk art exhibition, known as the **Folk Art Park** ㉓.

Return to Peachtree Center, and take the subway back one stop to **Five Points MARTA Station** ㉔, or follow Ralph McGill Boulevard west one block to Peachtree Street; continue walking south on Peachtree until you reach the **William-Oliver Building** ㉕, an award-winning restoration. Around the corner on Marietta Street at Broad Street is the handsome **NationsBank Building** ㉖, and nearby is the **Statue of Henry Grady** ㉗, right across from the building now housing the newspaper he founded, the **Atlanta Journal and Constitution** ㉘. A block west on Marietta Street is the **Federal Reserve Bank** ㉙, with its monetary museum. At Marietta Street and Techwood Drive, **Centennial Olympic Park** ㉚ hosts concerts and special events. Adjacent to the park is **CNN Center** ㉛, which you may tour by making an advance reservation. At the rear of the center is the **Georgia Dome** ㉜.

At the CNN Center/Georgia Dome station, take MARTA one station back to the Five Points Station, and exit at the sign for **Underground Atlanta** ㉝. After taking a rest and a restorative snack in its food court, wander the maze of subterranean streets here and exit the doors of Underground Atlanta, bearing slightly left toward the **Georgia Railroad Freight Depot** ㉞. Across the plaza from the Depot is the **World of Coca-Cola** ㉟, with fun memorabilia on display. Across Martin Luther King Jr. Drive at Central Avenue is the historic **Shrine of the Immaculate Conception** ㊱, one of many churches still operating in downtown. Just south of the Shrine are the neo-Gothic **City Hall** ㊲, with a modern addition housing a permanent art collection (✉ On Mitchell St.), and the Renaissance-style **Georgia State Capitol** ㊳ on Washington Street.

TIMING

This walk requires at least a day, assuming you don't spend much time at any one location. If you do plan to walk at a more leisurely pace, finish the first day at Woodruff Park and allow another half day for the rest of the walk. If you plan tours of CNN Center, the Georgia Dome, and World of Coca-Cola, you'll need yet an additional half day. If you wish to see everything in detail, including touring the King Center and Birth Home, Ebenezer Baptist Church, and the African-American Panoramic Experience, take the walk during Monday to Thursday; some sights are closed Friday, and Friday traffic downtown can be heavy. If you tour these sights at length, it will probably take two full days to cover the territory. The terrain is fairly level and not too taxing, with sidewalks the entire distance.

Sights to See

9 **African-American Panoramic Experience (APEX).** Housed in a restored downtown building, the museum chronicles the history of black people in America. The exhibits in this gem of a museum change quarterly. There is a gift shop, and videos illustrate the history of Sweet Auburn, the name bestowed upon Auburn Avenue by businessman John Wesley Dobbs, who fostered business development for African-Americans on this street. ✉ *135 Auburn Ave.*, ☎ *404/521–2739.* ✉ *$3.* ☺ *Tues.–Sat. 10–5.*

OFF THE
BEATEN PATH

Atlanta Cyclorama & Civil War Museum. In Grant Park, named for a New England–born Confederate colonel and not a U.S. president, you'll find a huge circular painting, completed by immigrant artists shortly after the Civil War, depicting the 1864 Battle of Atlanta. The *Texas*, a locomotive involved in the Great Locomotive Chase, is also exhibited. The museum has one of the best Civil War bookstores anywhere. To reach

Cyclorama by car, take I–20 east to Exit 26 and make a right into Grant Park; follow signs to Cyclorama. ⊠ *Grant Park, 800 Cherokee Ave.,* ☎ *404/624–1071 information.* ▧ *$5.* ☾ *June–Labor Day, daily 9:20– 5:30; 1st day after Labor Day–May, daily 9:20–4:30.*

❽ Atlanta Daily World Building. This simple two-story brick building, banded with a white frieze of lions' heads, was constructed in the early 1900s; it houses one of the nation's oldest black newspapers; despite its title, the publication is not a daily, although it was in the past. The newspaper was founded as a weekly in 1928. ⊠ *145 Auburn Ave.,* ☎ *404/659–1110.*

⓲ Atlanta-Fulton Public Library. The Marcel Breuer–designed building houses a large collection of *Gone With the Wind* memorabilia and newspapers from most major cities in the United States and elsewhere on its fourth floor. ⊠ *1 Margaret Mitchell Sq.,* ☎ *404/730–1700.* ☾ *Mon., Fri., Sat., 10–5; Tues., Wed., Thurs. 10–8, Sun. 2–6.*

★ **㉒ Atlanta International Museum of Art and Design.** Behind Peachtree Center in the Marriott Marquis Two Tower, this museum has mounted more than 20 major international exhibitions covering such subjects as textiles, puzzles, boxes, masks, and baskets. Exhibits focus on art and crafts from around the globe. ⊠ *285 Peachtree Center Ave.,* ☎ *404/688– 2467.* ▧ *Free.* ☾ *Tues.–Sat. 11–5.*

㉘ Atlanta Journal and Constitution. Within the building containing the business offices and printing plant for the city's—and the state's—dominant newspaper, the lobby displays front-page news of historic events, an old printing press, and photographs of famous former employees. ⊠ *72 Marietta St.,* ☎ *404/614–2688.* ☾ *Tours of plant available by prior arrangement at 11:30 AM and 12:30 PM.*

❿ Atlanta Life Insurance Company. The landmark enterprise founded by Alonzo Herndon, a former slave, was located in modest quarters at 148 Auburn Avenue until the modern complex at No. 100 was opened in 1980. The lobby holds an exhibition of art by black artists from the United States and Africa. ⊠ *100 Auburn Ave.,* ☎ *404/659–2100.* ☾ *Weekdays 8:30–5.*

⓫ Auburn Avenue Research Library on African-American Culture and History. This unit added to the ☞ **Atlanta-Fulton Public Library** system in 1994 is a noncirculating library housing about 23,000 volumes devoted to African-American subjects on the first floor alone. Special exhibits, programs, and tours are free and open to the public. The archives division contains rare books, manuscript collections, photographs, and memorabilia. ⊠ *101 Auburn Ave.,* ☎ *404/730–4001.* ☾ *Mon.–Thurs. noon–8, weekends 2–6.*

❼ Baptist Student Center. Adjacent to the **Georgia State University** campus, this restored Victorian building once contained the Coca-Cola Company's first bottling plant. ⊠ *125 Edgewood Ave.,* ☎ *404/659–8726.*

⓯ Candler Building. Asa G. Candler, founder of the Coca-Cola Company, engaged the local firm of Murphy and Stewart to design this splendid terra-cotta and marble building in 1906. The ornate bronze and marble lobby shouldn't be missed. ⊠ *84 Peachtree St.* ☾ *Daily 9–5 to public.*

㉚ Centennial Olympic Park. This 21-acre urban landscape, the largest urban park to be developed in this country in more than two decades, was the central venue for Olympics entertainment in summer 1996. The park's Fountain of Rings (the world's largest using the Olympic symbol) centers a court of 24 flags, each of them representing the Olympic

Games as well as the host countries of the modern Games. Seating in the fountain amphitheater allows visitors to enjoy the water and music spectacle (five tunes are programmed and timed to coincide with water displays). The park has a 6-acre great lawn and pathways formed by commemorative brick pavers. ⊠ *Marietta St. and Techwood Dr.,* ☎ *404/223–4412 or 404/223–4636 information.* ⊙ *Daily 8:30 AM–9 PM.*

㊲ City Hall. When the 14-story, neo-Gothic building, designed by Atlanta architect G. Lloyd Preacher, was erected in 1929, critics dubbed it "The Painted Lady of Mitchell Street." A modern addition as well as a restoration of the original building was completed in 1989. The new wing, with its five-story glass atrium and beautiful marble entryway, houses a splendid permanent collection of art. ⊠ *68 Mitchell St.,* ☎ *404/330–6000.* ⊙ *Weekdays 8:15–5.*

㉛ CNN Center. The home of Ted Turner's Cable News Network occupies all 14 floors of this dramatic structure on the edge of downtown. The 40-minute CNN studio tour begins with a ride up the world's longest escalator to an eighth-floor exhibit about Turner's global broadcasting empire. Tours are not open to children under age six. ⊠ *1 CNN Center,* ☎ *404/827–2300. Reservations must be made at least 1 day in advance using credit card (AE, MC, V); walk-up tickets for same day only, if available, go on sale at 8:30 AM.* ⊡ *$7.* ⊙ *Daily 9–6.*

❸ Ebenezer Baptist Church. A Gothic Revival–style building completed in 1922, the church became known as the spiritual center for the civil rights movement after Dr. King won the Nobel Peace Prize in 1964. Members of the King family have preached at the church for three generations; Dr. King's funeral was held here. A tour of the church includes an audiotape recorded by the pastor outlining the history of the building. ⊠ *407 Auburn Ave.,* ☎ *404/688–7263.* ⊡ *Tours free; donations accepted.* ⊙ *Tours of the sanctuary weekdays 9–5, Sat. 10–2.*

㉙ Federal Reserve Bank. This bank sits on the site once occupied by Thrasherville, a settlement that predates the 1837 establishment of Atlanta. An exhibit explains the story of money as a medium of exchange and the history of the U.S. banking system. Items displayed include rare coins, uncut sheets of money, and a gold bar. ⊠ *104 Marietta St.,* ☎ *404/521–8764.* ⊡ *Free.* ⊙ *Weekdays 9–4.*

㉔ Five Points MARTA Station. This MARTA station serves Underground Atlanta and nearby Woodruff Park, Georgia State University, and numerous businesses; the station is at the crossroads of MARTA's east–west and north–south lines. Stand on the corner of Peachtree and Alabama streets, outside the station, and notice the old-fashioned gas street light, with its historic marker proclaiming it the **Eternal Flame of the Confederacy.** ⊠ *Corner of Peachtree and Alabama Sts.*

⓮ Flatiron Building. The English-American Building, as it was originally known, was designed by Bradford Gilbert. Similar to the famous downtown New York City Flatiron Building, built after the turn of the century, this one dates from 1897, and is the city's oldest high-rise. Its distinguishing features include a knife-sharp point that looks proudly up Peachtree Street. The rounded facade gazes toward Woodruff Park, and interesting bays within protrude out of the facade about 3 ft. ⊠ *74 Peachtree St.* ⊙ *Weekdays 8:15–5:30.*

㉓ Folk Art Park. Revitalizing an ignored part of the city, the park pays homage to an important American art form by gathering works that reflect the diverse styles of American (especially Southern) folk art. Work by more than a dozen different artists is on display, among them

Harold Rittenberry, Howard Finster, and Eddie Owens Martin. Martin's brightly painted totems and snake-topped walls replicate portions of *Pasaquan* (Martin's visionary environment that he painted during his last years on the buildings at his farm near Columbus, Georgia). ⊠ *Ralph McGill Blvd. at Courtland St., Baker St., and Piedmont Ave.*

㉜ Georgia Dome. This arena accommodates 70,500 with good visibility no matter where the seat is located; it is the site of Atlanta Falcons football games, major rock concerts, conventions, and trade shows. The white, plum, and turquoise 1-million-square-ft facility is crowned with the world's largest cable-supported oval, giving the roof a circus-tent top. ⊠ *1 Georgia Dome Dr.,* ☎ *404/223–9200.* 🎫 *$4.* ☉ *Tours Tues.–Sun. every ½ hr, 10–4.*

⑯ Georgia-Pacific Building. The towering, 52-story structure occupies the site of the old Loew's Grand Theatre, where *Gone With the Wind* premiered in 1939. The red-marble high-rise from certain angles appears to be two-dimensional, or flat against the sky. The **High Museum of Art, Folk Art and Photography Galleries** is inside the building. ⊠ *133 Peachtree St., John Wesley Dobbs Ave. The Museum:* ⊠ *30 John Wesley Dobbs Ave.,* ☎ *404/577–6940.* 🎫 *Free.* ☉ *Mon.–Sat. 10–5.*

㉞ Georgia Railroad Freight Depot. After downtown's oldest extant building was built in 1869 to replace the one torched by Sherman's troops in 1864, it burned again in 1935 and was rebuilt in its present form. It is now used by several downtown companies as a banquet hall and for special events. It may be viewed only by appointment. ⊠ *65 Martin Luther King Jr. Dr.,* ☎ *404/656–3850.*

★ ㊳ Georgia State Capitol. A Renaissance-style edifice by Chicago architects Edbrooke and Burnham, the capitol building was dedicated on July 4, 1889. The gold leaf on its dome was mined in Dahlonega, a small town in north Georgia. In addition to housing politicos, it contains the **Museum of Science and Industry,** open to the public. State historical markers on the grounds commemorate the 1864 Battle of Atlanta, which destroyed 90% of the city. ⊠ *206 Washington St.,* ☎ *404/656–2844.* 🎫 *Free.* ☉ *Guided tours for groups every ½ hr, weekdays 9:30–3; for individuals, weekdays at 10, 11, 1, and 2.*

⑫ Hurt Building. Named for Atlanta developer Joel Hurt, this exquisitely restored 1913 Chicago-style high-rise, with its intricate grillwork and sweeping marble staircase, houses a lower level of shops and art galleries. The excellent City Grill (☞ *Dining, below*), a restaurant, is at the top of the sweeping staircase. ⊠ *50 Hurt Plaza.*

❹ John Wesley Dobbs Plaza. John Wesley Dobbs was an important civic leader whose legacy includes coining the name "Sweet Auburn," Atlanta's black business and residential neighborhood. A legacy of the 1996 Olympic Games, the plaza has a "life mask" of Dobbs himself; children playing in the plaza may look through the mask's eyes and view the street as Dobbs might have seen it. ⊠ *Auburn Ave. adjacent to I–75/85 overpass.*

⑰ Margaret Mitchell Park. With its cascading waterfall and columned sculpture, the park is named for Atlanta's most famous author, whose masterpiece is the novel *Gone With the Wind.* ⊠ *Margaret Mitchell Sq.*

★ ❶ Martin Luther King Jr. Birth Home. This modest Queen Anne–style bungalow is managed by the National Park Service, which also completed a visitor center across the street from the ☞ **Martin Luther King Jr. Center for Nonviolent Social Change** in the summer of 1996. The visitor center contains a multimedia exhibit focused on the civil rights movement and Dr. King's role in it. To sign up for tours, go to the Fire Station

(⊠ 39 Boulevard). ⊠ *501 Auburn Ave.,* ☎ *404/331–3920.* ⊠ *Tours free.* ☉ *Daily guided ½-hr tours every hr 10–5.*

❷ **Martin Luther King Jr. Center for Nonviolent Social Change.** The Martin Luther King Jr. National Historic District occupies several blocks on Auburn Avenue, a few blocks east of Peachtree Street in the black business and residential community of Sweet Auburn. The neighborhood was the birthplace of Martin Luther King Jr. in 1929. After his assassination in 1968, King's widow, Coretta Scott King, established the center, which contains a museum which displays King's Nobel Peace Prize, bible, and tape recorder, along with memorabilia and photos chronicling the civil rights movement. In the courtyard in front of Freedom Hall, on a circular brick pad in the middle of a rectangular "meditation" pool, is King's white marble tomb, where an eternal flame burns and the crypt's inscription reads, "Free at last!" A chapel of all faiths sits at one end of the reflecting pool. Tours of Sweet Auburn commence from the center. ⊠ *449 Auburn Ave.,* ☎ *404/524–1956.* ⊠ *Free.* ☉ *Daily 9–5.*

㉖ **NationsBank Building.** Originally known as the Chicago-style Empire Building, the handsome 1901 classic was designed by Atlanta architect Phillip Trammel Shutze. In 1929 Shutze refashioned the first three floors, bestowing upon them a decidedly Renaissance look. This is one of the city's first steel-frame structures, and at 14 stories one of its tallest, but during the renovation, Shutze resheathed the base with masonry. ⊠ *35 Broad St.*

❺ **Odd Fellows Building.** The Georgia Chapter of the Grand United Order of Odd Fellows was a trade and social organization for African-Americans. In 1912 the membership erected this handsome Romanesque Revival–style building housing meeting rooms, a theater, commercial spaces, and a community center. African-featured terra-cotta figures adorn the splendid entrance. Now handsomely restored, the building houses offices. ⊠ *250 Auburn Ave.*

㉔ **One Ninety One Peachtree Tower.** Designed by John Burgee with Philip Johnson as a consultant, the 50-story neo-Gothic skyscraper, built in 1990, has a dazzling lobby with a seven-story-high atrium. ⊠ *191 Peachtree St.*

㉑ **Peachtree Center.** John Portman designed this skyscraper complex, built between 1960–1992, which contains shops, offices, and a variety of restaurants. Across the street, connected to Peachtree Center by skywalks, is the massive **Atlanta Market Center.** Two additional Portman creations, the **Atlanta Marriott Marquis** and the **Hyatt Regency Hotel** are also connected to the center by skywalks. A MARTA stop is available at Peachtree Center. ⊠ *225 Peachtree St.,* ☎ *404/654–1255.*

㉒ **Ritz-Carlton, Atlanta.** The hotel has a fabulous collection of hunting art, both paintings and sculptures, in The Restaurant and The Bar. ⊠ *181 Peachtree St.,* ☎ *404/659–0400.*

㊱ **Shrine of the Immaculate Conception.** During the Battle of Atlanta, Fr. Thomas O'Reilly, the church's pastor, persuaded Union forces to spare his church and several others around the city. That 1848 structure was then replaced by this much grander building, whose cornerstone was laid in 1869. O'Reilly, a native of Ireland, was interred in the basement of the church. Now on the National Register, the church was nearly lost to fire in 1982 but has been exquisitely restored. The vestibule is always open, allowing visitors to view the interior, or contact the rectory for an appointment. ⊠ *48 Martin Luther King Jr. Dr., at Central Ave.,* ☎ *404/521–1866.* ☉ *Weekdays 8:30–5, Sat. 9–7, Sun. 7–3.*

27 Statue of Henry Grady. New York artist Alexander Doyle's bronze sculpture honors the post–Civil War editor of the *Atlanta Constitution* and early advocate of the so-called New South. Much about Grady reminds one of Ted Turner, contemporary Atlanta media mogul. Among other things, Grady was an early booster of baseball. The memorial was raised in 1891, after Grady's untimely death at age 39. ⊠ *Corner of Marietta and Forsyth Sts.*

6 Sweet Auburn Curb Market. An institution on Edgewood Avenue, established in 1923, the market sells vegetables, fish, flowers, prepared foods, and meat. Individual stalls are operated by separate owners, making this a true public market. ⊠ *209 Edgewood Ave.,* ☎ *404/659-1665.* ☉ *Mon.–Thurs. 8–5, Fri.–Sat. 8–7.*

33 Underground Atlanta. This six-block entertainment and shopping district, dotted with historic markers, was created from the web of underground brick streets, ornamental building facades, and tunnels that fell into disuse in 1929, when the city built viaducts over the train tracks. Merchants moved their storefronts to the new viaduct level, leaving the original street level for storage. Today, it houses restaurants, clubs, art galleries, shopping emporia, and a food court, making it a good stop on a walking tour. **Atlanta Heritage Row,** within the complex (⊠ 55 Upper Alabama St., ☎ 404/584-7879), is operated by the Atlanta History Center (☞ Buckhead, *below*) and has a multimedia presentation about the city and other historical exhibits. Admission is $3 and it's open Tuesday–Saturday 10–5, Sunday 1–5. ⊠ *50 Upper Alabama St.,* ☎ *404/523-2311.*

25 William-Oliver Building. Walk through the lobby of this Art-Deco gem and admire the ceiling mural, brass grills, and elevator doors. Formerly an office building, it has been renovated for luxury downtown residences, and won a 1997 award for historic preservation from the Atlanta Urban Design Commission. ⊠ *32 Peachtree St.*

13 Woodruff Park. Named for the city's great philanthropist, Robert W. Woodruff, the late Coca-Cola magnate, the triangular park fills during lunchtime on weekdays with executives, street preachers, politicians, Georgia State University students, and homeless people. It's a popular spot for enjoying brown-bag lunches and the sunshine. Occasionally, the park is the site of musical events. ⊠ *Bordered by Pryor, Houston, and Peachtree Sts.*

☺ 35 World of Coca-Cola. At this three-story, $15-million special-exhibit facility, you can sip samples of 38 Coca-Cola Company products from around the world and marvel over memorabilia from more than a century's worth of corporate archives. "Everything Coca-Cola," the renovated gift shop, sells everything from refrigerator magnets to evening bags. ⊠ *55 Martin Luther King Jr. Dr.,* ☎ *404/676-5151.* ☒ *$6.* ☉ *Sept.–May, Mon.–Sat. 10–8:30, Sun. noon–5; June–Aug., Mon.–Sat. 9–8:30, Sun. 11–5.*

OF THE
BEATEN PATH

ZOO ATLANTA – Named by *Good Housekeeping* magazine one of the top 10 zoos in the United States, the zoo, in Grant Park, has nearly 1,000 animals. An ongoing $35-million renovation program has already produced the Ford African Rain Forest, Flamingo Lagoon, Masai Mara (re-created plains of Kenya), and Sumatran Tiger Exhibit. Longtime resident gorilla, Willie B., and his child, Kudzoo, are always hits with zoo visitors. To reach the zoo by car, take I-20 east to Exit 26 and make a right into Grant Park; follow signs to the zoo. ⊠ *Grant Park, 800 Cherokee Ave.,* ☎ *404/624-5600.* ☒ *$7.50.* ☉ *Daily 10–4:30 (10–5:30 on weekends during daylight savings time).*

Midtown

Just north of downtown lies this thriving area, a hippie hangout in the late '60s and '70s, now home to a large segment of the city's gay population, along with young families, young professionals, artists, and musicians. Formerly in decline, Midtown has evolved into one of the city's most interesting neighborhoods. Its gleaming new office towers give it a skyline to rival downtown's, and the renovated mansions and bungalows in its residential section have made it a city showcase. *Numbers in the text correspond to numbers in the margin and on the Atlanta Neighborhoods map.*

A Good Drive

From downtown, take Piedmont Avenue about a half mile to **SciTrek** ㊴, a science museum all ages will enjoy. Turn left from Piedmont Avenue onto Ponce de Leon Avenue and drive two blocks to Peachtree Street, then turn right and find the 1929 **Fox Theatre** ㊵, and across the street, the **Georgian Terrace** ㊶, a luxury apartment building. From Peachtree Street, circle around the block, turning right on 3rd Street to Juniper Street; then turn right on Juniper and continue two blocks to North Avenue. Turn right again onto Peachtree Street to view the **Nations-BankPlaza Tower** ㊷. Next, turn right onto West Peachtree Street and drive 12 blocks to its intersection with 14th Street, where you'll find **One Atlantic Center** ㊸, built for IBM. Turn left onto 18th Street to reach the **Center for Puppetry Arts** ㊹. Take 18th Street east back to Peachtree Street, turn left, and continue on to the **Woodruff Arts Center** ㊺, which includes the **High Museum of Art** ㊻, an example of impressive modern architecture. From this point, travel two blocks north on Peachtree Street to **Rhodes Memorial Hall** ㊼. From here, take Beverly Road east off Peachtree Street for about ¼ mi to Montgomery Ferry Drive; turn a quick dogleg left then right, continuing on Beverly to Park Lane, then turn right on Park Lane about ¼ mi to where it intersects the Prado. Here, these two streets dead-end onto Piedmont Avenue, where you'll enter the **Atlanta Botanical Garden** ㊽, which adjoins **Piedmont Park** ㊾, bound by Piedmont Avenue, 10th Street, and Westminster Drive.

TIMING

This drive is best accomplished between mid-morning (about 9:30 AM) and mid-afternoon (3:30 PM) to avoid rush hour traffic. All the sights may be visited in between four and five hours. Parking is adjacent to or only a few steps away from all the sights, and often it is free.

Sights to See

㊽ **Atlanta Botanical Garden.** Occupying 30 acres inside ☞ **Piedmont Park**, the grounds contain 15 acres of display gardens, including a serene Japanese garden, a 15-acre hardwood forest with walking trails, and the Fuqua Conservatory, featuring unusual and threatened flora from tropical and desert climates. A permanent Fuqua Conservatory exhibit of tiny, bright-colored poison dart frogs is very popular, especially with children. ✉ *1345 Piedmont Ave., at the Prado,* ☎ *404/876–5859.* ☞ *$6; free Thurs. after 3.* ☉ *Tues.–Sun. 9–6; until 7 Apr.–Oct.*

★ ☕ ㊹ **Center for Puppetry Arts.** At this interactive museum, you can see puppets from around the world. Children can attend puppet-making workshops. Performances, which include original dramatic works for puppets and classics adapted for the museum theater, are presented by professional puppeteers who leave youngsters spellbound. ✉ *1404 Spring St., at 18th St.,* ☎ *404/873–3391.* ☞ *$5; special exhibits, programs, and performances may cost extra.* ☉ *Mon.–Sat. 9–5.*

40 **Fox Theatre.** One of a handful of classic movie palaces in the nation, the Fox was built in 1929 in a fabulous Moorish-Egyptian style to be the headquarters of the Shriner's Club. The interior's crowning glory is its "sky" ceiling—complete with clouds and stars above Alhambra-like minarets. Threatened by demolition in the 1970s, the Fox was saved from the wrecker's ball by concerted civic action and is still a prime venue for musicals, rock concerts, dance performances, and film festivals. ✉ *660 Peachtree St.,* ☎ *404/881–2100; 404/876–2041 Atlanta Preservation Center.* ▣ *Tour conducted by Atlanta Preservation Center $5.* ☉ *Tours Mon., Wed., Thurs. at 10 AM, Sat. at 10 and 11 AM.*

41 **Georgian Terrace.** Originally built in 1911 as a fine Beaux Arts-style hotel, the Georgian Terrace, designed by William L. Stoddart, housed the stars of the film *Gone With the Wind* when it premiered at the nearby Loew's Theater (now demolished) in 1939. President Calvin Coolidge also slept here. Stars of the Metropolitan Opera were housed at the hotel when the Met used to make its annual trek to Atlanta, and according to locals, Enrico Caruso routinely serenaded passersby from its balconies. Renovated with style and historic sensitivity, the building now houses luxury apartments and some interesting restaurants. ✉ *459 Peachtree St.*

46 **High Museum of Art.** Named for Mrs. Joseph High, whose generosity launched this high-tech showplace built in 1983, the museum draws from permanent holdings focused on American decorative arts and African art. In 1991 the American Institute of Architects listed the sleek museum, designed by Richard Meier, among the 10 best works of American architecture in the 1980s. ✉ *1280 Peachtree St., Woodruff Arts Center, MARTA Arts Center Station,* ☎ *404/733–4444 for recorded information.* ▣ *$6; free Thurs. after 1; special exhibits may cost extra.* ☉ *Tues.–Fri. 10–5, every 4th Fri. 10–9, Sat. 10–5, Sun. noon–5.*

42 **NationsBankPlaza Tower.** Built in 1992, the skyscraper has a graceful birdcage roof easily visible from the interstate, and is the South's tallest building at 1,023 ft. Its elegant marbled central lobby is worth seeing. ✉ *600 Peachtree St.*

43 **One Atlantic Center.** Also known as the **IBM Tower,** the pyramid-topped office building presents a unique profile that is visible from many parts of the city. It was built in 1987, designed by Philip Johnson. ✉ *1201 W. Peachtree St.*

49 **Piedmont Park.** The city's outdoor recreation center, this park is a major venue for special events. Tennis courts, a swimming pool, and paths for walking, jogging, and rollerblading are part of the attraction, but many retreat to the park's great lawn for picnics with a smashing view of the Midtown skyline. Each April the park hosts the popular Dogwood Festival. ✉ *Piedmont Ave. between 10th St. and the Prado.*

47 **Rhodes Memorial Hall.** Headquarters of the **Georgia Trust for Historic Preservation,** this former residence is one of the finest works of Atlanta architect Willis F. Denny II. Built at the northern edge of the city in 1904 for Amos Giles Rhodes, the wealthy founder of a local furniture chain, the hall features a series of stained-glass windows depicting the heroes of the Confederacy. ✉ *1516 Peachtree St.,* ☎ *404/881–9980.* ▣ *$3.* ☉ *Weekdays 11–4.*

★ ☾ **39** **SciTrek.** The Science and Technology Museum of Atlanta covers 96,000 square ft. and has rotating exhibitions and daily science demonstrations. About 150 hands-on exhibits occupy five environments: Simple Machines; Light, Color, and Perception; Electricity and Magnetism; Kidspace, for children ages two to seven; and Power Your Future. Recent additions include the Coca-Cola Science Show Theater and the Information Petting Zoo, exhibiting cybercritters. ✉ *395 Piedmont Ave.,* ☎ *404/522–5500.* 🎫 *$7.50.* ☉ *Mon.–Sat. 10–5, Sun. noon–5.*

④⑤ Woodruff Arts Center. Home to the world-renowned **Atlanta Symphony Orchestra,** the ☞ **High Museum of Art,** and the **Alliance Theatre,** the center also houses an intimate **Studio Theater.** Both theaters present contemporary dramas, classics, and frequent world premieres. ✉ *1280 Peachtree St.,* ☎ *404/733–4200.*

Buckhead

Atlanta's sprawl doesn't lend itself to walking between major neighborhoods, so take a car or MARTA to reach Buckhead. Many of Atlanta's trendy restaurants, music clubs, chic shops, and hip art galleries are concentrated in this neighborhood. Finding a parking spot on the weekends and at night can be a real headache, and waits of two hours or more are common in the hottest restaurants.

Numbers in the text correspond to numbers in the margin and on the Atlanta Neighborhoods map.

A Good Drive

While the adventurous and high spirited may elect to walk this tour, most will prefer to drive. For one thing, the distance between the Atlanta History Center and the Georgia Governor's Mansion, while not extreme, entails walking where there are no sidewalks, a tricky proposition with traffic zooming just inches away. So begin the drive at the intersection of two splendid shopping malls: The older and larger of the two, **Lenox Square** ㊿, sprawls from Peachtree Road down Lenox Road to East Paces Ferry Road. Across the street from Lenox Square is the **Ritz-Carlton, Buckhead** ㊶, one of two Ritz hotels in Atlanta; across the Buckhead Loop from the hotel, you'll find the elegant shops of **Phipps Plaza** ㊷. Leaving Phipps Plaza, exit onto Peachtree Road, and turn right (south), traveling about ⅓ mi to West Paces Ferry Road. At this intersection, turn right and proceed about ¼ mi to Andrews Drive. Turn left, and the entrance to the **Atlanta History Center** ㊳ is almost immediately on the left. Leaving the center, turn right from the entrance back to West Paces Ferry Road, then turn left driving about a half mile to reach the **Georgia Governor's Mansion** ㊴.

TIMING

As with other driving tours in this busy part of town, one is well advised to stick to the mid-morning to mid-afternoon hours, or about 9:30 AM to 3:30 PM. In Buckhead, an additional wrinkle is the lunchtime traffic, which can make the period from 11:30 AM to 1:30 PM additionally stressful. Shoppers will want to focus on the malls naturally, while anyone interested in local history and culture will want to spend time at the History Center and the Georgia Governor's Mansion. But simply driving the distance around the five sights, looking briefly at each one, will consume, generally, no more than 30 minutes. Otherwise, an in-depth tour of both the History Center and the Governor's Mansion may easily consume several hours.

Sights to See

★ **㊳ Atlanta History Center.** The museum highlights materials native to Georgia, with a floor of heart pine and polished Stone Mountain granite. Displays are provocative, juxtaposing *Gone With the Wind* romanticism with the grim reality of Ku Klux Klan racism. Also on the 33-acre site are the elegant 1928 **Swan House;** the **Tullie Smith Farm,** featuring a two-story plantation plain house (1840s) and **McElreath**

Hall, an exhibition space for artifacts from Atlanta's history. ✉ *130 W. Paces Ferry Rd.,* ☎ *404/814–4000.* ☞ *$7.* ☉ *Mon.–Sat. 10–5:30, Sun. noon–5:30.*

54 Georgia Governor's Mansion. Built in 1967 in Greek Revival style, the mansion contains American Federal-period antiques in its public rooms. Thomas Bradbury, a local architect, was the designer. The 24,000-square-ft mansion contains 30 rooms and sits on 18 acres originally belonging to the Robert Maddox family (no relation to famous Georgia governor Lestor Maddox, who was—ironically—its first occupant). ✉ *391 W. Paces Ferry Rd.,* ☎ *404/261–1858.* ☞ *Free.* ☉ *Guided tours Tues.–Thurs. 10–11:30 AM.*

50 Lenox Square. Local shoppers appreciate the more than 250 stores and several good restaurants at this mall. (☞ Shopping, *below.*) ✉ *3393 Peachtree Rd.,* ☎ *404/233–6767.*

52 Phipps Plaza. This mall is one of Atlanta's premier shopping areas, with more than 100 stores and restaurants and many specialty shops. It also includes a 14-screen movie theater. (☞ Shopping, *below.*) ✉ *3500 Peachtree Rd.,* ☎ *404/262–0992 or 800/810–7700.*

51 Ritz-Carlton, Buckhead. Considered one of the finest hotels in the country, the Ritz contains one of the South's most valuable private art collections, primarily 18th- and 19th-century American and European painting, sculpture, and porcelain. It's also home to one of Atlanta's top restaurants, the **Dining Room** (☞ Dining, *below*). ✉ *3434 Peachtree Rd.,* ☎ *404/237–2700.*

Virginia-Highland and the Emory Area

Restaurants and art galleries are the backbone of Virginia-Highland/Morningside, northeast of Midtown. Like Midtown, this residential area was down-at-the-heels only 25 years ago. Reclaimed by writers, artists, and a few visionary developers, Virginia-Highland today offers intriguing shopping and delightful walking. Nightlife hums here as well.

Numbers in the text correspond to numbers in the margin and on the Atlanta Neighborhoods map.

A Good Drive

This tour meanders through some unique residential areas, such as Druid Hills, location for the film *Driving Miss Daisy,* by local playwright Alfred Uhry. The neighborhood was designed by the firm of Frederick Law Olmsted, which also designed New York's Central Park. Begin at **Carter Presidential Center** 55, the central attraction in a subneighborhood called Poncey Highlands, because it lies south of Ponce de Leon Avenue and south of Virginia Highland. The former president's center is bounded by Freedom Parkway, which splits and encircles the facility. To reach it from downtown, drive on Ralph McGill Boulevard about 1 mi east of I–75/85 (Exit 97) to where the boulevard intersects with Freedom Parkway; or alternately, take North Avenue east from downtown about 1 mi to its intersection with North Highland Avenue, then turn right about ¹⁄₁₆ mi and follow the signs to the center.

From the center, take a left and drive only one short block on Highland Avenue to Ponce de Leon Avenue, and turn right (east), continuing for 1 mi to Clifton Road; next take a left on to Clifton and almost immediately enter the driveway for **Fernbank Museum of Natural History** 56. On the eastern end of this extensive forest and recreational/educational preserve lies **Fernbank Science Center** 57. To reach it, return via Clifton Road to Ponce de Leon Avenue and take a left. Drive east on Ponce de Leon Avenue about ½ mi to Heaton Road, and turn left. The center is on the left of Heaton Road about ¼ mi up the street. Leaving the center, turn left and take Heaton ⅛ mi to Coventry Road, where you should turn left again for about 1/16 mi until you see East Clifton Road. Turn right on East Clifton and follow it around to Clifton Road, and continue ¼ mi to North Decatur Road. The entrance to Emory University is directly in front of you. Enter the campus, bear right, and park in the lot if you wish to visit the **Michael C. Carlos Museum** (58), an exquisite contemporary structure.

TIMING

This tour may be driven in about 15 minutes without stops. It can easily take a full day if you spend a few hours at each sight.

Sights to See

★ (55) **Carter Presidential Center.** This worthwhile center occupies the site where Union General William T. Sherman orchestrated the Battle of Atlanta (1864). The museum and archives detail the political career of former president Jimmy Carter. The center itself, which is not open to the public, focuses on conflict resolution and human rights issues. It sponsors foreign-affairs conferences and projects on such matters as world food supply. Outside, the Japanese-style garden is a serene spot to unwind. ✉ *1 Copenhill Ave.,* ☎ *404/331–3942.* *$5.* *Mon.–Sat. 9–4:45, Sun. noon–4:45.*

(56) **Fernbank Museum of Natural History.** The largest natural history museum south of the Smithsonian Institution in Washington, DC, holds a permanent exhibit, "A Walk Through Time in Georgia." Visitors meander through 15 galleries to explore the earth's natural history. The museum's IMAX theater shows films about the natural world on a six-story screen. The café, with an exquisite view overlooking the forest, has really good food. ✉ *767 Clifton Rd.,* ☎ *404/370–0960; 404/370–0019 IMAX only; 404/370–0850 directions hot line.* *$9.50; prices vary for IMAX.* *Mon.–Thurs. and Sat. 10–5, Fri. 10–10, Sun. noon–5.*

(57) **Fernbank Science Center.** The museum focuses on geology, space exploration, and ecology; it may bore older children. Special seasonal programs, offered for 50¢, for children under five are offered four times a year on the weekends. ✉ *156 Heaton Park Dr.,* ☎ *404/378–4311.* *Museum free, planetarium shows $2.* *Mon. 8:30–5 (except planetarium), Tues.–Fri. 8:30 AM–10 PM, Sat. 10–5, Sun. 1–5.*

★ (58) **Michael C. Carlos Museum.** Housing a permanent collection that embraces 15,000 objects, this excellent museum designed by renowned American architect Michael Graves exhibits artifacts from Egypt, Greece, Rome, the Near East, the Americas, and Africa. European and American prints and drawings cover the Middle Ages through the 20th century. The gift shop has rare art books and art-focused items for children. ✉ *Emory University, 571 Kilgo St.,* ☎ *404/727–4282.* *Suggested donation $3.* *Mon.–Sat. 10–5, Sun. noon–5.*

Other Area Attractions

Atlanta's suburbs offer excellent entertainment opportunities, especially for anyone staying in the outskirts. It is essential to drive to any of these venues, so plan the times carefully in view of Atlanta's notorious rush hours.

American Adventures/White Water/Foam Factory. This complex is really three different theme parks. American Adventures has 15 indoor and outdoor rides, an 18-hole miniature golf course, an arcade, and a race-car track. White Water features more than 40 water attractions, including the largest kids' water playground in the country. Foam Factory is a three-story fun house containing interactive games and 50,000 foam balls coming at you from every direction. ⊠ *250 N. Cobb Pkwy., Marietta,* ☎ *770/424–9283 or 800/928–9283.* 🖃 *Call for pricing as it varies among parks; parking $2.* ⊘ *American Adventures and Foam Factory year-round. White Water May weekends, Memorial Day– Labor Day daily; hrs vary and weather determines operation, so call ahead.*

Chateau Elan. A 16th-century-style French château accommodates Georgia's best-known winery, set in 2,400 rolling acres just 30 minutes north of Atlanta. Winery tours and tastings are free. More than a winery, Chateau Elan is a complete resort. European luxury blends with southern hospitality at the 276-room inn and spa with private villas, golf courses, fishing, tennis, an equestrian center, an art gallery, and six dining areas. ⊠ *100 Rue Charlemagne, Braselton, I–85 to GA 211, Exit 48 (Chestnut Mountain/Winder),* ☎ *770/932–0900 or 800/ 233–9463,* 🅵🅰🆇 *770/271–6005.*

☾ **Chattahoochee Nature Center.** Birds and animals in their natural habitats may be seen from nature trails and a boardwalk winding through 124 acres of woodlands and wetlands. A gift shop, indoor exhibits, birds-of-prey aviaries, and a picnic area are on the property. ⊠ *9135 Willeo Rd., Roswell,* ☎ *404/992–2055.* 🖃 *$3.* ⊘ *Mon.–Sat. 9–5, Sun. noon–5.*

Chestnut Mountain Winery. Across the expressway from ☞ **Chateau Elan,** this Georgia winery makes all its wines from Georgia-grown grapes, including the Bordeaux varietals Chardonnay and Cabernet Sauvignon, or the American hybrids, such as Chambourcin. ⊠ *Hwy. 124, I–85, Exit 48 (Chestnut Mountain/Winder), Braselton,* ☎ *770/867– 6914.* 🖃 *Free tours and tastings.* ⊘ *Wed.–Sun. noon–5.*

☾ **Six Flags Over Georgia.** Atlanta's major theme park, with eight themed sections, heart-stopping roller coasters, and water rides (best saved for last to prevent being damp all day) is a kid's ideal playground. Especially popular is the Batman Stunt Show Spectacular. The park also features well-staged musical revues, concerts by top-name artists, and other performances. Take MARTA's west line to Hightower Station and then the Six Flags bus. ⊠ *I–20W at 7561 Six Flags Pkwy., Austell,* ☎ *770/739–3400.* 🖃 *All-inclusive 1-day pass $32, 2-day pass $37, $6 parking fee.* ⊘ *June–Aug., daily 10* AM*–11* PM*; Mar.–May and Sept.– Oct., park open weekends only from 10* AM*; closing times vary.*

☾ **Stone Mountain Park.** This 3,200-acre state park has the largest exposed granite outcropping on earth. The Confederate Memorial on the north face of the 825-ft-high domed mountain is the world's largest sculpture. The park has a skylift to the mountaintop, a steam locomotive ride around the mountain's 5-mi-diameter base, an antebellum plantation, a swimming beach, a campground, a hotel, a resort, six restaurants, a paddle-wheel steamboat, and two Civil War museums. The **Road to Tara Museum** houses an impressive collection of *Gone With the Wind* memorabilia. Summer nights are capped with a laser light show, and annual events like the Yellow Daisy Festival and the Scottish Highland Games are well attended. ⊠ *U.S. 78 E, Stone Mountain Pkwy.,* ☎ *770/ 498–5600.* 🖃 *$6 per car; $25 annual pass; additional fees for attractions and special events.* ⊘ *Daily 6* AM*–midnight.*

Dining

By Jane
Garvey

From a million-dollar Patrick Kuleto–designed diner to a humble meat-and-three establishment, one can find almost anything in the capital of the New South: prestigious kitchens run by world-class chefs; a multitude of ethnic restaurants; and such regional favorites as fried chicken, Brunswick stew, fried catfish, and hush puppies. Traditional Southern fare—including Cajun and Creole, country-style and plantation cuisine, coastal and mountain dishes—continues to thrive.

The local taste for things sweet and fried holds true for restaurants serving traditional Southern food. To taste Southern iced tea, order it sweet. (When ordering tea in the South, it is assumed you want iced tea; to get hot tea, specify hot.) Don't pass up desserts in the South; they're legendary. And fried chicken, seafood, collard greens, and okra are the staples of Southern cooking for all Southerners. Catch the flavor of the South at breakfast and lunch in modest establishments that serve only these meals. Reserve evenings for culinary exploration, including some of the new restaurants that present regional dishes and traditional ingredients in fresh and inventive ways. Recently arrived Asian immigrants in Atlanta have assured the prosperity of myriad Thai, authentic Chinese, Vietnamese, and Japanese establishments.

Downtown

$$$$ ✕ **The Abbey.** Established in 1968, the restaurant is housed in a for-
★ mer church. Stained-glass windows and celestial music played by a harpist in the former choir loft reinforce the ambience. Chef Richard Lindamood deals in serious cuisine. Muscovy duck breast glazed with lavender honey will come rare, as will certain fish and other meats, unless you specify otherwise. Southern flavors are found in such treats as grilled Georgia quail and grilled venison with caramelized apple. The weighty wine list has mostly French and American wines. ⊠ *163 Ponce de Leon Ave.,* ☎ *404/876–8532. Reservations essential. AE, D, DC, MC, V. No lunch.*

$$$$ ✕ **City Grill.** This posh but breezy restaurant has made the most of its
★ grand location in the elegantly renovated historic Hurt Building. The regional American menu changes frequently. The excellent wine list covers the world. Signature dishes include Southern fried quail with cream gravy and raspberry black-pepper biscuits. Carolina barbecued duck, using a vinegar-based barbecue sauce in true Carolina tradition, also reflects the region. City Grill is a top Atlanta "power lunch" spot. ⊠ *50 Hurt Plaza,* ☎ *404/524–2489. AE, D, DC, MC, V. Closed Sun. No lunch Sat.*

$$$$ ✕ **The Restaurant, The Ritz-Carlton, Atlanta.** Chef Daniel Schaffhauser, a native of Alsace, presents an international menu with regional American touches. Foie gras and game are always present on the menu, but American Southern tastes might be reflected in such dishes as sweet potato chowder. Consider the well-composed tasting menu. Compelling desserts include a Valrhona Dark Chocolate Tart. The well-selected wine list is ably administered by a knowledgeable sommelier. ⊠ *181 Peachtree St.,* ☎ *404/659–0400, ext. 6450. Jacket and tie. AE, D, DC, MC, V. Closed Sun. No lunch.*

$$–$$$ ✕ **Mumbo Jumbo.** A long bar skirts the left side of the establishment,
★ guiding the eye to the rear dining room. Sleek young staffers conduct guests to tables. Gunther Seeger, formerly with the Ritz-Carlton, Buckhead Dining Room and chef/owner of his own recently opened establishment, is the consulting chef. Manilla clams in an aromatic broth, an unusual crab salad on puffed phyllo dough, cardamom-crusted sea bass with curry-scented green lentils, and a chocolate/chestnut timbale

for dessert make downtown dining adventurous. ⊠ *89 Park Pl.,* ☎ *404/523–0330, AE, D, DC, MC, V. No lunch weekends.*

$$ ✕ **Food Studio.** Ensconced within a former plow factory, now turned
★ into a studio and performance space, this stylish restaurant gleams with hi-tech and industrial touches. From the same group that made South City Kitchen (☞ Midtown Dining, *below*) a success, the restaurant does innovative American food with a Southern twist: grilled turkey breast with fig and thyme compote and wheat berries, slow-roasted baby back ribs, and grilled venison with sweet potato Napoleon and turnip/apple compote. ⊠ *887 W. Marietta St., Studio K-102, King Plow Arts Center,* ☎ *404/815–6677. AE, DC, MC, V.*

$ ✕ **Delectables.** Don't let the location (inside the central branch of the Atlanta-Fulton Public Library) or the format (cafeteria) deter you. This sophisticated little operation serves ravishing salads, wholesome soups, yummy cookies, and freshly baked cakes. Enjoy your meal to the strains of classical music on the patio. ⊠ *Atlanta-Fulton Public Library, Margaret Mitchell Sq. and Carnegie Way (enter through Carnegie Way),* ☎ *404/681–2909. AE, MC, V. Closed weekends. No dinner.*

$ ✕ **French Quarter Food Shop.** A scruffy interior with seating both inside and outdoors might turn off the timid, but the place is worth a special trip. Sit down to some crawfish étouffée (in season), the biggest boiled crawfish on the planet, jambalaya, gumbo, a huge muffuletta that could easily serve two, or a shrimp or oyster po'boy; take-out is also available. Save room for the whiskey-sauced bread pudding. ⊠ *923 Peachtree St.,* ☎ *404/875–2489. Reservations not accepted. AE, D, DC, MC, V. Closed Sun.*

$ ✕ **Thelma's Kitchen.** After losing her original location to the Centennial Olympic Park, Thelma Grundy moved her operation down the road to the street level of a somewhat renovated Roxy Hotel. Brighter, spiffier, and more cheerful than the earlier spot, it still has some of the best Southern food in town. Unique okra pancakes should not be missed. Fried catfish, "cold" slaw, macaroni and cheese, homemade cakes, and to-die-for pecan pie are all special. ⊠ *768 Marietta St. NW,* ☎ *404/688–5855. No credit cards. Closed Sun.*

Midtown

$$$ ✕ **Ciboulette.** French-bistro food and atmosphere from Tom Coohill
★ have Atlantans lining up for hot smoked salmon with wild mushrooms and ginger; and herb-crusted rack of lamb and potato-crusted lamb loin with haricots verts, mashed potatoes and garlic jus. Fish dishes bear innovative touches, and game dishes are frequent specials in season. The wine list is well chosen and embraces many good selections by the glass. The dining room is a bit tight, making intimate conversation difficult, but the counter seats, with their kitchen view, provide a true bistro ambience. ⊠ *1529 Piedmont Ave.,* ☎ *404/874–7600. AE, D, DC, MC, V. Closed Sun. No lunch.*

$$$ ✕ **Veni Vidi Vici.** Gleaming woods, contemporary styling, and an out-
★ door boccie court and dining patio create a unique dining ambience, especially for Italian food. Piatti piccoli are savory small dishes, such as veal meatballs or herbed goat cheese in marinara sauce, that may be ordered as appetizers or combined as lunch. Pasta dishes, such as gnocchi with Gorgonzola cheese, may be ordered in half portions. From the rotisserie, savor duck, salmon, lamb, pork, or chicken. ⊠ *41 14th St.,* ☎ *404/875–8424. AE, D, DC, MC, V. No lunch weekends.*

$$–$$$ ✕ **Indigo Coastal Grill.** Trendy coastal cuisine packs them in at this lively Virginia-Highland eatery. Popular here are conch fritters and heavy-cream biscuits at brunch, lobster corn chowder, and fish with fresh herbs in a twist of parchment. Don't miss the refreshing key lime pie. Sunday brunch is served. ⊠ *1397 N. Highland Ave.,* ☎ *404/876–0676.*

Dining
The Abbey, **2**
City Grill, **9**
Delectables, **7**
Food Studio, **13**
French Quarter Food Shop, **1**
Mumbo Jumbo, **8**
The Restaurant, The Ritz-Carlton, Atlanta, **6**
Thelma's Kitchen, **12**

Lodging
Atlanta Marriott Marquis, **3**
Hyatt Regency, Atlanta **4**
Omni Hotel at CNN Center, **11**
Quality Hotel Downtown, **10**
Ritz-Carlton, Atlanta, **6**
Westin Peachtree Plaza, **5**

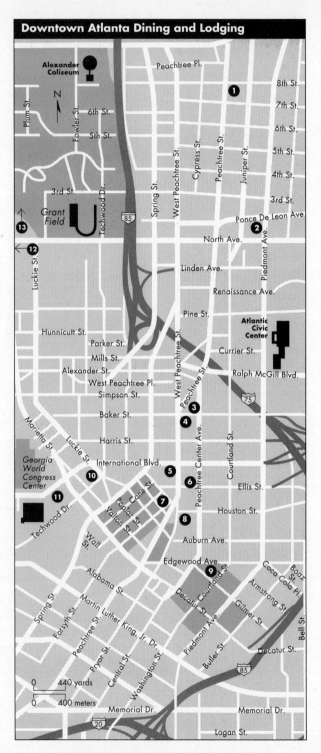

Downtown Atlanta Dining and Lodging

Atlanta Neighborhoods Dining and Lodging

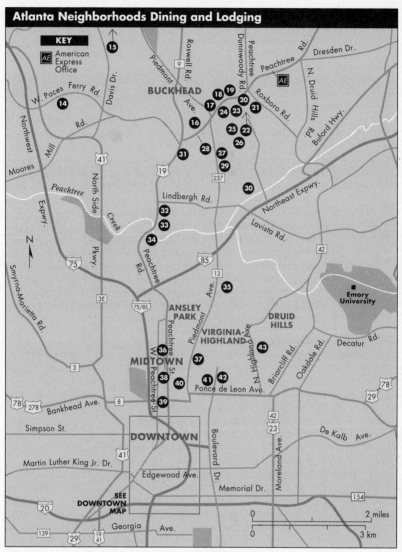

KEY

AE American Express Office

Dining

Abruzzi Ristorante, **32**
Annie's Thai Castle, **16**
Atlanta Fish Market, **25**
Bacchanalia, **27**
Bone's, **28**
Brasserie Le Coze, **20**
Buckhead Diner, **29**
Ciboulette, **35**
The Dining Room,
The Ritz-Carlton,
Buckhead, **19**
Horseradish Grill, **15**

Indigo Coastal
Grill, **43**
La Grotta, **31**
Luna Sí, **34**
Mary Mac's
Tea Room, **41**
Pano's and Paul's, **14**
Pricci, **26**
South City Kitchen, **38**
Tortillas, **42**
Toulouse, **33**
Veni Vidi Vici, **39**

Lodging

Buckhead Bed &
Breakfast Inn, **30**
Colony Square
Sheraton, **40**
Embassy Suites
Hotel, **24**
Four Seasons Hotel,
Atlanta, **36**
Grand Hyatt
Atlanta, **17**
JW Marriott, **22**

Ritz-Carlton,
Buckhead, **19**
Shellmont, **37**
Swissôtel, **23**
Terrace Garden
Hotel, **21**
Wyndham Garden
Hotel, **18**

Reservations not accepted. AE, DC, MC, V. No sit-down lunch, but take-out service available.

$$–$$$ ✕ **South City Kitchen.** The food traditions of South Carolina's Low-
★ country inspire the cooking at this bright in-town restaurant. The clean, spare, art-filled interior attracts a hip crowd. This is the place for catfish, prepared in a variety of intriguing ways. Sautéed shrimp and scallops with a sweet garlic gravy over a bed of stone-ground grits is one of the best dishes anywhere. Chocolate pecan pie is the best dessert in the house. ✉ *1144 Crescent Ave.,* ☎ *404/873–7358. AE, MC, V.*

$ ✕ **Mary Mac's Tea Room.** Local celebrities and ordinary folk line up for the country-fried steak, fried chicken, and fresh vegetables. Here, in the Southern tradition, lunch is called "dinner," and the evening meal is referred to as "supper." Waitresses will call you honey, and pat your arm to assure you that everything's all right. It's a great way to plunge into Southern food and hospitality all at once. ✉ *224 Ponce de Leon Ave.,* ☎ *404/876–1800. Reservations not accepted. No credit cards. No dinner Sun.*

$ ✕ **Tortillas.** This funky California-Spanish joint rates raves from the business and student crowd it attracts at lunch. Weekends and evenings find it packed with twenty-somethings. The burritos stuffed with pork, chicken, spinach, mushrooms, potato, or shrimp, the cheese-stuffed que-sadillas, and freshly prepared extras like green salsa, guacamole, and potatoes taste authentic. ✉ *774 Ponce de Leon Ave.,* ☎ *404/892–0193. Reservations not accepted. No credit cards.*

Buckhead

$$$$ ✕ **Bone's.** In this brash, New York–style steak house, sports celebs and fast-track businesspeople rub egos over excellent prime beef, chops, Maine lobster, and potatoes baked in a crust of salt. Silky, aromatic lobster bisque warms the heart. The award-winning wine list strikes a balance between French and American wines, and includes a fair num-ber of Italian vintages. Good wines are available by the glass. Most patrons wear jackets, but they're not required. Private dining rooms are available. ✉ *3130 Piedmont Rd.,* ☎ *404/237–2663. Reserva-tions essential. AE, D, DC, MC, V. No lunch weekends.*

$$$$ ✕ **Dining Room, The Ritz-Carlton, Buckhead.** This elegant, restrained dining room, with formal hunt scenes on the walls, romantic lighting, and generously spaced tables, comes across like an old gentleman's club. During the past decade, under the command of Chef Guenter Seeger, the Dining Room gained an international reputation. At press time, the new chef had not been announced; by all reports, however, the change will only mean fine new culinary achievements for this establishment. ✉ *3434 Peachtree Rd.,* ☎ *404/237–2700. Reservations essential, sev-eral days ahead for weekend dining. Jacket and tie. AE, D, DC, MC, V. Closed Sun. No lunch.*

$$$$ ✕ **La Grotta.** Despite its odd location in the basement of a posh con-dominium, this is one of the best-managed dining rooms in town. The kitchen, directed by Spanish chef Antonio Abizanda, experiments cau-tiously with new concepts and trendy ingredients, but old Northern Italian favorites remain at the core of the menu. Don't miss the warm grilled Portobello mushrooms, the baby quail on polenta, or the tiramisu. Veal and fresh pasta are outstanding. There's an excellent wine list. ✉ *2637 Peachtree Rd.,* ☎ *404/231–1368. Jacket required. Reser-vations essential. AE, D, DC, MC, V. Closed Sun. No lunch.*

$$$ ✕ **Abruzzi Ristorante.** "Understated elegance" is the buzz phrase for this modern yet traditional restaurant frequented by the city's old guard. If you're not taken with one of the myriad menu offerings, have managing partner Nico Petrucci suggest a specialty. Excellent dishes include salmon carpaccio, pappardelle (broad noodles) with game sauce, green-and-white gnocchi in pesto, sautéed sweetbreads, veal chop, baked fish with rosemary, and ricotta cheesecake. ✉ *2355 Peachtree Rd.,* ☎ *404/261–8186. AE, DC, MC, V. Closed Sun. No lunch Sat.*

$$$ ✕ **Bacchanalia.** In a modest former residence, comfortably spaced ta-
★ bles accommodate eager diners in an understated decor. Dazzling dishes take inspiration chiefly from Mediterranean sources, with occasional Asian touches. The four-course prix-fixe menu—$40 without wine; $54 chef's tasting menu—has plenty of options. The dishes change weekly, and may include, for starters, a roasted butternut squash and apple soup or blue crab fritters. Vegetarians enjoy offerings tailored to their requirements, with a four-course vegetarian menu for $40. ✉ *3125 Piedmont Rd.,* ☎ *404/365–0410. Reservations essential. AE, DC, MC, V. No smoking. Closed Sun.–Mon. No lunch.*

$$$ ✕ **Pano's and Paul's.** This Atlanta classic is known for stylish pampering. Pano Karatassos and Paul Albrecht hit gold with their single-minded devotion to their customers' needs, from whims to dietary restrictions. Many new ideas percolate through the kitchen; state-of-the-art dishes are introduced as specials and eventually included in the menu. Look for foie gras; soft-shell crab in season; lemon-roasted, farm-raised chicken with a crisp celery-potato cake; sautéed gulf red snapper fillet; and jumbo cold-water lobster tail fried in a light batter and served with Chinese honey mustard. ✉ *1232 W. Paces Ferry Rd.,* ☎ *404/261–3662. Reservations essential (days, sometimes weeks ahead for a prime slot). Jacket required. AE, D, DC, MC, V. Closed Sun. No lunch.*

$$–$$$ ✕ **Atlanta Fish Market.** An overwhelming selection of fresh seafood is served in this cavernous space, reminiscent of an old train station. Swordfish with roasted-cashew and cracked-pepper crust, served with white-corn cheese grits, exemplifies the kitchen's creativity and its respect for regional flavors. The raw oyster selection covers the waterfront. Oreo cheesecake for dessert is the perfect finish. The wine list has many good choices by the glass. The more intimate Geechee Porch is quieter than the main dining room. ✉ *265 Pharr Rd.,* ☎ *404/262–3165. AE, D, DC, MC, V. No lunch Sun.*

$$–$$$ ✕ **Buckhead Diner.** This million-dollar fantasy by the owners of Pano's
★ and Paul's is one of the hottest restaurants in town, a shimmering faux-diner wrapped in luscious hues of neon. Inlaid wood, Italian leather, hand-cut marble, and mellow lights establish a languorous ambience reminiscent of the *Orient Express*. The cuisine is anything but diner: Salt-and-pepper squid, fresh goat cheese and tomato fondue, veal-and-wild-mushroom meat loaf, and white chocolate banana cream pie are a sampling. ✉ *3073 Piedmont Rd.,* ☎ *404/262–3336. Reservations not accepted; expect a long wait. AE, D, DC, MC, V.*

$$–$$$ ✕ **Pricci.** The stamp of acclaimed designer Patrick Kuleto is apparent in the chic mirrored and windowed decor of this high-style hot spot. Deceptively simple Italian fare is accompanied by Pricci's own freshly baked breads. The homemade spinach-filled tortellini are delicious, as are the risottos, *cacciuco* (seafood stew in a light tomato broth), and tiramisu. ✉ *500 Pharr Rd.,* ☎ *404/237–2941. AE, D, DC, MC, V. No lunch weekends.*

$$ ✕ **Brasserie Le Coze.** Shoppers stream into this glowing, wood-pan-
★ eled space with comfortable banquettes and comforting bistro-style fare. Traditional dishes include quiche, onion tarte, mussels, coq au vin, and warm chocolate soufflé cake. Tuna carpaccio is a super starter or light luncheon. Vanilla *vacherin* (meringue rings placed on a pastry base) filled with ice cream and topped with meringue is just one of many extravagant desserts. The wine list offers a good number of by-the-glass selections. ✉ *3393 Peachtree Rd., Lenox Sq., near Neiman Marcus, Buckhead,* ☎ *404/266–1440. AE, DC, MC, V. Closed Sun.*

$$ ✕ **Horseradish Grill.** Once a red horse barn, this establishment, reno-
★   vated in 1994, is painted gray with white trim and made brighter with
     arched windows across the front. Some find it a bit noisy, but this place
     is a must for upscale Southern dishes that retain authenticity. Shrimp
     on grits and pecan pie tart are just two examples from a menu that
     changes with the seasons. ✉ *4320 Powers Ferry Rd., ☎ 404/255–7277.
     No reservations. AE, D, DC, MC, V.*

$$ ✕ **Toulouse.** Open spaces enclosed by warm, rough-brick walls char-
     acterize this attractive dining spot. The food is theoretically inspired
     by the cooking of southwestern France, but seems more American in
     execution. The grilled vegetable plate will please vegetarians or any-
     body else. Especially wonderful are the roast chicken, duck confit, lamb
     shank with mashed potatoes in the fall, and crème brûlée. ✉ *2293-B
     Peachtree Rd., Peachtree Walk, ☎ 404/351–9533. AE, D, DC, MC,
     V. No smoking. No lunch.*

$ ✕ **Annie's Thai Castle.** This small restaurant is lovingly decorated with
     objets d'art from Annie's native Thailand. Soups are perfectly flavored
     with spices and lemon grass, and the seafood salad, aromatic with gar-
     lic and lime, dazzles. *Nam sod,* chicken satay, and spicy catfish are ex-
     cellent choices. Traditional curries and noodle dishes seem to have an
     extra dash of finesse. ✉ *3195 Roswell Rd., ☎ 404/264–9546. AE,
     MC, V.*

$ ✕ **Luna Sí.** The emphasis is on fun at this New York loft–style restau-
     rant where Latin music blares and customers are encouraged to write
     on the walls. The menu, which changes weekly, is dominated by
     seafood. Signature dishes include salmon with a ginger crust, Cornish
     hen and mashed potatoes, excellent foie gras and pasta, and homemade
     biscotti that are made in heaven. ✉ *1931 Peachtree Rd., ☎ 404/355–
     5993. AE, DC, MC, V. No smoking.*

Lodging

One of America's three most popular convention destinations, Atlanta offers a broad range of lodgings. More than 12,000 rooms are
in the compact downtown area, close to the Georgia World Congress
Center, Atlanta Civic Center, Atlanta Merchandise Mart, and Omni
Coliseum. Other clusters are in Buckhead, in the north I–285 perimeter, and around Hartsfield Atlanta International Airport.

Downtown

$$$$ ▥ **Atlanta Marriott Marquis.** Immense and coolly contemporary, the
       Marquis seems to go on forever as you stand under the lobby's huge
       fabric sculpture that appears to float from the skylit roof 47 stories
       above. Each guest room—of average size and with standard-issue hotel
       decor—opens onto this atrium. ✉ *265 Peachtree Center Ave., 30303,
       ☎ 404/521–0000, ℻ 404/586–6299. 1,671 rooms, 71 suites. 5
       restaurants, 2 bars, indoor-outdoor pool, health club, concierge, busi-
       ness services. AE, D, DC, MC, V.*

$$$$ ▥ **Hyatt Regency, Atlanta.** The Hyatt's 23-story lobby launched the
       chain's "atrium look." Easily identified at night by its brightly lit blue
       bubble dome over the rooftop Polaris restaurant, it remains one of At-
       lanta's more unusual hotels. The adjacent IRS building was imploded
       in 1995, allowing a significant expansion, including meeting space, an
       exhibition facility, and grand ballroom. All atrium rooms were reno-
       vated at the same time. The hotel has 34 ADA rooms for guests using
       wheelchairs. ✉ *265 Peachtree St. (connected by skywalk to Peachtree
       Center), 30303, ☎ 404/577–1234 or 800/233–1234, ℻ 404/588–
       4137. 1,166 rooms, 98 suites. 3 restaurants, bar, pool, exercise room,
       concierge, business services. AE, D, DC, MC, V.*

$$$$ 🏨 **Omni Hotel at CNN Center.** The hotel is adjacent to the home of Ted Turner's Cable News Network. The lobby combines Old World and modern accents, with marble floors, Oriental rugs, and exotic floral and plant arrangements. Rooms have large windows and contemporary-style furniture, including a sofa in each room. Guests have access to the Downtown Athletic Club. ⊠ *100 CNN Center (MARTA's Omni rail station is adjacent to CNN Center), 30305,* ☎ *404/659–0000 or 800/843–6664,* FAX *404/525–5050. 455 rooms, 3 suites. 2 restaurants, lobby lounge. AE, D, DC, MC, V.*

$$$$ 🏨 **Ritz-Carlton, Atlanta.** The mood here is set by traditional afternoon
★ tea served in the intimate, sunken lobby beneath an 18th-century chandelier. Notice the 17th-century Flemish tapestry when you enter from Peachtree Street. Some guest rooms are luxuriously decorated with marble writing tables, plump sofas, four-poster beds, and white-marble bathrooms. **The Cafe**'s Sunday brunch spread is spectacular. In the evenings, live jazz music is performed at **The Bar** upstairs. ⊠ *181 Peachtree St. (entrance to MARTA's Peachtree Center rail station is across the street), 30303,* ☎ *404/659–0400 or 800/241–3333,* FAX *404/577–8366. 435 rooms, 15 suites. 2 restaurants, bar, exercise room, concierge, business services. AE, D, DC, MC, V.*

$$$$ 🏨 **Westin Peachtree Plaza.** Every photograph of Atlanta's skyline taken in the last 10 years features this cylindrical glass tower, the tallest hotel in North America. Designed by John Portman, the hotel has a five-story atrium and a narrow glass elevator attached to the outside of the building. For the best views of Atlanta, have a drink or meal in the revolving, multilevel **Sun Dial Restaurant & Lounge** atop the hotel. ⊠ *210 Peachtree St., at International Blvd., 30303,* ☎ *404/659–1400 or 800/937–8461,* FAX *404/589–7424. 1,068 rooms, 48 suites. 3 restaurants, 3 bars, coffee bar, indoor-outdoor pool, health club, concierge, business services. AE, D, DC, MC, V.*

$$ 🏨 **Quality Hotel Downtown.** This quiet, older downtown hotel, two blocks off of Peachtree Street, was renovated in 1996. A marble lobby lit by crystal chandeliers and modest-size rooms done in teal and navy make the hotel inviting. The restaurant is a '50s-style diner with red leatherette booths. ⊠ *89 Luckie St., 30303,* ☎ *404/524–7991,* FAX *404/ 524–0672. 75 rooms. Restaurant, pool. AE, D, DC, MC, V.*

Midtown

$$$$ 🏨 **Colony Square Sheraton.** Theatricality and opulence are epitomized by the dimly lit lobby with overhanging balconies, piano music, and fresh flowers. Rooms are modern and done in muted tones; those on higher floors have nice city views. Coffeemakers, irons, and ironing boards are in each room. The hotel is two blocks from MARTA's Art Center station and two blocks from the Woodruff Arts Center and the High Museum of Art (☞ *Midtown, above*); it anchors the Colony Square office/residential/retail complex. ⊠ *188 14th St., 30361,* ☎ *404/892–6000 or 800/422–7895,* FAX *404/872–9192. 436 rooms, 31 suites. Restaurant, lobby lounge, pool, exercise room, concierge, business services. AE, D, DC, MC, V.*

$$$$ 🏨 **Four Seasons Hotel, Atlanta.** Formerly the Grand Hotel, this hotel occupies the first 19 floors of a 50-story structure that also contains residences and offices. An elegant entrance leads up to a marble-enclosed world. The plush bar is an ideal spot to relax and take a breather, perhaps while enjoying afternoon tea. Stylish traditional furnishings fill the opulently designed rooms; baths and entrance areas are floored in marble. ⊠ *75 14th St., 30309,* ☎ *404/881–9898 or 800/952–0702,* FAX *404/873–4692. 220 rooms, 25 suites. 2 restaurants, bar, pool, health club, concierge, business services. AE, D, DC, MC, V.*

INNS AND GUEST HOUSES

$$–$$$$ 🏠 **Shellmont.** The Shellmont is named for the shell motif that adorns the house. Designed in 1891 by Massachusetts-born, Atlanta-reared architect Walter T. Downing for Dr. William Perrin Nicholson, the house has classical architectural elements and finely detailed stained-glass windows. Reproduced original stenciling is a Victorian detail. Fine American Victorian antiques fill the guest rooms. The price includes a full gourmet breakfast and turndown service with gourmet chocolates. ⊠ *821 Piedmont Ave., 30306,* ☎ *404/872–9290 or 404/872–5379. 2 rooms, 2 suites, 1 carriage house with suite (steam shower). AE, DC, MC, V.*

Buckhead

$$$$ 🏨 **Grand Hyatt Atlanta.** A dual-height lobby facing a courtyard with Japanese garden and cascading 35-ft waterfall is the opening statement of this modern, towering hotel. The understated decor features mainly hues of black, gray, and purple. Rooms are spacious and comfortable, with a style that's more American than Japanese. All baths are marble. Fax machines, irons and ironing boards, data ports, and robes are available in every room. Japanese and Mediterranean cuisine are served in the hotel's two restaurants. ⊠ *3300 Peachtree Rd., 30305,* ☎ *404/ 365–8100 or 800/233–1234,* 𝖥𝖠𝖷 *404/233–5686. 416 rooms, 22 suites. 2 restaurants, bar, pool, health club, concierge, business services, 14 meeting rooms. AE, D, DC, MC, V.*

$$$$ 🏨 **JW Marriott.** This elegant 25-story hotel, connected to Lenox Square Mall, is decorated traditionally with reproduction furniture and accents of brass and crystal. Irregularly shaped rooms have spacious baths with separate shower stall and tub. ⊠ *3300 Lenox Rd., 30326,* ☎ *404/262– 3344 or 800/228–9290,* 𝖥𝖠𝖷 *404/262–8689. 361 rooms, 10 suites. Restaurant, bar, lobby lounge, indoor pool, health club, concierge, business services, meeting rooms. AE, D, DC, MC, V.*

$$$$ 🏨 **Ritz-Carlton, Buckhead.** Decorated with the Ritz's signature 18th-
★   and 19th-century antiques and art, this elegant gem bids a discreet welcome to locals and visitors alike. Shoppers from nearby Lenox Mall and Phipps Plaza often revive here over afternoon tea or cocktails in the richly paneled Lobby Lounge. **The Dining Room** (☞ Dining, *above*) is one of the city's finest restaurants. The spacious rooms are furnished with traditional reproductions and have luxurious white-marble baths. From the hotel's club floors you get a view of Buckhead and an understanding of why Atlanta is known as a city of trees. Weekend musical performances are a delight. ⊠ *3434 Peachtree Rd., 30326,* ☎ *404/237–2700 or 800/241–3333,* 𝖥𝖠𝖷 *404/239–0078. 524 rooms, 29 suites. 2 restaurants, bar, indoor pool, hot tub, health club, concierge, business services. AE, D, DC, MC, V.*

$$$$ 🏨 **Swissôtel.** Sleek and efficient, this stunner boasts a chic, modern glass and white-tile exterior with curved walls and sophisticated Biedermeier-style interiors. Handy to Lenox Square Mall, a prime location for shopping and dining, the hotel is a favorite with business travelers. A VIP lounge enhances the hotel's business convenience. ⊠ *3391 Peachtree Rd., 30326,* ☎ *404/365–0065 or 800/253–1397,* 𝖥𝖠𝖷 *404/365–8787. 348 rooms, 17 suites. Restaurant, bar, indoor pool, health club, concierge, business services, meeting rooms. AE, D, DC, MC, V.*

$$$ 🏨 **Embassy Suites Hotel.** This modern high-rise in Buckhead is just blocks from the Phipps Plaza and Lenox Square malls. A variety of suites ranging from deluxe presidential (with wet bars) to more basic sleeping- and sitting-room combinations are available. ⊠ *3285 Peachtree Rd., 30305,* ☎ *404/261–7733 or 800/362–2779,* 𝖥𝖠𝖷 *404/261–6857. 313 suites, 4 suites for guests using wheelchairs. Restaurant, indoor-outdoor pool, exercise room, concierge. AE, D, DC, MC, V.*

$$$ 🏨 **Terrace Garden Hotel.** Renovated in 1996, this modern eight-floor hotel has the singular advantage of being right across from Lenox Square, making shopping there a breeze. Rooms have green decor and traditional Chippendale-style furnishings, with a desk and chair in some rooms and sofas in others. Complimentary full breakfast buffet is offered in the café. Within a 3-mi radius, complimentary transportation is available. ✉ *3405 Lenox Rd., 30326,* ☎ *404/261–9250 or 800/241–8260,* 𝔽𝔸𝕏 *404/848–7391. 355 rooms, 7 suites. Restaurant, bar, exercise room, pool. AE, D, DC, MC, V.*

$$$ 🏨 **Wyndham Garden Hotel.** This hotel has spacious rooms decorated with botanical prints, and rates are reasonable given the excellent location. Service is adequate, but doesn't compare with the luxury establishments in the area. Guests have access to a health club. ✉ *3340 Peachtree Rd., 30326,* ☎ *404/231–1234 or 800/996–3426,* 𝔽𝔸𝕏 *404/231–5236. 217 rooms, 4 suites. Restaurant, concierge. AE, D, DC, MC, V.*

INNS AND GUEST HOUSES

$$ 🏨 **Buckhead Bed & Breakfast Inn.** Built in 1996, the inn sits on a busy corner but provides intimacy and coziness lacking in the large hotels. The small rooms are painted in muted tones, and furnishings—some traditional and some contemporary—are comfortable. Baths are strictly utilitarian. Breakfast, substantial but not gourmet, is included. ✉ *70 Lenox Pointe, 30324,* ☎ *404/261–8284 or 888/224–8797,* 𝔽𝔸𝕏 *404/237–9224. 19 rooms. AE, MC, V.*

Nightlife and the Arts

Nightlife

The pursuit of entertainment—from Midtown to Buckhead—is known as the "Peachtree Shuffle." Atlanta's vibrant nightlife can mean anything from coffee bars to sports bars, from country line dancing to high-energy dance clubs. Atlanta has long been known for having more bars than churches, and in the South, that's an oddity.

Most bars and clubs are open seven nights, until 2–4 AM. Those with live entertainment usually have a cover charge. Consult *Creative Loafing* and the *Atlanta Journal and Constitution.*

ACOUSTIC

Eddie's Attic (✉ 515B N. McDonough St., Decatur, ☎ 404/377–4976) is a good spot for catching local and some national acoustic, folk, pop, and country-music acts; it is easily reached by MARTA, because it's right near the Decatur station. There's a full bar and restaurant.

BARS

The Bar at the Ritz-Carlton, Atlanta (✉ 182 Peachtree St., ☎ 404/659–0400) is a quiet spot, except for Friday nights, when the "martini and jazz" hour is in full swing. On those occasions, local blues vocalist Francine Reed is often in for a lively session of sophisticated music.

Limerick Junction (✉ 822 N. Highland Ave., ☎ 404/874–7147), a lively Irish pub, features singers from the large Atlanta community interested in and ably rendering traditional Irish music, as well as performers from the Old Sod itself. It has a rollicking, good-time atmosphere. Parking is dreadful, so consider a cab. A small cover may be charged.

Manuel's Tavern (✉ 602 N. Highland Ave., ☎ 404/525–3447) is a neighborhood saloon in the truest sense. Families, politicians, writers, students, professionals, and blue-collar workers enjoy drinks and very good food, ranging from beer-steamed hot dogs to a veggie soy burger.

When the Atlanta Braves play, the crowd gathers around the wide-screen TVs to cheer them on.

The Vortex (✉ 1041 W. Peachtree St., ☎ 404/875–1667), popular for its hamburgers, friendly atmosphere, and long beer list, is a classic Atlanta neighborhood bar.

COMEDY

The Punchline (✉ 280 Hilderbrand Dr., Sandy Springs, Balconies Shopping Center, ☎ 404/252–5233), Atlanta's longest-lived comedy club, books major national acts, among them Paula Poundstone and local yuckster Jeff Foxworthy. The small club is popular, and lines form early for reserved seats. Cover charges vary, and can hit high levels (upwards of $20 for some acts), but it's usually worth it.

COUNTRY

Buckboard Country Music Showcase (✉ 2080 Cobb Pkwy., Windy Hill Plaza, ☎ 770/955–7340), a 425-seat house, has a large dance floor, pool tables, and two full bars; it serves food of the hamburgers, nachos, and chicken fingers variety. The house band is the Buckboard Bandits, now with Ben Holley doing the vocals. Nashville-based bands and recording artists highlight on Thursday nights. The cover charge is $5–$10.

Cowboys Concert Hall (✉ 1750 N. Roberts Rd., Kennesaw, ☎ 770/426–5006) attracts national talent twice monthly on Friday. On Wednesday, Thursday, Friday, and Sunday, line dancing classes and couple dancing lessons are taught. This interesting venue, encompassing 44,000 square ft, is north of the city. The cover is $5, unless an unusually high-profile act is slated.

DANCE

Cajun dancing is rapidly gaining favor as a weekend frolic. The **Atlanta Cajun Dance Association** (✉ 2704 Laurelwood Rd., ☎ 770/451–6611) offers a one-hour lesson prior to beginning the party, called a *fais do-do*. While two local Cajun bands frequent the stage, nationally known bands from Louisiana often take over. Weekend dances usually take place at the Knights of Columbus Hall (✉ 2620 Buford Hwy.).

JAZZ AND BLUES

Blind Willie's (✉ 828 N. Highland Ave., ☎ 404/873–2583) showcases New Orleans– and Chicago-style blues that sends jam-packed crowds into a frenzy. The name honors Blind Willie McTell, a native of Thomson, Georgia, whose original compositions include "Statesboro Blues" made popular by the Macon, Georgia–based Allman Brothers. Cajun and zydeco are also on the agenda from time to time. Cover charges run in the $10 range.

Dante's Down the Hatch (✉ 3380 Peachtree Rd., Buckhead, ☎ 404/266–1600; ✉ Underground Atlanta, Lower Pryor St., ☎ 404/577–1800) has two of the city's most popular venues for both music and mood; entertainment varies. In Buckhead, the Paul Mitchell Trio conjures silky-smooth jazz sounds in the "hold" of a make-believe sailing ship. Downtown, jazz entertainers perform nightly.

Fuzzy's Place (✉ 2015 N. Druid Hills Rd., ☎ 404/321–6166), a crowded and smoke-filled neighborhood bar, begins the day by serving lunch to the denizens of nearby office buildings. By night, the place turns restaurant, sports bar, and blues room. The finest local talent holds forth on the stage. Usually no cover is charged.

Lou's Blues Review (✉ 736 Ponce de Leon Ave., ☎ 404/249–7311) is a classic urban and urbane blues room featuring musicians from around the South, but the place is at its best when the house band, Lou's Blues Review, takes to the stage and delivers some stunning music. Cover charges range up to $10.

Whiskers (✉ 8371 Roswell Rd., in shopping center at Roswell and Northridge Rds., ☎ 770/992–7445) features blues and rock groups, focusing on some of the best local talent. No cover.

ROCK

Masquerade (✉ 695 North Ave., ☎ 404/577–8178) is a grunge hang-out featuring just about everything in popular music, from disco to techno to industrial rock. Crowds are an odd mix that reflects the club's three separate spaces, dubbed Heaven, Hell, and Purgatory. A cover of $2 to $8 is charged.

The Point (✉ 420 Moreland Ave., ☎ 404/659–3522), in Little Five Points, headlines up-and-coming rock and progressive music groups in an intimate setting known for its excellent acoustics and sight lines. Opened in the mid-1980s, patrons are an eclectic mix, including some real characters. Sunday is for disco. Covers range from $3 to $10.

Smith's Olde Bar (✉ 1578 Piedmont Ave., ☎ 404/875–1522) sched-ules a wide variety of talent, both local and regional, in its acoustically fine performance space. Covers vary widely, depending on the act, but are usually in the $5–$10 range.

The Arts

For the most complete schedule of **cultural events,** check the *Atlanta Journal and Constitution*'s Friday "Weekend Preview" or Saturday "Leisure" sections. Also, check *Creative Loafing,* a lively community weekly distributed free at Atlanta restaurants, bars, and stores. You can also call the 24-hour **Arts Hotline** (☎ 404/853–3278) or connect with **Access Atlanta** via computer modem (☎ 800/224–5285, ext. 79 for hookup).

Tickets for the Fox Theatre, Atlanta Civic Center, and other locations are handled by **TicketMaster** (☎ 404/249–6400 or 800/326–4000) and **Ticket-X-Press, Inc.** (☎ 404/231–5888). However, most compa-nies sell tickets through their own box offices.

CONCERTS

The **Atlanta Symphony Orchestra (ASO),** under the musical direction of Yoel Levi, is now more than a half century old, with 14 Grammy Awards to its credit. It performs its fall-spring subscription series in the 1,800-seat Symphony Hall at **Woodruff Arts Center** (✉ 1280 Peachtree St., ☎ 404/733–5000). During the summer, the orchestra regularly performs with big-name popular and country artists in Chas-tain Park's outdoor amphitheater (✉ 4469 Stella Dr.).

Emory University (✉ N. Decatur Rd. at Clifton Rd., ☎ 404/727–6187, FAX 404/727–6421), an idyllic suburban campus, is the site of numer-ous musical performances, by both internationally renowned guest artists, and faculty/student performance groups. Expect a high level of per-formance quality from a variety of ensembles, such as woodwinds, brass, jazz, and vocal. Performances take place at four different venues.

Georgia State University (✉ Art and Music Bldg., Peachtree Center Ave. and Gilmer St., ☎ 404/651–4636 or 404/651–3676), with the entrance on Gilmer Street and fee parking at the corner of Edgwood and Peachtree Center Avenues, sponsors many concerts (about 80%)

that are free and open to the public. Performances by faculty/student/local artist groups and guest artists focus on jazz and classical.

DANCE

The country's oldest continuously operating ballet company (founded in 1929), the **Atlanta Ballet** (⌧ 1400 W. Peachtree St., ☎ 404/873–5811) has received international recognition for its high-quality productions of classical and contemporary works. Performances are usually at the Fox Theatre but may also take place at other venues. Artistic director John McFall, only the third in the company's history, brings new ideas and vision to the group.

FESTIVALS

The **Arts Festival of Atlanta** (⌧ 999 Peachtree St., Suite 140, 30309, ☎ 404/885–1125) combines performance and visual art; it has cutting-edge art and an artists' market, making it one of the most unusual such festivals in the country. More than 300 visual artists exhibit work for sale. The nine-day September festival was held in 1997 at Centennial Olympic Park. At press time, the 1998 venue had not been finalized.

The **Atlanta Jazz Festival,** held Memorial Day weekend, gathers the best local, national, and international musicians to give mostly free concerts at Atlanta's Piedmont Park. For information, contact the Atlanta Bureau of Cultural Affairs (⌧ 675 Ponce de Leon Ave., Atlanta 30308, ☎ 404/817–6815, FAX 404/817–6827).

The **Montreux/Atlanta International Music Festival** began in 1988, when Atlanta joined with Montreux, Switzerland, to cohost a music festival featuring a variety of styles: jazz, blues, gospel, reggae, and classical. The festival typically starts during Labor Day weekend, with performances in Piedmont Park (free) and Chastain Park (expensive). For information, call the Atlanta Bureau of Cultural Affairs (⌧ 675 Ponce de Leon Ave., Atlanta 30308, ☎ 404/817–6815, FAX 404/817–6827).

OPERA

The **Atlanta Opera** (⌧ 1800 Peachtree St., ☎ 404/355–3311) usually mounts three main-stage productions each year in the spring and summer at the Fox Theatre. Major roles are performed by national and international guest artists, while the chorus and orchestra come from the local community. Call TicketMaster (☎ 404/249–6400 or 800/326–4000) for information.

PERFORMANCE VENUES

Atlanta Civic Center (⌧ 395 Piedmont Ave., ☎ 404/523–6275) presents touring Broadway musicals, pop music, and dance concerts.

Fox Theatre (⌧ 660 Peachtree St., ☎ 404/881–2100), a fine faux-Moorish theater (☞ Midtown, *above*), is the principal venue for touring Broadway shows and national productions, as well as the home of the Atlanta Opera and the Atlanta Ballet (☞ *above*).

Georgia Tech Center for the Performing Arts (⌧ 349 Ferst Dr., ☎ 404/894–9600), which opened in 1992 at the Georgia Institute of Technology, offers performances that run the gamut, from classical to jazz, from dance to theater (in the **Robert Ferst Theatre**). The highly regarded student-operated theater, DramaTech, is in the **James E. Dull Theatre.** There's ample free parking on site.

Spivey Hall (☎ 404/733–4800) is a gleaming, modern, acoustically magnificent performance center at Clayton State College 15 mi south of Atlanta in Morrow. The hall is widely considered to be one of the finest concert venues in the country. Internationally renowned musicians perform everything from chamber music to jazz.

Woodruff Arts Center (⊠ 1280 Peachtree St., ☎ 404/733–4200) is home to the Alliance Theater and the Atlanta Symphony Orchestra (☞ Midtown, *above*).

Variety Playhouse (⊠ 1099 Euclid Ave., ☎ 404/524–7354), a former movie theater, is one of the cultural anchors of the hip Little Five Points neighborhood. Its denizens do not don fancy frocks to attend performances, which focus on rock, bluegrass and country, blues, reggae, folk, jazz, and pop.

THEATER

Atlanta's theatrical life is rich and varied. Check local listings in newspapers for information on some of the outstanding companies that operate throughout the metropolitan Atlanta area, including the suburbs. Consult *Creative Loafing* and the *Atlanta Journal and Constitution* for performance information.

Actor's Express (⊠ 887 W. Marietta St., ☎ 404/607–7469), an award-winning theater, presents an eclectic selection of classic and cutting-edge productions that take place in the 150-seat theater of the King Plow Arts Center, a stylish artists' complex hailed by local critics as a showplace of industrial chic.

Atlanta Shakespeare Tavern (⊠ 499 Peachtree St., ☎ 404/874–5299) produces plays by the Bard and more modern works, as well as plays by other dramatists who were Shakespeare's contemporaries, such as Molière. Performances vary in quality but are always fun.

Alliance Theatre (⊠ 1280 Peachtree St., ☎ 404/733–4200), Atlanta's premier professional theater, performs everything from Shakespeare to the latest Broadway and off-Broadway shows in the Woodruff Arts Center (☞ Midtown, *above*).

14th Street Playhouse (⊠ 175 14th St., ☎ 404/733–4750 or 404/733–4754) is part of the Woodruff Arts Center (☞ Midtown, *above*). The house has three stages, including a main stage (400-seat capacity), a second stage (200-seat capacity), and a third stage (80–90 seat capacity, which are rented for special productions). There is no resident theater. Musicals, plays, and sometimes opera are presented.

Horizon Theatre Co. (⊠ 1083 Austin Ave., Little Five Points, ☎ 404/584–7450) is a professional troupe that was established in 1983; it produces premieres of provocative and entertaining contemporary plays in a 185-seat theater.

Outdoor Activities and Sports

In a city where outdoor recreation is possible almost year-round, sports play a major role. At almost any time of the year, in parks, private clubs, and neighborhoods throughout the city, you'll find Atlantans pursuing everything from tennis to soccer to rollerblading. *Atlanta Sports & Fitness Magazine* (☎ 404/842–0359), available free at many grocery stores and health clubs, is a good link to Atlanta's athletic community.

Aerobics

Jeanne's Body Tech (⊠ 334 E. Paces Ferry Rd., ☎ 404/261–0227) has classes including step and spinning, done on special stationary bicycles. Exercise equipment of a wide variety also is available. The drop-in fee is $10.

Biking and Rollerblading

Piedmont Park (⊠ Piedmont Ave. between 10th St. and the Prado) is closed to traffic and popular for rollerblading and other recreational activities. **Skate Escape** (⊠ 1086 Piedmont Ave., across from the park, ☎ 404/892–1292) has rental bikes, Rollerblades, and skates.

Golf

Golf is enormously popular here, as the many courses will attest. The only public course within sight of downtown Atlanta is the **Bobby Jones Golf Course** (⊠ 384 Woodward Way, ☎ 404/355–1009), named after the famed golfer and Atlanta native and located on a portion of the site of the Battle of Peachtree Creek. Despite having some of the city's worst fairways and greens, the immensely popular 18-hole, par-71 course is always crowded. The **Alfred Tup Holmes Club** (⊠ 2300 Wilson Dr., ☎ 404/753–6158) is built upon a former Confederate breastworks; golf-wise, it's known for numerous doglegs and blind shots. The **Browns Mill Golf Course** (⊠ 480 Cleveland Ave., ☎ 404/366–3573) lies within the perimeter of I–285 and is considered the best operated course by the City of Atlanta. **North Fulton Golf Course** (⊠ 216 W. Wieuca Rd., ☎ 404/255–0723) offers one of the best layouts and lies within the perimeter.

Lakeside Country Club (⊠ 3600 Old Fairburn Rd., ☎ 404/344–3620), just outside I–285 in southwest Atlanta, offers many challenges. The **Sugar Creek Golf Course** (⊠ 2706 Bouldercrest Rd., ☎ 404/241–7671), straddling I–285 (11 holes on one side, seven on the other) in southeast Atlanta, is a challenging course with several long drives and good Bermuda greens. Outside I–285 in the suburbs, the best public course is the **Southerness Golf Club** (⊠ 4871 Flat Bridge Rd., Stockbridge, ☎ 770/808–6000), with a great variety of challenging holes—from long par fours to shots over water requiring pinpoint accuracy. **Stone Mountain Park** (⊠ U.S. 78, ☎ 770/498–5715) has several courses; Stonemont, an 18-hole course, is the best, with several challenging and scenic holes. Lakemont and Woodmont are both nine-hole courses, played as 18.

Health Clubs

SportsLife (⊠ 3340 Peachtree Rd., ☎ 404/262–2120), with six other locations, has equipment and amenities that vary from one location to another. The Cobb location (⊠ 1775 Water Pl., ☎ 770/952–2120), for instance, has indoor and outdoor tennis courts. Single visits cost $10. Selected hotels, such as the Wyndham (☞ Lodging, *above*), offer complimentary visits to guests.

Jogging and Running

Chattahoochee National Recreation Area contains different parcels of land which lie in separate units along the banks of the Chattahoochee River, much of which has been protected from development. The area is crisscrossed by 70 mi of trails in diverse sections. Some park trails are more appropriate to hiking than to jogging or running. For instance, the Johnson Ferry Unit, at Riverside Drive and Johnson Ferry Road, has a fairly level trail running along the riverbank and floodplain. Check with park personnel before deciding where to jog or run. ⊠ *1978 Island Ford Pkwy.*, ☎ 770/952–4419. ◷ *Daily 7–7.*

Peachtree Road Race 10K (⊠ 3097 E. Shadowlawn Ave., ☎ 404/231–9064) is held annually on July 4. Atlanta's hills provide joggers with plenty of challenges. On the plus side, most streets are heavily shaded, offering some respite from the miserable summer humidity. The race is sponsored by the Atlanta Track Club (☎ 404/231–9064), which can offer suggestions on where to run or jog.

Swimming

Dynamo Community Swim Center (⊠ 3119 Shallowford Rd., Chamblee, ☎ 770/451–3272) has an eight-lane, 165-ft outdoor pool; a 10-lane, 25-yard pool; and a five-lane, 25-yard pool. Locker facilities and a weight room are on site. The cost is $3 per visit. Take I–85 to Exit 33.

Tennis

Bitsy Grant Tennis Center (⊠ 2125 Northside Dr., ☎ 404/351–2774), named for one of Atlanta's best-known players, is the area's best public facility, with 13 clay courts and 10 hard courts.

Piedmont Park, Atlanta's most popular park, has 12 hard courts with lights. Access the tennis center from Park Drive off Monroe Drive; even though the sign says "Do Not Enter," the security guard will show you the parking lot. Courts are always open, but personnel keep specific hours. ⊠ *Piedmont Ave. between 10th St. and the Prado.* ☉ *Weekdays noon–9, weekends 9–5.*

Shopping

Atlanta is second only to Chicago in space devoted to shopping areas, and its department stores, specialty shops, large enclosed malls, and antiques markets draw shoppers from across the Southeast. Most stores are open Monday–Saturday 10–9, Sunday noon–6. Many downtown stores close Sunday. Sales tax is 6% in the city of Atlanta and Fulton County, and 4%–5% in the suburbs.

Shopping Centers

Brookwood Square (⊠ 2140 Peachtree Rd.) is a nifty arrangement of unusual shops, including **Vespermann Gallery** (☞ Art Galleries, *below*) and **The Piano Gallery,** Atlanta's Steinway dealership.

Buckhead has many interesting shops scattered throughout its specialty and small strip malls. At **Peachtree Plaza,** at the intersection of Peachtree Road and Mathieson Drive, you'll find **Beverly Bremer's Silver Shop,** devoted to fine antique silver, and **Irish Crystal Co.,** offering fine cut glass and linens. Down Maple Drive off Peachtree Road you'll find **Yesteryear,** dealing in antique books (☞ Books, *below*), next to **Atlanta Guitar Center.** A raft of boutiques and gift shops, along with some fine restaurants, is found down **Grandview Avenue,** also off Peachtree, and another similar collection runs down **East Shadowlawn Avenue.** **East Village Square** (⊠ Buckhead Ave. and Bolling Way) is honeycombed with art galleries and restaurants. Across from Lenox Square, the **Around Lenox Shopping Center** includes **Tower Records–Video–Books,** a masterful collection of such material. Over on East Andrews Drive, **Andrews Square** is a treasure trove of shops, eateries, nightspots, and galleries. Next to it, **Cates Center** has similar stores.

Lenox Square Mall (⊠ 3393 Peachtree Rd., ☎ 404/233–6767), one of Atlanta's oldest and most popular shopping centers, has branches of **Neiman Marcus, Rich's** (the local department store), **Crate & Barrel,** and **Macy's** looming next to specialty shops such as **Geode** (fine art jewelry) and **Mori's** (luggage and travel gifts). Several good restaurants are located in Lenox Square, preferable even for quick meals to the fare available in the food court.

Peachtree Center Mall (⊠ 231 Peachtree St., ☎ 404/524–3787) is a downtown mall that does steady business. Stores here are chiefly specialty shops, such as **International Records and Tapes,** the **Architectural Book Center,** and the **Atlanta International Museum** gift shop.

Perimeter Mall (⌧ 4400 Ashford Dunwoody Rd.), known for upscale family shopping, has such shops such as the **High Museum of Art Gift Shop, Gap Kids,** and the **Nature Company,** as well as branches of **Rich's, Sears,** and **JCPenney,** and a very good food court.

Phipps Plaza (⌧ 3500 Peachtree Rd., ☎ 404/262–0992 or 800/810–7700) contains branches of **Tiffany & Co., Saks Fifth Avenue,** Birmingham-based **Parisian, Lord & Taylor,** and **Abercrombie & Fitch** alongside such neighbors as **Skippy Musket** (unique jewelry, collectibles, decorative items for the home) and **Illumina** (fine art jewelry).

Underground (⌧ 50 Upper Alabama St., ☎ 404/523–2311) offers a wide assortment of retail shops, from galleries such as **Silver Sun** (Native American art) to apparel shops such as **Hats Under Atlanta** and even **Habersham Vineyard & Winery,** a tasting room for Georgia wines. There's a good food court.

Outlets

The **Dalton Factory Stores** (⌧ 80 mi north of Atlanta; Exit 136 off I–75) offer **Jones New York, West Point Pepperell,** and more. **Outlet Square Mall** (⌧ 4166 Buford Hwy.) is anchored by the **Burlington Coat Factory, Rack Room Shoes,** and **Marshall's.** Two locations of **Tanger Factory Outlet Center** (⌧ Exit 68, Hampton/Locust Grove, off I–75, about 30 mi south of the city, ☎ 770/957–0238; ⌧ Exit 53, Commerce, off I–85, 60 mi north of Atlanta, ☎ 706/335–4537) feature a collection of excellent discount shops including **Mikasa, L'Eggs, Casual Corner,** and **Corning.**

North Georgia Premium Outlets (⌧ GA 400 at Dawson Forest Rd.) is worth the 45 minutes it takes to get there from Atlanta's northern perimeter; this shopping center has more than 70 stores, including **Music for a Song** (discount CDs and tapes of all kinds), a **Barneys New York Outlet,** and **Stone Mountain Handbags.**

Specialty Shops

ANTIQUES

Buckhead is home to several antiques shops, with most of them along or near Peachtree Road. Expect rare goods and high prices in many stores, but don't limit yourself to this part of town. Venture into Virginia-Highland and the city's suburban towns to find treasures galore.

Bennett Street (⌧ 116 Bennett St., ☎ 404/352–4430) has numerous art galleries (e.g., **Out of the Woods**), antiques shops (**Kelim**), and a good restaurant (**Fratelli di Napoli**) (⌧ 2101-B Tula St., ☎ 404/351–1533), making it easy to spend a whole day here. **The Stalls** is a fine antiques market.

Chamblee Antique Row (⌧ 3519 Broad St., ☎ 770/455–0751), a browser's delight in the suburb of Chamblee, about 8 mi from downtown, has developed a reputation for good antiquing that lures visitors seeking to discover treasures in the dust.

Little Five Points (⌧ Intersection of Moreland and Euclid Aves.) attracts "junking" addicts who find nirvana in Atlanta's version of Greenwich Village, characterized by vintage clothing stores, art galleries, used record and book shops, and some stores that defy description.

Miami Circle, off Piedmont Road, is an enclave for antiques and decorative arts lovers. Drop in for a snack at **Eclipse di Luna** (⌧ Miami Circle, ☎ 404/846–0449).

Stone Mountain Village (⌧ Main St., Stone Mountain, ☎ 770/879–4971 visitor center) is a 19th-century village beside a railroad track at the foot of Stone Mountain (☞ Other Area Attractions, *above*). Storefronts are exquisitely decorated at holiday time. Shops of note include **Stone Mountain Handbags Factory Store** (☎ 770/498–1316), **Handcrafted Dulcimers** (☎ 770/496–5529), and the General Store (☎ 770/469–9331). The village is 17 mi from downtown.

2300 Peachtree Road, one of Buckhead's most stylish complexes, has more than 25 antiques shops, art galleries, and accessories enough to fill multiple mansions.

ART GALLERIES

Berman Gallery (✉ 3261 Roswell Rd., Buckhead, ☎ 404/261–3858) specializes in American studio ceramics and work by Southern artists. **Camille Love Gallery** (✉ 309 E. Paces Ferry Rd., Suite 120, ☎ 404/841–0446) deals in work by minority artists. **Fay Gold Gallery** (✉ 247 Buckhead Ave., East Village Sq., ☎ 404/233–3843) shows nationally renowned contemporary artists. **Jackson Fine Art Gallery** (✉ 3115 E. Shadowlawn Ave., ☎ 404/233–3739) exhibits fine art photography. **Modern Primitive** (✉ 1393 N. Highland Ave., Virginia-Highland, ☎ 404/892–0556) has a fascinating assembly of Folk and Visionary art from around the state and the region. **Ray's Indian Originals** (✉ 90 N. Avondale Rd., Avondale Estates, ☎ 404/292–4999) shows exquisite original work by Native American artists. **Vespermann Gallery** (✉ 2140 Peachtree Rd., Brookwood Sq., ☎ 404/350–9698) has lovely hand-blown glass objects.

BOOKS

Chapter 11 (✉ 6305 Roswell Rd., ☎ 404/252–4478) is a great place to find recently published titles at good prices. **Oxford Books at Buckhead** (✉ 360 Pharr Rd., ☎ 404/262–3333) has Atlanta's largest selection of books and newspapers; it's a local institution with frequent book signings. **Yesteryear** (✉ 3201 Maple Dr., ☎ 404/237–0163) is the destination of choice for antiquarians. Strengths include military history, Georgiana, and old cookbooks.

FOOD

DeKalb Farmers Market (✉ 3000 E. Ponce de Leon Ave., Decatur, ☎ 404/377–6400) has 175,000 square ft of exotic fruits, cheeses, seafood, sausages, breads, and delicacies from around the world. **East 48th St. Market** (✉ 2462 Jett Ferry Rd., at Mt. Vernon Rd., Williams at Dunwoody Shopping Center, ☎ 770/392–1499) sells Italian deli meats, fabulous breads (among the city's best), cheeses, and Italian prepared foods. **Harry's Farmers Markets** (✉ 1180 Upper Hembree Rd., Roswell, ☎ 770/664–6300; ✉ 2025 Satellite Pointe, Duluth, ☎ 770/416–6900; ✉ 70 Powers Ferry Rd., Marietta, ☎ 770/578–4400) consists of three markets north of the city, spun off from the original (☞ DeKalb Farmers Market, *above*) by the owner's brother; they sell quality fish, cheese, wine, and deli items.

Spectator Sports

Baseball

Atlanta Braves (✉ Turner Field, I–75/85, Exit 91/Fulton St.; I–20, westbound Exit 24, Capitol Ave.; eastbound Exit 22, Windsor St./Spring St., ☎ 404/522–7630). The beloved Braves now play in Turner Field, formerly the 1996 Olympic Stadium.

Basketball

Atlanta Hawks (✉ Omni Coliseum, 100 Techwood Dr., ☎ 404/827–3865). The NBA's Hawks had a proud Olympics moment when Coach Lenny Wilkenson was selected to coach the U.S. Olympic Men's Basketball Team.

Football

Atlanta Falcons (⊠ Georgia Dome, 1 Georgia Dome Dr., ☎ 404/223–9200). New Coach Dan Reeves, a native of Americus, Georgia, took over last year, bringing on board many impressive new personnel both on the coaching staff and on the team. The Falcons have made the play-offs seven times, most recently in 1995.

Atlanta A to Z

Arriving and Departing

BY BUS

Greyhound Bus Lines (⊠ 232 Forsyth St., ☎ 404/584–1728 or 800/231–2222) provides transportation to downtown Atlanta.

BY CAR

Some refer to Atlanta as the Los Angeles of the South, because travel by car is virtually the only way to get to most parts of the city. Although the congestion isn't comparable to L.A.'s yet, Atlantans have grown accustomed to frequent delays at rush hour. Beware: The South as a whole may be laid back, but Atlanta drivers are not; they tend to drive faster than drivers in other Southern cities. Visiting drivers should be vigilant.

The city is encircled by I–285. Three interstates—I–85, running northeast–southwest from Virginia to Alabama; I–75, north–south from Michigan to Florida; and I–20, east–west from South Carolina to Texas—also crisscross Atlanta.

BY PLANE

Hartsfield Atlanta International Airport (⊠ Off I–85 and I–285, ☎ 404/530–6600), 13 mi south of downtown, is served by the following airlines: Aero Costa Rica, AeroMexico, Air Jamaica, Air South, ALM Antillean, AMC, ASA, America West, American, British Airways, Cayman Airways, Continental, Delta, GP Express, Japan Airlines, Kiwi International, KLM, Korean Air, Leisure Air, Lufthansa, Markair, Midwest Express, National, Northwest, Sabena, Swissair, TWA, United, US Airways, ValuJet, and VARIG Brazilian.

Atlanta Airport Shuttle (☎ 404/766–5312) operates vans every half hour between 7 AM and 11 PM daily. The downtown trip, $8 one-way, $14 round-trip, takes about 20 minutes and stops at major hotels. Vans also go to Emory University and the Lenox area; $12 one-way, $20 round-trip.

If your luggage is light, take **MARTA** (Metropolitan Atlanta Rapid Transit Authority) (☎ 404/848–4711) high-speed trains between the airport and downtown and other locations. Trains operate 5:30 AM–1:17 AM (weekdays) and 5:30 AM–1:30 AM (weekends). The trip downtown takes about 15 minutes to the Five Points station, and the fare is $1.50.

From the airport to downtown, the **taxi** fare is $18 for one person, $20 for two, and $24 for three or more, including tax. From the airport to Buckhead, the fare is $28 for one and $30 for two or more. With a reasonable advance reservation, **Carey-Executive Limousine** (☎ 404/223–2000) normally can provide 24-hour service. **Checker Cab** (☎ 404/351–1111) and **Buckhead Safety Cab** (☎ 404/233–1152) offer 24-hour service.

BY TRAIN

Amtrak (⊠ 1688 Peachtree St., ☎ 404/881–3060 or 800/872–7245) has the *Crescent* train which operates daily to Atlanta from New York; Philadelphia; Washington, DC; Baltimore; Charlotte; and Greenville, arriving at Atlanta's Brookwood Station. It also goes daily from New Orleans to New York through Atlanta.

Getting Around

BY BUS

The **Metropolitan Atlanta Rapid Transit Authority (MARTA)** (☎ 404/848–4711), with a fleet of 667 buses, operates 150 routes covering 1,500 mi. The fare is $1.50, and exact change is required. Weekly and monthly *TransCards,* giving you a slight ride discount, are available, too. Outside the perimeter set by I–285, except for a few important areas of Clayton, DeKalb, and Fulton counties, service is very limited.

Amtrak (✉ 1688 Peachtree St., ☎ 404/881–3060 or 800/872–7245) operates "Thru-Way" bus service daily from Birmingham and Mobile, Alabama, to Atlanta's Brookwood Station. Another bus goes daily from the station to Macon.

BY SUBWAY

MARTA (☎ 404/848–4711) has clean and safe rapid-rail subway trains with somewhat limited routes that link downtown with many major landmarks. The rail system's two main lines cross at the **Five Points Station** downtown, where TransCards and information on public transportation are available at the **Ride Store,** open weekdays 7–7 and Saturday 8:30–5. The stores are at the airport, the Five Points Station, the headquarters building by the Lindbergh Station, and the Lenox Station. Trains run 5:30 AM–1:17 AM, and large parking lots (free) are at most stations beyond downtown. Tokens, costing $1.50 each, are required to enter the station, and can be bought from machines outside the station entrance or at the Ride Store. Free transfers, needed for some bus routes, are available by pressing a button on the subway turnstile or requesting one from the bus driver.

BY TAXI

Taxi service in Atlanta can be a mixed experience. Drivers often do not have correct change even for a small bill, so be prepared either to charge your fare (many accept credit cards) or insist that the driver obtain change. Drivers also appear as befuddled as visitors by Atlanta's notoriously winding and hilly streets, so if your destination is something other than a major hotel or popular sight, come armed with directions.

Taxi fares start at $1.60 for the first mile, with 20¢ for each additional ½ mi, 50¢ per extra passenger, and $12 per hour waiting time. Each additional person is charged another $1. Within the Downtown Convention Zone a flat rate of $5 for one person or $1 for each additional passenger will be charged for any destination. **Checker Cab** (☎ 404/351–1111) and **Buckhead Safety Cab** (☎ 404/233–1152) offer 24-hour service.

Contacts and Resources

B&B RESERVATIONS

Great Inns of Georgia (✉ 541 Londonberry Rd., Atlanta 30327, ☎ 404/843–0471 or 800/823–7787, FAX 404/252–8886) has the lowdown on inns for the entire state, including Atlanta.

EMERGENCIES

For **assistance,** dial 911. For **24-hour emergency rooms,** contact **Grady Memorial Hospital** (✉ 80 Butler St., ☎ 404/616–4307), **Georgia Baptist Medical Center** (✉ 303 Parkway Dr., ☎ 404/265–4000), **Northside Hospital** (✉ 1000 Johnson Ferry Rd., ☎ 404/851–8000), and **Piedmont Hospital** (✉ 1968 Peachtree Rd., ☎ 404/605–5000).

GUIDED TOURS
Gray Line of Atlanta (✉ 2541 Camp Creek Pkwy., College Park 30337, ☎ 404/767–0594) gives tours of Downtown Atlanta, Midtown, Buckhead, Stone Mountain, and the King Center. A four-hour tour costs $30; a full-day tour, $50.

The **Atlanta Preservation Center** (✉ 156 7th St., Suite 3, ☎ 404/876–2041; 404/876–2040 tour hot line) offers 10 walking tours of historic areas and neighborhoods for $5 each. Especially noteworthy are tours of Sweet Auburn, the neighborhood associated with Martin Luther King Jr. and other leaders in Atlanta's African-American community; Druid Hills, the verdant, genteel neighborhood where *Driving Miss Daisy* was filmed; and the Fox Theatre, the elaborate 1920s picture palace.

RADIO STATIONS
AM: WPLO 610, country; WGST 640, news/talk; WCNN 680, sports/talk; WQXI 790, music/talk. **FM:** WABE 90.1, National Public Radio/classical; WCLK 91.9, jazz/soul; WZGC 92.9, classic rock; WPCH 94.9, light rock; WKHX 101.5, country.

24-HOUR PHARMACIES
Big B Drug (✉ 1061 Ponce de Leon Ave., ☎ 404/876–0381). **Drug Emporium** (✉ 2625 Piedmont Rd., ☎ 404/233–1048). **Kroger Store Pharmacies,** selected locations.

VISITOR INFORMATION
To plan your trip, write to the **Georgia Department of Industry, Trade, and Tourism** (✉ Box 1776, 30301, ☎ 404/656–3590 or 800/847–4842, FAX 404/651–9063). For Atlanta only, contact the **Atlanta Convention & Visitors Bureau** (ACVB; ✉ 233 Peachtree St., Suite 2000, 30303, ☎ 404/222–6688 or 800/285–2682, FAX 404/584–6331). Once in Atlanta, the ACVB has several visitor information centers: **Hartsfield Atlanta International Airport,** in north terminal at west crossover; **Peachtree Center Mall** (✉ 233 Peachtree St.); **Underground Atlanta** (✉ 65 Upper Alabama St.); **Georgia World Congress Center** (✉ 285 International Blvd.); and **Lenox Square Mall** (✉ 3393 Peachtree Rd.).

SAVANNAH

The very sound of the name Savannah conjures up misty images of mint juleps, live oaks dripping with Spanish moss, handsome mansions, and a somewhat decadent city moving at a lazy Southern pace. Why, you can hardly say "Savannah" without drawling. Well, brace yourself. The mint juleps are there all right, along with the moss and the mansions and the easygoing pace, but this Southern belle rings with surprises. Take, for example, St. Patrick's Day: Why on earth does Savannah, of all places, have a St. Patrick's Day celebration second only to New York's? The greening of Savannah began more than 164 years ago, and nobody seems to know why, although everybody in town talks a blue (green) streak about St. Patrick's Day. Everything turns green on March 17, including the faces of startled visitors when green scrambled eggs and green grits are put before them.

Savannah's beginning was February 12, 1733, when English General James Edward Oglethorpe and 120 colonists arrived at Yamacraw Bluff on the Savannah River to found the 13th and last colony in the New World. As the port city grew, Englishmen, Scottish Highlanders, French Huguenots, Germans, Austrian Salzburgers, Sephardic and Ashkenazic Jews, Moravians, Italians, Swiss, Welsh, Greeks and the Irish all arrived to create what could be called a rich gumbo.

In 1793 Eli Whitney of Connecticut, who was tutoring on a plantation near Savannah, invented a mechanized means of "ginning" seeds from cotton bolls. Cotton soon became king, and Savannah, already a busy seaport, flourished under its reign. Waterfront warehouses were filled with "white gold," and brokers trading in the Savannah Cotton Exchange set world prices. The white gold brought in solid gold, and fine mansions were built in the prospering city.

In 1864 Savannahians surrendered their city to Union General Sherman rather than see it torched. Following World War I and the collapse of the cotton market, the city's economy virtually collapsed, and its historic buildings languished for more than 30 years. Elegant mansions were either razed or allowed to decay, and cobwebs replaced cotton in the dilapidated riverfront warehouses.

But in 1955, Savannah's spirits rose again. News that the exquisite Isaiah Davenport home (⊠ 324 E. State St.) was to be destroyed prompted seven outraged ladies to raise enough money to buy the house. They saved it the day before the wrecking ball was to swing. Thus was born the Historic Savannah Foundation, the organization responsible for the restoration of downtown Savannah, where more than 1,000 restored buildings form the 2½-square-mi Historic District, the nation's largest. Many of these buildings are open to the public during the annual tour of homes, and today Savannah is recognized as one of the top 10 cities in the United States for walking tours.

John Berendt's wildly popular *Midnight in the Garden of Good and Evil,* published in 1994, has dispatched many new visitors to Savannah. A nonfiction account of a notorious murder that took place in the city in the 1980s, the book brings to life such Savannah sites as Monterey Square, Mercer House, and Bonaventure Cemetery.

Georgia's founder, General James Oglethorpe, designed the original town of Savannah and laid it out in a perfect grid. The Historic District is neatly hemmed in by the Savannah River, Gaston Street, East Street, and Martin Luther King Jr. Boulevard. Streets are arrow-straight, public squares of varying sizes are tucked into the grid at precise intervals, and each block is sliced in half by a lane. Bull Street, anchored on the north by City Hall and the south by Forsyth Park, charges down the center of the grid and lunges around the five public squares that stand in its way.

Numbers in the text correspond to numbers in the margin and on the Savannah Historic District map.

The Historic District

A Good Walk and Drive

Historic Savannah may be covered completely on foot but to save some energy and time, it is best to combine walking with driving. Start at the **Savannah Visitors Center** ⑤⑨, on Martin Luther King Jr. Boulevard. Housed in the same building, the **Savannah History Museum** ⑥⓪ is an ideal introduction to the city's history. There is public parking next to the center and museum.

Exit the parking lot and turn left (north), walking or driving two short and one very long blocks on Martin Luther King Jr. Boulevard to the **Scarborough House** ⑥①, which contains the Ships of the Sea Museum. Cross Martin Luther King Jr. Boulevard and continue two blocks east on West Congress Street, past Franklin Square to **City Market** ⑥②. Skirting around Franklin Square north on Montgomery Street, go two blocks to West Bay Street, and turn right.

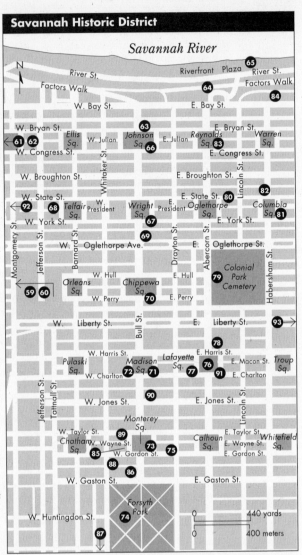

Savannah Historic District

From this point, continue east on West Bay Street four blocks to Bull
Street. On your left, you'll see **City Hall** ⑥③. Continue east down West
Bay Street (which now becomes East Bay Street) to **Factors Walk** ⑥④,
which lies south of River Street and the Savannah River. If you're driving, leave your car here to continue on foot (be sure to park in long-
term parking, as the short-term meters are carefully watched and
tickets dispensed expeditiously). Next, visit **Riverfront Plaza** ⑥⑤, which
steps down from Factors Walk toward the river, which can only be seen
on foot. At this point, if you're driving, you'll probably want to get in
your car again to continue the tour.

Return to East Bay Street and head west two long blocks back to Bull
Street; turn left going south two blocks on Bull Street to **Johnson
Square** ⑥⑥. Twenty-one of Savannah's original 24 squares survive and

are restored; they are spaced at four-block intervals in either compass direction.

Walk or drive four blocks south on Bull Street to **Wright Square** ⑥⑦, then turn right (west) two blocks to Telfair Square, where you can stop at the **Telfair Mansion and Art Museum** ⑥⑧. Stroll around Telfair Square, and then continue east on West York Street back toward **Wright Square**, and turn right on Bull Street, walking two blocks south to the **Juliette Gordon Low Birthplace** ⑥⑨. Two more short blocks south from the Low House on Bull Street, you'll reach **Chippewa Square** ⑦⓪. Continue south on Bull Street to **Madison Square** ⑦①, where you may stop to take in the Gothic Revival **Green-Meldrim House** ⑦②. Next, walk four blocks south on Bull Street to **Monterey Square** ⑦③. Proceed two blocks farther south from Monterey Square to **Forsyth Park** ⑦④, the divide between East and West Gaston streets.

From the park, walk east on East Gaston Street and go one block to Abercorn Street; then turn left (north) on Abercorn, to Calhoun Square, and note the **Wesley Monumental Church** ⑦⑤. Continue north on Abercorn eight blocks to **Lafayette Square** ⑦⑥. Walk left a few steps and view the **Andrew Low House** ⑦⑦. Northeast of Lafayette Square looms the **Cathedral of St. John the Baptist** ⑦⑧ on East Harris Street. One block north at the intersection of Abercorn and East Oglethorpe streets is the huge **Colonial Park Cemetery** ⑦⑨. Proceeding two blocks north on Abercorn from the cemetery takes you to Oglethorpe Square; across from the square is the **Owens-Thomas House and Museum** ⑧⓪. From the house, walk east on East President Street two blocks to **Columbia Square** ⑧①. Northwest of the square on East State Street stands the **Isaiah Davenport House** ⑧②. From here, continue north up Habersham Street two blocks to Warren Square; turn left (west) and go two blocks to **Reynolds Square** ⑧③, on Abercorn. Head north on Abercorn to East Bay Street, turn right and then walk one block to **Emmet Park** ⑧④, a splendid park to relax in at the end of your tour.

TIMING

This is a long but comfortable walk, as Savannah has no hills or inclines to tax the casual stroller. Allow a full day to see everything along this route, especially to read all the historic markers and explore all the sights thoroughly, including stopping at selected ones for tours within. Driving around the squares can be slow—but the entire drive can be done in two hours, a pace that allows for some stopping along the way. Allow extra time if Riverfront Plaza delights you enough to detain you for a half hour or so.

Sights to See

 Andrew Low House. This residence was built in 1848 for Andrew Low, one of Savannah's merchant princes and an investor in the SS *Savannah,* the first steamship to cross the Atlantic Ocean in 1819. The home later belonged to his son William, who married Juliette Gordon. After her husband's death, she founded the Girl Scouts in this house on March 12, 1912. Robert E. Lee and William Thackeray were both entertained here. In addition to its historical significance, the house has some of the finest ornamental ironwork in Savannah, fine 19th-century antiques, and stunning silver. ✉ *329 Abercorn St.,* ☎ *912/233–6854.* 🎫 *$6.* ☉ *Mon.–Wed. and Fri.–Sat. 10:30–4, Sun. noon–4; last tour at 3:30.*

 Cathedral of St. John the Baptist. Soaring like a hymn over the city, the French Gothic–style cathedral, with characteristic pointed arches and free-flowing traceries, is the seat of the Diocese of Savannah. It is the oldest Roman Catholic church in Georgia, having been founded in 1799

by the first French colonists. Fire destroyed the early structures, and the present cathedral dates from 1873. Most of the cathedral's impressive stained-glass windows were made by Austrian glassmakers and imported around the turn of the century. The high altar is of Italian marble, and the Stations of the Cross were imported from Munich. ⊠ *222 E. Harris St.,* ☎ *912/233–4709.*

⓻ Chippewa Square. Daniel Chester French's imposing bronze statue of General James Edward Oglethorpe, founder of Savannah and Georgia, anchors the square. Also note the **Savannah Theatre** on Bull Street which claims to be the oldest continuously operated theater site in North America.

⓺ City Hall. Built in 1905 on the site of the Old City Exchange (1799–1904), this imposing structure anchors Bay Street. Notice the bench commemorating Oglethorpe's landing on February 12, 1733. ⊠ *1 Bay St.,* ☎ *912/651–6444.* ⊙ *Weekdays 8:15–5.*

⓺ City Market. This popular area encompasses pedestrian-accessed galleries, nightclubs, restaurants, and shops. ⊠ *Between Franklin Sq. and Johnson Sq. on W. Saint Julian St.*

★ ⓻ Colonial Park Cemetery. This park is the final resting place for Savannahians buried here from 1750 to 1853. Shaded pathways lace through the cemetery, and you may want to stroll through and read some of the old inscriptions. There are several historical plaques to look at, one of which marks the grave of Button Gwinnett, a signer of the Declaration of Independence. ⊠ *Oglethorpe and Abercorn Sts.*

⓼ Columbia Square. When Savannah was a walled city (1757–1790), Bethesda Gate (one of six) was located here. The square was laid out in 1799.

⓼ Emmet Park. The lovely tree-shaded park is named for Robert Emmet, a late-18th-century Irish patriot and orator. ⊠ *Borders Bay St.*

⓺ Factors Walk. Cobblestone ramps lead pedestrians down to River Street. (These are serious cobblestones, and you will suffer if you wear anything but the most comfortable shoes you own.) A network of iron walkways connects Bay Street with the multistoried buildings that rise up from the river level, and iron stairways descend from Bay Street to Factors Walk.

⓻ Forsyth Park. The park forms the southern anchor of Bull Street. With 20 luxuriant acres and a glorious white fountain dating from 1858 and restored in 1988, it contains Confederate and Spanish-American War memorials, and the Fragrant Garden for the Blind, a project of Savannah garden clubs. There are tennis courts and a tree-shaded jogging path. The park is often the scene of outdoor plays and concerts. At the northwest corner of Forsyth Park, in **Hodgson Hall,** a 19th-century Italianate–Greek Revival building, you'll find the **Georgia Historical Society,** which shows selections from its collection of artifacts and manuscripts, chiefly concentrating on Georgia history. ⊠ *501 Whitaker St.,* ☎ *912/651–2128.* ⊡ *Free.* ⊙ *Tues.–Fri. 10–5, Sat. 9–3.*

★ ⓻ Green-Meldrim House. Designed by New York architect John Norris and built in 1852 for cotton merchant Charles Green, this splendid Gothic Revival mansion cost $90,000 to build—a princely sum back then. The house was bought in 1892 by Judge Peter Meldrim, whose heirs sold it to **St. John's Episcopal Church,** for which it is now the working parish house. General Sherman lived here after taking the city in 1864. Sitting on **Madison Square,** the mansion is complete with crenelated roof, oriel windows, and an external gallery with filigreed ironwork. Inside, the mantels are Carrara marble, the woodwork is carved black walnut, and the doorknobs and hinges are silver-plated. The house is furnished with donated 16th-, 17th-, and 18th-century antiques. ⊠ *14 W. Macon St.,* ☎ *912/233–3845.* ⊡ *$4.* ☼ *Tues. and Thurs.–Sat. 10–4; closed Dec. 15–Jan. 15 and 2 wks before Easter.*

★ 82 **Isaiah Davenport House.** This residence was the historic Savannah structure whose imminent demolition galvanized the city's residents into action to save their treasured buildings. Semicircular stairs with wrought-iron trim lead to the recessed doorway of the redbrick Federal mansion that master builder Isaiah Davenport built for himself in 1815. Three dormer windows poke through the sloping roof of the stately house, and the interior has polished hardwood floors, fine woodwork and plasterwork, and a soaring elliptical staircase. The furnishings are Hepplewhite, Chippendale, and Sheraton. In the attic, don't miss the collection of antique dolls. ⊠ *324 E. State St.,* ☎ *912/236–8097.* ⊡ *$5.* ☼ *Daily 10–4.*

66 **Johnson Square.** The oldest of James Oglethorpe's original 24 squares was laid out in 1733 and named for South Carolina Governor Robert Johnson. A monument marks the grave of Nathanial Greene, a hero of the Revolutionary War. The square was once a popular gathering place, where Savannahians came to welcome President Monroe in 1819, to greet the Marquis de Lafayette in 1825, and to cheer for Georgia's secession in 1861.

69 **Juliette Gordon Low Birthplace/Girl Scout National Center.** This majestic Regency town house, attributed to William Jay (built 1818–1821), was designated in 1965 as Savannah's first National Historic Landmark. "Daisy" Low, founder of the Girl Scouts, was born here in 1860, and the house is now owned and operated by the Girl Scouts of America. Mrs. Low's paintings and other artwork are on display in the house, restored to the style of 1886, the year of Mrs. Low's marriage. ⊠ *142 Bull St.,* ☎ *912/233–4501.* ⊡ *$5; discounts for Girl Scouts.* ☼ *Mon.–Tues. and Thurs.–Sat. 10–4, Sun. 12:30–4:30.*

76 **Lafayette Square.** Named for the Marquis de Lafayette, the square contains a graceful three-tier fountain donated by the Georgia chapter of the Colonial Dames of America. ⊠ *Abercorn St. between E. Harris and E. Charlton.*

71 **Madison Square.** A statue on the square, laid out in 1839 and named for President James Madison, depicts Sergeant William Jasper hoisting a flag and is a tribute to his bravery during the Siege of Savannah. Though mortally wounded, Jasper rescued the colors of his regiment in the assault on the British lines. ⊠ *Bull St. between W. Harris and W. Charlton.*

73 **Monterey Square.** Commemorating the victory of General Zachary Taylor's forces in Monterrey, Mexico, in 1846, this is the fifth and southernmost of Bull Street's squares. A monument honors General Casimir Pulaski, the Polish nobleman who lost his life in the Siege of Savannah during the Revolutionary War. **Temple Mickve Israel,** a splendid Gothic Revival synagogue on Monterey Square, is home to the third-oldest Jewish congregation in the United States; its founding members settled in town five months after the establishment of Savannah in 1733. The synagogue's collection includes documents and letters (some from George Washington, James Madison, and Thomas Jefferson) pertaining to early Jewish life in Savannah and Georgia. ⊠ *20 E. Gordon St.,* ☎ *912/233–1547.* ⊡ *Free.* ☼ *Weekdays 10–noon and 2–4.*

★ ⑧ **Owens-Thomas House and Museum.** English architect William Jay's first Regency mansion in Savannah is the city's finest example of that architectural style. Built in 1819, the thoroughly English house was constructed largely with local materials. Of particular note are the curving walls of the house, Greek-inspired ornamental molding, half-moon arches, stained-glass panels, and Duncan Phyfe furniture. You'll find canopied beds, a pianoforte, and displays of ornate silver. From a wrought-iron balcony, in 1825, the Marquis de Lafayette bade a two-hour au revoir to the crowd below. ⊠ *124 Abercorn St.,* ☎ *912/233–9743.* ☜ *$6.* ☉ *Tues.–Sat. 10–4:30, Sun. 2–4:30.*

OFF THE
BEATEN PATH   **RALPH MARK GILBERT CIVIL RIGHTS MUSEUM –** In Savannah's stellar historic district, this history museum, opened in 1996, houses a series of 15 exhibits covering segregation from Emancipation through the civil rights movement. The museum has touring exhibitions. ⊠ *460 Martin Luther King Jr. Blvd.,* ☎ *912/231-8900.* ☜ *$4.* ☉ *Mon.–Sat. 9–5, Sun. 1–5.*

⑧ **Reynolds Square.** John Wesley, who preached in Savannah and wrote the first English hymnal in Savannah in 1736, is remembered here. A monument to the founder of the Methodist Church is shaded by greenery and surrounded by park benches. The **Olde Pink House** (⊠ 23 Abercorn St.), built in 1771, is one of the oldest buildings in town. Now a restaurant (☞ Dining, *below*), the porticoed pink stucco Georgian mansion has been a private home, a bank, and headquarters for a Yankee general during the Civil War.

⑥ **Riverfront Plaza.** Here you can watch a parade of freighters and pug-nosed tugs; youngsters can play in the tugboat-shape sandboxes. River Street is the main venue for many of the city's celebrations, including the First Saturday festivals when flea marketeers, artists, and artisans display their wares, and musicians entertain the crowds.

⑥ **Savannah History Museum.** Housed in a restored railway station, the museum provides an excellent introduction to the city. Exhibits range from old locomotives to a tribute to Savannah-born songwriter Johnny Mercer. The nearby **site of the Siege of Savannah** marks the spot where, in 1779, the Colonial forces, led by Polish Count Casimir Pulaski, laid siege to Savannah in an attempt to retake the city from the Redcoats. They were beaten back, and Pulaski was killed while leading a cavalry charge against the British. ⊠ *303 Martin Luther King Jr. Blvd.,* ☎ *912/238–1779.* ☜ *$3.* ☉ *Weekdays 8:30–5, weekends 9–5.*

⑤ **Savannah Visitors Center.** Come here for free maps and brochures, lots of friendly advice, and an audiovisual overview of the city. The center is also the starting point for a number of guided tours. The center is in a big 1860 redbrick building with high ceilings and sweeping arches. It was the old Central of Georgia railway station. ⊠ *301 Martin Luther King Jr. Blvd.,* ☎ *912/944–0455.* ☉ *Weekdays 8:30–5, weekends 9–5.*

⑥ **Scarborough House.** This exuberant Greek Revival mansion, built during the 1819 cotton boom for Savannah merchant Prince William Scarborough, was designed by English architect William Jay. Scarborough was a major investor in the steamship *Savannah.* The house features a Doric portico capped by one of Jay's characteristic half-moon windows. Four massive Doric columns form a peristyle in the atrium entrance hall. The owner of the house, the **Ships of the Sea Museum,** relocated to the Scarborough House in 1996; ship models are on display, including steamships, a nuclear-powered ship (the *Savannah*), China clippers with their sails unfurled, and Columbus's ships. ⊠ *41 Mar-*

tin Luther King Jr. Blvd., ☎ *912/232–1511.* 🖃 *$5.* ☉ *Tues.–Sun. 10–5.*

68 **Telfair Mansion and Art Museum.** The oldest public art museum in the Southeast was designed by William Jay in 1819 for Alexander Telfair, and sits across the street from **Telfair Square.** Within its marbled rooms are American, French, and Dutch Impressionist paintings; German Tonalist paintings; a large collection of works by Kahlil Gibran; plaster casts of the Elgin Marbles, the Venus de Milo, and the Laocoön, among other classical sculptures; and some of the Telfair family furnishings, including a Duncan Phyfe sideboard and Savannah-made silver. ⊠ *121 Barnard St.,* ☎ *912/232–1177.* 🖃 *$5; free Sun.* ☉ *Tues.–Sat. 10–5, Sun. 2–5.*

75 **Wesley Monumental Church.** This Gothic Revival–style church memorializing the founders of Methodism is patterned after Queen's Kirk in Amsterdam. Noted for its magnificent stained-glass windows, the church celebrated a century of service in 1968. In the Wesley Window there are busts of John and Charles Wesley. ⊠ *429 Abercorn St.,* ☎ *912/232–0191.*

67 **Wright Square.** Named for James Wright, Georgia's last Colonial governor, the square has an elaborate monument in its center which honors William Washington Gordon, founder of the Central of Georgia Railroad. A slab of granite from Stone Mountain honors the grave of Tomo-Chi-Chi, the Yamacraw chief who befriended General Oglethorpe and the colonists.

Midnight in the Garden of Good and Evil

Town gossips can give you the best introduction to a city and, as author John Berendt discovered, Savannah's not short on them. In his 1994 best-seller, *Midnight in the Garden of Good and Evil,* Berendt shares the juiciest of tales imparted to him during the eight years he spent here wining and dining with Savannah's high society and dancing with her Grand Empress drag queen, The Lady Chablis, among others. By the time he left, there had been a scandalous homicide and several trials.

Before you set out, find a copy of the book, pour yourself a cool drink, and enter an eccentric world of cutthroat killers and society back stabbers, voodoo witches, and garden-club ladies. Next, slip on a pair of comfortable shoes and head over to the historic district to follow the characters' steps to their homes and haunts. By the end of this walking tour, you'll be hard-pressed to find the line between Berendt's creative nonfiction and Savannah's reality. Note: Unless otherwise indicated, the sights on this tour are not open to the public.

A Good Walk and Drive

Begin at the southwest corner of Monterey Square, site of the **Mercer House** ⑧⑤, whose construction was begun by songwriter Johnny Mercer's great grandfather just before the Civil War. Two blocks south on Bull Street is the **Armstrong House** ⑧⑥, an earlier residence of Jim Williams, the main character in the book. Walk south through Forsyth Park to the corner of West Gaston and Whitaker streets (or, if driving, turn right on East Gaston to West Gaston Street, then left onto Whitaker). The **Forsyth Park Apartments** ⑧⑦, where author John Berendt lived, are on the southwest corner of Forsyth Park. Then, if you're walking, turn back north through the park (and if driving, turn left down Drayton Street at the park's southeast corner, then left onto East Gaston Street). At the midpoint of the park's northern edge, turn north up Bull Street in the direction of Monterey Square. Turn left on West

Gordon Street at Bull Street and walk toward the corner of West Gordon and Whitaker, where you'll reach **Serena Dawes's House** ⑧. Next, cross West Gordon Street, walk north on Bull Street in front of Mercer House, cross Wayne Street, and the first house on the left facing Bull at Wayne is **Lee Adler's Home** ⑧, which sits across from Monterey Square's northwest corner. (If you're driving, proceed around Monterey Square to West Taylor Street, and at its intersection with Whitaker Street, take a left and go two blocks to West Gordon. Take a left onto West Gordon; the house is on the right.)

Continue walking north on Bull Street, and take a right (east) on East Jones Street. **Joe Odom's first house** ⑨ is the third house on the left before Drayton Street. (If you're driving, go around the square again onto Bull Street, and go north on Bull to East Jones Street. Take a right, and the house will be on the left.)

Continue on East Jones Street to Abercorn Street, and turn left (north), walking two blocks on Abercorn to East Charlton Street and the **Hamilton-Turner House** ⑨. Then, swing around Lafayette Square to East Harris Street, and take it about six blocks west to Pulaski Square at Barnard Street; turn right (north) on Barnard through Orleans Square back north to Telfair Square. On foot, you may elect to head west down West York Street on the south side of Telfair Square to find the **Chatham County Courthouse** ⑨, scene of all those trials, two blocks away. Drivers will have to continue around the square to take a left (west) onto West State Street, two blocks from the courthouse. Finally, whether walking or driving, you may conclude the tour by driving east on Liberty Street and Wheaton Street for about 4 mi to Bonaventure Road. Turn left to **Bonaventure Cemetery** ⑨.

TIMING

Allow a leisurely two hours to walk the main points of the tour, plus another hour to visit the cemetery. If driving, this tour is easily accomplished in an hour, but remember to add additional time to meander around Bonaventure Cemetery.

Sights to See

⑧ **Armstrong House.** Jim Williams lived and worked in this residence before purchasing the Mercer House. On a late-afternoon walk past the mansion, Berendt met Mr. Simon Glover, an 86-year-old singer and porter for the law firm of Bouhan, Williams, and Levy, occupants of the building. Glover confided that he earned a weekly $10 for walking one of the firm's former partner's deceased dogs up and down Bull Street. Baffled? So was the author. Behind the house's cast-iron gates are the offices of Frank Siler, Jim Williams's attorney, who doubles as keeper of Uga, the Georgia Bulldog mascot. ✉ *447 Bull St.*

⑨ **Bonaventure Cemetery.** Drive on Wheaton Street east out of downtown to Bonaventure Road. Once the grounds of a magnificent live oak–shaded plantation, whose mansion burned to the ground in the midst of a dinner party, Bonaventure is the final resting place for songwriter Johnny Mercer, poet Conrad Aiken, and also Danny Hansford (Greenwich Cemetery section). While you may be able to find Danny's marker, don't look too hard for the haunting female tombstone figure from the book's cover. Apparently, Berendt fans beat too tough a path to her feet, and she was removed. (Note: Get there before sundown, when it closes.)

⑨ **Chatham County Courthouse.** The courthouse was the scene of the three Williams murder trials, which took place over the course of about eight years. An underground tunnel leads from the courthouse to the jail where

Williams was held in a specially modified cell that allowed him to conduct his antiques business. ⊠ *133 Montgomery St.*

87 **Forsyth Park Apartments.** Here was Berendt's second home in Savannah; from his fourth-floor rooms he pieced together the majority of the book. While parking his newly acquired 1973 Pontiac Grand Prix outside these apartments, Berendt met The Lady Chablis coming out of her nearby doctor's office, freshly feminine from a new round of hormone shots. ⊠ *Whitaker and Gwinnett Sts.*

91 **Hamilton-Turner House.** After one too many of Odom's deals went sour, Mandy left him and took over his third residence, a Second Empire–style mansion dating from 1873. Mandy (or Nancy Hillis, as her driver's license reads) filled it with 17th- and 18th-century antiques; she has since transformed it into a successful museum through which she sometimes leads tour groups. The sturdily elegant towering hulk is at the southeastern corner of Lafayette Square. ⊠ *330 Abercorn St.,* ☎ *912/233–4800.* ▱ *$5.* ◷ *Daily 10–4.*

90 **Joe Odom's First House.** At this stucco town house, Odom, a combination tax lawyer, real-estate broker, and piano player, played host to a 24-hour stream of visitors. The author met Odom through his fourth fiancée-in-waiting, Mandy Nichols, a former Miss Big Beautiful Woman, who stopped by to borrow ice when their power had been cut off, a frequent occurrence. ⊠ *16 E. Jones St.*

89 **Lee Adler's Home.** Just north of the Mercer House, in half of the double town house facing West Wayne Street, Lee Adler, the adversary of Jim Williams (the main character of the book) runs his business of restoring historic Savannah properties. Adler's howling dogs drove Williams to his pipe organ, where he churned out a deafening version of César Franck's *Pièce Heroique.* Later, Adler stuck reelection signs in his front lawn, showing his support for the District Attorney who prosecuted Williams three times before he was finally found not guilty. ⊠ *425 Bull St.*

85 **Mercer House.** This redbrick Italianate mansion on the southwest corner of Monterey Square became the Taj Mahal of the book's main character, Jim Williams; here he ran a world-class antiques dealership and held *the* Christmas party of the season; here also his sometime house partner Danny Hansford was shot and died. Williams himself died here in 1990, near the very spot where Hansford fell. Today, his sister lives quietly among the remnants of his Fabergé collection and his Joshua Reynolds paintings, in rooms lit by Waterford crystal chandeliers. ⊠ *429 Bull St.*

88 **Serena Dawes's House.** Near the intersection of West Gorden and Bull streets, this house was owned by Helen Driscoll, also known as Serena Dawes. A high-profile beauty in the 1930s and '40s, she married into a Pennsylvania steel family. After her husband accidentally and fatally shot himself in the head, she retired here, in her hometown. Dawes, Berendt writes, "spent most of her day in bed, holding court, drinking martinis and pink ladies, playing with her white toy poodle, Lulu." Chief among Serena's gentlemen callers was Luther Driggers, rumored to possess a poison strong enough to wipe out the entire city. ⊠ *17 W. Gordon St.*

Other Area Attractions

Ebenezer. When the Salzburgers arrived in Savannah in 1734, Oglethorpe sent them up the Savannah River to establish a settlement. The first effort was assailed by disease, and they sought his permission to move to better ground. Not receiving it, they moved anyway and established Ebenezer. There, they engaged in silkworm production and, in 1769, built their Jerusalem Church, which still stands. Following the Revolution, the silkworm operation never resumed, and the town faded into history. Descendants of these original Protestant religious refugees have preserved the church, perhaps Georgia's oldest in continuous use by the same sect, and have assembled a few of the remaining buildings, moving them to this site from other locations. Be sure to follow GA 275 to its end and see Ebenezer Landing, where the Salzburgers came ashore. ⊠ *Ebenezer Rd., Rincon, U.S. 21 to GA 275, Rincon.*

Fort Jackson. About 3½ mi outside Savannah, you'll see a sign for the fort, located on Salter's Island. The Colonial building was purchased in 1808 by the federal government and is the oldest standing fort in Georgia. It was garrisoned in 1812 and was the Confederate headquarters of the river batteries. The brick edifice is surrounded by a tidal moat, and there are 13 exhibit areas. Battle reenactments, blacksmithing demonstrations, and programs of 19th-century music are among the fort's schedule of activities. ⊠ *1 Ft. Jackson Rd.,* ☎ *912/232–3945.* ☒ *$2.50.* ☉ *Daily 9–5.*

★ ☺ **Fort Pulaski National Monument.** Just 14 mi east of downtown Savannah, this must-see sight for Civil War buffs was built on Cockspur Island between 1829 and 1847 and named for Casimir Pulaski, a Polish count who was a Revolutionary War hero. Robert E. Lee's first assignment after graduating from West Point was as an engineer here. During the Civil War the fort fell on April 11, 1862, after a mere 30 hours of bombardment by newfangled rifled cannons. The restored fortification, operated by the National Park Service, is complete with moats, drawbridges, massive ramparts, and towering walls. You'll see the entrance on your left just before U.S. 80E reaches Tybee Island. The park has self-guided trails and ample picnic areas. ⊠ *U.S. 80,* ☎ *912/786–5787.* ☒ *$2.* ☉ *Daily 8:30–5; extended summer hrs.*

King-Tisdell Cottage. Tucked behind a picket fence is this museum dedicated to the preservation of African-American history and culture. The Negro Heritage Trail Tour (☞ Guided Tours *in* Savannah A to Z, *below*) visits this little Victorian house. Broad steps lead to a porch, and dormer windows pop up through a steep roof. The interior is furnished to resemble a middle-class African-American coastal home of the 1890s. To reach the cottage by car, go east on East Bay Street to Price Street, and turn south (right) on this street; continue for about 30 blocks to East Huntington Street, and take a left (east). The building is in the middle of the block. ⊠ *514 E. Huntingdon St.,* ☎ *912/236–5161.* ☒ *$2.50.* ☉ *Tues.–Fri. noon–4:30, weekends 1–4.*

Mighty Eighth Air Force Museum. The famous World War II squadron, the Mighty Eighth Air Force, was formed in Savannah in January 1942 and moved to the United Kingdom. Flying borrowed aircraft, it became the largest air force in the history of aviation, with some 200,000 combat crew personnel. Many lost their lives or were interned as prisoners of war. Opened in 1996, a sleek modern building houses memorabilia from the unit's heyday and the era in which it served. ⊠ *I–95 and U.S. 80, 175 Bourne Ave., Exit 18, Pooler,* ☎ *912/748–8888 or 800/421–9428.* ☒ *$7.50.* ☉ *Daily 10–6.*

🐾 **Oatland Island Education Center.** This 175-acre maritime forest five minutes from downtown is a natural habitat for coastal wildlife, including timber wolves and panthers. ⊠ *711 Sandtown Rd.,* ☎ *912/ 897–3773.* 🎫 *$1 donation requested.* ⊙ *Weekdays 8:30–5; special events and programs Oct.–May, 2nd Sat. of month 11–5.*

🐾 **Skidaway Marine Science Complex.** This center on the grounds of the former Modena Plantation has a 12-panel, 12,000-gallon aquarium with marine and plant life of the continental shelf. Other exhibits highlight coastal archaeology and fossils of the Georgia coast. Nature trails overlook marsh and water. ⊠ *30 Ocean Science Circle, Skidaway Island,* ☎ *912/598–2496.* 🎫 *$1.* ⊙ *Weekdays 9–4, Sat. noon–5.*

Tybee Island. Lying 18 mi east of Savannah on the Atlantic Ocean, Tybee has all manner of water and beach activities. Take Victory Drive (U.S. 80), sometimes called Tybee Road, onto the island. There are two historic forts to visit on the way (☞ Fort Jackson and Fort Pulaski National Monument, *above*). "Tybee" is an Indian word meaning salt. The Yamacraw Indians came to the island to hunt and fish, and legend has it that pirates buried their treasure here. The island is about 5 mi long and 2 mi wide, with a plethora of seafood restaurants, chain motels, condos, and shops, most of which sprung up during the 1950s and haven't changed much since. The entire expanse of white sand is divided into a number of public beaches, where visitors shell and crab, play on water slides, charter fishing boats, swim, and build sand castles. Nearby "Little" Tybee Island, actually larger than Tybee Island, is entirely undeveloped, making it ideal for pitching a dome tent and getting away from it all. Contact **Tybee Island Beach Visitor Information** (⊠ Box 1628, Savannah 31402, ☎ 800/868–2322).

Tybee Museum and Lighthouse. On the northern end of Tybee Island, across the way from Fort Screven, this museum displays Indian artifacts, pirate pistols, powder flasks, old prints tracing the history of Savannah, and even some sheet music of Johnny Mercer songs. The Civil War Room has old maps and newspaper articles pertaining to Sherman's occupation of Savannah. The 150-ft-high lighthouse across the road is Georgia's oldest and tallest, dating from 1773, with an observation deck 145 ft above the sea. Bright red steps—178 of them—lead to the deck and the awesome Tybee Light. ⊠ *30 Meddin Dr.,* ☎ *912/ 786–4077 museum, 919/786–5801 lighthouse.* 🎫 *Both lighthouse and museum $3.* ⊙ *Both summer, Wed.–Mon. 10–6; winter, Mon. and Wed.–Fri. noon–4, weekends 10–4.*

Dining

On a river, 18 mi inland from the Atlantic Ocean, Savannah naturally has excellent seafood restaurants. Locals also have a passion for spicy barbecue. The Historic District yields culinary treasures among its architectural diamonds—especially along River Street. Several of the city's restaurants—such as Elizabeth on 37th, 45 South, the Olde Pink House, and Il Pasticcio—can easily compete with the best of Atlanta's dining establishments. Savannahians also like to drive out to eat in Thunderbolt and on Skidaway, Tybee, and Wilmington islands.

$$$$ ✕ **Elizabeth on 37th.** Elizabeth Terry is the chef, and in 1995 she was
★ named James Beard Best Chef/Southeast. The restaurant is in the city's Victorian District, in an elegant turn-of-the-century mansion with hardwood floors and spacious rooms. Among the seasonal specialties are grouper with sesame seeds, tiny Bluffton oysters with leeks and country ham in the fall and winter, and stuffed Vidalia onions. While the emphasis is on sea creatures served in delicate sauces, there are other

excellent offerings, including beef tenderloin, quail, lamb, game, and chicken dishes. The Savannah Cream Cake is a study in layered extravagance. ⊠ *105 E. 37th St.,* ☎ *912/236–5547. Reservations essential. AE, D, DC, MC, V. Closed Sun. No lunch.*

$$$$ ✗ **45 South.** This popular southside eatery is small and stylish, with
★   contemporary decor in lush mauve and green. The ever-changing menu includes seared breast of duck with wild rice, ginger beets, and a Port wine and pear reduction sauce; and grilled ahi tuna with spinach, seared Hudson Valley foie gras, and a truffle vinaigrette. The wine list offers more than a dozen by the glass. ⊠ *20 E. Broad St.,* ☎ *912/233–1881. Reservations essential. AE, D, DC, MC, V. Closed Sun. No lunch.*

$$$ ✗ **Olde Pink House.** The brick Georgian mansion was built for James
★   Habersham, one of the wealthiest Americans of his time, in 1771. The elegant tavern, one of Savannah's oldest buildings, has original Georgia pine floors, Venetian chandeliers, and 18th-century English antiques. The owners have introduced Colonial cooking style to the menu where appropriate. Signature dishes are a Colonial version of crisp roast duck with a savory wild-berry compote, and black grouper stuffed with blue crab. The restaurant has one of the largest wine cellars in the state— fitting, as the Habersham family dominated the Madeira trade for years. ⊠ *23 Abercorn St.,* ☎ *912/232–4286. AE, MC, V. No lunch.*

$$–$$$ ✗ **River House.** This stylish restaurant sits over the spot where the SS *Savannah* set sail for her maiden voyage across the ocean in 1819. The mesquite-grilled entrées, including swordfish topped with vegetables and grouper Florentine, served with creamed spinach and a fresh dill and lemon-butter sauce, are good choices. Entrées are served with freshly baked loaves of sourdough bread, and fish dishes come with homemade angel-hair pasta. The extensive wine list favors California selections. ⊠ *125 W. River St.,* ☎ *912/234–1900. AE, D, DC, MC, V.*

$$ ✗ **Bistro Savannah.** Wicker-basket chairs, high ceilings, burnished heart-pine floors, and Savannah gray-brick walls lined with artwork by local artists all contribute to the true bistro atmosphere. Low-country dishes form the heart of the inventive menu, such as tasso ham and shrimp on stone-ground grits and pecan-crusted chicken. More modern tastes are represented, too, in such treats as shallot-marinated grilled tuna served with roasted seasonal vegetables. The restaurant is near City Market. ⊠ *309 W. Congress St.,* ☎ *912/233–6266. AE, MC, V. No lunch.*

$$ ✗ **Il Pasticcio.** Sicilian Pino Venetico turned this former department store
★   into his dream restaurant. Also a deli, the bistro-style spot gleams with steel, glass, and tile, and is lively with the buzz of a young, hip crowd. The menu changes frequently, but fresh pastas with inventive sauces are a constant. Don't miss the second-floor art gallery. Excellent homemade desserts (a superior tiramisu) and a good wine list make this one worth seeking out. ⊠ *2 E. Broughton St.,* ☎ *912/231–8888. AE, D, DC, MC, V. Deli closed Sun. No lunch.*

$–$$ ✗ **Shrimp Factory.** Like all of Savannah's riverfront restaurants, this was once an old warehouse. Now it's a light and airy place with exposed brick, wood paneling, beamed ceilings, and huge windows that let you gaze at the passing parade of ships. A house specialty is Pine Bark Stew—five native seafoods simmered with potatoes, onions, and herbs. Blackened mahimahi fillet is smothered with herbs and julienned sweet red peppers in butter sauce. Baked deviled crabs are served with chicken-baked rice, and seafood bisque comes with a tiny cruet of sherry. ⊠ *313 E. River St.,* ☎ *912/236–4229. AE, D, DC, MC, V.*

$ ✗ **Crystal Beer Parlor.** This comfortable family tavern is famed for hamburgers, thick-cut french fries, huge onion rings, and frosted mugs of draft beer. The menu also offers fried oyster sandwiches, gumbo, and

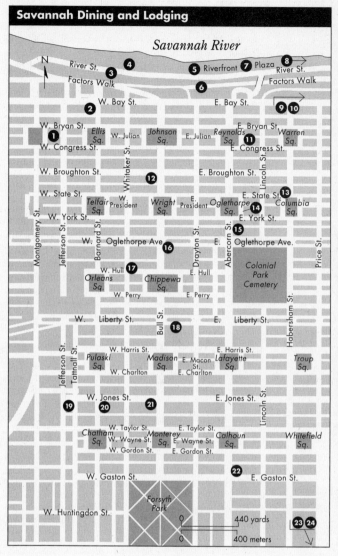

Savannah Dining and Lodging

shrimp salad. ✉ *301 W. Jones St., at Jefferson St.,* ☎ *912/232–1153. Reservations not accepted. MC, V. Closed Sun.*

$ ✕ **Johnny Harris.** What started as a small roadside stand in 1924 has grown into one of the city's mainstays, with a menu that includes steaks, fried chicken, seafood, and a variety of meats spiced with the restaurant's famous sauce. ✉ *1651 E. Victory Dr.,* ☎ *912/354–7810. AE, D, DC, MC, V. Closed Sun.*

$ ✕ **Mrs. Wilkes Dining Room.** At breakfast time and noon (no dinner
★ is served), folks line up for a culinary orgy. Charles Kuralt and David Brinkley are among the celebrities who have feasted on the fine Southern food, served family-style at big tables. For breakfast there are eggs, sausage, piping hot biscuits, and grits. At lunch, try fried or roast chicken, collard greens, okra, mashed potatoes, corn bread—the dishes just keep coming. ✉ *107 W. Jones St.,* ☎ *912/232–5997. Reservations not accepted. No credit cards. Closed weekends. No dinner.*

$ ✕ **Nita's Place.** Opened in 1993 just a half block from the Colonial Cemetery, this little steam-table operation offers nothing in decor. But Juanita Dixon has established a reputation for perfectly prepared down-home Southern cooking; locals and tourists alike come for salmon patties, baked chicken, perfectly cooked okra, outstanding squash casserole, freshly made lemonade—you can see the seeds!—and homemade desserts. The vegetables, always fresh, alone are worth the trip. ⊠ *40 Abercorn St.,* ☎ *912/238–8233. Reservations not accepted. MC, V. Closed Sun. No dinner.*

Lodging

While Savannah has its share of chain hotels and motels, the city's most distinctive lodgings are the more than two dozen historic inns, guest houses, and bed-and-breakfasts gracing the Historic District.

If "historic inn" brings to mind images of roughing it in shabbily genteel mansions with slightly antiquated plumbing, you're in for a surprise. Most of the inns are in mansions with the requisite high ceilings, spacious rooms, and ornate carved millwork. Most have canopied, four-poster, or Victorian brass beds. And amid antique surroundings, modern luxury: enormous baths, many with whirlpool baths or hot tubs; film libraries for in-room VCRs; and turndown service with a chocolate, praline, or even a discreet brandy on your nightstand. Continental breakfast and afternoon refreshments are often included in the rate.

Inns and Guest Houses

$$$$ **Ballastone Inn.** This sumptuous inn occupies a mansion dating from
★   1838 that once served as a bordello. Each room has a different decor. Scarborough Fair is a deep China blue and yellow with two four-poster beds. Mulberry Tulips has two queen-size antique iron beds. On the garden level, rooms are small and cozy, with exposed brick walls, beamed ceilings, and, in some cases, windows at eye level with the lush courtyard. Most rooms have fireplaces, and three have whirlpool tubs. Guests can exercise for free at the First City Club nearby. ⊠ *14 E. Oglethorpe Ave., 31401,* ☎ *912/236–1484 or 800/822–4553,* ℻ *912/236–4626. 15 rooms, 3 suites. In-room VCRs, concierge. AE, MC, V.*

$$$$ **Eliza Thompson House.** Eliza Thompson was a socially prominent widow when she built her fine town house around 1847. Restored and operating as a bed-and-breakfast in the 1980s, the property declined once more. But in 1995 Carol and Steve Day purchased the house and repainted, refinished, and refurnished it in period style. Continental breakfast and complimentary afternoon wine and cheese are served on the patio, with its fine Ivan Bailey sculpture. ⊠ *5 W. Jones St., 31401,* ☎ *912/236–3620 or 800/348–9378,* ℻ *912/238–1920. 23 rooms. Concierge. AE, MC, V.*

$$$$ **Foley House Inn.** Two town houses, built 50 years apart, form this
★   elegant bed-and-breakfast inn. Named for an Irish immigrant who made a fortune in Savannah, the house was built by his widow for her five grandchildren, whose parents had died leaving them in her care. Inge and Mark Moore purchased the inn in 1994 and have completely renovated it, adding fine antiques and reproductions. Continental breakfast may be served in your room, the lounge, or outdoors in the courtyard. Afternoon wine is available for an extra charge. Five rooms have whirlpool tubs. ⊠ *14 W. Hull St., 31401,* ☎ *912/232–6622 or 800/647–3708,* ℻ *912/231–1218. 19 rooms. In-room VCRs, concierge. AE, MC, V.*

$$$$ 🏨 **Gastonian.** Recently purchased by Decaturite Ann Landers, the
★ mansion was built in 1868, and each of its 10 rooms and three sumptuous suites is done up in vivid Scalamandre colors. The Caracalla Suite
is named for the marble bath with an 8-ft whirlpool tub. The huge bedroom has a king-size canopy bed, two working fireplaces, and a lounge
with a mirrored wet bar. All rooms have working fireplaces and antiques from the Georgian and Regency periods; most have whirlpool
tubs or Japanese soak tubs. In the morning, a full breakfast is served
in the kitchen or formal dining room—or you can opt for a Continental
breakfast in your room. ⊠ *220 E. Gaston St., 31401,* ☎ *912/232–
2869 or 800/322–6603,* 𝔽𝔸𝕏 *912/232–0710. 16 rooms. Outdoor hot
tub, concierge. AE, MC, V.*

$$$$ 🏨 **Kehoe House.** A fabulously appointed bed-and-breakfast inn, the
★ Victorian-style Kehoe House is furnished with brass-and-marble chandeliers, a courtyard garden, a music room, and a sense of the luxurious that defines opulence. On the main floor, a double parlor holds
two fireplaces and sweeps the eye upward with its 14-ft ceilings. Here,
guests enjoy sumptuous breakfasts. Turndown service includes chocolates, a Kehoe House robe, wine, and bottled water. Complimentary
visits to the Downtown Athletic Club are included. ⊠ *123 Habersham
St., 31401,* ☎ *912/232–1020 or 800/820–1020,* 𝔽𝔸𝕏 *912/231–0208.
15 rooms, including 3 at adjacent town house. Concierge, 2 meeting
rooms. AE, D, DC, MC, V.*

$$$$ 🏨 **Presidents' Quarters.** Each room in this classic Savannah inn is named
★ for an American president. Guests are greeted with wine and fruit in
their rooms, and complimentary afternoon tea tempts them with sumptuous cakes. Continental breakfast is served in the rooms, the lobby,
or the courtyard. Turndown service includes a glass of port or sherry.
The third floor is no-smoking. ⊠ *225 E. President St., 31401,* ☎ *912/
233–1600 or 800/233–1776,* 𝔽𝔸𝕏 *912/238–0849. 16 rooms. Outdoor
hot tub, concierge, parking. AE, D, DC, MC, V.*

$$$–$$$$ 🏨 **Olde Harbour Inn.** The building dates from 1892, when it was built
on the riverfront as an overall factory, but the old inn is actually a thor-
oughly modern facility. Each suite has a fully equipped kitchen, including
dishwasher and detergent. All suites overlook the river and have wall-
to-wall carpeting, exposed brick walls painted white, and a four-poster
bed. Each evening an ice-cream treat is brought to your room and placed
in the freezer. Cereal, fruit, hot muffins and biscuits, juice, tea, and cof-
fee are served in a cozy breakfast room each morning. ⊠ *508 E. Fac-
tors Walk, 31401,* ☎ *912/234–4100 or 800/553–6533,* 𝔽𝔸𝕏 *912/
233–5979. 24 suites. Laundry service, concierge, parking. AE, D,
DC, MC, V.*

Hotels and Motels

$$$$ 🏨 **DeSoto Hilton.** Three massive chandeliers glisten over the jardinieres
and discreetly placed conversation areas of the spacious lobby. The chan-
deliers are from the historic DeSoto Hotel that stood on this site long
ago. Guest rooms are on the cushy side in a burgundy and deep for-
est green color scheme, with wall-to-wall carpeting, traditional furni-
ture, and king-size or two double beds. (The best view is from the corner
king-size rooms.) Suites come with refrigerators upon request. Golf,
tennis, and athletic club privileges in the area are available to guests.
A major 1997 renovation freshened up the public and private rooms
and enhanced the number of suites. ⊠ *15 E. Liberty St., 31401,* ☎
912/232–9000 or 800/426–8483, 𝔽𝔸𝕏 *912/231–1633. 237 rooms, 7
suites. Restaurant, lobby lounge, pool, concierge. AE, D, DC, MC. V.*

$$$$ 🏨 **Hyatt.** When this riverfront hotel was built in 1981, preservation-
ists opposed a seven-story modern structure in the historic district. The
main architectural features are the towering atrium and a pleasant cen-

tral lounge, as well as glass elevators. Rooms have modern furnishings, marble baths, and balconies overlooking the atrium and the Savannah River. **MD's Lounge** is the ideal spot to have a drink and watch the river traffic drift by. **Windows,** the hotel's restaurant, is a great spot for Sunday buffet. ⊠ *2 W. Bay St., 31401,* ☎ *912/238–1234 or 800/ 233–1234,* FAX *912/944–3678. 325 rooms, 21 suites. Restaurant, lobby lounge, indoor pool, concierge, business services. AE, D, MC, V.*

$$$$ ☷ **Mulberry Inn.** This Holiday Inn property is filled with so many ob-
★ jets d'art in the public rooms that the management has obligingly provided a walking tour brochure. Treasures include 18th-century oil paintings. The restaurant is a sophisticated affair, with crystal chandeliers and mauve velvet Regency furniture. More of an inn in style than a hotel, the Mulberry has an elegant lobby with a grand piano. Daily afternoon tea service is offered here. The spacious courtyard is lushly landscaped. The guest rooms are in a traditional motif; suites have king-size beds and wet bars. ⊠ *601 E. Bay St., 31401,* ☎ *912/ 238–1200 or 800/465–4329,* FAX *912/236–2184. 96 rooms, 26 suites. Restaurant, bar, pool, outdoor hot tub. AE, D, DC, MC, V.*

$$$$ ☷ **River Street Inn.** This elegant hotel offers panoramic views of the Savannah River. Rooms are furnished with antiques and reproductions from the era of King Cotton. Amenities include turndown service. The interior is so lavish, it's difficult to believe it was once a vacant warehouse dating back to 1817. One floor includes charming shops and a New Orleans–style restaurant. Complimentary breakfast is included. ⊠ *115 E. River St., 31401,* ☎ *912/234–6400 or 800/253–4229,* FAX *912/234–1478. 44 rooms. 3 restaurants, 3 bars, concierge, business services. AE, DC, MC, V.*

$$$$ ☷ **Savannah Marriott Riverfront.** In the Historic District, the eight-story property with rounded balconies facing the river occupies a choice spot, adjacent to River Street and Factors Walk. ⊠ *100 Gen. McIntosh Blvd., 31401,* ☎ *912/233–7722 or 800/228–9290,* FAX *912/233–3765. 337 rooms, 46 suites. 2 restaurants, lobby lounge, indoor-outdoor pools, hot tub, health club. AE, D, DC, MC, V.*

$$$ ☷ **Days Inn/Days Suites.** This downtown hotel is in the Historic District near the City Market, only a block off River Street. Its compact rooms have modular furnishings and most amenities. Interior corridors and an adjacent parking garage minimize its motel qualities. Guests have access to a nearby health club. ⊠ *201 W. Bay St., 31401,* ☎ *912/236–4440 or 800/325–2525. 196 rooms, 57 suites. Restaurant, pool. AE, D, DC, MC, V.*

Nightlife and the Arts

Savannah's nightlife is a reflection of the city's laid-back, easygoing personality. Some clubs feature live reggae, hard rock, and other contemporary music, but most stay with traditional blues, jazz, and piano-bar vocalists. After-dark merrymakers usually head for watering holes on Riverfront Plaza or the south side.

Bars and Nightclubs

The **Bar Bar** (⊠ 312 W. Saint Julian St., ☎ 912/231–1910), a neighborhood hangout, has pool tables, games, and a varied beer selection; the place is popular with locals. **Club One** (⊠ 1 Jefferson St., ☎ 912/ 232–0200), a gay bar, is where The Lady Chablis (☞ *Midnight in the Garden of Good and Evil, above*) still bumps and grinds her way down the catwalk, lip-syncing disco tunes in a shimmer of sequin and satin gowns; admission is $5. **Kevin Barry's Irish Pub** (⊠ 117 W. River St., ☎ 912/233–9626) has a friendly atmosphere and traditional Irish music; it's *the* place to be on St. Patrick's Day. The rest of the year there's a mixed bag of tourists and locals, young and old. **Malone's** (✉ 27 Barnard St., ☎ 912/234–3059 or 912/237–9862), a sports bar, has 13 TV screens and monitors. Pool tables and a bar are downstairs. On the third level a dance floor with live entertainment attracts another crowd. **Velvet Elvis** (✉ 127 W. Congress St., ☎ 912/236–0665) has a selection of music (modest cover) ranging from punk to jazz. **The Zoo** (✉ 121 W. Congress St., ☎ 912/236–6266) is a mix of entertainments: four levels, with industrial and techno music on one; live entertainment on another; Top 40 and dance music on a third; and in the basement, pool tables and video screens.

Jazz and Blues Clubs
Bayou Café and Blues Bar (✉ 14 N. Abercorn St., at River St., ☎ 912/233–6411) has acoustic music during the week, while on the weekend the Bayou Blues Band plays numbers by the Allman Brothers and Eric Clapton. The food has a definite Cajun tone. **Crossroads** (✉ 219 W. Saint Julian St., ☎ 912/234–5438), Savannah's sole blues nightclub, features live performances by local and national talent Monday through Saturday. **Hard Hearted Hannah's East** (✉ 20 E. Broad St., ☎ 912/233–2225) showcases Emma Kelly, the undisputed "Lady of 6,000 Songs," who performs Tuesday through Saturday.

Outdoor Activities and Sports

Boating
Lake Mayer (✉ Lake Mayer Park, Sallie Mood Dr. and Montgomery Crossroads Dr., ☎ 912/652–6780) has paddle boats rented by the facility, sailing (there's a sailing center), and canoeing (the Red Cross teaches classes). **Saltwater Charters** (✉ 111 Wickersham Dr., ☎ 912/598–1814) provides packages ranging from two-hour sightseeing tours to 13-hour deep-sea fishing expeditions. Water taxis to the Barrier Islands are also available. **Public boat ramps** are found at **Bell's Landing** (✉ Apache Ave. off Abercorn St.) on the Forest River, **Islands Expressway** (✉ Islands Expressway adjacent to Frank W. Spencer Park) on the Wilmington River, and **Savannah Marina** on the Wilmington River in the town of Thunderbolt.

Golf
Bacon Park (✉ 1 Shorty Cooper Dr., ☎ 912/354–2625) is a public course with 27 holes. **Mary Calder** (✉ W. Lathrop Ave., ☎ 912/238–7100) has nine holes. **Henderson Golf Club** (✉ 1 Al Henderson Dr., at I–95 and GA 204, [Exit 16], ☎ 912/920–4653) is an 18-hole course about 15 mi from downtown Savannah.

Health Clubs
Jewish Educational Alliance has racquetball courts, a gymnasium, weight room, sauna, whirlpool, outdoor Olympic-size pool, and aerobic dance classes. Open to members of Jewish centers. ✉ *5111 Abercorn St.,* ☎ *912/355–8111.* ▣ *Guest fee $10 1st visit, then $8 per visit.*

Savannah Downtown Athletic Club offers Lifecycles, StairMasters, Body Master, Nautilus and free-weight equipment, sauna, swimming pool, aerobics, tanning beds, and tae kwon do classes. ✉ *7 E. Congress St.,* ☎ *912/236–4874.* ▣ *Guest fee $7 daily, $25 weekly, $50 monthly.*

YMCA Family Center has a gymnasium, aerobics, racquetball, and pool. ✉ *6400 Habersham St.,* ☎ *912/354–6223.* ▣ *Guest fee $5.*

Jogging and Running
Low-lying coastal terrain is ideal for jogging. **Forsyth Park** (✉ Bull St. between Whitaker and Drayton Sts.), which is flat as a benne seed wafer,

is an especially pleasant environment for walking, jogging, or running.
Tybee Island (☞ *above*) has a white-sand beach that is hard packed
and relatively debris free, making it a favorite with runners. For **suburban jogging trails,** head for **Daffin Park** (⊠ 1500 E. Victory Dr.) with
level sidewalks available during daylight hours and **Lake Mayer Park**
(⊠ Montgomery Crossroads Rd. at Sallie Mood Dr.) with a mile and
a half of level asphalt available 24 hours a day.

Tennis

Bacon Park (⊠ 6262 Skidaway Rd., ☎ 912/351–3850) has 16 lighted
asphalt courts. **Forsyth Park** (⊠ Drayton St. and Park Ave., ☎ 912/
351–3850) contains four lighted courts available until about 10 PM.
Lake Mayer Park (⊠ Montgomery Crossroads Rd. and Sallie Mood
Dr., ☎ 912/652–6780) has eight asphalt lighted courts.

Shopping

Find your own Lowcountry treasures among a bevy of handcrafted
wares—handmade quilts and baskets; wreaths made from Chinese
tallow trees and Spanish moss; preserves, jams, and jellies. The favorite
Savannah snack, and a popular gift item, is the benne wafer. It's about
the size of a quarter and comes in a variety of flavors.

Shopping Districts

City Market, on West Saint Julian Street, between Ellis and Franklin
squares, has sidewalk cafés, jazz haunts, shops, and art galleries. **Riverfront Plaza/River Street** is nine blocks of shops housed in the renovated
waterfront warehouses, where you can find everything from popcorn
to pottery. **Oglethorpe Mall** (⊠ 7804 Abercorn Extension, ☎ 912/354–
7038) has four department stores (Sears, JCPenney, Belks, Steinmart,
and Rich's) and more than 140 specialty shops and restaurants. **Savannah Festival Factory Stores** (⊠ 11 Gateway Blvd. S, I–95, Exit 16,
☎ 912/925–3089) sells manufacturers' merchandise at 25%–75% off
retail. **Savannah Mall** (⊠ 14045 Abercorn St., at Rio Rd., just off I–
95, ☎ 912/927–7467) has four major stores (JB White, Belk, Parisian,
and Montgomery Ward), along with more than 100 specialty shops
and restaurants. Kids delight in its old-fashioned carousel.

Specialty Shops

ANTIQUES

Arthur Smith Antiques (⊠ 1 W. Jones St., ☎ 912/236–9701) has four
floors showcasing 18th- and 19th-century European furniture, porcelain, rugs, and paintings. **Claire West Fine Linen and Antiques** (⊠ 411–
413 Whitaker St., ☎ 912/236–8163) fills two buildings with fine
European linens, antiques, prints, infants' christening gowns and receiving blankets, engravings, and old and new decorative tabletop objects.

ART GALLERIES

Compass Prints, Inc./Ray Ellis Gallery (⊠ 205 W. Congress St., ☎ 912/
234–3537) sells original artwork, prints, and books by internationally acclaimed artist Ray Ellis. **Gallery Espresso** (⊠ 6 E. Liberty St.,
☎ 912/233–5348) has great coffee and a new show every two weeks
focusing on work by local artists. A true coffee house, it's open until
the wee hours. **Gallery 209** (⊠ 209 E. River St., ☎ 912/236–4583) is
a co-op gallery, with paintings, watercolors, pottery, jewelry, batik,
stained glass, weavings, and sculpture by local artists. **Off the Wall** (⊠
412 Whitaker St., ☎ 912/233–8840) exhibits artists from the region,
the nation, and the world, rather than from Savannah. **Southern Images** (⊠ 132 E. Oglethorpe Ave., ☎ 912/234–6449) displays the

work of Jack Leigh, whose photograph of Bonaventure Cemetery graces the cover of *Midnight in the Garden of Good and Evil.*

Savannah College of Art and Design (✉ 342 Bull St., ☎ 912/238–2480), a privately owned school, has restored at least 40 historic buildings in the city, some of them housing galleries. Work by faculty and students is often for sale. Stop by **Exhibit A, Pinnacle Gallery,** and the **West Bank Gallery,** but also ask about other student galleries. **Garden for the Arts,** developed on a vacant lot next door to the West Bank Gallery, is a collaboration between the college's architecture and foundation departments. It presents rotating exhibitions by faculty and visiting artists.

BENNE WAFERS

Byrd Cookie Company (✉ 6700 Waters Ave., ☎ 912/355–1716), founded in 1924, is the best place to get the popular cookies that are also sold in numerous gift shops around town.

COUNTRY CRAFTS

Charlotte's Corner (✉ 1 W. Liberty St., ☎ 912/233–8061) carries expensive and moderately priced Savannah souvenirs, children's clothes and toys, and beach wear. **Georgia Gifts** (✉ 217 W. Saint Julian St., ☎ 912/236–1220) is the place to find Georgia-made country crafts and such products as jams, jellies, and preserves.

Savannah A to Z

Arriving and Departing

BY BUS

Greyhound/Trailways (✉ 610 W. Oglethorpe Ave., ☎ 912/232–2135 or 800/231–2222).

BY CAR

I–95 slices north–south along the Eastern Seaboard, intersecting 10 mi west of town with east–west I–16, which dead-ends in downtown Savannah. U.S. 17, the Coastal Highway, also runs north–south through town. U.S. 80, which connects the Atlantic to the Pacific, is another east–west route through Savannah.

BY PLANE

Savannah International Airport (☎ 912/964–0514), 18 mi west of downtown, is served by Delta, US Airways, and ValuJet for domestic flights. Despite the name, international flights are nonexistent. The foreign trade zone, a locus for importing, is responsible for the "international" aspect.

Vans operated by **McCall's Limousine Service** (☎ 912/966–5364 or 800/673–9365) leave the airport daily for downtown locations. The trip takes 15 minutes, and the one-way fare is $15 for one person; $25 round-trip for one person; two-person rate is $10 per person one way. Routes can include other destinations in addition to downtown. Advance reservation is required.

Taxi fare from the airport to downtown is $18 for one person, $5 for each additional person.

By car, take I–95 south to I–16 east into downtown Savannah.

BY TRAIN

Amtrak has regular service along the Eastern Seaboard, with daily stops in Savannah. The Amtrak station (✉ 2611 Seaboard Coastline Dr., ☎ 912/234–2611 or 800/872–7245) is 4 mi southwest of downtown. Cab fare into the city is $5–$10, depending on the number of passengers.

Getting Around

Despite its size, much of downtown Historic District can easily be explored on foot. Its grid shape makes getting around a breeze, and you'll find any number of places to stop and rest.

BY BUS

Chatham Area Transit (CAT; ☎ 912/233–5767) operates buses in Savannah and Chatham County Monday–Saturday from 6 AM to midnight, Sunday 7 to 7. Some lines may stop running earlier or may not run on Sunday. The CAT Shuttle operates throughout the Historic District; 50¢ one way or $1.50 all-day pass. Buses require $1.20 in exact change, and 5¢ extra for a transfer.

BY TAXI

Adam Cab Co. (☎ 912/927–7466) is a reliable, 24-hour taxi service. Calling ahead for reservations could yield a discount. Taxis start at 60¢ and cost $1.20 for each mile.

Contacts and Resources

EMERGENCIES

Dial 911 for **police** and **ambulance** in an emergency.

GUIDED TOURS

Carriage Tours of Savannah (✉ 10 Warner St., ☎ 912/236–6756 or 800/442–5933) takes you through the Historic District by day or by night at a 19th-century clip-clop pace, with coachmen spinning tales and telling ghost stories along the way. A romantic evening champagne tour in a private carriage will set you back $60, and, although champagne can no longer be included in the cost, guests may bring whatever refreshment they wish; regular tours are a more modest $13. Midnight tours are $15.

Gray Line (✉ 215 W. Boundary St., 31401, ☎ 912/234–8687) conducts a three-hour tour to Isle of Hope and the Lowcountry, including Thunderbolt (a shrimping community) and Wormsloe Plantation Site. Options include walking tours, minibus tours, and trolley tours. Cost ranges from $13 to $23.

Historic Savannah Foundation (✉ 212 W. Broughton St., 31401, ☎ 912/234–4088 or 800/627–5030), a preservation organization, leads three-hour excursions to the fishing village of Thunderbolt; the Isle of Hope, with stately mansions lining Bluff Drive; the much-photographed Bonaventure Cemetery on the banks of the Wilmington River; and Wormsloe Plantation Site, with its mile-long avenue of arching oaks. The cost depends on the number of people on tour; it costs $15 per person for a minimum of four persons, but private tours may be arranged, with prices beginning at $40 per hour.

Old Town Trolley Tours (☎ 912/233–0083) has narrated 90-minute tours traversing the Historic District, with on-and-off privileges. Trolleys come by 11 designated stops every half hour 9–4:30; cost is $15.

SPECIAL-INTEREST TOURS

Beach Institute African American Cultural Center (✉ 502 E. Harris St., ☎ 912/234–8000), the first private school built (1867) for African-American children in Savannah after emancipation, is headquarters for the **Negro Heritage Trail Tour.** A knowledgeable guide traces the city's more than 250 years of black history. Tours begin at the Savannah Visitors Center (☞ The Historic District, *above*). Tours are at 1 PM and 3 PM and cost $12.

Garden Club of Savannah (⊠ Box 13892, 31416, ☎ 912/238–0248) takes you during the spring to selected private gardens tucked behind old brick walls and wrought-iron gates.

A Ghost Talk Ghost Walk Tour (⊠ 127 E. Congress St., ☎ 912/233–3896) should send chills down your spine during an easy 1-mi jaunt through the Old Colonial City. Tours, lasting an hour and a half, leave from Reynolds Square (⊠ Congress and Abercorn Sts.) at the John Wesley Memorial, in the middle of the square. Call for dates, times, and reservations; cost is $10.

Square Routes (⊠ 60 E. Broad St., Suite 11, ☎ 912/232–6866 or 800/868–6867) provides customized strolls and private driving tours that wend through the Historic District and other parts of the Lowcountry. In-town tours focus on the city's architecture and gardens, and specialized tours include the Midnight in the Garden of Good and Evil walk based on the best-seller. Tours usually last two hours and cost from $15 to $25.

HOSPITALS

The following area hospitals have 24-hour emergency rooms: **Candler Hospital** (⊠ 5353 Reynolds St., ☎ 912/354–9211). **Memorial Medical Center** (⊠ 4700 Waters Ave., ☎ 912/350–8000).

24-HOUR PHARMACY

Revco Drug Center (⊠ Medical Arts Shopping Center, 4725 Waters Ave., ☎ 912/355–7111).

VISITOR INFORMATION

Savannah Area Convention & Visitor's Bureau (⊠ 222 W. Oglethorpe Ave., 31401, ☎ 912/944–0456 or 800/444–2427, FAX 912/944–0468) can provide maps and brochures about Savannah.

THE GOLDEN ISLES AND THE OKEFENOKEE

Jekyll, St. Simons, and Sea Islands

The Golden Isles are a string of lush, subtropical barrier islands meandering lazily down Georgia's Atlantic coast from Savannah to the Florida border. They have a long history of human habitation; Native American relics have been found on these islands that date from about 2500 BC. According to legend, the Indian nations agreed that no wars would be fought there and that tribal members would visit only in a spirit of friendship. In a similar spirit today, all Georgia beaches are in the public domain.

Each Golden Isle has a distinctive personality, shaped by its history and ecology. Three of them—Jekyll Island, Sea Island, and St. Simons Island—are connected to the mainland by bridges in the vicinity of Brunswick; these are the only ones accessible by automobile. The Cumberland Island National Seashore is accessible by ferry from St. Marys. Little St. Simons Island, a privately owned retreat with guest accommodations, is reached by a private launch from St. Simons. About 50 mi inland is the Okefenokee Swamp National Wildlife Refuge, which has a character all its own.

Numbers in the margin correspond to points of interest on the Golden Isles map.

Cumberland Island

94 *100 mi from Savannah to St. Marys via I–95, 45 mins by ferry from St. Marys.*

The largest, most southerly, and most accessible of Georgia's primitive coastal islands is Cumberland, a 16- by 3-mi sanctuary of marshes, dunes, beaches, forests, lakes and ponds, estuaries, and inlets. Waterways are home to 'gators, sea turtles, otters, snowy egrets, great blue herons, ibis, wood storks, and more than 300 other species of birds. In the forests are armadillos, wild horses, deer, raccoons, and an assortment of reptiles.

After the ancient Guale Indians came 16th-century Spanish missionaries, 18th-century English soldiers, and 19th-century planters. During the 1880s, the Thomas Carnegie family of Pittsburgh built several lavish homes here, but the island remained largely as nature created it. In the early 1970s, the federal government established the **Cumberland Island National Seashore** and opened this natural treasure to the public. There is no transportation on the island itself, and the only public access to the island is on the *Cumberland Queen,* a reservations-only, 146-passenger ferry based near the National Park Service Information Center at St. Marys. Ferry bookings are heavy in summer, but cancellations and no-shows often make last-minute space available. Reservations may be made as early as 11 months in advance. ✉ *Cumberland Island National Seashore, Box 806, 31558,* ☎ *912/882–4335,* 🖷 *912/673–7747.* 🎫 *Round-trip $10.07.* ☽ *Mid-May–Sept., ferry departure from St. Marys daily at 9 AM and 11:45 AM, from Cumberland at 10:15 AM and 4:45 PM. No ferry service Tues.–Wed. Oct.–May 14.*

From the Park Service docks at the island's southern end, you can follow wooded nature trails, swim and sun on 18 mi of undeveloped beaches, go fishing and bird-watching, and view the ruins of Carnegie's great estate, **Dungeness.** You can also join history and nature walks led by Park Service rangers. Bear in mind that summers are hot and humid, and that you must bring your own food, soft drinks, sunscreen, and a reliable insect repellent. All trash must be transported back to the mainland by campers and picnickers. Nothing can be purchased on the island.

Dining and Lodging

MAINLAND

$$ ✗ **Seagle's Waterfront Cafe.** The Riverview Hotel, a small seaside lodging, hosts an interesting restaurant that has been recently upgraded, renovated, and converted to a fine dining establishment. Along with renovation came a new menu and more elegant service. Rock shrimp, the local delicacy, comes blackened, fried, steamed, grilled, or broiled. Pecan-crusted grouper fillets in coconut rum sauce and topped with rock shrimp is a weekend special. ✉ *105 Osborne St., St. Marys,* ☎ *912/882–4187. AE, D, DC, MC, V. Closed Sun.–Mon. No lunch.*

$$ 🏨 **Spencer House Inn.** This comfortable Victorian-style inn dates from 1872. Perfect for walking historic St. Marys and visiting the waterfront, the inn is also handy for boarding the ferry to Cumberland Island. A hefty breakfast is included in the rate. This is a good selection for anyone needing wheelchair access, as there is an elevator. ✉ *101 E. Bryant St., St. Marys 31558,* ☎ *912/882–1872,* 🖷 *912/882–9427. 14 rooms. AE, D, MC, V.*

The Golden Isles

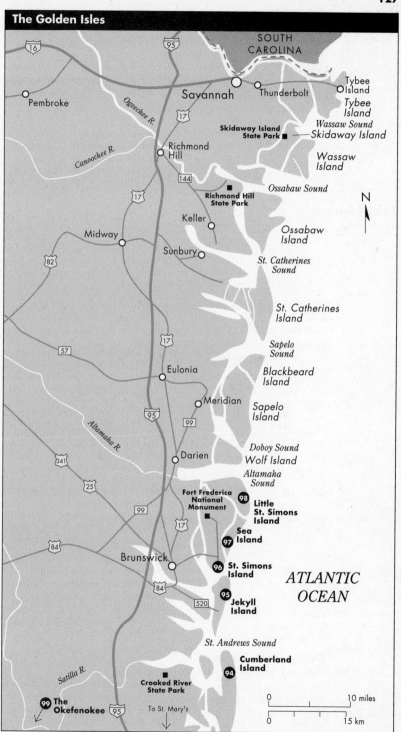

SOUTH CAROLINA

Pembroke

Savannah

Thunderbolt

Tybee Island

Tybee Island

Ogeechee R.

Richmond Hill

Skidaway Island State Park

Wassaw Sound

Skidaway Island

Wassaw Island

Canoochee R.

144

Richmond Hill State Park

Ossabaw Sound

Keller

Ossabaw Island

Midway

Sunbury

St. Catherines Sound

St. Catherines Island

Sapelo Sound

Blackbeard Island

Eulonia

Meridian

Sapelo Island

Altamaha R.

Darien

Doboy Sound

Wolf Island

Altamaha Sound

Fort Frederica National Monument

98

Little St. Simons Island

97

Sea Island

Brunswick

96

St. Simons Island

ATLANTIC OCEAN

95

Jekyll Island

520

St. Andrews Sound

94

Cumberland Island

Satilla R.

Crooked River State Park

99 The Okefenokee

To St. Mary's

0   10 miles

0   15 km

N

ISLAND

$$$$ ✕🖬 **Greyfield Inn.** Cumberland Island's only accommodations are in
a turn-of-the-century Carnegie family home. Greyfield's public areas
are filled with family mementos, furnishings, and portraits (you may
feel as though you've stepped into one of Agatha Christie's mysterious Cornwall manors). Prices include all meals, transportation, tours
led by a naturalist, and bike rentals. ⊠ *Box 900 Fernandina Beach,
FL 32035,* ☎ *904/261–6408. 13 rooms. MC, V.*

$ �glyph **Sea Camp.** A five-minute walk from the *Cumberland Queen* dock,
with rest rooms and showers adjacent to campsites, Sea Camp is the
ideal spot for novice campers ($8 per person per day). The beach is
just beyond the dunes. Experienced campers can hike 3–10 mi to several areas where cold-water spigots are the only amenities.

Jekyll Island

95 *90 mi from Savannah, 10 mi from Brunswick.*

For 56 winters, between 1886 and 1942, America's rich and famous
faithfully came south to Jekyll Island. Through the Gilded Age, the Great
War, the Roaring '20s, and the Great Depression, Vanderbilts and
Rockefellers, Morgans and Astors, Macys, Pulitzers, and Goodyears
shuttered their 5th Avenue castles and retreated to the serenity of their
wild Georgia island. There they built elegant "cottages," played golf
and tennis, and socialized. Early in World War II, the millionaires de-
parted for the last time. In 1947 the state of Georgia purchased the
entire island for the bargain price of $675,000.

Jekyll Island Welcome Center offers tram tours of the Jekyll Island National Historic Landmark District. Tours originate at the Historic District Visitors Center on Stable Road and include several restored
buildings in the 240-acre historic district. Faith Chapel, illuminated by
Tiffany stained-glass windows, is open for meditation Sunday–Friday
2–4. ⊠ *I–95 to Exit 6, Box 13186, Jekyll Island 31527,* ☎ *912/635–
3636 or 800/841–6586,* FAX *912/635–4004.* 💳 *$10.* ☉ *Daily 9:30–
4, tours daily 10–3.*

Jekyll Island is still a 7½-mi playground, but no longer restricted to
the rich and famous. The golf, tennis, fishing, biking, jogging, water
park, and picnic grounds are open to all. One side of the island is lined
by nearly 10 mi of hard-packed Atlantic beaches; the other, by the Intracoastal Waterway and picturesque salt marshes. Deer and wild
turkeys inhabit interior forests of pine, magnolia, and moss-veiled live
oaks. Egrets, pelicans, herons, and sandpipers skim the gentle surf. Jekyll's
clean, mostly uncommercialized public beaches are free and open year-
round. Bathhouses with rest rooms, changing areas, and showers are
open at regular intervals along the beach. Beachwear, suntan lotion,
rafts, snacks, and drinks are available at the **Jekyll Shopping Center,**
facing the beach at Beachview Drive.

Dining and Lodging

$$$ ✕ **Grand Dining Room.** In the Jekyll Island Club Hotel the dining
room sparkles with silver and crystal. Lowcountry cuisine is the culi-
nary focus, with shrimp, fish, veal, Georgia quail, and lamb. Much of
the raw material comes from local sources. California wines dominate
the wine list, with a few offerings by the glass. The restaurant has its
own label Pinot Noir and Chardonnay, made by Mountain View Vine-
yards. ⊠ *371 Riverview Dr.,* ☎ *912/635–2600, ext. 1002. Reserva-
tions essential. Jacket required at dinner. AE, D, DC, MC, V.*

$$$–$$$$ ⊡ **Jekyll Inn.** On a landscaped 15-acre site, these oceanfront units, the largest facility on the island, recently underwent an extensive renovation. Rooms were redecorated with new lighting and carpeting. Units include some villas with kitchenettes. ⊠ *975 N. Beachview Dr., Jekyll Island 31527,* ☎ *912/635–2531 or 800/736–1046. 264 units. Restaurant, pool, bicycles, playground. AE, D, DC, MC, V.*

$$$–$$$$ ⊡ **Jekyll Island Club Hotel.** Built in 1886, the four-story clubhouse with wraparound verandas and Queen Anne–style towers and turrets once served as the winter hunting retreat for wealthy financiers. In 1985 a group of Georgia businessmen spent $17 million restoring it. The guest rooms and suites are custom-decorated with mahogany beds, armoires, and plush sofas and chairs. Some have flowery views of the Intracoastal Waterway, Jekyll River, and the hotel's croquet lawn. The nearby Sans Souci Apartments, built in 1896 by William Rockefeller, have been converted into spacious guest rooms. The island itself has 22 mi of bicycle trails, and the hotel operates a free shuttle to area beaches. ⊠ *371 Riverview Dr., Jekyll Island 31527,* ☎ *912/635–2600 or 800/535–9547,* ℻ *912/635–2818. 134 units. 2 restaurants, pool, 9 tennis courts, croquet, bicycles. AE, D, DC, MC, V.*

$$–$$$ ⊡ **Holiday Inn Beach Resort.** Nestled amid natural dunes and oaks in a secluded oceanfront setting, this hotel has a private beach, but its rooms with balconies still don't have an ocean view. Bicycles are available for rent. ⊠ *200 S. Beachview Dr., Jekyll Island 31527,* ☎ *912/635–3311 or 800/753–5955. 206 rooms. Restaurant, lobby lounge, pool, 2 tennis courts, playground. AE, D, DC, MC, V.*

RENTALS

Jekyll's more than 200 **rental cottages and condos** are handled by **Jekyll Realty** (⊠ Box 13096, Jekyll Island 31527, ☎ 912/635–3301, ℻ 912/635–3303) and **Parker-Kaufman Realty** (⊠ Box 13126, Jekyll Island 31527, ☎ 912/635–2512, ℻ 912/635–2190).

Outdoor Activities and Sports

GOLF

Jekyll has 63 holes of golf including three 18-hole courses with a main clubhouse (⊠ Capt. Wylly Rd., ☎ 912/635–2368) and a nine-hole course known as the Historic Oceanside Nine (⊠ Beachview Dr., ☎ 912/635–2170), where millionaires used to play.

TENNIS

The **Jekyll Island Tennis Center** (⊠ Capt. Wylly Rd., ☎ 912/635–3154) has 13 clay courts, with seven lighted for nighttime play; it hosts eight U.S.T.A.-sanctioned tournaments throughout the year.

WATER PARK

Summer Waves, an 11-acre water park, has an 18,000-square-ft wave pool, water slides, a children's activity pool with two slides, and a circular river for tubing and rafting, but outside equipment is not permitted. ⊠ *210 S. Riverview Dr.,* ☎ *912/635–2074.* ▭ *$12.50.* ☉ *Memorial Day–Labor Day, plus selected weekends in May and Sept., Sun.–Fri. 10–6, Sat. 10–8.*

St. Simons Island

96   *6 mi from Brunswick.*

As large as Manhattan, with more than 14,000 year-round residents, St. Simons is the Golden Isles' most complete resort destination. Fortunately, the accelerated development in recent years has failed to spoil the natural beauty of the island's regal live oaks, beaches, and salt marshes. Visits are highlighted by swimming and sunning, golf, biking, hiking, fishing, horseback riding, touring historic sites, and feasting on fresh local seafood at more than 50 restaurants.

The **Brunswick and the Golden Isles Visitors Center** (⊠ 2000 Glynn Ave., Brunswick 31520, ☎ 912/264–5337, 912/265–5338, or 800/ 933–2627) provides helpful information.

Many sights and activities are in the **village** area along Mallery Street at the more developed south end of the island, where there are shops, several restaurants, pubs, and a popular public pier. A quaint "trolley" takes visitors on a 1½-hour guided tour of the island, leaving from near the pier, several times a day in high season, less frequently in winter; cost is $10.

Neptune Park (⊠ 550 Beachview Dr., ☎ 912/638–2393), on the island's south end, has picnic tables, a children's play park, miniature golf, and beach access. A swimming pool, with showers and rest rooms, is open each summer in the **Neptune Park Casino.**

St. Simons Lighthouse, a beacon since 1872, is virtually the symbol of St. Simons. The **Museum of Coastal History** in the lightkeeper's cottage has a permanent exhibit of coastal history. ⊠ 101 12th St., ☎ 912/638–4666. ◻ $3, including lighthouse. ☉ Mon.–Sat. 10–5, Sun. 1:30–5.

At the burgeoning north end of the island there's a marina, a golf club, and a housing development, as well as **Fort Frederica National Monument,** the ruins of a fort built by English troops in the mid-1730s as a bulwark against a Spanish invasion from Florida. Around the fort are the foundations of homes and shops. Start at the **National Park Service Visitors Center,** which has a film and displays. ⊠ Off Frederica Rd. just past Christ Episcopal Church, ☎ 912/638–3639. ◻ $4 per car. ☉ Daily 9–5.

Consecrated in 1886 following an earlier structure's desecration by Union troops, the white-frame Gothic-style **Christ Episcopal Church** is surrounded by live oaks, dogwoods, and azaleas. The interior has beautiful stained-glass windows. ⊠ Frederica Rd., St. Simons, ☎ 912/ 638–8683. ◻ Donations welcome.

Dining and Lodging

$$ ✕ **Blanche's Courtyard.** In the village, this lively restaurant/nightclub is done in "Bayou Victorian" style, with lots of antiques and nostalgic memorabilia. The menu features seafood as well as basic steak and chicken. Blue crab soup is a local favorite, and the huge seafood platter could easily feed two. Be sure to taste the popular apple fritters. A ragtime band plays for dancers on Saturday. ⊠ 440 Kings Way, ☎ 912/ 638–3030. AE, DC, MC, V. No lunch.

$–$$ ✕ **Alfonza's Olde Plantation Supper Club.** Down-home versions of seafood, superb steaks, and plantation fried chicken are served in a gracious and relaxed environment. ⊠ 171 Harrington La., ☎ 912/638– 9883. Reservations essential. D, DC, MC, V. Closed Sun. No lunch.

$ ✕ **CJ's.** This tiny village-area restaurant serves the island's best Italian food. Deep-dish and thin-crust pizzas, pastas, and all of the menu's sandwiches draw a faithful local clientele. The limited seating capacity creates lengthy waits, but the cuisine is worth your patience, and take-out is available. ⊠ 405 Mallory St., ☎ 912/634–1022. Reservations not accepted. No credit cards. Lunch served late Mar.–late Sept.

$ ✕ **Crab Trap.** One of the island's most popular spots, the Crab Trap offers a variety of fried, blackened, grilled, and broiled fresh seafood; oysters on the half shell; blue crab soup; heaps of batter fries; and hush puppies. The atmosphere is rustic-casual—every table has a hole in the middle for depositing corncobs and shrimp shells. ⊠ *1209 Ocean Blvd.,* ☎ *912/638–3552. Reservations not accepted. MC, V.*

$$$$ 🏨 **Sea Palms Golf and Tennis Resort.** A contemporary resort complex with fully furnished villas, most with kitchens, nestles on an 800-acre site. Bicycles are available for rent. ⊠ *5445 Frederica Rd., St. Simons Island 31522,* ☎ *912/638–3351 or 800/841–6268,* 𝔽𝔸𝕏 *912/634–8029. 154 rooms. 2 pools, 27-hole golf course, tennis court, children's programs. AE, DC, MC, V.*

$$–$$$$ 🏨 **King and Prince Beach and Golf Resort.** This hotel faces the beach. Guest rooms are spacious, and villas offer two or three bedrooms. The villas are owned by private individuals, so the total number available for rent varies from time to time. ⊠ *Box 20798, 201 Arnold Rd., St. Simons Island 31522,* ☎ *912/638–3631 or 800/342–0212,* 𝔽𝔸𝕏 *912/634–1720. 139 rooms, 42 villas. 2 restaurants, lounge, indoor pool, 4 outdoor pools, golf privileges, 4 tennis courts, bicycles. AE, D, MC, V.*

$$ 🏨 **Island Inn.** On wooded land just off one of the island's main streets, this newer antebellum-style motel offers convenience and privacy with its efficiency accommodations. Continental breakfast is included, and complimentary wine and cheese are served Monday through Thursday from 5:30 to 6:30 PM. ⊠ *Plantation Village, 301 Main St., St. Simons Island 31522,* ☎ *912/638–7805 or 800/673–6323. 74 rooms. Pool, hot tub, convention center, meeting rooms. AE, D, MC, V.*

$$ 🏨 **Queen's Court.** This family-oriented complex in the village has clean, modest rooms with shower-baths, some with kitchenettes. The grounds, with their ancient live oaks, are beautiful. ⊠ *437 Kings Way, St. Simons Island 31522,* ☎ *912/638–8459. 23 rooms. Pool. MC, V.*

RENTALS

For St. Simons **condo and cottage rentals,** contact **Golden Isles Realty** (⊠ 330 Mallory St., St. Simons Island 31522, ☎ 912/638–8623 or 800/337–3106, 𝔽𝔸𝕏 912/638–8624) and **Trupp–Hodnett Enterprises** (⊠ 520 Ocean Blvd., St. Simons Island 31522, ☎ 912/638–5450 or 800/627–6850).

Sea Island

❼ *5 mi from St. Simons Island.*

Separated from St. Simons Island by a narrow waterway and a good many steps up the social ladder, Sea Island has been the domain of the
★ well-heeled and the **Cloister Hotel** since 1928. The Cloister still lives up to its celebrity status. Guests lodge in spacious, comfortably appointed rooms and suites in the Spanish Mediterranean hotel, designed by Florida architect Addison Mizner. The owners of the 180 or so private cottages and villas treat the hotel like a country club, and their tenants may use the hotel's facilities. Contact **Sea Island Cottage Rentals** (⊠ Box 30351, Sea Island 31561, ☎ 912/638–5112 or 800/732–4752, 𝔽𝔸𝕏 912/638–5824).

For recreation, there are 54 holes of golf, tennis, swimming in pools or at the beach, skeet shooting, horseback riding, sailing, biking, lawn games, and surf and deep-sea fishing. After dinner, guests dance to live music in the lounge. All meals are included in the rate.

Like a person of some years, the Cloister has its eccentricities. Credit cards are not honored, but personal checks are accepted. Gentlemen must cover their arms in the dining rooms. A complete and superb spa facility opened in 1989 in a beautiful building of its own; it has a fully equipped workout room, daily aerobics classes, personal trainers, facials and massages, and other beauty treatments. There is no entrance gate, and nonguests are free to admire the beautifully planted grounds and to drive past the mansions lining Sea Island Drive. Space permitting, they may also play at the Sea Island Golf Course (on St. Simons) and dine in the main dining room.

✉ *The Cloister, Sea Island 31561,* ☎ *912/638–3611 or 800/732–4752 reservations,* FAX *912/638–5823. 262 rooms. 4 restaurants, 2 pools, spa, health club, 54-hole golf course, 18 tennis courts, concierge, business services, airport shuttle. No credit cards. High season (Mar. 15–May): $324–$638 for 2, including 3 meals daily; low season (Dec.–Feb. 14— excluding holiday times): $248–$366.*

Little St. Simons Island

★ ⑨⑧ *10–15 mins by ferry from the Hampton River Club Marina on St. Simons Island.*

Six miles long, 2 to 3 mi wide, skirted by Atlantic beaches and salt marshes teeming with birds and wildlife, this privately owned resort is custom-made for Robinson Crusoe–style getaways. The island's only development is a rustic but comfortable guest compound. Rates include all meals. Guided tours, horseback rides, canoe trips, fly-fishing lessons, and other extras can be arranged, some for no additional charge. Inquire about children, as there are some limitations. In summer, day tours may be arranged.

The island's forests and marshes are inhabited by deer, armadillos, horses, raccoons, 'gators, otters, and more than 200 species of birds. Guests are free to walk the 6 mi of undisturbed beaches, swim in the mild surf, fish from the dock, and seine for shrimp and crabs in the marshes. There are also horses to ride, nature walks with experts, and other island explorations via boat or the back of a pickup truck. From June through September, up to 10 nonguests per day may visit the island by reservation; the $70 cost includes the ferry to the island, an island tour by truck, lunch at the lodge, and a beach walk.

Dining and Lodging

$$$$ ✕☆ **Inn at Little St. Simons.** Up to 24 guests can be accommodated in the lodge and house. Each has four bedrooms with twin or king-size beds, private decks, and private baths. In cool weather, a huge fireplace in each lodge's central living room dispels any chill. A large screened porch across the back permits beautiful views of the glorious sunsets. Two other lodges have two bedrooms each; one with private and the other with shared bath. None of the rooms is air-conditioned, but ceiling fans make sleeping comfortable. The rates include all meals and dinner wines (complimentary cocktails available). Meals often include fresh fish, pecan pie, and home-baked breads. The properties also provide transportation from St. Simons Island, transportation on the island, and interpretive guides. ✉ *21078 Little St. Simons Island 31522,* ☎ *912/638–7472,* FAX *912/634–1811. 8 rooms. Pool, horseback riding, fishing. MC, V.*

Okefenokee National Wildlife Refuge

40 mi from Brunswick, 38 mi from St. Marys.

⑨⑨ Covering 730 square mi of southeast Georgia and spilling over into northeast Florida, **The Okefenokee,** with its mysterious rivers and lakes, bristles with seen and unseen life. Scientists agree that the Okefenokee, the largest intact freshwater wetlands in the contiguous United States, is not duplicated anywhere else on earth. The impenetrable Pinhook Swamp to the south, part of the same ecosystem, adds another

100 square mi. If the term swamp denotes a dark, dank place, the Oke-fenokee is never that. Instead, it is actually a vast peat bog with nu-merous and varied landscapes, including aquatic prairies, towering virgin cypress, sandy pine islands, and lush subtropical hammocks. During the last Ice Age 10,000 years ago, it was part of the ocean flow. Peat began building up 7,000 years ago atop of a mound of clay, now 120 ft above sea level. Two rivers, the St. Marys and the Suwanee, flow out of it. It provides at least a part-time habitat for myriad species of birds, mammals, reptiles, amphibians, and fish.

As you travel by canoe or speedboat among the water lilies and the great stands of live oaks and cypress, be on the lookout for, among many others, alligators, otters, bobcats, raccoons, opossums, white-tailed deer, turtles, bald eagles, red-tailed hawks, egrets, muskrats, herons, cranes, and red-cockaded woodpeckers. The black bears tend to be more reclusive.

Seminole Indians, in their migrations south toward Florida's Everglades, once took refuge in the Okefenokee. The last Native Americans to oc-cupy the area, they were evicted by the Army and Georgia's militia in the 1830s. When the Okefenokee acquired its present status of federal preserve (1937), the white homesteaders on its fringe were forced out.

Noting the many floating islands, the Seminole named this unique com-bination of land and water "Land of the Quivering Earth." If you have the rare fortune to walk one of these bogs, you will find the earth does indeed quiver, rather like fruit gelatin in a bowl.

The Okefenokee Swamp Park (☞ *below*), 8 mi south of Waycross, is a nonprofit development. The northern entrance to the refuge is here. There are two other gateways to the swamp: an eastern entrance at U.S. Fish & Wildlife Service Headquarters in the Suwanee Canal Recre-ation Area (☞ *below*), near Folkston; and a western entrance at Stephen C. Foster State Park (☞ *below*), outside the town of Fargo. You may take an overnight canoe/camping trip into the interior, but the Okefenokee is a wildlife refuge and designated national wilderness, not a park. Access is restricted by permit. The best way to see the Oke-fenokee up close is to take a day trip at one of the three gateways. Plan your visit between April and September to avoid the biting insects that emerge in May, especially in the dense interior.

South of Waycross, via U.S. 1, **Okefenokee Swamp Park** has orienta-tion programs, exhibits, observation areas, wilderness walkways, an outdoor museum of pioneer life, and boat tours into the swamp that reveal its ecological uniqueness. A boardwalk and 90-ft tower are ex-cellent places to glimpse cruising 'gators and a variety of birds. You may arrange for guided boat tours at an additional cost. ⊠ *5700 Swamp Park Rd., Waycross 31501,* ☎ *912/283–0583,* FAX *912/283–0023.* ☞ *$8, additional costs for tour packages.* ☉ *Summer, daily 9–6:30; spring, fall, and winter, 9–5:30.*

Stephen C. Foster State Park, 18 mi from Fargo via Route 177, is an 80-acre island park entirely within the Okefenokee National Wildlife Refuge. The park encompasses a large cypress and black gum forest, a majestic backdrop for one of the thickest growths of vegetation in the southeastern United States. Park naturalists leading boat tours will spill out a wealth of Okefenokee lore while you observe alligators, birds, and native trees and plants. You may also take a self-guided excursion in rental canoes and a motorized, flat-bottomed boat. Camping and cabins also are available here (☞ Camping, *below*). ⊠ *Fargo 31631,* ☎ *912/637–5274.* ☞ *$4 per vehicle to National Wildlife Refuge.* ☉ *Mar.–Sept. 15, daily 6:30 AM–8:30 PM; Sept. 16–Feb., daily 7–7.*

Suwanee Canal Recreation Area, 8 mi south of Folkston via GA 121/ 23, is administered by the U.S. Fish and Wildlife Service. Stop first at the Visitor Information Center, with exhibits on the Okefenokee's flora and fauna. A boardwalk takes you over the water to a 50-ft observation tower. The concession has equipment rentals and daily food service; you may sign up here for one- or two-hour guided boat tours. Hikers, bicyclists, and private motor vehicles are welcome on the Swamp Island Drive; several interpretive walking trails may be taken along the way. Picnicking is allowed. Wilderness canoeing and camping in the Okefenokee's interior is by reserved fee permit only. Permits are hard to get especially in cool weather. Call refuge headquarters (☎ 912/496–3331) when it opens at 7 AM EXACTLY two months in advance of the desired starting date. Guided overnight canoe trips can be arranged by refuge concessionaire Carl E. Glenn Jr. ⊠ *Rte. 2, Box 3325, Folkston 31537,* ☎ *912/496–7156 or 800/792–6796. Refuge headquarters:* ⊠ *Rte. 2, Box 3330, Folkston, 31537,* ☎ *912/496–7836.* 🖼 *Park is free; $4 per car; 1-hr tours $8; 2-hr tours $16.* ☼ *Refuge Mar.–Sept. 10, daily 7 AM–7:30 PM; Sept. 11–Feb., daily 8–6.*

Camping

$–$$ ⚸ **Stephen C. Foster State Park.** The park has furnished two-room cottages and campsites with water, electricity, rest rooms, and showers. Because of roaming wildlife and poachers, and because the park is inside the refuge, the gates close between sunset and sunrise. If you're staying overnight, stop for groceries before you get there. ⊠ *Fargo 31631,* ☎ *912/637–5274 or 800/864–7275.*

$ ⚸ **Laura S. Walker State Park.** Named for a Waycross teacher who championed conservation, the park, 9 mi from Okefenokee Swamp Park, offers campsites for $12, with electrical and water hookups. Be sure to pick up food and supplies on the way to the park. Boating and skiing are permitted on the 100-acre lake, and there's an 18-hole championship golf course, with all amenities. Cost is $17; carts $16. ⊠ *5653 Laura Walker Rd., Waycross 31503,* ☎ *912/287–4900. Picnic areas, pool, fishing, playground.*

The Golden Isles and Okefenokee A to Z

Arriving, Departing, and Getting Around

BY CAR

From Brunswick by car, take the Jekyll Island Causeway for $2 per car to Jekyll Island, and the Torras Causeway to St. Simons and Sea Island. You can get by without a car on Jekyll Island and Sea Island, but you'll need one on St. Simons. You cannot bring a car to Cumberland Island or Little St. Simons.

BY FERRY

Cumberland Island and Little St. Simons are accessible only by ferry or private launch (☞ *above*).

BY PLANE

The Golden Isles are served by **Glynco Jetport,** 6 mi north of Brunswick, which is served in turn by Delta affiliate **Atlantic Southeast Airlines** (☎ 800/282–3424) with flights from Atlanta.

Visitor Information

Georgia has centralized park reservations (Reservation Resource) for the state's **Department of Natural Resources** parks. For reservations, call 800/864–7275. In metropolitan Atlanta, the reservation number is 770/398–7275. For general park information, call 404/656–3530.

ELSEWHERE IN GEORGIA

Andersonville National Historic Site

From Atlanta, take I–75 south to GA 49.

Andersonville, which opened in 1864, was the Civil War's most notorious prisoner-of-war site: 13,000 prisoners died here, and at war's end the Swiss-born commandant Captain Henry Wirz was tried, convicted, and hanged when he refused to exculpate himself by blaming Confederate President Jefferson Davis for the brutal treatment of the prisoners. Each state that had prisoners at Andersonville has a monument to their memory, and it is a place of active burial for U.S. veterans and their spouses. The site's living history event ("Andersonville Revisited") takes place the last weekend in February. The tiny nearby town of Andersonville hosts many Civil War memorial events. Now under construction at the site is the National Prisoner of War Memorial, scheduled to open in April 1998. *Andersonville Welcome Center:* ⊠ *114 Church St.,* ☎ *912/924–2558;* ⊠ *Box 800, Andersonville 31711,* ☎ *912/924–0343.* ⊡ *Free.* ⊙ *Daily 8–5.*

Athens

Take I–85 north from Atlanta to GA 316.

The home of the University of Georgia, Athens has an appeal that's a cross between Mayberry R.F.D. and MTV—the latter owing to its reputation as a breeding ground for new and alternative music. Athens has several splendid Greek Revival buildings, including, on campus, the **University Chapel,** built in 1832, and the **University President's House** (⊠ 570 Prince Ave.), built in the late 1850s. The **Taylor-Grady House** (⊠ 634 Prince Ave., ☎ 706/549–8688), down the street, was constructed in 1844. The **Franklin House** (⊠ 480 E. Broad St.), also built in 1844, was recently restored and reopened as an office building. Contact the **Athens Convention and Visitors Bureau** (⊠ 300 N. Thomas St., 30601, ☎ 706/357–4430 or 800/653–0603, ℻ 706/546–8040) or the **Athens Welcome Center** (⊠ 250 E. Dougherty St., ☎ 706/353–1820), in the town's oldest surviving residence, the Church-Waddel-Brumby House.

Augusta

From Atlanta, take I–20 east to Exit 66 (River Watch Pkwy.).

Augusta is Georgia's third-oldest city, having been founded in 1736 by James Edward Oglethorpe, who also founded Savannah in 1733. The city was named for Augusta, Princess of Wales, wife of the future Frederick Louis, Prince of Wales. Augusta served as Georgia's capital from 1785 to 1795. **Riverwalk** (⊠ Between 5th and 10th Sts.) curves along the Savannah River, providing a leisurely paced stroll on well-maintained paths. **Olde Town,** lying along Telfair and Greene streets, is a restored neighborhood of Victorian homes.

Many antebellum and Victorian homes of interest lie throughout the city. The **Morris Museum of Southern Art** (⊠ 1 10th St., ☎ 706/724–7501) houses a splendid collection of Southern art, from early landscapes and portraits through neo-Impressionism and naive and modern art. **Meadow Garden** (⊠ 1320 Independence Dr., ☎ 706/724–7501) was the home of George Walton, one of Georgia's three signers of the Declaration of Independence and its youngest signer at age 26. It is documented as Augusta's oldest extant residence. The **Ezekiel Harris House** (⊠ 1840 Broad St., ☎ 706/724–0436) dates from the late 18th century and is notable for its exterior staircase, a space-saving feature, and its gambrel roof.

The 1845 tree-lined **Augusta Canal** is a pleasant place for a stroll.

Barnsley Gardens

Take I–75 north from Atlanta to Exit 128W (Adairsville).

The Civil War halted construction of Godfrey Barnsley's 26-room Italianate house, and in 1988 the estate and its gardens lay in ruins. A German prince, Hubertus Fugger-Babenhausen, and his wife, Princess Alexandra, bought it and started work on restoration of the gardens. (The house will remain in ruins as it is today.) Today there are 30 acres of shrubbery, trees, ponds, fountains, and flowers, designed in the style of Barnsley's time. The attractive restaurant serves breakfast and lunch, mainly salads and light dishes. ⊠ *Barnsley Gardens Rd. off Hall Station Rd.,* ☎ *770/773–7480.* ☞ *$6.50.* ☉ *Tues.–Sun. 10–6.*

Callaway Gardens, in Pine Mountain

Take I–85 south from Atlanta to U.S. 27S.

This 14,000-acre family-style golf and tennis resort is best known for its impressive gardens and its not-to-be-missed butterfly conservatory. The gardens were developed in the 1930s by a couple determined to breathe new life into the area's dormant cotton fields. On the grounds are four nationally recognized golf courses, 17 tennis courts, bicycling trails, and a lakefront beach. The **Day Butterfly Center** contains more than 1,000 varieties flying free. **Mountain Creek Lake** is well stocked with largemouth bass and bream. If you visit here in the height of the spring season or during the garden's annual holiday light spectacular in December, you may find yourself in a traffic jam. ⊠ *U.S. 27S, Pine Mountain 31822,* ☎ *706/663–2281 or 800/282–8181.* ☞ *$10.* ☉ *Sept.–May, daily 8–7; June–Aug., daily 8–8.*

In the nearby **Pine Mountain Wild Animal Park,** a 500-acre wilderness habitat, more than 3,000 animals from 300 species roam free. ⊠ *1300 Oak Grove Rd., Pine Mountain 31822,* ☎ *706/663–8744 or 800/367–2751.* ☞ *$11.* ☉ *Daily 10–5:30.*

Chickamauga and Chattanooga National Military Park

Take I–75 north from Atlanta.

Established in 1890 as the nation's first military park, this was the site of one of the Civil War's bloodiest battles; casualties totaled more than 30,000. Though the Confederates routed the Federals early, General Ulysses Grant eventually broke the siege of Chattanooga and secured the city as a base for Sherman's march through Atlanta and on to the sea. Monuments, battlements, and weapons adorn the road that traverses the 8,000-acre park, with markers explaining the action. ⊠ *U.S. 27 off I–75, south of Chattanooga,* ☎ *706/866–9241.* ☞ *Free.* ☉ *Mid-Aug.–mid-June, daily 8–4:45; mid-June–mid-Aug., daily 8–5:45.*

To capture the feeling of the era, stay overnight at the **Gordon-Lee Mansion** (⊠ 217 Cove Rd., Chicamauga 30707, ☎ 706/375–4728), which during the war stood on the edge of the battlefield and served as a field hospital.

Clayton

Take I–985 north from Atlanta to U.S. 23.

An unassuming mountain town, Clayton is near spectacular Tallulah Gorge, the deepest canyon in the United States after the Grand Canyon, and a popular turn-of-the-century destination for Atlantans. The state of Georgia recently acquired the site for a state park, and vast improvements are planned. In Clayton, the **Main Street Gallery** (⊠ 641 Main St., ☎ 706/782–2440), one of the state's best sources for folk art, features works by regional artists such as Sarah Rakes, O. L. Samuels, Jay Schuette, and James Harold Jennings. The **Dillard House** (⊠ Old Dillard Rd., Dillard, ☎ 706/746–5348 or 800/541–0671) is famous for its country food served family style. As much as a two-hour wait can make getting in a bit of a chore. D/r

Dahlonega

Take GA 400 north from Atlanta.

Gold was mined in Dahlonega before the Civil War, and a U.S. mint operated in this modest boomtown from 1838 to 1861. In the present-day courthouse on the town square is the Gold Museum, with coins, tools, and a 5½-ounce nugget. The square is ringed with a mixture of tourist-oriented boutiques, restaurants, and old small-town businesses. ⊠ GA 400 to GA 16 north into downtown; about 55 mi northeast of Atlanta, ☎ 706/864–2257. ☜ $2. ☉ Mon.–Sat. 9–5, Sun. 10–5.

Helen

Take I–985 to Cleveland (Exit 7) and continue 9 mi on GA 75.

Alpine Helen (⊠ Helen Welcome Center, Box 730, 30545; 726 Bruckenstrasse, ☎ 706/878–2181 or 800/858–8027, FAX 706/878–4032) simulates an Alpine village in the Georgia mountains. The look is Bavaria, and attractions are mostly of the fun-and-fudge variety. The town's annual Oktoberfest draws crowds. Take I–85 to I–95 to GA 365, then take Exit 7.

Macon

90 mi south of Atlanta on I–75.

This antebellum town has more than 100,000 flowering cherry trees. Founded in 1823, it occupies the geographic center of the state. Its antebellum and Victorian homes are among the state's best preserved. Besides its numerous historic sites, Macon is a music center, and home to Otis Redding, the Allman Brothers Band, Little Richard, and many more fine musicians.

Georgia Music Hall of Fame is appropriately located in Macon as a tribute to the city's extensive contribution to American music; the official state museum for music opened in 1996. The project, a joint effort of state and private resources, is dedicated to Georgians who have helped define America's musical culture. Among those remembered here are Ma Rainey and Ray Charles (blues), Otis Redding and James Brown (soul), Little Richard, the Allman Brothers Band, Chet Atkins, and groups such as R.E.M. and the B-52s. Those honored from the classical world are Robert Shaw (director emeritus, Atlanta Symphony Orchestra), Jessye Norman (from Augusta), Robert McDuffie (Macon), and James Melton (Moultrie). ⊠ 200 Martin Luther King Jr. Blvd., ☎ 912/750–8555. ☜ $7.50. ☉ Mon.–Sat. 9–4:30, Sun. 1–4:30.

Hay House, one of the South's finest Italianate villas (1855–1859), was designed by Thomas & Sons, a New York architectural firm, and is renowned for its fine architectural and decorative detailing. In addition, the house is outstanding for its technology, which included indoor plumbing, a ventilation system, gas lighting, a dumbwaiter, and a basic speaker tube intercom system. Preservation efforts are ongoing. ⊠ *934 Georgia Ave.,* ☎ *912/742–8155.* ☞ *$6.* ⊙ *Mon.–Sat. 10–5, Sun. 1–5; last tour at 4:30.*

Jarrell Plantation, about 20 mi north of Macon, allows visitors to view the way of life of a well-to-do family in rural Georgia in the mid-19th to early 20th centuries. The collection of rustic dwellings and outbuildings is linked by a well-marked trail. Period machinery and equipment and farm animals are part of the exhibit. ⊠ *From Macon, I–75N to Exit 55 (U.S. 23); from I–75S, Exit 60 (Hwy. 18/Gray); Rte. 2, Box 220, Juliette, 31046,* ☎ *912/986–5172.* ☞ *$2.* ⊙ *Tues.–Sat. 9–5, Sun. 2–5:30.*

The **Museum of Aviation,** about 20 mi south of Macon at Robins Air Force Base, has an extraordinary collection of vintage aircraft including a MIG, a U-2, and assorted flying machines from past campaigns. From Macon, take I–75 south to Exit 45 (Centerville/Warner Robins), and turn left onto Watson Blvd., 7 mi to Hwy. 247, then right for 2 mi. ⊠ *Hwy. 247 at Russell Pkwy., Warner Robins 31098,* ☎ *912/926–6870.* ☞ *Free; special film $2.* ⊙ *Daily 10–5.*

Ocmulgee National Monument lies just east of Macon, 3 mi from the city limits. This archaeological site, occupied for more than 10,000 years, was at its peak under the Mississippian peoples who lived here between AD 900 and 1100. There's a reconstructed earth lodge and displays of pottery, effigies, and jewelry of copper and shells discovered in the burial mound. ⊠ *Rte. 80 east of Macon, 1207 Emery Hwy.,* ☎ *912/752–8257,* FAX *912/752–8259.* ☞ *Free.* ⊙ *Daily 9–5.*

The **Tubman African American Museum** is a tribute to the former slave who led more than 300 people to freedom as one of the "conductors" on the Underground Railroad. A mural that spans two walls and several centuries depicts black history and culture. The museum also has an African artifacts gallery. ⊠ *340 Walnut St.,* ☎ *912/743–8544.* ☞ *$3.* ⊙ *Weekdays 9–5, Sat. 10–5, Sun. 2–5.*

Madison

60 mi east of Atlanta via I–20.

Madison is a well-preserved antebellum town with splendid examples of antebellum and Victorian architecture. The Madison-Morgan Cultural Center is housed in a turn-of-the-century schoolhouse built in Romanesque Revival style. Besides a restored classroom of the period, the center contains artifacts, information, and printed guides for other historic sites in town. ⊠ *434 S. Main St.,* ☎ *706/342–4743.* ☞ *$3.* ⊙ *Tues.–Sat. 10–4:30, Sun. 2–5.*

New Echota State Historic Site

Take I–75 north to Rte. 225.

From 1825 to 1838, **New Echota** was the capital of the Cherokee nation, whose constitution was patterned after that of the United States. There was a council house, a printing office, a Supreme Court building, and the *Cherokee Phoenix,* a newspaper that utilized the Cherokee alphabet developed by Sequoyah. Some buildings have been reconstructed. ⊠ *Rte. 225, 1 mi east of I–75N, near Calhoun,* ☎ *706/ 629–8151.* 🎫 *$2.* ◷ *Tues.–Sat. 9–5, Sun. 2–5:30.*

The two-story brick **Chief Vann House,** just a few miles north of New Echota, was built in 1805 by a leader of the Cherokee Nation, who hired Moravian artisans to construct it. Chief Vann's slaves also worked on the house. The interior is intricately carved and beautifully restored. ⊠ *Rte. 52A west of Chatsworth, 82 Hwy. 225 N, Chatsworth,* ☎ *706/695–2598.* 🎫 *$2.* ◷ *Tues.–Sat. 9–5, Sun. 2–5:30.*

Warm Springs

From Atlanta, take I–85 south to Exit 8.

President Franklin Delano Roosevelt first visited Warm Springs in 1924 to take the therapeutic hot waters. In 1932 he built the "Little White House," a simple, three-bedroom cottage. Now restored, it contains his personal effects, and looks much as it did the day he died here. ⊠ *Rte. 1, Box 10, GA 85W, Warm Springs 31830,* ☎ *706/655–5870.* 🎫 *$4.* ◷ *Daily 9–4.*

Washington

100 mi east of Atlanta via I–20 (Exit 56).

For a glimpse into the past, visit this former state capital, a showcase of antebellum and Victorian architecture. Incorporated in 1780, it was the first city in the nation to be named for George Washington. Don't miss **Callaway Plantation** (⊠ Washington–Wilkes Chamber of Commerce, Box 661, 104 E. Liberty St., Washington 30673, ☎ 706/ 678–2013, FAX 706/678–1932), 5 mi outside town on U.S. Highway 78, for an authentic view of 19th-century life.

GEORGIA A TO Z

Arriving and Departing

By Bus
Greyhound Bus Lines (⊠ 232 Forsyth St., ☎ 404/584–1728 or 800/ 231–2222) serves Atlanta and many towns across the state, large and small. Instructions are available in both English and Spanish.

By Car
Georgia is traversed east and west by several interstate highways. North and south are covered by I–75, running from northwest through the center of the state to the Florida line; I–85 runs from the northeastern part of the state through the west to Alabama; I–95 runs along the Georgia coast from South Carolina to Florida. I–85 and I–75 converge in Atlanta near its downtown; this nexus is called the Connector. Running east and west, I–20 stretches from Birmingham, Alabama, to Augusta, Georgia, running through the center of downtown Atlanta on its way. From Macon, I–16 leads directly east to Savannah, where it ends; along its route lie several interesting towns, including Vidalia (home of the famous onion). Scenic routes include GA 76, a good highway running east–west through the north Georgia mountains, and U.S. 441, running north–south from the mountains to the Florida line. Along the way, U.S. 441 links numerous charming small towns and is lined with barbecue joints of worth. On the western side of the state, various pleasant small towns are connected by U.S. 19, the north–south route of choice prior to development of the interstate and still a good option if I–75 comes to a standstill, as it routinely does Thanksgiving Eve. I–75 also runs through a number of quaint small towns.

By Plane

Numerous international and domestic airlines serve **Hartsfield Atlanta International Airport** (⌑ I–85 and I–285, ☎ 404/530–6600), 13 mi south of downtown (☞ Atlanta A to Z, *above*).

By Train

Amtrak serves Atlanta and the state from the Brookwood Station (⌑ 1688 Peachtree St., ☎ 404/881–3060 or 800/872–7245). The *Crescent* operates daily to Atlanta from New York; Philadelphia; Washington, DC; Baltimore; Charlotte; and Greenville, and daily from New Orleans to New York through Atlanta. The "Thru-Way" bus service operates daily from Birmingham and Mobile, Alabama, to Atlanta's Brookwood Station. Another bus goes from the train station to Macon.

Getting Around

By Bus

Greyhound (☎ 800/231–2222) serves selected cities and towns around the state.

By Car

The speed limit on interstates is 50 mph in metropolitan areas and 70 mph elsewhere. Right turns on red lights are permitted unless otherwise indicated. Call the **Georgia Department of Industry, Trade, and Tourism** (⌑ Box 1776, Atlanta 30301, ☎ 404/656–3545 or 800/847–4842, FAX 404/651–9063) for copies of its brochures and maps. Especially useful is its "Georgia On My Mind," published annually, which includes a map and much valuable information.

By Plane

Numerous regional airports serve the state. The **Macon Municipal Airport** (⌑ 4000 Terminal Dr., GA 247 and I–75, ☎ 912/788–3760) is served by Atlantic Southeast Airlines. Eighteen miles west of downtown, **Savannah International Airport** (☎ 912/964–0514) is served by Delta, US Airways, and ValuJet for domestic flights. To reach the Golden Isles by air, **Glynco Jetport** (☎ 800/282–3424), 6 mi north of Brunswick, is served by Delta affiliate Atlantic Southeast Airlines, with flights from Atlanta.

By Train

Amtrak has regular service along the Eastern Seaboard, with daily stops in Savannah (⌑ 2611 Seaboard Coastline Dr., ☎ 912/234–2611 or 800/872–7245), where a station is 4 mi southwest of downtown.

Contacts and Resources

B&B Reservations

Georgia Bed & Breakfast (☎ 770/493–1930) is an agency that can connect you with area lodging (homes, resorts, and inns), while **Bed & Breakfast Atlanta** (☎ 404/875–0525 or 800/967–3224) represents 80–100 homes. **Great Inns of Georgia** (☎ 404/252–8886 or 800-664-7328) can connect you to numerous bed-and-breakfast inns around the state as well as in the metro Atlanta area. In addition the bimonthly *Georgia Journal* (⌑ Box 1604, Decatur 30031-1604, ☎ 404/377–4275 or 800/268–6942) has extensive lists of restaurants and bed-and-breakfast inns throughout the state.

Biking

With a membership of about 4,000, the **Southern Bicycle League** (⌑ Box 1360, Roswell 30077, ☎ 770/594–8350) for more than 20 years has promoted bicycling across Georgia and the South. The **Bicycle Ride Across Georgia (BRAG)** (☎ 770/921–6166) is an annual event.

Emergencies

For **ambulance and fire emergencies statewide,** call 911.

Fishing

The **Georgia Department of Natural Resources, Game and Fish Division** (✉ 2070 U.S. Hwy. 278, Social Circle 30279, ☎ 770/918–6400) has free pamphlets covering Georgia's regulations and maps suggesting good fishing spots.

Road Conditions

For road information, call the **Georgia Department of Transportation** (☎ 404/656–1267).

State Parks

Housed under the Georgia Department of Natural Resources, the **Parks, Recreation & Historic Sites** division (✉ 205 Butler St. SE, 30334, ☎ 404/656–3530 or 800/864–7275 reservations; 770/389–7275 local reservations) has information on Georgia's parks.

Visitor Information

The **Georgia Department of Industry, Trade and Tourism** (✉ Box 1776, Atlanta 30301, ☎ 404/656–3590 or 800/847–4842, FAX 404/651–9063) is the best source for visitor information around the state.

4 Louisiana

Louisiana is a state divided, both physically and philosophically. North Louisiana, with its rolling hills and piney woods, is strongly Southern in flavor and appeal. The flatter, marshy land in South Louisiana is Cajun Country, with sharp differences in food, music, and even language. Riverboats ply the mighty Mississippi and antebellum homes line the wayside in both regions, but it's New Orleans, home of the famous Mardi Gras festivities, that garners the lion's share of attention, drawing most visitors to South Louisiana.

By Honey
Naylor

LOCALS GENERALLY DESCRIBE REGIONS of their states as "upstate," "to the south," and so on, but in Louisiana (also known as "Sportsman's Paradise," the "Bayou State," and the "Pelican State"), the land is clearly divided. Louisianians almost to a person say "North Louisiana" and "South Louisiana," and even in conversation you can detect the capitalized distinction. North Louisiana is Southern, and South Louisiana is not. (A South Louisiana exception is the area north of Baton Rouge, in the Feliciana Parishes, where both terrain and customs are akin to those in North Louisiana.) Peace reigns 'twixt the twain, of course, but it is no accident that construction of I–49, the north–south interstate, dragged on for years. Now, at least the North and the South are physically—though not philosophically—connected.

Louisiana's Mason-Dixon line cuts through Alexandria, in the state's mid-section, known as Alex and pronounced "Elleck" by most. North of Alexandria are rolling hills and piney woods, acres of hiking and happy hunting grounds, and lakes where you can fish and camp. The terrain flattens out and becomes marshy south of Alexandria. In Cajun Country (also known as "Acadiana" and "French Louisiana"), Cajun fiddles tune up for fais-do-do (dances); tables are laden with crawfish, jambalaya, and gumbo; and pirogues (small, flat-bottom boats) are poled through bayous. Gracious antebellum homes decorate the Great River Road between Baton Rouge and New Orleans, frilly riverboats play upon the Mississippi, and tour boats sneak beneath lacy gray Spanish moss into mysterious cypress swamps and sloughs.

Pleasures and Pastimes

Biking
Bicycle trails honeycomb the state. The Kisatchie National Forest, near Natchitoches, has miles of trails through the piney woods. In flat-as-a-pancake South Louisiana, the area around Lafayette has more than 60 mi of marked trails. Some of the streets in New Orleans's French Quarter are blocked to all but bikers and pedestrians during the day. City Park and Audubon Park are great places for biking.

Birding, Boating, and Fishing
From north to south, the state is laced with waterways, making it an ideal destination for boaters and fisher folk. Birders and fishers like to stalk the coastal marshes, and the Gulf of Mexico beckons those in search of big guys like blue marlin and wahoo.

Dining
Louisiana is perhaps the only state in the country that has a distinctive regional cuisine. The famed French Creole cuisine cooked up in New Orleans kitchens has blended over the years with Cajun cuisine born in the bayous and popularized by celebrity chef Paul Prudhomme, to produce what's known as "South Louisiana Cooking." Cajun cooking, in particular, which usually means hot and spicy, has turned up on tables all over the world, but nobody does it like South Louisianians. Graced as the state is with waterways, Louisiana tables are also laden with seafood in every imaginable and innovative variety. Dress in restaurants is informal unless otherwise noted.

Louisiana

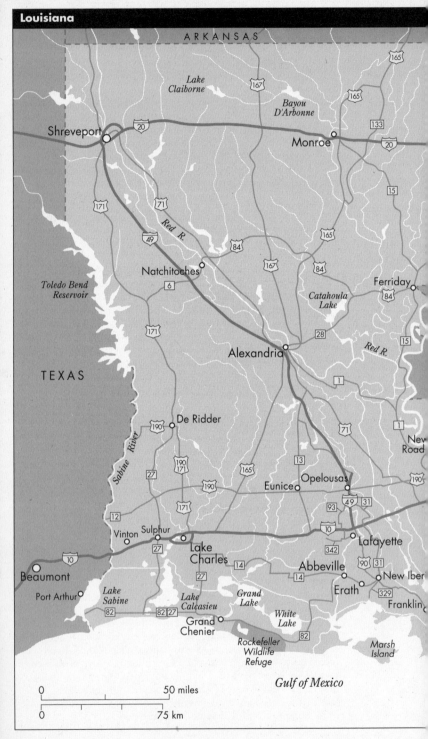

ARKANSAS

Lake Claiborne

Bayou D'Arbonne

Shreveport

Monroe

Red R.

Natchitoches

Toledo Bend Reservoir

Ferriday

Catahoula Lake

Red R.

Alexandria

TEXAS

Sabine River

De Ridder

New Road

Eunice

Opelousas

Lafayette

Vinton

Sulphur

Lake Charles

Abbeville

New Iber

Erath

Franklin

Beaumont

Port Arthur

Lake Sabine

Lake Calcasieu

Grand Chenier

Grand Lake

White Lake

Rockefeller Wildlife Refuge

Marsh Island

Gulf of Mexico

0   50 miles

0   75 km

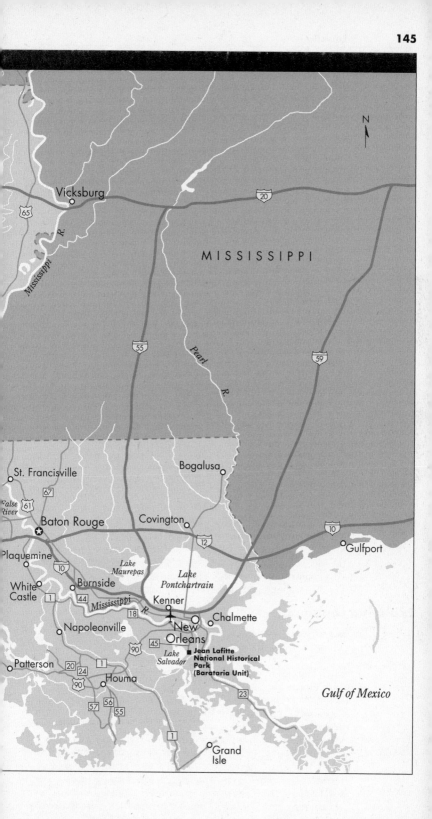

CATEGORY	COST*
$$$$	over $40
$$$	$30–$40
$$	$20–$30
$	under $20

per person for a three-course meal, excluding drinks, service, and 9% sales tax

Festivals

Hardly a day goes by in Louisiana without a festival of some sort, saluting everything from the tomato to petroleum. New Orleans is home to North America's biggest bash—Mardi Gras—but Lafayette celebrates the same holiday with a Cajun flair. The New Orleans Jazz and Heritage Festival is a world-class event, as is the Festival International de la Louisiane in Lafayette.

Lodging

Sleeping accommodations in Louisiana run from homey bed-and-breakfasts to chain motels to luxury hotels to elegant antebellum mansions open for overnighters. Louisiana has well over 100 bed-and-breakfasts; Cajun Country is loaded with charming ones, and Natchitoches alone has 16. Old and new blend in New Orleans, which also has many B&Bs in or near the city. Its French Quarter particularly has a plethora of guest houses that occupy 19th-century town houses and carriage houses, in which the emphasis is on Old World ambience. As one of the nation's favorite convention cities, New Orleans has a Central Business District that is dominated by a host of big and brassy high-rise, high-tech convention hotels.

CATEGORY	COST*
$$$$	over $120
$$$	$90–$120
$$	$50–$90
$	under $50

All prices are for a standard double room, excluding 6% tax.

Music

About a century ago, New Orleans gave birth to jazz, and the music has scarcely missed a beat since. It pours out of clubs along Bourbon Street in the French Quarter and floods the sightseeing riverboats on the Mississippi. It's everywhere. Southern as it is, North Louisiana favors country-and-western music, while in South Louisiana feet fly to the intoxicating Cajun and zydeco rhythms.

Exploring Louisiana

For most Louisianians, the state has two clearly defined regions: north and south. South Louisiana—Louisianians never say "southern Louisiana"—encompasses all of the region south of Alexandria and extending east to the "instep" of this boot-shape state. Paradoxically, only North Louisiana is Southern in flavor. Almost all of South Louisiana is considered Cajun Country, or French Louisiana, except for the region north of Baton Rouge, whose residents cherish their British heritage. Even the terrain changes above Alexandria, with flat marshlands and Spanish moss–draped live oaks giving over to rolling hills and piney woods. By the time you reach Natchitoches, you're deep into North Louisiana, although the town also boasts rich Creole and Cajun textures. The state's main attraction, New Orleans, is in a class by itself, being characteristic of neither north nor south Louisiana. The city is a paradox in that it is both a major international port and an overgrown small town with an insouciant Caribbean flavor.

Great Itineraries

Most visitors to Louisiana go first to New Orleans and, specifically, to the French Quarter. You can spend weeks exploring the Quarter and still not see all of it. One of the "problems" about seeing New Orleans on a short visit is the city's vast number of outstanding restaurants. If you don't spend too much time in restaurants, you can hit the high spots of the Quarter in three days. Allow a half day each to visit the Aquarium of the Americas and to stroll around and see the Garden District mansions. You can get a taste of Plantation Country, to the west of the city, by visiting two in a single day. However, if you plan to visit all of them you'll need at least two days; some of the plantations offer overnight accommodations in handsome mansions.

You can get a tempting taste of Cajun Country on a one-day jaunt from New Orleans to Lafayette, but in order to fully savor its considerable attractions you should plan to spend at least one night in the area. A three- to four-night trip will enable you to explore as far as Lake Charles and environs. Allow at least a week if you want to combine some of Cajun Country with a trip up into Natchitoches, the oldest permanent European settlement in the entire Louisiana Territory. While Natchitoches can be seen in a day and a half, it lies 142 mi north of Lafayette, and Cane River Country, south of Natchitoches, has several sites that should be seen leisurely. The return to New Orleans from Natchitoches is a long haul, at 264 mi, so your last day will be devoted almost exclusively to driving.

IF YOU HAVE 3 DAYS

Spend this time in ⊞ **New Orleans.** Many visitors never leave the French Quarter, even if they stay a week or more. On a short trip, at least see the sights in and around **Jackson Square,** tour the **Old Ursuline Convent,** and stroll along Bourbon street to hear the music pouring out of the jazz clubs. On your last day, spend a morning at the **Aquarium of the Americas,** and in the afternoon take the St. Charles Avenue streetcar to the Garden District and the Audubon Zoo.

IF YOU HAVE 5 DAYS

After a couple of days in ⊞ **New Orleans** (☞ *above*), travel 80 mi northwest to ⊞ **Baton Rouge,** the capital of Louisiana, with its museums and sites that pertain to state lore. Baton Rouge is in the heart of the area called Plantation Country; drive north of the city to quaint little **St. Francisville,** especially to see Rosedown Plantation. Your last day can be spent touring the River Road plantations that lie between Baton Rouge and New Orleans, particularly **Nottoway, Madewood,** and **Laura.**

IF YOU HAVE 10 DAYS

Get to know ⊞ **New Orleans** and ⊞ **Baton Rouge** for a few days (☞ *above*), then take 1–10 west out of Baton Rouge to spend at least a day in ⊞ **Lafayette,** whose many attractions focus on Cajun culture. Within a short drive of Lafayette are colorful small towns and villages, such as **Erath** and **Abbeville,** that are typical of Cajun Country. On your last day, drive up to see the historic district in Natchitoches.

When to Tour Louisiana

The best times to visit Louisiana are in October and in the spring. During those times of the year temperatures and humidity are at bearable levels. Summers are scorchers throughout the state, with the mercury hovering above 90 degrees for much of June, July, and August. During those months, weather forecasters routinely predict "hot and humid, with a chance of afternoon thunder showers." In South Louisiana, hurricane season runs from June 1 through November 30, and the coastline is sometimes battered with high winds and heavy rain. An ideal time for a first visit to New Orleans is Spring Fiesta (the weekend following Easter), when the city is dressed in springtime finery and many of the handsome homes are open for tours. Mardi Gras (February or March) is not recommended for a first visit to New Orleans. All of the city is given over to raucous revelry, and its quiet charms are buried beneath the mighty hordes of merrymakers.

NEW ORLEANS

When Rhett Butler took Scarlett O'Hara to New Orleans on their honeymoon, the city was scarred by war, carpetbaggers were looting the town, and decent folk feared for their lives. But gone with the wind the city wasn't. Captain Butler and his bride were entertained at a continuous round of lavish parties, suppers, and plays.

Since the 1980s, New Orleans, like most other U.S. cities, has had problems with crime and its economy. But its reputation as a good-time town remains intact, and the city is forever finding something to celebrate. World-famous Mardi Gras aside, new festivals crop up at the drop of a Panama hat. New Orleans party animals even celebrate each new addition to the main zoo. The city's most famous party place is the French Quarter, bordered by Canal Street, Esplanade Avenue, North Rampart Street, and the Mississippi River. Also called the Vieux Carré (Old Square), the Quarter is the original colony, founded in 1718 by French Creoles. As you explore its famous restaurants, antiques shops, and jazz haunts, try to imagine a handful of determined early 18th-century settlers living in crude palmetto huts and battling swamps, floods, hurricanes, and yellow fever. Two cataclysmic fires in the late 18th century virtually leveled the town. The Old Ursuline Convent on Chartres Street is the only remaining original French Colonial structure. Survival was a struggle for the Creoles, and the sobriquet "The City That Care Forgot" stems from a determination not only to live life but to celebrate it.

The French Quarter is a carefully preserved historic district. It's also home to some 3,600 residents, some of the most famous French Creole restaurants, and many a jazz club. An eclectic crowd, which includes some of the world's best jazz musicians, ambles in and out of small two- and three-story frame, old-brick, and pastel-painted stucco buildings. Baskets of splashy subtropical plants dangle from the eaves of buildings with filigreed galleries, dollops of gingerbread, and dormer windows. Built flush with the banquettes (sidewalks), the houses, most of which date from the early to mid-19th century, front secluded courtyards awash with greenery and brilliant blossoms.

In the early 19th century, the American Sector was just upriver of the French Quarter. For that reason, street names change as you cross Canal Street from the French Quarter: Bourbon Street to Carondelet Street, Royal Street to St. Charles Avenue, and so on.

The nerve center of the nation's second-largest port and main parade route during Mardi Gras, the CBD (Central Business District) cuts a wide swath between Uptown and Downtown, with Canal Street the official dividing line. Bordered by Canal Street, the river, Howard Avenue, and Loyola Avenue, the CBD has the city's newest convention hotels along with ritzy shopping malls, old department stores, international trade agencies and consulates, fast-food chains, monuments, and the monumental Superdome.

Nestled in between St. Charles Avenue, Louisiana Avenue, Jackson Avenue, and Magazine Street, the Garden District is aptly named. The Americans who built their estates upriver surrounded their homes with lavish lawns, forgoing the Creoles' preference for secluded courtyards. Many of the elegant Garden District homes were built during New Orleans's Golden Age, from 1830 until the Civil War. Magazine Street is heaven on earth for shoppers. Joggers, golfers, tennis buffs, and horseback riders head for Audubon Park.

Directions in New Orleans are described with respect to the Father of Waters. The Mississippi River moves in mysterious waves, looping around the city and wreaking havoc with ordinary routes. New Orleanians, ever resourceful, refer instead to lakeside (toward Lake Pontchartrain), riverside (toward the Mississippi), upriver (also called uptown), and downriver (downtown).

Some words of caution are necessary. Beneath New Orleans's exotic veneer is a high-crime city. The French Quarter and the Garden District can be very dangerous, even in broad daylight; walks at night can be particularly risky. Stay alert and streetwise, wherever and whenever you go—especially if you're carrying such obvious tourist trappings as cameras and opened maps.

Numbers in the text correspond to numbers in the margin and on the Downtown New Orleans map.

The French Quarter

A Good Walk

A good place to begin a stroll around the Quarter is **Jackson Square** ①, which has been the heart and soul of the French Quarter. A flagstone pedestrian mall borders three sides of the square. As you face the statue, the **New Orleans Welcome Center** ② is to your left, a few steps across the flagstones.

Turn right as you leave the visitor center to see the three historic buildings that sit on Chartres Street, facing the square. The white church in the middle is the late 18th-century **St. Louis Cathedral** ③. The two Spanish Colonial buildings flanking the church are the **Cabildo** ④, on the left as you face the church, and the **Presbytère** ⑤ on the right. Alongside the church are Pirate's Alley and Père Antoine's Alley, cracked-flagstone passageways redolent of infamous plots and pirate intrigue—but, alas, the streets were laid long after Jean Lafitte and his Baratarian band had vanished. William Faulkner wrote his first novel, *A Soldier's Pay,* while living at 624 Pirate's Alley.

Lining Jackson Square, on St. Peter and St. Ann Streets, the Pontalba Buildings are among the nation's oldest apartment buildings, built between 1849 and 1851. In the lower Pontalba ("lower" because it's downriver of the square) is the **1850 House** ⑥.

The promenade of **Washington Artillery Park** ⑦, opposite Jackson Square on Decatur Street, affords a splendid perspective of the square and the Mississippi River. On the Moon Walk promenade, across the tracks from the park, you can sit on a bench or stroll down the steps to the water's edge.

Washington Artillery Park is anchored on the upriver side by the Jackson Brewery and Millhouse, and downriver by the French Market. Jax Beer used to be made in the Brewery, and the market is on the site of a late-17th-century Indian trading post. Both sights are now filled with boutiques and restaurants, with Planet Hollywood hogging most of the Brewery space. Two blocks toward Canal Street on Decatur Street

Downtown New Orleans

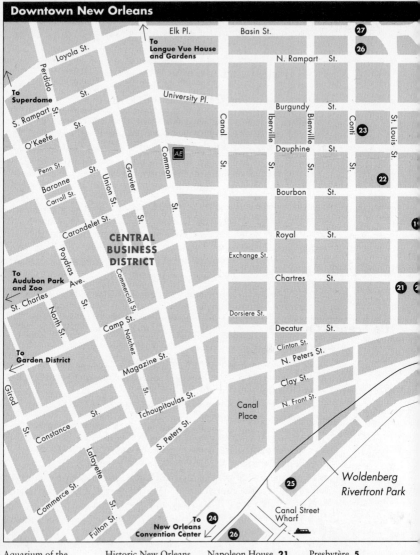

Aquarium of the Americas, **25**

Beauregard-Keyes House, **10**

Cabildo, **4**

Cornstalk Fence, **13**

1850 House, **6**

First Skyscraper, **17**

Gallier House, **11**

Hermann-Grima House, **22**

Historic New Orleans Collection, **19**

Jackson Square, **1**

LaBranche Houses, **16**

Lafitte's Blacksmith Shop, **12**

Madame John's Legacy, **15**

Musée Conti Wax Museum, **23**

Napoleon House, **21**

New Orleans Historic Voodoo Museum, **14**

New Orleans Pharmacy Museum, **20**

New Orleans Welcome Center, **2**

Old U.S. Mint, **8**

Old Ursuline Convent, **9**

Presbytère, **5**

Preservation Hall, **18**

Spanish Plaza, **26**

St. Louis Cathedral, **3**

Washington Artillery Park, **7**

World Trade Center, **24**

Louis Armstrong Park

25

N. Rampart St.

St. Ann

Dumaine

St.

St.

Burgundy St.

Toulouse

St. Peter

Orleans

St.

St.

St. Philip

Ursulines

Gov. Nicholls St.

Barracks

Esplanade

St.

St.

St.

FRENCH QUARTER (VIEUX CARRÉ)

Dauphine St.

Ave.

St.

St.

St.

12

Bourbon St.

18

14

13

17

16

Père Antoine's Alley

Royal St.

11

rate's Alley

15

10

4

3

5

Chartres St.

9

Wilk Row

1

Madison St.

2

Jackson Square

6

Decatur St.

7

French Market Pl.

8

Moon Walk

N. Peters St.

Esplanade Wharf

Mississippi River

Algiers Point

KEY

AE American Express Office

Ferry

Rail line

Z

0   440 yds

0   400 m

is the Jackson Brewery Corporation's Marketplace, home of yet more restaurants and retail outlets.

On the same site for more than 100 years, Café du Monde at 800 Decatur Street is the upriver anchor for the French Market, and is in one of its oldest buildings. Stretching from St. Ann Street downriver to Barracks Street, the market is alive with shops, outdoor cafés, and ice cream and candy stores. The downriver anchor of the French Market is the Old Farmers Market, where farmers from the countryside have been bringing their produce for more than 170 years, and where a Community Flea Market flourishes daily from dawn till dusk.

The area on the Esplanade Avenue fringe of the Quarter should be avoided at night, but you'll be safe during the day when you visit the Jazz and Mardi Gras Exhibits in the **Old U.S. Mint** ⑧. From the Mint, walk up tree-lined Esplanade Avenue to Chartres Street and turn left to reach the **Old Ursuline Convent** ⑨, within a walled complex at the corner of Chartres and Ursulines streets; it was built in 1749. The Greek Revival house across the street from the Ursuline Convent is the **Beauregard-Keyes House** ⑩. From the house, turn right onto Ursuline Street, walk one block to Royal Street and turn right again, where you'll find the **Gallier House** ⑪, built around 1857.

Turn right at the corner of Royal and St. Philip Streets to see the 18th-century **Lafitte's Blacksmith Shop** ⑫, which now houses a neighborhood bar. Near the intersection of Royal Street and St. Philip Street, look to the right at **Cornstalk Fence** ⑬. Around the corner is the **New Orleans Historic Voodoo Museum** ⑭ on Dumaine Street. From the museum, walk south on Dumaine Street, crossing Royal Street. On Dumaine, between Royal and Chartres streets, is **Madame John's Legacy** ⑮, a West Indies–style raised cottage that is similar to those built by the early planters in this area.

Turn right after leaving Madame John's Legacy, walk down to Chartres Street, and make another right. Continue on Chartres Street through Jackson Square to St. Peter Street, turn right again and walk one block up to Royal Street. Here you'll see the 19th-century **LaBranche Houses** ⑯. Directly across St. Peter Street from the LaBranche Houses is the four-story **First Skyscraper** ⑰, constructed between 1795 and 1811.

Next, walk up St. Peter Street, away from Jackson Square. About midway between Royal and Bourbon Streets, behind weathered walls is **Preservation Hall** ⑱, where old-time legends of traditional jazz hold forth nightly. Not much happens here during the day, but you can peer through the gate to see the carriageway and the courtyard beyond it. Return to Royal Street, turn right, and cross Toulouse Street to reach the old Merieult House, which contains the **Historic New Orleans Collection** ⑲.

Walk toward the Mississippi River on Toulouse Street and turn right to find the **New Orleans Pharmacy Museum** ⑳. On the same side of the street, at the corner of Chartres and St. Louis streets is **Napoleon House** ㉑, a longtime favorite haunt of artists and writers.

Wrench yourself from the Napoleon House, walk away from the river, and cross Bourbon Street to reach the **Hermann-Grima House** ㉒, an American-style town house–museum dating from the early 19th-century. After you leave the residence, walk less than a block and turn left on Dauphine Street. Turn right at Conti Street to the **Musée Conti Wax Museum** ㉓.

TIMING

Properly done, a tour of the French Quarter should take weeks, so much is there to see. Be prepared for crowds: The neighborhood is almost always full of tourists and/or conventioneers, except perhaps during the worst dog days of summer. Autumn and early spring offer mild temperatures and low humidity. This old historic district is only about 1 square mi, and it can be walked easily in half a day. But that would mean you'd miss peeking into the plethora of shops and knocking back a Dixie beer, brewed locally, at Lafitte's Blacksmith Shop or a Pimm's Cup (a gin-based drink) at the Napoleon House. Allow yourself at least a full day to enjoy the Quarter's main attractions: the Cabildo and St. Louis Cathedral at Jackson Square, the Old Ursuline Convent, and Gallier House. April and October are ideal times for strolling around the neighborhood. Summers are brutal, and ambling is simply impossible during Mardi Gras, when the streets are paved with people.

Sights to See

⑩ Beauregard-Keyes House. A raised cottage with a Greek Revival portico, this house was built in 1826. For a brief period after the Civil War, it was home to Confederate General Pierre Gustav Toutant Beauregard, the Creole New Orleanian who ordered the first shot fired at Fort Sumter. In the mid-1940s the house was bought by novelist Frances Parkinson Keyes (author of *Dinner at Antoine's*), whose office was in the former slave quarters. Some of Keyes' books are sold in the gift shop. The pretty French garden adjacent to the house is part of the tour. ⊠ *1113 Chartres St.,* ☎ *504/523–7257.* ⊠ *$4.* ☺ *Mon.–Sat. 10–3; tours on the hr.*

❹ Cabildo. There has been a *cabildo* (Spanish governing council) in New Orleans since the 1700s. Transfer papers for the Louisiana Purchase of 1803 were signed on the second floor, in the Sala Capitular, and in 1825, Lafayette stayed here on a triumphal tour. Exhibits trace the multicultural historic contributions to the region. Among the artifacts is a death mask of Napoleon, who was a hero for many a New Orleanian. The Cabildo—along with the ☞ **Presbytère,** the ☞ **1850 House,** and the ☞ **Old U.S. Mint**—is a property of the Louisiana State Museum. ⊠ *Jackson Sq.,* ☎ *504/568–6968.* ⊠ *$4.* ☺ *Tues.–Sun. 10–5.*

⑬ Cornstalk Fence. This heavy cast-iron fence, with its design of morning glories and ears of corn, is one of three such fences in the city; it dates from 1859. ⊠ *915 Royal St.*

❻ 1850 House. You can see what life was like for upscale 19th-century Creole apartment dwellers on a guided tour of this restored apartment, which belongs to the Louisiana State Museum; it is filled with period furnishings, antique dolls, and plenty of evidence of cushy Creole living. ⊠ *523 St. Ann St., Jackson Sq.,* ☎ *504/568–6968.* ⊠ *$4.* ☺ *Tues.–Sun. 10–5.*

⑰ First Skyscraper. Also known as Maison LeMonnier, this "skyscraper" was so-called because it was once the tallest building in the French Quarter. It was built between 1795 and 1811 for Dr. Yves LeMonnier, whose initials can be seen worked into the second-floor balcony. The edifice was originally a three-story high-rise; rumor has it that the fourth floor was added later so that it might retain its towering name. Shops on the ground floor are open to the public. ⊠ *640 St. Peter St.*

⑪ Gallier House. Born in Ireland, James Gallagher Sr. changed his name to Gallier before moving to New Orleans in order to fit in with the Creoles. This handsome house, which is exquisitely furnished, was designed by his renowned architect son, James Gallagher Jr., around

1857; he lived here with his family. The house has early Louisiana and Victorian antique furnishings upholstered in rich brocades and velvets, living room chandeliers made of etched glass and brass, marble mantels, and elaborate ceiling medallions. The residence was one of the settings used in the 1994 film *Interview with the Vampire*. (☞ Anne Rice's New Orleans, *below*). ✉ *1118 Royal St.,* ☎ *504/523–6722.* ▧ *$5.* ☉ *Tours Mon.–Sat. 10–3:30.*

㉒ Hermann-Grima House. Architect William Brand designed this American-style town house in 1831 for a wealthy merchant named Samuel Hermann. Hermann sold the house in 1844 to Felix Grima, an attorney. A guided tour takes in the first floor and the ancient rear kitchens, where Creole cooking demonstrations take place on Thursdays October through March. ✉ *820 St. Louis St.,* ☎ *504/525–5661.* ▧ *$5.* ☉ *Mon.–Sat. 10–4; last tour at 3:30.*

⑲ Historic New Orleans Collection. One of the nation's largest private collections of documents, paintings, blueprints, and artifacts is contained in the 18th-century Merieult House, one of the few buildings to survive the fire of 1794. The ground floor Williams Gallery, with changing exhibits relating to the city's past, is free to the public; other galleries can be seen on a guided tour. ✉ *533 Royal St.,* ☎ *504/523–4662.* ▧ *House tour $4, galleries tour $4.* ☉ *Tues.–Sat. 10–4:45.*

★ ✋ ❶ **Jackson Square.** Jackson Square was called Place d'Armes by the Creoles and was the center of all Colonial life, home to parading militia, religious ceremonies, social gatherings, food vendors, entertainers, and pirates. The square's focal point is a massive equestrian statue of General Andrew Jackson, hero of the 1815 Battle of New Orleans which was fought 5 mi downriver at Chalmette. In the mid-19th century the area was renamed to honor the man who defeated the British and saved the city. Today the square remains a social hub. Pirate attire is not uncommon in the colorful crowd that flocks here. The only thing missing is the militia.

The **Pontalba Buildings** that line either side of Jackson Square on St. Ann and St. Peter streets are among the oldest apartment houses in the country. Built between 1849 and 1851, they were constructed under the supervision of the baroness Micaela Pontalba, who occasionally lent the laborers a helping hand. ✉ *Jackson Square: bordered by Chartres, St. Ann, Decatur, and St. Peter Sts.*

⑯ LaBranche Houses. This complex of lovely town houses, built in the 1830s by widow LaBranche, fills the half block between Pirate's Alley, Royal, and St. Peter streets behind the ☞ **Cabildo.** The one at 700 Royal Street (on the corner of Royal and St. Peter streets) is one of the most photographed residences in the French Quarter. Its filigreed double balconies bedecked with flowering plants are cast iron with an oak-leaf-and-acorn motif. Cast iron such as this was introduced into New Orleans in about 1850, so the balconies would have been a later addition. All the houses are privately owned. There are shops and restaurants on the ground floor.

⑫ Lafitte's Blacksmith Shop. In the mid-19th century, notorious freebooters Jean and Pierre Lafitte are said to have operated a blacksmith shop in this tattered cottage, which served as a front for their slave trading, smuggling, and sundry nefarious deeds. The building dates back to 1772. For many years, it has served as a popular neighborhood bar, especially favored by artists and writers, both famous and obscure. ✉ *941 Bourbon St.,* ☎ *504/523–0066.*

⓯ **Madame John's Legacy.** The 19th-century writer George Washington Cable, who lived in the Garden District, wrote often about New Orleans Creoles. He used several French Quarter homes as settings for his stories. This house is named for a character in his short story " 'Tite Poulette." The West Indies–style house was built in 1788 on the site of the birthplace of Renato Beluche, a Lafitte lieutenant who helped Andrew Jackson in the Battle of New Orleans. Owned by the Louisiana State Museum, the house is not open to the public. It played a role in the film *Interview with the Vampire.* (☞ Anne Rice's New Orleans, *below.*) ⊠ 632 *Dumaine St.*

🐚 ㉓ **Musée Conti Wax Museum.** For a great introduction to New Orleans history, be sure to visit New Orleans's answer to Madame Tussaud's. Each of the 100 colorful tableaux depicts an event in the city's history, beginning with the 1682 arrival of LaSalle. Among the Louisiana luminaries captured in wax are Andrew Jackson, Jean Lafitte, Marie Laveau, and former governor Edwin Edwards. ⊠ 917 *Conti St.,* ☏ 504/525–2605. ⊠ $6. ☽ *Mon.–Sat. 10–5, Sun. noon–5.*

★ ㉑ **Napoleon House.** Arguably the most popular bar of New Orleanians, this is a wonderfully atmospheric place with peeling sepia walls and Napoleonic memorabilia; the classical music, however, is canned. Napoleon never visited New Orleans, but he had many admirers. Among them was mayor Nicholas Girod, whose house this was. Girod and cronies formed a syndicate whose purpose was to rescue the Little Corporal from incarceration on St. Helena and bring him to this house to live in an apartment Girod had added for that purpose. Alas, Napoleon died before the rescue could take place. ⊠ 500 *Chartres St.,* ☏ 504/524–9752. ☽ *Mon.–Sat. 11 AM–1 AM, Sun. 11–7.*

⓮ **New Orleans Historic Voodoo Museum.** An only–in–New Orleans attraction, this is a dimly lit place with a prominently featured portrait of 19th-century voodoo queen Marie Laveau, a voodoo altar, sundry potions, and information about voodoo as it is practiced today in the Crescent City. ⊠ 724 *Dumaine St.,* ☏ 504/523–7685. ⊠ $5.25. ☽ *Daily 10–6.*

⓴ **New Orleans Pharmacy Museum.** In 1823 Louis Dufilho, said to be the nation's first licensed pharmacist, had his pharmacy on the ground floor and lived upstairs. He grew medicinal herbs in the courtyard. This is a musty old place, full of ancient, mysterious medicinal items; there's also an Italian marble fountain used by 19th-century soda jerks. ⊠ 514 *Chartres St.,* ☏ 504/565–8027. ⊠ $2. ☽ *Tues.–Sun. 10–5.*

❷ **New Orleans Welcome Center.** Before sallying forth on sightseeing forays, the New Orleans Welcome Center should be one of your first stops for maps, brochures, and friendly advice about the city. The Welcome Center shares space with an outlet of the Louisiana Office of Tourism, which offers information about attractions statewide. ⊠ 529 *St. Ann St.,* ☏ 504/566–5068. ☽ *Daily 9–5.*

❽ **Old U.S. Mint.** Built in 1835, the massive Greek Revival building was the first branch of the U.S. Mint, and it turned out money hand over fist from 1838 until 1861 and the War for Southern Independence. During the War, Confederate coins were stamped here, until the Confederate States of America went broke, and afterward the Mint continued currency production until 1909. It's now a part of the Louisiana State Museum, housing Jazz and Mardi Gras exhibits. Among many other artifacts, the Jazz exhibit displays the first horn used by native son Louis Armstrong, and some of his famous white handkerchiefs. Glittering Carnival gowns, crowns, and scepters are among the colorful Mardi

Gras exhibits. ✉ *400 Esplanade Ave.,* ☎ *504/568–6968.* 💲 *$4.* ☉
Tues.–Sun. 10–5.

❾ Old Ursuline Convent. This handsome Greek Revival building is the oldest structure in the Lower Mississippi Valley, and the only undisputed
survivor of the late 18th century fires. It was erected in 1749 by order
of Louis XV, the second convent built on this site. The first Sisters of
Ursula arrived in the colony in 1727, after surviving a torturous five-
month voyage from France. The iron cross on the convent grounds came
with the nuns from Rouen. The Ursulines stayed in another building
until this one was completed; they occupied this convent from 1749
to 1824. The hand-hewn cypress spiral stairs inside are from the original convent. Guided tours of the complex include the lovely restored
St. Mary's Church. ✉ *1100 Chartres St.,* ☎ *504/529–3040.* 💲 *$4.*
☉ *Tours Tues.–Fri. 10, 11, 1, 2, and 3; weekends 11:15, 1, and 2.*

❺ Presbytère. This building was constructed in 1795 to house priests of
the church but was never used for this purpose. Like the ☞ **Cabildo,**
it is also a museum, with changing exhibits of photographs, paintings,
documents, and artifacts that pertain to the state. The odd-shape structure in the arcade of the Presbytère is a Confederate submarine. ✉ *Jackson Sq.,* ☎ *504/568–6968.* 💲 *$4.* ☉ *Tues.–Sun. 10–5.*

★ ⑱ Preservation Hall. The Hall, as it is known locally, may be the best-
known attraction in town. Preservation Hall Jazz Bands tour around
the world, ambassadors for New Orleans, for traditional jazz, and for
the sight itself (☞ Nightlife and the Arts, *below*). In the years prior to
World War I, the city was full of places like this, but over a period of
time after that war they disappeared. In the 1960s, Allen Jaffe—Penn-
sylvanian, tuba player, and jazz aficionado—opened Preservation Hall,
providing a place for musicians to play and tourists to throng. Jaffe
was revered by musicians; at his death in 1987 thousands came from
all over the world to pay their last respects and to march in a traditional jazz funeral. ✉ *726 St. Peter St.,* ☎ *504/522–2841.* 💲 *$4
cover.* ☉ *Daily 7:30 PM–midnight.*

❸ St. Louis Cathedral. Soaring above the earthly activity taking place right
in its front yard, the small white church is a quiet reminder of the spiritual life of New Orleans citizens. The first church on this site was built
in 1724 and named for Louis IX, France's saint-king. The present church
dates from 1794, and was restored and enlarged in 1849. It was elevated to the status of minor basilica in 1964, and in honor of Pope
John Paul II's 1987 visit, the mall in front of the cathedral was chris-
tened Place Jean Paul Deux. ✉ *Jackson Sq., on 700 block of Chartres
St.,* ☎ *504/525–9585.* ☉ *Services daily every ½ hr 9–5.*

❼ Washington Artillery Park. Named for the 141st Artillery, which has
fought in every war since 1845 when its commander was General
Zachary Taylor, this small "park" is formed mostly of concrete. Ramps
and steps lead from Decatur Street up to a promenade, where there
are park benches, box trees, and a grand view of Jackson Square on
one side and Old Man River on the other. Steps leading up to the promenade from Decatur Street form an amphitheater, with sundry jugglers
and mimes entertaining on the sidewalk below. If you go down the steps
on the riverside of the park and cross the streetcar tracks, you'll reach
Moon Walk. This promenade that stretches right along the Mississippi
is lined with park benches, and stone steps lead down into the muddy
water. Street musicians often play here. Beware the panhandlers. ✉ *Decatur St. between St. Peter and St. Ann Sts.*

Foot of Canal

A Good Walk

At the foot of Canal Street in the Central Business District (CBD), you can begin your walk at the **World Trade Center** ㉔, where the observation deck on the 31st floor affords a 360-degree overview of the city. From the Center, turn right, walk past the Canal Street Ferry landing, and cross Canal Street to reach the **Aquarium of the Americas** ㉕ in the 16-acre Woldenberg Riverfront Park.

To reach **Spanish Plaza** ㉖ behind the World Trade Center, backtrack across Canal Street to the ferry landing. Just to the right of the ferry landing is a large equestrian statue of Bernardo de Galvez, a governor of the Louisiana Territory during the Spanish colonial period. Behind the governor, a broad arch heralds Riverwalk. Spanish Plaza is across the tracks (watch out for the Riverfront Streetcar!), up the steps, and to the right.

The large unfinished structure across from the World Trade Center was begun in 1995, and was to be the home of Harrah's New Orleans Casino. At press time, Harrah's was sorting out sundry financial problems, while the city and the casino try to hammer out an agreement.

TIMING

Allow at least a full morning or afternoon for a leisurely stroll around this riverfront area. The World Trade Center's observation deck can be done in less than a half hour. You can easily devote two hours to the aquarium. Spanish Plaza is a broad open area smack by the Mississippi River, where the Riverwalk shopping mall can take up a few more hours of your time.

Sights to See

🔆 ㉕ **Aquarium of the Americas.** Visitors have close-up encounters with 7,000 aquatic creatures here. There are 60 separate displays in four major environments. A $25 million wing contains galleries and an IMAX movie theater. The beautifully landscaped 16-acre **Woldenberg Riverfront Park** around the aquarium is a tranquil spot with many excellent views of the river. ✉ *Foot of Canal St.,* ☎ *504/861–2538 aquarium, 504/581–4629 theater.* 🎟 *Aquarium $10.50, IMAX $7; combination ticket $15.* ☺ *Aquarium Sun.–Thurs. 9:30–6, Fri.–Sat. 9:30–7; IMAX daily 10–8, shows on the hr.*

OFF THE BEATEN PATH

LOUISIANA CHILDREN'S MUSEUM – This is an excellent museum with a host of educational hands-on exhibits, including a market, a TV station, and a small port. You can reach the museum from Spanish Plaza (☞ *below*) by walking through Riverwalk and exiting at Julia Street. ✉ *420 Julia St., Warehouse District,* ☎ *504/523–1357.* 🎟 *$5.* ☺ *Tues.–Sat. 9:30–4:30, Sun. noon–4:30.*

㉖ **Spanish Plaza.** A gift to the city from the Spanish government in the 1970s, this broad open expanse paved with mosaic tile stretches from behind the World Trade Center to the Mississippi River. The centerpiece of the plaza is a splendid fountain emblazoned with Spanish coats of arms. Several excursion boats take on passengers at the plaza, and there are often food vendors. The area is anchored downriver by the ferry landing and upriver by **Riverwalk**, a ½-mi-long shopping mall that stretches right along the river from the plaza to Julia Street in the Warehouse District. There are some 200 shops and restaurants, along with local specialty shops, such as Yvonne LaFleur and Louisiana Opal. *Riverwalk:* ✉ *Poydras St. at the River,* ☎ *504/522–1555.* ☺ *Mon.–Sat. 10–9, Sun. 11–7.*

㉔ **World Trade Center (WTC).** This skyscraper contains offices of foreign consulates and trade agencies. In the lobby, you'll find a gallery of regional artwork, and on the third floor a moderately priced cafeteria. A glass elevator on the side of the building glides up to **Viewpoint,** a 31st-floor observation deck with coin-operated telescopes, where you have a grand vista of the city. The **Top of the Mart,** a revolving cocktail lounge, resides on the 33rd floor. ✉ *2 Canal St., Viewpoint:* ☎ *504/525–2185.* 🎟 *$2.* ◷ *Daily 9–5. Top of the Mart:* ☎ *504/522–9795.* ◷ *Weekdays 10 AM–midnight, Sat. 11 AM–1 AM, Sun. 2 PM–midnight.*

The Garden District

The Americans who flocked to New Orleans after the 1803 Louisiana Purchase settled upriver of the French Quarter and built fine homes surrounded by luxuriant gardens. One of the nation's loveliest residential districts, it is an easily walkable area that is now known as the Garden District, bounded by Jackson, Louisiana, and St. Charles avenues and Magazine Street. Its grand mansions are private homes and closed to the public, but they are worth seeing from the outside.

A Good Walk

This walk begins following a short streetcar ride from Canal Street. Get off at 4th Street (stop No. 16) and walk toward the river one block to Prytania Street. At the corner of 4th and Prytania, Colonel Short's Villa (✉ 1448 4th St.) is a stunning Greek Revival/Italianate mansion. Walk down 4th Street to Coliseum Street, turn left and go one block to 3rd Street. The Robinson House (✉ 1415 3rd St.) is a lovely white house, said to have been among the first in New Orleans to have indoor plumbing. Continue on Coliseum Street to 1st Street. The home of novelist Anne Rice and husband Stan (✉ 1239 1st St.) is a handsome Greek Revival house, which the writer restored and used as the setting for her novel, *The Witching Hour.* Like other Garden District mansions, it is not open to the public, but there are often fans hanging out on the sidewalk, hoping for an author sighting. ☞ Anne Rice's New Orleans, *below.*

Walk toward St. Charles Avenue on 1st Street; at the corner of 1st and Prytania streets is Toby's Corner (✉ 2340 Prytania St.), which is said to be the oldest house in the Garden District, dating from about 1838. Across the street from it, the Bradish Johnson House (✉ 2343 Prytania St.), now the Louise McGehee School, was built in the late 1860s.

TIMING

Allow about an hour and a half to leisurely stroll around the Garden District. The walk suggested above is highly selective; the neighborhood is filled with stunning mansions, and you might want to allow extra time for picture taking.

OFF THE BEATEN PATH

AUDUBON PARK AND ZOO – To reach Audubon Park and Zoo from the Garden District, board the St. Charles streetcar once again to head Uptown. The park rolls out across St. Charles Avenue from Tulane and Loyola Universities. The 340-acre Audubon Park, with live oaks and lush tropical plants, was once part of the plantation of Etienne de Boré, the father of Louisiana's granulated-sugar industry. In addition to the 18-hole golf course, there is a 2-mi jogging track with 18 exercise stations along the way, a stable that offers guided trail rides, and 10 tennis courts.

The Friends of the Zoo operate a free shuttle that boards in front of Tulane every 15 to 20 minutes for a ride to the zoo, which lies on the 58 acres of the park nearest the river. A wooden walkway strings through the zoo, a miniature train rings around a part of it, and it can take an entire day to explore. More than 1,800 animals roam about in natural habitats, such as the Australian exhibit, where kangaroos hob-nob with wallabies. ⊠ *St. Charles Ave. (main entrance),* ☎ *504/861–2537.* 🖃 *$8.* ⊙ *Oct.–Mar., weekdays 9:30–5, weekends 9:30–6; Apr.–Sept., weekdays 9:30–5:30, weekends 9:30–6.*

Mid-City

This section of town stretches roughly lakeward from the French Quarter to City Park, and from Esplanade Avenue to I–10. The early French Creole settlers made camp near Bayou St. John, which forms the eastern border of City Park. The sights to be seen here are spread out, and you'll need a car to get from one to the other.

A Good Drive

To reach the **Pitot House** from the French Quarter drive straight out Esplanade Avenue. Just before the Esplanade Avenue Bridge, turn left on Moss Street. Bayou St. John will be on your right, the Pitot House on your left. To reach the **New Orleans Museum of Art,** backtrack to Esplanade Avenue, cross the Esplanade Avenue Bridge, and go to the right of the equestrian statue of General P. G. T. Beauregard. At this entrance to **City Park,** Lelong Avenue, a long oak-lined drive, leads to the museum's entrance at Collins-Diboll Circle. Behind the museum, a half circle to the right and over a bridge takes you to the park's Victory Avenue. The New Orleans Botanical Garden is on the right, and past the garden is Storyland, a children's playground. Next door is Carousel Gardens, whose star attraction is the restored 1906 merry-go-round. Driving away from Carousel Gardens, you'll see tennis courts on the left. Turn left at the end of the courts, and left again onto Dreyfous Drive. On this drive, the casino building houses a snack shop and rentals for pedalboats and canoes; fishing licenses are also issued here (you can't fish in the park without one). Turn left at the end of the road, then right onto Lelong Avenue and right again onto City Park Avenue. At I–10, City Park Avenue becomes Metairie Road. Continue on Metairie Road to the sign indicating **Long Vue House and Gardens.**

TIMING

Plan to spend a minimum of two hours each at the New Orleans Museum of Art and Longue Vue House and Gardens. Both facilities hold treasures and should not be glossed over. A tour of the Pitot House takes about an hour. As for City Park, you can do a drive-through in a half hour or so, but this is a place to return time and again, for golfing, tennis, fishing, canoeing, and riding the carousel.

Sights to See

City Park. With 1,500 luxuriant acres, this is one of the nation's largest urban parks. You can spend a great deal of time simply admiring the lagoons and majestic live oaks, whose gnarled branches bow and scrape to Mother Earth. But there is plenty to keep you busy if you are not an idler. There are four 18-hole golf courses, a double-deck driving range, 39 lighted courts in the Wisner Tennis Center, baseball diamonds, stables, and the New Orleans Botanical Garden. The latter has a tropical conservatory, a water-lily pond, a formal rose garden, and azalea and camellia gardens. At the casino on Dreyfous Avenue you can rent bikes, boats, and canoes—or just have a bite to eat. Storyland, a children's playground, has puppet shows, talking storybooks, story-book exhibits, and storytelling. Next door, Carousel Gardens has the Last Carousel, a restored 1906 merry-go-round replete with wooden horses, zebras, and other exotic creatures. Unfortunately, City Park is not safe at night. ⊠ *Main entrance at Lelong Ave.,* ☎ *504/482–4888. Botanical Garden:* ▩ *$3.* ☉ *Tues.–Sun. 10–4:30. Storyland:* ▩ *$1.50.* ☉ *Daily 10–4:30. Carousel Gardens:* ▩ *$1, rides $1.* ☉ *Wed.–Fri. 10–2:30, weekends 11–5:30.*

★ **Longue Vue House and Gardens.** Right on the border between Orleans and Jefferson parishes, the elegant estate was patterned after the great country manor houses of England. Once a private home, it is now a museum of decorative arts, furnished with European and Oriental antiques. The house sits on 8 acres of landscaped gardens. ⊠ *7 Bamboo Rd.,* ☎ *504/488–5488.* ▩ *$7.* ☉ *Mon.–Sat. 10–4:30, Sun. 1–5; last tour 45 mins before closing.*

OFF THE
BEATEN PATH

LOUISIANA NATURE AND SCIENCE CENTER – You can get a good in-town look at the surrounding swamps and bayous at this facility. There are nature trails, a children's discovery center, an interpretive center, and a planetarium. To reach it from City Park, take I–10 East toward Slidell to Exit 244 (Read Boulevard) and turn right. At the third traffic light on Read Boulevard, turn left onto Nature Center Boulevard, which dead-ends at the facility. ⊠ *11000 Lake Forest Blvd. (E. New Orleans),* ☎ *504/246–5672.* ▩ *$4.* ☉ *Tues.–Fri. 9–5, Sat. 10–5, Sun. noon–5.*

New Orleans Museum of Art (NOMA). Housed in a white neoclassical building, this facility is large enough for the exhibition of virtually all of the museum's vast collections of Italian paintings from the 13th to 18th centuries, 20th-century European and American paintings and sculptures, Chinese jades, and the imperial treasures by Peter Carl Fabergé. ⊠ *City Park at 1 Collins Diboll Circle,* ☎ *504/488–2631.* ▩ *$6; free to LA residents with valid ID Thurs. 10–noon.* ☉ *Tues.–Sun. 10–5.*

Pitot House. This charming West Indies–style house was built in the late 18th century and bought in 1810 by New Orleans mayor James Pitot as a country home. It is furnished with Louisiana and other American 19th-century antiques. ⊠ *1440 Moss St.,* ☎ *504/482–0312.* ▩ *$3.* ☉ *Wed.–Sat. 10–3; last tour at 2:15; sometimes closed Sat.*

Anne Rice's New Orleans

The eccentric charm and mystique of New Orleans have inspired many great fiction writers, but none has even approached the colossal commercial success enjoyed by Anne Rice. Her occult classics have spawned a cottage industry within New Orleans's tourist trade as devoted readers seek to retrace the steps of her characters. Fans sporting vampire garb with pale makeup and black lipstick are just part of the scenery in this city with a penchant for pageantry. True diehards hang out in front of Rice's house waiting for a glimpse of their idol. Even if you eschew fangs and cape, the following tips may enhance your visit to the land of red beans and Rice. Each site appears in Rice's books and/or the 1994 film version of *Interview with the Vampire,* or relates to Rice herself.

Two neighborhoods predominate in Rice's writing set in New Orleans. The French Quarter, the figurative and literal center of the city, is both a bustling tourist area and a residential section. The Garden District is primarily residential, some 3 mi upstream and ½ mi or so in from the river. The French Quarter sights discussed below are best visited on foot.

The Garden District sights may be visited on foot or by car; traffic and parking are both quite manageable. Several tour companies have Garden District tours, but Anne Rice's Very Own New Orleans (☞ Guided Tours *in* New Orleans A to Z, *below*) is the only one that focuses on Garden District Rice sites per se.

Anne Rice has two ways to keep her fans updated on her busy life: her Web site is http://www.annerice.com and her phone line, on which she keeps a recorded message that she changes periodically, is 504/522–8634.

French Quarter

In the French Quarter, New Orleans's sensory barrage reaches overload. There's live music on the streets and in the nightclubs, exquisite food at some of the world's best restaurants, and a visually intoxicating array of 17th- and 18th-century architecture, both public and residential. At night these old buildings—many of which are said to be haunted—take on a mysterious air that provides a plausible backdrop for the arcane activities of Anne Rice's fictional characters.

A GOOD WALK

Start at **Gallier House** at 1132 Royal Street, a mid-19th-century mansion that is perhaps the model for the fictional home of the vampires Lestat, Louis, and Claudia in the novel *Interview with the Vampire*. From Gallier House, turn left and walk two blocks along Royal Street to **Dumaine Street,** which often appears in Rice's writing. The house at 632 Dumaine Street, also known as Madame John's Legacy, appears in *Interview with the Vampire*. In Jackson Square, Lestat had his first encounter with Raglan James in *The Tale of the Body Thief,* and Lasher first appeared here in *The Witching Hour.* In *Interview with the Vampire*, Lestat drank the blood of a priest at St. Louis Cathedral.

The upper end of the French Quarter near Canal Street has several points of interest for Rice readers. Various characters in her books dine at **Galatoire's** and **Desire Oyster Bar.** The **St. Louis Hotel** is possibly the influence for the "new Spanish hotel" featured in *Interview with the Vampire*. Dolls used in the film *Interview with the Vampire* were handmade in the Upper Quarter by Karl Boyer of Boyer Antiques and Doll Shop (⊠ 241 Chartres St., ☎ 504/522–4513); some interior footage was shot here as well.

Just outside the French Quarter are the historic and labyrinthine **St. Louis Cemeteries #1 and #2,** mentioned in both *Interview with the Vampire* and *Queen of the Damned.*

Timing. Allow a good three or four hours to take in the French Quarter sights. Anne Rice readers may well want to come for Halloween, when the author throws an annual bash that includes thousands of costumed guests. Bear in mind that New Orleans has a serious crime problem. You need to be careful strolling through the French Quarter, even during the day; at night, cemetery visits or walks, which may have special appeal for Rice readers, can be particularly dangerous. Remain alert and streetwise at all times.

SIGHTS TO SEE

Desire Oyster Bar. In *The Witching Hour,* Michael Curry and Rowan Mayfair grab a bite here, as do Aaron Lightner and Rita Mae Lonigan. ⊠ *300 Bourbon St.,* ☎ *504/586–0300.*

Dumaine Street. The French Quarter segment of Dumaine Street figures prominently in Rice's work: In *Interview with the Vampire,* a musician friend of Lestat lives there; Lestat has digs on Dumaine in *The Vampire Lestat,* as does Julien Mayfair in *Lasher.* The house at **632**

Dumaine Street, also known as Madame John's Legacy, was finished in 1789 and is notable for its elements of West Indies plantation architecture; it appears in the film *Interview with the Vampire* during a voice-over by Louis, who describes Lestat's habit of dining on entire families, one member at a time. The home is not open to the public.

Galatoire's. This is one of the best of the city's old-line restaurants (☞ Dining, *below*). Aaron Lightner and Llewelyn dine here in *The Witching Hour.* ⊠ *209 Bourbon St.,* ☎ *504/525–2021.*

Gallier House. A restored mid-19th-century mansion, this residence is reputed to be the model for the fictional home of the vampires Lestat, Louis, and Claudia, as described in *Interview with the Vampire, The Queen of the Damned,* and *The Tale of the Body Thief.* A tour of the house may help Rice readers visualize scenes from these books and daily life in old New Orleans. ⊠ *1132 Royal St.,* ☎ *504/525–5661.* 💰 *$5.* ☼ *Tours Mon.–Sat. 10:30–4 on ½ hr.*

St. Louis Cemeteries #1 and #2. These historic and labyrinthine cemeteries lie just outside the French Quarter. St. Louis Cemetery #1 is mentioned in both *Interview with the Vampire* and *Queen of the Damned*; in the latter book it is the site of Louis's empty tomb. It's easy to get lost in the cemeteries' maze of aboveground graves; for this and other security reasons, as well as maximum information, it's well worthwhile to take a guided tour (☞ Guided Tours *in* New Orleans A to Z, *below*). ⊠ *400 Basin St.,* ☎ *504/482–5065 or 504/596–3050.* ☼ *Mon.–Sat. 9–3, Sun. 9–noon.*

St. Louis Hotel. This is the reported prototype of the "new Spanish hotel" where several vivid blood-imbibing scenes unfold in *Interview with the Vampire.* For those who tire of a steady diet of crimson and claret, the hotel's restaurant **Louis XVI** serves exquisite French haute cuisine, at haute prices; if your budget allows splurging, this is a good place for it. ⊠ *730 Bienville St.,* ☎ *504/581–7300.*

Garden District

This area is the other New Orleans neighborhood most closely associated with Anne Rice's novels. Several miles upriver from the French Quarter, the Garden District is one of the most beautiful residential sections in America. This is where Anne Rice grew up; she left the city around 1957 and lived in Dallas and San Francisco before returning to her hometown in 1988.

A GOOD WALK OR DRIVE

Start at Anne Rice's house, the Greek Revival–Italianate mansion at **1239 1st Street.** Next, walk one block on 1st Street in the direction of the streetcar tracks and turn left on Coliseum Street. Go four blocks on Coliseum to Washington Avenue and **Lafayette Cemetery #1,** which plays an important part in *Interview with the Vampire.* Across the street from the cemetery is **Commander's Palace,** another site appearing in Anne Rice's work. Just down the street, at the downtown-lake corner of Washington and Prytania streets, is an upscale mini-mall known as the Rink. This is the home of the Garden District Book Shop (⊠ 2727 Prytania St., ☎ 504/895–2266), which specializes in Rice's work and is the venue for the author's first signings of her new books.

Timing. Two to three hours should be ample here. One pleasant way to make the trip is via the St. Charles Avenue streetcar, stepping off around 1st Street. As in the French Quarter, you should be alert and streetwise when walking the streets, day or night; walking around at night, especially in the Lafayette Cemetery, can be dangerous.

SIGHTS TO SEE

Commander's Palace. This landmark restaurant is one of the city's more renowned spots for elegant regional cuisine. It is also the site of various Mayfair family dinners, especially after funerals, in *The Witching Hour*. ⊠ *1403 Washington Ave.,* ☎ *504/899–8221.*

Lafayette Cemetery #1. From the gates of the cemetery, you can see the lavish aboveground vaults and tombs of the families who built the surrounding Garden District mansions. Although the gates are generally open during working hours, it is not advisable to wander among the unguarded tombs. This sight serves as the burial ground for the fictional Mayfairs in *The Witching Hour*. The cemetery is also a major setting in *Interview with the Vampire*. Claudia Feeling requests a visit there to "roam the high marble tombs" in hopes of feasting on a sleeping vagrant, while Lestat uses the graveyard as a secret hiding place for his valuables. ⊠ *1400 Washington Ave.,* ☎ *504/588–9357.* ☉ *Weekdays 7–2:30, Sat. 7–noon; closed Sun. except for Mother's Day and Father's Day.*

1239 1st Street. Aspiring writers who gaze at Anne Rice's residence, a 19th-century Greek Revival–Italianate mansion, can imagine the potential rewards of creating a best-seller. Rice readers regard it as the obvious model for the Mayfair home in *The Witching Hour*. The building is not open to the public.

OFF THE
BEATEN PATH

ST. ELIZABETH'S HOME – In Uptown New Orleans, a mile upriver from the Garden District, St. Elizabeth's Home is a 19th-century three-building complex that Anne Rice owns. Rice has her extensive doll collection on display here. The former orphanage is not usually open to the public—except to people on tours with her own tour company. ⊠ *1314 Napoleon Ave.*

Scattered Grains of Rice

Although the French Quarter and Garden District are the main centers for Rice ramblings around town, some other neighborhoods and outlying rural areas are also significant. The swamps and bayous that surround New Orleans have a distinct aura of mystery—making them ideal backdrops for such scenes as Claudia and Louis's dumping the body of Lestat—although the fictional plantation homes, such as Oak Haven, Pointe du Lac, and Riverbend are based on a number of real-life residences. In or near town, these include the Pitot House and Destrehan Plantation.

Destrehan Plantation. The 1787 West Indies–style house was one of the film locations in *Interview with the Vampire*. The plantation is 23 mi from New Orleans. (☞ Destrehan, *below.*) ⊠ *9999 River Rd. (LA 48),* ☎ *504/764–9315 or 504/524–5522.* ☜ *$6.* ☉ *Daily 9:30–4. Tours on the ½ hr.*

Madewood Plantation. Seventy miles southwest of New Orleans near Napoleonville, the impressive 21-room Greek Revival Madewood is the prototype for the Mayfair family's country home, Fontrevault in *The Witching Hour* (☞ Napoleonville, *below*). There are many other plantations up and down both sides of the river—some in idyllic settings and others butting up against oil refineries. The rural roads that lead to them are perfect for unloading those pesky corpses you've been lugging around. ⊠ *4250 Hwy. 308, Napoleonville,* ☎ *800/375–7151.* ☜ *$6.* ☉ *Daily 10–5.*

Oak Alley. Some 60 mi up and across the river near the town of Vacherie, this grand 1839 home was used as a film location in *Inter-*

view with the Vampire. (☞ *Vacherie, below.*) ⊠ *3645 Hwy. 18, Vacherie,* ☎ *800/442–5539.* ☞ *$7.* ☉ *Daily 9–5, tours on the hr and ½ hr.*

Pitot House. This late 18th-century West Indian cottage on Bayou St. John inspired Louis's Pointe du Lac in *Interview with the Vampire.* ⊠ *1440 Moss St.,* ☎ *504/482–0312.* ☞ *$3.* ☉ *Wed.–Sat. 10–3. Final tour begins at 2.*

Dining

By Gene Bourg

New Orleans usually means excellent dining. The Big Easy is recognized almost as much for zestily seasoned culinary delights as it is for hot and steamy jazz. Louisiana styles of cooking are becoming increasingly popular worldwide—but what is a fad elsewhere is a tradition here.

New Orleans is most renowned for Creole cuisine. A Creole, by definition, is a person of French or Spanish ancestry born in the New World. However, Creole is also a word of elastic implications, and in culinary terms, Creole refers to a distinctive cuisine indigenous to New Orleans with roots in European, African, and Caribbean dishes, enhanced by the liberal usage of local seasonings such as cayenne pepper and filé. The French influence is also strong, but the essence of Creole is in sauces, herbs, and the prominent use of seafood.

In recent years the term "Nouvelle Creole" has been popularized by local restaurateurs. Instead of gumbo or jambalaya, a nouvelle menu might include hickory-grilled items, seafood served with pasta, or smoked meats and fish. There has also been a strong Italian influence in Creole cuisine, creating yet another marriage of styles.

The initial restaurant listings here are divided into four Creole categories: Classic Creole, restaurants devoted to traditional Louisiana cuisine with minimal French overtones; French Creole, indicating a more expansive Continental accent; Soul Creole, black cuisine of Creole origin; and Creole-inspired, meaning the newer breed of cooking styles that incorporate Nouvelle Creole dishes, new American cooking, and classic Creole. Please note that the above categories often overlap; it is not unusual to find a blend of varying Creole cuisines on any given menu.

Cajun cuisine evolved from the farmhouse cooking brought from Nova Scotia to the bayou country by the Acadians more than 200 years ago, along with influences from the same French, African, Caribbean, and Spanish settlers who influenced Creole cookery. Cajun cooks generally use less expensive ingredients than their Creole counterparts, and they rely heavily on pork, game, and wild fowl. Cajun cuisine is rarely served in its purest form in New Orleans; rather it is often blended with Creole to create what's known as "New Orleans–style" cooking. There is a difference, though, between the two: Creole is distinguished by its classical French-inspired sauces; Cajun, by its tendency to be hearty and rustic.

The following terms will appear frequently throughout this section:

Andouille (an-dooey)—a smoked Cajun sausage made with pork blade meat, onion, garlic, and other seasonings.

Bananas Foster—a dessert of bananas sautéed with butter, brown sugar, and cinnamon, flambéed in white rum and banana liqueur, and served on ice cream.

Barbecue shrimp—large shrimp baked in the shell, covered with butter, rosemary, herbs, and spices. They are not barbecued at all.

Boudin (boo-dan)—hot, spicy pork with onions, rice, and herbs stuffed in sausage casing.

Court-bouillon (coo-bee-yon)—a thick, hearty soup made with a roux, vegetables, and fish, and served over rice.

Crawfish—also known as "mud-bugs," because in the wild state they live in the mud of freshwater streams. They resemble miniature lobsters and are served in a great variety of ways.

Étouffée (ay-too-fay)—crawfish étouffée is made with crawfish "fat" (actually, the liver), celery, and onion, then cooked for a short period of time and served over rice. Shrimp étouffée is heartier, made with an oil-and-flour roux or tomato paste, celery, onion, bell pepper, tomatoes, and chicken stock, cooked for approximately an hour and served over rice.

Filé (fee-lay)—ground sassafras, used to season gumbo and many other Creole and Cajun specialties.

Grillades (gree-yads)—bite-size pieces of veal rounds or beef chuck, braised in red wine, beef stock, garlic, herbs, and seasoning, served for breakfast with grits and with rice for dinner.

Gumbo—a hearty soup prepared in a variety of combinations (okra gumbo, shrimp gumbo, chicken gumbo, to name a few).

Jambalaya (jum-bo-lie-yah)—a spicy rice dish cooked with stock and chopped seasoning, and made with any number of ingredients including sausage, shrimp, ham, and chicken.

Muffuletta—a large, round loaf of bread filled with cheese, ham, salami, and a garlicky olive salad.

Praline (praw-leen)—candy patty most commonly made from sugar, water or butter, and pecans. There are many different flavors and kinds.

Rémoulade—a cold dressing that accompanies shrimp (sometimes crabmeat) over shredded lettuce, traditionally made of oil, Creole mustard, vinegar, horseradish, paprika, cayenne, celery, and green onion.

Reservations

Apart from Galatoire's, where reservations are accepted only three days a week for groups of eight or more, you are strongly advised to make reservations and to book well in advance for weekends, particularly during holiday periods or conventions.

Mealtimes

Lunch hours are 11:30 AM to 2:30 PM. Dinner is almost always served from 6 to 10 PM, although some restaurants offer early-bird dinner specials for those who don't mind eating about 5:30 or 6.

The Bill

As a general rule, expect to tip from 15% to 20%. Most establishments do not automatically add a service charge. Credit cards are accepted in most, but not all, dining establishments; it's wise to check in advance.

What to Wear

Pricey restaurants adhere to a moderate dress code—jackets for men, and in some places, a tie. New Orleans is a conservative city; dining out is an honored ritual, and people are expected to dress the part. A man in faded jeans and sports coat may be turned away, and even if he isn't, he may not feel entirely welcome.

Louisiana Cuisine

CAJUN-INSPIRED

$$$ ✕ **K-Paul's Louisiana Kitchen.** Chef Paul Prudhomme started the blackening craze and added "Cajun" to America's culinary vocabulary in this rustic French Quarter café. Almost a decade later, thousands still consider a visit to New Orleans partly wasted without a trip to K-Paul's, where a recent, extensive renovation has added a waiting area indoors, making the once-familiar queues outside the entrance virtually extinct. One also can book a table for the chef's inventive gumbos, fried crawfish tails, blackened tuna, roast duck with rice dressing, and sweet potato–pecan pie. Although servings are generous, the prices are steep at dinner; lunch prices are more moderate. The jalapeño-laced martinis are served in canning jars. ⊠ *416 Chartres St., French Quarter,* ☎ *504/596–2530. AE. Closed Sun.–Mon.*

CLASSIC CREOLE

$$$$ ✕ **Arnaud's.** This is a grande dame of classic Creole restaurants. The main dining room's outside wall of ornate etched glass reflects light from the charming old chandeliers. When that room fills up, the overflow spills over into a labyrinth of plush banquet rooms and bars. The big, ambitious menu includes classic dishes, as well as some new, more contemporary creations. Always reliable are the cold shrimp Arnaud in a superb rémoulade, the creamy oyster stew, and rich shrimp bisque, as well as the fine crème brûlée. Expect hurried service on especially crowded nights. ⊠ *813 Bienville St., French Quarter,* ☎ *504/523–5433. Reservations essential. Jacket required. AE, D, DC, MC, V.*

$$$ ✕ **Brigtsen's.** Owner-chef Frank Brigtsen's fusion of Creole refine-
★ ment and Acadian earthiness reflects his years as a protégé of Paul Prudhomme. His ever-changing menus add up to some of the best South Louisiana cooking you'll find anywhere. Everything is fresh and filled with the deep and complex tastes that characterize Creole-Cajun food. Rabbit and chicken dishes, usually involving rich sauces and gravies, are full of robust flavor. Fish dishes are elaborate, often showing up as crawfish, shrimp, or oysters in buttery, seasoned sauces. The simple surroundings remain as they were when this was a long, narrow-frame cottage at the turn of the century, although the walls have gained charming little trompe l'oeil murals. ⊠ *723 Dante St., Uptown,* ☎ *504/ 861–7610. Reservations essential (wk or more in advance). AE, MC, V. Closed Sun.–Mon.*

$$$ ✕ **Clancy's.** Easy, sophisticated charm and a consistently classy menu have made this minimally decorated bistro a favorite with professional and business types from nearby uptown neighborhoods. Most of the dishes are imaginative treatments of New Orleans favorites. Some of them, like the fresh sautéed fish in cream sauce flavored with crawfish stock and herbs, are exceptional. Simpler dishes such as fettucine Alfredo and filet mignon in Madeira sauce benefit from careful and knowledgeable preparation. The decor is neutral, with gray walls and a few ceiling fans above bentwood chairs and white linen cloths. ⊠ *6100 Annunciation St., Uptown,* ☎ *504/895–1111. Reservations essential. AE, MC, V. Closed Sun. No lunch Mon.–Tues.*

$$$ ✕ **Gabrielle.** A bright and energetic restaurant, about five minutes by
★ taxi from the French Quarter, has remained a hit with locals thanks to chef Greg Sonnier's marvelous interpretations of earthy and spicy South Louisiana dishes. Spaces are tight, even in the recently expanded dining spaces, their pale walls hung with pleasant pastel still lifes. Regulars come for the spicy rabbit and veal sausages, buttery oysters gratinéed with artichoke and Parmesan, a slew of excellent gumbos and

étouffées, and Mary Sonnier's fresh-fruit cobblers and shortcakes. Servings are generous and sauces are rich. ⊠ *3201 Esplanade Ave., Mid-City,* ☎ *504/948–6233. AE, DC, MC, V. Closed Sun.–Mon. No lunch Tues.–Thurs. and Sat.*

$$ ✕ **Mandich's.** This many-faceted locals' favorite resists categorizing. It occupies a neat but unremarkable building in a blue-collar neighborhood. The decor—a mix of bright yellow paint, captain's chairs, and wood veneer—won't win prizes. The food ranges from straightforward and home-style to ambitious trout and shellfish dishes. Fried oysters are swathed in a finely balanced butter sauce with garlic and parsley. The breaded trout Mandich has become a classic of the genre. Prices are steep for a restaurant that invests little in decoration, accepts no reservations, and opens for dinner only two nights a week. ⊠ *3200 St. Claude Ave., Ninth Ward,* ☎ *504/947–9533. MC, V. Closed Sun.–Mon. No dinner Tues.–Thurs.; no lunch Sat.*

CREOLE-INSPIRED

$$$$ ✕ **Emeril's.** For many seasoned restaurant goers in New Orleans, ★ Emeril's is the pacesetter for endlessly creative New Orleans cooking, much of it with Creole antecedents. Proprietor-chef Emeril opened this large, noisy, and decidedly contemporary restaurant in early 1990 with an ambitious menu that gives equal emphasis to Creole and modern American cooking. On the plate, this translates as a fresh corn crepe topped with Louisiana caviar, a sauté of crawfish over jambalaya cakes, and a cornucopia of other creative dishes. The looks of the place are appropriately avant-garde—brick and glass walls, gleaming wood floors, burnished-aluminum lamps, and a huge abstract-expressionist oil painting. ⊠ *800 Tchoupitoulas St., Warehouse District,* ☎ *504/528–9393. Reservations essential (at least several days in advance). AE, DC, MC, V. Closed Sun. No lunch Sat.*

$$$ ✕ **Nola.** Fans of chef Emeril Lagasse's who can't get a table at Emeril's have this sassy and vibrant French Quarter restaurant as an alternative. Lagasse has not lowered his sights with Nola's menu, as lusty and rich as any in town. He stews boudin sausage with beer, onions, cane syrup, and Creole mustard before landing it all onto a sweet-potato crouton. Trout is swathed in a horseradish-citrus crust before it's plank-roasted in a wood oven. The combinations seem endless. For dessert, go for the coconut cream or apple-buttermilk pie with cinnamon ice cream. ⊠ *534 St. Louis St., French Quarter,* ☎ *504/522–6652. AE, D, DC, MC, V. No lunch Sun.*

$$ ✕ **Mr. B's Bistro.** The energy never subsides in this attractive, smart French Quarter restaurant, with waiters darting between the wood and glass screens that reduce the vastness of the dining room. In the green vinyl banquettes, diners choose from a dependable contemporary-Creole menu centering on meats and seafood from a grill fueled with hickory and other aromatic woods. The barbecue shrimp is one of the best versions in town. Pasta dishes, especially the pasta jambalaya with andouille sausage and shrimp, are fresh and imaginative. The traditional-style bread pudding with Irish whiskey sauce is excellent, too. ⊠ *201 Royal St., French Quarter,* ☎ *504/523–2078. AE, D, DC, MC, V.*

$$ ✕ **Palace Café.** Members of the Commander's Palace branch of the Brennan family operate this big and colorful restaurant on Canal Street just a few blocks from the Mississippi riverfront. Crafted from a multistory building that was the city's oldest music store, the two-level Palace is a convivial spot to try some of the more imaginative contemporary Creole dishes. The crab chops, rabbit ravioli in sauce piquante, grilled shrimp with fettuccine, and seafood Napoleon represent the best in both traditional and modern New Orleans cookery. Desserts, especially the white-chocolate bread pudding and Mississippi mud pie, are luscious. Out

The French Quarter Dining and Lodging

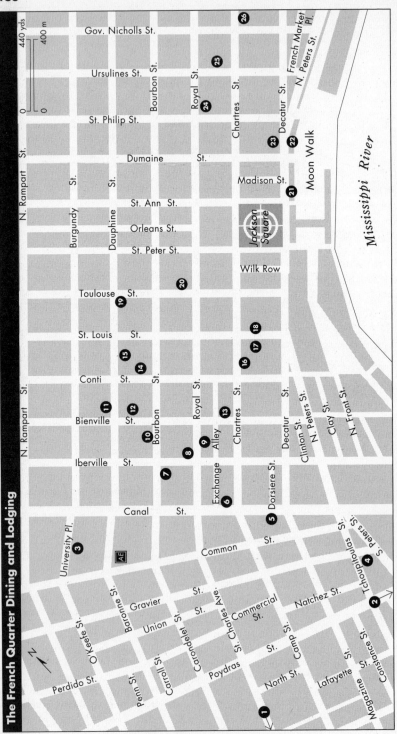

New Orleans Dining and Lodging

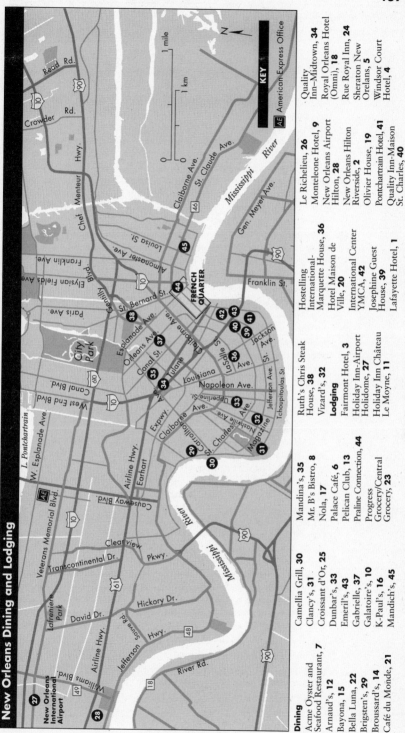

169

KEY

AE American Express Office

Dining

Acme Oyster and Seafood Restaurant, **7**
Arnaud's, **12**
Bayona, **15**
Bella Luna, **22**
Brigtsen's, **29**
Broussard's, **14**
Café du Monde, **21**
Camellia Grill, **30**
Clancy's, **31**
Croissant d'Or, **25**
Dunbar's, **33**
Emeril's, **43**
Gabrielle, **37**
Galatoire's, **10**
K-Paul's, **16**
Mandich's, **45**
Mandina's, **35**
Mr. B's Bistro, **8**
Nola, **17**
Palace Café, **6**
Pelican Club, **13**
Praline Connection, **44**
Progress Grocery/Central Grocery, **23**
Ruth's Chris Steak House, **38**
Vizard's, **32**

Lodging

Fairmont Hotel, **3**
Holiday Inn-Airport Holidome, **27**
Holiday Inn Château Le Moyne, **11**
Hostelling International-Marquette House, **36**
Hotel Maison de Ville, **20**
International Center YMCA, **42**
Josephine Guest House, **39**
Lafayette Hotel, **1**
Le Richelieu, **26**
Monteleone Hotel, **9**
New Orleans Airport Hilton, **28**
New Orleans Hilton Riverside, **2**
Olivier House, **19**
Pontchartrain Hotel, **41**
Quality Inn-Maison St. Charles, **40**
Quality Inn-Midtown, **34**
Royal Orleans Hotel (Omni), **18**
Rue Royal Inn, **24**
Sheraton New Orleans, **5**
Windsor Court Hotel, **4**

front, the sidewalk tables are an excellent vantage point for people-watching. ⊠ *605 Canal St., Central Business District,* ☎ *504/523–1661. AE, DC, MC, V.*

FRENCH CREOLE

$$$ ✕ **Broussard's.** No French Quarter restaurant surpasses Broussard's for old-fashioned spectacle. A complete overhaul in the 1970s turned a dowdy Creole bistro into a soft-edged, glittery mix of elaborate wall coverings, chandeliers, porcelain, and polished woods, with a manicured courtyard to boot. If the menu blazes no trails, it contains respectable renditions of the fancier Creole standbys further upgraded with Continental touches. The savory cheesecake of crab and shrimp with dill and roasted sweet peppers is a star among the appetizers, along with lumps of backfin crab in a spicy sauce. Other luxurious sauces crown fillets of fresh pompano, braised quail, and a rack of lamb. ⊠ *819 Conti St., French Quarter,* ☎ *504/581–3866. AE, D, DC, MC, V. No lunch Sat.–Thurs.*

$$ ✕ **Galatoire's.** Almost as old as the century, this restaurant seems as fresh as it was at 20, epitomizing the old-style French-Creole bistro. The lengthy menu is filled with sauces that can be humdrum in lesser restaurants but somehow escape staleness in this one. Fried oysters and bacon en brochette court excess but are worth every calorie. Lumps of crabmeat, served either cold in a seasoned mayonnaise or warm atop buttery broiled pompano, never tasted better. The setting is close to perfect—a single, narrow dining room lit with glistening brass chandeliers, swathed in white-framed mirror panels, and bordered with polished brass coat hooks. Reservations are accepted for groups of eight or more on Tuesday, Wednesday, and Thursday. On other days, a long line outside sometimes can be avoided by eating early. ⊠ *209 Bourbon St., French Quarter,* ☎ *504/525–2021. Jacket required at dinner. AE, MC, V. Closed Mon.*

SOUL CREOLE

$ ✕ **Dunbar's.** Red tufted booths and homey, brightly colored paintings perk up the atmosphere at this diamond-in-the-rough, where home-style Creole cooking is king. Owner-chef Tina Dunbar's fried chicken takes a backseat to none other, and her stuffed sweet peppers, red beans, fried-seafood po'boys, and mustard greens are state-of-the-art as well. Prices are the next best thing to free, and students who produce ID cards get free iced tea. You're not likely to spend more than $5 or $6 for a very filling dinner here, and substantial breakfasts can be had for about $2. Table service is rudimentary at best. ⊠ *4927 Freret St., Uptown,* ☎ *504/899–0734. Reservations not accepted. MC, V.*

$ **Praline Connection.** Down-home, the Southern-Creole–style cooking
★ is the forte of this laid-back and likeable restaurant a couple of blocks from the French Quarter (there's a branch in the Warehouse District, too). The food is the no-nonsense kind that has fueled generations of Southern families urban and rural, rich and poor. The fried or stewed chicken, smothered pork chops, barbecued ribs, and collard greens are definitively done. Add to this some of the lowest prices anywhere, a congenial service staff, and a neat-as-a-pin dining room and the sum is a fine place to spend an hour or two. ⊠ *542 Frenchmen St., Faubourg Marigny,* ☎ *504/943–3934;* ⊠ *901 S. Peters St., Warehouse District,* ☎ *504/523–3973. MC, V. Closed Sun. No lunch Sat.*

Avant-Garde

$$$$ ✕ **Bella Luna.** If luxurious surroundings, imaginative food, and a knockout view of the Mississippi River are high on your list, this elegantly turned-out restaurant in the French Market complex should fill the bill. Handsome French-style windows line one wall in the plush main dining room, offering overhead views of the riverbank and the ships and excursion boats gliding by. The second dining space is enclosed on three sides by even more glass. The kitchen takes an eclectic approach, although the strongest accent is Italian. Good bets are the pastas. The robust osso buco is a straightforward delight. ⊠ *French Market complex, near corner of Decatur and Dumaine Sts., French Quarter,* ☎ *504/529–1583. AE, DC, MC, V. No lunch.*

$$$ ✕ **Bayona.** "New World" is the label chef Susan Spicer applies to her
★ cooking style—such dishes as turnovers filled with spicy crawfish tails; a bisque of corn, leeks, and chicken; or fresh salmon fillet in white-wine sauce with sauerkraut. These and myriad other imaginative dishes are served in an early 19th-century Creole cottage on a quiet French Quarter street. The chef herself supervised the renovation of the handsome building, fairly glowing with oversize flower arrangements, elegant photographs, and, in one small dining room, trompe l'oeil murals suggesting Mediterranean landscapes. ⊠ *430 Dauphine St., French Quarter,* ☎ *504/525–4455. Reservations essential. AE, DC, MC, V. Closed Sun.*

$$$ ✕ **Pelican Club.** Sassy New York flourishes are found throughout the
★ menu of this smartly decorated but eminently comfortable place in the heart of the French Quarter. Chef Richard Hughes spent seven years in Manhattan as the top chef of the acclaimed Memphis, but evidence of his South Louisiana origins also keeps popping up. In three handsome dining rooms inside a balconied old town house, he turns out a stew of shellfish that's a clever improvisation on both San Francisco's cioppino and Louisiana's bouillabaisse. A touch of saffron in his jambalaya of chicken, sausage, and shellfish makes it a cousin of Spain's paella. Closer to home are red snapper stuffed with crabmeat and a bisque of bourbon, crab, and corn. ⊠ *615 Bienville St., French Quarter,* ☎ *504/523–1504. AE, D, DC, MC, V. No lunch.*

$$ ✕ **Vizard's.** This newcomer to the Uptown section's bustling Magazine Street has quickly become a neighborhood favorite, for its comfortably uncluttered atmosphere and owner-chef Kevin Vizard's moderate-size but always engaging menu. Beyond the antique, stained-wood bar against the far wall, white-clothed tables hold modern treatments of such longtime local favorites as duck roasted with thyme, skewers of fried oysters and prosciutto ham with sage on toast points, and filet mignon with fried oysters. The wine list's modest size (and pricing) is offset by its selectivity and interesting varietals from small California wineries. ⊠ *5538 Magazine St., Uptown,* ☎ *504/895–5000. D, DC, MC, V. Closed Sun.–Mon. No lunch.*

Back to Basics

DESSERT

$ ✕ **Croissant d'Or.** Locals compete with tourists for a table in this col-
★ orful and pristine pastry shop that serves excellent and authentic French croissants, pies, tarts, and custards, as well as an imaginative selection of soups, salads, and sandwiches. Wash them down with real French breakfast coffee, cappuccino, or espresso. In good weather, the cheerful courtyard, with its quietly gurgling fountain, is the place to sit. A filling lunch can be had for less than $10. ⊠ *617 Ursulines St., French Quarter,* ☎ *504/524–4663. No credit cards.*

GRILLS AND COFFEE SHOPS

$ ✕ **Café du Monde.** For most visitors, a cup of chicory-laced café au
★ lait and a few sugar-dusted beignets in this venerable Creole institution are essential to their trip to New Orleans. The dozens of tables, inside or out in the open air, are jammed at almost any hour with locals and tourists feasting on the views of Jackson Square and the hubbub on Decatur Street. The magical time to go is just before dawn, when

the bustle subsides and you can almost hear the birds in the crepe myrtles across the way. ⊠ *French Market, Decatur and St. Ann Sts., French Quarter,* ☎ *504/525–4544. No credit cards.*

$ ✕ **Camellia Grill.** Every diner should be as classy as Camellia Grill, a
★   one-of-a-kind eatery that deserves its following. Locals vie until early morning hours for one of the 29 stools at the gleaming counter, each place supplied with a large, fresh linen napkin. The hamburger—four ounces of excellent beef on a fresh bun with any number of embellishments—is unsurpassed in the city. Other blue-ribbon dishes are the chili, the fruit and meringue pies, the garnished omelets, and the "cannibal special"—uncooked hamburger and egg with chopped onion on rye. Everything's made on the premises and served by bow-tied, white-waistcoated waiters with the fastest feet in the business. ⊠ *626 S. Carrollton Ave., Uptown,* ☎ *504/866–9573. No credit cards.*

$ ✕ **Progress Grocery and Central Grocery.** These two old-fashioned Italian grocery stores in the French Quarter produce authentic muffulettas, one of the greatest gastronomic gifts of the city's Italian immigrants. They're good enough to challenge the po'boy as the local sandwich champ, and are made by filling soft round loaves of seeded bread with ham, salami, mozzarella, and a salad of marinated chopped green olives. Each sandwich, about 10 inches in diameter, is sold in quarters and halves. Central is better known, but Progress comes up with a sandwich that many locals prefer because it's cheaper, more generous, and available in several varieties. *Progress:* ⊠ *915 Decatur St., French Quarter,* ☎ *504/525–6627.* ⊙ *Mon.–Sat. 8 AM–5:30 PM. Central:* ⊠ *923 Decatur St.,* ☎ *504/523–1620.* ⊙ *Daily 8 AM–5:30 PM.*

SEAFOOD

$ ✕ **Acme Oyster and Seafood Restaurant.** A rough-edged classic in every way, this no-nonsense eatery at the entrance to the French Quarter is a prime source of cool and salty raw oysters on the half shell; great shrimp, oyster, and roast-beef po'boys; and state-of-the-art red beans and rice. Table service is offered in the front dining room. If all tables are taken, expect lengthy queues at the marble-topped oyster bar and cafeteria-style sandwich counter. Crowds are sparser in the late afternoon. Don't expect coddling. ⊠ *724 Iberville St., French Quarter,* ☎ *504/522–5973. Reservations not accepted. AE, DC, MC, V.*

$ ✕ **Mandina's.** The interior of this white-clapboard corner building is a study in 1940s nostalgia, with its functional bar facing a roomful of laminated tables set with sugar shakers, hot sauce, and salt and pepper. Regulars—a cross section of the population—endure a ¼-hour wait for a table under a 30-year-old newspaper clipping or the latest artwork from a St. Louis brewery. Butter, hearty seasonings, and tomato sauce are the staples. The shrimp rémoulade and old-fashioned gumbo are the logical appetizers. Broiled trout and shrimp, wading in seasoned butter, are tasty, as are the fried oysters and shrimp, the seafood or Italian-sausage po'boys, and the super-sweet bread pudding. ⊠ *3800 Canal St., Mid-City,* ☎ *504/482–9179. Reservations not accepted. No credit cards.*

STEAKS

$$$ ✕ **Ruth's Chris Steak House.** Ruth's Chris is sacred to New Orleans
★   steak lovers. The all-American menu fairly drips with butter, and the main draw is aged U.S. prime beef in he-man portions, charbroiled and served atop a sizzling seasoned butter sauce. The hefty filet mignon is often taller than it is wide, the New York strip is usually packed with flavor, and a monstrous porterhouse serves several. If the salads lack sparkle, the copious potato dishes are consistently first-rate. The large plush but unfussy dining rooms of the flagship Mid-City restaurant are lined in pale wood paneling and understated landscape paintings.

Politicians, both actual and aspiring, are everywhere. ✉ *711 N. Broad St., Mid-City,* ☎ *504/486–0810;* ✉ *3633 Veterans Blvd., Metairie,* ☎ *504/888–3600. Reservations essential on weekends. AE, D, DC, MC, V.*

Lodging

Visitors to New Orleans have a wide variety of accommodations to choose from: posh high-rise hotels, antiques-filled antebellum homes, Creole cottages, or old slave quarters. Always try to reserve well ahead, especially during Mardi Gras or other seasonal events. Hotels frequently offer special packages at reduced rates, but during Mardi Gras almost every accommodation doubles its rates and many require a three- to five-day minimum stay.

Hotels

CENTRAL BUSINESS DISTRICT

Staying in the Central Business District will appeal to visitors who prefer accommodations in luxurious high-rise hotels. Hotels listed here are within walking distance of the French Quarter, but shuttles, taxis, buses, and the streetcar are available. Walking in this area after dark is not recommended.

$$$$ ⊞ **Fairmont Hotel.** The Fairmont, which is one of the oldest grand hotels in America, had a $38 million face-lift in 1996. The blue-and-gold Victorian splendor of the massive lobby evokes a more elegant and gracious era. The hotel is composed of three connected historic buildings. Special touches in every room include down pillows, terry-cloth robes, and bathroom scales. Suites have fax machines. Impressive murals depicting life in the South enliven the walls of the famed **Sazerac Bar.** The **Sazerac Restaurant** has a romantic ambience. ✉ *123 Baronne St., 70140,* ☎ *504/529–7111 or 800/527–4727,* ℻ *504/529–4775. 685 rooms, 50 suites. 3 restaurants, 2 bars, room service, pool, beauty salon, 2 tennis courts, health club, parking (fee). AE, D, DC, MC, V.*

$$$$ ⊞ **Lafayette Hotel.** This small brick dwelling has housed a Lafayette
★ Hotel ever since it was built in 1916. Special features are the handsome millwork, brass fittings, and marble baths throughout. The lobby is tiny but chic; rooms are spacious and sunny. Some have four-posters; each has cushy easy chairs and ottomans, an in-room safe, terrycloth robes, and closets with full-length mirrors; there are even books on the bookshelves. Though there's no pool, guests receive reduced admission to a nearby health club where they can swim and work out. ✉ *600 St. Charles Ave., 70130,* ☎ *504/524–4441 or 800/733–4754,* ℻ *504/523–7327. 24 rooms, 20 suites. Restaurant, no-smoking rooms, dry cleaning, laundry service, concierge, parking (fee). AE, D, DC, MC, V.*

$$$$ ⊞ **Windsor Court Hotel.** Exquisite, gracious, elegant, eminently civi-
★ lized—these words are frequently used to describe Windsor Court, but all fail to capture its wonderful quality. **Le Salon**'s scrumptious high tea is served each afternoon in the lobby. Plush carpeting, canopy and four-poster beds, stocked wet bars, marble vanities, oversize mirrors, dressing areas—all contribute to the elegance and luxury of the Windsor Court. The hotel is across from the new Canal Street casino site and four blocks from the French Quarter. ✉ *300 Gravier St., 70130,* ☎ *504/523–6000 or 800/262–2662,* ℻ *504/596–4513. 58 rooms, 266 suites. 2 restaurants, lobby lounge, pool, hot tub, sauna, steam room, health club, laundry service, parking (fee). AE, DC, MC, V.*

$$–$$$$ ⊞ **New Orleans Hilton Riverside.** The property is on the banks of the Mississippi, with Riverwalk sprawled out around it, sightseeing riverboats docked virtually at its door, the New Orleans Convention Center just down the street, and Pete Fountain's Club inside. The River Center Tennis & Racquetball Club is a handy spot for working off calories. VIPs check into the Tower suites, where a concierge looks after things, but the best views of the river are in the appropriately named Riverside section. ⊠ *Poydras St. at Mississippi River, 70140,* ☎ *504/561–0500 or 800/445–8667,* FAX *504/568–1721. 1,600 rooms, 78 suites. 4 restaurants, 4 bars, 3 lobby lounges, no-smoking floors, 2 pools, beauty salon, outdoor hot tub, massage, saunas, 8 tennis courts, aerobics, health club, jogging, racquetball, squash, nightclub, business services, parking (fee). AE, D, DC, MC, V.*

\$\$–\$\$\$\$
★ 🏨 **Sheraton New Orleans.** On Canal Street, across from the French Quarter, the Sheraton has an impressive lobby, decked out with a spiral staircase and player grand piano. A tropical atmosphere permeates its **Gazebo Lounge,** which features jazz nightly. **Café Promenade** encircles the second level. Executive rooms on the top floors come with many special amenities. The Waterbury Health Club is a superb facility. Usually bustling with conventioneers, this upscale Sheraton gets high marks for above-average rooms and top-quality service. ⊠ *500 Canal St., 70130,* ☎ *504/525–2500 or 800/325–3535,* FAX *504/492–5615. 1,100 rooms, 72 suites. 3 restaurants, bar, lobby lounge, no-smoking rooms, pool, health club, parking (fee). AE, D, DC, MC, V.*

\$\$
🏨 **Quality Inn–Midtown.** As you would expect from a Quality Inn, rooms are motel-modern. This is too far to walk but only a short drive from the French Quarter. ⊠ *3900 Tulane Ave., 70119,* ☎ *504/486–5541 or 800/228–5151,* FAX *504/561–5858. 102 rooms. Restaurant, bar, no-smoking rooms, pool, airport shuttle. AE, D, DC, MC, V.*

FRENCH QUARTER

Most people who visit New Orleans stay in the Quarter, and the 96-square-block area abounds with every type of guest accommodation. The selections that follow are all quality establishments chosen to provide variety in location, atmosphere, and price. Reservations are usually a must.

\$\$\$\$
★ 🏨 **Monteleone Hotel.** The grande dame—and oldest hotel—of the Quarter, with its ornate Baroque facade, liveried doormen, and shimmering lobby chandeliers, was built in 1886 and had a multimillion dollar face-lift at age 110. Rooms are extra large and luxurious, each decorated differently. Fabrics are rich, and there is a mix of four-posters, brass-frame beds, and beds with traditional headboards. Junior suites have a spacious combo bedroom and living room; for extra pampering, stay in one of the opulent VIP suites. Some bathrooms are too small, but many have phones. The exercise room and pool are on the roof. The lobby's slowly revolving **Carousel Bar** is a New Orleans landmark. ⊠ *214 Royal St., 70140,* ☎ *504/523–3341 or 800/535–9595,* FAX *504/528–1019. 600 rooms, 35 suites. 3 restaurants, 2 bars, pool, barbershop, beauty salon, exercise room, concierge, business services, meeting rooms. AE, DC, MC, V.*

\$\$\$–\$\$\$\$
★ 🏨 **Hotel Maison de Ville.** This small, romantic hotel lies in seclusion amid the hustle and bustle of the French Quarter. Tapestry-covered chairs, a fire burning in the sitting room, and antiques-furnished rooms all contribute to a 19th-century atmosphere. Some rooms are in former slave quarters in the courtyard; others are on the upper floors of the main house. The Continental breakfast is served with a rose on a silver tray, either in your room, in the parlor, or on the patio. Other meals can be enjoyed at **Le Bistro.** Visitors who seek a special hideaway will love the fully equipped Audubon cottages—in a private, enclosed area, with statuary and individual patios—two blocks from the hotel. ⊠ *727 Toulouse St., 70130,* ☎ *504/561–5858 or 800/634–1600,* FAX *504/528–*

9939. *14 rooms, 2 suites, 7 cottages. Restaurant, pool at cottage location, parking (fee). AE, D, MC, V.*

$$$–$$$$
★ 🏨 **Royal Orleans Hotel (Omni).** Though it was built in 1960, this elegant, white-marble hotel re-creates an aura that reigned in New Orleans more than a century ago. Rooms, though not large, are well appointed with marble baths (telephone in each) and more marble on dressers and tabletops. Balcony rooms cost the most. The well-known **Rib Room Restaurant** makes its home on the lobby level. ⊠ *621 St. Louis St., 70140,* ☎ *504/529–5333 or 800/843–6664,* 𝖥𝖠𝖷 *504/529–7089. 350 rooms, 16 suites. Restaurant, 2 bars, lobby lounge, pool, barbershop, beauty salon, exercise room, parking (fee). AE, D, DC, MC, V.*

$$–$$$$
★ 🏨 **Le Richelieu.** Here the friendly, personal atmosphere of a small hotel is accented with such luxury touches as generous bath-amenity packages and hair dryers—and mostly at a moderate rate. Some rooms have mirrored walls and walk-in closets, many have refrigerators, and all have brass ceiling fans. Luxury suites (like the one Paul McCartney stayed in while cutting a record in New Orleans) are also available. An intimate bar and café off the courtyard has tables on the terrace by the pool. ⊠ *1234 Chartres St., 70116,* ☎ *504/529–2492 or 800/535–9653,* 𝖥𝖠𝖷 *504/524–8179. 69 rooms, 17 suites. Restaurant, bar, pool, free parking. AE, D, DC, MC, V.*

$$–$$$$
🏨 **Olivier House.** The entrance of this small hotel, in two 1836 town houses, contains an enormous mirror in a carved frame and chandeliers that are original to the house. Room design and decor vary; some rooms have lofts, many have complete kitchens with microwaves; gas-burning fireplaces and a comfortable mix of antiques and traditional decor are found throughout. Some rooms have a tropical feeling, with wicker furnishings and sunny colors. Pets are welcome and could perhaps be entertained by the noisy birds that inhabit the two tropical plant–filled courtyards. Don't expect a spic-and-span luxury hotel; in this family-owned and -operated charmer, the homey, casual atmosphere is the thing. ⊠ *828 Toulouse St., 70112,* ☎ *504/525–8456,* 𝖥𝖠𝖷 *504/529–2006. 42 rooms. Pool. AE, D, DC, MC, V.*

$$–$$$
★ 🏨 **Holiday Inn Château Le Moyne.** Old World atmosphere and decor pervade; eight suites occupy Creole cottages off a tropical courtyard. Here you'll find the familiar Holiday Inn standards, basic and clean, along with a good dose of French Quarter ambience in the structural decor. ⊠ *301 Dauphine St., 70112,* ☎ *504/581–1303 or 800/465–4329,* 𝖥𝖠𝖷 *504/523–5709. 160 rooms, 11 suites. Restaurant, bar, pool. AE, D, DC, MC, V.*

$$–$$$
🏨 **Rue Royal Inn.** This circa-1850 home has balcony rooms overlooking a courtyard and Royal Street. Some rooms have kitchenettes, and two suites have whirlpool baths. Great location is the main appeal. ⊠ *1006 Royal St., 70116,* ☎ *504/524–3900 or 800/776–3901,* 𝖥𝖠𝖷 *504/558–0566. 17 rooms. AE, D, DC, MC, V.*

GARDEN DISTRICT/UPTOWN

The Garden District, lined with magnificent mansions, is one of the city's ritziest residential areas. It's five minutes from the CBD via St. Charles Streetcar.

$$–$$$$
★ 🏨 **Pontchartrain Hotel.** Maintaining the grand tradition is the hallmark of this quiet, elegant European-style hotel that has reigned on St. Charles Avenue for more than 60 years. Accommodations range from lavish sun-filled suites to small pensione-style rooms with showers. The internationally known **Caribbean Room** provides memorable dining. ⊠ *2031 St. Charles Ave., 70140,* ☎ *504/524–0581 or 800/777–6193,* 𝖥𝖠𝖷 *504/529–1165. 60 rooms, 42 suites. 2 restaurants, piano bar, concierge, parking (fee). AE, D, DC, MC, V.*

$$ ⊞ **Josephine Guest House.** In this restored Italianate mansion, built
★ in 1870, European antiques fill the rooms and Oriental rugs cover gleam-
ing hardwood floors. Four rooms and a parlor are in the main house;
there are two smaller but still spacious rooms in the garçonnière (quar-
ters where the original owners' sons stayed). The bathrooms are im-
pressive in both size and decor. A complimentary Creole breakfast of
orange juice, café au lait, and homemade biscuits can be brought to
your room (Wedgwood china on a silver tray) or served on the secluded
patio. ⊠ *1450 Josephine St., 70130, 1 block from St. Charles Ave.,* ☎
504/524–6361 or 800/779–6361, ℻ *504/523–6484. 6 rooms. AE,
D, DC, MC, V.*

$$ ⊞ **Quality Inn–Maison St. Charles.** This lovely property consists of five
★ historic buildings along St. Charles Avenue set amid well-kept grounds.
Rooms here are larger than average, and the hotel is conveniently located on the St. Charles streetcar line. ⊠ *1319 St. Charles Ave., 70130,*
☎ *504/522–0187 or 800/831–1783,* ℻ *504/525–2218. 112 rooms,
20 suites. Restaurant, bar, no-smoking rooms, pool, hot tub, parking
(fee). AE, D, DC, MC, V.*

KENNER/AIRPORT

$$–$$$ ⊞ **New Orleans Airport Hilton & Conference Center.** This sleek, mod-
ern facility is directly opposite the New Orleans International Airport.
The upmarket hotel, whose guest list has included former president
Ronald Reagan, offers spacious, sunny rooms. ⊠ *901 Airline Hwy.,
Kenner 70062,* ☎ *504/469–5000 or 800/445–8667,* ℻ *504/466–5473.
317 rooms, 2 suites. Restaurant, lobby lounge, pool, tennis court, ex-
ercise room, business services, airport shuttle, free parking. AE, DC,
MC, V.*

$$ ⊞ **Holiday Inn–Airport Holidome.** Some of the motel-modern rooms
here face the dome-covered pool area, and there are plenty of other
recreational activities found on the sprawling grounds. This is a good
choice for families. ⊠ *2929 Williams Blvd., Kenner 70062,* ☎ *504/
467–5611 or 800/465–4329,* ℻ *504/469–4915. 302 rooms, 1 suite.
Restaurant, lobby lounge, indoor pool, hot tub, sauna, exercise room,
airport shuttle, free parking. AE, D, DC, MC, V.*

Hostels

$ ⊞ **Hostelling International–Marquette House, New Orleans.** Formerly
called Marquette House, this is the fourth-largest youth hostel in the
country. Budget-priced rooms are very simple but clean. There are two
equipped community kitchens open to guest use, lockers, and a gar-
den patio with picnic tables. ⊠ *2253 Carondelet St., 70130,* ☎ *504/
523–3014,* ℻ *504/529–5933. 160 dorm beds, 5 private rooms with
shared bath, 12 apartments with private bath. Dining room, 2 lobby
lounges, coin laundry. AE, MC, V.*

$ ⊞ **International Center YMCA.** Accommodations (for both men and
women) are spartan, though rooms have color TVs, and guests have
free use of the excellent health club. The St. Charles streetcar line is
nearby. For a ringside view of the Mardi Gras parade, reserve a room
on the St. Charles Avenue side (several months in advance). ⊠ *920 St.
Charles Ave., 70130,* ☎ *504/568–9622,* ℻ *504/568–9622, ext. 268.
50 rooms with shared baths. Restaurant, indoor pool, health club, park-
ing (fee). MC, V.*

Mardi Gras

North America's biggest bash takes place in February or March (the
date depends upon when Easter falls). Carnival season begins January
6 (Twelfth Night) and ends at midnight of Fat Tuesday, with the ad-
vent of Ash Wednesday and Lent. Mardi Gras means giant and fan-

tastic floats rolling through downtown streets (though not in the French Quarter), eye-popping costumes, and the occasional exposed body parts. The last great push of the Carnival season is the weekend before Fat Tuesday (Mardi Gras Day), when parades roll day and night and the city is given over to flat-out partying.

Nightlife and the Arts

Nightlife

New Orleans is a 24-hour town, meaning that there are no legal closing times and it ain't over till it's over. Last call, especially on Bourbon Street, depends on how business is. Your best bet is to phone ahead before tooling out to bar-hop at 2 AM. It is also smart to ask ahead about current credit-card policy, cover, and minimum.

Gambit, the free weekly newspaper, has a complete listing of who's doing what where. Things can change between press and performance times, so if there's an artist you're especially eager to hear, it's wise to call and confirm before turning up.

BARS

With imbibing a favorite local pastime, New Orleans is loaded, so to speak, with good bars. The French Quarter has at least one in every block; touristy Bourbon Street is lined with bars of every sort, from oyster to bottomless. The University section, around Loyola and Tulane, is also a great place for bar-hopping.

One of the world's best-known bars and not incidentally home of the Hurricane (a sweetly potent concoction of rum and fruit juices) is **Pat O'Brien's** (⊠ 718 St. Peter St., ☎ 504/525–4823). There are three bars, including a lively piano bar and a large courtyard bar, and mobs of collegians and tourists line up to get in. Very lively, very loud, very late. The **Napoleon House** (⊠ 500 Chartres St., ☎ 504/524–9752), with sepia walls, taped classical music, and Napoleonic memorabilia, is a favored local haunt. **Lafitte's Blacksmith Shop** (⊠ 941 Bourbon St., ☎ 504/523–0066), in a tattered 18th-century cottage, has been a hangout for artists and writers for ages.

CASINOS

Virtually everything regarding gambling in New Orleans is a crapshoot, and the situation changes almost moment-to-moment. At press time, the riverboat casinos listed below were operating; each is open 24 hours daily, and has a lounge and/or grill, live music, plus slots, video poker, and gaming tables for roulette, craps, blackjack, and big six.

Belle of Orleans (⊠ 1 Stars & Stripes Blvd., ☎ 504/248–3200 or 800/ 572–2559) is on Lake Pontchartrain adjacent to Lakefront Airport. **Boomtown Belle Casino** (⊠ 4132 Peters Rd., on the Harvey Canal, Westbank, ☎ 504/366–7711 or 800/366–7711) has a Wild West theme. **Flamingo** (⊠ Poydras St. Wharf, behind Hilton Hotel, ☎ 504/587– 7777; 800/587–5825 outside New Orleans) is the closest floating casino to the French Quarter and the CBD. **Treasure Chest** (⊠ 5050 Williams Blvd., Kenner, ☎ 504/443–8000 or 800/298–0711) is docked on Lake Pontchartrain, across from the Pontchartrain Center. In 1995 a glitzy entertainment complex was added.

DANCING

Two-stepping to a Cajun band is billed as the "spécialité de la maison," but the **Maple Leaf Bar** moves with rock, R&B, reggae, and gospel as well. (Cajun nights are special.) ⊠ 8316 Oak St., ☎ 504/866–9359. ☞ $5 cover. ☉ 3 PM; closing time varies.

This is New Orleans, so it shouldn't surprise you that even a bowling alley has live music. Locals flock to the **Mid-City Lanes Rock-N-Bowl** to dance to homegrown bands. ✉ *4133 S. Carrollton Ave.,* ☎ *504/ 482–3133.* 🎟 *$5.* ◷ *Fri.–Tues. noon–midnight, Wed.–Thurs. noon– 2 AM.*

JAZZ

Jazz was born in New Orleans, and the music isn't always at night. Weekend jazz brunches are enormously popular and pop up all over town. But a stroll down Bourbon Street will give you a taste of the city's eclectic rhythms—Cajun, gutbucket, R&B, rock, ragtime, New Wave— you name it, and you'll hear it almost around the clock.

Aboard the ***Creole Queen*** you'll cruise on the river with a Dixieland jazz band, and there's a buffet to boot. If you've an ounce of romance racing through your veins, do it. ✉ *Poydras St. Wharf,* ☎ *504/524– 0814. Daytime cruise:* 🎟 *$14.* ◷ *Daily 10:30 and 2. Dinner cruise:* 🎟 *$39.* ◷ *8–10, boards 7–8.*

There's live music five nights a week at the **Palm Court Jazz Cafe.** Traditional jazz is the rule, with blues thrown in on Wednesday. The fine Creole and international kitchen stays open until the music stops. ✉ *1204 Decatur St.,* ☎ *504/525–0200.* 🎟 *$4 cover to sit at the tables, free at the bar.* ◷ *7–11 PM; live music Wed., Thurs., and Sun. at 8 PM; Fri.–Sat. at 7 PM. Closed Mon.–Tues.*

Pete Fountain's Club is a New Orleans legend with Pete's clarinet and his band that plays in a plush 500-seat room on the third floor of the Hilton Hotel. This is Pete's home base, and the man's on the stand Tuesday, Wednesday, Friday, and Saturday when he's in town (he makes frequent appearances around the country, so it's wise to call ahead). ✉ *2 Poydras St.,* ☎ *504/523–4374.* 🎟 *$19 cover.* ◷ *Shows daily 10 PM–11:15 PM.*

Speaking of legends, the old-time jazz greats lay out the best traditional jazz in the world in a musty, funky hall that's short on comfort, long on talent. **Preservation Hall** is the place for traditional jazz. You may have to stand in line to get in (and it's often standing-room-only inside), but it will help if you get here about 7:30. ✉ *726 St. Peter St.,* ☎ *504/522–2841.* 🎟 *$4 cover.* ◷ *Daily 7:30 PM–midnight.*

Rambling, rustic, and raucous **Snug Harbor** is where graybeards and undergrads get a big bang out of the likes of the Dirty Dozen, Charmaine Neville, the David Torkanowsky Trio, and Maria Muldaur. ✉ *626 Frenchmen St.,* ☎ *504/949–0696.* 🎟 *Weekdays $8–$10 cover, weekends $12–$15 cover.* ◷ *Daily 5 PM–2 AM; show times 8 and 11 PM.*

During the annual **Jazz and Heritage Festival,** held from the last weekend in April through the first weekend in May, musicians from all over the world pour in to mix it up with local talent. Called by its devotees the Jazzfest, this festival draws thousands of fans and internationally acclaimed musicians. The weekend venue is the infield of the Fair Grounds; the week in between sees music venues all over town bursting. In addition to homegrown talent such as Wynton and Branford Marsalis, Harry Connick Jr., Allen Toussaint, and the Neville Brothers, look for such luminaries as B. B. King, Al Green, and Ray Charles.

R&B, CAJUN, ROCK, NEW WAVE

Industrial-strength rock rolls out of the sound system at the **Hard Rock Cafe.** Hard Rock Hurricanes are dispensed at a guitar-shape bar, and the place is filled with rock-and-roll memorabilia. Hamburgers, salads, and steaks are served. There's no cover. ✉ *440 N. Peters St.,* ☎ *504/529–8617.* ⊘ *Weekdays 11–11, weekends 11–midnight.*

House of Blues is a $7 million music venue with an awesome sound system where local and nationally known artists perform. There's also a recording studio, restaurant, and a shop. The cover and closing time vary depending on the show. ✉ *225 Decatur St.,* ☎ *504/529–2624.* ⊘ *Restaurant daily 11–midnight; nightclub daily 8 PM, sets begin 9:30 PM.*

The college crowd raises the rafters at **Jimmy's Music Club.** The music, by national as well as local groups, is rock, New Wave, reggae, R&B, whatever. ✉ *8200 Willow St.,* ☎ *504/861–8200.* ✍ *$8–$15 cover.* ⊘ *Tues.–Sat. 9 PM, shows begin 9:30 PM; closing time varies.*

Fans of Jimmy Buffett flock to **Margaritaville Café,** where local funk and R&B acts perform, as does Buffett himself, occasionally. The cover varies. ✉ *1104 Decatur St.,* ☎ *504/592–2565.* ⊘ *Daily 11 AM, live band sets daily 2 PM, main stage weekend shows 10:30 PM; closing time varies.*

An institution, **Tipitina's** is sort of a microcosm of the Jazzfest, featuring progressive jazz, reggae, R&B, rock, New Wave, and blues. Its name comes from a song by Professor Longhair, who was posthumously awarded a Grammy for Best Traditional Blues Recording, and the place is dedicated to his memory. It's funky, mellow, and loaded with laid-back locals. ✉ *501 Napoleon Ave.,* ☎ *504/897–3943.* ✍ *$3–$10 cover.* ⊘ *Daily 5 PM; closing time varies.*

The Arts

Comprehensive listings of events can be found in the weekly newspaper *Gambit,* which is distributed free at newsstands, supermarkets, and bookstores. The Friday edition of the daily *Times-Picayune* carries a "Lagniappe" tabloid that lists weekend events. The monthly *New Orleans Magazine* also has a Calendar section. Credit-card purchases of tickets for events at the Theatre for Performing Arts, the Saenger Performing Arts Center, the Orpheum Theater, and Kiefer UNO Lakefront Arena can be made through TicketMaster (☎ 504/522–5555).

CONCERTS

Free **jazz concerts** are held on weekends during the day in Dutch Alley. Pick up a schedule at the **French Market Visitor Center** (✉ French Market at Dumaine St., ☎ 504/596–3424). The **Louisiana Philharmonic Orchestra** (☎ 504/523–6530) performs at the Orpheum Theatre (✉ 129 University Pl.).

DANCE AND OPERA

The city has no resident professional **ballet or opera** company. The **New Orleans Ballet Association** (✉ 639 Loyola Ave., 70112, ☎ 504/522–0996) and the **New Orleans Opera Association** (✉ 333 St. Charles Ave., 70112, ☎ 504/529–2278) produce performances of visiting companies. Both ballet and opera productions take place at the New Orleans Theatre for the Performing Arts in Armstrong Park.

THEATER

The avant-garde, the offbeat, and the satirical are among the theatrical offerings at **Contemporary Arts Center** (✉ 900 Camp St., ☎ 504/523–1216). At **Le Petit Théâtre du Vieux Carré** (✉ 616 St. Peter St., ☎ 504/522–9958), classics, contemporary drama, children's theater, and musicals are presented. Touring Broadway shows, dance companies, and top-name talent appear at the **Saenger Performing Arts Center** (✉ 143 N. Rampart St., ☎ 504/524–2490). The **Kiefer UNO**

Lakefront Arena (✉ 6801 Franklin Ave., ☎ 504/286–7222) is a venue for major concerts.

Outdoor Activities and Sports

Baseball

The **AAA New Orleans Zephyrs** (☎ 504/734–5155), a farm team of the Houston Astros, play ball at the 10,000-seat Zephyr Field (✉ 6000 Airline Hwy. [Hwy. 61]), near David Drive and Transcontinental Drive, in Jefferson Parish, a 15-minute drive west of New Orleans. The **University of New Orleans Privateers** take on foes at the Lakefront (☎ 504/286–7240). **Tulane Green Wave** teams play home games at the school's St. Charles Avenue campus (☎ 504/861–3661).

Basketball

The **Sugar Bowl Basketball Classic** (☎ 504/525–8573) is played in the Superdome the week preceding the annual football classic.

Biking

Rentals are available at **Bicycle Michael's** (✉ 622 Frenchmen St., ☎ 504/945–9505) at $3.50 per hour and $12.50 per day. **French Quarter Bicycles** (✉ 522 Dumaine St., ☎ 504/529–3136) has mountain bikes ($4.50 per hour, $14 and up per day), baby strollers and baby carriages ($1 per hour, $4 per day), and one wheelchair ($4.50 per hour, $14 per day) for rent.

Football

The **New Orleans Saints** (☎ 504/522–2600) play NFL games in the Superdome. Home games of **Tulane University** (☎ 504/861–3661) are played in the Dome. The annual **Sugar Bowl Football Classic** (☎ 504/525–8573) takes place in the Dome on New Year's Day. In late November the **Bayou Classic** (☎ 504/587–3663) pits Southern University against Grambling University. In 1997 the Superdome hosted the **Super Bowl** for the eighth time, more than any other city, and undoubtedly will do so again.

Horseback Riding

Cascade Stables (✉ 6500 Magazine St., ☎ 504/891–2246) has guided 45-minute trail rides, costing $20 per person, in Audubon Park.

Tennis

There are 39 courts in the **City Park Wisner Tennis Center** (✉ 1 Dreyfous Ave., in City Park, ☎ 504/483–9383). **Audubon Park** (☎ 504/895–1042) has 10 courts near Tchoupitoulas Street.

Shopping

Pralines, chicory coffee, Mardi Gras masks, vintage clothing, and jazz records are usually hot tickets for tourists (as well as for locals). The packaging of New Orleans food to go is a growing trend.

Shopping Districts

New Orleans shops string along the Mississippi all the way from the French Quarter to beyond Riverbend (at the Uptown bend in the river). The **French Quarter** is the place to search for antiques shops, art galleries, designer boutiques, bookstores, and all sorts of unique shops in all sorts of edifices. Among **Canal Place's** (✉ 333 Canal St.) lofty tenants you'll find Saks Fifth Avenue, Laura Ashley, Gucci, Brooks Brothers, and the wares of New Orleans jewelry designer **Mignon Faget**. **Riverwalk** (✉ 1 Poydras St.) is a long, tunnel-like marketplace brightened by more than 200 splashy shops, restaurants, food courts, and huge windows overlooking the Mississippi. The tony **New Orleans Centre,** between the Hyatt Regency Hotel and the Superdome on Poydras St., has more than 100 occupants, including **Macy's** and **Lord & Taylor.** Along 6 mi of **Magazine Street** are Victorian houses and small cottages filled with antiques and collectibles. Stop at the **New Orleans Welcome Center** for a copy of the shopper's guides published by the Magazine Street Merchants Association and the Royal Street Guild. Turn-of-the-century Creole cottages cradle everything from toy shops to designer boutiques and delis in the **Riverbend** (✉ Maple St. and Carrollton Ave.). **Macy's** and **Mervyn's** are among the 155 shops in Metairie's glittering three-level **Esplanade Mall** (✉ 1401 W. Esplanade Ave.). The **Warehouse District** (✉ Bounded roughly by Girod St., Howard Ave., Camp St., and the river), particularly Julia Street, has become a major center for the visual arts, not unlike New York City's SoHo.

Department Stores

Maison Blanche department store (✉ 901 Canal St., ☎ 504/566–1000) is in the CBD, with branches in the suburban shopping centers. It carries designer labels as well as full lines of appliances and home furnishings.

Specialty Stores

ANTIQUES

Shoulder to shoulder along **Royal Street** are some of the finest—and oldest—antiques stores in New Orleans. **Adler & Waldhorn** (✉ 343 Royal St., ☎ 504/581–6379), the city's oldest antiques store, was established in 1881; specialties are English furniture, Victorian and Early American jewelry, and antique English porcelain and silver. **French Antique Shop** (✉ 225 Royal St., ☎ 504/524–9861) has a large selection of European chandeliers and furniture, as well as some Creole and local designs. **Lucullus** (✉ 610 Chartres St., ☎ 504/528–9620) carries fine Continental and English 17th- to 19th-century furniture, art, and cookware. **Manheim Galleries** (✉ 403–409 Royal St., ☎ 504/568–1901) has the city's largest collection of antique English, Continental, and Asian furnishings; porcelains; paintings; silver; and jade. This is the agent for Boehm Birds. **Moss Antiques** (✉ 411 Royal St., ☎ 504/522–3981) has a large selection of antique and estate jewels, as well as fine French and English furnishings, paintings, and bric-a-brac. **Patout Antiques** (✉ 920 Royal St., ☎ 504/522–0582) has high-quality antiques from Louisiana plantation houses. **Rothschild's Antiques** (✉ 241 Royal St., ☎ 504/523–5816; ✉ 321 Royal St., ☎ 504/523–2281) has a large collection of furniture, silver, jewelry, mantels, and clocks from the 18th through the 20th centuries. **Whisnant Galleries** (✉ 222 Chartres St., ☎ 504/524–9766) has delightfully eclectic antique jewelry, African sculptures, clocks, and unusual pieces.

ART

The **French Quarter** is known for its many art galleries, most of which are on Royal Street. **Bergen Galleries** (✉ 730 Royal St., ☎ 504/523–7882) offers posters and collectibles by local artists. The **Black Art Collection** (✉ 309 Chartres St., ☎ 504/529–3080) displays and sells works by local and national African-American artists. **Dyansen Gallery** (✉ 433 Royal St., ☎ 504/523–2902) features the work of modern and contemporary artists. **Merrill B. Domas American Indian Art** (✉ 824 Chartres St., ☎ 504/586–0479) offers antique and contemporary art and crafts by Native American artists. **Southern Expressions** (✉ 521 St. Ann St., at Jackson Sq., ☎ 504/525–4530) shows the work of regional artists.

FLEA MARKET

Jazz is within earshot and "junque" at your fingertips, at the **French Market Flea Market** (⊠ French Sq., ☎ 504/522–2621) daily from 7 to 7.

FOOD TO GO

Bayou To Go (⊠ New Orleans International Airport, Concourse C, ☎ 504/468–8040) has a full line of Louisiana food products, including fresh, frozen, and cooked seafood packed to check or carry on the plane. **Battistella's Sea Foods, Inc.** (⊠ 910 Touro St., ☎ 504/949–2724) carries packaged seafoods to go. The **New Orleans School of Cooking** (⊠ Jax Brewery, 620 Decatur St., ☎ 504/525–2665) stocks packaged red beans and rice, beignet mix, Cajun spices, pecans, and other Louisiana specialties.

JAZZ RECORDS

You'll find the hard-to-find vintage stuff at **Record Ron's** (⊠ 1129 Decatur St. and 407 Decatur St., ☎ 504/524–9444).

MASKS

For exotic handmade masks to decorate your face or your wall, try **Rumors** (⊠ 513 Royal St., ☎ 504/525–0292).

PRALINES

For the best pralines in town, try **Old Town Praline Shop** (⊠ 627 Royal St., ☎ 504/525–1413).

Side Trip from New Orleans

Jean Lafitte National Historical Park

20 mi south of downtown.

Just 45 minutes by car from the French Quarter, you can sample Louisiana's exotic natural splendors in the park's 8,000-acre Barataria Unit. Paved walkways lace alongside bayous, over which hang frayed canopies of Spanish moss, and in which alligators, snakes, and other critters slither. Park rangers conduct free walking tours daily, but you can also wander along the trails on your own. At the **Bayou Barn** (⊠ Intersection of Rtes. 31, 34, and 45, ☎ 504/689–2663 or 800/862–2968, FAX 504/689–4554), the intrepid can rent a canoe and paddle off alone; $7.50 per person for two hours. The less adventuresome can take a Bayou Barn guided tour, $20 for two hours; and all can enjoy the fresh gumbo and jambalaya dished up by the friendly folks at the shop. To reach the park, take U.S. 90 over the Crescent City Connection (bridge) across the river and turn left on Route 45. ⊠ *Just below Marrero on Lake Salvador (via U.S. 90, south of New Orleans, and Rte. 45),* ☎ 504/589–2330.

New Orleans A to Z

Arriving and Departing

BY BOAT

You can arrive from northern ports in grand 19th-century style aboard one of the authentic overnight steamboats of the **Delta Queen Steamboat Company**—the *Delta Queen,* the *Mississippi Queen,* or the *American Queen*—which home port in New Orleans (⊠ 30 Robin St. Wharf, ☎ 800/543–1949, FAX 504/585–0630).

BY BUS

Greyhound (☎ 800/231–2222) operates out of Union Passenger Terminal (☞ By Train, *below*).

BY CAR
I–10 runs from Florida through New Orleans and on to California. I–55 is the north–south route, connecting with I–12 west of Ponchatoula and with I–10 a touch west of New Orleans; I–59 runs northeast into Mississippi and Alabama; and I–49 slashes diagonally through the state's midsection, from Lafayette to Shreveport. U.S. 61, from the west, and U.S. 90, from the east, also run through New Orleans.

BY PLANE
New Orleans International Airport (Moisant Field), 15 mi west of New Orleans, in Kenner, is served by American (☎ 800/433–7300), Continental (☎ 800/525–0280), Delta (☎ 800/221–1212), Northwest (☎ 800/225–2525), Southwest (☎ 800/531–5601), TWA (☎ 800/221–2000), United (☎ 800/241–6522), and US Airways (☎ 800/428–4322). Foreign carriers serving the city include Aeromexico (☎ 800/237–6639), Aviateca (☎ 800/327–9832), Lacsa (☎ 800/225–2272), Sahsa (☎ 800/327–1225), and Taca (☎ 800/535–8780).

Buses operated by **Louisiana Transit** (☎ 504/737–9611) run every 22 minutes between the airport and Elk Place in the CBD. Hours of operation are 6 AM to 6:20 PM; the last bus leaves the airport at 5:40 PM. The $1.10 trip downtown takes about an hour.

The **Airport Shuttle** (☎ 504/522–3500 or 800/543–6332) leaves the airport every 5–10 minutes, 24 hours a day, for the 20- to 30-minute trip into town. Small vans drop passengers off at their hotels, so arrival time at your destination depends upon the van's number of stops. The fare is $10 per person.

Taxi fare is $21 for one or two passengers, $8 per additional person. The driver may offer three or four strangers together a rate comparable to the airport shuttle.

By **car,** you can drive to New Orleans from Kenner via Airline Highway (U.S. 61) or I–10. Hertz, Avis, Budget, and other major car-rental agencies have airport outlets (☞ Car Rental, *below*).

BY TRAIN
Amtrak (☎ 800/872–7245) trains pull into the CBD's Union Passenger Terminal (✉ 1001 Loyola Ave., ☎ 504/528–1610). New Orleans is connected via rail to California, Chicago, Florida, New York, and points in between.

Getting Around
BY BICYCLE
The flat terrain of the French Quarter invites bikers, and Royal and Bourbon streets in the Quarter are closed off during the day to all but bikers and pedestrians. Many cyclists make the trek from the Quarter to City Park or Audubon Park, both good places for easy wheeling.

BY BOAT AND FERRY
The **Canal Street Ferry** will take you across the Mississippi from the Canal Street Wharf to Algiers Ferry Landing; the ride takes 25 minutes round-trip. ☎ *504/364–8114.* ▧ *Free to pedestrians; motorists pay $1 for the return to Canal Street Wharf.* ☉ *Daily 5:30 AM–9:30 PM.*

The **New Orleans Steamboat Company** runs the mighty steamboat *Natchez,* which has two-hour cruises of the harbor during the day and two-hour dinner-jazz cruises in the evening; and the little *John James Audubon,* which cruises between the Aquarium and the Audubon Zoo. Aside from the view of the city and the water lapping at the sides of the boats, kids (and some adults) love to watch the big stern wheel turning. ☎ *504/586–8777 or 800/233–2628.* ✎ *Natchez harbor cruise $14.75. Natchez evening cruise $22.50, $42.50 with dinner. John James Audubon cruise $13.50 round-trip.* ☯ *Natchez harbor cruise daily 11:30, 2:30. Natchez evening cruise daily 7–9, boarding 6–7. John James Audubon cruise daily 10, noon, 2, and 4 from aquarium; daily 11, 1, 3, and 5 from zoo.*

BY BUS

Buses require $1 exact change or a token (sold only in banks). Transfers are 10¢ extra. The Vieux Carré shuttle operates weekdays from 5 AM to 7:30 PM. The Regional Transit Authority (RTA) has a 24-hour information service (☎ 504/248–3900, TTY 504/248–3838). One- and three-day visitor passes cost $4 and $8 respectively and allow unlimited travel on buses and streetcars.

BY STREETCAR

The **St. Charles Streetcar** (☎ 504/248–3900, TTY 504/248–3838), New Orleans's mobile Historic Landmark, clangs up St. Charles Avenue through the Garden District, past the Audubon Park and Zoo and other Uptown sights. The streetcar can be boarded in the CBD at Canal and Carondelet streets; $1 fare. A round-trip self-guided sightseeing jaunt covers just over 13 mi and takes 90 minutes. The streetcar operates daily, every five minutes from 7:30 AM to 6 PM, every 15–20 minutes from 6 PM to midnight, and hourly from midnight to 7 AM.

The **Riverfront Streetcar** (☎ 504/248–3900, TTY 504/248–3838) follows the river between Esplanade Avenue and the Robin Street Wharf. It makes 10 stops, five above and five below Canal Street. The fare is $1.25, and it operates weekdays 6 AM–midnight; weekends 8 AM–midnight.

BY TAXI

Taxi fares start at $1.70, plus 50¢ per additional passenger and $1 per mile or 40 seconds stopped in traffic. For trips to special events, such as a ride to the Fairgrounds during Jazzfest, cabs charge $3 per person. Try **United Cabs** (☎ 504/522–9771) or **Yellow-Checker Cabs** (☎ 504/525–3311).

Contacts and Resources

B&B RESERVATION AGENCIES

Bed & Breakfast, Inc.–Reservations Service has a variety of accommodations in all areas of New Orleans. Some are 19th-century historic homes. Guest cottages, rooms, and suites are also available. Prices range from $40 to $150. Write or call Hazel Boyce: ✉ *1021 Moss St., Box 52257, New Orleans 70152,* ☎ *504/488–4640 or 800/729–4640,* FAX *504/488–4639. No credit cards.*

New Orleans Bed & Breakfast. Among 300 properties citywide are private homes, apartments, and condos. Prices range from $45 to $250. Contact Sarah-Margaret Brown: ✉ *Box 8163, New Orleans 70182,* ☎ *504/838–0071 or 504/838–0072,* FAX *504/838–0140. AE, D, MC, V.*

CAR RENTAL

National **car rental services** in New Orleans include Avis (☎ 800/831–2847), Budget (☎ 800/527–0700), Enterprise (☎ 800/325–8007), Hertz (☎ 800/654–3131), and National (☎ 800/227–7568).

EMERGENCIES

Police and ambulance: 911. All-night **hospital emergency rooms** include Tulane Medical Center (✉ 220 Lasalle St., ☎ 504/588–5711), in the CBD near the French Quarter, and Touro Infirmary (✉ 1401 Foucher St., ☎ 504/897–8250), near the Garden District.

GUIDED TOURS

Orientation. If you prefer a "known" in an unknown city, hop aboard an air-conditioned, 45-passenger **Gray Line** bus (☎ 504/587–0861) for a two-hour tour of New Orleans's major sights. Gray Line also offers a Loop Tour in small vans, with unlimited on-and-off privileges for an entire day. Pickups are every other hour at 12 spots in the French Quarter, CBD, and Garden District. **Tours by Isabelle** (☎ 504/391–3544) uses air-conditioned, 14-passenger vans for a multilingual and more intimate three-hour tool around town.

Special-Interest. Anne Rice's Very Own New Orleans (☎ 800/733–7423), a company owned by the famous author, conducts walking and bus tours in and around New Orleans featured in Rice's writings. Tours cover attractions in the French Quarter and the Garden District, as well as Destrehan Plantation and Pitot House. Cost: $20–$80. **Heritage Tours** (☎ 504/949–9805) conducts literary and historical walking tours of the French Quarter. **Le 'Ob's Tours** (☎ 504/288–3478) runs a daily African-American heritage/city tour, as well as plantation and bayou tours. **Pat Bernard's Classic Tours** (☎ 504/899–1862) is operated by a native New Orleanian who is in love with the city. Her chatty tours cover art, antiques, architecture, and history. **Save Our Cemeteries** (☎ 504/588–9357) conducts lively guided tours of some of the city's aboveground graveyards. Statistics for the **Superdome** (☎ 504/587–3810) are staggering and you can learn all about the huge facility during daily tours. **Tours by Isabelle** (☎ 504/391–3544) takes you around town, to plantations, and to the bayous for a visit with a Cajun alligator hunter. **Voodoo haunts** and such are covered by both **Magic Walking Tours** (☎ 504/593–9693) and the **New Orleans Historic Voodoo Museum** (☎ 504/523–7685). On the flatboats of **Wagner's Honey Island Swamp Tours** (☎ 504/641–1769), steered by a professional wetland ecologist, you can tour one of the country's best-preserved river swamps.

RADIO STATIONS

AM: WWL 870, talk, news; KGLA 1540, Spanish-language; WNOE 101.1, country music, news, weather; WGSO 990, CNN radio; WWNO 89.9, NPR, classical music, jazz. **FM:** WCKW 92.3, classic rock; WWOZ 90.7, community radio, New Orleans jazz; WNOE 101.1, country music, news, weather.

24-HOUR PHARMACIES

Eckerd (✉ 3400 Canal St., ☎ 504/488–6661). **Walgreen's** (✉ 3057 Gentilly Blvd., ☎ 504/282–2621; ✉ 9999 Lake Forest Blvd., ☎ 504/242–0981).

VISITOR INFORMATION

Write to the **New Orleans Metropolitan Convention and Visitors Bureau** (✉ 1520 Sugar Bowl Dr., New Orleans 70112, ☎ 504/566–5011 or 800/672–6124). The **Tourist Commission** staffs a desk near the customs desk at New Orleans International Airport; its main outlet is the **The Louisiana State Office of Tourism**, which shares space with the city at the **New Orleans Welcome Center**. ✉ 529 St. Ann St., French Quarter, ☎ 504/566–5068. ☼ Daily 9–5.

CAJUN COUNTRY
Lafayette, Abbeville, Lake Charles, Opelousas

Acadiana, also called French Louisiana, is the cradle of the Cajun craze that's swept the nation. Cajuns are descendants of 17th-century French settlers who established a colony they called l'Acadie in the present-day Canadian provinces of Nova Scotia and New Brunswick. The Acadians—"Cajun" is a corruption of "Acadian"—were expelled by the British in the mid-18th century. Their exile was described by Henry Wadsworth Longfellow in his epic poem "Evangeline." They eventually found a home in South Louisiana, and there they have been since 1762, imbuing the region, the state, and the nation with their unique cuisine and culture. The flavor of the region is summed up in the Cajun phrase *Laissez les bons temps rouler!* (Let the good times roll!). Cajun Country is made for meandering. There are scenic routes and state highways, and you're encouraged to take to the country roads along the way to further explore the back roads and byways of bayou country.

U.S. 90 drops down from New Orleans into the marshlands of Houma, an area that abounds with campgrounds and charter fresh- and salt-water fishing boats. This route will take you through Morgan City, where the first Tarzan film was made; Franklin, an official Main Street USA town; and one of the state's Native American reservations. We'll follow the rambling Bayou Teche (pronounced tesh) into St. Martinville in Evangeline Country, and next you'll head for Lafayette, which proudly calls itself, with some justification, the capital of French Louisiana. LA 14 is the scenic route to Lake Charles, which is fishing, camping, and bird-watching territory. Looping back toward Baton Rouge, you'll go through the area famed for the Courir de Mardi Gras, or Mardi Gras Run, during which masked and costumed horseback riders make a mad dash through the countryside. The trip ends near Baton Rouge on the Mississippi River, where you'll begin the second tour.

While you're in Cajun Country, try to experience chank-a-chanking at a *fais do-do*. The little iron triangles in most Cajun bands make a rhythmic "chank-a-chank" sound, and most folks call dancing to the rhythm chank-a-chanking. As for fais do-do (pronounced fay doh-doh), that's the dance, or party, where you go to chank-a-chank. Fais do-dos crop up all over Cajun Country, sometimes in the town square, sometimes at somebody's house. There are also restaurants, dance halls, and lounges that regularly feature live Cajun music. The **Times of Acadiana** is a free newspaper that comes out every Wednesday and is available in hotels, restaurants, and shops. Check the "On the Town" section to see what's doing in the area.

Many restaurants and lounges regularly feature music for two-stepping, waltzing, and chank-a-chanking. ("Regularly" does not necessarily mean every night.) Sunday afternoon is often devoted to dancing. Be sure to call to find out the schedule.

Numbers in the margin correspond to points of interest on the Cajun Country map.

Houma

27 *57 mi south of New Orleans on U.S. 90.*

Houma, in Terrebonne Parish, dates from 1795 and is in the heart of the old Hache Spanish Land Grant. The town is named for the Houmas Indians (the stressed first syllable of Houma sounds like "home"). Terrebonne Parish is a major center for shrimp and oyster fisheries, and the blessing of the shrimp fleets in Chauvin and Dulac is a colorful April event.

OFF THE BEATEN PATH

WILDLIFE GARDENS – To get a real feel for the area, take the guided walking tour through this 30-acre park. All sorts of critters slither, slink, and fly in the natural-habitat facility. There is a working alligator farm and a snack bar (though the two are unrelated). Nature lovers can B&B in a trapper's cabin. ✉ *14 mi west of Houma on U.S. 90 in Gibson,* ☎ *504/575-3676.* 🎫 *$8.* ⊗ *Sept.–May, Mon.–Sat. tours at 10, 1, and 3:30; June–Aug., Mon.–Sat. tours 10 and 3:30.*

Morgan City

28 *37 mi northwest of Houma on U.S. 90.*

Morgan City, smack on the Atchafalaya River, struck it rich when the first oil-producing offshore well was completed on November 14, 1947, and the Kerr-McGee Rig No. 16 ushered in the "black gold rush." Front Street runs alongside the 22-mi-long flood wall.

Atop the Great Wall, **Moonwalk** is a lookout with a great view of the Atchafalaya, as well as displays depicting the history of the region. At the **Morgan City Information Center** you can see a video of the first Tarzan movie, which was filmed here in 1917. ✉ *725 Myrtle St.,* ☎ *504/384–3343.* ⊗ *Weekdays 8–4, weekends 9–4.*

Across from the information center, you can take a guided tour of 3½-acre **Swamp Gardens,** a heritage park that depicts the settlement of Atchafalaya Basin; displays include pirogues and other aspects of bayou life. ✉ *725 Myrtle St.,* ☎ *504/384–3343.* 🎫 *$3.* ⊗ *Daily 10–4.*

Franklin

29 *20 mi northwest of Morgan City on U.S. 90.*

If you're of a nostalgic bent, you'll love Franklin's **Main Street,** which was named an official Main Street USA by the National Trust for Historic Preservation. The street rolls out beneath an arcade of live oaks, and old-fashioned street lamps with NO HITCHING signs line the boulevard. Franklin is nestled along a bend in the bayou, and there is a splendid view of it from **Parc sur le Teche.** (To reach the park as you drive north through town, turn right on Willow Street by the courthouse square.)

For information about this pretty town and its environs, stop at the **St. Mary Parish Tourist Commission** (✉ 1600 Northwest Blvd., ☎ 318/828–2555).

We recommend traveling to Franklin via LA 182, which you pick up just outside of Patterson. This is **Bayou Teche** country, and the state highways follow the writhing bayou along some stretches. Teche is a Native American word meaning snake. According to an ancient Indian legend, the death throes of a giant snake carved the bayou.

Cajun Country

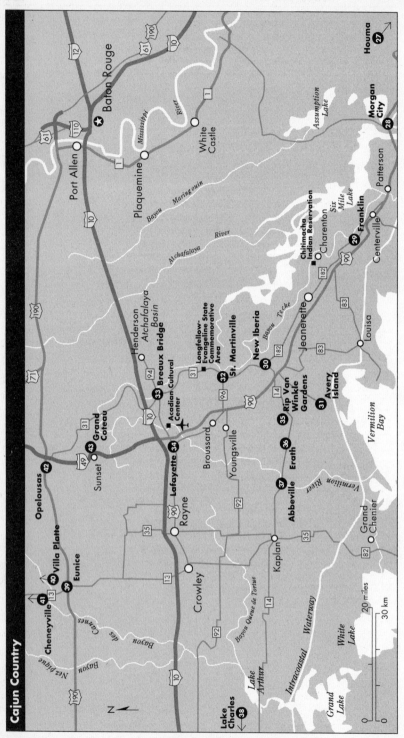

Baton Rouge
Port Allen
Plaquemine
White Castle
Houma 27
Morgan City 28
Patterson
Franklin 29
Centerville
Charenton
Chitimacha Indian Reservation
Six Mile Lake
Assumption Lake
Atchafalaya River
Bayou Maringouin
Mississippi River
Henderson
Atchafalaya Basin
Breaux Bridge
Acadian Cultural Center
Longfellow-Evangeline State Commemorative Area
St. Martinville
New Iberia 30
Bayou Teche
Jeanerette
Louisa
Avery Island 31
Rip Van Winkle Gardens 35
Erath 36
Abbeville 37
Broussard
Youngsville
Lafayette 34
Grand Coteau 43
Sunset
Opelousas 42
Villa Platte
Eunice 39 40
Cheneyville 41
Bayou Nez Piqué
Bayou des Cannes
Rayne
Crowley
Kaplan
Grand Chenier
Vermilion River
Vermilion Bay
White Lake
Grand Lake
Lake Arthur
Intracoastal Waterway
Bayou Queue de Tortue
Lake Charles 38

N

20 miles
30 km

OFF THE
BEATEN PATH

CHITIMACHA INDIAN RESERVATION – For centuries the Chitimacha flour-ished along the shores of Bayou Atchafalaya. The tribe's main settlement was in Charenton, site of the present-day reservation. The tribe is fa-mous for its weaving, and Chitimacha baskets as well as other small craft items are sold in the reservation's crafts shop. ✉ *LA 326, Charen-ton, 3 mi north of Franklin,* ☎ *318/923–4830.* 🎟 *Free.* ☼ *Daily 8– 4:30.*

The Chitimacha's main attraction these days is the busy **Cypress Bayou Casino** (✉ 832 Martin Luther King Rd., Charenton, ☎ 800/284–4386). The large and seemingly ever-expanding facility is awash with slots, video poker, and gaming tables.

New Iberia

30 *25 mi northwest of Franklin via U.S. 90 or LA 182.*

New Iberia—the "Queen City of the Teche"—was founded in 1779 by Spanish settlers, who named the town after the Iberian Peninsula. The town is a blend of Spanish, French, and Acadian cultures.

Set in 2 lush acres on the bank of the bayou, in the shadows of moss-draped oaks, **Shadows-on-the-Teche** is one of the South's best-known plantation homes. Built in 1834 for sugar planter David Weeks, this fine old home epitomizes what went with the wind. ✉ *317 E. Main St.,* ☎ *318/369–6446.* 🎟 *$6.* ☼ *Daily 9–4:30.*

✋ **City Park** is a 45-acre grassy playground across the Teche from Main Street, with tennis courts, playgrounds, baseball and softball fields, a fishing pond, boat ramps, and picnic shelters with barbecue facilities. 🎟 *Free.* ☼ *Weekdays 8 AM–9 PM, Sat. 1–9, Sun. 1–5.*

Dining and Lodging

$ ✕ **Cafe Lagniappe Too.** Just one block from Shadows-on-the-Teche is Elaine and Al Landry's charming, affordable restaurant. Not only does Elaine do the cooking, she also makes the huggable, oversize stuffed dolls with funny faces that perch here and there; Al creates the color-ful paintings that hang on the walls. For lunch there are salads, soups, and sandwiches, as well as stuffed eggplant and mirliton stuffed with shrimp and beef; the cuisine moves haute for dinner. ✉ *204 E. Main St.,* ☎ *318/365–9419. AE, MC, V. Closed Sun. No lunch Sat.*

$$$ ✕🛏 **leRosier.** Across the street from Shadows-on-the-Teche, set behind an antique rose garden, leRosier is a small family-run bed-and-break-fast whose dining room has won national acclaim. Chef Hallman Woods III has prepared his five-course crawfish degustation for the James Beard Foundation in New York. In addition to seafood are such spe-cialties as grilled marinated duck breast and tournedos of beef tenderloin with herbs. Rooms are quite small but are decorated with good-qual-ity fabrics. ✉ *314 E. Main St., 70560,* ☎ *318/367–5306. 4 rooms. AE, MC, V.*

Avery Island

31 *7 mi southwest of New Iberia via LA 329.*

Avery Island (it's actually a salt dome) is the birthplace of Tabasco sauce, and descendants of Edmund McIlhenny continue making the hot sauce he invented in the mid-1800s. Other attractions are the 200-acre **Jun-gle Gardens,** lush with tropical plants, and **Bird City,** a sanctuary with flurries of snow-white egrets. ✉ *Off LA 329,* ☎ *318/369–6243 Jun-*

gle Gardens, 318/365–8173 Tabasco factory. 🖾 *Gardens and sanctuary $5.50, Tabasco factory free.* ☉ *Gardens daily 8–5; factory weekdays 9–4, Sat. 9–noon.*

St. Martinville

32 *10 mi north of New Iberia via LA 31.*

St. Martinville is awash with legends. Longfellow's poem "Evangeline" was based on the story of Emmeline Labiche and Louis Arceneaux, two young lovers separated for years during Canada's Acadian exile (St. Martinville was a major entry point of Acadian refugees in the mid-18th century). Louis arrived in the town first and waited years hoping to find Emmeline, but eventually despaired of ever seeing her again and became engaged to another woman. Emmeline finally did reach St. Martinville, and, the story is told, Louis saw her by chance as she stepped ashore. Pale with shock, he told her that he was betrothed to another, turned on his heel, and disappeared. Their last, unhappy meeting place was beneath the Evangeline Oak (🖾 Evangeline Blvd. at Bayou Teche). The Romance of Evangeline was filmed in St. Martinville in 1929. Dolores Del Rio starred as Evangeline, and posed for the bronze statue that the cast and crew donated to the town. You can see the statue in the cemetery behind the church of St. Martin de Tours (☞ *below*), near the grave of Emmeline Labiche. In the late 18th century, St. Martinville was known as Petit Paris because it was a major refuge for royalists who fled the French Revolution. "Little Paris" was the scene of many regal balls, soirees, and operas.

St. Martin de Tours (🖾 123 S. Main St., ☎ 318/394–2233), Mother Church of the Acadians, is one of the oldest Catholic churches (circa early 18th century) in the country. Inside there is a replica of the Lourdes Grotto and a baptismal font said to have been a gift from Louis XVI.

La Remise, the St. Martinville visitor center, is adjacent to the Evangeline Oak park, just behind the Church Square. 🖾 *120 Market St.,* ☎ *318/394–2233.* ☉ *Daily 9–5.*

La Maison Duchamp is a Classic Revival structure built as a private home in 1876. Here you can see a bedroom furnished with period antiques and turn-of-the-century photographs of the town. Tours are conducted in French and English. 🖾 *Main St. at Evangeline Blvd.,* ☎ *318/394–2229.* 🖾 *Free.* ☉ *Daily 9–3.*

OFF THE BEATEN PATH
LONGFELLOW–EVANGELINE STATE COMMEMORATIVE AREA – Just north of the city limits, on LA 31 and the banks of the Teche, this 157-acre park is shaded by majestic, moss-draped live oaks. The park contains picnic tables and pavilions, a boat launch, and early Acadian houses. ☎ *318/394-3754.* 🖾 *Grounds $2.* ☉ *Daily 9-5.*

Dining and Lodging

$$ ✕🖼 **La Place d'Evangeline.** In the historic redbrick Old Castillo Hotel,
★ on the banks of the Bayou Teche beneath the branches of the Evangeline Oak, dine in high-ceilinged rooms where 18th-century royalists once held lavish balls and operas. Seafood is king here, with the menu listing the likes of corn and crab bisque, red snapper (broiled, fried, stuffed, and blackened), and frogs' legs. Don't pass up the homemade bread. Proprietors Peggy and Gerald Hulin have renovated the upstairs part of the old hotel, and antiques-filled rooms are open for guests. 🖾 *220 Evangeline Blvd., 70582,* ☎ *318/394–4010 or 800/621–3017,* 🖷 *318/394–7983. 5 rooms. AE, MC, V.*

Breaux Bridge

㉝ *13 mi north of St. Martinville on LA 31.*

The little town of Breaux Bridge is the home of world-famous **Mulate's** restaurant and the self-proclaimed Crawfish Capital of the World. The **Crawfish Festival,** held in May, draws upwards of 100,000 people.

Dining

$$ ✕ **Mulate's.** A roadhouse with flashing yellow lights outside and plas-
★ tic checkered cloths inside, Mulate's is an eatery, a dance hall, an age-old family gathering spot, and a celebrity, having been featured on the *Today Show* and *Good Morning, America,* among other appearances. A dressed-down crowd digs into the likes of stuffed crabs and the Super Seafood Platters. There's live music at lunch and dinner. ✉ *325 Mills Ave.,* ☎ *800/634–9880; 800/422–2586 outside LA. AE, MC, V.*

Nightlife and the Arts

La Poussière (✉ 1301 Grand Pointe Rd., Breaux Bridge, ☎ 318/332–1721) is one of the oldest dance halls around.

Lafayette

㉞ *9 mi west of Breaux Bridge on LA 94.*

Lafayette is a major center of Cajun lore and life. Stop in at the **Lafayette Convention and Visitors Bureau** (✉ Willow St. and Evangeline Thruway) and load up your tote bag with maps and brochures.

☺ The **Acadian Village,** a re-creation of an early 19th-century bayou settlement nestled in 10 wooded acres, has a general store, a blacksmith shop, a chapel, and houses representing different styles of Acadian architecture. ✉ *200 Greenleaf Rd. (LA 342),* ☎ *318/981–2364.* ✑ *$5.50.* ☉ *Daily 10–5.*

The Louisiana Live Oak Society, founded in Lafayette more than 50 years ago, is on the grounds of the **Cathedral of St. John the Evangelist** (✉ 914 St. John St.), a Romanesque church with Byzantine touches. A charter member of that silent but leafy set of trees dominates the 900 block of St. John Street. The **St. John Oak** is 400 years old and has a matronly waistline of about 19 ft.

☺ The **Lafayette Natural History Museum** is a busy place, with workshops, movies, concerts, and planetarium programs. It's also the venue for the annual September **Louisiana Native & Contemporary Crafts Festival.** ✉ *637 Girard Park Dr.,* ☎ *318/291–5544.* ✑ *Free.* ☉ *Mon. and Wed.–Fri. 9–5, Tues. 9–9, weekends 1–5.*

☺ The natural history museum's sister facility is the **Acadiana Park Nature Station,** a three-story cypress pole structure with an interpretive center and discovery boxes to help children get acquainted with the wildflowers, birds, and other things they'll see along a 3½-mi trail. ✉ *E. Alexandre St.,* ☎ *318/291–8448.* ✑ *Free.* ☉ *Weekdays 9–5, weekends 11–3.*

The **Lafayette Art Gallery** gives visitors a close look at local arts and crafts. ✉ *412 Travis St.,* ☎ *318/269–0363.* ✑ *Free.* ☉ *Tues.–Fri. noon–5, Sat. by appointment.*

OFF THE
BEATEN PATH

ACADIAN CULTURAL CENTER – The center, a unit of the Jean Lafitte National Historical Park and Preserve, traces the history of the Acadians through numerous audiovisual exhibits of Cajun music, food, and folklore. ✉ *501 Fisher Rd.,* ☎ *318/232–0789 or 318/232–0961.* ✉ *Free.* ⊙ *Daily 8–5.*

Dining and Lodging

$$ ✕ **Cafe Vermilionville.** This 19th-century inn with crisp white napery, old-brick fireplaces, and a casual elegance serves French and Cajun cuisine. Among the specialties are fried soft-shell crab with crawfish fettuccine, smoked turkey and andouille gumbo, and Kahlua grilled shrimp. ✉ *1304 W. Pinhook Rd.,* ☎ *318/237–0100. AE, MC, V.*

$$ ✕ **Prejean's.** Housed in a cypress cottage, this local favorite has a cozy oyster bar, red-checkered cloths, and live music nightly. Specialties include Prejean's Platter (seafood gumbo, fried shrimp, oysters, catfish, and seafood-stuffed bell peppers), as well as Cajun rack of elk, American buffalo au poivre, and steak and chicken in various costumes. ✉ *3480 U.S. 167 N, next to Evangeline Downs,* ☎ *318/896–3247. AE, DC, MC, V.*

$$ ✕ **Prudhomme's Cajun Café.** In a suburb of Lafayette, celebrity chef
★ Paul Prudhomme's sister Enola—a major contributor to the Prudhomme Family Cookbook—has her country kitchen in a cypress cottage. Her specialties are blackened fish dishes, eggplant pirogue, and panfried rabbit in cream sauce—plus homemade jalapeño-and-cheese bread. ✉ *4676 N.E. Evangeline Thruway,* ☎ *318/896–7964. AE, MC, V. Closed Mon.*

$ ✕ **Dwyer's Café.** Come here for highly affordable Cajun plate lunches, burgers, and sandwiches. ✉ *323 Jefferson St.,* ☎ *318/235–9364. AE, MC, V. Closed Sun. No dinner.*

$$–$$$$ 🏨 **Holiday Inn Central–Holidome.** These 17 acres contain virtually everything you'd ever need for a relaxing stay. Rooms with modern furnishings surround the large entertainment area. ✉ *2032 N.E. Evangeline Thruway, 70509,* ☎ *318/233–6815 or 800/942–4868,* 𝔽𝔸𝕏 *318/225–1954. 244 rooms, 6 suites. Restaurant, lobby lounge, indoor pool, hot tub, sauna, 2 tennis courts, jogging, recreation rooms, airport shuttle. AE, D, DC, MC, V.*

$–$$ 🏨 **Best Western Hotel Acadiana.** This centrally located hotel has stan-
★ dard rooms with marble-top dressers, mini-refrigerators, and wet bars. Rooms on the concierge floor have such perks as Continental breakfast, evening hors d'oeuvres, and turndown service. The hotel has rooms equipped for people with disabilities. Even-numbered rooms face the pool. ✉ *1801 W. Pinhook Rd., 70508,* ☎ *318/233–8120 or 800/ 826–8386; 800/874–4664 in LA;* 𝔽𝔸𝕏 *318/234–9667. 301 rooms, 3 suites. Restaurant, bar, pool, 2 hot tubs, airport shuttle. AE, D, DC, MC, V.*

Nightlife and the Arts

Randol's (✉ 2320 Kaliste Saloom Rd., Lafayette, ☎ 318/981–7080) has hot dancing in a greenhouse setting. Major **concerts** are held at the **Cajundome** (✉ 444 Cajundome Blvd., ☎ 318/265–2100) and at the **Heymann Performing Arts Center** (✉ 1373 S. College Rd., ☎ 318/291–5540). **Lafayette Community Theatre** (✉ 529 Jefferson St., ☎ 318/235–1532) offers contemporary plays with a Cajun flair. The **Theatre 'Cadien** (☎ 318/893–5655) performs plays in French in various venues.

Outdoor Activities and Sports

BIKING

These flatlands and lush parks make for easy riding. There are 60 mi of marked bike trails in Lafayette. Guides, rental bikes, and maps are available at **Pack & Paddle** (✉ 601 E. Pinhook Rd., Lafayette, ☎ 318/ 232–5854).

GOLF

Play golf at **City Park Golf Course** (⊠ Mudd Ave. and 8th St., Lafayette, ☎ 318/268–5557).

Rip Van Winkle Gardens

🖑 ③⑤ *15 mi south of Lafayette on U.S. 90, off LA 675.*

The 20 acres of formal and informal gardens that comprise Rip Van Winkle Gardens (formerly known as Live Oak Gardens) are part of a 5,000-acre tract that was purchased in the late 19th century by an American actor, Joseph Jefferson, who toured the country portraying Rip Van Winkle. On a hunting trip to South Louisiana, Jefferson fell in love with the area's groves of live oaks and lush countryside, and in 1870 he bought the land on which he built a winter home. His land came to be called **Jefferson Island.** In 1980 the salt dome on which the "island" rested collapsed, causing severe damage. The area has been completely restored. **Jefferson's house** is a three-story, comfortably opulent, Southern Gothic home with Moorish touches. ⊠ *5505 Rip Van Winkle Rd., off LA 14,* ☎ *318/365–3332.* ⊡ *$7.50.* ☉ *Daily 9–5.*

Erath

③⑥ *24 mi south of Lafayette via U.S. 90 and LA 89.*

In Erath, you can poke through all sorts of Acadiana at the **Acadian Museum.** The several rooms are filled to the rafters with memorabilia donated by local folks—everything from antique radios and butter churns to patchwork quilts and yellowed newspaper clippings. ⊠ *203 S. Broadway,* ☎ *318/233–5832 or 318/937–5468.* ⊡ *Free, but donations welcome.* ☉ *Weekdays 1–4.*

Abbeville

③⑦ *5 mi west of Erath on LA 14.*

Abbeville is a charming town whose picturesque village square boasts a gazebo and moss-hung live oak trees. The vicinity of the square is the scene of the annual Giant Omelette Festival each November, when some 5,000 eggs go into the concoction. Pick up a self-guided walking tour brochure at the **Abbeville Main Street Program Office** in City Hall (⊠ 101 N. State St., ☎ 318/898–4110). Many buildings in the 20-block Main Street district are on the National Register of Historic Places. **St. Mary Magdalen Catholic Church,** adjacent to the village square, is a fine Romanesque Revival building with stunning stained glass windows.

On an earthy note, Abbeville is home to **Cajun Downs** (⊠ On LA 338 off the LA 14 bypass, ☎ 318/893–8160 or 318/893–0421), a "bush" track cut smack through a cane field where all manner of critters race—horses, mules, maybe even pigs or chickens. The track is more than 100 years old and draws a Cajun Runyonesque crowd that cheers on the favorite with great enthusiasm. The track is open only on Sunday, when a half dozen or so races are run. Call first to see if the races are on; schedules tend to be pretty informal here.

OFF THE
BEATEN PATH

ROCKEFELLER WILDLIFE REFUGE – Fifty-eight miles southwest of Abbeville via LA 82, you'll find an 84,000-acre tract where thousands of ducks, geese, 'gators, wading birds, otters, and others while away the winter months. ⊠ *On LA 82 between villages of Little Pecan Island and Grand Chenier (information center),* ☎ *318/538–2165.* ⊡ *Free.* ☉ *Refuge daily sunrise–sunset, information center daily 7–4.*

Lake Charles

38   *74 mi west of Abbeville via La 14, LA 13, and I–10.*

Lake Charles, the state's third-largest seaport, dates from the 1760s, when the first French settlers arrived. The first home was built by Charles Sallier on the shell beach by the lake, and the town was originally called Charlie's Lake. The city is blessed with more than 50 mi of rivers, lakes, canals, and bayous, making it a paradise for sailing, fishing, canoeing, shrimping, and crabbing. **North Beach** is a white-sand beach on the north shore of the lake, where you can loll in the sun, swim, or rent a wave runner during summer months. ✉ *$1 per vehicle June–Aug.; free other times.*

Twelve miles north of the city, **Sam Houston Jones State Park** is a 1,068-acre recreation area that beckons sports and nature enthusiasts. ✉ *LA 378,* ☎ *318/855–2665.* ✉ *$2 per vehicle.* ☉ *Daily 7 AM–8 PM.*

The **Imperial Calcasieu Museum,** on the site of Charles Sallier's home, has an extensive collection pertaining to Lake Charles and Calcasieu Parish. The museum includes an old-fashioned pharmacy, an Audubon collection, a Gay Nineties barbershop, and an art gallery featuring works by local craftspeople. ✉ *204 W. Sallier St., Lake Charles,* ☎ *318/439–3797.* ✉ *$1.* ☉ *Tues.–Fri. 10–5, weekends 1–5.*

The **Children's Museum** features interactive computers, a nature center, a TV station, a grocery store, and other hands-on exhibits as well as a toddlers' area. ✉ *925 Enterprise Blvd., Lake Charles,* ☎ *318/433–9420 or 318/433–9421.* ✉ *$3.* ☉ *Tues.–Sat. 10–5.*

Dining and Lodging

$$–$$$ ✕ **Café Margaux.** Think candlelight, soft pinks, white linens, tuxedoed
★   waiters, and a 5,000-bottle mahogany wine cellar. Specialties include a marvelous lobster bisque, rack of lamb en croute, good steaks, and fillet of flounder with lump crabmeat and brown meunière sauce. ✉ *765 Bayou Pines E,* ☎ *318/433–2902. Jacket and tie. AE, D, MC, V. Closed Sun.*

$$ 🏨 **Holiday Inn, Lake Charles.** Between the lake and the interstate, hotel guests can stroll through a "casinowalk" to board the Players Riverboat Casino, which docks next door. The Holiday Inn has traditional furnishings in rooms done in soothing earth tones, including five for guests with disabilities. ✉ *505 N. Lakeshore Dr., 70601,* ☎ *318/433–7121 or 800/367–1814; 800/433–8809 in LA;* 🅵🅰🆇 *318/436–8459. 262 rooms, 7 suites. Restaurant, coffee shop, no-smoking rooms, room service, pool, video games, airport shuttle. AE, D, DC, MC, V.*

$–$$ 🏨 **Chateau Charles Hotel and Conference Center.** A New Orleans–style structure with wrought-iron trim and beamed ceilings, the hotel is on 25 acres, minutes from downtown. There are two-bedroom suites with wet bars, microwaves, and mini-refrigerators; six apartments; and rooms for people with disabilities in the all-ground-level hotel. ✉ *Box 1269, 70602,* ☎ *318/882–6130 or 800/324–7647,* 🅵🅰🆇 *318/882–6601. 212 rooms, 13 suites. Restaurant, lobby lounge, no-smoking rooms, laundry, meeting rooms, airport shuttle. AE, D, DC, MC, V.*

$ 🏨 **Players Riverboat Casino Hotel.** Virtually an extension of the floating casino (the riverboat docks at the hotel's dock on Lake Charles), this hotel is for folks who want plenty of gambling action. ✉ *507 N. Lakeshore Dr., 70601,* ☎ *318/433–0541 or 800/977–7529,* 🅵🅰🆇 *318/437–1612. 132 rooms, 2 suites. Restaurant, bar, lobby lounge, room service, airport shuttle. AE, D, DC, MC, V.*

Nightlife and the Arts

Wildly successful since it opened in 1994, **Grand Casino Coushatta** (☎ 800/584–7263), 20 minutes north of I–10 on U.S. 165, is on the Coushatta Indian Reservation near Lake Charles. **Players Island Hotel-Casino-Entertainment Complex** (✉ 507 N. Lakeshore Dr., Lake Charles, ☎ 800/977–7529), done up like a tropical island, has two riverboat casinos with 1,600 one-armed bandits, 100 table games, and 24-hour entertainment. The **Isle of Capri** (✉ Exit 27 off I–10, ☎ 800/843–4753) is a 26,000-square-ft three-decker, open 24 hours, with table games and more than 900 slots.

Major concerts are held at the **Lake Charles Civic Center** (✉ 900 Lakeshore Dr., ☎ 318/491–1256). The **Lake Charles Little Theater** (✉ 813 Enterprise Blvd., Lake Charles, ☎ 318/433–7988) puts on a variety of plays and musicals.

Outdoor Activities and Sports

CANOEING

Paddling is almost a breeze on the easygoing **Whisky Chitto Creek.** Canoes can be rented at **Arrowhead Canoe Rentals** (☎ 318/639–2086 or 800/637–2086) and at **White Sand Canoe Rental** (☎ 800/621–9306), both in the Lake Charles area.

GOLF

You can tee off at the 18-hole **Pine Shadows Golf Center** (✉ 750 Goodman Rd., Lake Charles, ☎ 318/433–8681). The 18-hole **Mallard Cove** (✉ Chennault Airpark, Lake Charles, ☎ 318/491–1241) is popular with locals.

HIKING AND NATURE TRAILS

The Old Stagecoach Road in **Sam Houston Jones State Park** (✉ 12 mi north of Lake Charles on LA 378, ☎ 318/855–2665) is a favorite for hikers who want to explore the park and the various tributaries of the Calcasieu River.

En Route The **Creole Nature Trail,** a 180-mi loop through exotic subtropical scenery, is one of only 14 rural roads in the country to be designated a National Scenic Byway by the Federal Highway Administration. Beginning on LA 27 in Sulphur, the state road dips down along the Gulf of Mexico on LA 82, and winds up back in Lake Charles. Beautiful in the spring, this drive takes you to the **Sabine Wildlife Refuge,** where interpretative displays include a diorama featuring the Cajun Man, an animated talking mannequin. Admission is free. Three miles south of the center, a 1½-mi marsh trail leads right into the wilds, and at its end an observation tower affords excellent views of the wilderness. Bring insect repellent. For information, call the Southwest Louisiana Convention and Visitors Bureau (☎ 318/436–9588 or 800/456–7952). The Sabine Wildlife Refuge has an interpretative center (☎ 318/762–3816) that is open weekdays 7–4, weekends noon–4.

Eunice

③⑨ *66 mi northeast of Lake Charles via I–10 and LA 13.*

The tiny town of Eunice is home of the Cajun radio show *Rendez-Vous des Cajuns* (☞ Nightlife and the Arts, *below*). The **Eunice Museum** is in a former railroad depot and contains displays on Cajun culture, including Cajun music and Cajun Mardi Gras. ✉ *220 South C. C. Duson Dr., Eunice,* ☎ *318/457–6540.* ☜ *Free.* ☉ *Tues.–Sat. 8–noon and 1–5.*

The **Prairie Acadian Cultural Center,** a large facility that's part of the Jean Lafitte National Historical Park, traces the history and culture of the Prairie Acadians, whose lore and mores differ from those of the Bayou Acadians around Lafayette. Food, craft, and music demonstrations are held from time to time. ⊠ *250 W. Park Ave., Eunice,* ☎ *318/457–8490 or 318/457–8499.* ☞ *Free.* ☉ *Daily 8–5.*

A number of places in Cajun country make not just Cajun music but instruments. Among them is the **Savoy Music Center Accordion Factory,** its front half a music store, its back a Cajun accordion workshop. Proprietor Marc Savoy says his factory turns out about five accordions a month and fills orders all the way from Alaska to New Zealand. On Saturday mornings, accordions and other instruments tune up during the weekly jam sessions held in the shop. There's beer, two-stepping, and musicians from all over the area dropping over to sit in on the informal sessions. ⊠ *U.S. 190, 3 mi east of Eunice,* ☎ *318/457–9563.* ☞ *Free.* ☉ *Tues.–Fri. 9–5, Sat. 9–noon.*

The area surrounding Eunice is the major stomping grounds for an annual event **Courir de Mardi Gras,** which takes place the Sunday before Fat Tuesday (Mardi Gras Day). Le Capitain leads a band of masked and costumed horseback riders on a mad dash through the countryside, stopping at farmhouses along the way to shout, *"Voulez-vous recevoir cette bande de Mardi Gras?"* (Do you wish to receive the Mardi Gras band?) The answer is always "Yes," and the group enlarges and continues, gathering food for the street festivals that wind things up. For information, contact Lafayette Convention and Visitors Bureau (☎ 800/346–1958).

Nightlife and the Arts

Rendez-Vous des Cajuns, a live radio show, mostly in French, has been described as a combination of the "Grand Ole Opry," the "Louisiana Hayride," and the "Prairie Home Companion." ⊠ *Liberty Theatre, Park Ave. at 2nd St.,* ☎ *318/457–6577.* ☞ *$2.* ☉ *Sat. 6–8 PM.*

Ville Platte

❹ *20 mi northeast of Eunice via LA 13 and LA 10.*

Ville Platte is home to the annual Cotton Festival, held in October, which features a medieval-style Tournoi with knights, steeds, and jousting.

The **Louisiana State Arboretum** is a 600-acre facility with 2½ mi of nature trails leading past a variety of plants native to the state. ⊠ *8 mi north of Villa Platte,* ☎ *318/363–2503.* ☞ *Free.* ☉ *Dawn–dusk.*

Cheneyville

❹ *44 mi north of Eunice via LA 13 and I–49.*

At the turn of the 19th century, a group of immigrants, mostly of British ancestry, came from South Carolina to the area. Among them was a
★ chap named Cheney, and the town was named for him. **Lloyd Hall Plantation** is the perfect place for a quiet getaway. Adjacent to a historic plantation mansion, accommodations are in a rustic replica of a 19th-century farmhouse; a three-room cottage that once housed the commissary; or two suites in the restored kitchens overlooking the pool. All units are furnished with a blend of antiques and modern comforts: wood-burning fireplaces, rockers on the porches, four-poster or tester beds, air-conditioning, TV, and modern kitchens stocked with breakfast fixings. ⊠ *292 Lloyd Bridge Rd., 71325,* ☎ *318/776–5641 or 800/240–8135,* ℻ *318/776–5886. Housekeeping cottage (2 bedrooms share bath), housekeeping cottage with bath, 2 suites. Kitchen, pool. AE, MC, V.*

Opelousas

42 *51 mi south of Cheneyville on I–49.*

Opelousas is the third-oldest town in the state—Poste de Opélousas was founded in 1720 by the French as a trading post. The town is named for the Appalousa Indians, who lived in the area centuries before the French and Spanish arrived. For a brief period during the Civil War, Opelousas served as the state capital. At the intersection of I–49 and U.S. 190, look for the **Opelousas Tourist Information Center** (☎ 318/948–6263), where you can get plenty of information; arrange for tours of historic homes; and see memorabilia pertaining to Jim Bowie, the Alamo hero who spent his early years in Opelousas.

The **Opelousas Museum and Interpretive Center** has among its eclectic exhibits a washbasin in which celebrity chef (and native son) Paul Prudhomme bathed as a babe, a Civil War Room, adorable dollhouses, and an old-time barbershop replete with antique accoutrements. ⊠ *329 N. Main St.,* ☎ *318/948–2589.* ☛ *Free.* ☺ *Tues.–Sat. 9–5.*

Dining

$ ✕ **Palace Café.** A down-home coffee shop on the town square and operated by the same family since 1927, this locals' favorite is famous for its homemade baklava. Among the eclectic specialties are cold fried-chicken salad, baked eggplant stuffed with Alaskan king crabmeat dressing, and Greek salad with feta cheese, black and green olives, and anchovies. There are also steaks, fried chicken, sandwiches, burgers, and seafood. ⊠ *167 W. Landry St.,* ☎ *318/942–2142. Reservations not accepted. MC, V.*

Nightlife and the Arts

Louisiana Life magazine rated **Slim's Y-Ki-Ki** (⊠ LA 167, Washington Rd., ☎ 318/942–9980), a rural club, the best zydeco dancing place in the state.

Grand Coteau

43 *10 mi south of Opelousas via I–49, exiting on LA 93.*

Virtually every structure in peaceful little Grand Coteau, a religious and educational center, is on the National Register of Historic Places. The **Church of St. Charles Borromeo** is a simple wooden structure with an ornate High Baroque interior. There are 36 works of art inside, most of which were done by Erasmus Humbrecht, whose works can also be seen in St. Louis Cathedral in New Orleans. The church's unusual bell tower is one of the area's most-photographed sights. ☎ *318/662–5279.* ☛ *Tours $1 donation.* ☺ *Tours weekdays, but you must call to make arrangements in advance.*

Established in 1821, the **Academy of the Sacred Heart** is the second-oldest institution of learning west of the Mississippi, remaining in operation through fire, epidemics, and war. The academy contains the **Shrine of St. John Berchmans,** in which the Miracle of Grand Coteau occurred. You'll hear all about the miracle on a guided tour. For tour information, contact Wendy Ortego. ☎ *318/662–5275.* ☛ *$5.*

Chretien Point Plantation is noted not only for its grandeur but also for the role it played in *Gone With the Wind.* In the 1930s, a photographer infatuated with the house took pictures of it and sent them to Hollywood. As a result, its staircase was the model for the one in Scarlett O'Hara's Tara. The house takes bed-and-breakfast guests. ⊠

About 4 mi from Sunset on the Bristol/Bosco Rd., ☎ 318/662–5876.
⌨ *$5.50.* ☉ *Daily 10–5; last tour at 4.*

Cajun Country A to Z

Arriving and Departing

BY BUS

Greyhound Southeast Lines (☎ 800/231–2222) has frequent daily departures from New Orleans to Franklin, Houma, Lafayette, Lake Charles, Morgan City, New Iberia, Opelousas, and Thibodaux.

BY CAR

The fastest route from New Orleans through Cajun Country to Lafayette and Lake Charles is via I–10, which cuts coast-to-coast across the southern United States. However, if you have time, take the leisurely scenic drives for exploring.

Great Drives. LA 56 to LA 57 is a circular drive out of Houma, along which you can see shrimp and oyster boats docked along the bayous from May through December. Another circular drive is the Creole Nature Trail (LA 27) out of Lake Charles (☞ En Route, *above*). LA 82 (Hug-the-Coast Highway) runs through the coastal marshes along the Gulf of Mexico.

BY PLANE

Lafayette Regional Airport (☎ 318/232–2808) is served by American Eagle, Continental, Atlantic Southeast (a Delta connection), and Northwest Airlink. **Lake Charles Regional Airport** (☎ 318/477–6051) is served by American Eagle and Continental.

BY TRAIN

Amtrak (☎ 800/872–7245) serves Franklin, Schriever (12 mi from Houma), Lafayette, New Iberia, and Lake Charles.

Contacts and Resources

EMERGENCIES

Dial **911** for assistance. **Emergency rooms** include the **Medical Center of Southwest Louisiana** (✉ 2810 Ambassador Caffery Pkwy., Lafayette, ☎ 318/981–2949); in Lake Charles: **Lake Charles Area Medical Center** (✉ 4200 Nelson Rd., ☎ 318/474–6370).

GUIDED TOURS

Acadiana to Go (☎ 318/981–3918) gives guided tours of Acadiana, as well as the rest of Louisiana. **Allons à Lafayette** (☎ 318/269–9607) offers customized tours, with bilingual guides and itinerary planning for Lafayette and Cajun Country. **Terrebonne Swamp & Marsh Tours** (☎ 504/879–3934) is especially popular with the kids. Annie Miller, who gets along great with 'gators, conducts daily tours March 1–November 1 out of Houma into the swamps. **Coerte Voorhies** (☎ 318/233–7816), based in Lafayette, conducts tours into the 800,000-acre Atchafalaya Basin for photographers, ornithologists, and all nature lovers. **Hammond's Flying Service** (☎ 504/876–0584) has air tours, which soar out of Houma over the swamps, marshlands, and the Gulf of Mexico. **McGee's Landing** (☎ 318/228–2384) conducts pontoon-boat tours from the levee in Henderson into the Atchafalaya Basin. **Airboat Tours** (☎ 318/229–4457) skims through the remote swamps, bayous, and sloughs of Lake Fausse Pointe.

Trips to fish, sightsee, or bird-watch can be arranged at **Gator Guide Service** (✉ Box 9224, New Iberia, ☎ 318/365–6400). **Sportsman's Paradise** (☎ 504/594–2414) is a charter-fishing facility 20 mi south of Houma, with eight boats available year-round. **Salt, Inc. Charter Fishing Service** (✉ Coco Marina, LA 56 south of Houma, ☎ 504/594–

6626 or 504/594–7581) offers fishing trips in the bays and barrier islands of lower Terrebonne Parish, as well as into the Gulf of Mexico.

In the far southwestern part of the state, **Burgess Offshore, Inc.** (☎ 800/
932–5077) conducts offshore fishing trips. **Hackberry Rod & Gun Club**
(☎ 318/762–3391) is a charter saltwater fishing service.

RADIO STATIONS
AM: KROF 960, French/Cajun; KPEL 1420, news/talk; KEUN 1490,
country/news/sports. **FM:** KROF 105.1, oldies; KTDY 99.9, adult contemporary; KYKZ 96.1, country.

24-HOUR PHARMACIES
In Lafayette, **Eckerd** (✉ 4406 Johnston St., ☎ 318/984–5220). In Lake
Charles, **Walgreen's** (✉ 300 18th St., ☎ 318/433–4178).

VISITOR INFORMATION
The **Iberia Parish Tourist Commission** (✉ 2690 Centre St., New Iberia,
☎ 318/365–1540). The **Lafayette Convention and Visitors Commission** (✉ 1400 N.W. Evangeline Thruway, ☎ 318/232–3808 or 800/
346–1958; 800/543–5340 in Canada; FAX 318/232–0161). For information from the visitors commission via fax, call 800/884–7329,
main menu ext. 610. The **Southwest Louisiana Convention and Visitors Bureau** (✉ 1211 N. Lakeshore Dr., Lake Charles, ☎ 318/436–
9588 or 800/456–7952, FAX 318/494–7952); open weekdays 8–5,
weekends 9–3.

BATON ROUGE AND
PLANTATION COUNTRY

St. Francisville, Livonia,
White Castle, Napoleonville

Baton Rouge, one of South Louisiana's major cities, is the state capital. Legend has it that in 1699 French explorers observed that a red
stick planted in the ground on a high bluff overlooking the Mississippi
served as a boundary between two Indian tribes. Sieur d'Iberville,
leader of the expedition, noted le baton rouge—the red stick—in his
journal, and voila! Baton Rouge.

This is the city from which colorful, cunning Huey P. Long ruled the
state; it is also the site of his assassination. Even today, more than a
half century after Long's death, legends about the controversial governor and U.S. senator abound.

The parishes to the north of Baton Rouge are quiet and bucolic, with
gently rolling hills, high bluffs, and historic districts. John James
Audubon lived in West Feliciana Parish in 1821, tutoring local children and painting 80 of his famous bird studies. In both terrain and
traits, this region is more akin to North Louisiana than to South
Louisiana—which is to say, the area is very "Southern."

The area designated Plantation Country begins with a reservoir of fine
old homes north of Baton Rouge that cascades all the way down the
Great River Road to New Orleans. After touring the state capital, we
recommend taking LA 61 to the historic districts and plantations in
the parishes north of Baton Rouge, overnighting in one of the plantation bed-and-breakfasts. From St. Francisville, take the ferry for $1 at
the tip of town and start south on LA 1 to the antebellum gems that
decorate the Great River Road between Baton Rouge and New Orleans.

Numbers in the margin correspond to points of interest on the Baton Rouge and Plantation Country map.

Baton Rouge

❹ *80 mi northwest of New Orleans via I–10.*

Start your tour at the **Visitor Information Center,** which is loaded with maps and brochures; it's in the lobby of the **State Capitol Building.** You can tour the first floor of the building, which includes the spot where Huey Long was shot. At 34 stories, this is America's tallest state capitol. There is an observation deck on the 27th floor that affords a spectacular view of the Mississippi River and the city. ✉ *State Capitol Dr.,* ☎ *504/342–7317.* 🎫 *Free.* ⊙ *Daily 8–4:30; last tour at 4.*

A museum in the **Pentagon Barracks** has exhibits that acquaint visitors with the Capitol complex. The barracks were originally built in 1823–24 to quarter U.S. Army personnel, and when Louisiana State University moved from Pineville to Baton Rouge in 1869, it was to these buildings. ✉ *959 3rd St., on State Capitol grounds,* ☎ *504/342–1866.* 🎫 *Free.* ⊙ *Mon.–Sat. 10–4, Sun. 1–4.*

Only one Revolutionary War battle was fought outside the 13 original colonies, and it was fought on the State Capitol grounds. One of the historic buildings, the **Old Arsenal Museum,** a restored heavy-duty structure dating from about 1838, now houses a museum. A terrific place for children, the museum has hands-on exhibits set up inside powder kegs, displays on Louisiana's Native American history, and a giant jigsaw puzzle meant to compare the capitol grounds as they appear today to 1865. ✉ *State Capitol grounds,* ☎ *504/342–0401.* 🎫 *$1.* ⊙ *Weekdays 9–4, Sat. 10–4, Sun. 1–4.*

★ In 1994 a $17 million renovation was completed at the castlelike, Gothic Revival **Old State Capitol,** restoring the building to its original grandeur. When it was built in 1849, the structure was considered by some to be a masterpiece, by others a monstrosity. No one can deny that it's colorful and dramatic. In the entrance hall a stunning purple, gold, and green spiral staircase winds toward a stained-glass atrium. The building now houses the **Louisiana Center for Political and Government History,** an education and research facility with audiovisual exhibits. In the House Chamber a multimedia show plays every hour beginning at 10:15, with the last show at 4. ✉ *100 North Blvd., at River Rd.,* ☎ *504/342–0500.* 🎫 *$4.* ⊙ *Tues.–Sat. 10–4, Sun. noon–4.*

Ⓒ Across the street from the Old State Capitol is the **Louisiana Arts & Science Center Riverside Museum,** housed in a 1925 Illinois Central railroad station. There is a fine-arts museum with changing exhibits, an Egyptian tomb exhibit, restored trains from the 1890s to the 1950s, and a Discovery Depot with a children's art gallery and workshop. Once a month the museum presents a hands-on Challenger simulated space flight. Call for specific times. ✉ *100 S. River Rd.,* ☎ *504/344–5272.* 🎫 *$3; Sun. $1.* ⊙ *Tues.–Fri. 10–3, Sat. 10–4, Sun. 1–4.*

At press time, the **Old Governor's Mansion,** which was built in 1930 during Huey Long's administration, was closed for extensive restoration. It is expected to reopen as an elegant house museum sometime in 1998, under the auspices of the Foundation for Historical Louisiana. ✉ *502 North Blvd.,* ☎ *504/387–2464 for information about restoration and reopening.*

★ The **USS** *Kidd,* a Fletcher-class destroyer, is a World War II survivor restored to its V-J Day configuration. A brochure details a self-guided tour that takes in more than 50 inner spaces of this ship, including one

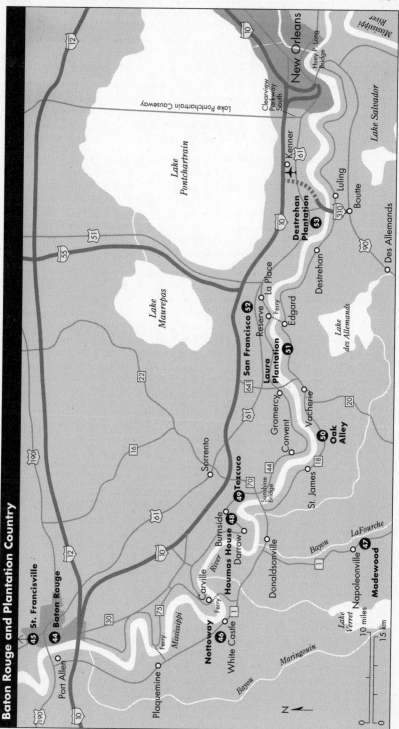

Baton Rouge and Plantation Country

set up as a **Nautical History Museum.** Among its exhibits are articles from the 175 Fletcher-class ships that sailed for the United States, a collection of ship models, and a restored P-40 fighter plane hanging from the ceiling. ⊠ *305 S. River Rd. (Government St. at the levee),* ☎ *504/342–1942.* ⊠ *$5.* ☉ *Daily 9–5.*

About 1½ mi from the center of town, **Magnolia Mound Plantation** (circa 1791) is a raised cottage furnished with Federal antiques and Louisiana artifacts. On Tuesday and Thursday from October through May cooking demonstrations are conducted in the outbuildings. ⊠ *2161 Nicholson Dr.,* ☎ *504/343–4955.* ⊠ *$3.50.* ☉ *Tues.–Sat. 10–4, Sun. 1–4.*

Louisiana State University (LSU) (⊠ 1 mi south of Magnolia Mound Plantation on Nicholson Dr., ☎ 504/388–3202) was founded in Pineville in 1860 as the Louisiana State Seminary of Learning and Military Academy. Its president was William Tecumseh Sherman, who resigned when war broke out and four years later made his famous march through Georgia. The 200-acre campus has several museums as well as Indian burial mounds that are of particular interest to archaeologists and archaeology buffs.

Spread over 5 acres of the 450-acre Burden Research Plantation, the LSU **Rural Life Museum** is an outdoor teaching and research facility. With three major areas (the Barn, the Working Plantation, and Folk Architecture), the compound's 20 or so rustic 19th-century structures represent the rural life of early Louisianians. Hundreds of items are displayed in the enormous barn, including a "prairie schooner," ancient surreys and sulkies, antique cars, tools and dental implements, and African artifacts and masks. The working plantation's several buildings include a gristmill, a blacksmith's shop, and several outbuildings. ⊠ *In Baton Rouge on Essen La., just off I–10,* ☎ *504/765–2437.* ⊠ *$5.* ☉ *Daily 8:30–5.*

Baton Rouge's major institution of higher learning other than LSU is **Southern University** (⊠ About 5 mi north of town on U.S. 61., ☎ 504/771–4500). Founded in 1880, Southern U. is the nation's largest predominantly black university.

OFF THE
BEATEN PATH

PORT HUDSON STATE COMMEMORATIVE AREA – Fourteen miles north of Baton Rouge on U.S. 61, you'll come to this 650-acre park on the site of a fiercely fought Civil War battle that was the longest siege in American military history. There are high viewing towers, gun trenches, and, on the first Sunday of each month, small arms demonstrations. Seven miles of hiking trails wend peacefully throughout the park. ⊠ *756 W. Plains-Port Hudson Rd. (U.S. 61),* ☎ *504/654-3775.* ⊠ *$2.* ☉ *Wed.–Sun. 9–5.*

Dining and Lodging

$$ ✕ **Drusilla's.** The several large rooms that comprise this rambling restaurant are decorated with murals and paintings of sea scenes and sea creatures, setting the mood for the seafood served here. Munch on plump, seasoned hush puppies while you study the extensive menu. Standout appetizers include escargot in mushroom caps, fried crab fingers, and oysters on the half shell. "A Taste of Louisiana"—a sampling of seafood gumbo, seafood eggplant casserole, shrimp au gratin, fried shrimp, fried catfish, french fries, and salad—is a good choice. There are several Cajun fried sea critters and a lengthy list of broiled dishes. ⊠ *3482 Drusilla La. (Drusilla Shopping Center),* ☎ *504/923–0896. AE, DC, MC, V.*

$$ ✕ **Juban's.** An upscale bistro with a lush courtyard and walls adorned
★ with art, Juban's is a family-owned and -operated restaurant that
proudly presents its house specialty—hallelujah crabs, a delectable
concoction of stuffed soft-shell crabs dressed in a Creole sauce. The
sophisticated menu lists, among the starters, oysters Rockefeller and
Bienville, and for the main course a tempting assortment of seafood,
beef, and veal dishes, as well as roasted duck, rabbit, and quail. Veg-
etables are exceptionally tasty here, and Juban's own mango tea is de-
licious. The warm bread pudding is something to write home about.
✉ 3739 Perkins Rd. (Acadiana Shopping Center), ☎ 504/346–8422.
AE, DC MC, V. Closed Sun. No lunch Sat.

$ ✕ **Christina's.** Downtown businesspeople flock here for hearty, inex-
pensive breakfasts (two-fisted biscuits, pancakes, and the like) and
lunches (spaghetti and meatballs is usually one of the specials). Only
the name has changed; everything else is the same: The atmosphere could-
n't be more casual, and the most expensive item on the menu is $6.50.
✉ 320 St. Charles St., ☎ 504/336–9512. AE, MC, V. Closed Sun. No
dinner.

$ ✕ **Mamacita's.** Gussied up with splashy murals of Mexican scenes, bright
hues of pink and green, and sombreros hanging here and there, Ma-
macita's is very popular with locals. A whole raft of combination plat-
ters, fajitas, burritos, tacos, and enchiladas are on the list, and portions
are huge. Gringos can get mesquite-grilled burgers, a grilled red snap-
per, or barbecued pork ribs. ✉ 7524 Bluebonnet Blvd. (Bluebonnet
Village), ☎ 504/769–3850. AE, D, DC, MC, V.

$$$ 🏨 **Embassy Suites.** This centrally located property opened as Crown
Sterling Suites in 1989, and, in 1992, reverted back to Embassy Suites.
Nothing has changed except the name. Each two-room suite, with com-
plexions of peaches and greens, has a galley kitchen with microwave
and coffeemaker, and custom-made mahogany furniture. The complimentary full breakfast is cooked to order. ✉ 4914 Constitution Ave.,
70808, ☎ 504/924–6566 or 800/433–4600, FAX 504/923–3712. 224
suites. Restaurant, bar, room service, indoor pool, sauna, steam room,
shop, laundry service, airport shuttle. AE, D, DC, MC, V.

$$–$$$ 🏨 **Baton Rouge Hilton.** Conveniently located at I–10 and College
Drive, this high-rise hotel has somewhat formal rooms and public
spaces, with traditional furnishings. Of the six suites, two are split-level;
the top two floors offer VIP perks such as Continental breakfast and
afternoon hors d'oeuvres and cocktails. ✉ 5500 Hilton Ave., 70808,
☎ 504/924–5000 or 800/621–5116; 800/221–2584 in LA; FAX 504/
925–1330. 292 rooms, 6 suites. Restaurant, coffee shop, lobby lounge,
no-smoking rooms, room service, sauna, 2 tennis courts, health club,
jogging, laundry service, concierge, business services, airport shuttle.
AE, D, DC, MC, V.

$$ 🏨 **Marriott's Residence Inn.** One- and two-bedroom suites in this cen-
★ trally located hotel come with dens, wood-burning fireplaces, dining
rooms, and fully equipped kitchens. The two-bedroom suites have
whirlpool tubs. Rooms have traditional furnishings. ✉ 5522 Corpo-
rate Blvd., 70808, ☎ 504/927–5630 or 800/331–3131, FAX 504/926–
2317. 80 suites. Pool, outdoor hot tub, laundry service, concierge. AE,
D, DC, MC, V.

Nightlife and the Arts

BARS AND NIGHTCLUBS

Housed in an old movie house, the **Varsity Theatre** (✉ 3353 Highland
Rd., ☎ 504/343–5267 or 504/383–7018) features live shows, live music,
and dancing. Live shows, music, dancing, and pool tables attract a
younger crowd to the **Caterie** (✉ Acadian Perkins Plaza, 3617 Perkins

Rd., ☎ 504/383–4178). **The Chimes** (✉ 3357 Highland Rd., next to Varsity Theatre, ☎ 504/383–1754) is a popular gathering place for the young crowd. **Gino's Restaurant** (✉ 4542 Bennington Ave., ☎ 504/927–7156) has a piano bar and occasionally a jazz trio. The young and not-so-young dance in a tropical setting at **TD's** (✉ Baton Rouge Hilton Hotel, ☎ 504/924–5000). There's live jazz at **Rick's Café Americain** (✉ 2363 College Dr., ☎ 504/924–9042).

CAJUN CLUBS

Mulate's (✉ 8322 Bluebonnet Rd., ☎ 504/767–4794) in Baton Rouge is a chip off the famed old Breaux Bridge block.

CONCERTS

Top-name stars such as Alabama and Neil Diamond are booked into the **Centroplex Theatre for the Performing Arts** (☎ 504/389–3030). Guest soloists perform frequently with the **Baton Rouge Symphony Orchestra** (✉ Centroplex Theatre for the Performing Arts, ☎ 504/387–6166). LSU's annual **Festival of Contemporary Music** (☎ 504/388–5128), which takes place in February, is more than 40 years old.

COUNTRY-WESTERN

The **Texas Club** (✉ 456 N. Donmoor Ave., ☎ 504/928–4655) is the hot spot for top-name country artists.

RIVERBOAT CASINOS

Carnival's *Casino Rouge* (☎ 800/447–6843) docks across from the capitol and is loaded up with games of chance and lively entertainment. **Argosy's** *Belle of Baton Rouge* (☎ 800/266–2692), a riverboat casino with all the games and entertainment you'd expect, is berthed at Catfish Town, Front and Government streets.

THEATER

The **Swine Palace Theatre** (✉ LSU Theater on Dalrymple Dr., LSU campus, ☎ 504/388–5128) is an Equity theater whose director is the estimable Barry Kyle. The **Baton Rouge Little Theatre** (✉ 7155 Florida Blvd., ☎ 504/924–6496) has been presenting musicals, comedies, and dramas for more than 40 years. **Cabaret Theatre** (✉ 3116 College Dr., ☎ 504/927–7529) presents productions by local groups.

Outdoor Activities and Sports

GOLF

Two 18-hole championship **golf courses** that are open to the public: **Santa Maria** (✉ 1930 Perkins Rd., ☎ 504/752–9667) and **Webb Park** (✉ 1351 Country Club Dr., ☎ 504/383–4919), which is close to most hotels.

SWIMMING

Blue Bayou Waterpark, the state's largest water park, has a wave pool, a seven-story slide, and a lazy river. For the little ones there's a 7,000-square-ft pollywog pool. There's also a seafood restaurant, a chicken restaurant, a pizzeria, and a fast-food facility. ✉ *18142 Perkins Rd., off I-10, Baton Rouge,* ☎ *504/753–3333.* ⛄ *$13.99 for anyone over 4', $10.95 for under 4'.* ☉ *June–Labor Day, daily 10–6.*

TENNIS

You can lob and volley at the tennis courts of **City Park** (✉ 1440 City Park Ave., ☎ 504/344–4501 or 504/923–2792), **Highland Road Park** (✉ Highland and Amiss Rd., ☎ 504/766–0247), and **Independence Park** (✉ 549 Lobdell Ave., ☎ 504/923–1792).

St. Francisville

45   *25 mi north of Baton Rouge on U.S. 61.*

Described as a town 2 mi long and 2 yards wide, much of long, skinny St. Francisville is listed on the National Register of Historic Places. Allow
★ plenty of time for your visit to **Rosedown Plantation and Gardens,** which may bring on a bad attack of hyperbole. Suffice it to say that the opulent house dates from 1835, is beautifully restored, and nestles in 28 acres of exquisite formal gardens. Rosedown offers bed-and-breakfast accommodations, though not in the main mansion. ✉ *12501 LA 10, just off U.S. 61,* ☎ *504/635–3332.* 🎟 *$10.* ☉ *Mar.–Oct., daily 9–5; Nov.–Feb., daily 10–4.*

The Myrtles is noted for its 110-ft gallery with Wedgwood-blue cast-iron grillwork, a lovely setting for the weddings and receptions that are frequently held here. The house was built around 1796 and has elegant formal parlors with rich molding and faux marble paneling. The house tour touches on the Myrtles's claim to the title, America's Most Haunted House. The Carriage House Restaurant is a fine place for lunch. ✉ *7747 U.S. 61, about 1 mi north of downtown St. Francisville on U.S. 61,* ☎ *504/635–6277.* 🎟 *$8.* ☉ *Daily 9–5.*

OFF THE   **AUDUBON STATE COMMEMORATIVE AREA –** A few miles south of St.
BEATEN PATH   Francisville, off U.S. 61, you'll find the 100-acre park where Audubon did a major portion of his "Birds of America" studies. The three-story Oakley Plantation House on the grounds is where Audubon tutored the young Eliza Pirrie. ✉ *LA 956,* ☎ *504/635–3739.* 🎟 *Park and plantation $2.* ☉ *Daily 9–5.*

Golf

The Bluffs (✉ LA 965, 6 mi east of U.S. 61, ☎ 504/634–5222) is an 18-hole Arnold Palmer course that visitors are welcome to play.

En Route   Drive aboard the **ferry** ($1 per car) just outside St. Francisville for a breezy ride across the Mississippi. Pick up LA 1 in New Roads and head south. You'll be driving right alongside False River, which was an abandoned riverbed that became a lake. In contrast to the muddy Mississippi, the waters of False River are dark blue. This is an excellent fishing area, and you'll see long piers and fishing boats tied up all along the route.

Livonia

24 mi west of Baton Rouge via U.S. 190 and LA 77.

In this part of the state, Cajun Country lies to the west and English Louisiana is to the east in St. Francisville. Livonia and environs were settled by French Creoles who moved north from New Orleans in the early 18th century.

Dining

$$ ✕ **Joe's "Dreyfus Store."** This restaurant—off the beaten track, 35 mi
★   west of Baton Rouge—is simply one of Louisiana's best. The rustic frame house contained the Dreyfus Store from 1920 until 1989; shelves along the wall are still lined with relics from its general store days, and the restaurant still uses many of the store's original chairs and cabinets. The atmosphere is quite casual. The highly creative cuisine includes sherry-spiked turtle soup; charbroiled, bacon-wrapped quail; and a superb pork tenderloin, charbroiled, marinated, and served on a bed of braised red cabbage. B&B accommodations are available in the nearby **Dreyfus House,** a quaint Victorian cottage brimming with antiques.

⊠ 2731 Maringouin Dr. (Rte. 77 S), ☎ 504/637–2625. *No reservations. No credit cards. Closed Mon. No dinner Sun.*

White Castle

18 mi south of Baton Rouge on LA 1 on the east bank of the Mississippi.

㊻ White Castle is best known for **Nottoway,** the South's largest plantation home, built in 1859 by famed architect Henry Howard. Legend has it that the town, founded in 1885, was named for the plantation, which looked to residents like a magnificent castle. In fact, some say that the town was named for another grand plantation that no longer exists. The Greek Revival/Italianate mansion has 64 rooms filled with antiques and is especially noted for its white ballroom, which has original crystal chandeliers and hand-carved Corinthian columns. Some of the rooms are open for overnighters. Before you leave the lush grounds, walk across the road and go up on the levee for a splendid view of Old Man River. ⊠ 30970 LA 405, 2 mi north of White Castle, ☎ 504/545–2730. ▧ $8. ☉ Daily 9–5.

Lodging

$$$–$$$$ 🏠 **Nottoway.** A massive Italianate mansion with antiques-filled rooms, this is reputed to be one of the most stunning B&Bs in the nation. Elegant rooms are let to overnight guests, who are welcomed with complimentary sherry upon arrival. Your first breakfast of croissants, juice, and coffee is served in your room; the second breakfast a short while later is a full feast in the Magnolia Room. ⊠ 30970 LA 405, 2 mi north of White Castle, 70788, ☎ 504/545–2730. 13 rooms. AE, D, MC, V.

Donaldsonville

17 mi south of White Castle on LA 1.

In 1770 there was a settlement on this site called Fourche de Chitimacha. A town with the present name was founded in 1806; for a brief period in 1825 it was the state capital. A newspaper reporter at the time wrote that the capital was moved from New Orleans to Donaldsonville because the Crescent City was considered a "modern Sodom."

Dining

$$$ ✕ **Lafitte's Landing.** Pirate Jean Lafitte is said to have frequented this
★   raised Acadian cottage, which dates from 1797. Chef John Folse, who is renowned the world over in culinary circles, prepares such delicacies as shrimp Anne (pecan-smoked shrimp served on fried zucchini) and pecan-smoked tournedos finished with a pecan tasso glace. ⊠ *Sunshine Bridge Access Rd.,* ☎ 504/473–1232. *Reservations essential. Jacket required. D, MC, V.*

Napoleonville

16 mi southeast of Donaldsonville: Take LA 70 and Spur 70 from Donaldsonville south to LA 308, and proceed southeast on LA 308 to Napoleonville.

Contrary to what many people think, Napoleonville was named not for the Little Corporal, but for a family of Napoleons who were early settlers. The town now has a population of just over 800.

★ ㊼ Henry Howard, of Nottoway fame, was also the architect for **Madewood,** a magnificent 21-room Greek Revival mansion with double galleries and white columns. *A Woman Called Moses,* starring Cicely Tyson, was filmed in the house. Like Nottoway, this is an elegant antebellum bed-and-breakfast. ⊠ *4250 LA 308, 2 mi south of Napoleonville,* ☎ *504/369–7151.* ☜ *$6.* ⊙ *Daily 10–5.*

Lodging

$$$$ ☆ **Madewood.** Expect gracious Southern hospitality in this antiques-filled Greek Revival mansion. What sets Madewood apart is its warmth as well as its elegance. As the weekend country home of the Marshall family, it exudes a comfortably lived-in ambience lacking at other plantation mansions. There are five rooms in the main mansion, and three suites in a cottage behind it. The room or suite rate includes not only a full breakfast but wine and cheeses in the parlor, followed by a candlelit Southern dinner in the stately dining room. ⊠ *4250 LA 308, 2 mi south of Napoleonville, 70390,* ☎ *504/369–7151 or 800/375–7151. 5 rooms, 3 suites. AE, D, MC, V.*

Burnside

20 mi northwest of Napoleonville: Go 16 mi on LA 308 to Donaldsonville, then cross the Sunshine Bridge to LA 44 on the west bank and continue west for 4 mi.

The town is named for John Burnside who, in 1840, bought 20,000 acres of land and built Houmas House. On the east bank of the Mississippi River, docents in antebellum garb guide you through **Houmas House,** a Greek Revival masterpiece famed for its three-story spiral staircase. *Hush Hush, Sweet Charlotte,* with Bette Davis and Olivia de Haviland, was filmed here. ⊠ *LA 942, ½ mi off LA 44,* ☎ *504/522–2262.* ☜ *$8.* ⊙ *Feb.–Oct., daily 10–5; Nov.–Jan., daily 10–4.*

49 Built in 1835, **Tezcuco** is a graceful raised cottage with delicate wrought-iron galleries, ornate friezes, an antiques shop, a restaurant, and overnight cottages. Tezcuco is also home to the **River Road African American Museum and Gallery,** which examines this region's slave culture. ⊠ *LA 44, about 7 mi above Sunshine Bridge,* ☎ *504/562–3929.* ☜ *$6.* ⊙ *Mar.–Oct., daily 10–5; Nov.–Feb., daily 10–4.*

Vacherie

24 mi southeast of Burnside via the Sunshine Bridge and LA 18.

Although "vacherie" is a French word meaning pasturelands, this area was originally settled by Germans who came here shortly after the 1718 founding of New Orleans. Later inhabitants were Acadians.

50 Like many of its neighbors, the plantation **Oak Alley** is a movie star, having served as the setting for the Don Johnson–Cybill Shepherd TV remake of *The Long Hot Summer* and more recently for scenes in the Tom Cruise film *Interview with the Vampire.* The house dates from 1839, and the 28 gnarled and arching live oaks trees that give the house its name were planted in the early 1700s. There is a splendid view of those trees from the upper gallery. The plantation also has a restaurant and overnight accommodations on the grounds. ⊠ *LA 18, 7½ mi upriver of the Gramercy/Wallace Bridge,* ☎ *504/265–2151 or 800/442–5539.* ☜ *$7.* ⊙ *Nov.–Feb., daily 9–5; Mar.–Oct., daily 9–5:30.*

51 Different from the dressed-up River Road mansions, **Laura Plantation** is an in-progress restoration of the main house and six slave cabins of a former sugar plantation. The $1.3 million project, scheduled for completion in 2005, will include bed-and-breakfast accommodations. Opened for tours in 1994, it is named for the 1805 owner/manager Laura Locoul, and the restoration is based on historical documents that include 100 pages of her diary. The Br'er Rabbit stories are said to have first been told here by Senegalese slaves. ✉ *2247 Hwy. 18, Vacherie,* ☎ *504/265–7690.* 🎟 *$6.* ⊙ *Daily 9–5.*

Reserve

12 mi east of Vacherie on the west bank: From Vacherie, take LA 18 on the east bank 4 mi to the Veterans Memorial Bridge; cross the bridge to LA 44 on the west bank and go 5 mi east to Reserve.

Local lore has it that a 19th-century peddler who went from plantation to plantation selling trinkets and such was turned away from a particular home (not San Francisco) and vowed he'd "reserve" it for his own. The story (probably apocryphal) continues that the plantation was later sold at auction, and the peddler purchased it for little more than a song.

52 **San Francisco,** completed in 1856, is an elaborate Steamboat Gothic house noted for its ornate millwork and ceiling frescoes. ✉ *LA 44 near Reserve,* ☎ *504/535–2341.* 🎟 *$7.* ⊙ *Daily 10–4.*

Destrehan

5 mi east of San Francisco via LA 44 and LA 48 (the Great River Road), 23 mi from New Orleans via LA 48.

This town was named in the 18th century for one d'Estrehan des Tours, who was a royal treasurer when Louisiana was a French colony. **53** **Destrehan Plantation** is the oldest plantation left intact in the lower Mississippi Valley. The simple West Indies–style house, dating from 1787, is typical of the homes built by the earliest planters in the region. ✉ *9999 River Rd.,* ☎ *504/764–9315.* 🎟 *$7.* ⊙ *Daily 9:30–4.*

Baton Rouge and Plantation Country A to Z

Arriving and Departing

BY BUS
Greyhound Southeast Lines (☎ 800/231–2222) has frequent daily service from New Orleans to Baton Rouge and surrounding towns.

BY CAR
I–10 and U.S. 190 run east–west through Baton Rouge. I–12 heads east, connecting with north–south I–55 and I–59. U.S. 61 leads from New Orleans to Baton Rouge and north. Ferries across the Mississippi cost $1 per car; most bridges are free.

Great Drives. LA 1 travels along False River, which is a blue oxbow lake created ages ago when the mischievous, muddy Mississippi changed its course. The route wanders past gracious homes and small lakeside houses.

BY PLANE
Baton Rouge Metropolitan Airport (☎ 504/355–0333), 12 mi north of downtown, is served by American, Continental, Delta, and Northwest.

Contacts and Resources

EMERGENCIES
Dial **911** for assistance. Hospital **emergency rooms** are open 24 hours a day: **Baton Rouge General Medical Center** (✉ 3600 Florida Blvd., ☎ 504/387–7000) and **Our Lady of the Lake Medical Center** (✉ 5000 Hennessy Blvd., ☎ 504/765–6565).

GUIDED TOURS
Tiger Taxi & Tours (☎ 504/921–9199 or 504/635–4641) runs Baton Rouge city tours, tours of plantation country, and swamp tours. **Rachel**

Hall's St. Francisville Tours (☎ 504/635−6283) conducts van tours of the Feliciana parishes north of Baton Rouge and of Cajun Country.

RADIO STATIONS
AM: KBRH 1260, CNN news/talk; WIBR 1300, news/talk/sports. **FM:** WYNK 101.5, country; WBRH 90.3, jazz/alternative.

24-HOUR PHARMACIES
Eckerd (⊠ 4530 S. Sherwood Forest Blvd., ☎ 504/291−0596). **Walgreen's** (⊠ 4747 S. Sherwood Forest Blvd., ☎ 504/292−8975).

VISITOR INFORMATION
Louisiana Visitor Information Center (⊠ Louisiana State Capitol Bldg., State Capitol Dr., Box 94291, Baton Rouge 70808-9291, ☎ 504/342−7317). **Baton Rouge Area Convention and Visitors Bureau** (⊠ 730 North Blvd., Box 4149, Baton Rouge 70804, ☎ 504/383−1825 or 800/527−6843). **West Feliciana Historical Society Information Center** (⊠ 364 Ferdinand St., St. Francisville, ☎ 504/635−6330).

NATCHITOCHES AND CANE RIVER COUNTRY

Natchitoches and environs have characteristics of both North and South Louisiana in terms of culture and cuisine. In this part of the state, barbecue is as popular as Cajun food, and country-western beats vie with zydeco for dancing feet. The terrain, however, is decidedly different. Here, the hills are alive with the scent of pine trees. Natchitoches is on the fringe of the Kisatchie National Forest, and while the area isn't exactly mountainous—the highest peak in all the state, "Driskill Mountain," farther north, soars to a dizzying 535 ft above sea level— it appears so after flat-as-a-pancake South Louisiana.

Natchitoches

264 mi northwest of New Orleans via I−10, U.S. 190, and I−49.

The earliest permanent European settlement in the Louisiana Purchase territory was not New Orleans but the little town of Natchitoches (pronounced Nak-uh-tish), which predates the Crescent City by four years. Nestled in rolling green hills and thick pine forests, Natchitoches has two other claims to fame. The town hosts a sparkling Christmas Festival of Lights, which was featured in the film *Steel Magnolias,* and it's the hometown of that film's screenwriter, Robert Harling. The friendly residents are happy to point out where Dolly Parton, Sally Field, Julia Roberts, and the other magnolias hung out during filming.

Front Street, which is lined with small, wrought iron−faced buildings, lies alongside pretty Cane River Lake. The lake's sloping grass-green banks are shaded by giant live oak trees. The downtown area is part of a 33-block historic landmark district, which contains a number of homes open to the public. Trolley and boat tours, which focus on *Steel Magnolias* sites, are available through Cane River Cruises (☎ 318/352−2557).

The **Museum of Historic Natchitoches** examines the colorful history of the area. Rooms are devoted to the 1803 Louisiana Purchase, the prehistoric Caddo Indians (with artifacts from 5000 BC), the French and Spanish influence of the 1700s, and to the movies *Steel Magnolias* and *The Horse Soldiers*, both of which were filmed in Natchitoches. ⊠ 840 Washington St., ☎ 318/357−0700. ☞ $2. ☉ Daily 9−5.

Fort St. Jean Baptiste is a reconstruction of the outpost that stood near this site in 1716. The several replica buildings were constructed using 18th-century hardware, including hand-forged door latches and hinges. Structures include a church, powder magazine, and kitchen. ⊠ *Morrow and Jefferson Sts.,* ☎ *318/357–3101.* ⊡ *$2.* ⊙ *Daily 9–5.*

Natchitoches is on the fringe of the 100,000-acre **Kisatchie National Forest** (☎ 318/352–2568). In addition to its hardwood and pine forests, it offers equestrian, hiking, and nature trails; picnic and camping sites; and splendid vistas.

Dining and Lodging

$$ ✕ **Landing.** This large, noisy bistro with white tablecloths is one of the
★   town's most popular restaurants. The extensive menu includes such starters as shrimp rémoulade, potato skins, and fried cheese sticks. Pasta, steak, chicken, and seafood are prepared a number of different ways. The spicy, country-fried steak is distinctive; the garlic bread is superb, as is the bread pudding. ⊠ *530 Front St.,* ☎ *318/352–1579. AE, MC, V. Closed Mon.*

$ ✕ **Lasyone's Meat Pie Kitchen.** Natchitoches is famed for its succulent meat pies, and the best place to sample them is this ultracasual country-kitchen café. Other offerings include meat, chicken, and seafood; for dessert, select from a display of Cane River cream pies. ⊠ *622 2nd St.,* ☎ *318/352–3353. Reservations not accepted. No credit cards. Closes at 7 PM. Closed Sun.*

$ ✕ **Open Hearth Deli & Pub.** On the ground floor of the Cloutier Townhouse, this casual eatery has Cajun and Creole soups, po'boys, salads, and deli sandwiches. A trio entertains Wednesday evenings. You can call in orders for take-out, or dine in. ⊠ *8 Ducournau Sq., Front St.,* ☎ *318/352–3197. Reservations not accepted. AE, DC, MC, V.*

$$ ⊡ **Cloutier Townhouse.** On Front Street, overlooking Cane River Lake, this elegant three-story town house offers B&B accommodations. The exterior is adorned with filigreed cast-iron galleries, and the interior has high ceilings, hardwood floors, and Louisiana Empire antiques. The larger and quieter of the two bedrooms is the master bedroom, which has a tester bed, gas fireplace, wing chairs, and a settee. The master bath has a whirlpool bath and lighted shower stall. Breakfast includes homemade multigrain bread, fresh fruit, and traditional Natchitoches meat pies. ⊠ *8 Ducournau Sq., 71457,* ☎ *318/352–5242. 2 rooms. Deli. MC, V.*

$$ ⊡ **Holiday Inn.** Comfortable and predictable rooms are available in this link of the familiar chain. On the outskirts of town, it offers a restaurant, outdoor pool, and cable TV. ⊠ *Hwy. 1 South Bypass, 71457,* ☎ *318/357–8281 or 800/465–4329,* ⊞ *318/352–9907. 143 rooms, 2 suites. Restaurant, bar, pool. AE, D, DC, MC, V.*

$$ ⊡ **Jefferson House.** A B&B near the historic district, Jefferson House is a split-level frame structure in a serene setting. Guests occupy the entire first floor, which is decorated in a tasteful blend of traditional furnishings and East Asian objets d'art. A large, stately parlor has a high beamed ceiling, brick fireplace, and doors opening to a veranda with rocking chairs and a view of Cane River Lake. Bedrooms have quilted spreads and matching drapes; baths are large and modern. ⊠ *229 Jefferson St., 71457,* ☎ *318/352–3957. 2 rooms. MC, V.*

$ ⊡ **Fleur-de-Lis.** The granddaddy of local B&Bs is an unpretentious turn-of-the-century house with a front porch and swing. The downstairs family room looks and feels lived-in. A friendly golden retriever named Moose helps Tom and Harriette Palmer make guests feel at home. Full breakfast is served family-style in an adjacent dining room. Guest rooms have a four-poster or a brass bed and wicker furnishings; baths are small but modern. ✉ *336 2nd St., 71457,* ☎ *318/352–6621 or 800/489–6621. 5 rooms. AE, MC, V.*

Nightlife and the Arts

The **Melrose Plantation Arts and Crafts Festival,** an annual event held the second weekend in June, showcases 135–150 regional craftsmen and -women displaying their arts beneath the canopy of live oaks on the picturesque grounds of Melrose Plantation. There are also food booths galore featuring Natchitoches meat pies and oodles of home-made desserts. For information, call the Natchitoches Parish Tourist Commission at 318/352–8072 or 800/259–1714.

Cane River Country

South of Natchitoches and nestled amid lush gardens is **Beau Fort Plantation,** constructed in the early 1800s of hand-hewn cypress and bousillage (an insulating material made of Spanish moss and mud). The handsome home, which is also a B&B, has an 84-ft gallery, and French doors line the front. The house is furnished with 19th-century Louisiana antiques and family heirlooms. ✉ *Rte. 119, Bermuda, about 11 mi south of Natchitoches.* ☎ *318/352–5340 or 318/352–9580.* 🎟 *$4.* ☉ *Daily 1–4.*

The Cane River Lake drifts southward from Natchitoches, lined by tall trees, stately plantations, and humble cottages. Several plantation homes are open for tours. Eight miles south of Beau Fort Plantation, **Melrose Plantation** was the home of the late self-taught artist Clementine Hunter, who was known as the "black Grandma Moses." The first owner of Melrose was a black freed slave who, with her family, began construction of the seven buildings in 1796. In this century, Melrose was the home of a patron of the arts whose guests included Erskine Caldwell, Lyle Saxon, and Alexander Woollcott. The African House, an unusual Congo-style structure, the second floor of which is decorated with Hunter's murals, is of particular interest. ✉ *Rte. 119, Melrose,* ☎ *318/379–0055.* 🎟 *$5.* ☉ *Daily noon–4.*

The still-working **Magnolia Plantation** is 6.2 mi south of Melrose. It is one of only two National Bicentennial Farms west of the Mississippi River. The mansion's 27 rooms are furnished with an extensive collection of Louisiana and Southern Empire antiques. The outbuildings, which include brick cabins and a barn containing the only cotton press in the United States still in its original location, will become part of a projected Cane River Creole National Historical Park. ✉ *Hwy. 119 near Derry, 22 mi south of Natchitoches,* ☎ *318/379–2221.* 🎟 *$5.* ☉ *Daily 1–4 by appointment.*

Handmade bricks, heart cypress, and wood pegs were used to build the Kate Chopin House, which houses the **Bayou Folk Museum.** Completed in 1813, in the 1880s this raised cottage was the home of Kate Chopin, author of *The Awakening.* The museum contains photographs and memorabilia and a first edition of *Bayou Folk,* a collection of Chopin's short stories about Cane River Country. ✉ *LA 491, 4 mi south of Magnolia Plantation in Cloutierville,* ☎ *318/379–2233.* 🎟 *$5.* ☉ *Mon.–Sat. 9–5, Sun. 1–5.*

OFF THE
BEATEN PATH

LECOMPTE – This small town, 45 mi south of Cloutierville via I-49 and U.S. 71, was named for a racehorse famed in these parts in the 19th century. The horse's name was Lecomte (the town is pronounced le-count); according to an oft-told tale, an inebriated sign painter inserted the "p," and the town became Lecompte.

Louisianians who make the trek from North to South Louisiana often plan to arrive in Lecompte at lunchtime. At **Lea's Lunch Room,** there's nothing fancy—just a huge sun- and noise-filled room where country food has been served since 1928. The corn bread and homemade pies are legendary. Expect brusqué service and plate lunches of prodigious proportions. ☒ *U.S. 71S, Lecompte,* ☎ *318/776-5178. Reservations not accepted. MC, V. Closed Mon.*

Natchitoches and Cane River Country A to Z

Arriving and Departing

BY BUS

Natchitoches is served by **Greyhound** (☎ 800/231–2222).

BY CAR

Route 1 and I–49, which cut north–south through the state's midsection, bisect Natchitoches.

Contacts and Resources

EMERGENCIES

Dial **911** for police and ambulance in an emergency. The **Natchitoches Parish Hospital** (☒ 501 Keyser, ☎ 318/352–1200) offers help in medical emergencies.

GUIDED TOURS

Cane River Cruises (☎ 318/352–2557) offers tours of Natchitoches by boat and by trolley. The boat tour is romantic; kids love the tours on the little trolley. **Tours by Jan** (☎ 318/352–2324 or 318/352–3802, FAX 318/352–0666), **Ducournau Square, Inc.** (☎ 318/352–5242), and **UniqueTours of Natchitoches** (☎ 318/357–8698) all offer walking and driving tours of Natchitoches and the Cane River region.

RADIO STATION

KNWD 91.7, rock and alternative (FM).

VISITOR INFORMATION

The **Natchitoches Parish Tourist Office** (☒ 781 Front St., ☎ 318/352–8072 or 800/259–1714) provides information about the region, including self-guided walking/driving-tour brochures.

LOUISIANA A TO Z

Arriving and Departing

By Bus

Greyhound-Trailways (☎ 800/231–2222) provides both interstate and intrastate bus service.

By Car

Major east–west arteries through the state are Interstate 20 (I–20), which parallels U.S. 80 through North Louisiana, and Interstate 10 (I–10), which goes coast to coast, cutting through downtown New Orleans along the way. North–south routes include Interstate 49 (I–49), which goes diagonally through the state from Lafayette in the south through Shreveport and into Arkansas. Interstate 55 (I–55) comes south from Chicago and connects with I–10 about 20 mi west of New Orleans. LA Hwy 1 is a scenic route, often over substandard roads, that goes diagonally from Grand Isle on the Gulf of Mexico to the farthest northwest tip of the state.

By Plane

All major domestic carriers, as well as AeroMexico, British Airways, and Lacsa, fly into **New Orleans International Airport** (☎ 504/464–3547), the state's largest airport.

By Train

Amtrak trains (☎ 800/872–7245) from Miami, New York, Chicago, Los Angeles, and points in between pull into New Orleans's' Union Terminal in the Central Business District.

Getting Around

By Bus

Greyhound-Trailways (☎ 800/231–2222) provides bus service between the state's cities and towns.

By Car

The speed limit on interstates is 70 mph. Right turns on red lights are permitted unless otherwise indicated. The Official State Map, available from the Louisiana Office of Tourism (☞ Visitor Information, *below*) and visitor centers, has a mileage chart as well as directories for each tourist area.

By Plane

There are **regional airports** served by commuter carriers in Baton Rouge (☎ 504/357–4165), Lafayette (☎ 318/232–2808), Alexandria (☎ 318/449–4642), Lake Charles (☎ 318/477–6051), Shreveport (☎ 318/673–5370), and Monroe (☎ 318/329–2461).

By Train

Amtrak (☎ 800/872–7245) serves South Louisiana with stops in Schreiver (between Thibodaux and Houma), New Iberia, Lafayette, and Lake Charles. There is one train that operates westbound on Monday, Wednesday, and Saturday, and an eastbound train Tuesday, Thursday, and Sunday.

Contacts and Resources

Bed-and-Breakfasts

For a free illustrated brochure of statewide bed-and-breakfasts, contact **Louisiana Bed & Breakfast** (✉ Box 4003, Baton Rouge 70821–4003, ☎ 800/677–5597).

Emergencies

For **ambulance and fire** emergencies statewide, call 911.

Fishing

For information about licenses and lake maps, contact the **Louisiana Department of Wildlife & Fisheries** (✉ Box 98000, Baton Rouge 70898, ☎ 504/765–2800).

Road Conditions

Cal the **24-hour Highway Safety Hotline** (☎ 800/259–4929 or 504/379–1541) for information.

Shopping

Louisiana is the first state to grant a sales tax rebate to non-U.S. shoppers. Look for shops, restaurants, and hotels that display the tax-free logo, then ask for a voucher for the tax, which varies from parish to parish, that's tacked onto most purchases. Present vouchers with your passport and airline ticket at the tax rebate office in New Orleans International Airport, and receive up to $500 cash back. Rebates exceeding $500 will be mailed to your home address.

State Parks

Detailed information about campsites and facilities in the state parks can be obtained from the **Louisiana Office of State Parks** (⊠ Box 44426, Baton Rouge, LA 70804, ☎ 504/342–8111).

Visitor Information

For a copy of the free "Louisiana Tour Guide" brochure, contact the **Louisiana Office of Tourism** (⊠ Box 94291, Baton Rouge 70804-9291, ☎ 504/342–8119 or 800/334–8626).

5 Mississippi

Dotted with Civil War battlegrounds, Mississippi is a gold mine for history buffs and offers some of the best-preserved examples of antebellum architecture in the South. The Natchez Trace Parkway, strung with magnolia trees and hilltop vistas, cuts across the heart of Dixie, passing through Tupelo, Jackson, and antebellum Natchez. The mighty Mississippi forms the western border of the state, winding slowly through the Delta past the port towns of Greenville and Vicksburg. Even the riverboat casinos along the Gulf Coast evoke the past.

Updated by
Charlotte
Durham

AS YOU ENTER THE LUSH AND LOVELY Magnolia State, slow down, look around, and listen carefully so as not to miss a single one of the South's great treasures. Mississippi is, indeed, deep in the heart of Dixie, and Dixieland is steeped in legend and lore.

Listen, and hear the soft, gentle drawl of an authentic Southern welcome. Stop in small towns, rich with historic houses and museums, busy with locals eager to regale you with slightly partisan tales of the Civil War. Sit quietly and catch snippets of the gossip that permeates the air of any eatery redolent with country cooking. Gossip and good food get on famously down South.

Mississippians eat, sleep, and breathe history—so much so that they subconsciously perpetuate the presence of ancestors. Dyed-in-the-wool Mississippians honor tradition, which manifests itself in everything from the meticulous upkeep of stately old homes—you can tour many of them during special pilgrimage times—to the painstaking preservation of colorful front-porch stories passed down from generation to generation.

You'll feel exalted reading William Faulkner's Nobel Prize address, you'll laugh at the characters in Eudora Welty's short stories, and you'll find pathos aplenty in Tennessee Williams's plays, and thrills in John Grisham's best-sellers. Hear the Delta Blues music of Robert Johnson and B. B. King, and roll to the rock of Tupelo native Elvis Presley. Mississippians all, they've contributed to a mystique no other state can touch.

Pleasures and Pastimes

Dining

Fresh Gulf seafood, particularly redfish, flounder, and speckled trout, stars in coast restaurants. Soft-shell crab is a coast specialty, and crab claws are a traditional appetizer. Coast locals are fond of quaffing Barq's root beer with their seafood. In Tupelo, Jackson, and Natchez you can find everything from caviar to chitlins. Jackson has several elegant restaurants. Tupelo specializes in down-home cooking, but blue-plate dinners of fresh Mississippi vegetables are a widely available alternative. Southern breakfasts served in antebellum opulence are a Natchez trademark. All in all, good food and drink are required in the South; fancy surroundings aren't. Dress is casual unless otherwise noted.

CATEGORY	COST*
$$$$	over $20
$$$	$15–$20
$$	$10–$15
$	$5–$10

*per person for a three-course meal, excluding drinks, service, and 8%–10% sales tax (depending on the area)

Gambling

Sip a cocktail, enjoy a show, or maybe even strike it rich at the splashy, Las Vegas–style casinos permanently docked along the waterfront in Gulfport, Biloxi, Bay St. Louis, and Waveland on the Gulf Coast, or in the Delta's Tunica County. The casinos, with their numerous bars, lounges, and restaurants, are open 24 hours a day, so night owls are never at a loss for a place to go.

Lodging

With the advent of dockside casinos, the Gulf Coast hotel business is booming. Reserve a couple of weeks ahead—as gambling aficionados say, the "coast is cookin'." National hotel and motel chains are found

Mississippi

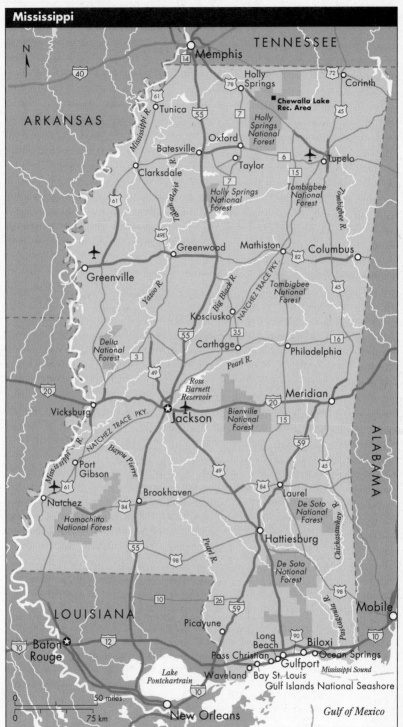

throughout the Natchez Trace region, though Jackson's historic mansions add variety. In Natchez, travelers will find plantation homes that open their doors in bed-and-breakfast courtesy.

CATEGORY	COST*
$$$$	over $70
$$$	$50–$70
$$	$30–$50
$	$20–$30

All prices are for a standard double room, excluding 8%–9% tax (depending on the area).

Pilgrimage Tours

Mississippians love to show their Southern hospitality by opening their antebellum and Victorian homes to the public in the form of spring and fall, and, in Natchez, December pilgrimages. Annual or biannual pilgrimages take place in Biloxi, Columbus, Holly Springs, Ocean Springs, Port Gibson, Natchez, and Vicksburg, with tours in Natchez being the crown jewel. Dates change year to year, so call the visitor centers in the towns for details.

Exploring Mississippi

Mississippi is a state of contrasts. The Gulf Coast and the areas as far north as Vicksburg and Natchez have a decidedly New Orleans flavor, while the Delta—the rich area of farmland periodically delivered by Mississippi River floods—is more like Memphis: genteel, polite, but all business. A trip along the Natchez Trace, which stretches from Natchez northeast through Jackson and Tupelo, then on to Nashville, will carry you back to a time of settlers, outlaws, traveling preachers, and post riders. Holly Springs and Oxford are sophisticated courthouse towns in northern Mississippi that don't fit neatly under the Gulf Coast, Delta, or Natchez Trace banners. They exemplify yet another dimension of Mississippi's diversity.

Great Itineraries

How you tour Mississippi depends largely on whether you start at the top or the bottom. You can experience a section of the Natchez Trace whether you're in north, central, or south Mississippi, since it cuts diagonally through the state. Driving the entire Trace takes about seven hours, but you could spend seven days if you have the time. The same goes for the rest of Mississippi. You could drive from top to bottom in six hours, but your only memory might be row after row of roadside pine trees. Instead, take at least three days to explore any one of Mississippi's areas, or span the state for a nine-day vacation.

IF YOU HAVE 3 DAYS

Casinos docked all along the Gulf Coast have kept the area from Ocean Springs to Bay St. Louis packed with tourists, and there are other activities besides gambling to keep you busy. A day and a half here is a minimum. **Ocean Springs** is worth at least an afternoon, with its Walter Anderson Museum of Art, Shearwater Pottery, and unique shops. Move westward to ☒ **Biloxi**, for sand, sun, and fishing, and by all means take an excursion to one of the barrier islands that separate the Gulf of Mexico from Mississippi Sound. The second day, head for ☒ **Natchez**, where you might want to stay at one of the antebellum town's bed-and-breakfast establishments. Leave a full day for touring Natchez, more if you come during a pilgrimage time, when many of Natchez's lovely old homes are opened to visitors.

IF YOU HAVE 6 DAYS

Start out on the Gulf Coast where you'll dine on some of the finest seafood in the states. Overnight at either ⊞ **Ocean Springs** or ⊞ **Biloxi.** On day two, head to ⊞ **Natchez,** worth at least an afternoon of exploration. On the third day, enjoy a leisurely drive through **Port Gibson** to ⊞ **Vicksburg,** at the southern end of the Delta. Civil War history buffs could easily spend a day here, and perhaps a night before going on to ⊞ **Jackson,** which is filled with notable architecture and small museums. On the fifth day, drive a long stretch of the Natchez Trace, being sure to stop and explore **Tupelo.** If time allows, drive on to ⊞ **Oxford** to spend the night.

IF YOU HAVE 9 DAYS

With nine days you'll have time to experience the Gulf Coast and a good portion of the Natchez Trace; see the itineraries above for suggested routes. Set aside the last three days to explore the Delta. You'll want to spend part of a day in ⊞ **Oxford,** soaking up the literary vibes set forth by such Southern heros as William Faulkner, Eudora Welty, and Tennessee Williams. Visit Faulkner's Rowan Oak and the campus of the University of Mississippi, more commonly called Ole Miss, but be sure to stop by the Eudora Welty Library where the region's rich literary history is felt most strongly. Try to fit in a trip north to ⊞ **Holly Springs,** which survived more than 50 raids during the Civil War. Next morning, start toward **Clarksdale.** You'll pass the casinos of **Tunica County** on your right as you head into blues country. A hot tamale at Doe's in **Greenville** will let you know you've entered another phase of Mississippi.

When to Tour Mississippi

To be part of the action, hit the Gulf Coast's Mardi Gras celebrations in late January and February, Biloxi's Blessing of the Fleet in May, and Jackson's Jubilee! JAM, also in May. Fall brings historic house tours and antiques browsing in Natchez. The Mississippi Division of Tourism Development (☞ Visitor Information *in* Mississippi A to Z, *below*) will gladly send you a travel planner.

Prepare for the weather—Mississippi's fairly fickle. Spring and fall are glorious, while lazy summer days call for cool drinks on a shady veranda. Now and then, a winter cold snap sends porch-sitters scurrying inside. Locals say it's tolerable here year-round, but be prepared for a few mood swings.

THE GULF COAST

Ocean Springs, Biloxi, Gulfport

The Mississippi Gulf Coast runs along U.S. 90 from Alabama to Louisiana. Restaurants, bars, hotels, motels, and souvenir shops jostle for space along U.S. 90's busy four lanes, and the riverboat casinos permanently docked at the water's edge welcome travelers seeking a good time. But don't let the clamor of this neon strip hide the coast's quieter treasures: the ancient land, sculpted by wind and water, continually changing; serene beachfront houses set on green and shady lawns; the teeming wildlife of Mississippi Sound and its adjacent bayous and marshes; the unspoiled natural beauty of the seven barrier islands that separate the Gulf of Mexico from Mississippi Sound.

On a clear day, if you have good eyesight or a good imagination, you can see these islands. Their names (from east to west) are Petit Bois (anglicized as "Petty Boy"), Horn, East and West Ship, and Cat. Two others, Round and Deer, lie within Mississippi Sound.

Three hundred years ago, France, England, and Spain ruled the area, according to their fortunes in international wars. Street names, family names, and traditions still reflect this colorful heritage. In the late 19th and early 20th centuries, the coast became a fashionable vacation spot for wealthy New Orleanians and Delta planters eager to escape yellow fever epidemics. Elegant hotels, imposing beachfront mansions, and smaller summer homes sprang up. Today the homes that have endured the vagaries of time and hurricanes stand along the beach—brave and beautiful survivors. Many of the homes along the coast are open for tours during pilgrimage time. The dates vary, so call the Mississippi Beach Convention and Visitors Bureau (☞ Visitor Information *in* the Gulf Coast A to Z, *below*).

Today, the coast's people are known to be easygoing and tolerant, artistic and hardy. Add the local love of fun and frolic, and you'll understand why Las Vegas–style gaming has been a major coastal to-do since its inception in August 1992. Dockside gambling's replica ships recall the days of riverboat gambling once rampant along the mighty Mississippi. Casino vessels today, however, are permanently moored and open round-the-clock. Restaurants, dockside cafés, and Southern hospitality are among the offerings.

Enjoy wondrous walks along the water, but take your cue from the locals and ignore any urge to swim in the Sound. It's murky (at best). Instead, admire the stately live oaks and frolic on the white sands. Go floundering and spear your supper. Above all, slow down. On the Mississippi Coast only the traffic on U.S. 90 moves quickly.

Ocean Springs

35 mi west of Mobile, 90 mi east of New Orleans.

To begin at the beginning, at least as far as Mississippi is concerned, start in Ocean Springs. Here, in 1699, the French commander Pierre LeMoyne Sieur d'Iberville established Fort Maurepas to shore up France's claim to the central part of North America. This first colony was temporary, but it's fondly remembered by Ocean Springs in its spring festival celebrating d'Iberville's landing. Magnificent oaks shade the sleepy town center, a pleasant area of small shops to explore on foot.

Walter Anderson (1903–65), an artist of genius and grand eccentricity, made his home in Ocean Springs. Drawings and watercolors, some not discovered until after his death, are on display at the **Walter Anderson Museum of Art,** built as an attachment to the **Old Community Center** where Anderson painted murals in 1951 (before it became the "Old" Community Center). The **Little Room** was extracted from Anderson's cottage home, loaded on a flatbed truck, and moved to the museum, with its murals intact. Anderson painted the intricate murals in the Community Center for a fee of $1; they are now appraised at $1 million. *Museum:* ⊠ *510 Washington Ave.,* ☎ *601/872–3164.* ⊠ *$3.* ☉ *Mon.–Sat. 10–5, Sun. 1–5.*

The **Shearwater Pottery and Showroom** offers a wide selection of original Anderson family hand-thrown and cast pottery. Visitors can watch the pottery being made in the Anderson family workshop. ⊠ *102 Shearwater Dr.,* ☎ *601/875–7320.* ☉ *Showroom Mon.–Sat. 9–5:30, Sun. 1–5:30; workshop weekdays 9–noon, 1–4.*

A brochure from the **Ocean Springs Chamber of Commerce** (⊠ 1000 Washington Ave., ☎ 601/875–4424) will guide you on a driving tour of the d'Iberville Trail, shaded by moss-draped trees and bordered by weathered but lovely summer houses. The route, which begins at

Ocean Springs' train station, winds through the area first explored 300 years ago by Pierre LeMoyne Sieur d'Iberville.

🕭 The **Doll House** accommodates a collection of contemporary and antique dolls, stuffed animals, and dollhouses. ⊠ *1201 Bienville Blvd. (U.S. 90), Ocean Springs,* ☎ *601/872–3971.* ⊇ *$1 donation requested for YMCA Pet Shelter.* ⊙ *Tues.–Sun. 1–5.*

★ **Gulf Islands National Seashore** (⊠ 3500 Park Rd., Ocean Springs, ☎ 601/875–9057)—which includes Ship, Horn, and Petit Bois islands—has its headquarters on Ocean Springs's Davis Bayou. When the heat and humidity aren't overwhelming, have a picnic and explore the nature trails. Wilderness camping is available on Horn and Petit Bois islands, accessible by charter and private boat. Call for a list of charter boat operators. Gulf Islands National Seashore offers 50 campsites for trailers and RVs, with electrical hookups available.

Dining

$$$ ✕ **Germaine's.** Formerly Trilby's, this little house surrounded by live oaks has served many a great meal to its faithful clientele. The atmosphere is reminiscent of New Orleans, with unadorned wooden floors, walls decked in local art for sale, fireplaces, and attentive service. Specialties include crabmeat au gratin, broiled trout served with mushrooms and sautéed crabmeat, and sautéed veal served with a creamy port wine sauce. ⊠ *1203 Bienville Blvd., U.S. 90E,* ☎ *601/875–4426. AE, DC, MC, V. Closed Mon. No dinner Sun.*

$$–$$$ ✕ **Jocelyn's Restaurant.** Jocelyn scandalized Mississippians when she
★ left Trilby's kitchen (now Germaine's, *above*), but they love her cooking just as much in this old frame house. This is as good as coast seafood gets. Specialties are fresh crabmeat fixed three or four ways. Trout, flounder, and, when available, snapper are subtly seasoned and served with garnishes as bright and original as modern art. Stuffed eggplant is another specialty. ⊠ *U.S. 90E, opposite Sunburst Bank,* ☎ *601/875–1925. Reservations not accepted. No credit cards.*

Shopping

At **Ballard's Pewter** (⊠ 1110 Government St., Ocean Springs, ☎ 601/875–7550) you can find necklaces and earrings made from sand dollars or have the pewterer fashion a "bespoke" (custom-made) piece.

Biloxi

2 mi west of Ocean Springs.

Biloxi (pronounced bi-*lux*-i) is the oldest continuous settlement on the Gulf Coast and the third-largest city in Mississippi. When Pierre LeMoyne Sieur d'Iberville met the Native Americans who called themselves Biloxi, or "first people," he gave their name to the area and to the bay. The French constructed Fort Louis here; it served as the capital of the Louisiana Territory from 1720 to 1722, when the capital was moved to New Orleans.

Visit the **J. L. Scott Marine Education Center and Aquarium,** which has 41 live exhibits and aquariums brimming with reptiles and fish. The centerpiece is a spectacular 42,000-gallon tank. ⊠ *115 Beach Blvd.,* ☎ *601/374–5550.* ⊇ *$3.50.* ⊙ *Mon.–Sat. 9–4.*

Across U.S. 90 is **Point Cadet Plaza,** a waterfront complex which, in the 1880s, housed European immigrants who flocked to Biloxi to work in seafood canneries. Exhibits at the **Seafood Industry Museum** depict the growth and development of the Gulf Coast seafood industry. A re-created **schooner,** which docks at Point Cadet's marina, is available for short trips and charters; call for fees and schedules. ⊠ *Point*

Cadet Plaza, Hwy. 90 and 1st St., ☎ 601/435–6320. ▣ Museum $2.50. ☉ *Mon.–Sat. 9–4:30.*

Biloxi's **Small Craft Harbor,** off U.S. 90 on the Sound, captures the atmosphere of a lazy fishing village. Catch the **Sailfish Shrimp Tour** boat and experience 70 minutes as a shrimper as you cast your nets upon the waters. ✉ *Hwy. 90 and Main St., ☎ 601/385–1182. ▣ $9.* ☉ *Call for schedule.*

Erected in 1848, Biloxi's 65-ft-tall **lighthouse,** on U.S. 90, is a landmark. During the Civil War, Federal forces, operating from Ship Island, blockaded Mississippi Sound and cut Biloxi off from much-needed supplies. When the Yankees demanded that Biloxi submit or starve, the reply was that the Union would have to "blockade the mullet" first. Ever since, mullet has been known as "Biloxi bacon" and honored with its own festival each October. The city defended itself with what appeared to be a formidable cannon array near the lighthouse but was actually only two cannons and many logs painted black. ✉ *U.S. 90 at Porter Ave., ☎ 601/435–6293. ▣ $1.50.* ☉ *By appointment.*

Mardi Gras is almost as grand a celebration in Biloxi as in nearby New Orleans, and the Krewe costumes are equally festive. Costumes and crowns are housed in the **Mardi Gras Museum,** in the old Magnolia Hotel, an 1847 structure listed on the National Register of Historic Places. ✉ *119 Rue Magnolia, ☎ 601/435–6245. ▣ $1.* ☉ *Weekdays 11–4.*

The **George Ohr Arts & Cultural Center** houses a collection of pottery crafted by the eccentric Ohr, known as "the mad potter of Biloxi." ✉ *136 G.E. Ohr St., ☎ 601/374–5547. ▣ $2.* ☉ *Mon.–Sat. 9–5.*

En Route   On U.S. 90 between Biloxi and Gulfport is **Beauvoir,** the antebellum beachfront mansion where Jefferson Davis spent the last 12 years of his life. Here the president of the Confederacy wrote his memoirs and his book *The Rise and Fall of the Confederate Government.* The serene, raised cottage–style house, with its sweeping front stairs, is flanked by pavilions and set on a broad lawn shaded by ancient live oaks. A Confederate cemetery on the grounds includes the Tomb of the Unknown Soldier of the Confederacy. ✉ *2244 Beach Blvd., ☎ 601/ 388–1313. ▣ $6.* ☉ *Daily 9–4.*

Dining and Lodging

$$$$ ✕ **Mary Mahoney's Old French House Restaurant.** Locals swear by it, perhaps more for the comfort of its old brick and age-darkened wood (the mansion Mary Mahoney's calls home dates back to 1737) and for the memory of Mary herself (who always went from table to table, chatting with customers) than for the food. Start off with a bowl of gumbo. The lightly breaded panfried Veal Antonio, topped with cheese sauce and plenty of fresh crabmeat, the stuffed red snapper, and the sautéed shrimp are excellent main choices. Don't leave the table without sampling the mouthwatering bread pudding drenched in rum sauce. ✉ *110 Rue Magnolia, ☎ 601/374–0163. AE, DC, MC, V. Closed Sun.*

$$–$$$ ✕ **Fisherman's Wharf.** A neighboring shrimp factory perfumes the parking lot here, but inside there's fresher air and views of oyster shuckers at work on the pier. You'll find soft-shell crab, gumbo, and oyster po'boys among the lunch specials; broiled catch-of-the-day for dinner; and always, the only dessert, the mysterious Fisherman's Wharf pie. ✉ *315 E. Beach Blvd., ☎ 601/436–4513. Reservations not accepted. AE, D, DC, MC, V.*

$–$$$ ✕ **McElroy's Harbor House Restaurant.** Biloxi locals and real shrimpers eat hearty breakfasts, lunches, and dinners as fishing boats come and go and fisherfolk load and unload their nets just outside. Notable are the po'boys, oysters on the half shell, broiled stuffed flounder, and stuffed crabs. ✉ *Biloxi Small Craft Harbor, 695 Beach Blvd.,* ☎ *601/435–5001. Reservations not accepted. AE, D, DC, MC, V.*

$ ✕ **Ole Biloxi Schooner.** Coast residents flock to this family-run restaurant on Biloxi's serene back bay. It's tiny—little more than a shack—but the food is good, especially the gumbo and the po'boys, which come "dressed" and wrapped in paper. ✉ *159 E. Howard,* ☎ *601/374–8071. Reservations not accepted. No credit cards.*

$$$$ 🏨 **President Broadwater Beach Resort.** This sprawling property comes complete with golf courses, tennis courts, a casino, and a marina. Accommodations vary depending on which of the two hotels in the resort you choose, and rates vary according to room size and location. ✉ *2110 Beach Blvd., 39533,* ☎ *601/388–2211 or 800/647–3964,* ᴲᴬˣ *601/385–1801. 540 rooms, 10 suites. 4 restaurants, 3 lounges, 4 pools, 2 18-hole golf courses, 10 tennis courts, basketball, exercise room, volleyball, boating, casino, playground. AE, D, DC, MC, V.*

$$$–$$$$ 🏨 **Treasure Bay.** Formerly the Royal d'Iberville, the hotel has spacious rooms now bright with chintz, along with a casino. The furniture is hotel-functional; the large public areas are comfortably contemporary. ✉ *1980 W. Beach Blvd., 39530,* ☎ *601/385–6000. 268 rooms. Restaurant, lounge, 2 pools, casino, meeting rooms. AE, D, DC, MC, V.*

Gulfport

12 mi west of Biloxi.

A variety of activities for children plus access to one of the Gulf's most historic islands makes Gulfport a nice stop for families. If you have time for only one activity on the coast, make it a getaway to **Ship Island** on the passenger ferry from the **Gulfport Small Craft Harbor;** the ferry runs March–October. At Ship Island, a part of Gulf Islands National Seashore, a U.S. Park Ranger will guide you through **Fort Massachusetts,** built in 1859 and used by Federal troops to blockade Mississippi Sound during the Civil War. The rangers will treat you to tales of the island's colorful past, including the story of the *filles aux casquettes—* young women sent by the French government as brides for the lonely early colonists. Each girl (*fille*) carried a small hope chest (*casquette*). Spend the day sunning, swimming in the clear green water, and beach-combing for treasures washed up by the surf. ✉ *Ticket office at Gulfport Harbor in Joseph T. Jones Memorial Park, east of intersection of U.S. 49 and U.S. 90,* ☎ *601/864–3797; 601/864–1014 after hrs for ferry schedule.* 🎫 *Fees vary; call ahead.* ☉ *Ferry runs Mar.–Oct.*

☾ With a playground, bumper boats and cars, and more than 100 arcade games, **Funtime USA** provides hours of entertainment for children. ✉ *U.S. 90 and Cowan Rd.,* ☎ *601/896–7315.* 🎫 *Grounds free; 75¢– $3 for rides and games.* ☉ *Summer months, daily 9 AM–midnight; rest of yr, daily 9–4.*

☾ **Marine Life Oceanarium** puts on continuous shows with performing dolphins, sea lions, and macaws. ✉ *Joseph T. Jones Memorial Park, east of intersection of U.S. 49 and U.S. 90,* ☎ *601/863–0651.* 🎫 *$11.75.* ☉ *Daily 9 AM–sunset.*

Dining

$$$ ✕ **Chappy's.** Special-occasion dining for Coast residents often means a visit to this pleasant restaurant in Long Beach, just outside Gulfport. Specialties include rich gumbo, redfish panfried Cajun style, and barbecued shrimp. The fish, fresh from the Gulf, is cooked by Chef Chappy himself. ⊠ *624 E. Beach,* ☎ *601/865–9755. AE, D, DC, MC, V.*

$$–$$$ ✕ **Vrazel's.** The interior of this charming brick building has a soothing intimacy about it, with soft lighting and dining nooks with large windows facing the beach. Choose from a substantial list of coastal water fare: red snapper, Gulf trout, flounder, and shrimp prepared every which way. Try the Eggplant La Rosa: baby Gulf shrimp and fresh crabmeat blended with eggplant, herbs, spices, and cheese in a casserole, topped with Parmesan and baked. ⊠ *3206 W. Beach Blvd. (U.S. 90),* ☎ *601/863–2229. AE, D, DC, MC, V. Closed Sun. No lunch Sat.*

Shopping

Gulfport Factory Shops (⊠ Exit 34A off I–10, 10000 Factory Shops Blvd., ☎ 601/867–6100) has more than 70 famous-brand shops offering factory-outlet prices. The shops are connected by a covered walkway. A food court, a tourist information booth, and a playground are also on premises.

En Route The landscape grows increasingly broad, wild, and lovely west of Gulfport. From Long Beach through to Pass Christian, **Ocean Boulevard** (MS 90) bisects stretches of stately homes to the north and shimmering water to the south.

Pass Christian

10 mi west of Gulfport.

Sailboat racing in the South began here, and consequently, the second yacht club in the country was formed (it still exists today)—Louisiana landowner Zachary Taylor was at the yacht club when he was persuaded to run for the presidency. Twenty-six miles of man-made beach extend from Biloxi to Pass Christian. Toward the west the beaches become less commercialized and crowded; Pass Christian's is the best of all. Tan, sail, jet ski, or beachcomb, but *don't swim:* The waters are shallow and murky.

Dining

$$$$ ✕ **Blue Rose Restaurant & Lounge.** This antiques-filled West Indian–
★ style house (circa 1848), with a wonderful view of the Pass Christian Yacht Harbor and the Gulf of Mexico, is known in these parts for its Sunday champagne brunch featuring eggs Benedict and Creole platter (redfish, crab cakes, and barbecued shrimp). Other times, the kitchen turns out beautifully prepared and presented traditional New Orleans cuisine including a thick gumbo, pasta Orleans with oyster sauce, and trout roulades with crabmeat dressing and cayenne cream. ⊠ *120 W. Scenic Dr.,* ☎ *601/452–9402. AE, DC, MC, V. Closed Sun. after 3.*

OFF THE BEATEN PATH
CROSBY ARBORETUM – Well worth a 30-mi detour to the town of Picayune, the arboretum, with its 64-acre Interpretive Center Pinecote, focuses on the ecosystems of the 16,000-square-mi Pearl River Drainage Basin of southern Mississippi and Louisiana. ⊠ *I–59, Exit 4 at Picayune, 370 Ridge Rd.,* ☎ *601/799–2311.* ☞ *$3.* ☉ *Wed.–Sun. 9–5.*

Shopping

Hillyer House (⊠ 207 E. Scenic Dr., ☎ 601/452–4810) sells handmade jewelry, pottery, glass, and brass made by local and regional artists, plus packaged Southern delicacies.

Waveland

15 mi west of Pass Christian.

Travelers who think of Waveland as just a spot to get onto I–10 for New Orleans are missing one of the most accessible tourist information offices on the Gulf Coast. Waveland also offers great camping, and the residents throw a pretty snazzy Mardi Gras parade.

Camping

Turn south on Nicholson Avenue, and follow the signs to **Buccaneer State Park** (✉ 1150 S. Beach Blvd., ☎ 601/467–3822), which conceals 129 campsites in a grove of live oaks streaming with moss. An Olympic-size wave pool may lure you from the nature trail and picnic sites. There are no cabins, but toilet and shower facilities are available. The park, open year-round, also has two tennis courts with lights, two basketball courts, and a seasonal camp store.

Dining

$ ✕ **Lil Ray's.** Though the appointments are limited to trestle tables and benches, this is a place to dream about when you're hungry for seafood platters and po'boys. A waitress, asked by a customer for a diet drink, said it best: "Mister, this ain't no diet place." ✉ *613 Hwy. 90,* ☎ *601/ 467–4566. Reservations not accepted. D, MC, V.*

The Gulf Coast A to Z

Arriving, Departing, and Getting Around

BY BUS

Coast Area Transit (✉ 333 DeBuys Rd., Gulfport, ☎ 601/896–8080) provides coast-wide public transportation. **Greyhound** (☎ 800/231–2222) connects the coast with Jackson, New Orleans, and Mobile. Local service exists in Biloxi (✉ 166 Main St., ☎ 601/436–4335); Gulfport (✉ 2805 13th St., ☎ 601/863–1022); and Bay St. Louis (✉ 512 Ulman Ave., ☎ 601/467–4272).

BY CAR

You can drive across the Gulf Coast in 1½ hours via I–10 and U.S. 90. From Gulfport, it takes just over an hour to reach New Orleans, and less than three hours to get to Jackson via U.S. 49.

BY PLANE

Fly into the **Gulfport-Biloxi Regional Airport** (✉ Airport Rd., off Washington Ave., Gulfport, ☎ 601/863–5953), 15 minutes from the beach. Try American Eagle, ASA/The Delta Connection, Casino Airlink (scheduled charter service), Continental Express, or Northwest Airlink.

Contacts and Resources

EMERGENCIES

Dial 911 or go to the emergency room at **Gulf Coast Medical Center** (✉ 180 DeBuys Rd., Biloxi, ☎ 601/388–6711).

GUIDED TOURS

Celebrity Limousine and Tours Service (✉ 2421 South Shore Dr., Biloxi, ☎ 601/388–1384) charters bus tours of the coastal area and New Orleans. **Magnolia Tours & Transportation** (✉ 111 Rue Magnolia, Suite 103, Biloxi 39530, ☎ 601/374–7423 or 800/642–4684) custom-plans group tours in buses or vans.

OUTDOOR ACTIVITIES AND SPORTS

For **floundering** you'll need nighttime, a flashlight, and a gig. Just head for Mississippi Sound, roll up your jeans, and spear your supper with the gig. A chicken neck on a string will put you in the **crabbing** business at any public pier. If you're feeling lazy (or queasy), substitute a crab trap for the string and chicken neck.

Charter boats for half-day, full-day, and overnight deep-sea **fishing** can be found at marinas and harbors all along the Gulf Coast. Prices start around $30 per person; group rates are usually available. The Mississippi Beach Convention and Visitors Bureau (☞ Visitor Information, *below*) can assist you. Unless you're on a chartered boat (where the captain's license will cover you), you'll need a fishing license. Three-day licenses are available in many bait shops and other stores along the harbor.

The coast's climate allows for year-round **golfing,** and golf packages are offered by many coast hotels and motels. Diamondhead's **Pine** and **Cardinal courses** (✉ 7600 Country Club Circle, ☎ 601/255–3910) offers 36 holes that challenge even the pros. Wooded, gently rolling, and well kept, they are ringed by the large, elegant houses and condominiums of Diamondhead resort community. **Mississippi National Golf Club** (✉ 900 Hickory Hill Dr., Gautier, ☎ 601/497–2372 or 800/538–3155) offers visitors fairways lined with whispering pines, tall oaks, magnolias, and dogwoods on an 18-hole course. Flowers surround the teeing areas. **Pine Island Golf Course** (✉ Gulf Park Estates, 2¼ mi east of Ocean Springs, 3 mi south of U.S. 90, ☎ 601/875–1674) was designed by Pete Dye, who created the tournament players course in Jacksonville. This 18-hole course spans three islands, and its abundant wildlife, beautiful setting, and clubhouse can console you for any double bogeys. **Windance Country Club** (✉ 19385 Champion Circle, Gulfport, ☎ 601/832–4871) has an 18-hole golf course ranked by *Golf Digest* among the top 100 in the United States; nonmembers can play here through hotel golf packages.

PHARMACY
Talvert Gamble (✉ 2561 Pass Rd., Biloxi, ☎ 601/338–1411).

RADIO STATIONS
FM: KNN 99.1, country; WMJY 93.7, adult contemporary.

VISITOR INFORMATION
Get a free *Attractions and Accommodations* guide to the Gulf Coast area at the **Mississippi Beach Convention and Visitors Bureau** (✉ Box 6128, Gulfport 39506, ☎ 601/896–6699 or 800/237–9493), open weekdays 8–5.

THE NATCHEZ TRACE
Corinth, Tupelo, Jackson, Natchez

The flower-sprigged and forested Natchez Trace Parkway is a vast and verdant history lesson. This enchanted path between Nashville and Natchez is said to be about 8,000 years old. It follows the early trails worn by Choctaw and Chickasaw Native Americans, itinerant preachers, post riders, soldiers, and settlers. Landscaped by the National Park Service, the Trace winds through straight pines, haunting cypresses, peaceful vistas of reeds, and still waters with dense woodlands, and grows increasingly wild and mysterious as it nears Natchez.

Now virtually complete, the Trace is almost 450 mi long, with 313 mi in Mississippi. The Mississippi segment of the Natchez Trace begins as you enter the state's northeast corner, between Iuka and Belmont. Mile markers are posted along the way to help drivers navigate. There are no billboards on the parkway and commercial vehicles are forbidden to use it. Park rangers are serious about the 50 mph speed limit; you'll probably get acquainted with one if you drive any faster.

Numbers in the margin correspond to points of interest on the Natchez Trace map.

Corinth

1 *90 mi southeast of Memphis.*

Settled just seven years before the war, Corinth assumed military importance because of its Memphis and Charleston Railroad. In April 1862, after the bloody battle of Shiloh, near Shiloh Church in Tennessee, 21 mi to the north, the Confederates retreated to Corinth and turned it into a vast medical center. In May 1862, the Confederates, under General P. G. T. Beauregard, were forced to withdraw farther. Their retreat involved the most ingenious hoax of the war: To fool the Federal forces, campfires were lighted, dummy cannoneers were placed at fake cannons, empty trains were cheered as if they were carrying reinforcements, and buglers moved along the deserted works, playing taps. The ploy worked and was hailed as a triumph for Beauregard and a hollow victory for the Union forces who occupied the town. In October 1862, a Confederate attempt to recapture the town failed.

Markers and displays throughout town commemorate the Battles of Shiloh and Corinth. The **Northeast Mississippi Museum** displays Civil War artifacts and distributes a free self-guided tour brochure to help you explore the historic town. ⊠ *4th St. at Washington St.,* ☎ *601/ 287–3120.* ⌹ *Free.* ☉ *Mar.–Oct., daily 10–5; Nov.–Feb., daily 10:30–4:30.*

J. P. Coleman State Park

2 *13 mi north of Iuka off U.S. 25.*

With accommodations aplenty for overnighters, J. P. Coleman State Park (⊠ 613 County Rd. 321, Iuka 38852, ☎ 601/423–6515) allows nature lovers ample time for exploring its various nature trails and playing in its waters. There are wooded campsites for tents and RVs, and 10 secluded cabins, some of them old and rustic, others from the 1970s with fireplaces and central air and heat. Rooms at the balconied lodge overlook the shale beaches of serene Pickwick Lake. Visitors can rent canoes and boats, fish, swim, and water-ski.

Jacinto

3 *9 mi east of U.S. 45.*

Between Corinth and Tupelo on MS 356 is Jacinto, with its restored Federal-style courthouse (1854) surrounded by pre-1870 buildings that are slowly being restored. Jacinto also has nature trails that lead to mineral springs, and a swinging bridge. For more information on Jacinto, call 601/286–8662.

Tishomingo State Park

4 *15 mi south of Iuka.*

In the Appalachian foothills, Tishomingo State Park (⊠ Natchez Trace mile marker 304, Box 880, Tishomingo 38873, ☎ 601/438–6914) has a unique terrain for Mississippi. If you're feeling peppy, a 13-mi nature trail winds through a canyon along steep hills by waterfalls, granite outcrops, and a swinging bridge; otherwise, take the winding roads through shady forests. Eight-mile canoe trips and float trips are offered

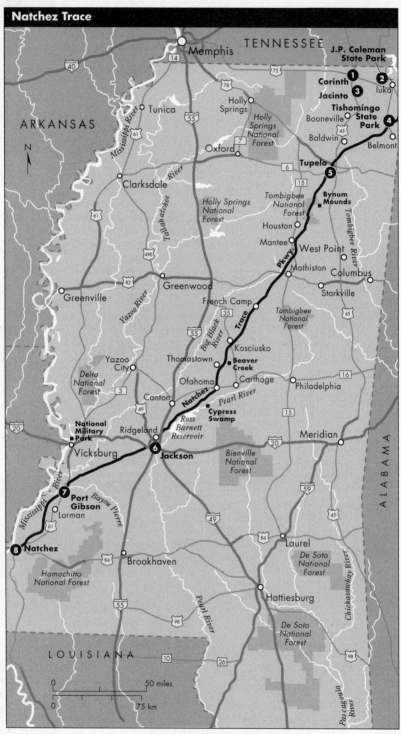

Natchez Trace

from mid-March through October. Around Ha[...]
campsites and hookups. Rustic cabins are an[...]
own food. The park has an outdoor swim[...]
warmer months; there's a $2 charge.

En Route The **Natchez Trace Parkway Visitor Center** [...]
the Trace. The Visitor Center offers exhibits, a 12-min[...]
on area for children, and the 4-ft *Official Map and Guide*, with mi[...]
by-mile information from Nashville to Natchez.

Tupelo

❺ *90 mi southeast of Memphis, 70 mi east of Oxford.*

The largest city in north Mississippi, Tupelo (named after the tupelo gum tree), was founded in 1859 and is a city of accomplishment—it's here, after all, that Elvis Presley was born. Progressive leaders have successfully lured business and industry to an area that only 30 years ago was predominantly agricultural. The arts flourish here, and the medical center is among the largest in the state. The scenic hill country provides beautiful places to camp, swim, fish, jog, and bike.

★ The **Elvis Presley Park and Museum** is anchored by the tiny, two-room "shotgun" house built by Presley's father, Vernon, for just $180. Elvi[...] Aaron Presley was born here on January 8, 1935. The home has bee[...] restored and furnished much as it was when the Presleys lived in [...] The house is now surrounded by Elvis Presley Park, land purchas[...] with proceeds from Elvis's 1956 concert at the Mississippi–Alaba[...] Fair. The park includes a swimming pool, tennis courts, a playgrou[...] a youth center with a gift shop (stocked with Elvis souvenirs), an[...] Elvis Presley Museum, which stores more than 3,000 pieces of [...] memorabilia. The **Elvis Presley Memorial Chapel,** suggested by the s[...] in 1971 as a place for his fans to meditate, was dedicated in 1979, tw[...] years after Presley's death. ⊠ *Off E. Main St., at 306 Elvis Presley Dr.,* ☎ *601/841–1245.* ⊠ *Birthplace $1, museum $4.* ☉ *May–Sept., Mon.–Sat. 9–5:30, Sun. 1–5; Oct.–Apr., Mon.–Sat. 9–5, Sun. 1–5.*

The **Tupelo Museum** displays Presley memorabilia along with other exhibits, including a turn-of-the-century Western Union office, a working sorghum mill, a train depot and caboose, and an old-time country store. ⊠ *James J. Ballard Park, off MS 6W,* ☎ *601/841–6438.* ⊠ *$1.* ☉ *Weekdays 8–4, weekends 1–5.*

The **Tupelo National Battlefield** (⊠ W. Main St. [MS 6]), inside the city limits, commemorates the Civil War Battle of Tupelo with monuments and displays. In 1864 Union General A. J. Smith marched 14,000 troops against Nathan Bedford Forrest's forces near Tupelo. Smith's goal was to end the constant Confederate harassment of supply lines to Sherman's army, and thereby secure the Union invasion of Atlanta. The battle, on July 14, 1864, was the last major battle in Mississippi and one of the bloodiest.

Dining and Lodging

$$$ ✕ **Jefferson Place.** This austere 19th-century house is lively inside, with red-checked tablecloths and bric-a-brac. The place is popular with the college crowd; short orders and steaks are the specialties. ⊠ *823 Jefferson St.,* ☎ *601/844–8696. Reservations not accepted. AE, MC, V. Closed Sun.*

$$ ✕ **Harvey's.** It's a favorite in four cities, and here's why: Harvey's restaurants have based their reputation on consistency and quality in food and service. Try the prime rib, seafood, steak, or, for lighter fare, the chicken Alpine or great garden salad. Lots of plants and warm wood

tones add to the appeal. ⊠ *424 S. Gloster St.,* ☎ *601/842–6763. AE, MC, V. Closed Sun.*

$ ✕ **Vanelli's.** Family pictures and scenes of Greece adorn the walls, and tables are draped in traditional red-and-white checkered tablecloths at this comfortable restaurant. Lunch and dinner buffets include both Greek specialties and lighter fare. Vanelli's own bakery produces breads, strudels, and pastries. ⊠ *1302 N. Gloster St.,* ☎ *601/844–4410. AE, D, DC, MC, V.*

$$$–$$$$ ✕🏠 **Mockingbird Inn Bed & Breakfast.** Each of the seven rooms in this tiny inn is decorated with the theme of a different country. The Athens room comes with Greek columns and statues and sheer flowing fabrics. Some rooms have fireplaces, and one has a whirlpool tub. You're welcome to sit out in the gazebo or on the porch swing and watch the world go by. ⊠ *305 N. Gloster, 38801,* ☎ *601/841–0286,* ℻ *601/840–4158. 7 rooms. AE, D, MC, V.*

$$$$ 🏠 **Rex Plaza Suites.** This four-building hotel offers a variety of suites for short or long-term stays. Some rooms have kitchens and washers and dryers. ⊠ *619 N. Gloster, 38801,* ☎ *601/840–8000 or 800/203–5917,* ℻ *601/840–1116. 64 suites. Restaurant, lounge, pool, exercise room, meeting rooms. AE, D, DC, MC, V.*

$$$ 🏠 **Executive Inn.** Guest rooms in this large, contemporary hotel are plain and functional, but clean. ⊠ *1011 N. Gloster St., 38801,* ☎ *601/841–2222 or 800/533–3220,* ℻ *601/844–7836. 115 rooms. Restaurant, lounge, indoor pool, hot tub, sauna. AE, DC, MC, V.*

$ 🏠 **Ramada Inn.** This modern hotel caters to business travelers and conventions as well as families. There is dancing nightly except Sunday in Bogart's Lounge. Breakfast and lunch buffets are served. ⊠ *854 N. Gloster, 38801,* ☎ *601/844–4111 or 800/228–2828. 230 rooms, 10 suites. Restaurant, pool, barbershop. AE, DC, MC, V.*

$–$$ 🏠 **Trace Inn.** This old motel on 15 acres near the Natchez Trace offers neat rooms and friendly service. ⊠ *3400 W. Main St., 38801,* ☎ *601/842–5555,* ℻ *601/844–3105. 134 rooms. Restaurant, pool, playground. AE, MC, V.*

From Tupelo to Jackson

From Tupelo, the trip to Jackson takes three hours if you don't stop. It can easily take an entire day, however, if you pause to read the brown wooden markers, explore nature trails, and admire the neat fields, trees, and wildflower meadows. If you have the time, don't miss Columbus and environs, an hour or so east of the parkway near the Alabama line. The parkway is incomplete from mile marker 101.5 to 87.0. I–55, I–20, and I–220 are connecting routes. To reach Jackson, follow I–55 south from the Trace.

Bynum Mounds (mile marker 232.4) are ceremonial hills that were constructed between 100 BC and AD 200 by prehistoric people. Exhibits describe their daily existence.

At **French Camp** (mile marker 180.7), where Frenchman Louis LeFleur established a stand in 1812, you can watch sorghum molasses being made on Saturday in late September and October. And you can see Native American and French artifacts inside the authentic "dogtrot-style" cabin.

Cypress Swamp (mile marker 122.0), a pleasure today, was once a treacherous, mosquito-infested morass for early travelers. A 20-minute self-guided nature walk takes you through the tree-canopied tupelo/bald cypress swamp.

The **Mississippi Crafts Center at Ridgeland** (mile marker 102.4) displays and sells high-quality crafts in a dogtrot log cabin. Members of the Craftsmen's Guild of Mississippi have created pewter and silver jewelry, pottery, handwoven and hand-screened clothing, whimsical wooden toys, highly prized Choctaw baskets, and other interesting items. The Center sponsors free demonstrations (usually on weekends) of basket weaving, wood carving, pottery, and quilting. There are rest rooms and picnic tables on site. ⊠ *Natchez Trace at Ridgeland,* ☎ *601/856–7546.* 🖭 *Free.* ☉ *Daily 9–5.*

OFF THE
BEATEN PATH

COLUMBUS – Forty-five miles east of the Natchez Trace on U.S. 82 is one of Mississippi's most undisturbed antebellum towns. This river city (on the Tombigbee) contains 100 pre–Civil War mansions—some of which are open to the public as bed-and-breakfasts or for tours—and many historic sites. Columbus is called the town "where flowers healed a nation" because of a group of gracious women who, in 1866, placed flowers on the graves of both Confederate and Union soldiers. The gesture inspired the poem "The Blue and the Gray," and Columbus's Decoration Day at Friendship Cemetery is now observed as the nation's Memorial Day.

WAVERLY MANSION – This privately owned, immaculately restored showplace has been around since 1852. Outstanding antiques adorn each spacious room. It's 10 mi northwest of Columbus off MS 50. ⊠ Rte. 2, West Point, ☎ 601/494-1399. 🖭 $7.50. ☉ Apr.–Oct., daily 9–sunset; Nov.–Mar., daily 9–5.

Jackson

❻ *180 mi southwest of Tupelo, 45 mi west of Vicksburg.*

At its spangled edges, Jackson has little to distinguish it, but the state capital becomes increasingly original toward its shady heart. The downtown area has many small museums and most of the city's notable architecture.

The city is named for Andrew Jackson, who was popular with Mississippians long before he became president. As Major General Jackson, he helped negotiate the Treaty of Doak's Stand by which the Choctaw ceded large chunks of Mississippi to the United States on October 18, 1820. President Thomas Jefferson recommended that the town be laid out in a checkerboard pattern of alternating squares of buildings and parks. Peter A. Vandorn proposed the plan for Jackson and submitted a map for the new city in April 1822; today the Old Capitol Building and the Capitol Green on which it sits is one of the few remaining examples of Vandorn's brainchild.

The City of Jackson is also the county seat of Hinds County, named for another negotiator, Major General Thomas Hinds, an enterprising and daring hero of the Battle of New Orleans in the War of 1812.

The **Jim Buck Ross Mississippi Agriculture and Forestry Museum** is home to the **Jackson Visitor Information Center,** located in the Chimneyville Crafts Gallery (☞ *Shopping, below*) on the museum grounds. The museum complex looks like an old farm marooned in the midst of expanding suburbs, but the city was actually here first. The 10 farm buildings were brought here to stand exactly as they once did in Jefferson Davis County, Mississippi. A crossroads town, similar to small Mississippi towns in the 1920s, has been assembled with a working blacksmith's shop and a cotton gin; meetings are held in the old Masonic Lodge, and weddings can be arranged at the 1897 Epiphany Episcopal church building. The general store sells soft drinks, snacks, and souvenirs. A complete tour of the museum, which has fine exhibits on agriculture, forestry, and farm-related aviation, takes about 90 minutes. ⊠ *1150 Lakeland Dr., 39216,* ☎ *601/354–6113 or 800/844–8687.* ☞ *$4.* ☉ *Mon.–Sat. 9–5, Sun. 1–5.*

The **Old Capitol Building,** flanked by the **War Memorial Building** (1940) to the north and the **Mississippi Archives Building** (1971) to the south, served as the state capitol from 1839 to 1903. Built between 1833 and 1838, the Old Capitol, with its simple columns and elegant proportions, is a tribute to Greek Revival architecture. The building was restored in 1959–61 to house the **State Historical Museum.** The Vandorn map, a blueprint of the city's original design, and other exhibits depicting Mississippi's history are on display in the museum. ⊠ *100 S. State St.,* ☎ *601/359–6920.* ☞ *Free.* ☉ *Weekdays 8–5, Sat. 9:30–4:30, Sun. 12:30–4:30. Guided tours available.*

The **Jackson Zoological Park** uses more than 100 acres to re-create a natural habitat for about 500 animals. Children love the petting zoo, complete with hands-on exhibits, and the miniature train ride. ⊠ *2918 W. Capitol St.,* ☎ *601/352–2580.* ☞ *$4.* ☉ *Daily 9–5.*

Since its opening in 1847, **City Hall** (⊠ 219 S. President St., ☎ 601/960–1035) has served continuously as Jackson's center of government. A Masonic Hall originally occupied the third floor of this stately white Greek Revival Building. During the Civil War, City Hall was used as a hospital. Peek into the tiny City Council Chamber with its black-and-white floors and heavy red-velvet curtains. On the west side of the building is the formal Josh Halbert Garden, with a 1968 statue of Andrew Jackson.

Within the **Mississippi Arts Center** is the **Mississippi Museum of Art,** dedicated to preserving Mississippi's artistic heritage. With its impressive permanent collection of both regional and national paintings, plus changing exhibits and a sculpture garden, you'll want to allow plenty of time to explore each and every corner. ⊠ *201 E. Pascagoula St.,* ☎ *601/960–1515.* ☞ *$3.* ☉ *Tues.–Sat. 10–5.*

Davis Planetarium is the largest planetarium in the Southeast and one of the world's best-equipped, but its shows vary wildly in quality and scope. ⊠ *201 E. Pascagoula St.,* ☎ *601/960–1550.* ☞ *$4.* ☉ *Hrs vary; call ahead.*

The **U.S. Federal Courthouse** (⊠ 245 E. Capitol St.), in concrete and sandstone, exemplifies the streamlined Art Deco style that was popular between the world wars, a time when many Jackson buildings were constructed. This building was completed in 1934 and served as Jackson's post office and as a Federal court building until 1988, when a new post office was built. The motifs of eagles, stars, and geometric designs on the exterior are repeated throughout the interior and on the freestanding light fixtures around the building.

St. Andrew's Episcopal Cathedral is an important example of Gothic Revival architecture enhanced by fine stained-glass windows. ⊠ *305 E. Capitol St.,* ☎ *601/354–1535.* ☉ *Weekdays 8:30–5.*

The **Mississippi Governor's Mansion** has been the official home of the state's first family since its completion in 1842. At that time, Jackson was a tiny city and this grand Greek Revival dwelling was an optimistic statement. General Sherman presumably lived here in 1863. The mansion is one of only two executive residences to be designated a National Historic Landmark. Invest 30 minutes in the lively tours, strong on leg-

In case you want to see the world.

At American Express, we're here to make your journey a smooth one. So we have over 1,700 travel service locations in over 120 countries ready to help. What else would you expect from the world's largest travel agency?

do more

AMERICAN
EXPRESS

Travel

In case you want to be welcomed there.

We're here to see that you're always welcomed at establishments everywhere. That's why millions of people carry the American Express® Card – for peace of mind, confidence, and security, around the world or just around the corner.

do more

AMERICAN EXPRESS

Cards

In case you're running low.

We're here to help with more than 118,000 Express Cash locations around the world. In order to enroll, just call American Express before you start your vacation.

do more

AMERICAN EXPRESS

Express Cash

And just in case.

We're here with American Express® Travelers Cheques and Cheques *for Two*® They're the safest way to carry money on your vacation and the surest way to get a refund, practically anywhere, anytime.

Another way we help you...

do more ®

AMERICAN
EXPRESS

Travelers Cheques

end as well as fact. ✉ *300 E. Capitol St.*, ☎ *601/359–6421.* ▣ *Free.*
◷ *Tours Tues.–Fri. 9:30–11:30.*

Smith Park (✉ At center of Smith Park Historic District) is the only
public square that remains from the 1822 checkerboard plan of the
city. The park was named after James Smith, a former Jacksonian
(originally from Glasgow, Scotland), who donated $100 to fence and
beautify the area. Eudora Welty used the park as the setting for her
short story "The Winds." The park hosts frequent concerts, festivals,
picnics, and art exhibits.

The **Cathedral of St. Peter the Apostle** (✉ 203 N. West St.), built between 1897 and 1900, is the third building of the congregation, which
organized in 1846. Their first building was burned by Federal troops
in 1863, as were many others in the city. Their second building, now
in the very center of the downtown area, at the site of the present rectory (✉ 123 N. West St.), was considered too remote from town. The
cathedral is only open to the public for church services.

Mynelle Gardens is a 7-acre botanical showplace, where you're invited
to stroll along colorful paths surrounded by Southern flora and gentle streams. ✉ *4736 Clinton Blvd.*, ☎ *601/960–1894.* ▣ *$2.* ◷ *Mar.–*
Oct., daily 9–5:15; Nov.–Feb., daily 8–4:15.

The **Galloway House** (✉ 304 N. Congress St.) is a two-story Second
Empire house. Completed in 1889, this house was built for Methodist
Bishop Charles Galloway, a distinguished churchman of international
renown. In 1983 it was renovated for use as a law office.

The **New Capitol** sits in Beaux Arts splendor at the junction of Mississippi and North Congress streets, its dome surmounted by a goldplated copper eagle with a 15-ft wingspan. Completed in 1903 at a
cost of $1 million, the Capitol underwent a $19-million renovation from
1979 to 1983. It was designed by the German architect Theodore C.
Link, who was influenced by the design of the Capitol in Washington,
D.C. Among the elaborate architectural details inside the building is
a Tiffany window. ✉ *400 High St.*, ☎ *601/359–3114.* ▣ *Free.* ◷ *Week-*
days 8–5; guided tours weekdays at 9, 10, 11, 1:30, 2:30, 3:30.

Eudora Welty Library, the largest public library in Mississippi, is named
in honor of the city's famed short-story writer and novelist (*The Pon-*
der Heart, Losing Battles, The Optimist's Daughter). Opened in 1986,
it houses a 42-ft-long circulation desk, handcrafted in rosewood and
maple by local craftsman Fletcher Cox. The Mississippi Writers' Room
pays homage to the South's rich literary history with exhibits on Miss
Welty, as well as William Faulkner, Tennessee Williams, Margaret
Walker Alexander, Ellen Douglas, and many others. ✉ *300 N. State*
St., ☎ *601/968–5811.* ◷ *Mon.–Thurs. 9–9, Fri.–Sat. 9–6, Sun. 1–*
5.

On North State Street between College and Fortification streets stand
a few **Victorian homes,** the survivors of the many large houses that lined
this street in its heyday as Jackson's best address. The **Morris House**
(✉ 505 N. State St.) is a Classic Revival house built about 1900. The
Virden-Patton House (✉ 512 N. State St.), built about 1849, went un-
damaged through the Civil War, suggesting that Union officers may have
used it as headquarters. The **Millsaps-Buie House** (✉ 628 N. State St.),
built in 1888, has been restored as a bed-and-breakfast inn (☞ Lodging, *below*). Two doors north is the **Garner Green House** (1910), with
an imposing portico of Corinthian columns. This house was moved
across the street from its original location and restored in 1988 as an
office building. **Greenbrook Flowers** (✉ 705 N. State St.), circa 1895–

97, occupies the former St. Andrew's Episcopal rectory; it has been greatly altered. With the exception of the bed-and-breakfast, none of these homes are open to the public.

The **Manship House** was built about 1857 by Charles H. Manship, the Jackson mayor who surrendered the city to General William Tecumseh Sherman on July 16, 1863. The museum is a careful restoration of a small Gothic Revival cottage with wood graining painted by Manship himself. ⊠ *420 E. Fortification St. (enter parking area from Congress St.),* ☎ *601/961–4724.* 🎫 *Free.* ⊘ *Tours Tues.–Fri. 9–4, Sat. 1–4.*

C. W. Welty and his wife, Chestina, built the house at **741 North Congress Street** in 1907. Their daughter Eudora was born in the master bedroom on the second floor in 1909. Welty used images of this house and neighborhood in many of her literary works, including *The Golden Apples.* It is now a law office.

The **Smith Robertson Museum and Cultural Center** has artifacts and exhibits depicting the history of black life in Mississippi. The building housed the first public school for black children in Jackson. ⊠ *528 Bloom St.,* ☎ *601/960–1457.* 🎫 *$1.* ⊘ *Weekdays 9–5, Sat. 9–noon, Sun. 2–5.*

Jackson's oldest house, **The Oaks,** was built by James Hervey Boyd, mayor of Jackson between 1853 and 1858. ⊠ *823 N. Jefferson St.,* ☎ *601/353–1742.* 🎫 *$2.* ⊘ *Tues.–Sat. 10–3.*

Jackson's neat, tree-shaded neighborhoods are excellent for walking, jogging, or Sunday driving, especially the **Belhaven area** bounded by Riverside Drive, I–55, Fortification Street, and North State Street. **Carlisle, Poplar, Peachtree,** and **Fairview streets** are distinguished by fine homes.

Dining and Lodging

$$$ ✕ **Nick's.** Seafood is the main fare at this casually elegant restaurant.
★   Grilled blackfish with crabmeat is one of the many luncheon specials, while dinner brings out more elaborate seafood masterpieces. Soup or salad, and vegetable du jour are included with the entrée. Desserts are wonderful, too, especially the white-chocolate mousse with raspberry sauce. ⊠ *1501 Lakeland Dr.,* ☎ *601/981–8017. Reservations not accepted weekend nights. AE, D, DC, MC, V. Closed Sun.*

$$$ ✕ **Ralph & Kacoo's.** Ralph & Kacoo's originated in South Louisiana,
★   so Cajun fare is naturally de rigueur. Crawfish étouffée is prepared to perfection, for a good price. ⊠ *100 Dyess Rd. (County Line Rd. and I–55),* ☎ *601/957–0702. AE, MC, V.*

$$ ✕ **Iron Horse Bar & Grill.** Near downtown, this fern-filled restaurant in a converted factory serves Southwestern fare, including fajitas and mesquite-grilled seafood or steak. ⊠ *320 W. Pearl St.,* ☎ *601/355–8419. Reservations not accepted. AE, D, MC, V. Closed Sun.*

$$ ✕ **Primos.** In this spot since 1964, after spending its first 15 years in another Jackson location, this cozy and comfy eatery has much experience pleasing local palates. The main dining room recalls a French country inn, while the patio is pure American South. House specialties are fresh seafood and prime ribs. ⊠ *4330 N. State St.,* ☎ *601/982–2064. AE, DC, MC, V. Closed Sun.*

$–$$ ✕ **Palette.** This restaurant, in a gallery in the Mississippi Museum of Art, is one of the state's finest lunch spots. Everybody likes the large, light-filled spaces, the art on the white walls, the friendly bustle of the arts and business communities, the piano music, and, most of all, the food—carefully prepared and beautifully presented. Try the Whine Country Pie: eight layers of meats, cheeses, and vegetables under a flaky crust.

But note that the delicacies change frequently. ⊠ *201 E. Pascagoula St.,* ☎ *601/960–2003. AE, D, MC, V. Closed Mon.*

$ ✕ **Gridley's.** Mexican tile tables and floors enhance small, sunny dining areas. Gridley's is famous for its spicy barbecued pork and ribs served with all the trimmings—coleslaw, baked beans, and potatoes. ⊠ *1428 Old Square Rd.,* ☎ *601/362–8600. AE, D, MC, V.*

$$$$ 🏨 **Fairview.** Listed on the National Register of Historic Places, this stately Colonial Revival mansion is in Jackson's prestigious Belhaven section, conveniently situated near many of the major attractions, yet secluded enough to suggest a country retreat. Period antiques fill the public rooms, and the guest rooms are decked out in chintz and Laura Ashley fabrics. A full breakfast is included in the rate. ⊠ *734 Fairview St., 39202,* ☎ *601/948–3429. 8 rooms. AE, D, MC, V.*

$$$$ 🏨 **Millsaps-Buie House.** This Queen Anne–style home, with its cor-
★ ner turret and tall-columned porch, was built in 1888 for Jackson financier and philanthropist Major Reuben Webster Millsaps, founder of Millsaps College. It is listed on the National Register of Historic Places. Restored as a B&B in 1987, its guest rooms are individually decorated with antiques. A full Southern breakfast is served in the Victorian dining room. ⊠ *628 N. State St., 39202,* ☎ *800/784–0221,* F͞A͞X͞ *601/352–0221. 11 rooms. AE, DC, MC, V.*

$$$ 🏨 **Edison Walthall Hotel.** The cornerstone and huge brass mailbox near the elevators are almost all that remain of the original Walthall Hotel. The dismal motel that occupied the site next door was transformed into the present hotel. The marble floors, gleaming brass, paneled library/writing room, and cozy bar almost fool you into thinking this is a restoration of a 19th-century home. ⊠ *225 E. Capitol St., 39201,* ☎ *601/948–6161 or 800/932–6161,* F͞A͞X͞ *601/948–0088. 208 rooms, 6 suites. Restaurant, bar, barbershop, hot tub, exercise room, gift shop, airport shuttle. AE, DC, MC, V.*

$$$ 🏨 **Ramada Plaza Hotel.** This high-rise convention motel is sleekly contemporary and conveniently located just off I–55N. Rooms are comfortable and clean but nothing to write home about. ⊠ *1001 County Line Rd., 39211,* ☎ *601/957–2800,* F͞A͞X͞ *601/957–3191. 294 rooms. Restaurant, bar, pool, barbershop, exercise room, shop, airport shuttle. AE, DC, MC, V.*

Nightlife

Live rock and roll and rhythm and blues beckon a mix of young and old to the **Dock** (⊠ Main Harbor Marina at Ross Barnett Reservoir, ☎ 601/856–7765) Thursday through Sunday. **Hal and Mal's** (⊠ 200 S. Commerce St., ☎ 601/948–0888) often has live music and there's always plenty of room to dance. **Poet's** (⊠ 1855 Lakeland Dr., ☎ 601/982–9711) presents food, drink, and dance bands in an old-fashioned atmosphere created by antiques, old signs, and a pressed-tin ceiling. **Rodeo's** (⊠ 6107 Ridgewood Rd., ☎ 601/957–9300) is an "in" spot, where live music and dancing attract big crowds.

Outdoor Activities and Sports

GOLF

Lefleur's Bluff Golf Course has nine holes and a driving range. ⊠ *Highland Dr. at Lakeland Dr.,* ☎ *601/987–3998.* 🎫 *$5 weekdays, $6 weekends.*

JOGGING

Jog on paths that curve under tall pines and stretch down to a sunny meadow in **Parham Bridges Park** (⊠ 5055 Old Canton Rd.).

TENNIS

Volley and lob at the 14 outdoor hard courts at **Tennis Center South** (⊠ 2827 Oak Forest Dr., off McDowell Rd., ☎ 601/960–1712) and **Bridges Tennis Center** (⊠ 5055 Old Canton Rd., ☎ 601/956–1105), where there are 15 outdoor hard courts. Both centers have lights for night play.

Shopping

ANTIQUES

Bobbie King's (⊠ Woodland Hills Shopping Center, Old Canton Rd. at Duling Ave., ☎ 601/362–9803) specializes in new and heirloom textiles and exhibits them in lavish displays with one-of-a-kind accessories. **C. W. Fewel III & Co., Antiquarians** (⊠ 840 N. State St., ☎ 601/355–5375) specializes in fine 18th- and 19th-century furnishings and accessories.

BOOKS

Books by Mississippi authors and about Mississippi are available from knowledgeable booksellers at **Lemuria** (⊠ 202 Banner Hall, 4465 I–55N, ☎ 601/366–7619). **Choctaw Books** (⊠ 926 North St., ☎ 601/352–7281) stocks first editions of Southern writers' works.

FLEA MARKET

If you're in the mood for a treasure hunt, the **Fairground Antique & Flea Market,** with 220 dealers, often harbors some fine pieces among the simply fun stuff. ⊠ 900 High St., ☎ 601/353–5327. ☉ Sat. 8–5, Sun. 10–5.

GIFTS

The **Chimneyville Crafts Gallery** (⊠ 1150 Lakeland Dr., ☎ 601/981–2499) sells the work of members of the Craftsmen's Guild of Mississippi, who have raised crafts from their "arts and crafts" status to "craft as art." Pottery, jewelry, woodwork, glasswork, quilts, and paper are among the offerings. The Craftsmen's Guild's objets d'art can also be found in the Mississippi Crafts Center at Ridgeland (☞ From Tupelo to Jackson, *above*).

The **Everyday Gourmet** (⊠ 2905 Old Canton Rd., ☎ 601/362–0723; ⊠ 1625 County Line Rd., ☎ 601/977–9258) stocks state products, including pecan pie, bread, and biscuit mixes; muscadine jelly; jams and chutneys; cookbooks; fine ceramic tableware; and a complete stock of kitchenware and gourmet foods.

En Route Post riders stopped during the early 1800s at the Natchez Trace's **Rocky Springs** (mile marker 54.8). General Grant's army camped here on its march to Jackson and Vicksburg during the Civil War. Trails meander through the woods and up a steep hill to a tiny old cemetery and **Rocky Springs Methodist Church** (1837), where services are still held Sunday.

At mile marker 41.5 is a portion of the **Old Trace,** a short section of the original Native American Trace of loess soil (easily eroded and compacted earth). You can park and walk along it for a short way.

Port Gibson

❼ *Mile marker 39.2; 60 mi southwest of Jackson.*

This is the earliest still-existent town on the Trace, with a large concentration of antebellum homes. **Grand Gulf Military Monument** commemorates the town of Grand Gulf, site of an 1862 Civil War naval battle. On a steep hill, the old town site has become a museum with an 1863 cannon, a collection of carriages, an 1820s dogtrot cabin, an old Catholic church, and a Spanish house from the 1790s. ⊠ *North of Port Gibson off U.S. 61, Rte. 2, Port Gibson,* ☎ *601/437–5911.* ☜ *$1.50.* ☉ *Mon.–Sat. 8–noon and 1–5, Sun. 9–noon and 1–6.*

Aptly named **Church Street** is a shady main thoroughfare lined with churches and stately homes. You won't want to miss the **First Presbyterian Church**, 1859, with its spire topped by a 10-ft hand pointing heavenward. Also on Church Street are **Gage House** (⊠ 602 Church St.), 1830, with double galleries and a handsome brick dependency; **Temple Gemiluth Chassed** (⊠ 706 Church St.), 1892, a synagogue with Moorish Byzantine architecture unique in Mississippi; **St. James Episcopal Church** (⊠ 808 Church St.), circa 1897, a high Victorian Gothic structure designed by a Boston architect; **Port Gibson Methodist Church** (⊠ 901 Church St.), 1860, Romanesque Revival in style; the **Hughes Home** (⊠ 907 Church St.), 1825, once owned by Henry Hughes, author of the first sociology textbook, and once the residence of poet Irvin Russell; and **St. Joseph's Catholic Church** (⊠ 909 Church St.), 1849, Gothic in style, with pointed arches and buttresses.

Gibson's Landing (⊠ 1002 Church St.) is called the "Disharoon House" by locals. Built in the 1830s, it's now a bed-and-breakfast, as is the palatial mid-19th century, 30-room mansion **Oak Square** (☞ Lodging, *below*). This classic Greek Revival treasure is open for tours by appointment.

The Chamber of Commerce (☎ 601/437–4351), where you can get maps to local historic sites, is housed in a small 1805 home built by Port Gibson's founder Samuel Gibson and moved to this site in 1980.

Lodging

$$$$ 🏨 **Oak Square.** Constructed about 1850, this home, with its numerous outbuildings and lovely gardens, occupies an entire block on historic Church Street. Now a bed-and-breakfast, it offers a full Southern breakfast. Rooms are comfortable and have a private bath and color TV. ⊠ *1207 Church St., Port Gibson 39150,* ☎ *601/437–4350 or 800/729–0240,* 🖷 *601/437–5768. 12 rooms. AE, MC, V.*

Shopping

Mississippi Cultural Crossroads (⊠ 507 Market St., ☎ 601/437–8905) has an enviable collection of quilts on display and for sale.

Lorman and Environs

12 mi south of Port Gibson.

Handmade bonnets swing in the breeze on the porch of the **Old Country Store** (⊠ U.S. 61, in Lorman, ☎ 601/437–3661), which was a plantation store built in 1875. Its longleaf-pine flooring is jammed with display cases, most installed when the store was built. You can buy souvenirs here, including mellow hoop cheese.

About 12 mi southwest of Lorman is the restored **Rodney Presbyterian Church.** The town of Rodney, once home to wealthy plantation owners and river merchants, became a ghost town when the Mississippi River shifted its course. Your visit to Rodney will be enhanced by reading Eudora Welty's powerful essay "Some Notes on River Country" and her short story "At the Landing."

Northwest of Lorman, on MS 552, are 23 vine-clad columns that are the romantic ruins of **Windsor,** a huge Greek Revival mansion that was built in 1861 and burned down in 1890. The ruins were featured in *Raintree County,* a late '50s film starring Elizabeth Taylor.

En Route   **Emerald Mound** (Natchez Trace mile marker 10.3) is the second-largest Native American mound in the country, covering almost 8 acres. It was built around 1300 for religious ceremonies practiced by ancestors of the Natchez Native Americans.

The Parkway abruptly ends, putting you on U.S. 61 as you near Natchez. You'll pass through the little town of Washington, capital of the Mississippi Territory from 1802 to 1817. In 1802 **Jefferson College** (☎ 601/442–2901) was chartered as the territory's first educational institution; its historic buildings have been meticulously restored.

Natchez

★ **8** *40 mi southwest of Port Gibson.*

Antebellum Natchez is named for the Natchez Native Americans who lived here and worshipped the sun in small villages before the French built Fort Rosalie in 1716. Later the city came under British rule (1763–79), and the district known today as **Natchez-under-the-Hill** grew up at the Mississippi River landing beneath the bluff. The Spanish took control in 1779 and left their mark on the city by establishing straight streets—which intersect at right angles, atop the bluff—and green parkland that overlooks the river. The United States claimed Natchez by treaty, and the U.S. flag first flew over Natchez in March 1798. The city gave its name to the Natchez Trace and prospered as travelers heading for Nashville passed through with money in their pockets and a willingness to spend it on a rowdy good time.

Between 1819 and 1860, wealthy planters built stylish town houses and ringed the city with opulent plantation homes. Though Natchez survived the Civil War virtually unscathed, its economy suffered. Ironically, it was the city's decline that saved its architectural treasures—no one could afford to remodel or tear houses down. In 1932 the women of Natchez originated the idea of a pilgrimage, in which plantation families offered their homes for touring in hopes of raising money for preservation. The Natchez Pilgrimage is now held three times a year, in spring, fall, and around Christmas. During Pilgrimage, between 24 and 30 houses are open, and crowds flock to see them. Some houses are open year-round.

The following three **antebellum homes,** open daily from 9 to 5, are of particular note. All charge a $5 admission fee. The 1857 **Stanton Hall** (✉ 401 High St., ☎ 601/442–6282 or 800/647–6742) is one of the most palatial and most photographed houses in America. Four giant fluted columns support double porticos enclosed by delicate, lacy wrought-iron railings. This magnificent preservation project of the Pilgrimage Garden Club is furnished with Natchez antiques.

Rosalie (✉ 100 Orleans St., ☎ 601/445–4555), circa 1823, established the ideal form of the "Southern mansion" with its white columns, hipped roof, and red bricks. Furnishings purchased for the house in 1858 include a famous Belter parlor set.

Magnolia Hall (✉ 215 S. Pearl St., ☎ 601/442–6672), circa 1858, was shelled by the Union gunboat *Essex* during the Civil War. The shell reportedly exploded in a soup tureen, scalding several diners at the table. The Greek Revival mansion has stucco walls and fluted columns topped with curving Ionic capitals. Note the plaster magnolia blossoms on the parlor ceiling. There is a costume museum on the second floor.

Natchez National Historical Park was established in 1988 to help preserve the city. Park headquarters are in **Fort Rosalie,** established in 1716 by French colonists. Currently, only one park property is open to the public: **Melrose,** circa 1845, a planter's estate that symbolizes the cotton era. A second property, the **William Johnson House,** circa 1841, is undergoing extensive renovation and can be viewed only from the outside. Johnson's house will eventually open as a museum dedicated to African-American history. *Park headquarters:* ⊠ *210 State St.,* ☎ *601/442–7047. Melrose:* ⊠ *1 Melrose–Montebello Pkwy.,* ☎ *601/446– 5790.* ☞ *$5.* ⊙ *Daily 8:30–5. Tours on the hr.*

Longwood, circa 1860–61, is the largest octagonal house in the United States. Under construction during the Civil War, it was never completed. Preserved in its unfinished state, Longwood is now a museum for the Pilgrimage Garden Club and a National Historic Landmark. ⊠ *140 Lower Woodville Rd.,* ☎ *601/442–5193.* ☞ *$5.* ⊙ *Daily 9–5; hrs during spring, fall, and Christmas pilgrimages vary, so call ahead.*

Natchez in Historic Photographs offers a pictorial history of the city in the late 19th and early 20th centuries through the photography of Henry and Earl Norman. Several hundred prints made from the original glass negatives portray everything from river scenes to street scenes, leaving little to imagine about life in early Natchez. ⊠ *117 S. Pearl St., 2nd floor,* ☎ *601/442–4741.* ☞ *$3 suggested donation.* ⊙ *Mon.–Sat. 10–5, Sun. 1–5.*

Grand Village of the Natchez Indians. This archaeological park and museum depicts the culture of the Natchez Native Americans, which reached its zenith in the 1500s. ⊠ *400 Jefferson Davis Blvd.,* ☎ *601/ 446–6502.* ☞ *Free.* ⊙ *Mon.–Sat. 9–5, Sun. 1:30–5.*

Dining and Lodging

$$$ ✕ **Liza's.** Since it opened in October 1993 this restaurant, in a historic
★ house (circa 1852) with a view of the Mississippi River, has consistently attracted a loyal following. The menu features regional New American cuisine, rare fare for a small Southern town. Roast breast of duck with tart cherry sauce served with pecan wild rice, and sautéed veal medallions with smoked garlic Alfredo are popular choices. ⊠ *657 S. Canal St.,* ☎ *601/446–6368. MC, V. No lunch.*

$$ ✕ **Carriage House Restaurant.** On the grounds of Stanton Hall (☞ Natchez, *above*), the Carriage House serves up fried chicken, baked ham, and its famous mouthwatering miniature biscuits. The Victorianparlor ambience is delightful. ⊠ *401 High St.,* ☎ *601/445–5151. AE, MC, V. No dinner except during Pilgrimage weeks.*

$$ ✕ **Natchez Landing.** The porch tables provide a view of the Mississippi
★ River, which is at its very best when both the *Delta Queen* and *Mississippi Queen* steamboats dock. Specialties are barbecue (pork ribs, chicken, beef) and fried and grilled catfish. ⊠ *35 Silver St., Natchez-Under-the-Hill,* ☎ *601/442–6639. Reservations not accepted. AE, MC, V.*

$$ ✕ **Pearl Street Pasta.** This intimate restaurant with minimalist decor is known for its fresh pasta and daily specials. Favorites on the menu are the Cajun shrimp pasta, Italian chicken salad pasta, and pasta jambalaya. ⊠ *105 S. Pearl St.,* ☎ *601/442–9284. AE, MC, V. No lunch Sun.*

$$ ✕ **Scrooge's.** This old storefront-cum-restaurant has a pub atmosphere downstairs and a more subdued and intimate ambience upstairs. The menu includes red beans and rice, and mesquite-grilled chicken or shrimp with angel-hair pasta. ⊠ *315 Main St.,* ☎ *601/446–9922. Reservations not accepted. AE, MC, V. Closed Sun.*

$ ✕ **Cock of the Walk.** The famous original of a regional franchise, this marvelous old train depot overlooking the Mississippi River specializes in fried catfish fillets, fried dill pickles, hush puppies, mustard greens, and coleslaw. There's also blackened or grilled catfish and chicken. ⊠

200 N. Broadway, on bluff, ☎ *601/446–8920. AE, D, DC, MC, V. No lunch.*

$$$$ ✕🏠 **Monmouth.** This plantation mansion (circa 1818) was owned by
★ Mississippi governor John A. Quitman from 1826 to his death in
1858. Guest rooms are decorated with tester beds and antiques. The
grounds are tastefully landscaped, with a New Orleans–style courtyard, a pond, and a gazebo. The plantation dinner, featuring true-to-
period foods, is unforgettable. ⊠ *36 Melrose Ave., 39120,* ☎ *601/
442–5852 or 800/828–4531,* FAX *601/446–7762. 13 rooms, 14 suites.
Reservations essential for dinner. AE, D, DC, MC, V.*

$$$$ 🏠 **Briars.** Once the home of Varina Howell, the wife of Jefferson
Davis, the Briars sits on a promontory overlooking the Mississippi River.
The 19 acres of landscaped grounds are a perfect place for peaceful
strolling, and the inn's rooms are beautifully decorated with period furnishings imparting a gracious plantation feel. ⊠ *31 Irving La. (behind
the Ramada Hilltop), 39121,* ☎ *601/446–9654 or 800/634–1818. 14
rooms. Dining room. AE, D, MC, V.*

$$$$ 🏠 **The Burn.** This elegant 1836 mansion offers a seated plantation breakfast, private tour of the home, and swimming pool. The guest rooms
are quiet and comfortable, and furnished throughout with antiques.
The Burn's verdant surroundings lend it the atmosphere of a country
home, despite its size. ⊠ *712 N. Union St., 39120,* ☎ *601/442–1344
or 800/654–8859,* FAX *601/445–0606. 7 rooms. Dining room, pool.
AE, D, MC, V.*

$$$$ 🏠 **Dunleith.** Stately, colonnaded Dunleith is a popular Natchez bed-
and-breakfast whose elegant, plantation-style rooms are furnished
with four-poster beds and antiques. Guests are served lemonade upon
arrival. The breakfast room is a former poultry house with old brick
walls. Beautiful gardens enhance the grounds. ⊠ *84 Homochitto St.,
39120,* ☎ *601/446–8500 or 800/433–2445. 11 rooms. Dining room.
No children under 18. AE, MC, V.*

$$$$ 🏠 **The Guest House Historic Inn.** A renovated home built in 1840, this
cozy inn is in the heart of Natchez, on Antique Row. Its rooms are decorated with antiques and reproductions, giving the place the feel of a
small European hotel. ⊠ *201 N. Pearl St., 39120,* ☎ *601/442–1054,*
FAX *601/446–1374. 16 rooms. Meeting room. AE, D, DC, MC, V.*

$$$ 🏠 **Natchez Eola Hotel.** This beautifully restored 1920s hotel has an el-
egant, formal lobby and small guest rooms with antique reproduction
furniture. Many rooms afford views of the river. ⊠ *110 N. Pearl St.,
39120,* ☎ *601/445–6000 or 800/888–9140,* FAX *601/446–5310. 125
rooms, 5 suites. 2 restaurants, 2 lounges, shop. AE, DC, MC, V.*

Nightlife

King's Tavern (⊠ 619 Jefferson St., ☎ 601/446–8845) is in the old-
est house in the Natchez Territory (1789). The lounge is rustic yet invit-
ing, especially if you're an "Old Natchez" aficionado. **Under-the-Hill
Saloon** (⊠ 25 Silver St., ☎ 601/446–8023) has live entertainment—
from blues to folk—on weekends in one of the few original buildings
left in Natchez-Under-the-Hill.

Outdoor Activities and Sports

There are eight tennis outdoor courts in **Duncan Park** (⊠ Duncan St.
at Auburn Ave., ☎ 601/442–1589), with lights for night play.

Natchez Trace A to Z

Arriving, Departing, and Getting Around

BY BUS

Greyhound (☎ 800/231–2222) offers daily service to Tupelo (⊠ 201 Commerce St., ☎ 601/842–4557), Corinth (⊠ 204 U.S. 72E, ☎ 601/287–1466), Columbus (⊠ 904 Main St., ☎ 601/328–4732), Philadelphia (⊠ West Side Finance and Insurance Bldg., 270B W. Beacon St., ☎ 601/656–2851), Jackson (⊠ 201 S. Jefferson St., ☎ 601/353–6342), Port Gibson (⊠ 17 Church St., ☎ 601/431–5751), and Natchez (⊠ 103 Lower Woodville Rd., ☎ 601/445–5291).

BY CAR

A car is the only way to tour the Natchez Trace properly, though you can reach major cities by plane and by bus. Corinth is at the intersection of U.S. 72 and U.S. 45, and Tupelo is 5 mi south of the Natchez Trace Parkway at the intersection of U.S. 45 and U.S. 78.

The Natchez Trace Parkway breaks at Jackson; pick up either I–55 or I–20, which run through the city. Jackson is accessed by U.S. 49 and U.S. 51. Natchez, the beginning of the Natchez Trace Parkway, is served by U.S. 61.

BY PLANE

Golden Triangle Regional Airport (⊠ U.S. 82, 10 mi west of Columbus, ☎ 601/327–4422) is served by Northwest Airlink, American Eagle, and Atlantic Southeast Airlines, with connections nationwide through Memphis and Atlanta.

American Eagle, Continental Express, Delta, and Northwest Airlink offer nonstop daily flights to Dallas, Atlanta, and New Orleans, with direct service available nationally. The **Jackson International Airport** (⊠ East of Jackson off I–20, ☎ 601/939–5631) is 10 minutes from downtown.

Tupelo Municipal Airport (⊠ 631 Jackson Extended, 5 mi west of Tupelo, ☎ 601/841–6570) is served by Northwest Airlink and American Eagle.

Contacts and Resources

B&B RESERVATION AGENCIES

Natchez Pilgrimage Tours (☞ Guided Tours, *below*) can answer questions and handle reservations for bed-and-breakfasts.

EMERGENCIES

In towns and cities, dial 911 for **police** or **ambulance.** For help on the Natchez Trace Parkway, dial 0 and ask for the nearest Park Ranger. Seek medical help at **North Mississippi Regional Medical Center** (⊠ 830 S. Gloster St., Tupelo, ☎ 601/841–3000), **Mississippi Baptist Medical Center** (⊠ 1225 N. State St., Jackson, ☎ 601/968–1776), and **Jefferson Davis Hospital** (⊠ 54 Sgt. Prentiss Dr., Natchez, ☎ 601/442–2871).

GUIDED TOURS

Jackson Tour & Travel (⊠ 1801 Crane Ridge Dr., Jackson 39216, ☎ 601/981–8415 or 800/873–8572), one of the South's premier tour operators, arranges independent departures to the state's prime attractions; Natchez and New Orleans are popular destinations.

Natchez Pilgrimage Tours, Inc. (⊠ 200 State St., Natchez 39121, ☎ 601/446–6631 or 800/647–6742) takes groups of 20 or more to tour about a dozen antebellum homes year-round. Carriage rides through downtown Natchez are also offered. Tours are conducted mornings and afternoons, and bus tickets can be bought at six of the area's hotels. Tour tickets can be bought at the Pilgrimage Tour office on the corner of Canal and State streets.

AM: WKTS 95.5, country; WTUP 1490, all-sports talk. **FM:** WJMI 99.7, urban contemporary; WQNZ 95.1, country; WTRC 97.3, adult contemporary/news/sports.

Eckerd's (✉ Deville Plaza, I–55, E. Frontage Rd., Jackson, ☎ 601/956–5143) and **Super D Drugs** (✉ 327 Meadowbrook, Meadowbrook Shopping Center, Jackson, ☎ 601/366–1449).

The **Alliance** (✉ 810 Tate St., Corinth 38834, ☎ 601/287–5269 or 800/748–9048); open weekdays 8–5. **Metro Jackson Convention and Visitors Bureau** (✉ Box 1450, Jackson 39215, ☎ 601/960–1891 or 800/354–7695); open weekdays 8:30–5. **Natchez Trace Parkway Visitor Center** (✉ 2680 Natchez Trace Pkwy., Tupelo 38801; on the Natchez Trace Pkwy., mile marker 266; ☎ 601/680–4025 or 800/305–7417); open weekdays 8–5. **Natchez Convention & Visitors Bureau** (✉ 422 Main St., Natchez 39120, ☎ 601/446–6345 or 800/647–6724); open weekdays 8–5. **Natchez Pilgrimage Tours** (tickets for tours and activities: ✉ Canal St. at State St., Box 347, Natchez 39120, ☎ 601/446–6631 or 800/647–6742); open weekdays 8:30–5:30. **Tupelo Convention and Visitors Bureau** (✉ 399 E. Main St., Box 47, Tupelo 38802, ☎ 601/841–6521 or 800/533–0611); open weekdays 8–5, Saturday 9–5, Sunday 1–5.

HOLLY SPRINGS AND OXFORD

Holly Springs and Oxford, just east of I–55 in north Mississippi, are sophisticated versions of the Mississippi small town; both are courthouse towns incorporated in 1837. They offer visitors historic architecture, arts and crafts, literary associations, a warm welcome, and those unhurried pleasures of Southern life that remain constant from generation to generation—entertaining conversation, good food, and nostalgic walks at twilight.

Holly Springs

40 mi southeast of Memphis.

Holly Springs arose from a crossroads of old Native American trails originally called Spring Hollow. Chickasaw and travelers stopped to rest here and bathe in medicinal spring waters sheltered by holly trees. After the Chickasaw Cession in 1832, settlers came from the Carolinas, Virginia, and Georgia. Holly Springs became an educational, business, and cultural center as the newly arrived planters began to rake in profits. Cotton barons built palatial mansions and handsome commercial buildings. Today Holly Springs has more than 200 structures (61 of which are antebellum homes) listed on the National Register of Historic Places.

At least 50 raids befell Holly Springs during the Civil War. The worst took place in December 1862, when the Confederate army, under General Earl Van Dorn, destroyed $1 million worth of Union supplies intended to aid General Grant in his march against Vicksburg. Bent on reprisals against the city, Grant ordered General Benjamin Harrison Grierson to burn it to the ground. However, a clever Holly Springs matron, Maria Mason, invited the general into her home to chat. They discovered that they shared a love of music and that they had studied piano under the same teacher; so instead of destroying Holly Springs, Grierson enjoyed its hospitality at a series of afternoon gatherings and piano concerts.

Montrose (1858), owned by the Holly Springs Garden Club, has an elegant spiral staircase as well as elaborate cornices and plaster ceiling medallions. ✉ *307 E. Salem Ave.,* ☎ *601/252–2943.* ☞ *$5.* ⊙ *By appointment with Chamber of Commerce.*

Rust College (✉ N. Memphis St., ☎ 601/252–4661), founded in 1866, contains **Oak View** (circa 1860), one of the oldest buildings in the area. Metropolitan Opera star Leontyne Price, a native of Laurel, Mississippi, gave a brief concert in 1966 which raised money to build the library named for her. It houses the extensive memorabilia of Civil Rights leader Roy Wilkins. The **Yellow Fever House** (✉ 104 E. Gholson Ave.), built in 1836, was Holly Springs's first brick building. It was used as a hospital during the 1878 yellow fever epidemic. **Hillcrest Cemetery** (✉ 380 S. Maury St.) contains the graves of 13 Confederate generals. Many of the iron fences surrounding the graves were made locally before the Civil War.

The **Kate Freeman Clark Art Gallery** is dedicated solely to the work of Holly Springs resident Kate Freeman Clark, who was trained as a painter in New York City during the 1890s. Clark completed more than 1,000 works on canvas and paper, including landscapes and portraits. She returned to Holly Springs in the 1920s and never painted again. Many of her friends did not know of her talent until her paintings were discovered after her death. In her will she left funds to establish a museum. ✉ *292 E. College Ave.,* ☎ *601/252–4211.* ☞ *$2.* ⊙ *By appointment.*

Many of Holly Springs's **historic homes** are open only during Spring Pilgrimage (the last weekend in April), but even the briefest visit to Holly Springs should include a look at the exteriors of several of them. **Oakleigh,** on Salem Avenue across the street from Montrose (☞ *above*), is a mansion with fine details. Also on Salem Avenue are **Cedarhurst** and **Airliewood,** brick houses constructed in the Gothic style popularized in the 1850s by Andrew Jackson Downing. General Grant used Airliewood as his headquarters during his occupation of Holly Springs.

Dining

$ ✕ **Phillips Grocery.** The building housing Phillips was constructed in 1882 as a saloon for railroad workers. Today it's decorated with antiques and crafts, and serves big, old-fashioned hamburgers. ✉ *541A Van Dorn St., across from old depot,* ☎ *601/252–4671. Reservations not accepted. No credit cards. Closed Sun.*

Outdoor Activities and Sports

Holly Springs's **Chewalla Lake and Recreation Area** are part of Holly Springs National Forest and have nature trails, picnic areas, swimming, boating, camping, and fishing (license required). ✉ *MS 4 to Higdon Rd. then turn east; drive 7 mi to entrance. Information:* ✉ *National Forests Mississippi, 100 W. Capitol St., Suite 1141, Jackson 39269,* ☎ *601/965–4391.*

Oxford

60 mi southeast of Memphis, 50 mi east of Tupelo.

Oxford and Lafayette County were immortalized as "Jefferson" and "Yoknapatawpha County" in the novels of Oxford native William Faulkner, but even if you're not a Faulkner fan, this is a great place to experience small-town living. You won't be bored: The characters who fascinated Faulkner still live here, and the University of Mississippi keeps things lively.

Faulkner received the Nobel Prize for Literature in 1949, and his readers will enjoy exploring the town that inspired *The Hamlet, The Town,* and *The Mansion.* "I discovered that my own little postage stamp of native soil was worth writing about, and that I would never live long enough to exhaust it," said Faulkner. "I created a cosmos of my own."

Many people who knew the eccentric "Mr. Bill" still live in Oxford and are willing to share stories about him. You may encounter them around **Courthouse Square,** a National Historic Landmark in the center of town. At the center of the square is the white sandstone **Lafayette County Courthouse** (pronounced luh-*fay*-it), named for the French Revolutionary War hero the Marquis de Lafayette. The courthouse was rebuilt in 1873 after Union troops burned it down; on its south side is a monument to Confederate soldiers. The courtroom on the second floor is original.

University Avenue, which runs from South Lamar Boulevard just south of the Courthouse Square to the University of Mississippi, is one of the state's most beautiful sights when the trees flame orange and gold in the fall, or when the dogwoods blossom in the spring.

The **University Museums** display the brightly colored paintings of local artist Theora Hamblett. Hamblett gained international fame for her works depicting dreams and visions, Mississippi landscapes, and scenes from her childhood. Here, too, is a collection of Greek and Roman antiquities and what may perhaps be the country's quirkiest exhibit—a collection of fully dressed fleas! ✉ *University Ave. at 5th St.,* ☎ *601/ 232–7073.* 🎟 *Free.* ☉ *Tues.–Sat. 10–4:30, Sun. 1–4.*

The state's beloved "Ole Miss," or the **University of Mississippi,** opened in 1848 with 80 students. The **Grove,** the tree-shaded heart of the campus, is almost as important a meeting place as Courthouse Square (☞ *above*). (Supposedly, it was here that Faulkner, just fired from his position as postmaster for writing novels on the job, said, "Never again will I be at the beck and call of every son-of-a-bitch who's got two cents to buy a stamp.") Contact the school's **Public Relations Department** (☎ 601/232–7236) for information about university plays, lectures, sporting events, and special events.

The **Center for the Study of Southern Culture** (☎ 601/232–5993) is housed in antebellum Barnard Observatory, facing the Grove. The center has exhibits on Southern music, folklore, and literature, and the world's largest blues archive (40,000 records). Its annual Faulkner seminar attracts Faulkner scholars from around the world, and its Oxford Conference for the Book (☞ Nightlife and the Arts, *below*), held each April, draws book lovers from all across the United States. The center's remarkable *Encyclopedia of Southern Culture* is on sale here.

The **Mississippi Room** (☎ 601/232–5855) in the John Davis Williams Library contains both a permanent exhibit on Faulkner, including his Nobel Prize medal, and first editions of other Mississippi authors.

★ **Rowan Oak** was William Faulkner's home from 1930 until his death in 1962. Although this is one of Mississippi's most famous attractions, there are no signs to direct you and only an unobtrusive historic marker at the site. The house and its surrounding 32 acres are as serene and private as they were when Faulkner lived and wrote here. Built about 1848 by Colonel Robert Sheegog, the two-story, white-frame house with square columns represents the primitive Greek Revival style of architecture common to many Mississippi antebellum homes. After the

Civil War it fell into disrepair and, in 1930, it was purchased by Faulkner and his bride of one year, Estelle Oldham Franklin.

The house was both a sanctuary and a financial burden to the author; it is now a National Historic Landmark owned by the University of Mississippi. Faulkner made improvements and additions to the house, including a brick wall to shield him from curious strangers. After winning the Nobel Prize, he added the study where his bed, typewriter, desk, and other personal items—such as his sunglasses, a Colgate shave stick refill, an ink bottle, and a can of dog repellent—still evoke his presence. Faulkner wrote an outline for his novel *The Fable* on the walls of the study, which is reputed to be the most photographed room in the state. The days of the week are neatly printed over the head and length of the bed, and to the right of the door leading into the room is the notation "Tomorrow." ⊠ *Old Taylor Rd.,* ☎ *601/234–3284.* ⌨ *Free.* ☉ *Tues.–Sat. 10–noon and 2–4, Sun. 2–4.*

Faulkner's funeral was held at Rowan Oak, and he was buried in the family plot in **St. Peter's Cemetery** at Jefferson and North 16th streets, beside his relatives. Also buried here is Caroline Barr, "Mammy Callie," Faulkner's childhood nurse. The tomb of the author's brother, Dean Faulkner, who was killed in an airplane crash, bears the same epitaph as the one Faulkner had given to John Sartoris in the novel *Pylon.*

OFF THE
BEATEN PATH

COLLEGE HILL PRESBYTERIAN CHURCH – William Faulkner was married at this little church 8 mi northwest of Oxford on College Hill Rd. on June 20, 1929. The original pews are intact, although it's believed that Sherman stabled horses here during his occupation of College Hill in 1862. Behind the church is one of north Mississippi's oldest cemeteries.

Dining and Lodging

$$$–$$$$
★

✕ **City Grocery Store.** What was once a grocery store is now a trendy bistro on Oxford's historic Courthouse Square. The chef's innovative menu is more suggestive of New Orleans than north Mississippi. A signature dish is the shrimp and grits, and the bananas Foster bread pudding is a showstopper. ⊠ *1118 Van Buren Ave.,* ☎ *601/232–8080. AE, MC, V. Closed Sun. No lunch.*

$$

✕ **Downtown Grill.** With its comfortable plaid chairs and dark walls, the Grill's bar could be a club in Oxford, England. But then there's the light and airy balcony overlooking the square—pure Oxford, Mississippi. Downstairs in the restaurant, specialties include famous seafood gumbo; Mississippi catfish either grilled or Lafitte (topped with shrimp, julienned ham, and a savory cream sauce); and an array of rich desserts. ⊠ *110 Courthouse Sq.,* ☎ *601/234–2659. AE, D, MC, V. Closed Sun.*

$

✕ **Bottletree Bakery.** This is the closest to crusty European-style bread that you'll find in Mississippi and perhaps in all of the South. If that isn't reason enough to stop in, check out the saucer-size cinnamon rolls. The bakery serves breakfast and lunch, as well as pastries and specialty coffees, all day. Thursday through Saturday the bakery extends its hours for coffee and dessert. ⊠ *923 Van Buren Ave.,* ☎ *601/236–5000. MC, V. Closed Mon.*

$

✕ **Smitty's.** Home-style cooking features red-eye gravy and grits, biscuits with blackberry preserves, fried catfish, chicken and dumplings, corn bread, and black-eyed peas. The menu reads, "If'n You Need Anything That Ain't on Here, Holler at the Cook." ⊠ *208 S. Lamar Blvd., south of square,* ☎ *601/234–9111. MC, V.*

$$$$ 🏨 **Puddin Place.** Near the Ole Miss campus, this Victorian house has a wonderful back porch with swings and rockers. The two suites—each with sitting room, separate bedroom, and private bath—are thoughtfully furnished with antiques and collectibles. The downstairs suite has its own washer and dryer as well as two working fireplaces; the upstairs suite has four working fireplaces—including one in the bathroom. ✉ *1008 University Ave., 38655,* ☎ *601/234–1250. 2 suites. Breakfast included. No credit cards.*

$$$ 🏨 **Alumni Center Hotel.** The modern, hotel-style rooms bring a fresh look to a unique location on the Ole Miss campus. All rooms are done in rich dark colors, giving them a distinguished feel. ✉ *Alumni Dr., University of Mississippi, 38677,* ☎ *601/234–2331. 96 rooms. Snack bar, pool, 6 meeting rooms. MC, V.*

$$$ 🏨 **Holiday Inn.** These functional rooms have no surprises. The restaurant, however, can do a remarkably good breakfast, though you'll probably choose nearby Smitty's (☞ *above*) for the biscuits. ✉ *400 N. Lamar, 38655,* ☎ *601/234–3031,* 🖷 *601/234–2834. 123 rooms. Restaurant, lounge, pool. AE, DC, MC, V.*

$$$ 🏨 **Oliver-Britt House.** Each comfortable, pleasant room has its own bath and color TV in this restored home built about 1900 and run as a casual B&B. The location, midway between the university and Courthouse Square, is convenient. ✉ *512 Van Buren Ave., 38655,* ☎ *601/ 234–8043,* 🖷 *601/281–8065. 5 rooms. Breakfast included weekends. AE, DC, MC, V.*

Nightlife and the Arts

Local Oxford bands play Cajun, country, reggae, and Motown Tuesday through Saturday at the **Gin** (✉ E. Harrison St. and S. 14th St., ☎ 601/234–0024). The **Hoka** (✉ 304 S. 14th St., ☎ 601/234–3057), a warehouse–turned–movie theater/restaurant, has been called the "only Bohemian café in Mississippi" by author Barry Hannah. It has hard wooden booths, a jukebox, and is unbelievably cluttered. BYOB to wash down short-order food.

The **Faulkner and Yoknapatawpha Conference,** held the first week in August, includes lectures by Faulkner scholars and field trips in "Yoknapatawpha County." The annual **Elvis Conference** is also held here in August. There's also the annual **Oxford Conference for the Book,** a meeting of bibliophiles with an emphasis on Southern authors. For information on all three conferences, contact the Center for the Study of Southern Culture (✉ University of Mississippi, Oxford 38677, ☎ 601/232–5993).

Outdoor Activities and Sports

Oxford's Avent Park (✉ Park Dr., the continuation of Bramlett Rd., which runs north of E. Jackson Ave.) has tennis courts, a playground, picnic areas, and a jogging trail.

OFF THE
BEATEN PATH
TAYLOR – From Oxford take Old Taylor Road to the town of Taylor. Downtown Taylor is comprised of three buildings—two grocery stores and a potter's shop. The old Taylor Grocery has a restaurant in back where catfish and trimmin's are served Thursday through Sunday nights (☎ 601/236–1716). (At press time Taylor Grocery was closed for renovations, so be sure to call ahead.) In sculptor William Beckwith's studio you can see his statue of Temple Drake, the character who waited for the train in Taylor in Faulkner's novel *Sanctuary.* Small as it is, Taylor is achieving cult status; it's proper to brag about coming here!

Holly Springs and Oxford A to Z

Arriving, Departing, and Getting Around

BY BUS

Greyhound (☎ 800/231–2222) has a station in Holly Springs (✉ 490 Craft St., ☎ 601/252–1353).

BY CAR

A 30-minute drive from Memphis, Holly Springs is in north Mississippi near the Tennessee state line on U.S. 78 and MS 4, MS 7, and MS 311.

Contacts and Resources

EMERGENCIES

In Holly Springs, dial 0 for assistance. In Oxford, dial 911. Medical help is available at **Baptist Memorial North Mississippi Hospital** (✉ Off I–55; take Batesville exit, 1 mi south of Oxford Sq. on S. Lamar Ave., ☎ 601/232–8100).

RADIO STATIONS

AM: WSUH 1420, news/talk. **FM:** WOXD 95.5, oldies; WWMS 97.5, contemporary and country.

VISITOR INFORMATION

Holly Springs Chamber of Commerce (✉ 154 S. Memphis St., ☎ 601/252–2943); open weekdays 9–5. **Oxford Information Center** (✉ Cottage next to City Hall, ☎ 601/232–2419); open daily 9–5. **Oxford Tourism Council** (✉ 111 Courthouse Sq., Box 965, Oxford 38655, ☎ 601/234–4680 or 800/758–9177); open weekdays 9–5. **Oxford-Lafayette County Chamber of Commerce** (✉ 299 W. Jackson Ave., ☎ 601/234–4651); open weekdays 8:30–4.

THE DELTA

Clarksdale, Greenville, Vicksburg

"The Delta begins in the lobby of the Peabody Hotel in Memphis and ends on Catfish Row in Vicksburg," said Greenville journalist David Cohn. In between is a vast agricultural plain created by the Mississippi River. If life should give you only one day in the Delta, use it to cruise down U.S. 61 and the Great River Road (MS 1) from Memphis to Vicksburg. Gamble your way through Tunica. Time it right for lunch in Clarksdale, Merigold, or Boyle, and dinner at Doe's in Greenville. Then on a Saturday night you'll be able to pick up public radio's "Highway 61," which will be playing the blues about the time you glimpse the first kudzu near Vicksburg.

Numbers in the margin correspond to points of interest on the Mississippi Delta map.

Tunica County

30 mi south of Memphis off U.S. 61.

This region is a gambler's paradise. Las Vegas–style casinos have sprung up all along the otherwise empty and somewhat barren strip of Delta highway. The view of these garish entertainment and hotel complexes emerging from the cotton fields can seem quite surreal, but step inside and you'll never know you're not in Vegas or Atlantic City. Spend the morning at the blackjack tables, then continue down U.S. 61 to **Coahoma County.**

Mississippi Delta

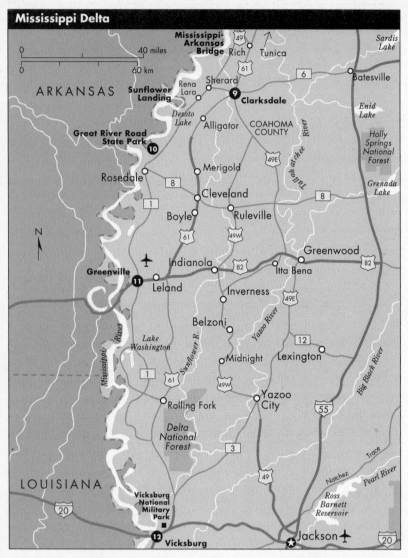

En Route At Rich, swing west on U.S. 49 for a spectacular view of the Mississippi River from the **Mississippi–Arkansas Bridge.** Continue south on
MS 1 to skirt serene Moon Lake and Friars Point. The levee parallels
MS 1 for most of the southbound trip; park and climb up for a look
at the "Father of Waters."

At Rena Lara, turn west to **Sunflower Landing** on Desoto Lake. Near
here, in May 1541, Hernando DeSoto "discovered" the Mississippi River.

Clarksdale

⑨ *60 mi southwest of Memphis.*

As a child, author Tennessee Williams spent time in Clarksdale, visiting his grandfather, the rector of St. George's Episcopal Church. (In
Williams's *Cat on a Hot Tin Roof,* Brick was running high hurdles at
nearby Friars Point when he broke his leg.)

The **Delta Blues Museum** is a testament to the important role played by Clarksdale and Coahoma County in the history of the blues. The museum highlights the history of the blues in exhibits and programs, tracing its influence on rock, jazz, and pop music through videotapes, slides, records, and books. At press time, there was talk of moving the museum from the recently renovated Carnegie Public Library, so call the library for current information. ⊠ *114 Delta Ave.,* ☎ *601/627–6820.* 🎫 *Free.* ☉ *Weekdays 9–5, Sat. 10–5.*

Dining

$ ✕ **Rest Haven.** The Delta's large Lebanese community influences the food, which is considered regional fare. Among the favorites are *kibbe* (seasoned lean ground lamb with cracked wheat), spinach and meat pies, and cabbage rolls. Daily plate-lunch specials include chicken and dumplings, and red beans and sausage over rice. ⊠ *419 State St. (Hwy. 61),* ☎ *601/624–8601. No credit cards. Closed Sun.*

En Route The McCartys of **Merigold** are famous throughout the state for their pale stoneware. Their shop showcases their pottery and handcrafted jewelry; in the spring and summer you may get a peek at their gardens. The shop also includes an eatery called The Gallery where a choice of two entrées is offered for lunch. ⊠ *Corner Goff and St. Mary Sts.,* ☎ *601/748–2293.* ☉ *Feb.–Dec., Tues.–Sat. 10–4.*

Cleveland

30 mi southwest of Clarksdale.

Home to 15,000 residents plus the students at Delta State University, Cleveland is said to have inspired W. C. Handy's music. There's little danger of confusing it with New York City, except when you're eating at KC's.

Dining

$$$$ ✕ **KC's Restaurant.** A hidden treasure in the heart of the Delta, this funky but fabulous restaurant can hold its own anywhere. The eclectic and sophisticated menu changes every two weeks, and has French, Italian, Asian, and Southwestern influences. Count on seeing wild game, fresh fish, free-range meats, and organic vegetables. There's a walk-in wine cellar (with a table for those who like to dine among the bottles) that offers evidence of the restaurant's amazing wine list. ⊠ *U.S. 61 N. at 1st St., Cleveland,* ☎ *601/843–5301. AE, MC, V. No lunch Sat., no dinner Sun.*

Rosedale

18 mi west of Cleveland.

This pastoral town on MS 8 offers sweeping views of the Mississippi River, and an 800-acre park with the state's largest campground inside the levee. The **Great River Road State Park,** on the bluffs of the Mississippi River, has a 75-ft-high overlook tower. There's also a boat ramp, both developed and primitive campsites, canoeing and tubing, fishing, nature trails, and picnic shelters. ⊠ *Off MS 1, Box 292, Rosedale 38769,* ☎ *601/759–6762.* ☉ *Daily 8–5.*

Greenville

🕚 *35 mi southwest of Cleveland.*

Greenville, the seat of Washington County, is named for Revolutionary War hero General Nathaniel Greene, a close friend of George Washington. The city's history has been dominated by the Mississippi River. The river created the rich soil in which cotton flourished, and

Greenville was—and is—the port used by the massive Delta plantations to ship their bales to market. During the Civil War battle for Vicksburg, Union troops burned Greenville to the ground. The citizens rebuilt the town only to suffer a yellow fever epidemic in 1877. Then, in 1890, the city experienced disastrous flooding; levees finally solved the problem after the great flood of 1927. At the turn of the century Greenville developed into a major river port.

Greenville probably has produced more writers than any other city of its size in the country. These include William Alexander Percy (*Lanterns on the Levee*), his nephew Walker Percy (*The Last Gentleman, The Moviegoer*), Ellen Douglas (*A Family's Affair, The Magic Carpet*), Hodding Carter (Pulitzer Prize–winning, crusading journalist), Shelby Foote (*The Civil War, Love in a Dry Season*), and Hodding Carter III (television news commentator and journalist). The best reason to visit Greenville, however, is to eat at Doe's (☞ *Dining, below*).

The **Birthplace of the Frog Exhibit** in Leland, on the outskirts of Greenville, is a tribute to the late Muppet creator Jim Henson and a must for Kermit fans. In the same building as the Leland Chamber of Commerce, the exhibit includes Henson family memorabilia, videos of Henson's first attempts at kiddie TV, three original Muppets on loan, and more. Henson was born in Greenville, but grew up in Leland. ⊠ *MS 82 at S. Deer Creek Dr. E,* ☎ *601/686–2687.* ☞ *Free.* ☼ *Weekdays 10–4, tours on weekends by appointment.*

Dining

$$$$ ✕ **Doe's.** This is a tumbledown building, visually as uninspiring as any restaurant you'll find—Formica-top tables, mismatched chairs, mismatched cutlery, mismatched plates—and you're practically eating in the kitchen. But when you see that huge steak hanging off your plate, you'll know why this place is famous. Hot tamales and the house salad dressing (olive oil, lemon juice, garlic) are specialties. ⊠ *502 Nelson St.,* ☎ *601/334–3315. MC, V. No lunch.*

OFF THE BEATEN PATH

FLOREWOOD RIVER PLANTATION STATE PARK – This living-history park 2 mi west of Greenwood on Hwy. 82 is worth straying from the Delta path. Near Greenwood, it's an exact replica of an 1850s working plantation, complete with reenactments in the school, blacksmith shop, plantation store, and more. ⊠ *Box 680, Greenwood 38930,* ☎ *601/455–3821.* ☞ *$3.50.* ☼ *Tues.–Sat. 9–5, Sun. 1–5; park closes noon–1.*

MAMA'S DREAM WORLD – In Belzoni, 35 mi southeast of Greenville, Mama's Dream World contains pictures embroidered by the late Ethel Wright Mohamed, who took up needlework in her sixties to record her life in the Delta with her storekeeper husband and eight children. Some of Mrs. Mohamed's work is in the Smithsonian's permanent collection. The gallery is in the Mohamed family home, and more than 125 pictures cover every wall. ⊠ *307 Central St.,* ☎ *601/247-1433.* ☞ *$2.* ☼ *By appointment.*

Vicksburg

⑫ *75 mi south of Greenville, 35 mi west of Jackson.*

Vicksburg began as a mission founded by the Reverend Newitt Vick in 1814. He chose a spot high on the bluffs above a bend in the Mississippi River, a location that would have important consequences for the young city during the Civil War.

In June 1862, the Union had control of the Mississippi River, with the exception of Vicksburg, which was in Confederate hands. Ulysses S. Grant's men doggedly slogged through canals and bayous in five futile attempts to capture the city, which was called the Gibraltar of the Confederacy because of its impregnable natural defenses. Then, in a series of raids and battles, Grant laid waste the area between Vicksburg and Jackson to the east and Port Gibson to the south, before returning to Vicksburg. His attacks were repulsed once again; he then laid siege to the city for 47 days as its citizens, hiding in caves, slowly starved. On July 4, 1863, the city surrendered, giving the Union control of the river and sounding the death knell for the Confederacy.

★ The **Vicksburg National Military Park,** which nearly surrounds Vicksburg, keeps the city's past close to today's constituents. The park comprises 1,800 acres of fortifications and earthworks lined with monuments and markers tracing battle positions. The Visitor Center offers orientation programs and exhibits. A guided tour is a good investment, should time and money ($20 for two hours) permit. The self-guided driving tour is well marked, however, and a cassette tape may be rented for $4.50. About 7 mi into the park is the USS *Cairo,* a Union gunboat raised from the Yazoo River and restored. Civil War artifacts recovered from the *Cairo* are on display at the adjacent USS *Cairo* Museum. ⊠ *3201 Clay St.,* ☎ *601/636–0583 main switchboard, 601/636–2199 USS* Cairo. ☜ *$4 per car.* ◎ *National Military Park grounds fall–spring, daily 8–5; summer, daily 8–6; USS* Cairo *fall–spring, daily 9–5; summer, daily 9–6.*

The Vanishing Glory is a multimedia, 15-projector show portraying the sights and sounds of Vicksburg under siege. ⊠ *717 Clay St.,* ☎ *601/634–1863.* ☜ *$5.* ◎ *Daily 10–5.*

Vicksburg's **historic homes** may have cannonballs imbedded in their walls, but they have been beautifully restored. Visit **Cedar Grove** (⊠ 2200 Oak St.; ☞ Dining and Lodging, *below*), **Balfour House** (⊠ Crawford and Cherry Sts.), and the **Martha Vick House** (⊠ 1300 Grove St.), built by the daughter of the founder of Vicksburg, Newitt Vick.

Narrated, one-hour **Hydro-Jet Boat Tours** depart from Vicksburg for those longing for a Mississippi River adventure. ⊠ *Box 506, 39181,* ☎ *601/638–5443 or 800/521–4363.* ☜ *$16.* ◎ *Mar.–Nov., daily at 10, 2, 5.*

In 1894 Coca-Cola was bottled at the **Biedenharn Candy Company,** which is now a Coke museum. The history of one of the world's favorite soft drinks is documented through Coca-Cola advertisements and memorabilia. There's also an old-fashioned soda fountain on site. ⊠ *1107 Washington St.,* ☎ *601/638–6514.* ☜ *$1.75.* ◎ *Mon.–Sat. 9–5, Sun. 1:30–4:30.*

Dining and Lodging

$$$ ✕ **Delta Point.** This elegant restaurant sits high on a bluff—admire the views of the Mississippi River through picture windows. China, crystal, and flowers contribute to the gracious mood. Specialties are beef tenderloin stuffed with marinated Bing cherries; shrimp and fettuccine; and cherries jubilee and bananas Foster. ⊠ *4144 Washington St.,* ☎ *601/636–5317. Reservations essential. AE, DC, MC, V. Closed Sun.–Mon. No lunch.*

$ ✕ **Walnut Hills.** If you're yearning for authentic regional cooking, this restaurant is a must. Don't miss the outstanding fried chicken, served with fresh snap beans or purple-hull peas. For dessert, try the black-

berry cobbler. ⊠ *1214 Adams St., at Clay St.,* ☎ *601/638–4910.*
Reservations essential for large groups. AE, DC, MC, V. Closed Sat.
No dinner Sun.

$$$$ 🏨 **Cedar Grove.** This 1840s mansion and its grounds cover an entire
★   city block. All rooms are furnished with period antiques, the most impressive of which is the Union cannonball still lodged in the parlor wall.
Hear nearby river traffic from the quiet, gaslit grounds, or survey the
watery scene from the rooftop garden. A house tour and hearty Southern breakfast are included. ⊠ *2200 Oak St., 39180,* ☎ *601/636–1000*
or 800/862–1300, 𝖥𝖠𝖷 *601/634–6126. 35 rooms. Restaurant, piano*
bar, pool, tennis court, croquet, bicycles. AE, D, DC, MC, V.

$$$$ 🏨 **Duff Green Mansion.** This 1856 mansion was used as a hospital dur-
★   ing the Civil War. Each guest room is decorated with antiques, including
half-tester beds. A large, Southern-style breakfast and a tour of the home
are included. ⊠ *1114 1st East St., 39180,* ☎ *601/636–6968 or 800/*
992–0037. 5 rooms, 2 suites. Pool. AE, MC, V.

Nightlife

Beechwood Restaurant & Lounge (⊠ 4449 Hwy. 80E, ☎ 601/636–
3761) is a hot spot for Monday Night Football fans. Other nights, country-and-western bands bring crowds to their feet. **Maxwell's** (⊠ 4702
Clay St., ☎ 601/636–1344 or 800/418–7379) offers live entertainment in its lounge most weekends.

Outdoor Activities and Sports

JOGGING

The hilly roads in the **Vicksburg National Military Park** (⊠ I–20, Exit
4-B, Clay St.) are a challenging course for joggers.

TENNIS

Clear Creek (⊠ I–20, Bovina Exit 7, Vicksburg) has public courts.

Shopping

Climb up into the **Attic Gallery** (⊠ 1406 Washington St., Vicksburg,
☎ 601/638–9221) to see regional art and fine crafts chosen with a dis-
criminating eye—a Southern rival to New York galleries.

Delta A to Z

Arriving, Departing, and Getting Around

BY BUS

Greyhound (☎ 800/231–2222) stops in Belzoni (⊠ West Side Gro-
cery, 711 Francis St., ☎ 601/247–2150), Clarksdale (⊠ 1604 State
St., ☎ 601/627–7893), Cleveland (⊠ U.S. 61N, ☎ 601/843–5113),
Columbus (⊠ 904 Main St., ☎ 601/328–4732), Greenville (⊠ 1849
U.S. 82E, ☎ 601/335–2633), and Vicksburg (⊠ 1295 S. Frontage Rd.,
☎ 601/638–8389).

BY CAR

U.S. 61 runs from Memphis through the Delta to Vicksburg, Natchez,
and Baton Rouge, Louisiana. The Great River Road (MS 1) parallels
U.S. 61 and the river through part of this route.

BY PLANE

The **Greenville Municipal Airport** (⊠ Air Base Rd., ☎ 601/334–3121)
is served by Northwest Airlink.

Contacts and Resources

EMERGENCIES

In Greensville and Vicksburg, dial 911 for **police** and **ambulance** in emergencies. Seek medical help at **Delta Regional Medical Center** (⊠ 1400

E. Union St., Greenville, ☎ 601/378–3783) and at **Vicksburg Medical Center** (✉ 1111 N. Frontage Rd., Vicksburg, ☎ 601/636–2611).

RADIO STATIONS
FM: WAID 106.5, urban contemporary; WBBV 101.1, country.

VISITOR INFORMATION
Clarksdale-Coahoma County Chamber of Commerce (✉ 1540 De Soto Ave., Box 160, Clarksdale 38614, ☎ 601/627–7337). **Cleveland–Bolivar County Chamber of Commerce** (✉ 600 3rd St., Box 490, Cleveland 38732, ☎ 601/843–2712). **Greenville–Washington County CVB** (✉ 410 Washington Ave., Greenville 38701, ☎ 601/334–2711 or 800/467–3582). **Greenwood Convention & Visitors Bureau** (✉ 1902 Le Flore Ave., Box 739, Greenwood 38935-0739, ☎ 601/453–9197 or 800/748–9064). **Mississippi Welcome Center** (✉ 4210 Washington St., Vicksburg 39180, ☎ 601/638–4269). **Vicksburg Convention & Visitors Bureau** (✉ Clay St. and Old Hwy. 27, Box 110, Vicksburg 39181, ☎ 601/636–9421 or 800/221–3536). **Washington County Welcome Center** (✉ U.S. 82 at Reed Rd., Box 6022, Greenville 38701, ☎ 601/332–2378).

MISSISSIPPI A TO Z

Arriving and Departing

By Bus
Greyhound (☎ 800/231–2222) serves most major cities in Mississippi.

By Car
The state's main north–south artery is I–55. I–20 crosses the state east–west from Meridian through Jackson to Vicksburg. I–10 crosses the Gulf Coast and I–59 links Meridian with Picayune.

By Plane
Most visitors use **Jackson International Airport** (☎ 601/939–5631) or **Memphis International Airport** (☎ 901/544–3495).

Getting Around

By Bus
Coast Area Transit (✉ 333 DeBuys Rd., Gulfport, ☎ 601/896–8080) provides a coast-wide public transportation system.

By Car
The speed limit on Mississippi interstate highways is 70 mph unless otherwise posted. The speed limit on the Natchez Trace Parkway is 50 mph. There's one service station on the Parkway at mile marker 193.1. Right turns on red lights are permitted throughout the state unless otherwise indicated. Crash helmets approved by the American Association of Motor Vehicle Administrators are required for motorcycle riders. Drivers and front-seat passengers in any vehicle designed to carry 10 riders or less must wear seat belts. Children under four years of age must be in an approved child passenger restraint device.

By Train

Amtrak (☎ 800/873–7245) serves Batesville, Biloxi, Brookhaven, Canton, Durant, Grenada, Gulfport, Hattiesburg, Hazlehurst, Jackson, Laurel, McComb, Meridian, Pascagoula, Picayune, and Winona.

Contacts and Resources

Emergencies

In towns and cities, dial 911 for **police** or **ambulance.** Cellular calls to the Highway Patrol are free by dialing HP (47).

Visitor Information

The **Mississippi Division of Tourism Development** (✉ Box 1705, Ocean Springs, MS 39566, ☎ 601/359–3297 or 800/927–6378) will gladly send you a travel planner.

6 North Carolina

Historical sites and natural wonders are plentiful in North Carolina, from Old Salem in Winston-Salem, where the 1700s spring to life today, to the Great Smoky and Blue Ridge mountains. On the Cape Hatteras and Cape Lookout national seashores, lighthouses stand as they have for 200 years, and unspoiled beaches stretch for miles. You'll find sophisticated shopping and dining in Charlotte; first-class golf in the Sandhills; and high technology, health care, and culture within the Triangle, a shape traced by Raleigh, Durham, and Chapel Hill.

By Lisa H.
Towle

IN 1524 EXPLORER GIOVANNI DE VERRAZANO landed on what is now eastern North Carolina's shore and wrote in his log, ". . . as pleasant and delectable [a land] to behold as is possible to imagine." That early visitor was on to something. The state has mountains, some of the tallest in the East, laced with waterfalls that tumble into verdant gorges. It has Cape Hatteras and Cape Lookout national seashores, where tides wash over the wooden beams of ancient shipwrecks. Its largest city, Charlotte, draws national attention thanks to its banking industry and professional basketball team. And in the Piedmont, there's the internationally respected Research Triangle Park, where pharmaceutical researchers working to develop lifesaving drugs are down the road from cutting-edge telecommunications companies.

North Carolina has three distinct geographical regions: the mountains, the Piedmont, and the coast. The Great Smoky and Blue Ridge mountain ranges create the rough, slanted border of western North Carolina. The mountains taper into foothills and then become the Piedmont, a gently rolling landscape characterized by farmlands to the north, red clay soil in the center, and sandy pine forests to the south. Most major cities have grown up in the center of the state, built primarily by the textile, furniture, and tobacco industries. The rolling hills of the Piedmont level off into the rich soil of the coastal plain. Much of eastern North Carolina remains agricultural and rural. Wilmington is a bustling port city, in sharp contrast to the tranquil villages along the Outer Banks.

Golf is the recreational focus in the Sandhills, while skiing has taken hold in the High Country (Alleghany, Ashe, Avery, Mitchell, and Watauga counties). Asheville has maintained its status as a resort city for more than 100 years and continues to grow in popularity.

North Carolina has courted visitors since the first English settlers arrived in 1584. Since the Great Depression of the 1930s, when the state began to realize the importance of tourism, the welcome mat has been out. The Blue Ridge Parkway was built largely by the CCC (Civilian Conservation Corps), as were many state park facilities. Cape Hatteras was declared a national seashore—the country's first—in 1953. A good highway system and several airports were built, and now eight welcome centers greet you at state borders. You'll discover the state's historic sites and natural beauty, its sports, resorts, and down-home cooking, including its legendary barbecue.

Pleasures and Pastimes

Beaches
From the thin band of barrier islands known as the Outer Banks, along the northern coastline, to the area around Wilmington and the Cape Fear Coast, North Carolina's beaches are a year-round destination. You can visit national seashores or wildlife refuges, go fishing, hiking, hang gliding, or bird-watching—or just watch the waves roll in. North Carolinians are proud that the nation's first national seashore, Cape Hatteras, is in their state, as is Roanoke Island, where the country's first European settlers landed over 400 years ago.

Dining
If there is one sure indication of Charlotte's transformation from Southern town to big city, it's the restaurant scene. Risotto and dim sum are becoming as common as grits and corn bread. Ethnic specialties of all kinds are available, as well as American nouvelle cuisine and chain

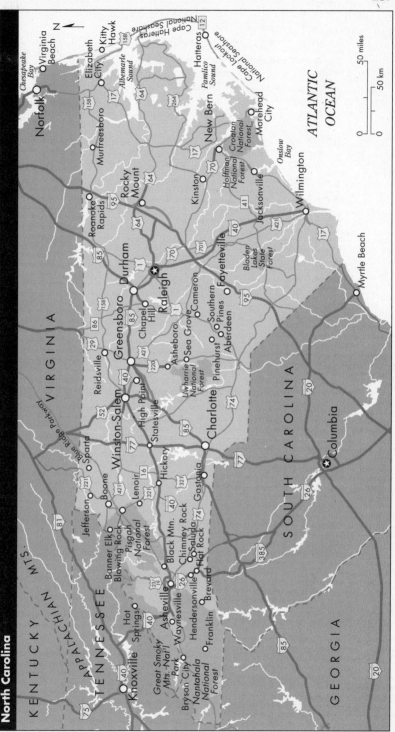

restaurant fare. But if it's good old-fashioned Southern cooking you want, you can still find that, too.

Traditional fare in the Triad (Greensboro, Winston-Salem, High Point) is Southern-fried chicken, ham, vegetables, biscuits, fruit cobblers, and the like. Chopped or sliced pork barbecue is still a big item. Nowadays, however, your dining choices include gourmet fare. Dining in the Triangle (Raleigh/Durham/Chapel Hill) is both sophisticated and down-home. There are many upscale restaurants, as well as informal places where barbecue, Brunswick stew, fried chicken, and lots of country vegetables are served in great quantities for very low prices. No particular local cuisine typifies the Sandhills, but the area has a number of sophisticated restaurants. Casual but neat clothing and golfwear are suitable anywhere.

By far the best fare around the Outer Banks is the fresh seafood. There are plenty of raw bars serving oysters and clams on the half shell, and seafood houses offering fresh crabs (soft-shells in season, early in the summer) and whatever local fish—tuna, wahoo, mahimahi—have been hauled in that day. Local cuisine in the Wilmington area is simply seafood. Shrimp (this is where the shrimp boats come in), oysters, Atlantic blue crab, and king mackerel are prepared in a variety of ways. Homegrown fruits and vegetables, too, are used extensively. Barbecued pork is another popular dish. International cuisines—from Mexican to Japanese to German—are also represented.

From Cherokee County to Asheville and Buncombe County, the dining choices are many: upscale gourmet restaurants, middle-of-the-road country fare, and fast-food eateries. In the past 30 years, High Country towns outside Asheville have seen a tremendous increase in restaurants. Fresh mountain trout, as well as such game meats as pheasant and venison, are regional specialties. Beer, wine, and liquor by the drink are permitted in Blowing Rock, Banner, Elk, and Beech Mountain; beer and wine only in Boone.

Unless otherwise noted, neat, casual wear is acceptable throughout North Carolina.

CATEGORY	COST*
$$$$	over $25
$$$	$15–$25
$$	$8–$15
$	under $8

*per person for a three-course meal, excluding drinks, service, and 6%–7% sales tax (depending on county)

Historic Places
Opportunities abound to get out of the fast lane and onto the back roads that lead to places where history is kept alive. Whether it's the site of a key battle in the Revolutionary War or the largest troop surrender of the Civil War, a Quaker settlement, or studios where artisans carry on a 200-year-old tradition in pottery, North Carolina cherishes its past. Places to visit are as varied as the site of man's first flight and the architectural legacies of America's industrial barons.

Lodging
In North Carolina's cities, you'll find everything from economy motels to convention hotels to bed-and-breakfasts in lovely historic districts. Most of the major chains are represented, and some hotels offer great weekend packages. A few warnings, though: During the twice-a-year furniture market in High Point, when 75,000 people from all over the world descend on the city, empty hotel rooms and rental cars

are almost impossible to find. May is graduation time for all of the Triangle's colleges and universities. Hotel rooms and restaurant seats are booked, in some cases, years in advance.

Most lodging options in the Sandhills are in the luxury resort category, with full amenities and services. Many of the prices quoted are for golf packages. However, there are a few chain motels in Southern Pines, as well as several bed-and-breakfasts in the area.

There are motels and hotels clustered up and down the Outer Banks, with rental properties in all the towns that dot the Cape Hatteras National Seashore. There are 60 cottages for rent on Ocracoke Island, plus a dozen or so motels and inns. Visitors to Wilmington and the Cape Fear Coast can choose from among a variety of chains, condos, and resorts overlooking the ocean, and in-town guest houses. There are also many accommodations at Carolina, Kure, and Wrightsville beaches.

Lodging options in the western mountains range from posh resorts to mountain cabins, country inns, and economy chain motels. There's a bed for virtually every pocketbook.

CATEGORY	COST*
$$$$	over $100
$$$	$60–$100
$$	$30–$60
$	under $30

*All prices are for a standard double room, excluding 6%–12% tax (depending on county).

Exploring North Carolina

Charlotte, the state's largest city, is known as a center of high finance in the South and prides itself on its cosmopolitan flair. The cities of the Triad (Greensboro, Winston-Salem, and High Point), in the upper Piedmont, showcase the diverse legacies of some of the state's founding families. The Triangle (Raleigh, Durham, and Chapel Hill), in the central Piedmont, is the hub of higher education, scientific research, and state-sponsored cultural resources. The Sandhills, on the coastal plain, offers finds for antiques lovers and is recognized worldwide as a golf mecca. On the Outer Banks comes solitude in the form of miles of pristine shore, sand, and sea oats. Wilmington and the Cape Fear Coast aren't just resort vacation spots—they're a thriving business and cultural center for the eastern portion of North Carolina. And in the mountains to the west, anchored by the city of Asheville, you'll find everything from hiking and Southern crafts to boot-scoot music and Brahms.

Great Itineraries

North Carolina is a large state and touring it comfortably from end to end could easily take two weeks, although you could whiz through in a week. Many people concentrate each trip on one region: mountains, Piedmont, or coast. A week could be spent in each of these, but there are many worthwhile trips of shorter duration.

IF YOU HAVE 3 DAYS

Start your tour of the Outer Banks from the northern end, coming in on U.S. 158. Drive north on NC 12 your first morning there to spend time in **Corolla,** visiting the Currituck Beach Lighthouse. Continue south after lunch through **Kitty Hawk, Kill Devil Hills,** and **Nags Head,** with a stop at the Wright Brothers National Memorial. Stay the night on ⊞ **Roanoke Island,** where you'll spend all of the second day visiting historical locations and the North Carolina Aquarium. On day three, leave Roanoke and spend the day along the **Cape Hatteras National Seashore,** visiting sights on **Hatteras Island** in the morning and ⊡ **Ocracoke Island** in the afternoon.

IF YOU HAVE 5 DAYS

⊡ **Asheville** is the logical starting point for a tour of the North Carolina mountains. It will take a full first day to cover the Biltmore Estate and neighboring village. Day two should be devoted to the attractions south of Asheville, including **Chimney Rock** and the Carl Sandburg Home National Historical Site. Another day back in Asheville will allow you to visit the remaining area attractions, including Pack Place and the Thomas Wolfe Memorial. On the fourth morning begin your journey up the **Blue Ridge Parkway,** lingering at the many scenic stopping points along the way, and arrive in the ⊡ **Boone** area for the night. Day five will be occupied with High Country activities, including the Tweetsie Railroad.

IF YOU HAVE 7 DAYS

With a full week at your disposal a whirlwind tour from one end of North Carolina to the other is possible. Start your journey in ⊡ **Asheville,** touring the Biltmore Estate and Thomas Wolfe Memorial. Next head for ⊡ **Charlotte**; be sure to visit Discovery Place during your day here. The Triad and the historical attractions of Old Salem are the focus of the third day; overnight in ⊡ **Winston-Salem.** The next two days will allow time for a taste of the Triangle, including the Duke University campus and Sarah Duke Gardens in **Durham,** the Morehead Planetarium and Franklin Street shopping in **Chapel Hill,** and the museums and capitol area of ⊡ **Raleigh.** Your sixth day should be spent in the Sandhills area enjoying antiquing and the world-class golf in ⊡ **Pinehurst.** Wind up your visit in ⊡ **Wilmington,** where you can visit the historic downtown and U.S.S. *North Carolina* Battleship Memorial or just head for the nearby beaches.

When to Tour North Carolina

North Carolina particularly shines in the spring (April) and fall (October), when the weather is especially temperate and the trees and flowers burst with color. An added plus is that you avoid the peak tourist season and stand a better chance of missing the crowds. Summer trips are best spent in the mountains or at the coastal beaches, where temperatures are significantly cooler. In winter it's wise to avoid the mountains, because many attractions close until late spring.

CHARLOTTE

Though Charlotte dates from Revolutionary War times (it is named for King George III's wife, Queen Charlotte), its Uptown is distinctively New South, complete with skyscrapers. Uptown encompasses all of downtown Charlotte, the business and cultural heart and soul. It's also home to the government center and some residential neighborhoods. New and popular attractions here are the sculptures at the four corners of Trade and Tryon streets. Erected at the Square, they symbolize Charlotte's beginnings: a gold miner (commerce), a mill worker (the city's textile heritage), an African-American railroad builder (transportation), and a mother holding her baby aloft (the future). Residents of the Queen City are proud that theirs is the largest city in the Carolinas and the second-largest banking center in the nation.

Heavy development has created some typical urban problems. Outdated road systems make traffic a nightmare during rush hour, and virtually all the city's restaurants are packed on weekends. But the Southern courtesy of the locals is contagious, and people still love the traditional plea-sure of picnicking in Freedom Park.

You'll be able to walk around Uptown and the Fourth Ward, and buses are adequate for getting around within the city limits; otherwise, you will need a car for touring.

Numbers in the text correspond to numbers in the margin and on the Charlotte map.

Uptown Charlotte

Uptown Charlotte is ideal for walking. The city was laid out in four wards around Independence Square, at Trade and Tryon streets. The Square, as it is known, is the center of the Uptown area.

A Good Walk

Stop first at Info! Charlotte (✉ 330 S. Tryon St., ☎ 704/331–2700) for information on a self-guided walking tour of the Fourth Ward (☞ *below*) and a historic tour of Uptown, as well as maps and brochures. You can park your car in an open lot a few blocks east of the Square. Take a stroll north on Tryon Street and enjoy the ambience of this re-vitalized area, noting the outdoor sculptures on the plazas and the cre-ative architecture of some of the newer buildings, including the **NationsBank Corporate Center** ①.

Walk two blocks west on Trade Street from the Square to the First Pres-byterian Church (✉ 200 W. Trade St.) and begin exploring the **Fourth Ward** ②, Charlotte's new "old" city. It offers a refreshing change from the newly developed parts of town. The brochure available at Info! Char-lotte leads you to 18 historic sites.

When you're done exploring the Fourth Ward, head south to North Tryon Street just above 6th Street, where you will find the science and technology museum **Discovery Place** ③, a leading attraction.

TIMING

You can spend a pleasant half-day to a day touring these areas. Allow an hour to browse NationsBank Corporate Center and Founders Hall. The Fourth Ward can be toured in an hour or so. The bulk of your time will be spent in Discovery Place, which can occupy as much of the day as you wish. You can avoid the workday bustle by visiting on the weekend, but note the Discovery Center's Sunday hours.

Sights to See

★ ☾ ❸ **Discovery Place.** At Charlotte's premier attraction, make the wonder-ful hands-on **Science Museum** a priority, and allow at least two hours for the **aquariums,** the **rain forest,** the **Omnimax theater,** and **Kelly Space Voyager Planetarium,** the largest in the United States. Check the sched-ule for special exhibits. ✉ *301 N. Tryon St.,* ☎ *704/372–6261 or 800/935–0553.* ✍ *$6.50–$12.50, depending on the number of attractions selected.* ☾ *Weekdays 9–5, Sat. 9–6, Sun. 1–6.*

❷ **Fourth Ward.** Charlotte's newly popular "old" neighborhood began as a political subsection created for electoral purposes in the mid-1800s. The architecture and atmosphere of this quiet, homespun neigh-borhood provide a feeling for life in a less hectic time. A brochure available at Info! Charlotte includes 18 historic places of interest here. Be sure to stop by **Old Settlers Cemetery,** behind the **First Presbyterian Church** (✉ 200 W. Trade St., ☎ 704/332–5123), which contains tombstones that date from the 1700s. The church, which takes up a city block and faces West Trade Street, reflects the prosperity of the early settlers and their descendants. By the turn of the last century, they

Charlotte

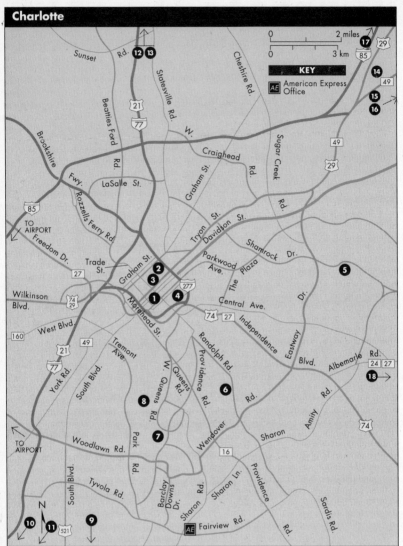

had built this Gothic Revival complex with stained glass to replace a much simpler meeting house. **Fourth Ward Park** is an oasis in the middle of the city. **Alexander Michael's** (✉ 401 W. 9th St., ☎ 704/332–6789) is a favorite eatery. **Poplar Street Books** is housed in the Victorian Young-Morrison House (✉ 226 W. 10th St.). U.S. President Taft spent the night in the **Liddell-McNinch House** (✉ 511 N. Church St.), now a restaurant, when he visited Charlotte in 1909. **Spirit Square** (✉ 345 N. College St.), in a former church, includes galleries, a performing arts center, and classrooms that used to be the sanctuary for the First Baptist Church. The **public library** (✉ 310 N. Tryon St.), which contains a mural reproducing a Romare Bearden painting, is open weekdays 9–9, Saturday 9–6, and Sunday 2–6.

❶ NationsBank Corporate Center. Built in 1992, this 60-story structure with a crownlike top designed by Pelli is one of the city's most striking buildings. Its main attraction is three philosophical frescoes by Ben Long that symbolize the city's past, present, and future. Also housed in the tower are the **North Carolina Blumenthal Performing Arts Center** and **Founders Hall,** a complex of restaurants and shops. ✉ *100 N. Tryon St.*

Greater Charlotte

Beyond Uptown, and farther flung, lie many of Charlotte's most interesting sights, from gardens to museums. You can reach the ones listed below by car or by city bus; for visits elsewhere, a car is essential.

A Good Tour

From Uptown, follow 7th Street east and turn north on North Myers Street to visit the galleries of the **Afro-American Cultural Center** ④. Continue east on 7th Street past I–277 to Central Avenue; go east on central Avenue to Eastway Drive, north to Shamrock Drive, and east to the **Hezekiah Alexander Homesite and Charlotte History Museum** ⑤, where you can capture the area's early days at the county's oldest building. Return west on Shamrock to Eastway Drive and travel south on Eastway until it becomes Wendover Road. Continue on Wendover to Randolph Road and then turn right on Randolph to the **Mint Museum of Art** ⑥, a wide-ranging collection in what was a mint. The next stop, **Wing Haven Gardens and Bird Sanctuary** ⑦, is in Myers Park, a handsome neighborhood. One approach to this area is to continue north on Randolph Road to South Laurel Avenue, which leads south to Providence Road (NC 16). Follow Providence south to Queens Road to Selwyn and then turn west on Ridgewood. More experience with nature can be found at the **Charlotte Nature Museum** ⑧, next to Freedom Park. To get here, continue west on Ridgewood to Westfield Road, take Westfield north to Sterling, and then follow Sterling north to the museum.

TIMING

You can spend a pleasant day touring these sights, which are only a few miles apart from one other.

Sights to See

❹ Afro-American Cultural Center. This arts center has galleries and a theater; it's housed in the former Little Rock AME Zion Church. ✉ *401 N. Meyers St.,* ☎ *704/374–1565.* ☞ *Free.* ☉ *Tues.–Sat. 10–6, Sun. 1–5.*

❽ Charlotte Nature Museum. Live animals, nature trails, hands-on exhibits, and nature films are highlights of this museum. ✉ *1658 Sterling Rd. (next to Freedom Park),* ☎ *704/337–2660.* ☞ *$1.* ☉ *Weekdays 9–5, Sat. 10–5, Sun. 1–5.*

⑤ Hezekiah Alexander Homesite and Charlotte History Museum. The stone house, built in 1774, is the oldest dwelling in the county. Here, Alexander and his wife, Mary, reared 10 children and farmed the land. Costumed docents give guided tours, and seasonal events commemorate the early days. ⊠ *3500 Shamrock Dr.,* ☎ *704/568–1774.* ⊉ *$4.* ⊙ *Tues.–Fri. 10–5, weekends 2–5.*

★ **⑥ Mint Museum of Art.** Built in 1837 as a U.S. Mint, this building has served as a home for art since 1936, attracting such visiting exhibits as "Classical Taste in America." ⊠ *2730 Randolph Rd.,* ☎ *704/337–2000.* ⊉ *$4.* ⊙ *Tues. 10–10, Wed.–Sat. 10–5, Sun. noon–5.*

⑦ Wing Haven Gardens and Bird Sanctuary. In Myers Park, one of Charlotte's loveliest neighborhoods, a 3-acre garden developed by the Clarkson family is home to more than 135 species of birds. ⊠ *248 Ridgewood Ave.,* ☎ *704/331–0664.* ⊉ *Free.* ⊙ *Sun. 2–5, Tues. 3–5, Wed. 10–noon or by appointment.*

Other Area Attractions

Ringing Charlotte are historical sites, gardens, offbeat museums, a speedway, and theme parks—plenty to explore, depending on your interest.

⑯ Backing Up Classics Memory Lane Motor Car Museum. At this museum (and we're not making the name up), you can see up close some of the '50s race and muscle cars that have been the workhorses of stock-car racing. ⊠ *4545 U.S. 29, Harrisburg,* ☎ *704/788–9494.* ⊉ *$4.50.* ⊙ *Weekdays 9–5:30, Sat. 9–5, Sun. 10–5.*

⑮ Charlotte Motor Speedway. Learn all about racing at this state-of-the-art facility, browse through the gift shop, or even take a lesson at the track through the Richard Petty Driving School (☎ 704/455–9443) or Fast Track Driving School (☎ 704/455–1700). ⊠ *5555 U.S. 29, Concord, northeast of Charlotte,* ☎ *704/455–3200.* ⊉ *Tour $3.* ⊙ *Mon.–Sat. 9–4, Sun. 1–4.*

⑬ Energy Explorium. At this center operated by Duke Power Company on Lake Norman, hands-on exhibits let you simulate the creation of nuclear power and other kinds of energy. ⊠ *McGuire Nuclear Site, 13339 Hagers Ferry Rd., off I–77 and NC 73, Huntersville,* ☎ *704/875–5600 or 800/777–0003.* ⊉ *Free.* ⊙ *Mon.–Sat. 9–5, Sun. noon–5.*

⑨ James K. Polk Memorial. A state historic site south of Charlotte marks the humble 1795 birthplace of the 11th president. Guided tours of the log cabins (replicas of the originals) are available, and exhibits depict early life in Mecklenburg County. ⊠ *U.S. 521, Pineville,* ☎ *704/889–7145.* ⊉ *Free.* ⊙ *Apr.–Oct., Mon.–Sat. 9–5, Sun. 1–5; Nov.–Mar., Tues.–Sat. 10–4, Sun. 1–4.*

⑫ Latta Plantation Park. This nature preserve centers on Latta Place, a Catawba River plantation house built by merchant James Latta in the early 1800s. Costumed guides give tours of the house. The park also has farm animals, an equestrian center, and the Carolina Raptor Center, a unique nonprofit facility where injured birds of prey are rehabilitated and then released. Those unable to return to the wild are cared for and used to educate visitors. ⊠ *5225 Sample Rd., Huntersville,* ☎ *704/875–2312 Latta Place, 704/875–1391 park, 704/875–6521 Carolina Raptor Center.* ⊉ *House tour $3, Raptor Center $4.* ⊙ *Park daily 7:30 AM–dark; Raptor Center Tues.–Sat. 10–5, Sun. noon–5; house tours Tues.–Fri. at 1:30 and 3:30, weekends at 2, 3, and 4.*

☕ **⑰ N.C. Transportation Museum.** At this former railroad repair facility, a restored train takes passengers on a 45-minute ride over the 57-acre

Pick up the phone.
Pick up the miles.

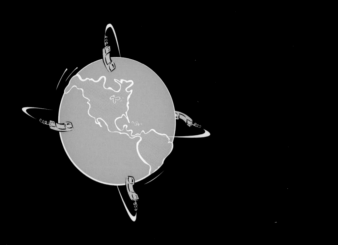

1-800-FLY-FREE

Is this a great time, or what? :-)

Now when you sign up with MCI
you can receive up to 8,000 bonus
frequent flyer miles on one of seven
major airlines.

Then earn another 5 miles for every
dollar you spend on a variety of
MCI services, including MCI Card®
calls from virtually anywhere in
the world.*

You're going to use these services
anyway. Why not rack up the miles
while you're doing it?

Urban planning.

CITYPACKS

The ultimate guide to the city—a complete pocket guide plus a full-size color map.

www.fodors.com

complex, with a stop at the round house. The museum, a state historic site, traces the development of transportation in North Carolina from Indian times to the present. The gift shop sells some unique train memorabilia. The museum is 40 mi northeast of Charlotte. ⊠ *411 S. Salisbury Ave., off I–85, Spencer,* ☎ *704/636–2889.* ⊠ *Free; train rides $4.* ☉ *Apr.–Oct., Mon.–Sat. 9–5, Sun. 1–5; Nov.–Mar., Tues.–Sat. 10–4, Sun. 1–4.*

👆 ⑪ **Paramount's Carowinds.** A 91-acre theme amusement park on the South Carolina state line has taken on a new image since its acquisition by the movie studio and the addition of new attractions based on films. Costumed movie characters and actors greet visitors to the park, and the Paladium offers musical concerts with star entertainers. A water park expansion in 1997 added to the fun. ⊠ *14523 Carowinds Blvd., off I–77,* ☎ *704/588–2600 or 800/888–4386.* ⊠ *$28.99.* ☉ *June–Aug., daily; mid-Mar.–May and Sept.–mid-Oct., weekends only; park usually opens around 10 AM; closing hrs vary.*

⑩ **Radisson Grand Resort.** This two-restaurant Radisson occupies property once owned by Jim and Tammy Bakker's PTL television ministry and formerly known as New Heritage USA. Changes have been made, but the water park—open mid-May–Labor Day—paddle boats, and bike rentals remain, as do some shops. Now found on the 600+ acres are tennis courts and an 18-hole championship golf course. You can also visit Billy Graham's boyhood home, previously moved to the site. To get here, head south from Charlotte on I–77 for about 12 mi to South Carolina. ⊠ *9700 Regent Pkwy., Fort Mill, SC,* ☎ *803/548–7800 or 800/333–3333.* ⊠ *Water park and other attractions $10, Graham house free.*

👆 ⑱ **Reed Gold Mine State Historic Site.** This area, east of Charlotte in Cabarrus County, is where America's first gold rush began, following Conrad Reed's discovery of a 17-pound nugget in 1799. You can explore the underground mine shaft and gold holes, pan for gold in summer, learn about gold mining, or enjoy a picnic. ⊠ *9621 Reed Mine Rd., north of NC 24/27, Locust (follow signs beyond town),* ☎ *704/786–8337.* ⊠ *Free, but gold panning is $2.* ☉ *Apr.–Oct., Mon.–Sat. 9–5, Sun. 1–5; Nov.–Mar., Tues.–Sat. 10–4, Sun. 1–4.*

⑭ **UNC Charlotte Botanical Garden and Sculpture Garden.** A rhododendron garden and greenhouse with a rain forest, orchids, carnivorous plants, and cacti create a peaceful atmosphere. ⊠ *NC 49 off I–85,* ☎ *704/547–2364.* ⊠ *Free.* ☉ *Gardens daylight–dark; greenhouse weekdays 9–4, Sat. 10–3.*

Dining

American

$$$–$$$$ ✕ **Townhouse.** American cuisine with a French twist is exquisitely prepared and served in an atmosphere of casual elegance. Choose among appetizers such as spinach lasagna with snails and garlic cream and entrées such as caramelized salmon, or let the chef compose a five-course "chef's choice" menu for $45 per person. ⊠ *1011 Providence Rd.,* ☎ *704/335–1546. AE, DC, MC, V.*

$$–$$$ ✕ **Atlantic Beer & Ice Co.** Here's an Uptown eatery in a sprawling three-story building with something for everyone. There's live entertainment, a cigar and Scotch bar, and five billiards tables. The menu is Floribbean—a combination of foods from southern Florida and the Caribbean. Try the breast of chicken rolled in crushed banana chips, sautéed and served with coconut rice, candied star fruit, and a light pistachio cream. ⊠ *330 N. Tryon St.,* ☎ *704/339–0566. AE, DC, MC, V.*

$$–$$$ ✕ **Providence Café.** Many of the dishes (especially the sandwiches) served in this chic, contemporary eatery decorated with neon and original art center around foccacia that is baked daily on the premises. The eclectic menu also includes chicken, steaks, and seafood grilled over green hickory wood. It's a great place for Sunday brunch and after-hours desserts with cappuccino or espresso. ⊠ *110 Perrin Pl.,* ☎ *704/376–2008. AE, D, DC, MC, V.*

$$–$$$ ✕ **South End Brewery & Smokehouse.** This restaurant and microbrewery has rapidly become a hot spot in the historic South End district. The decor is industrial chic, the music live, and the food regional American. Particularly popular is the pork tenderloin with applejack brandy sauce and Italian grits. ⊠ *2100 South Blvd.,* ☎ *704/358–4677. AE, D, MC, V.*

$ ✕ **College Place Restaurant.** You'll find down-home cookin' here for breakfast or lunch. Breakfasts, particularly, are big and offer any combination of eggs, pancakes, grits, bacon, and sausage, to name just a few items. Lunch has lots of vegetable choices (12), homemade corn bread, and cobblers. This cafeteria-style eatery is very close to the convention center. ⊠ *300 S. College St.,* ☎ *704/343–9268. No credit cards. Closed weekends. No dinner.*

$ ✕ **Landmark Restaurant-Diner.** This spacious New York–style eatery in the Eastland Mall neighborhood is a cut above most inexpensive restaurants, and it's open until 3 AM on weeknights and 24 hours on weekends. The Landmark is a good place for an informal meal or a late-night dessert; ask for the New York cheesecake. ⊠ *4429 Central Ave.,* ☎ *704/532–1153. Reservations not accepted. AE, MC, V.*

Continental

$$$$ ✕ **Lamplighter.** You don't have to go abroad to dine on fine Continental
★ cuisine served in an elegant setting. Just step into the softly lit, sophisticated atmosphere of the Lamplighter, in an old Dilworth home. The trio combination entrées (beef, veal, and lamb, or different seafood) are exceptional, and the wine list is extensive. There's a quiet, intimate lounge for cocktails. ⊠ *1065 E. Morehead St.,* ☎ *704/372–5343. Reservations essential. AE, DC, MC, V.*

$$ ✕ **Pewter Rose Bistro.** In a renovated textile mill in historic Dilworth,
★ five minutes from Uptown, the Pewter Rose Bistro is a favorite hangout for Charlotte's young professionals. Lace curtains and plants decorate the dining room, and the kitchen specializes in fresh seasonal foods, plus chicken and seafood dishes. You can order vegetarian pasta with feta cheese, sun-dried tomatoes, and olives, or add chicken for a heartier meal. Reservations are accepted for parties of six or more. ⊠ *1820 South Blvd.,* ☎ *704/332–8149. AE, D, DC, MC, V.*

Italian

$$$$ ✕ **Bravo!** Authentic classic Northern Italian cuisine is served in a Mediterranean-style atmosphere at this hotel restaurant, the "in" place for special celebrations and Sunday brunches. The professionally trained singing waitresses and waiters never seem to tire of performing or graciously serving. ⊠ *Adam's Mark Hotel, 555 S. McDowell St.,* ☎ *704/372–5440. Reservations essential except for Sun. brunch. AE, D, DC, MC, V.*

$$–$$$ ✕ **Cafe 521.** Put on your Doc Maartens and join the Generation X-ers for excellent Northern Italian cuisine at one of the city's coolest restaurants. Don't miss the zesty minestrone. Industrial-looking on the outside, the restaurant is painted with funky murals on the inside. ⊠ *521 N. College St.,* ☎ *704/377–9100. AE, D, MC, V.*

$–$$ ✕ **PizZarrelli Trattoria.** The secret to the flavor of the made-from-scratch pizzas is in the wood-burning brick ovens, built by Italian masons. The menu also includes calzone, lasagna, and other Southern Italian dishes—all family recipes. The walls display posters and photographs chronicling the professional singing career of owner Neal Zarrelli, a former opera star who often sings for his customers. ✉ *9101 Pineville-Matthews Rd., Pineville,* ☎ *704/543–0647. AE, D, MC, V.*

Thai

$$–$$$ ✕ **Thai House.** Fiery pleasure awaits the adventurous diner who samples from a selection of vegetarian, seafood, and classic Thai dishes at what many regard as the best Thai place in town. The satays and pad Thai noodles are mild enough for any taste buds, but many other dishes are seasoned as you request. ✉ *3210 N. Sharon Amity Rd.,* ☎ *704/532–6868. AE, D, DC, MC, V.*

Lodging

Hotels and Motels

$$$ 🏨 **Dunhill.** Charlotte's oldest and most historic hotel (built in 1929)
★ has artwork by Philip Moose and 18th- and 19th-century reproduction furniture in the lobby, restaurant, and guest rooms. The restaurant, **Monticello's,** gets rave reviews for its beautifully presented American cuisine. ✉ *237 N. Tryon St., 28202,* ☎ *704/332–4141 or 800/354–4141,* 🖷 *704/376–4117. 59 rooms, 1 penthouse. Restaurant, lounge. AE, D, DC, MC, V.*

$$$ 🏨 **Embassy Suites.** An eight-story atrium and three glass elevators distinguish this all-suite hotel, near the airport and the Coliseum. Regular suites have two rooms, with a coffeemaker, refrigerator, and microwave. You're served a cooked-to-order full breakfast and treated to an afternoon reception. ✉ *4800 S. Tryon St., 28217,* ☎ *704/527–8400 or 800/362–2779,* 🖷 *704/527–7035. 274 suites. Restaurant, lounge, indoor pool, hot tub, sauna, health club, meeting rooms, airport shuttle. AE, D, DC, MC, V.*

$$$ 🏨 **Hilton at University Place.** This high-rise fronts on a lake and dominates a European-style shopping and entertainment village near the University of North Carolina at Charlotte. Movies, restaurants, shops, a bank, and even a hospital are just steps from the hotel door. Dining is offered in the **Upper Deck Bar & Beach Club.** ✉ *8629 J. M. Keynes Blvd., 28262,* ☎ *704/547–7444 or 800/445–8667,* 🖷 *704/548–1081. 240 rooms, 3 suites. Restaurant, bar, pool, exercise room, beach, meeting rooms. AE, D, DC, MC, V.*

$$$ 🏨 **Hyatt Charlotte SouthPark.** The focal point of the four-story atrium is a Mexican water fountain surrounded by 25-ft olive trees. Guest rooms have data ports for laptop computers and fax machines. Meeting rooms and the lower lobby are by the open-air courtyard. **Scalini's,** one of the city's best restaurants, serves Northern Italian cuisine; the Club piano bar is a favorite. ✉ *5501 Carnegie Blvd., 28209-3462,* ☎ *704/554–1234 or 800/233–1234,* 🖷 *704/554–8319. 258 rooms, 4 suites. Restaurant, piano bar, indoor pool, hot tub, sauna, health club, meeting rooms, airport shuttle. AE, D, DC, MC, V.*

$$$ 🏨 **Radisson Plaza Hotel.** Convenience and contemporary elegance distinguish this property just steps from the Square and the center of Uptown. It's also connected via enclosed skywalks to the Overstreet Mall. Try dining at the **Azaleas American Grill.** ✉ *1 Radisson Plaza, 101 S. Tryon St., 28280,* ☎ *704/377–0400 or 800/333–3333,* 🖷 *704/347–0649. 361 rooms, 4 suites. Restaurant, bar, pool, sauna, health club, meeting rooms, airport shuttle. AE, D, DC, MC, V.*

$$$ ⊞ **Westin Hotel, Charlotte.** The pink marble used in the public rooms makes the Westin (formerly the Omni) one of Charlotte's classiest Uptown hotels. You can enjoy the ambience of **C. Banknight's Bistro and Bar,** then work out with Charlotte's movers and shakers in the adjoining 50,000-square-ft YMCA, which includes an indoor track and a lap pool. ⊠ *222 E. 3rd St., 28202,* ☎ *704/377–6664 or 800/843–6664,* FAX *704/377–4143. 392 rooms, 18 suites. Restaurant, bar, indoor pool, health club, meeting rooms. AE, D, DC, MC, V.*

$ ⊞ **Comfort Inn–Lake Norman.** This economy motel, north of Charlotte on I–77 near Lake Norman, offers complimentary breakfast and rooms with refrigerators and coffeemakers. Some rooms have VCRs, microwaves, and whirlpool baths. ⊠ *20740 Torrence Chapel Rd., Davidson 28036,* ☎ *704/892–3500 or 800/484–9751,* FAX *704/892–6473. 90 rooms. Refrigerators, pool, coin laundry. AE, D, DC, MC, V.*

Bed-and-Breakfasts

$$$–$$$$ ⊞ **Inn Uptown.** The inn, an 1891 brick château on the edge of the historic Fourth Ward neighborhood, is popular with business and leisure travelers because of its proximity to Uptown businesses and attractions. Deep green wallpaper and a green-and-white-striped bedspread lend formal elegance to one room; another has a whirlpool tub, and four have fireplaces. A full breakfast is served. ⊠ *129 N. Poplar St., 28202,* ☎ *704/342–2800 or 800/959–1990,* FAX *704/342–2222. 6 rooms. In-room modem lines. AE, D, DC, MC, V.*

$$$ ⊞ **Homeplace.** This spotless turn-of-the-century Victorian gem in a res-
★ idential neighborhood is now a B&B filled with antiques and memorabilia from yesteryear. Breakfast is prepared by owners Peggy and Frank Darien and served in the dining room. ⊠ *5901 Sardis Rd., 28270,* ☎ *704/365–1936. 2 rooms, 1 2-bedroom suite. AE, MC, V.*

$$$ ⊞ **Morehead Inn.** Though it's a commercial venture catering to corporate clients, this B&B in the Dilworth neighborhood has all the comforts of a beautiful home. Wedding parties find it ideal. The breakfast is Continental. ⊠ *1122 E. Morehead St., 28204,* ☎ *704/376–3357,* FAX *704/335–1110. 12 rooms. Meeting rooms. AE, DC, MC, V.*

Nightlife and the Arts

Nightlife

Bailey's Sports Bar & Grille (⊠ 5873 Albemarle Rd., ☎ 704/532–1005; ⊠ 8500 Pineville-Matthews Rd., ☎ 704/541–0794) offers billiards in an upscale setting, with a big-screen TV and deli-style food. **Comedy Zone** (⊠ 5317 E. Independence Blvd., ☎ 704/568–4242) showcases live comedy nightly except Monday, with two shows nightly Friday and Saturday. **Dilworth Brewing Company** (⊠ 1301 East Blvd., ☎ 704/377–2739) showcases rock bands on Friday and Saturday nights, plus several varieties of excellent beer made on the premises. The **Moon Room** (⊠ 433 S. Tryon St., ☎ 704/342–2003), a funky bar, presents a variety of entertainment. Thursdays range from psychic night to experimental music night. Fridays and Saturdays are reserved for live music. **Mythos** (⊠ 300 N. College St., ☎ 704/375–8765), an alternative dance club, doesn't open until 10 PM Tuesday through Sunday. DJs spin house, techno, and European dance music.

The Arts

The key venue for performing arts is the **North Carolina Blumenthal Performing Arts Center,** or PAC (⊠ 130 N. Tryon St., ☎ 704/372–1000). It's home to several resident companies, including the **Charlotte Symphony Orchestra, North Carolina Dance Theatre, Charlotte Repertory Theatre,** and **Opera Carolina.** PAC also presents national tours of Broadway musicals. The **Spirit Square Center for the Arts & Education** (✉ 345 N. College St., ☎ 704/376–8883 or 800/922–6431) is an interdisciplinary arts center that offers classes, exhibits, and national acts such as Wynton Marsalis and Jerry Jeff Walker.

Blockbuster Pavilion (✉ 707 Pavilion Blvd., ☎ 704/549–1292) spotlights a variety of concerts spring through fall. The **Paladium Amphitheater** at Paramount's Carowinds (✉ 14523 Carowinds Blvd., ☎ 704/588–2600 or 800/888–4386) present stars in concert mid-spring through mid-fall.

Outdoor Activities and Sports

Participant Sports

CAMPING

Near Charlotte, camping can be found at McDowell Park and Nature Reserve (✉ 15222 York Rd., ☎ 704/588–5224), Paramount's Carowinds (14523 Carowinds Blvd., off I–77, ☎ 704/588–2600 or 800/888–4386), and Duke Power State Park (✉ Rte. 2, Troutman, ☎ 704/528–6350).

CANOEING

Inlets on Lake Norman and Lake Wylie are ideal for canoeing, as are some spots of the Catawba River. The Pee Dee River east of Charlotte and the New River in the mountains offer other options.

FISHING

There's good fishing in Charlotte's neighboring lakes and streams. A mandatory state license can be bought at local bait and tackle shops or over the phone (with a credit card) from the North Carolina Wildlife Commission (☎ 919/715–4091).

GOLF

There are 23 public and 31 private courses in the Charlotte area. The *Metrolina Golf Guide,* a free publication available at Info! Charlotte (☞ Visitor Information *in* Charlotte A to Z, *below*), has a complete list. **Crystal Springs Golf Club** (✉ NC 51, Pineville, ☎ 704/588–2640) is an 18-hole championship course with a restaurant and lounge. **Highland Creek Golf Club** (✉ 7001 Highland Creek Pkwy., ☎ 704/875–9000), an 18-hole course with a driving range, is considered by some to be the best public course in Charlotte. **Larkhaven Golf Club** (✉ 4801 Camp Stewart Rd., ☎ 704/545–4653) is an 18-hole championship course with clubhouse and pro shop. **Paradise Valley Golf Center** (✉ 9309 N. Tryon St., ☎ 704/547–0222), in the university area, has a nine-hole regulation course and a nine-hole par-three course. The driving range is down the street (✉ 9615 N. Tryon St., ☎ 704/548–8114). The **Peninsula Club** (✉ 19101 Peninsula Club Dr., Davidson, ☎ 704/896–7080) has hosted the Carolinas LPGA. **Woodbridge Golf Links** (✉ 922 New Camp Creek Church Rd., Kings Mountain, ☎ 704/482–0353), an attractive course with covered cart bridges, has 18 holes and a driving range.

HIKING

Crowder's Mountain and Kings Mountain near Gastonia and the Uwharrie Mountains east of Charlotte offer plenty of varied terrain and challenge for hikers.

SWIMMING

The **Mecklenburg County Aquatic Center** (✉ 800 E. 2nd St., ☎ 704/336–3483) has a 50-meter lap pool, hydrotherapy pool, fitness room, and whirlpool. It is open daily to local residents and visitors; fee is $4.

TENNIS

Tennis courts are available in several Charlotte city parks, including Freedom, Hornet's Nest, Park Road, and Veterans. A growing number of hotels and motels provide courts as well. For details, call the Charlotte Park and Recreation Department (☎ 704/336–3854).

Spectator Sports

AUTO RACING

NASCAR races, such as the Coca-Cola 600 and Mello Yello 500, draw huge crowds at the **Charlotte Motor Speedway** (⊠ 12 mi north on U.S. 29, near Concord). For tickets, call 704/455–3200.

BASEBALL

The AAA minor league **Charlotte Knights** play from April through August at Knights Castle (⊠ 2280 Deerfield Dr., by I–77 and Gold Hill Rd., Fort Mill, SC, ☎ 704/357–8071 or 803/548–8050).

BASKETBALL

The **Charlotte Hornets** NBA team plays from November through April at the Charlotte Coliseum (⊠ Tyvola Rd. off Billy Graham Pkwy., ☎ 704/522–6500).

FOOTBALL

The **Carolina Panthers** NFL team plays September–January at the Carolinas Stadium (⊠ 800-1 S. Mint St., ☎ 704/358–7800).

HOCKEY

The **Charlotte Checkers** play from mid-October to mid-March at Independence Arena (⊠ 2700 E. Independence Blvd., ☎ 704/342–4423).

Shopping

Charlotte is the largest retail center in the Carolinas, with the majority of stores in suburban malls. Villages and towns in outlying areas have some regional specialties. Uptown shops are open 10–5:30 daily except Sunday. Malls are open Monday–Saturday 10–9 and Sunday 1–6. Sales tax is 6%.

Shopping Malls

Carolina Place Mall (⊠ 11025 Carolina Place Pkwy., off I–277 at Pineville, ☎ 704/543–9300) is the only Charlotte shopping center with five anchors and interstate access. It also offers visitor discount cards upon request. **SouthPark Mall** (⊠ 4400 Sharon Rd., ☎ 704/364–4411), in the most affluent section of the city, caters to upscale customers. **Eddie Bauer, Godiva Chocolatier, Caswell-Massey,** and **NordicTrack** are here. The main attraction at **Eastland Mall** (⊠ 5471 Central Ave., ☎ 704/537–2626), on the east side of town, is an ice-skating rink. **Belk, Dillards, JCPenney, Sears,** and other retail stores are also here.

You can buy well-known brands at a discount in outlets in **Midtown Square** (⊠ 401 S. Independence Blvd., ☎ 704/333–8205), near Uptown Charlotte, **Windsor Square** (⊠ 9915 E. Independence Blvd., ☎ 704/847–5533), near Matthews, or **Outlet Marketplace** (⊠ Off I–77, Fort Mill, SC, ☎ 704/377–8630).

Specialty Stores

ANTIQUES

The towns of Waxhaw, Pineville, and Matthews are the best places to find antiques. Waxhaw sponsors an annual antiques fair each February. Shops are usually open Monday through Saturday in Pineville and Matthews. In Waxhaw, some shops are open on Sunday but closed on

Monday. You can find a good selection of antiques at the **Metrolina Expo** (✉ Off I–77N at 7100 Statesville Rd., ☎ 704/596–4643) on the first and third weekends of the month.

BOOKS

Little Professor Book Center (✉ Park Road Shopping Center, 4139 Park Rd., ☎ 704/525–9239; ✉ South Lake Shopping Center, Lake Norman, ☎ 704/896–7323) has a nice selection of contemporary fiction and classics. **Barnes & Noble Bookstore** (✉ 5837 E. Independence Blvd., ☎ 704/535–9810; ✉ 10701 Centrum Pkwy., Pineville, ☎ 704/541–1425) carries more than 100,000 titles. **Borders Books & Music** (✉ 4500 Sharon Rd., ☎ 704/365–6261), the newest contender in the Charlotte book market, has 100,000 titles and an espresso bar where you can mull over the choices. **Newsstand International** (✉ 5636 E. Independence Blvd., ☎ 704/531–0199) carries 5,000 newspapers, maps, and magazines from around the world.

CRAFTS

The best Charlotte crafts buys are in the **Metrolina Expo** (☞ Antiques, *above*). At a number of shows, including the **Carolina Craft Shows,** held in the fall and spring at the Convention Center, as well as the **Southern Christmas Show** and the **Southern Spring Show** at the Merchandise Mart, you can buy a wide variety of items.

FOOD AND PLANTS

Try the **Charlotte Regional Farmers Market** (✉ 1801 Yorkmount Rd., ☎ 704/357–1269) for produce and fish, plants, and crafts. The **Harris-Teeter** grocery store in Morrocroft Village (✉ 6701 Morrison Blvd., ☎ 704/364–1245) is a white-columned showplace with a staff chef who oversees an elaborate dine-in deli and two other stores.

Charlotte A to Z

Arriving and Departing

BY BUS

Greyhound Trailways System (✉ 601 W. Trade St., ☎ 704/342–2506 or 800/231–2222) serves the Charlotte area.

BY CAR

Charlotte is a transportation hub; I–77 comes in from Columbia, South Carolina, to the south and then continues north to Virginia, intersecting I–40 on the way. I–85 arrives from Greenville, South Carolina to the southwest and then goes northeast to meet I–40 between Winston-Salem and the Triangle. From the Triangle, I–85 continues northeast to Petersburg, Virginia.

BY PLANE

Charlotte-Douglas International Airport (☎ 704/359–4013) is west of the city off I–85. Carriers include American, British Airways, Delta, Northwest, TWA, United, US Airways, and their local affiliates.

For **transportation from the airport,** taxis cost about $12 ($2 each additional person), and airport vans are approximately $5 per person. Most major hotels provide complimentary transportation. By car, take the Billy Graham Parkway, then Wilkinson Boulevard (U.S. 74) east to I–277, which leads to the heart of Uptown.

BY TRAIN

Amtrak (✉ 1914 N. Tryon St., ☎ 704/376–4416 or 800/872–7245) offers daily service from Charlotte to Washington, D.C., Atlanta, and points beyond, and there's daily service to Raleigh.

Getting Around

BY BUS

Charlotte Transit (℡ 704/336–3366) provides public transportation throughout the city. Fares are 80¢ for local rides and $1.15 for express service. Free service is available between Mint and Kings Drive on Trade and between Stonewall and 11th on Tryon, weekdays 9–3.

BY TAXI

Yellow Cab (℡ 704/332–6161) has cars and airport vans. The **University Shuttle** (℡ 704/553–2424) caters to business travelers. Passengers pay a set flat rate.

Contacts and Resources

DOCTORS

Care Connection (℡ 704/384–4111), operated by Presbyterian Hospital, will give physician referrals and make appointments weekdays 9–4. **Healthfinder,** run by Mercy Hospital, offers recorded physician referral information (℡ 704/379–6100). The **Mecklenburg County Medical Society** (℡ 704/376–0847), open weekdays 9–1, also gives physician referrals.

EMERGENCIES

Police (℡ 911). **Ambulance** (℡ 911).

GUIDED TOURS

The **Catawba Queen** paddle wheeler (✉ U.S. 150, Exit 36, ℡ 704/663–2628) gives dinner cruises and tours on Lake Norman. Reservations are essential.

Several balloon companies give **aerial tours,** which end with champagne: Balloons Over Charlotte (℡ 704/541–7058) and Adventures Aloft of Charlotte (℡ 704/398–8122).

LATE-NIGHT PHARMACY

Eckerd Drugs (✉ Park Road Shopping Center, ℡ 704/523–3031; ✉ 3740 E. Independence Blvd., ℡ 704/536–3600).

RADIO STATIONS

AM: WBT 1110, sports, talk, country; WGSP 1310, Christian. **FM:** WSOC 103.7, country; WFAE 90.7, National Public Radio; WWMG 96, oldies; WXRC 95.7, rock.

VISITOR INFORMATION

Info! Charlotte (✉ 330 S. Tryon St., ℡ 704/331–2700 or 800/231–4636) is open weekdays 8:30–5, Saturday 10–4, and Sunday 1–4. Parking is available.

THE TRIAD

Greensboro, Winston-Salem, High Point

North Carolinians have grouped six urban centers in the Piedmont into two threesomes: the Triad and the Triangle (☞ *below*). While this shorthand is a verbal convenience—Greensboro, Winston-Salem, and High Point is a mouthful—it's also testament to the fact that the whole can be greater than the sum of the parts. Make no mistake, though: While they share geography and are scattered along the major arteries of the region, the Triad's major cities have very distinct personalities. Greensboro, to the east, bustles as a business center. Smaller Winston-Salem, to the west, will catch you by surprise with its large and eclectic arts scene. High Point, to the south, has managed to fuse the simplicity of Quaker forebears with its role as a world-class furniture market.

Greensboro

96 mi northeast of Charlotte, 26 mi east of Winston-Salem, 58 mi west of Durham.

With a population of 200,000, Greensboro is the largest population center in the Triad, and thanks to spacious convention facilities it's increasingly a destination for business travelers. But this city, named in honor of General Nathanael Greene, a Revolutionary War hero, takes pride in the role it has played in American history and has taken great pains to preserve and showcase the sights of other eras.

With the exception of Old Greensborough and the downtown historic district, however, walking is not a comfortable sightseeing option. If you want to tour the grand historic homes, glimpse monuments to famous native sons and daughters—Dolley Madison, Edward R. Murrow, O. Henry—or visit one of the many parks and recreation areas, you'll need a car.

Start your tour of Greensboro in a place that memorializes one of the earliest events in the city's history. On March 15, 1781, the Battle of Guilford Courthouse so weakened British troops that they surrendered seven months later at Yorktown. Today **Guilford Courthouse National Military Park** offers a tour of the nation's first Revolutionary War park, with over 200 acres of wooded hiking trails, monuments, and military memorabilia. ⊠ *2332 New Garden Rd.,* ☎ *336/288–1776.* ☞ *Free.* ◷ *Daily 8:30–5.*

Tannenbaum Park, a hands-on history experience near Guilford Courthouse National Military Park, draws you into the life of early settlers. With advance notice costumed reenactors will escort you through exhibits at the **Colonial Heritage Center** in the visitors center. Don't overlook one of the most outstanding collections of original colonial settlement maps in the country. ⊠ *Visitors center, New Garden Rd. and Battleground Ave.,* ☎ *336/545–5315.* ☞ *Free.* ◷ *Tues.–Sat. 10–5, Sun. 1–5.*

Roam through a dinosaur gallery, learn about gems and minerals, and see the lemurs, snakes, and amphibians at the **Natural Science Center of Greensboro.** There's also a petting zoo. ⊠ *4301 Lawndale Dr., adjacent to Country Park,* ☎ *336/288–3769.* ☞ *$3.50.* ◷ *Science center Mon.–Sat. 9–5, Sun. 12:30–5; zoo Mon.–Sat. 10–4:30, Sun. 12:30–4:30.*

The **Greensboro Historical Museum** is housed in a Romanesque church built in 1892. Native son and daughter O. Henry and Dolley Madison are the subjects of exhibits, as is the Woolworth sit-in that helped launch the national civil rights movement. ⊠ *130 Summit Ave.,* ☎ *336/ 373–2043.* ☞ *Free.* ◷ *Tues.–Sat. 10–5, Sun. 2–5.*

Greensboro Cultural Center at Festival Park, an architectural showplace, houses 25 visual and performing arts organizations, five art galleries, rehearsal halls, a sculpture garden, a restaurant with outdoor café-style seating, and an outdoor amphitheater. **ArtQuest,** developed by educators and artists, is North Carolina's only permanent interactive children's art gallery, and one of only several in the country. ⊠ *200 N. Davie St.,* ☎ *336/373–2712.* ☞ *Free.* ◷ *Weekdays 8 AM–10 PM, Sat. 9–6, Sun. 1–6:30.*

Elm Street, with its turn-of-the-century architecture, is the heart of **Old Greensborough** (⊠ 100 block of N. Elm St. to 600 block of S. Elm St., with portions of several other streets), which is listed on the National Register of Historic Places. Stop by the William Fields House, headquarters for the **Old Greensborough Preservation Society** (⊠ 447 Arlington St., ☎ 336/272–6617), to collect your self-guided tour map. The entire tour may be walked in two hours.

In Old Greensborough, the elegant **Blandwood Mansion,** home of former governor John Motley Morehead, is considered the prototype of the Italian villa architecture that swept the country during the mid-19th century. Designed by noted architect Alexander Jackson Davis, the house still contains many of its original furnishings. ⊠ 447 W. Washington St., ☎ 336/272–5003. ☜ $5. ☉ Tues.–Sat. 11–2, Sun. 2–5.

Dining and Lodging

$$–$$$ ✕ **Lo Spiedo Di Noble.** Murals adorn some walls, and from the upstairs seating area you can see the wood-burning tile oven and the slowly turning spit that turn out Tuscan cuisine such as rack of pork with fresh peach-walnut-thyme compote on a bed of white beans and red chard. The piano bar on the lower level is a nice way to end the evening. ⊠ 172 Battleground Ave., ☎ 336/333–9833. AE, D, MC, V.

$$–$$$ ✕ **Paisley Pineapple.** The dining is formal in this romantic Old Greensborough restaurant in a restored 1920s building. The fare on the extensive menu—rack of lamb, grilled veal tenderloin, and sautéed beef tenderloin—tends toward the hearty. On the lighter side are the soups (try the berry bisque if it's available) and seafood. Don't miss the cinnamon-seared salmon. Upstairs there's a sofa bar with live jazz. ⊠ 345 S. Elm St., ☎ 336/279–8488. AE, MC, V.

$–$$ ✕ **Casaldi's Cafe.** Light gray-green is the predominant color in this sleek little trattoria, appearing in the tile floors as well as marble countertops. Wildflowers decorate the tables, and display cases provide a powerful lure to sample the myriad pasta dishes. Particularly popular are the spinach and walnut ravioli and the hat-shape pasta with chicken and mushrooms. ⊠ 1310 Westover Terr., ☎ 336/379–8191. Reservations not accepted. D, MC, V. Closed Sun.

$–$$ ✕ **Sunset Cafe.** The look is art deco, the feel is bohemian, the preparations straightforward. The chef stresses the use of high-quality fresh ingredients, which makes the vegetarian dishes here the best in the Triad. There's a definite Middle Eastern flavor to meat, seafood, and appetizers. ⊠ 4608 W. Market St., ☎ 336/855–0350. MC, V.

$$$ 🏨 **Biltmore Greensboro Hotel.** In the heart of the central business dis-
★ trict, the Biltmore is within walking distance of shopping, dining, and nightclubs. The crystal front doors create a feeling of luxury, as does the attentive guest service manager, who makes sure your bags are whisked to your room. Guest rooms have period furniture and brass and marble baths. A free Continental breakfast is offered, and complimentary wine and cheese are served from 6 to 8 every evening. ⊠ 111 W. Washington St., 27401, ☎ 336/272–3474 or 800/332–0303. 21 rooms, 4 suites. Meeting room. AE, D, DC, MC, V.

$$$ 🏨 **Greenwood Bed and Breakfast.** Eclectic antiques, art, and various other collections fill this 1905 Craftsman-style home in historic Fisher Park. A complete breakfast is served daily at the time of your choosing. The presentation is elegant, the flavor French: Café au lait, French bread, eggs Benedict, and crêpes suzette come with fresh-squeezed orange juice and fruit. There's no smoking in the rooms. ⊠ 205 N. Park Dr., 27401, ☎ 336/274–6350 or 800/535–9363, ℻ 336/274–9943. 4 rooms. AE, D, MC, V.

$$$ 🏨 **Holiday Inn Four Seasons/Joseph S. Koury Convention Center.** With over 1,000 guest rooms and 200,000 square ft of meeting space, this place is a minicity rather than an intimate retreat. For the most part the accommodations are standard fare. But if it's convenience you want, you've got it. Business travelers are the mainstay here. ✉ *3121 High Point Rd., 27407,* ☎ *336/292–9161 or 800/242–6556,* FAX *336/294– 3516. 935 rooms, 79 suites. Restaurant, bar, no-smoking rooms, pool, sauna, exercise room, meeting rooms. AE, D, DC, MC, V.*

Nightlife and the Arts

After sampling the buffet at the **Barn Dinner Theatre** (✉ 120 Stagecoach Trail, ☎ 336/292–2211), you see popular Broadway plays such as "Forever Plaid." Cost of admission and meal ranges from $22.50– $28.50. The **Broach Theatre** (✉ 520 S. Elm St., ☎ 336/378–9300) offers professional adult and children's theater in the Old Greensborough historic district. The adult season runs March–June and September– December. The children's theater runs September–June.

The **Carolina Theatre** (✉ 310 S. Greene St., ☎ 336/333–2600), a restored vaudeville theater that serves as one of the city's principal performing arts centers, showcases dance, concerts, films, and plays.

The vast **Greensboro Coliseum Complex** (✉ 1921 W. Lee St., ☎ 336/ 373–7474) hosts arts and entertainment events throughout the year as well as professional, college, and amateur sports. It's home to the **Greensboro Symphony** (☎ 336/333–7490) and the **Greensboro Opera Company** (☎ 336/273–9472).

Outdoor Activities and Sports

BASEBALL

The **Greensboro Bats,** the Class A farm club for the New York Yankees, play April through September at War Memorial Stadium (✉ Corner of Lindsay and Yanceyville Sts., ☎ 336/333–2287).

CAMPING

Some good choices are **Fields Campground** (✉ 2317 Campground Rd., ☎ 336/292–1381), **Greensboro KOA** (✉ 2300 Montreal Ave., ☎ 336/274–4143 or 800/562–4143), **Hagan-Stone Park** (✉ 5920 Hagan-Stone Rd., ☎ 336/674–0472), and **Outdoor Center YMCA** (✉ 4924 Tapawingo Tr., ☎ 336/697–0525).

GOLF

Golfers can choose from among 22 public courses and six driving ranges and practice facilities. **Bryan Park and Golf Club** (✉ 6275 Bryan Park Rd., Browns Summit, ☎ 336/375–2200) is a highly regarded course north of Greensboro. The **Greensboro National Golf Club** (✉ 330 Niblick Dr., Summerfield, ☎ 336/297–4653), 15 minutes north of Greensboro, has 18 holes. The **Grandover Resort/Grandover Golf Club** (✉ One Thousand Club Rd., ☎ 336/294–1800) has two 18-hole courses.

The **Greater Greensboro Chrysler Classic** is the third-oldest PGA tournament to be continually hosted in the same city. It's held in April at the Forest Oaks Country Club (✉ U.S. 421 S, ☎ 336/379–1570).

HIKING

The **Bog Garden** (✉ On Hobbs Rd. north of Friendly Ave., ☎ 336/ 373–2199) has an elevated wooden walkway that provides easy access through the swampy area with more than 8,000 individually labeled trees, shrubs, ferns, bamboo, and wildflowers. There are walking trails and an exercise course at the 120-acre **Oka T. Hester Park** (✉ 910 Ailanthus St., ☎ 336/373–2937).

HOCKEY

The **Carolina Monarchs,** members of the American Hockey League, play October–April at the Greensboro Coliseum Arena (✉ 1921 W. Lee St., ☎ 336/852–6170).

TENNIS

Greensboro Jaycee Park (⊠ Pisgah Church Rd. on Forest Lawn Dr. adjacent to Country Park, ☎ 336/545–5342) offers a wide variety of sports facilities including a tennis center with 13 championship courts.

Shopping

SHOPPING DISTRICTS AND MALLS

Four Seasons Town Centre (⊠ I–40 at High Point Rd., ☎ 336/292–0171) holds more than 200 major stores, specialty shops, and restaurants. There's also a first-run movie theater. In **Old Greensborough** (☞ Greensboro, *above*) there are more than a dozen antiques shops, a grocery and seed store, and numerous bookstores.

SPECIALTY STORES

Replacements, Ltd. (⊠ I–85/40 at Mt. Hope Church Rd., Exit 132, ☎ 800/737–5223) is the world's largest retailer of discontinued and active china, crystal, flatware, and collectibles. There are more than 3 million pieces of inventory and 65,000 patterns. Free tours of the showrooms and warehouse are given daily.

Side Trips from Greensboro

CHARLOTTE HAWKINS BROWN MEMORIAL STATE HISTORIC SITE
10 mi east of Greensboro.

On the site of the Palmer Institute, the memorial honors the African-American woman who founded the school in 1902. Before closing, this accredited preparatory school for African Americans was recognized as one of the country's best and had expanded to over 350 acres of land. There's a visitor center and gift shop. ⊠ *6136 Burlington Rd., Sedalia, off I–85, Exit 135,* ☎ *336/449–4846.* ☞ *Free.* ☉ *Oct.–Apr., Tues.–Fri. 10–4, Sun. 1–4; May–Sept., Mon.–Sat. 9–5, Sun. 1–5.*

CHINQUA-PENN PLANTATION
25 mi north of Greensboro.

★ The **Chinqua-Penn Plantation,** a National Historic Register English country mansion, was built by tobacco and utility magnates Jeff and Betsy Penn in 1925. The Penns filled the 27-room house with an eclectic collection of artifacts representing 30 countries. The estate also has a Chinese pagoda, a three-story clock tower, greenhouses, and formal gardens. ⊠ *2138 Wentworth St., Reidsville,* ☎ *336/349–4576.* ☞ *$10.* ☉ *Mar.–Dec., Tues.–Sat. 9–5, Sun. noon–5.*

Winston-Salem

81 mi north of Charlotte, 26 mi west of Greensboro.

The manufacture of cigarettes, textiles, and furniture built a solid economic base in the Winston-Salem area; major area employers today include US Airways, Wachovia Bank, the Bowman Gray School of Medicine, RJR Nabisco, Sara Lee Corporation, and Hanes. Winston-Salem residents' donations to the arts are among the highest per capita in the nation. The city bills itself as the "City of the Arts," and its museums show the benefits of this support. The North Carolina School of the Arts commands international attention. Salem College, the oldest women's college in the country, is here, as is Wake Forest University, where writer Maya Angelou teaches. Old Salem, a restored 18th-century Moravian town within the city, has been a popular attraction since the early 1950s.

Begin your sightseeing at the **Winston-Salem Visitor Center** (⊠ 601 N. Cherry St., ☎ 336/777–3796). The staff will not only assist with directions but will help you make dining and hotel reservations. You can munch on Moravian cookies while you watch a film on the area.

★ Founded in 1766 as a Moravian Congregation town and backcountry trading center, **Old Salem** has become one of the nation's most authentic and well-documented colonial sites. At this living history museum with more than 80 restored and original buildings, costumed interpreters re-create household activities and trades common in Salem in the late 18th and early 19th centuries. Guests can also participate in African-American programs that include a stop by St. Philip's Church, the state's oldest standing African-American church. Old Salem is home to museum shops, an Old Salem Furniture & Accessories Shop, the 1816 Salem Tavern restaurant, and the Winkler Bakery. The village is a few blocks from downtown Winston-Salem and only a stone's throw from Business I–40 (take the Old Salem/Salem College exit). ⊠ *600 S. Main St.*, ☎ *336/721–7300 or 888/653–7253.* ⊠ *$14; combination ticket with Museum of Early Southern Decorative Arts (☞ below) $19.* ☉ *Mon.–Sat. 9–5, Sun. 12:30–5.*

NEED A BREAK	**Winkler Bakery** (⊠ 525 S. Main St., ☎ 336/721–7302) will satisfy your craving for hot, freshly baked Moravian sugar cake.

★ The **Museum of Early Southern Decorative Arts (MESDA),** on the southern edge of Old Salem, is the only museum dedicated to exhibiting and researching the regional decorative arts of the early South. Twenty-one period rooms and six galleries showcase the furniture, painting, ceramics, and metalware made and used regionally through 1820. The bookstore carries current and hard-to-find books on Southern decorative arts, culture, and history. ⊠ *924 S. Main St.,* ☎ *336/721–7360 or 888/653–7253.* ⊠ *$6; combination ticket with Old Salem (☞ above) $19.* ☉ *Mon.–Sat. 10:30–4:30, Sun. 1:30–4:30.*

☺ The **SciWorks** complex includes a 120-seat planetarium, 15-acre Environmental Park, and 45,000 square ft of exhibits that are interactive or hands-on, including the Coastal Encounters wet lab. ⊠ *400 W. Hanes Mill Rd.,* ☎ *336/767–6730.* ⊠ *Museum $4; the "Works" (planetarium, park, and museum) $7.* ☉ *Mon.–Sat. 10–5, Sun. 1–5.*

You can take a guided tour through the exhibits on tobacco growing at **R. J. Reynolds Whitaker Park** and then move on to the factory floor, where 8,000 cigarettes are produced every minute. ⊠ *1100 Reynolds Blvd.,* ☎ *336/741–5718.* ⊠ *Free.* ☉ *Weekdays 8–6.*

☺ **Historic Bethabara Park,** set in a wooded 180 acres, is the site of the first Moravian settlement (1753) in North Carolina. Bethabara—meaning "house of passage"—was to be temporary until the town of Salem was established. You can tour restored buildings such as the 1788 congregation house and explore the foundations of the town. Kids love the reconstructed Native American fort. Strolling the greenways is a pleasant way to pass time. ⊠ *2147 Bethabara Rd.,* ☎ *336/924–8191.* ⊠ *Free.* ☉ *Exhibit buildings Apr.–Nov., weekdays 9:30–4:30, weekends 1:30–4:30; guided tours Apr.–Nov. or by appointment. Brochures for self-guided walking tour available year-round at visitor center.*

The **Museum of Anthropology** offers exhibits of peoples and cultures of the Americas, Asia, Africa, and Oceania. The Discovery Room is filled with hands-on activities for families. ⊠ *Wake Forest University, Wingate Rd.,* ☎ *336/759–5282.* ⊠ *Free.* ☉ *Tues.–Sat. 10–4:30.*

Reynolda House Museum of American Art, formerly the home of tobacco magnate Richard Joshua Reynolds and his wife Katherine, is filled with American paintings, prints, and sculptures by such artists as

Thomas Eakins, Frederic Church, and Georgia O'Keeffe. There's also a costume collection, and clothing and toys used by the Reynolds children. The museum is in **Reynolda Village,** a collection of shops and restaurants that fill the estate's original outer buildings. ⊠ *2250 Reynolda Rd.,* ☎ *336/725–5325.* 🏷 *$6.* ⊘ *Tues.–Sat. 9:30–4:30.*

The **Southeastern Center for Contemporary Art (SECCA),** near Reynolda House, has long been a hidden treasure. The exhibits, in a series of cascading galleries, now have a much broader scope than regional arts and crafts, showcasing nationally known artists as well. The Centershop sells many one-of-a-kind arts and crafts. ⊠ *750 Marguerite Dr.,* ☎ *336/725–1904.* 🏷 *$3.* ⊘ *Tues.–Sat. 10–5, Sun. 2–5.*

Just south of the city, **Tanglewood Park,** the home of the late William and Kate Reynolds, is now open to the public; in addition to boating, hiking, fishing, horseback riding, and swimming, it offers a holiday light festival, the largest such display in the Southeast. The **Tanglewood Festival of Lights** runs from mid-November to mid-January annually. ⊠ *U.S. 158 off I–40, Clemmons,* ☎ *336/778–6300.* 🏷 *$2 per car, plus separate fees for each activity.* ⊘ *Daily dawn–dusk.*

Dining and Lodging

$$$ ✕ **Leon's Café.** A casual eatery in a renovated building near Old Salem serves some of the best food in town—fresh seafood, chicken breasts with raspberry sauce, lamb, and other specialties. The restaurant's dark colors are set off by artwork and lacy window treatments. ⊠ *924 S. Marshall St.,* ☎ *336/725–9593. AE, MC, V.*

$$–$$$ ✕ **Noble's Grille.** This upscale Continental restaurant serves a variety of entrées grilled or roasted over an oak-and-hickory fire, such as braised rabbit with black-pepper fettuccine and Carolina *poussin* (young chicken) with polenta. The dining room, with tall windows and track lighting, has a view of the kitchen grill. ⊠ *380 Knollwood St.,* ☎ *336/777–8477. AE, DC, MC, V.*

$$–$$$ ✕ **Old Salem Tavern.** Here you can dine on Moravian food in a Moravian setting. Standard menu items are chicken pot pie, ragout of beef, and Wiener schnitzel. From April through October you can eat outside on the patio or have drinks under the arbor. ⊠ *736 S. Main St.,* ☎ *336/748–8585. AE, MC, V.*

$$ ✕ **Café Piaf.** Inside the Stevens Center, a restored Art Deco performing-arts space, the café offers pasta primavera, chicken Piaf (mushroom pâté and chicken breast in puff pastry with champagne or mushroom cream sauce), and other French entrées. Dessert and coffee follow performances. ⊠ *401 W. 4th St.,* ☎ *336/750–0855. Reservations essential. AE, DC, MC, V.*

$$ ✕ **Paul's Fine Italian Dining.** Don't be put off by the strip-mall location of this restaurant, which serves cuisine from both the south and north of Italy. Particularly notable are the veal dishes such as veal au cognac, and the full wine list. The green, white, and coral colors are soothing, and there's enough room between tables to allow private conversation. ⊠ *3443-B Robin Hood Rd.,* ☎ *336/768–2645. AE, DC, MC, V. No lunch weekends.*

$$ ✕ **The Vineyards.** Innovative American fare, such as chicken with black-eyed-pea salad or eggplant sandwiches, draws diners to this Reynolda Village restaurant. ⊠ *120 Reynolda Rd.,* ☎ *336/748–0269. AE, MC, V.*

$$$$ ▥ **Brookstown Inn.** Sleep under a handmade quilt, relax in the whirlpool tubs that come in some rooms, sample wine and cheese or freshly baked cookies in the lobby, and enjoy the complimentary Continental breakfast at this inn, built in 1837 as a textile mill. ⊠ *200 Brookstown Ave.,*

27101, ☎ 336/725–1120 or 800/845–4262, FAX 336/773–0147. 71 rooms. Meeting rooms. AE, DC, MC, V.

$$$–$$$$ 🏨 **Adam's Mark Winston Plaza Hotel.** Centrally located off I–40, this elegant hotel, the city's premier lodging, has a marble lobby, traditional furnishings, and almost 10,000 square ft of meeting space. ✉ *425 N. Cherry St., 27101, ☎ 336/725–3500 or 800/444–2326, FAX 336/721–2240. 317 rooms. 2 restaurants, bar, pool, sauna, steam room, recreation room, meeting rooms. AE, D, DC, MC, V.*

$$$–$$$$ 🏨 **Henry F. Shaffner House.** Accessible to downtown and Old Salem, this B&B is a favorite with business travelers and honeymooning couples. The rooms in the restored English Tudor house are furnished in 19th-century Victorian elegance. In addition to a complimentary Continental breakfast, there's afternoon tea and evening wine and cheese. ✉ *150 S. Marshall St., 27101, ☎ 336/777–0052, FAX 336/777–1188. 8 rooms. AE, MC, V.*

$$$–$$$$ 🏨 **Tanglewood Manor House Bed & Breakfast.** At this former home of a branch of the Reynolds family, your choices include the 10 rooms in the antiques-filled manor house, 18 rooms in a more contemporary motel behind the house, or four cottages on Mallard Lake in Tanglewood Park. Those staying in the motel can purchase the Continental breakfast served in the manor house. Admissions to the park, swimming pool, and fishing are included. Greens fees are discounted. ✉ *U.S. 158 off I–40, Clemmons 27012, ☎ 336/778–6300, FAX 336/766–1571. 28 rooms, 4 cottages. Pool, fishing. AE, DC, MC, V.*

$$$ 🏨 **Comfort Inn–Cloverdale.** Off I–40 near downtown and Old Salem, this immaculately kept property provides a free Continental breakfast. ✉ *110 Miller St., 27103, ☎ 336/721–0220 or 800/228–5150, FAX 336/723–2117. 122 rooms. Pool, health club, meeting room. AE, D, DC, MC, V.*

Nightlife and the Arts

NIGHTLIFE

In the Adam's Mark Winston Plaza, the **Cherry Street Bar** (✉ 425 N. Cherry St., ☎ 336/725–3500) has cozy chairs and a smart decor of hunter green furnishings and wood paneling. Downtown, **Shober's** (✉ 871 W. 4th St., ☎ 336/724–3510) is a bar and restaurant that allows you to sit by a warm fireplace in the winter and fall or sip under the stars on the tree-dotted patio. **Lucky 32** (✉ 109 S. Stratford Rd., ☎ 336/777–0032) is a fine bar adjoining a restaurant that caters to a professional crowd. **Beethoven's 4th** (✉ 638 W. 4th St., ☎ 336/773–1517) plays all the latest tunes in a great dance environment.

THE ARTS

The North Carolina School of the Arts presents musical performances and numerous dramatic performances year-round, including three major productions each academic year. Many of these are held at the **Stevens Center** (✉ 405 W. 4th St., ☎ 336/721–1945), a restored 1929 movie palace downtown that is part of the NCSA campus. The Broadway Preview Series showcases first-run productions before they move on to Broadway engagements.

Outdoor Activities and Sports

BASEBALL

The **Winston-Salem Warthogs**, a Class A affiliate of the Cincinnati Reds, play April–August at Ernie Shore Field (✉ 401 Deacon Blvd., ☎ 336/759–2233).

GOLF

Tanglewood Park Golf Club (✉ NC 158, Clemmons, ☎ 336/766–5082) has two fine 18-hole courses, the Reynolds Course and the Championship Course, where the Vantage Championship is played each year. **Reynolds Park Golf Course** (⊠ 2931 Reynolds Park Rd., ☎ 336/650–7660) has 18 holes with a view of the city skyline.

Shopping

SHOPPING DISTRICTS AND MALLS

Reynolda Village is near the Reynolda House Museum of American Art (☞ Winston-Salem, *above*). The **Art District** at 6th and Trade Streets (just behind the Winston-Salem Visitor Center) has several galleries and arts and crafts shops. **Stratford Place,** a collection of upscale shops, restaurants, and cafés, is off Business I–40 in the Five Points area, where Country Club, Miller Road, and 1st Street converge.

Hanes Mall (⊠ Silas Creek Pkwy. and Hanes Mall Blvd.) is the largest mall in the Carolinas, with major department stores such as **Hecht's** and **Dillards** and specialty stores such as **The Nature Company** and **Banana Republic.**

BOOKS

Again and Again (⊠ 704 Brookstown Ave., ☎ 336/724–0599) is a wonderful place where you can browse through a converted old home filled with new and used books. Next door, the **Rainbow News & Cafe** has a coffee and wine bar and a wide variety of magazines.

CRAFTS

All items at the **Piedmont Craftsmen's Shop and Gallery** (⊠ 1204 Reynolda Rd., ☎ 336/725–1516) are juried, making it what the *New York Times* called a "showcase for Southern crafts." An annual fair is held in October. The **Winston-Salem Emporium** (⊠ 217 W. 6th St., ☎ 336/722–7277), in the Art District (☞ Shopping Districts and Malls, *above*), is a collection of galleries, boutiques, and small shops under one roof. More than 50 vendors display their wares.

OUTLET CENTERS

This is a textile center, so many clothing outlets cluster along the interstates. **Marketplace Mall** (⊠ 2101 Peters Creek Pkwy., ☎ 336/722–7779) has 36 outlet stores under one roof, including specialty shops, shoes, and apparel. The 100 stores in **Burlington Manufacturers Outlet Center** (☎ 336/227–2872) make the area off I–85 near Burlington a mecca for dedicated shoppers. Most stores are open Monday–Saturday 10–9, Sunday 1–6.

High Point

76 mi northeast of Charlotte, 20 mi southwest of Greensboro.

Originally settled by Quakers in the 1700s, High Point was incorporated in 1859. Its name is derived from the fact that it was the highest point on the railroad between Goldsboro and Charlotte. Today when people think of High Point they think of furniture, for it is home to the twice-a-year (April and October) International Home Furnishings Market, the largest wholesale furniture market in the world (not open to the public). Tens of thousands of buyers and others associated with the trade "go to market" and in the process lend a sophistication to this warm and hospitable city.

The **High Point Museum/Historical Park,** focusing on Piedmont history, includes the 1786 Haley House and a mid-1700s blacksmith shop and weaving house. Exhibits highlight furniture, pottery, communication, transportation, and military artifacts. ⊠ *1805 E. Lexington Ave.,* ☎ *336/885–6859.* ☜ *Free.* ☺ *Museum Tues.–Sat. 10–4:30, Sun. 1–4:30; park buildings weekends 1–4:30.*

The **Furniture Discovery Center,** in a renovated fabric warehouse downtown, is a new museum simulating a modern furniture factory. Besides the Furniture Hall of Fame, there's an extensive miniature collection with displays such as 15 miniature bedrooms that detail settings from the 17th through the 20th centuries. ⊠ *101 W. Green Dr.,* ☎ *336/887–3876.* ⊡ *$5; combination ticket with Angela Peterson Doll and Miniature Museum (☞ below) $7.50.* ⊙ *Apr.–Oct., Mon.–Sat. 10–5, Sun. 1–5; Nov.–Mar., Tues.–Sat. 10–5, Sun. 1–5.*

The **Angela Peterson Doll and Miniature Museum** houses the lifelong collection of one woman and is said to be the South's largest doll museum, with more than 1,700 dolls, costumes, miniatures, and dollhouses. ⊠ *101 W. Green Dr.,* ☎ *336/885–3655.* ⊡ *$3; combination ticket with Furniture Discovery Center (☞ above) $7.50.* ⊙ *Apr.–Oct., Mon.–Sat. 10–5, Sun. 1–5; Nov.–Mar., Tues.–Sat. 10–5, Sun. 1–5.*

OFF THE BEATEN PATH   **MENDENHALL PLANTATION** – A few miles northwest of High Point you'll find this well-preserved example of 19th-century Quaker domestic architecture. The Mendenhalls opposed slavery, and one of the nation's few surviving false-bottomed wagons, used to help slaves to freedom on the Underground Railroad, is on the site. ⊠ *603 W. Main St., Jamestown,* ☎ *336/454–3819.* ⊡ *$5.* ⊙ *Tues.–Fri. 11–2, Sat. 1–4, Sun. 2–4.*

Dining and Lodging

$$$–$$$$ ✕ **J. Basul Noble's.** Locals hold Noble's in very high esteem, and it's not hard to see why. The atmosphere is cosmopolitan; Sinatra crooning in the background establishes the mood. Veal dishes are recommended, and you could make an entire meal out of the fine breads (baked daily on the premises) and desserts served here. There's live jazz on weekends. ⊠ *114 S. Main St.,* ☎ *336/889–3354. AE, D, MC, V.*

$$–$$$ ✕ **Atrium Cafe.** This restaurant manages to be casual and elegant at the same time. It really shines during the dinner hours. Veal, duck, and fish dishes are standouts, but the pasta and mushrooms with marinara sauce proves the Atrium can appeal to vegetarians and nonvegetarians alike. ⊠ *430 S. Main St.,* ☎ *336/889–9934. AE, D, DC, MC, V.*

$$$–$$$$ 🏨 **Radisson Hotel High Point.** Each room here is outfitted with furniture from the different manufacturers represented in the area. It's a favorite with people coming to town for weekend shopping trips. ⊠ *135 S. Main St., 27260,* ☎ *336/889–8888,* ℻ *336/885–2737. 235 rooms, 16 suites. Restaurant, bar, indoor pool, exercise room, meeting rooms, airport shuttle. AE, D, DC, MC, V.*

$$–$$$ 🏨 **Premier Bed & Breakfast.** A local furniture designer owns this three-story B&B that occupies a 1930s-era home in a historic neighborhood. It's conveniently located just a mile north of downtown, near the furniture outlets and shopping. The bridal suite on the first floor has a hand-stenciled four-poster canopied bed and a huge bathtub. After a long day of touring, you can relax while sipping wine by the fireplace or on the front porch swing. ⊠ *1001 Johnson St., 27262,* ☎ *336/889–8439. 6 rooms. Meeting room. MC, V.*

Nightlife and the Arts

Headquartered in High Point is the **North Carolina Shakespeare Festival,** which has performances August–October and in December at the High Point Theatre (⊠ 305 N. Main St., Suite 200, ☎ 336/841–2273).

Outdoor Activities and Sports

GOLF

There are four public golf courses in High Point; three have 18 holes, one has nine. At **Oak Hollow** (✉ 3400 N. Centennial St., ☎ 336/883–3260), Pete Dye designed the 18-hole course.

HIKING

The **Piedmont Environmental Center** (✉ 1220 Penny Rd., ☎ 336/883–8531) has 357 acres of hiking trails adjacent to City Lake, a nature preserve with a nature store and exhibits. There's also access to a 6-mi greenway trail. All trails are open sunrise to sunset daily.

SOCCER

Carolina Dynamo Soccer is played at the A. J. Simeon Stadium (✉ 2920 School Park Rd., ☎ 336/884–5255 or 800/396–2664) from April to August.

TENNIS

In Oak Hollow Lake Park, the **Reitzel Tennis Center** (✉ 3431 N. Centennial St., ☎ 336/883–3493) has two indoor courts and 12 outdoor courts.

Shopping

There are over 60 retail **furniture stores** in and around High Point. The **Atrium Furniture Mall** (✉ 430 S. Main St., ☎ 336/882–5599) carries only furniture and home accessories.

Oak Hollow Mall (✉ 921 Eastchester Dr., ☎ 336/886–6255) is High Point's newest shopping center, with over 90 specialty stores, boutiques, restaurants, and department stores, including **Dillards, Belk,** and **Sears.**

Art shows rotate through the three galleries of **Theatre Art Galleries** (✉ 220 E. Commerce Ave., ☎ 336/887–3415), open weekdays 12–5 and weekends by appointment.

The Triad A to Z

Arriving, Departing, and Getting Around

BY BUS

Contact the **Greyhound Trailways System** (☎ 800/231–2222) for area service.

BY CAR

Greensboro and Winston-Salem are on I–40, which runs from Asheville in the west to Wilmington in southeastern North Carolina. I–40 and I–85 are combined coming into the Triad from the east, but in Greensboro, I–85 splits off to head southwest to Charlotte. High Point is located off a business bypass of I–85 southwest of Greensboro.

BY PLANE

Just west of Greensboro, the **Piedmont Triad International Airport** (☎ 336/665–5666) is located off NC 68 north from I–40 West; it's served by American, Continental, Delta, Eastwind, Northwest, United, and US Airways.

BY TAXI

Taxi service to and from the airport is provided by **Airport Express** (☎ 800/934–8779).

BY TRAIN

The **Amtrak** station is in Greensboro (✉ 2603 Oakland Ave., ☎ 336/855–3382 or 800/872–7245).

Contacts and Resources

EMERGENCIES
Police (☎ 911). **Ambulance** (☎ 911).

GUIDED TOURS
Carolina Treasures and Tours (✉ 1031 Burke St., ☎ 336/631–9144) offers a look at historic Winston-Salem.

RADIO STATIONS
AM: WSJS 600, news, talk; WAAA 980, urban contemporary. **FM:** WFDD 88.5, National Public Radio; WKRR 92.3, rock; WJMH 102.1, urban contemporary; WTQR 104.1, country.

VISITOR INFORMATION
The following provide maps, brochures, and flyers on attractions, accommodations, and services.

Greensboro Area Convention & Visitors Bureau (✉ 317 S. Greene St., Greensboro 27401, ☎ 336/274–2282 or 800/344–2282). **High Point Convention & Visitors Bureau** (✉ 300 S. Main St., High Point 27260, ☎ 336/884–5255 or 800/720–5255). **Winston-Salem Convention & Visitors Bureau** (✉ Box 1408, Winston-Salem 27102, ☎ 336/725–2361 or 800/331–7018). In Winston-Salem, a visitor's **reception center** in the City Market building (✉ 601 N. Cherry St., ☎ 336/777–3796) is open daily.

THE TRIANGLE
Raleigh, Durham, Chapel Hill

The cities of Raleigh, Durham, and Chapel Hill make up the Triangle, with Raleigh to the east, Durham to the north, Chapel Hill to the west, and in the center, Research Triangle Park—a renowned complex of corporations and public and private research facilities set in 6,800 acres of lake-dotted pineland that attracts scientists, academicians, and businesspeople from all over the world. Politics and basketball are always hot topics throughout the Triangle. The NCAA basketball championship has traded hands among the area's three schools.

Raleigh

143 mi northeast of Charlotte, 104 mi east of Winston-Salem.

Raleigh is Old South and New South, down-home and upscale, all in one. Named for Sir Walter Raleigh (who established the first English colony on the coast in 1585), it's the state capital and the biggest of the three cities. The state's largest and best museums are here, as are North Carolina State University and six other universities and colleges.

The city is spread out, so a car is almost a necessity unless you limit your sightseeing to downtown, where the streets are laid out in an orderly grid fashion with the State Capitol as the hub. Most downtown Raleigh attractions are state government and historic buildings and are free to the public. You'll need several hours just to hit the high spots, and even more time if you tend to get hooked on museums (which are also free). The **Capital Area Visitor Center** (✉ 301 N. Blount St., ☎ 919/733–3456) is a good place to pick up maps and brochures.

A good place to begin a tour of downtown Raleigh is the **State Capitol,** a beautifully preserved example of Greek Revival architecture from 1840 that once housed all the functions of state government. Today it's part museum, part executive offices. The capitol contains, under the domed rotunda, a copy of Antonio Cannova's statue of George Washington depicted as a Roman general with tunic, tight-fitting body armor, and a short cape. ⊠ *Capitol Sq.,* ☎ *919/733–4994.* ⊙ *Weekdays 8–5, Sat. 9–5, Sun. 1–5.*

The **State Legislative Building,** one block north of the State Capitol, hums with lawmakers and lobbyists when the legislature is in session. It's fun to watch from the gallery. You can also take a free guided tour, available through the Capital Area Visitor Center (☞ *above*). ⊠ *Salisbury and Jones Sts.,* ☎ *919/733–7928.* ⊙ *Weekdays 8–5, Sat. 9–5, Sun. 1–5.*

At the **North Carolina Museum of Natural Sciences,** you can check out the skeletons of whales and dinosaurs or watch volunteers cleaning fossil bones. The gift shop sells some unusual souvenirs. ⊠ *102 N. Salisbury St.,* ☎ *919/733–7450.* ☎ *Free.* ⊙ *Mon.–Sat. 9–5, Sun. 1–5.*

★ The **North Carolina Museum of History,** adjacent to the Museum of Natural Sciences on Bicentennial Plaza, was founded in 1898 and is now housed in an airy, state-of-the-art facility. It combines artifacts, audiovisual programs, and interactive exhibits to bring the state's history to life. Exhibits include the N.C. Sports Hall of Fame, N.C. Folklife, and Women Making History. ⊠ *1 E. Edenton St.,* ☎ *919/715–0200.* ☎ *Free.* ⊙ *Tues.–Sat. 9–5:30, Sun. noon–5:30.*

★ The **Executive Mansion** (⊠ *200 N. Blount St.,* ☎ *919/733–3456*) is a brick turn-of-the-century Queen Anne cottage–style structure with gingerbread trim and manicured lawns. Tour hours vary; check with the Capital Area Visitor Center (☞ *above*). A stroll through the **Oakwood Historic District** will introduce you to many fine examples of Victorian architecture. The neighborhood encompasses a 20-block area bordered by Person, Edenton, Franklin, and Watauga/Linden Streets.

The revitalized **City Market** is home to specialty shops, art galleries, restaurants, and a comedy club. Trolleys shuttle between downtown and the market at lunchtime; the fare is only 10¢. ⊠ *Martin St. and Moore Sq.,* ☎ *919/828–4555.* ⊙ *Stores Mon.–Sat. 10–5:30; restaurants Mon.–Sat. 7 AM–1 AM and Sun. 11:30–10.*

Fayetteville Street Mall extends from the State Capitol to the Raleigh Civic and Convention Center. Open to pedestrians only, it has a variety of shops, restaurants, and a statue of Sir Walter Raleigh.

The **Wakefield/Joel Lane House,** the oldest dwelling in Raleigh, was the home of the "father of Raleigh" and dates from the 1760s. Joel Lane sold the state the property on which the capital city grew. ⊠ *720 W. Hargett, at St. Mary's St.,* ☎ *919/833–3431.* ☎ *Free.* ⊙ *Mar.–mid-Dec., Tues., Thurs., Fri. 10–1:30.*

At the **Mordecai Historic Park,** you can see the Mordecai family's plantation home and other structures, including the house where President Andrew Johnson was born. One-hour guided tours are given on the half hour. ⊠ *1 Mimosa St., at Wake Forest Rd.,* ☎ *919/834–4844.* ☎ *$4.* ⊙ *Mon. 10–3, Wed.–Sat. 10–3, Sun. 1–3.*

☾ **Pullen Park** (⊠ *520 Ashe Ave., near North Carolina State University,* ☎ *919/831–6468 or 919/831–6640*) attracts large crowds during the summer to its 1911 Dentzel carousel and train ride. You can swim here in a large public aquatic center, explore an arts and crafts center, and see a play at the Theater in the Park.

★ On the west side of Raleigh, the **North Carolina Museum of Art** is home to one of the nation's largest collections of Jewish ceremonial art. Other exhibits range from ancient Egyptian times to the present, from the Old World and the New. The glass-walled **Museum Café** looks out on a dramatic outdoor performance center cum sculpture that when viewed from above spells the words "Picture This." The café is open for lunch Tuesday–Sunday, with live entertainment Friday evening. ✉ *2110 Blue Ridge Blvd.,* ☎ *919/839–6262; 919/833–3548 restaurant.* 🎫 *Free.* ☉ *Tues.–Thurs. and Sat. 9–5, Fri. 9–9, Sun. 11–6.*

OFF THE BEATEN PATH

AVA GARDNER MUSEUM – This museum in the hometown of the legendary beauty and movie star has memorabilia that trace her life from childhood on the farm to Hollywood glory days. It's about 30 mi east of Raleigh in downtown Smithfield. ✉ *105 S. 3rd St., Smithfield,* ☎ *919/934-5830 or 919/934-0887.* 🎫 *$3.* ☉ *Daily 1-5.*

Dining and Lodging

$$$–$$$$ ✕ **Angus Barn, Ltd.** A Raleigh tradition that has won virtually every major dining award is housed in a huge rustic barn. The astonishing wine and beer list covers 35 pages of the menu. The restaurant serves the best steaks, baby back ribs, and prime rib, plus fresh seafood, for miles around. Desserts are heavenly. Reservations aren't accepted for Saturday dinner. ✉ *U.S. 70W (Glenwood Ave.) near Aviation Pkwy.,* ☎ *919/787–3505. AE, D, DC, MC, V.*

$$$–$$$$ ✕ **Margaux's.** Continental cuisine is the focus at this north Raleigh fixture, where a massive stone fireplace adds warmth to the intimate setting. A blackboard lists the diverse specials, such as red chili fettuccine with goat cheese, Angus beef shell steak and puff pastry, or grilled shrimp and crawfish tostada with roasted corn, black beans, and salsa verde. ✉ *8111 Creedmoor Rd.,* ☎ *919/846–9846. AE, MC, V.*

$$$–$$$$ ✕ **Tony's Bourbon Street Oyster Bar.** The wrought iron and street lamps and feather masks on the walls tell you that every day is Mardi Gras at Tony's. Cajun and Creole dishes such as gumbo, jambalaya, and crawfish étoufée are served in the large, open dining room, or you can sit at the oyster bar and savor the classic oyster stew. Cary, near the entrance to Research Triangle Park, is 25 minutes from downtown Raleigh. ✉ *107 Edinburgh Dr., MacGregor Village Shopping Center, Cary,* ☎ *919/462–6226. AE, MC, V.*

$$$ ✕ **Black Marlin.** The name is a giveaway: Seafood is the specialty here. The contemporary setting includes a series of undersea scenes with neon flashes of small orange fish. Fresh ingredients are emphasized, as in the grilled sushi-grade yellowfin tuna with wasabi-sesame butter and a shiitake mushroom salad. ✉ *428 Daniels St.,* ☎ *919/832–7950. AE, D, MC, V.*

$$$ ✕ **WickedSmile.** Everything in this renovated 1920s warehouse screams ★ chic: sconces of twisted iron and fiberglass, menus in rustic folders of anodized aluminum. The food, which owner Chris Bender labels "metro American," is influenced by French and Italian menus. A starter of Carolina deep-fried soft-shell crab or chilled artichoke, fusilli, and crab Caesar could be followed by herbed pan roast of Maine salmon with warm cilantro potato salad and champagne vinaigrette. You can also sip single malts and martinis at the bar while you listen to the live jazz. ✉ *511 W. Hargett St.,* ☎ *919/828–2223. AE, MC, V.*

$ ✕ **Big Ed's City Market Restaurant.** A must for breakfast, Big Ed's is filled with antique farm implements and the owner's political memorabilia, including pictures of presidential candidates who have made the requisite stop at this landmark. Come here for down-home cookin' and don't pass up the biscuits. ✉ *220 Wolfe St.,* ☎ *919/836–9909. Reservations not accepted. No credit cards. Closed Sun.*

$ ✕ **Greenshields Brewery & Pub.** Sip beer and ale brewed on the spot with your soups, salads, sandwiches, or such entrées as fish-and-chips, shepherd's pie, and steak in this multilevel English-type pub. Oak paneling and working fireplaces enhance the mood. ⊠ *214 E. Martin St., City Market,* ☎ *919/829–0214. AE, D, MC, V.*

$$$ 🏨 **Courtyard by Marriott–Airport.** Convenient to the airport and Research Triangle Park, this chain property offers many amenities, including a Continental breakfast, without hefty rates. Rooms are predictably modern, and some have refrigerators. The dining room is for guests only. ⊠ *2001 Hospitality Ct., 27560,* ☎ *919/467–9444 or 800/321–2211,* ⨳ *919/467–9332. 152 rooms. Dining room, pool, hot tub, exercise room, coin laundry, airport shuttle. AE, D, DC, MC, V.*

$$$ 🏨 **North Raleigh Hilton.** This is a favorite spot for corporate meetings. Rooms are done in mauve and green, and all have coffeemakers, ironing boards, and dataports for PCs. You can dine in **Lofton's** restaurant and listen to the piano afterward in the lobby bar. **Bowties** (☞ Nightlife and the Arts, *below*) is a popular nightspot. ⊠ *3415 Wake Forest Rd., 27609,* ☎ *919/872–2323 or 800/445–8667,* ⨳ *919/876–0890. 330 rooms, 7 suites. Restaurant, bar, indoor pool, health club, nightclub, meeting rooms, airport shuttle. AE, D, DC, MC, V.*

$$$ 🏨 **Oakwood Inn.** An alternative to hotel/motel living, this is in Historic Oakwood, one of the city's oldest downtown neighborhoods. Built in 1871 and now on the National Register of Historic Places, the pale lavender inn is furnished with Victorian period pieces. Guests are served a sumptuous complimentary breakfast. ⊠ *411 N. Bloodworth St., 27604,* ☎ *919/832–9712 or 800/267–9712,* ⨳ *919/836–9263. 6 rooms. AE, D, DC, MC, V.*

$$$ 🏨 **Raleigh Marriott Crabtree Valley.** In one of the city's most luxurious hotels, fresh floral arrangements adorn the elegantly decorated public rooms. Standard rooms have soft colors such as cream, Asian floral prints, and dark cherrywood furnishings. Guests can dine at **J. W.'s Steakhouse** and **Quinn's,** which serves light fare and drinks daily. ⊠ *4500 Marriott Dr. (U.S. 70W near Crabtree Valley Mall), 27612,* ☎ *919/781–7000 or 800/228–9290,* ⨳ *919/571–7445. 372 rooms, 4 suites. Restaurant, bar, indoor-outdoor pool, hot tub, exercise room, recreation room, airport shuttle. AE, D, DC, MC, V.*

$$$ 🏨 **Velvet Cloak Inn.** This brick-and-wrought-iron hotel is in a class of its own; the individually decorated rooms have a choice of traditional or contemporary furniture. Local brides have wedding receptions in the tropical garden around the enclosed pool, and politicians frequent the bar at **Baron's Lounge.** The **Charter Room,** an elegant restaurant, often has live entertainment. ⊠ *1505 Hillsborough St., 27605,* ☎ *919/828–0333 or 800/334–4372; 800/662–8829 in NC;* ⨳ *919/828–2656. 168 rooms, 4 suites. 2 restaurants, bar, meeting rooms, airport shuttle. AE, D, DC, MC, V.*

$$–$$$ 🏨 **Quality Suites Hotel.** Minutes from downtown, this hotel offers luxurious two-room suites equipped with cassette stereos, microwaves, and wet bars. The manager's evening reception and the cooked-to-order breakfast are included in the rate. ⊠ *4400 Capital Blvd., 27604,* ☎ *919/876–2211 or 800/543–5497,* ⨳ *919/790–1352. 114 suites. In-room VCRs, refrigerators, pool, exercise room, meeting rooms. AE, D, DC, MC, V.*

$$–$$$ 🏨 **Ramada Inn Crabtree.** Rooms are comfortable in familiar chain style at what may be the friendliest motel in town. It's also where football and basketball teams like to stay when they're here for a game, as evidenced by the sports memorabilia in the **Brass Bell Lounge.** ⊠ *3920 Arrow Dr. (U.S. 70 and Beltline), 27612,* ☎ *919/782–7525 or 800/441–4712. 157 rooms, 17 suites. Restaurant, lounge, pool, jogging, meeting rooms, airport shuttle. AE, D, DC, MC, V.*

$$ 🖭 **Hampton Inn North Raleigh.** You'll pay inexpensive rates without sacrificing quality at this budget motel. A Continental breakfast, local calls, and in-room movies are available at no extra charge. ✉ *1001 Wake Towne Dr., 27609,* ☎ *919/828–1813 or 800/426–7866,* 𝕱𝕬𝕏 *919/ 834–2672. 131 rooms. Pool, meeting rooms. AE, D, DC, MC, V.*

Nightlife and the Arts

NIGHTLIFE

Bowties (✉ North Raleigh Hilton, 3415 Wake Forest Rd., ☎ 919/878– 4917) is a popular after-hours spot. **Charlie Goodnight's Comedy Club** (✉ 861 W. Morgan St., ☎ 919/828–5233) combines dinner with a night of laughs. Alumni include Jay Leno, Jerry Seinfeld, and Brett Butler. The **Berkeley Cafe** (✉ 217 W. Martin St., ☎ 919/821–0777) is one of the hottest gathering places in the Triangle for live music: rock and roll, R&B, and blues.

THE ARTS

The **North Carolina Theatre** (✉ 1 E. South St., ☎ 919/831–6916 or 919/831–6060), the state's only professional nonprofit theater, produces five Broadway musicals a year. The **North Carolina Symphony** (✉ 2 E. South St., ☎ 919/733–2750) gives more than 200 concerts throughout the state annually, but its home venue is the elegant **Memorial Auditorium.**

Walnut Creek Amphitheatre (✉ 3801 Rock Quarry Rd., ☎ 919/831– 6666) claims to be the most-attended amphitheater on the East coast. Musical acts appear from spring through mid-fall and cover the spectrum.

Outdoor Activities and Sports

BASEBALL

The **Carolina Mudcats** (☎ 919/269–2287), the A´A affiliate of the Pittsburgh Pirates, play at Five County Stadium in Zebulon, about 20 mi east of Raleigh.

BASKETBALL

Raleigh's Atlantic Coast Conference entry is the North Carolina State University **Wolfpack** (☎ 919/515–2106).

BIKING

Raleigh has more than 25 mi of greenways for biking, and maps are available through **Raleigh Parks and Recreation** (☎ 919/831–6640).

CAMPING

Try the North Carolina State Fairgrounds, William B. Umstead State Park, Clemmons State Forest near Clayton, or Jordan Lake between Apex and Pittsboro. For details, call the Greater Raleigh Convention and Visitors Bureau (☞ *Visitor Information in* the Triangle A to Z, *below*) or the North Carolina Department of Commerce, Travel and Tourism Division (☞ *Visitor Information in* North Carolina A to Z, *below*).

FISHING

Jordan Lake, a 13,900-acre reservoir in Apex, is a favorite fishing spot. Others are Lake Wheeler in Raleigh and the Falls Lake State Recreation Area in Wake Forest.

FITNESS

The **YMCA** (✉ 1601 Hillsborough St., ☎ 919/832–6601) will permit visitors to use its facilities for a few dollars provided they have a YMCA membership elsewhere. The Y also accepts guests staying at certain local hotels.

GOLF

There are 14 golf courses within a half-hour drive of downtown Raleigh. **Cheviot Hills Golf Course** (⊠ 7301 Capitol Blvd., Raleigh, ☎ 919/876–9920) is an 18-hole championship course. **Devil's Ridge Golf Club** (⊠ Holly Springs Rd., Cary, ☎ 919/557–6100), about 15 mi from Raleigh, is a challenging course with large, rolling greens. The **Neuse Golf Club** (⊠ NC 42E, Clayton, ☎ 919/550–0550) is an attractive course on the banks of the Neuse River. **Lochmere Golf Club** (⊠ Kildaire Farm Rd., Cary, ☎ 919/851–0611) provides a friendly atmosphere and good value.

HIKING

Jordan Lake, Lake Wheeler, and William B. Umstead State Park near Raleigh offer thousands of acres for hiking. For trail information, call the **North Carolina Department of Commerce, Travel and Tourism Division** (☎ 919/733–4171 or 800/847–4862).

HOCKEY

The **Raleigh Icecaps** compete in Dorton Arena at the NC State Fairgrounds (☎ 919/755–0022).

JOGGING

Runners frequent Shelley Lake, the track at North Carolina State University, and the Capitol Area Greenway system (☎ 919/831–6640 for a system map).

SOCCER

The **Raleigh Flyers** (☎ 919/848–3063), the city's first professional soccer team, competes in the Interregional Soccer League, the nation's largest outdoor league.

TENNIS

More than 80 courts in Raleigh city parks are available for use; call 919/876–2616 for details.

Shopping

SHOPPING MALLS

Cameron Village Shopping Center (⊠ 1900 Cameron St.), Raleigh's oldest shopping center and one of the first in the Southeast, contains specialty shops and boutiques and restaurants. **Crabtree Valley Mall** (⊠ Glenwood Ave., U.S. 70) is one of the South's largest enclosed malls and has over 240 specialty stores, including **Brooks Brothers, Abercrombie & Fitch,** and **Williams-Sonoma.** Department stores include **Lord & Taylor, Hudson-Belk, Hecht's,** and **Sears. Magnolia Marketplace** (⊠ 651 Cary Towne Blvd., at Walnut St., Cary, ☎ 919/319–0505) stocks upscale home and garden accents (some of them one-of-a-kind), including furniture and antiques.

ART AND ANTIQUES

City Market (⊠ Martin St. at Moore Sq., ☎ 919/828–4555) is a revitalized shopping area with cobblestone streets and an array of shops and art galleries. Check out Artspace, a gallery where you can watch artists at work.

FLEA MARKETS

The **Raleigh Flea Market Mall** (⊠ 1924 Capital Blvd., ☎ 919/839–0038) offers antiques and knickknacks. It's open weekends 9–5.

FOOD

Open year-round, the 60-acre **State Farmer's Market** (⊠ Lake Wheeler Rd. and I–40, ☎ 919/733–7417 market; 919/833–7973 restaurants) includes a garden center, seafood restaurant, and a down-home-style restaurant. **Wellspring Grocery** (✉ 3540 Wade Ave., ☎ 919/828–5805) has outstanding fresh produce and a wide selection of health foods.

Durham

23 mi northwest of Raleigh on I–40 and NC 147 (Durham Freeway), 81 mi east of Winston-Salem.

Durham long ago shed its tobacco-town image and is now known as the City of Medicine, for the medical and research centers at Duke University, one of the top schools in the nation. With more than 20,000 employees, Duke is not only the largest employer in Durham but also one of the largest in the state. Warehouses and mills around the city have been converted to chic shops, offices, and condos.

A stroll along the beautiful tree-lined streets of the **Duke University** campus is a lovely way to spend a few hours. In all, the university encompasses 525 acres in the heart of Durham. There's the East Campus, off Broad Street, with its Georgian architecture. A mile or so away is the West Campus, dominated by Duke Chapel on Chapel Drive and late Gothic–style buildings. The sprawling medical school is on Erwin Road. A bus system and bike paths connect the campuses.

★ The 55-acre **Sarah P. Duke Gardens,** complete with a wisteria-draped gazebo and a Japanese garden with a lily pond teeming with fat goldfish, have more than 5 mi of pathways through formal plantings and woodlands. ✉ *Main entrance on Anderson St., West Campus of Duke University,* ☎ *919/684–3698.* 🎫 *Free.* ⊙ *Daily 8 AM–dusk.*

★ The Gothic-style **Duke Chapel,** built in the early 1930s, is the centerpiece of the campus. Modeled after Canterbury Cathedral, it has 77 stained-glass windows and a 210-ft bell tower. ✉ *Chapel Dr., West Campus of Duke University,* ☎ *919/681–1704.* ⊙ *Daily, daylight hrs.*

☞ At the **North Carolina Museum of Life and Science,** you can create a 15-ft tornado, encounter near-life-size models of dinosaurs on the prehistoric trail, and ride a train through a 78-acre wildlife sanctuary. The nature center has such native North Carolina animals as flying squirrels. A new addition is the seasonal Butterfly House. ✉ *433 Murray Ave., off I–85,* ☎ *919/220–5429.* 🎫 *$5.50.* ⊙ *Mon.–Sat. 10–5, Sun. 1–5.*

African-American art is showcased at the **North Carolina Central University Art Museum**; besides the permanent collection you can see works by students and local artists. ✉ *1801 Fayetteville St., south of Durham Freeway,* ☎ *919/560–6211.* 🎫 *Free.* ⊙ *Tues.–Fri. 9–5, Sun. 2–5.*

One of Durham's oldest ecclesiastical structures, St. Joseph's AME church, houses the **Hayti Heritage Center** for African-American art. In addition to exhibitions of traditional and contemporary art by local, regional, and national artists, the center hosts special events such as the Black Diaspora Film Festival. ✉ *804 Old Fayetteville St.,* ☎ *919/683–1709.* 🎫 *Free.* ⊙ *Weekdays 9–5, Sat. 10–2:30.*

A city park on the banks of the Eno River, **West Point on the Eno** has a 19th-century blacksmith shop, an 1880s home, and a restored mill dating from 1778. It's the site of an annual three-day folk-life festival surrounding the Fourth of July holiday; musicians, artists, and craftspeople come from around the region. ✉ *5101 N. Roxboro Rd. (U.S. 501 N),* ☎ *919/471–1623.* 🎫 *Free.* ⊙ *Daily 8 AM–sunset (historic buildings weekends only).*

The 2,064-acre **Eno River State Park** has hiking trails, historic homes and mills, and Class II rapids. ⊠ *6101 Cole Mill Rd.,* ☎ *919/383–1686.* ▨ *Free.* ☉ *Daily 8 AM–sunset.*

OFF THE BEATEN PATH

BENNETT PLACE STATE HISTORIC SITE – In this Durham farmhouse in April 1865, Confederate General Joseph E. Johnston surrendered to U.S. General William T. Sherman, 17 days after Lee's surrender to Grant at Appomattox. The two generals then set forth the terms for a "permanent peace" between the South and the North. Historic reenactments are held annually. ⊠ *4409 Bennett Memorial Rd., 10 mi from downtown,* ☎ *919/383-4345.* ▨ *Free.* ☉ *Apr.–Oct., Mon.–Sat. 9–5, Sun. 1–5; Nov.–Mar., Tues.–Sat. 9–5, Sun. 1–5.*

Dining and Lodging

$$$ ✕ **Magnolia Grill.** This award-winning bistro is consistently one of the
★   finest, most innovative places to dine in the state. On the daily menu you're likely to find grilled jumbo sea scallops on spicy black beans with blood-orange-and-onion marmalade, or grilled hickory-smoked pork tenderloin in a sun-dried cherry sauce with fresh horseradish, roasted beets, and a gratin of sweet potatoes and caramelized onions. ⊠ *1002 9th St.,* ☎ *919/286–3609. MC, V. Closed Sun. No lunch.*

$$$ ✕ **Pop's.** The roof is rough tin and the sculptures rusty industrial, while the lattice walls are covered in silk flowers and vines. Like the decor, the menu is eclectic, with Italian and new American cuisine. You can get a grilled pork chop with polenta or *fritto misto* calamari (batter-fried squid) at this eatery next to Brightleaf Square. ⊠ *810 W. Peabody St.,* ☎ *919/956–7677. MC, V.*

$$ ✕ **Cafe Parizäde.** This Erwin Square Mediterranean restaurant gets high marks for its food, service, and atmosphere. Soft lighting and white tablecloths give the place an elegant feel, even at lunch. Start with grilled bread soaked in garlic oil, fresh tomatoes and eggplant relish, or fried calamari with jalapeño-tomato salsa. Then choose among such entrées as fettuccine with fresh salmon and black pepper–dill cream, sesame pasta with scallops, and roasted duck with fresh vegetables. ⊠ *2200 W. Main St.,* ☎ *919/286–9712. AE, MC, V. Closed Sun.*

$$$$ ▤ **Washington Duke Hotel & Golf Club.** On the campus of Duke Uni-
★   versity, this luxurious hotel overlooks the Robert Trent Jones golf course. Rooms evoke the feeling of an English country inn, with floral bedspreads and creamy striped wallcoverings. On display in the public rooms are memorabilia belonging to the Duke family, for whom the hotel and university are named. ⊠ *3001 Cameron Blvd., 27706,* ☎ *919/490–0999 or 800/443–3853,* FAX *919/688–0105. 165 rooms, 6 suites. Restaurant, bar, pool, 18-hole golf course, jogging. AE, DC, MC, V.*

$$$–$$$$ ▤ **Arrowhead Inn.** Brick chimneys and tall Doric columns distinguish the Arrowhead, a bed-and-breakfast inn in an 18th-century white-clapboard farmhouse. It's a few miles outside Durham and offers a homelike setting with antiques, old plantings, and a log cabin in the garden. Breakfast is hearty. ⊠ *106 Mason Rd., 27712,* ☎ FAX *919/477–8430. 8 rooms, 6 with bath. AE, D, DC, MC, V.*

$$$–$$$$ ▤ **Blooming Garden Inn.** Truly a bright spot in the Holloway Historic District, this B&B has a yellow paint exterior. Inside, the inn explodes with color and warmth, thanks to exuberant hosts Dolly and Frank Pokrass. Breakfast might be walnut crepes with ricotta cheese and warm raspberry sauce. ⊠ *513 Holloway St., 27701,* ☎ *919/687–0801. 5 rooms. AE, D, DC, MC, V.*

Nightlife and the Arts

Durham's gorgeously renovated 1926 Beaux Arts **Carolina Theatre** (⊠ 309 Morgan St., ☎ 919/560–3060) hosts film festivals, symphony orchestras, musicals, and operas, as well as the International Jazz Festival in March and the American Dance Festival in June.

Outdoor Activities and Sports

BASEBALL

The **Durham Bulls,** a tradition since 1902, were immortalized in the hit movie *Bull Durham.* They play at their attractive, spacious stadium near downtown Durham (⊠ 409 Blackwell St., ☎ 919/687–6500).

BASKETBALL

Durham's Atlantic Coast Conference team is Duke's **Blue Devils** (☎ 919/681–2583).

CAMPING

Try the **Eno River State Park** (⊠ 6101 Cole Mill Rd., ☎ 919/383–1686). For details, call the North Carolina Department of Commerce, Travel and Tourism Division (☎ 919/733–4171 or 800/847–4862).

GOLF

Durham has four public golf courses. **Duke University** (⊠ Cameron Blvd. and Science Dr., Durham, ☎ 919/681–2288) has a Robert Trent Jones course. **Hillandale Golf Course** (⊠ Hillandale Rd., Durham, ☎ 919/286–4211) has an 18-hole George Cobb course.

HIKING

The **Eno River State Park** and **Duke Forest** in Durham both offer many acres for hiking. For trail information, call the North Carolina Department of Commerce, Travel and Tourism Division (☎ 919/733–4171 or 800/847–4862).

TENNIS

For information on Durham's six public tennis courts, call the **Parks and Recreation Department** (☎ 919/560–4355).

Shopping

SHOPPING DISTRICTS AND MALLS

Durham's **9th Street** has funky shops and restaurants that cater to the hip student crowd. **Brightleaf Square** (⊠ 905 W. Main St.) is an upscale shopping-entertainment complex housed in old tobacco warehouses in the heart of downtown. **Northgate Mall** (⊠ 1058 W. Club Blvd.) draws shoppers from all parts of the Triangle. Kids enjoy riding the old-fashioned carousel while adults choose from among three department stores and nearly 200 specialty stores, including **Ann Taylor** and **Urban Hype.**

CRAFTS

One World Market (⊠ 1918 Perry St., ☎ 919/286–2457) is a place to find unique, affordable gifts. It also appeals to the socially aware, as one goal of the establishment is to provide increased self-employment for low-income crafters from around the world.

FOOD

Fowler's Gourmet (⊠ 905 W. Main St., in Brightleaf Square, ☎ 919/683–2555) is an epicurean's delight. The assortment of items is stunning—everything from exotic spices to European chocolates and wines to cured hams and fresh seafood. **Wellspring Grocery** (⊠ 621 Broad St., ☎ 919/286–2290) has outstanding fresh produce, soups, salads, and sandwiches prepared daily, and the widest selection of health items in town.

Chapel Hill

12 mi southwest of Durham on U.S. 15–501, 28 mi northwest of Raleigh.

Chapel Hill may be the smallest city in the Triangle, but its reputation as a seat of learning—and of liberalism—looms large indeed. The home of the nation's first state university, the 208-year-old University of North Carolina, Chapel Hill retains the feel of a quiet, tree-shaded village while crowded with students and retirees.

Morehead Planetarium, where the original Apollo astronauts and many since have trained, was the first planetarium in the state. Visitors can learn about the constellations and take in laser light shows. ⊠ *250 E. Franklin St.,* ☎ *919/549–6863 or 919/962–1236.* ☞ *$3.50.* ☉ *Weekdays 12:30–5 and Tues.–Fri. 7–9:45, Sat. 10–5 and 7–9:45, Sun. 12:30–5 and 7–9:45.*

★ **Franklin Street,** in the heart of downtown Chapel Hill, is lined with bicycle shops, bookstores, clothing stores, restaurants and coffee shops, and sidewalk flower vendors. Franklin Street runs along the northern edge of the **University of North Carolina** campus, which is filled with oak-shaded courtyards and stately old buildings. The Louis Round Wilson Library (⊠ South St.) contains the **North Carolina Collection Gallery** (☎ 919/962–1172), which has exhibits of rare books, photographs, and oil portraits. Several historic rooms highlight topics in the state's history, such as the Walter Raleigh Rooms and the colonial Early Carolonia Rooms.

Ở The **ArtsCenter** (⊠ 300G E. Main St., in Carrboro near Chapel Hill, ☎ 919/929–2787) has exhibits and offers classes of all kinds for children, as well as entertainment.

From downtown Chapel Hill, follow U.S. 15–501 Bypass south to the **North Carolina Botanical Garden,** with the largest collection of native plants in the Southeast. Two miles of nature trails wind through a 300-acre Piedmont forest; there's also an impressive herb garden and a carnivorous plant collection. ⊠ *Old Mason Farm Rd.,* ☎ *919/962–0522.* ☞ *Free.* ☉ *Mid-Mar.–mid-Nov., weekdays 8–5, Sat. 9–6, Sun. 10–6; mid-Nov.–mid-Mar., weekdays 8–5.*

Dining and Lodging

$$$–$$$$ ✕ **Il Palio Ristorante.** Alternative Tuscan cuisine is the buzzword for this restaurant in the sumptuous Siena Hotel (☞ *below*). Winner of the Award of Excellence from the *Wine Spectator,* Il Palio doesn't hurry its patrons. It's a good thing, because it takes a while just to get through the antipasti *assortiti* while you anticipate your *filetto di branzino*—black grouper filled with summer greens and wrapped with prosciutto, in a saffron broth. ⊠ *1505 E. Franklin St.,* ☎ *919/929–4000. AE, DC, MC, V.*

$$–$$$ ✕ **Aurora.** In a historic textile mill in nearby Carrboro, Aurora specializes in Northern Italian cuisine. The changing menu sometimes includes succulent sea scallops and shiitake mushrooms sautéed in rosemary and white wine, fresh chive pasta stuffed with four cheeses and tossed with walnut sauce, and veal sautéed with apples. ⊠ *200 N. Greensboro St. (Carr Mill Mall), Carrboro,* ☎ *919/942–2400. AE, MC, V.*

$$–$$$ ✕ **Pyewacket Restaurant.** What began as a hole-in-the-wall vegetarian restaurant in 1977 has become one of Chapel Hill's most popular eateries. Now in bigger digs and offering courtyard dining, Pyewacket has added seafood and pasta specialties to its repertoire. Entrées range

from southwestern grilled seafood to spinach lasagna. ⊠ *431 W. Franklin St.,* ☎ *919/929–0297. AE, DC, MC, V.*

$$ ✕ **Crook's Corner.** This small, often noisy restaurant is the exemplar of Southern chic. It turns out such regional specialties as sautéed snapper with mint, pecans, and oranges, hot pepper jelly, collard greens, crab gumbo, cheese grits, and buttermilk pie. In summer you can lunch on Crook's patio, where a wall of bamboo and a waterfall fountain make for a delightful alfresco experience. ⊠ *610 W. Franklin St.,* ☎ *919/929–7643. AE, MC, V.*

$$$$ ✕⛫ **Fearrington House.** A member of the prestigious Relais & Châteaux ★ group, this French-style country inn is on a 200-year-old farm that has been remade into a residential community resembling a country village. The inn's modern guest rooms are furnished with English pine and floral print fabrics. The restaurant, done up in green ivy and delicate peach prints, serves regional food prepared in a classic manner; Carolina crab cakes with mustard mayonnaise and beef tenderloin with merlot and peppercorn sauce are favorites. Afternoon tea and breakfast are included in the rate. Guests can use the Fearrington Swim & Croquet club, too. ⊠ *8 mi south of Chapel Hill on U.S. 15–501; Fearrington Village Center, Pittsboro 27312,* ☎ *919/542–2121,* FAX *919/542–4202. 28 rooms. Restaurant. AE, MC, V.*

$$$$ ⛫ **Siena Hotel.** The love affair Sam and Susan Longiotti have with Siena, Italy, has carried over to their hotel. Every room has imported furniture, and the artwork is reminiscent of the Italian Renaissance. Handmade ceramic Contrada crests adorn the lobby walls, and you can purchase Italian silk and leather goods here. The Siena is small by most standards but it is first class all the way. Each room has a marble bath, and a complimentary breakfast buffet is served daily by Il Palio, the in-house restaurant (☞ *above*). ⊠ *1505 E. Franklin St., 27514,* ☎ *919/918–2545,* FAX *919/968–8527. 80 rooms. Restaurant, meeting rooms, airport shuttle. AE, MC, V.*

Nightlife and the Arts

NIGHTLIFE

The Chapel Hill area is the place to hear live rock and alternative bands. **Cat's Cradle** (⊠ 300 E. Main St., ☎ 919/967–9053) presents entertainment nightly. For comedy try **Comedy Sportz** (⊠ Omni Europa, U.S. 15–501, ☎ 919/968–4900).

THE ARTS

The **Dean E. Smith Center** (⊠ Skipper Bowles Dr., on the UNC campus, ☎ 919/962–7777) is home not only to the university's men's basketball games but is also a venue for special events and rock concerts. **Playmakers Repertory Company** (⊠ CB 3235 Graham Memorial, ☎ 919/962–7529) performs six plays annually at the **Paul Green Theatre.** Jazz and folk music, dance and theater are all offered at the **ArtsCenter** (⊠ 300G E. Main St., Carrboro, ☎ 919/929–2787).

Outdoor Activities and Sports

BASKETBALL

The Triangle is basketball heaven, with three Atlantic Coast Conference teams, including the University of North Carolina's **Tarheels** (☎ 919/962–2296).

BIKING

Chapel Hill is a great town for biking; for a bicycling map, contact the **Chapel Hill/Orange County Visitors Bureau** (☞ Visitor Information *in* the Triangle A to Z, *below*).

GOLF

Chapel Hill has one public golf course: **Finley Golf Course** (✉ Finley Golf Course Rd., ☎ 919/962–2349), on the UNC campus, has an 18-hole course, driving range, putting green, and lessons.

TENNIS

For information on tennis courts, call the **Chapel Hill Parks and Recreation Department** (☎ 919/968–2784) or the **Orange County Parks and Recreation Department** (☎ 919/732–8181).

Shopping

SHOPPING DISTRICTS

Fearrington Village, a planned community 8 mi south of Chapel Hill on U.S. 15–501 in Pittsboro, has upscale shops selling art, garden items, handmade jewelry, and more. **Franklin Street** in Chapel Hill has a wonderful collection of shops, including bookstores, art galleries, crafts shops, and clothing stores.

BOOKS

The **Intimate Bookshop** (✉ 119 E. Franklin St., ☎ 919/929–0411), a downtown mainstay for years, has a sister store at the Eastgate Mall (✉ 1800 E. Franklin St., ☎ 919/929–0414). At **McIntyre's Fine Books and Bookends** (✉ Fearrington Village, U.S. 15–501, Pittsboro, ☎ 919/542–3030) you can curl up and read in an armchair by the fire in one of the cozy library rooms.

FOOD

A Southern Season (✉ Eastgate Mall, ☎ 919/929–9466 or 800/253–3663) stocks everything from gourmet chocolates and wine to housewares to such Tarheel treats as cheese, wine, barbecue sauces, peanuts, turkeys, and hams. The **Weathervane Café** has indoor and alfresco dining. **Wellspring Grocery** (✉ 81 S. Elliott Rd., ☎ 919/968–1983) has outstanding fresh produce and a wide selection of health foods.

The Triangle A to Z

Arriving and Departing

BY BUS

Carolina Trailways/Greyhound Lines (☎ 800/231–2222) serves Raleigh, Durham, and Chapel Hill.

BY CAR

U.S. 1, which runs north–south through the Triangle and the Sandhills, also links to I–85 going northeast. U.S. 64, which makes an east–west traverse across the Triangle, continues eastward all the way to the Outer Banks. I–95 runs northeast–southwest to the east of the Triangle and the Sandhills, crossing U.S. 64 and I–40 on its way from Virginia to South Carolina.

BY PLANE

The **Raleigh-Durham International Airport** (☎ 919/840–2123), off I–40 between the two cities, is served by American, Continental, Delta, Northwest, TWA, United, US Airways, and Midway. If you're driving to Raleigh, take I–40 east to Exit 285; for Chapel Hill, take I–40 west to Exits 273, 270, and 266; for Durham, also take I–40 west to NC 147. It takes about 20 minutes to get to any of the three cities.

BY TRAIN

Amtrak (✉ 320 W. Cabarrus St., Raleigh, ☎ 919/833–7594 or 800/872–7245) has one daily train northbound and one southbound, with stops in Raleigh and Durham. Service to Charlotte is also offered twice daily.

Getting Around

BY BUS

Capital Area Transit (☎ 919/833–5701) is Raleigh's public transport system. Fares are 50¢. **Chapel Hill Transit** (☎ 919/968–2769) buses serve the city as well as Research Triangle Park and Duke University. **Durham Area Transit Authority** (☎ 919/688–4587) is Durham's intra-city bus system. Fares are 75¢; transfers 10¢.

Triangle Transit Authority (☎ 919/549–9999), which links downtown Raleigh with Cary, Research Triangle Park, Durham, and Chapel Hill, runs weekdays except major holidays. Fares are $1 for a 10-mi trip, $1.50 for 15 mi, and $2 for 20 mi.

BY TAXI

Approximately 28 taxi companies serve The Triangle; contact **City Taxi** (⊠ Raleigh, ☎ 919/832–1489), **National Cab** (⊠ Raleigh-Durham Airport, ☎ 919/469–1333), or **Orange Cab** (⊠ Durham, ☎ 919/ 682–6111) for service. Fares are calculated by the mile.

BY TROLLEY

For transportation around downtown Raleigh, try the trolley (☎ 919/ 833–5701), which begins at City Market. Trolleys run weekdays 11– 2, and the fare is 10¢.

Contacts and Resources

EMERGENCIES

Dial 911 for **police** or **ambulance** in an emergency. Hospital emergency rooms are open 24 hours a day. For minor emergencies, go to one of the many urgent-care centers in Raleigh, Durham, and Chapel Hill.

GUIDED TOURS

The **Capital Area Visitor Center** in Raleigh provides maps, brochures, and free tours of the executive mansion, state capitol, legislative building, and other government buildings. ⊠ *301 N. Blount St.,* ☎ *919/ 733–3456.* ☉ *Weekdays 8–5, Sat. 9–5, Sun. 1–5.*

From noon to 3 PM on the first and third Saturdays of each month, Mordecai Historic Park (☞ Raleigh, *above*) runs a **historic trolley tour** of Raleigh for $5, with pickup at the Amtrak station by advance arrangement.

The **Historic Chapel Hill/UNC Trolley Tour** (☎ 919/942–7818) operates April–November 15, Wednesday at 2. Fare is $5; call on weekdays for reservations.

LATE-NIGHT PHARMACIES

Kerr Drug Store (⊠ Lake Boone Shopping Center, Wycliff Rd., Raleigh, ☎ 919/781–4070) is open 24 hours. **Eckerd Drugs** (⊠ 3527 Hillsborough Rd., Durham, ☎ 919/383–5591) is open 8 AM–midnight weekdays and 9 AM–11 PM weekends.

RADIO STATIONS

AM: WPTF 680, news, talk; WKIX 850, country. **FM:** WCPE 89.7, classical; WUNC 91.5, National Public Radio; WRAL 101.5, adult contemporary; WDUR 104, urban contemporary.

VISITOR INFORMATION

Chapel Hill/Orange County Visitors Bureau (⊠ Box 600, Chapel Hill 27514, ☎ 919/968–2060). The **Downtown Chapel Hill Welcome Center** provides maps, brochures, and flyers on attractions, accommodations, and services. Volunteers are usually on hand to answer questions. ⊠ *113 W. Franklin St.,* ☎ *919/929–9700.* ☉ *Tues.–Sat. 10–4.*

The **Durham Convention & Visitors Bureau** (✉ 101 E. Morgan St., Durham 27701, ☎ 919/687–0288 or 800/446–8604). The **Durham Bullhorn** provides 24-hour recorded information on events and activities (☎ 919/688–2855 or 800/772–2855).

The **Greater Raleigh Convention and Visitors Bureau** (✉ 225 Hillsborough St., Suite 400, Raleigh 27603, ☎ 919/834–5900 or 800/849–8499).

THE SANDHILLS
Southern Pines, Pinehurst

Because of their sandy soil—they were once Atlantic beaches, although now they're over 100 mi from the sea—the Sandhills weren't of much use to early farmers, most of whom switched to lumbering and making turpentine for a livelihood. Since the turn of the century, however, this area with its gently undulating hills has proved ideal for golf and tennis. Today promoters call it the Golf Capital of the World; the Tufts Archives honors the sport and the founding of Pinehurst. First-class resorts are centered around more than three dozen golf courses, including the famed Pinehurst Number 2 and several spectacular new courses. Public tennis courts can be found in many Sandhills communities. For details, contact the Convention and Visitors Bureau or the Moore County Parks and Recreation Department (☞ Visitor Information *in* Sandhills A to Z, *below*).

The Highland Scots who settled the area left a rich heritage perpetuated through festivals and gatherings. In colonial times, English potters were attracted to the rich clay deposits in the soil, and today their descendants and others turn out beautiful wares that are sold in more than 40 local shops.

Southern Pines

104 mi east of Charlotte, 71 mi southwest of Raleigh.

Southern Pines, the center of the Sandhills, is a good place to start a visit of the area.

Sandhills Horticultural Gardens has a wetland area that can be observed from elevated boardwalks. It's part of a 15-acre series of gardens showcasing roses, fruits and vegetables, herbs, conifers, hollies, a formal English garden, pools, and a waterfall. ✉ *2200 Airport Rd., Sandhills Community College campus,* ☎ *910/695–3882 or 800/338–3944.* ☞ *Free.* ☉ *Year-round, daily sunrise–sunset.*

The **Shaw House,** the oldest structure in town (circa 1840), serves as headquarters for the Moore County Historical Association. ✉ *S.W. Broad St. and Morganton Rd.,* ☎ *910/692–2051.* ☞ *Free.* ☉ *Apr.–Dec., Wed.–Sun. 1–4.*

Weymouth Center, former home of author and publisher James Boyd, hosts numerous music, lecture, and holiday events. Boyd, who died in 1944, was visited by many well-known writers; his home served as a cultural center for the area. The North Carolina Literary Hall of Fame is here, and a writer-in-residence program has hosted more than 550 North Carolina writers. ✉ *555 E. Connecticut Ave.,* ☎ *910/692–6261.* ☞ *Free.* ☉ *Weekdays 10–noon, 2–4; call ahead to arrange tours.*

Weymouth Woods Nature Preserve, on the eastern outskirts of town, is a 571-acre wildlife preserve with 4 mi of hiking trails, a beaver pond, and a naturalist on staff. ⊠ *400 N. Ft. Bragg Rd. (off U.S. 1)*, ☎ *910/692–2167.* 🎦 *Free.* ☉ *Mon.–Sat. 9–6, Sun. noon–5.*

Dining and Lodging

$$–$$$ ✕ **Lob Steer Inn.** Come hungry for broiled seafood and prime rib dinners, complemented by salad and dessert bars. ⊠ *U.S. 1*, ☎ *910/692–3503. Reservations essential. AE, DC, MC, V. No lunch.*

$ ✕ **Whiskey NcNeill's Restaurant.** You can fill up on soups, sandwiches, salads, and a variety of entrées (from grilled sirloin to pork chops) over what used to be a downtown filling station but is now a fabulous spot for lunch and dinner. Stare closely at the building and you can practically imagine pulling up to the pump in your '57 Chevy. ⊠ *181 N.E. Broad St.*, ☎ *910/692–5440. MC, V.*

$$$–$$$$ 🏨 **Mid Pines Inn and Golf Club.** This resort community includes an 18-hole golf course designed by Donald Ross that has been the site of numerous tournaments. The spacious rooms in the inn are Wedgwood blue, with American antiques or good copies. ⊠ *1010 Midland Rd., 28387*, ☎ *910/692–2114 or 800/323–2114*, ℻ *910/692–4615. 66 rooms, 66 3- to 10-bedroom villas. Restaurant, bar, pool, 18-hole golf course, 4 tennis courts, recreation room, meeting rooms, airport shuttle. AE, D, DC, MC, V.*

$$$–$$$$ 🏨 **Pine Needles Resort and Country Club.** One of the bonuses of staying at this informal lodge is the chance to meet Peggy Kirk Bell, a champion golfer and golf instructor. She built the resort with her late husband and continues to help run it. The rooms are done in a rustic style; many have exposed beams. ⊠ *1005 Midland Rd., Box 88, 28387*, ☎ *910/692–7111 or 800/747–7272*, ℻ *910/692–5349. 72 rooms. Restaurant, pool, hot tub, sauna, 18-hole golf course, 2 tennis courts, meeting rooms, airport shuttle. AE, MC, V.*

Outdoor Activities and Sports

Club at Longleaf (⊠ 2001 Midland Rd., ☎ 910/692–6100 or 800/889–5323) was built on a former horse farm. The front nine plays through posts, rails, and turns of the old racetrack. **Pine Needles Resort** (⊠ 1005 Midland Rd., ☎ 910/692–7111) has a Donald Ross–designed golf course that hosted the 1996 U.S. Women's Open. **Mid-Pines Resort** (⊠ 1010 Midland Rd., ☎ 910/692–2114 or 800/323–2114) is another golf getaway with a Donald Ross–designed course. **Talamore at Pinehurst** (⊠ 1595 Midland Rd., ☎ 910/692–5884 or 800/552–6292), designed by Rees Jones, was ranked 14th in the state by *Golf Digest*.

Shopping

Country Bookshop (⊠ 140 N.W. Broad St., ☎ 910/692–3211), in the historic downtown district, often has regional authors to readings and signings; the store stocks lots of children's books.

Pinehurst

6 mi west of Southern Pines.

Pinehurst, a New England–style village with quiet, shaded streets and immaculately kept cottages, was laid out in the late 1800s in a wagon-wheel design by landscape genius Frederick Law Olmsted. It is a mecca for sports enthusiasts, retirees, and tourists.

Tufts Archives recounts the founding of Pinehurst in the letters, pictures, and news clippings, dating from 1895, of James Walker Tufts. Golf memorabilia are also on display. ⊠ *Given Memorial Library, 150 Cherokee Rd.*, ☎ *910/295–6022 or 910/295–3642.* ☉ *Weekdays 9:30–5, Sat. 9:30–12:30.*

Dining and Lodging

$ ✕ **Pinehurst Playhouse Restaurant.** This casual eatery in the shop-filled Theater Building is in the heart of the village. It's *the* place to meet for soups and sandwiches. ⊠ *W. Village Green,* ☎ *910/295–8873. Reservations not accepted. No credit cards. Closed Sun. No dinner.*

$$$$ ✕⊞ **Pinehurst Resort and Country Club.** The Pinehurst, a venerable re-
★   sort hotel in operation for nearly a century, has never lost the charm that founder James Tufts intended it to have. Civilized decorum rules in the spacious public rooms, on the rocker-lined wide verandas, and amid the lush gardens of the surrounding grounds. Guest rooms are elegantly traditional. You can tee off on one of eight signature golf courses. The **Carolina Dining Room** (jackets required) is known for its five-course gourmet cuisine; try the sautéed veal medallions with applejack cream sauce, grilled apples, and caramelized Vidalia onions. ⊠ *Carolina Vista, Box 4000, 28374,* ☎ *910/295–6811 or 800/487–4653,* 𝖥𝖠𝖷 *910/295–8503. 338 rooms, 130 condominiums. 2 restaurants, pool, 8 18-hole golf courses, 24 tennis courts, croquet, windsurfing, boating, fishing, bicycles, children's programs, meeting rooms, airport shuttle. AE, D, DC, MC, V.*

$$$ ⊞ **Holly Inn.** This renovated wooden inn, built in 1895, is testimony to James Tufts' success as a hotelier. It was so popular that he was forced to build a bigger structure—now the Pinehurst Resort. ⊠ *Cherokee Rd., Box 2300, 28374,* ☎ *910/295–2300; 800/682–6901 in NC;* 𝖥𝖠𝖷 *910/295–0988. 44 rooms, 32 suites. Restaurant, lounge, pool. AE, DC, MC, V.*

$$$ ⊞ **Inn at Eagle Springs.** A private girls' school during the 1920s, this B&B amid the pines in a remote area 15 mi from Pinehurst is great for golfers who want less action, more rest and quiet. A full breakfast is provided, and other meals can be arranged ahead. ⊠ *1813 Samarcand Rd., Box 186, Eagle Springs 27242,* ☎ *910/673–2722,* 𝖥𝖠𝖷 *910/673–7740. 6 rooms. AE, MC, V.*

$$$ ⊞ **Magnolia Inn.** Once just a hangout for golfing buddies, this Old South inn is now tastefully decorated with fresh paint and unusual antiques. The inn's dining room serves superb grilled Norwegian salmon and roasted herb-crusted rack of lamb—there's also an English pub, where you can discuss your golf game. ⊠ *Magnolia and Chinquapin Rds., Box 818, 28370,* ☎ *910/295–6900 or 800/526–5562,* 𝖥𝖠𝖷 *910/215–0858. 11 rooms. 2 restaurants, pub, pool. AE, MC, V.*

$$$ ⊞ **Pine Crest Inn.** Chintz and mahogany fill the rooms of a small village inn once owned by golfing great Donald Ross. Chefs Carl and Peter Jackson whip up some great dishes, including homemade soups, fresh seafood dishes, and the house special, stuffed pork chops. **Mr. B's Bar** is the liveliest nightspot in town. Guests have golf and tennis privileges at local clubs. Rates include two meals per day. ⊠ *Dogwood Rd., Box 879, 28370,* ☎ *910/295–6121,* 𝖥𝖠𝖷 *910/295–4880. 40 rooms. AE, D, DC, MC, V.*

Outdoor Activities and Sports

GOLF

Pinehurst Resort and Country Club (⊠ Carolina Vista, ☎ 910/295–6811 or 800/487–4653) will host the U.S. Open in June 1999. It has eight courses designed by masters such as Donald Ross, including the famed Number 2, rated second-best resort course in America by *Golf Digest.* Number 7 is also highly ranked.

The **Pit Golf Links** (⊠ NC 5, ☎ 910/944–1600 or 800/574–4653) is ranked among America's 75 best public courses by *Golf Digest.* The eighth hole is ranked by *Golf Magazine* as one of the 50 best holes open to the public.

HORSEBACK AND CARRIAGE RIDING

Riding instruction and carriage rides are available by appointment at **Pinehurst Stables** (⊠ NC 5, ☎ 910/295–8456).

TENNIS

The **Lawn and Tennis Club of North Carolina** (⊠ 1 Merrywood, ☎ 910/692–7270) and **Pinehurst Resort and Country Club** (⊠ Carolina Vista Rd., ☎ 910/295–8556) are known for their daily clinics.

Aberdeen

5 mi southeast of Pinehurst, 5 mi southwest of Southern Pines.

Aberdeen, a small town of Scottish ancestry, has a beautifully restored turn-of-the-century train station and plenty of shops with antiques and collectibles. The **Bethesda Presbyterian Church,** on Bethesda Road east of town, was founded in 1790. The present wooden structure, which is used for weddings, funerals, and reunions, was built in the 1860s and has bullet holes from a Civil War battle. The cemetery, where many early settlers are buried, is always open.

Malcolm Blue Farm has farm buildings and an old gristmill. A September festival recalls life here in the 1800s. ⊠ Bethesda Rd., ☎ 910/944–7558. ☉ By appointment only.

Lodging

$$–$$$ 🏠 **Inn at Bryant House.** Downtown, one block off U.S. 1, this charming B&B is a home away from home. The inn offers golf packages and arranges tennis and horseback riding. ⊠ 214 N. Poplar St., 28315, ☎ 910/944–3300 or 800/453–4019, FAX 910/944–8898. 9 rooms. AE, D, MC, V.

Outdoor Activities and Sports

Legacy Golf Links (⊠ U.S. 15–501 S, ☎ 910/944–8825 or 800/344–8825) has the first American course designed by Jack Nicklaus II.

Cameron

12 mi north of Southern Pines.

You can shop for antiques in Cameron, which hasn't changed much since the 19th century. Approximately 60 antiques dealers operate out of several stores. The town itself, off U.S. 1, has been declared a historic district. Most shops are open Wednesday–Saturday 10–5, Sunday 1–5; call the historic district office (☎ 910/245–7001) for information.

OFF THE   **SANDHILLS FARM –** Twelve mi east of Cameron is a one-of-a-kind opera-
BEATEN PATH   tion that raises miniature horses and also sells herbs, wildflowers, wreaths, crafts, and oils. ⊠ Off NC 24 E, ☎ 919/499–4753. ☉ Mar.–Dec., Mon.–Thurs. 1–5; Jan.–Feb. by appointment.

Dining

$ ✗ **Dewberry Deli.** Housed in the Old Hardware, this eatery is a wonderful place for a sandwich or salad after shopping for antiques. ⊠ Carthage St., ☎ 910/245–3697. *Reservations not accepted. No credit cards. Closed Sun.–Mon. No dinner.*

Seagrove

35 mi northwest of Pinehurst via NC 211 and U.S. 220.

★ Potters, some of whom are carrying on traditions that have been in their families for generations, and others who are newer to the craft, make mugs, bowls, pitchers, platters, and sometimes clay voodoo heads in the **Seagrove** area. More than 90 potteries are scattered along and off Route 705 and U.S. 220. The work of some local potters is exhibited in national museums, including the Smithsonian. A logical place to start is the **Friends of the North Carolina Pottery Center** (⊠ 124 E. Main St., ☎ 336/873–7887). Maps of the area locating the various studios are available here as well as at the guild headquarters in downtown Seagrove. Most shops are open Tuesday–Saturday 10–5.

Asheboro

13 mi north of Seagrove, 23 mi south of Greensboro.

Asheboro, the seat of Randolph County, sits in the Uwharrie National Forest, a haven for hikers, bikers, horseback riders, and fishermen. This part of the southern Piedmont is a lovely place to view scenery and visit crafts shops. You can also visit an excellent zoo, the **American Classic Motorcycle Museum** (⊠ 11740 U.S. 64 W, ☎ 336/629–6819), or the **Foundation for Aircraft Conservation Flying Museum** (⊠ 2222 Pilot View Rd., ☎ 336/625–0170).

★ The **North Carolina Zoological Park,** a 1,400-acre natural habitat for animals, is one of the country's up-and-coming zoos. The park includes the 300-acre African Pavilion, an aviary, a gorilla habitat, a Sonoran Desert habitat, and a 200-acre North American habitat with polar bears and sea lions. ⊠ 4401 Zoo Pkwy., ☎ 336/879–7000 or 800/488–0444. ☞ $8, including tram ride. ⊙ Apr.–Oct., daily 9–5; Nov.–Mar., daily 9–4.

Sandhills A to Z

Arriving, Departing, and Getting Around

BY CAR

U.S. 1 runs north–south through the Sandhills and is the recommended route from the Raleigh–Durham area, a distance of about 70 mi.

BY PLANE

You can get to Southern Pines via US Airways Express (☎ 800/428–4322) from **Charlotte-Douglas International Airport** (☎ 704/359–4013) or fly into the **Raleigh-Durham Airport** (919/840–2123) or the **Piedmont Triad International Airport** (☎ 336/665–5666) and rent a car.

BY TRAIN

Amtrak (☎ 910/692–6305 or 800/872–7245) southbound and northbound trains, one daily in each direction, stop in Southern Pines.

Contacts and Resources

EMERGENCIES

Dial 911 for **police** or **ambulance** in an emergency. For medical care, go to the emergency room of the **Moore Regional Hospital** (⊠ Memorial Dr., Pinehurst, ☎ 910/215–1111).

RADIO STATIONS

AM: WKHO 550, easy listening; WEEB 990, news, talk; WQNX 1350, talk. **FM:** WIOZ 107, easy listening.

VISITOR INFORMATION
Convention and Visitors Bureau (✉ 1480 U.S. 15–501 N, Box 2270, Southern Pines 28388, ☎ 910/692–3330 or 800/346–5362) serves the Pinehurst, Southern Pines, and the Aberdeen area. For details on local events, call the Events Hotline (☎ 910/692–1600). **Moore County Parks and Recreation Department** (☎ 910/947–2504) can provide recreational information.

THE OUTER BANKS
Cape Hatteras, Cape Lookout

North Carolina's Outer Banks, a series of barrier islands on the Atlantic Ocean, stretch from the Virginia state line south to Cape Lookout. Throughout history the nemesis of shipping, these waters have been called the "Graveyard of the Atlantic"; the network of lighthouses and lifesaving stations draws visitors today, and the many submerged wrecks attract scuba divers. English settlers landed here in 1587 and attempted to colonize the region, but the colony disappeared without a trace. The islands' coves and inlets offered privacy to pirates—the notorious Blackbeard lived and died here. For many years the Outer Banks remained isolated, home only to a few families who made their living by fishing. Today the islands, linked by bridges and ferries, have become popular destinations. Much of the area is included in the Cape Hatteras and Cape Lookout national seashores. The largest towns are Kitty Hawk, Kill Devil Hills, Nags Head, and Manteo.

On the inland side of the Outer Banks is the historic Albemarle region, a remote area of small villages and towns surrounding Albemarle Sound. Edenton was the colonial capital for a while, and many of its early structures are preserved.

You can tour the Outer Banks from the southern end, by taking a car ferry to Ocracoke Island, or, as in the following route, from the northern end. You can drive the 120-mi stretch of NC 12 from Corolla to Ocracoke in a day, but be sure to allow plenty of time in summer to wait for the ferry connecting the islands, and to explore the undeveloped beaches, historic lifesaving stations, and charming beach communities stretched along the Cape Hatteras and Cape Lookout national seashores. Rentals are available from Corolla to Ocracoke, with the highest concentration of accommodations in the area from Kill Devil Hills to Nags Head. Mile markers (MM) indicate addresses for sites where there aren't many buildings. Be aware that during major storms and hurricanes the roads and bridges become clogged with traffic. In that case, follow the blue-and-white evacuation signs.

Numbers in the margin correspond to points of interest on the Outer Banks map.

Corolla, Duck, and Kitty Hawk

Kitty Hawk: 87 mi south of Norfolk, Va., via U.S. 17 and U.S. 158; 215 mi east of Raleigh via U.S. 64 and NC 12. Duck: 7 mi north of Kitty Hawk. Corolla: 19 mi north of Duck.

The small settlements of **Corolla** and **Duck** are largely seasonal residential enclaves full of summer rental condominiums with, in Duck, a growing number of restaurants and shopping outlets. The Currituck Beach Lighthouse in Corolla is the northernmost lighthouse on the Outer Banks. Drive slowly in Corolla; wild ponies wander free here and always have the right of way. **Kitty Hawk,** with 1,672 permanent residents, is

The Outer Banks

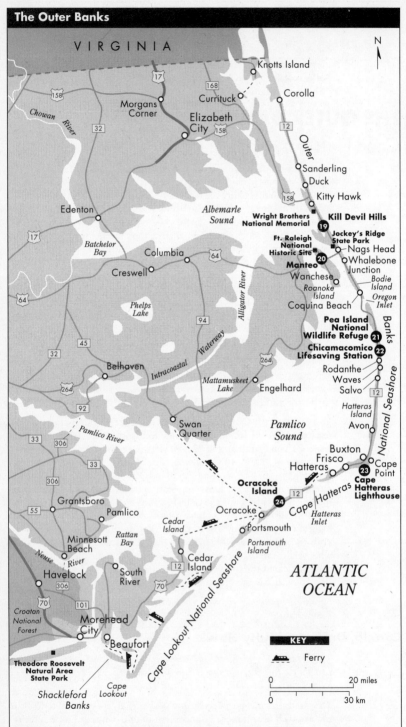

VIRGINIA

N

Chowan River

Knotts Island

Currituck

Corolla

Morgans Corner

Elizabeth City

17

168

158

32

158

Outer

12

Sanderling

Duck

Kitty Hawk

158

Albemarle Sound

Wright Brothers National Memorial

Kill Devil Hills

19

Jockey's Ridge State Park

Edenton

17

Batchelor Bay

Columbia

64

Ft. Raleigh National Historic Site

Manteo

20

Nags Head

Whalebone Junction

Creswell

Wanchese

Bodie Island

64

Phelps Lake

Roanoke Island

Coquina Beach

Oregon Inlet

45

94

Pea Island National Wildlife Refuge

21

32

Intracoastal Waterway

Alligator River

Banks

Chicamacomico Lifesaving Station

22

Belhaven

Mattamuskeet Lake

Rodanthe

264

Engelhard

Waves

Salvo

12

92

33

306

Pamlico River

Hatteras Island

Avon

33

Swan Quarter

National Seashore

306

Pamlico Sound

Buxton

Frisco

Hatteras

Cape Point

55

Grantsboro

Pamlico

Ocracoke Island

23

Cape Hatteras Lighthouse

Minnesott Beach

Rattan Bay

Cedar Island

12

Ocracoke

24

Cape Hatteras

Hatteras Inlet

Neuse River

Portsmouth

Havelock

South River

306

70

Cedar Island

12

Portsmouth Island

ATLANTIC OCEAN

70

101

Croatan National Forest

Morehead City

70

Beaufort

Cape Lookout National Seashore

Theodore Roosevelt Natural Area State Park

Shackleford Banks

Cape Lookout

KEY

Ferry

0   20 miles

0   30 km

among the quieter of the beach communities, with fewer rental accommodations.

Dining and Lodging

$$$$ ✕🏠 **Sanderling Inn Resort and Conference Center.** If you enjoy being pampered, come to this inn on a remote beach 5 mi north of Duck. For recreation you can play tennis, go swimming, or take a nature walk through the Pine Island Sanctuary. Though it was built in 1985 and has all the contemporary conveniences, the inn has the stately, mellow look of old Nags Head. Ceiling fans, wicker, and neutral tones give rooms a cool and casual feel. The ambitious restaurant (dinner reservations essential) is in a renovated lifesaving station; try the crab cakes, roast Carolina duckling with black cherry sauce, or fricassee of shrimp. ⊠ *1461 Duck Rd., Sanderling 27949,* ☎ *919/261–4111 or 800/701– 4111,* 🅵🅰🆇 *919/261–1638. 87 rooms, 26 efficiencies. Restaurant, lounge, pool, hot tub, 2 tennis courts, health club, library, meeting rooms. AE, D, MC, V.*

$$$ 🏠 **Advice 5¢.** The name may be quirky, but once you arrive at this B&B in the heart of Duck, just a short walk from downtown shops and restaurants, you'll find a quiet, casual, contemporary atmosphere. Beds in each room are dressed with crisp, colorful linens. All rooms have ceiling fans and shuttered windows. You can use a nearby pool and tennis courts. ⊠ *111 Scarborough La., 27949,* ☎ *919/255–1050 or 800/ 238–4235. 4 rooms, 1 suite. MC, V.*

Outdoor Activities and Sports

Sea Scape Golf Course (⊠ 300 Eckner St., MM 2¼, Kitty Hawk, ☎ 919/261–2158) is an authentic links course set amid the dunes.

OFF THE **MERCHANTS MILLPOND STATE PARK** – A 170-year-old millpond and an
BEATEN PATH ancient swamp form one of the state's rarest ecosystems. Cypress and gum trees hung with Spanish moss reach out of the still, dark waters, which are ideal for canoeing. Fishing, hiking, and camping are also available. The park is 80 mi west of Kitty Hawk, on the mainland. ⊠ *U.S. 158, Gatesville,* ☎ *919/357–1191.* 🎫 *Free.* ⊙ *Sept.–May, daily 8–8; June–Aug., daily 8 AM–9 PM.*

Kill Devil Hills

⓳ *4 mi south of Kitty Hawk.*

Kill Devil Hills, on U.S. 158 Bypass, has been the site of rapid development over the last decade. Its population explodes in summer, and though many businesses are seasonal, you can find anything you need here year-round. It's also the windswept site of man's first motorized

★ flight. The **Wright Brothers National Memorial,** a granite monument that resembles the tail of an airplane, stands as a tribute to Wilbur and Orville Wright, two bicycle mechanics from Ohio who took to the air on December 17, 1903. You can see a replica of *The Flyer* and stand on the spot where it made four takeoffs and landings, the longest being a distance of 852 ft. Exhibits and an informative talk by a National Park Service ranger bring the event to life. The Wrights had to bring in the unassembled airplane by boat, along with all their food and supplies for building a camp. They made four trips to the site, beginning in 1900. The First Flight is commemorated annually. ⊠ *Off U.S. 158, between MM 7 and MM 8,* ☎ *919/441–7430.* 🎫 *$4 per car or $2 per person.* ⊙ *Daily 9–5; extended hrs in summer.*

Kill Devil Hills has 5 mi of beach with 27 public access areas with limited parking off NC 12. Some have off-road vehicle access. Because of the large number of rental cottages and hotels, this beach tends to have a higher number of people, but it is seldom uncomfortably crowded, even at the height of the season.

Dining and Lodging

$$–$$$ ✕ **Etheridge Seafood Restaurant.** The fish comes straight from the boat to the kitchen at this family-owned seafood house, in operation for over a half century. Popular items are the seafood egg rolls and seafood au gratin. It's decorated with Etheridge family memorabilia, depicting their successful fishing and warehousing operation. ⊠ *U.S. 158 Bypass at MM 9.5,* ☎ *919/441–2645. Reservations not accepted. D, MC, V. Closed Dec.–Feb.*

$$$–$$$$ 🛏 **Ramada Inn.** Rooms in this convention-style hotel have private balconies with ocean views and come with refrigerators and microwave ovens. **Peppercorns** restaurant, overlooking the ocean, serves breakfast and dinner, and lunch is available on the sundeck next to the pool. ⊠ *NC 12, Box 2716, 27948,* ☎ *919/441–2151 or 800/635–1824,* 🗚 *919/441–1830. 172 rooms. Refrigerators, pool, hot tub, meeting rooms. AE, D, DC, MC, V.*

Nags Head

4 mi south of Kill Devil Hills.

Nags Head got its name because Outer Bankers hoping for shipwrecks would tie lanterns around the heads of their horses to lure merchant ships onto the shoals, thus profiting from the cargo that washed ashore. It is the most commercial section of the Outer Banks, with restaurants, motels, and hotels.

Nags Head has 11 mi of beach with 33 public access areas, all with parking and some with rest rooms and showers. One point of interest is mile marker 11.5, the first North Carolina Historic Shipwreck Site. The USS *Huron* lies in 20 ft of water off the Nags Head pier.

Coquina Beach (⊠ Off NC 12, 8 mi south of U.S. 158) in the **Cape Hatteras National Seashore** (☞ *below*) is considered by some to be the best swimming hole on the Outer Banks. The wide-beamed ribs of the shipwreck *Laura Barnes* rest in the dunes here. Picnic shelters are available.

Jockey's Ridge State Park has the tallest sand dune in the East and is a popular spot for hang gliding and kite flying. You can join in the activities and have a picnic here. ⊠ *Rte. 158 Bypass, MM 12,* ☎ *919/441–7132.* 🖾 *Free.* ☉ *Daily 8* AM–*sunset.*

Dining and Lodging

$$$ ✕ **Owens' Restaurant.** Housed in an old Nags Head–style clapboard cottage, Owens' has been in the same family since 1946. The seafood is outstanding—especially the coconut shrimp and lobster bisque. Nightly entertainment is offered in the brass-and-glass Station Keeper's Lounge. ⊠ *U.S. 158, MM 17,* ☎ *919/441–7309. Reservations not accepted. AE, D, DC, MC, V. Closed Jan.–Mar. No lunch.*

$$–$$$ ✕ **Lance's Seafood Bar & Market.** You can contemplate the fishing and hunting memorabilia while you dine on steamed or raw seafood and then drop the shells through the hole in the table. ⊠ *U.S. 158 Bypass, MM 14,* ☎ *919/441–7501. AE, D, MC, V.*

$$$–$$$$ 🏨 **First Colony Inn.** The rooms in this historic inn near the ocean are
★ furnished with four-poster and canopied beds, hand-crafted armoires,
and English antiques. Two rooms have wet bars, kitchenettes, and
whirlpool baths. A Continental breakfast and afternoon tea come with
the room. ⊠ *6720 S. Virginia Dare Trail, 27959,* ☎ *919/441–2343
or 800/368–9390,* 🆕 *919/441–9234. 26 rooms. Refrigerators, pool.
AE, D, MC, V.*

Outdoor Activities and Sports

GOLF

Nags Head Golf Links (⊠ 5615 S. Seachase Dr., MM 15, ☎ 919/441–
8074 or 800/851–9404) offers ocean views.

HANG GLIDING

Lessons are given by Kitty Hawk Kites (⊠ U.S. 158 at MM 13, ☎ 919/
441–4124 or 800/334–4777).

Roanoke Island

10 mi southwest of Nags Head.

On a hot July day in 1587, 117 men, women, and children left their
boat and set foot on Roanoke Island to make the first permanent En-
glish settlement in the New World. Three years later they disappeared
without a trace, leaving a mystery that continues to intrigue histori-
ans. Today Roanoke Island is a sleepy, well-kept place that hasn't suc-
cumbed to full-scale commercialism. Much of the 12-mi-long island
remains wild. In summer months, Roanoke and its two villages—pic-
turesque Manteo, whose waterfront provides a pleasant combination
of residential and commercial development, and Wanchese, a commercial
fishing community—come alive. The island is reached by U.S. 64/264
❷⓿ from U.S. 158 Bypass. **Manteo** has some attractions related to the is-
land's history; other sights include an aquarium.

By the waterfront is the **Elizabeth II State Historic Site,** a 16th-century
vessel re-created to commemorate the 400th anniversary of the land-
ing of the first English colonists on Roanoke Island. A visitor center
has exhibits on exploration and shipboard life. Historical interpreta-
tions are given by costumed guides during the summer. ⊠ *Downtown
Manteo,* ☎ *919/473–1144.* ▦ *$4.* ☽ *Nov.–Mar., Tues.–Sun. 10–4;
Apr.–Oct., daily 10–6.*

Clustered together on the outskirts of Manteo you'll find the lush **Eliz-
abethan Gardens,** established as a memorial to the first English
colonists. They are impeccably maintained by the Garden Club of
North Carolina and are a fine site for a leisurely stroll. ⊠ *U.S. 64/264,
3 mi north of downtown,* ☎ *919/473–3234.* ▦ *$2.* ☽ *Mar.–Nov.,
daily 9–5; Dec.–Feb., weekdays 9–4.*

Fort Raleigh National Historic Site is a reconstruction of what is thought
to be the original fort of the first Carolinian colonists. Be sure to see
the orientation film and then take a guided tour of the fort. A nature
trail leads to an outlook over Roanoke Sound. ⊠ *U.S. 64/264, 3 mi
north of Manteo,* ☎ *919/473–5772.* ▦ *Free.* ☽ *Daily 9–5; extended
hrs in summer.*

The ***Lost Colony,*** the country's first and longest-running outdoor drama
(60 years in 1997), reenacts the story of the first colonists who settled
here in 1587 and then disappeared. It is staged at the Waterside Am-
phitheatre. ⊠ *1409 U.S. 64/264,* ☎ *919/473–3414 or 800/488–5012.*
▦ *$14 (reservations essential).* ☽ *Performances June–Aug., Sun.–Fri.
at 8:30 PM.*

ⓒ **The North Carolina Aquarium/Roanoke Island,** next to the Dare County Regional Airport, is one of three aquariums in the state. The aquarium has a shark exhibit and a hands-on observation tank that is the aquatic equivalent of a petting zoo. ⊠ *Airport Rd. (off U.S. 64),* ☎ *919/473–3493.* ⌨ *$3.* ⊘ *Daily 9–5.*

Dining and Lodging

$$$ ✕ **Queen Anne's Revenge.** A stately old home in the woods of Wanchese has been expanded into a restaurant that serves some of the coast's best seafood. Nightly specials, like marinated grilled tuna, are fresh and well prepared; even the side dishes are impressive. ⊠ *1064 Old Wharf Rd., Wanchese (5 mi south of Manteo),* ☎ *919/473–5466. Reservations not accepted. AE, D, DC, MC, V. Closed Tues.*

$$ ✕ **Weeping Radish Brewery and Restaurant.** Waiters dressed in Bavarian costumes serve you while German music plays in the background. Tours of the brewery are given upon request. The beer is superb and goes well with the good German dishes; this isn't the place for seafood, though. ⊠ *U.S. 64, Manteo,* ☎ *919/473–1157. D, MC, V.*

$$$$ ✕▦ **Tranquil House Inn.** This 19th-century-style waterfront inn is only a few steps from shops, restaurants, and the **Elizabeth II State Historic Site** (☞ *above*). Handmade comforters in designer fabrics give rooms a cozy feel. A Continental breakfast and wine and cheese each evening are on the house. The restaurant, **1587,** serves inventive entrées such as sesame-crusted tuna with wasabi vinaigrette and shiitake mushrooms. ⊠ *Queen Elizabeth Ave., the Waterfront, Box 2045, Manteo 27954,* ☎ *919/473–1404 or 800/458–7069,* ☏ *919/473–1526. 25 rooms. Restaurant, bicycles. AE, D, MC, V.*

OFF THE BEATEN PATH | **SOMERSET PLACE** – The Collins family kept meticulous records on the 300 slaves who worked this plantation on Albemarle Sound (now a state historic site) in the 1800s. The slaves' descendants still hold family reunions here. The site is 45 mi west of Roanoke Island on the mainland. E *Off U.S. 64 at Creswell,* P *919/797–4560.* A *Free.* C *Apr.–Oct., Mon.–Sat. 9–5, Sun. 1–5; Nov.–Mar., Tues.–Sat. 10–4, Sun. 1–4.*

Cape Hatteras National Seashore

Extends 70 mi south of Nags Head.

★ **Cape Hatteras National Seashore** offers more than 70 mi of unspoiled beaches stretching from south Nags Head to Ocracoke Inlet across three narrow islands: Bodie, Hatteras, and Ocracoke. The islands are linked by NC 12 and the Hatteras Inlet ferry. This coastal area is ideal for swimming, surfing, windsurfing, diving, boating, and any number of water activities. It's easy to find a slice of beach all your own as you drive south down NC 12, but park only in designated areas. If you want to swim, beware of strong tides and currents—there are no lifeguard stations. Fishing piers can be found in Rodanthe, Avon, and Frisco. For information, *see* Visitor Information *in* the Outer Banks A to Z, *below*.

Hatteras Island

15 mi south of Nags Head.

The Herbert C. Bonner Bridge arches for 3 mi over Oregon Inlet and carries traffic to Hatteras Island, the "Blue Marlin Capital of the World." The island, a 33-mi-long ribbon of sand, juts out into the Atlantic Ocean; at its most distant point (Cape Hatteras), Hatteras is 25 mi from the mainland. About 85% of the island belongs to Cape Hatteras National Seashore, and the remainder is privately owned in seven small, quaint villages strung along the island's fragile lifeline to points north, NC 12.

㉑ Pea Island National Wildlife Refuge, between Oregon Inlet and Rodanthe, is made up of more than 5,000 acres of marsh. This birder's paradise is on the Atlantic Flyway: More than 265 species are spotted regularly, including endangered peregrine falcons and piping plovers. NC 12 routes you through marsh areas filled with birds; you can hike or drive, depending on the terrain. A visitor center, 5 mi south of Oregon Inlet, has an informational display. ✉ *Pea Island Refuge Headquarters, NC 12,* ☎ *919/473–1131.* ⊡ *Free.* ☉ *Apr.–Nov., weekdays 8–4.*

㉒ Rodanthe is the site of the 1911 **Chicamacomico Lifesaving Station.** Now restored, it has a museum that tells the story of the 24 stations that once lined the Outer Banks. Living-history reenactments are performed June–August. ✉ *Off NC 12,* ☎ *919/987–2203.* ⊡ *Free.* ☉ *May–Oct., Tues., Thurs., and Sat. 11–5.*

㉓ Cape Hatteras Lighthouse, about 30 mi south of Rodanthe, is a beacon to ships offshore. The 208-ft lighthouse is the tallest in the East, and is open for climbing in season, April–October. Offshore lie the remains of the *Monitor,* a Confederate ironclad ship that sank in 1862. The visitor center here offers information on the national seashore. ✉ *Hatteras Island Visitor Center, off NC 12 near Buxton,* ☎ *919/995–4474.* ⊡ *Free.* ☉ *Daily 9–5.*

Dining

$$$ ✕ **Great Salt Marsh.** This well-lighted place has a black-and-white checkered art-deco look. Entrées include Pamlico crab cakes with "absolutely no filler" and soft crabs served on a bed of garlic-laced spinach. The wine list is splendid. ✉ *Osprey Shopping Center, NC 12, Buxton,* ☎ *919/995–6200. Reservations essential. AE, D, DC, MC, V. Closed Sun.*

Ocracoke Island

㉔ *Southwest of Hatteras Island.*

Much of Ocracoke Island is part of Cape Hatteras National Seashore. A free ferry that leaves every hour during the day will take you from Hatteras to the island in 40 minutes; other ferries leave from the mainland. Ocracoke was cut off from the world for so long that locals still speak in quasi-Elizabethan accents; today, however, the island is a refuge for tourists. There is a village of shops, motels, and restaurants around Silver Lake Harbor, which is where the pirate Blackbeard met his death in 1718. The **Ocracoke Lighthouse** is a photographer's dream. The **Ocracoke Island Visitor Center** (✉ Ocracoke Village, southern end of NC 12 on Silver Lake, ☎ 919/928–4531), run by the National Park Service, can help you with information.

Ocracoke Trolley Tours (✉ NC 12, ☎ 919/928–6711) depart from Trolley Stop One in Ocracoke and tour the island. Tours run Easter–Labor Day, Monday to Saturday.

Ocracoke Island beaches are among the least populated and most beautiful on the Cape Hatteras National Seashore. There are four public access areas with parking, as well as off-road vehicle access. Be sure to stop at the **Ocracoke Pony Pen** (✉ NC 12, 6 mi southwest of the Hatteras–Ocracoke ferry landing), where you can observe from a platform the direct descendants of Spanish mustangs that once roamed wild on the island.

Dining and Lodging

$$–$$$ ╳⊞ **Island Inn and Dining Room.** The inn, built as a private lodge back in 1901, shows its age a bit but is full of Outer Banks character and is being upgraded gradually. Some rooms are in a modern wing. The large rooms in the Crow's Nest on the third floor are the best; they have cathedral ceilings and look out over the island. The restaurant is known for its oyster omelet, crab cakes, and hush puppies. ⊠ *Rte. 12, Box 9, 27960,* ☎ *919/928–4351 inn, 919/928–7821 dining room. 35 rooms. Restaurant, pool. D, MC, V.*

Cape Lookout National Seashore

Southwest of Ocracoke Island via Cedar Island.

★   **Cape Lookout National Seashore** extends for 55 mi from Portsmouth Island to Shackleford Banks and includes 28,400 acres of uninhabited land and marsh. The remote, sandy islands are linked to the mainland by private ferries. Ferry service is available from Harkers Island to the Cape Lookout Light area, from Davis to Shingle Point, from Atlantic to an area north of Drum Inlet, and from Ocracoke to Portsmouth Village. Portsmouth, a deserted village that was inhabited from 1753 until 1984, is being restored; to the south, wild ponies roam Shackleford Banks. Four-wheel-drives are allowed on the beach, and primitive camping is available. For information, *see* Visitor Information *in* the Outer Banks A to Z, *below.*

The Outer Banks A to Z

Arriving, Departing, and Getting Around

BY BOAT

Seagoing visitors travel the Intracoastal Waterway through the Outer Banks and Albemarle region. Boats may dock at Elizabeth City (☎ 919/338–2886), Manteo Waterfront Docks (☎ 919/473–3320), Park Service Docks at Ocracoke (☎ 919/928–5111), and other ports. For a complete list of facilities, see the *North Carolina Coastal Boating Guide* compiled by the North Carolina Department of Transportation (☎ 919/733–2520).

BY CAR

U.S. 158 links the Outer Banks with U.S. 17 leading to Norfolk, Virginia, and other places north. NC 12 goes north toward Corolla and south toward Ocracoke. From Ocracoke there are car ferries to Cedar Island and Swan Quarter on the mainland (☎ 800/293–3779 for reservations).

BY FERRY

For information about the state-run ferry system and its schedules and costs, call the **North Carolina Department of Transportation's Ferry Information Line** (☎ 800/293–3779).

BY PLANE

The closest commercial airports are the **Raleigh-Durham International Airport** (☎ 919/840–2123) and, in Virginia, **Norfolk International** (☎ 804/857–3340), both of which are served by major carriers, including American, Continental, Delta, and US Airways. Southeast Airlines (☎ 919/473–3222) provides charter service between the **Dare County Regional Airport** (☎ 919/473–2600) at Manteo and major cities along the East Coast.

Beach Cabs (☎ 919/441–2500), based in Nags Head, offers 24-hour service from Norfolk to Ocracoke and towns in between. **Outer Banks Limousine Service** (☎ 919/261–3133) serves the area.

Amtrak service (☎ 800/872–7245) is available to Norfolk, Virginia, about 75 mi to the north.

Contacts and Resources

Dial 911 for Oregon Inlet, Roanoke Island, Hatteras Island, and Ocracoke Island. The **Outer Banks Medical Center** (⊠ 425 W. Health Center Dr., Nags Head, ☎ 919/441–7111) is open 24 hours a day. For **Coast Guard** assistance, dial 919/995–6411.

Historic Albemarle Tour, Inc. (⊠ 1 Harding Sq., Washington, ☎ 800/734–1117) offers guided tours of Edenton and publishes a brochure on a self-guided tour of the Albemarle Region.

Kitty Hawk AeroTours leave from the First Flight Airstrip or from Manteo for Kitty Hawk, Corolla, Cape Hatteras, Ocracoke, Portsmouth Island, and other areas along the Outer Banks. ⊠ *Behind Wright Brothers Monument, MM 8, Kill Devil Hills,* ☎ *919/441–4460.* ☉ *Tours Mar.–Labor Day.*

The **North Carolina Aquarium/Roanoke Island** (⊠ Box 967, Airport Rd., Manteo, ☎ 919/473–3493) sponsors summer boat tours of the estuary and the sound.

Camping is permitted in designated areas all along the **Cape Hatteras National Seashore** (⊠ Rte. 1, Box 675, Manteo 27954, ☎ 919/473–2111). Be sure to take extra-long tent stakes for sand, and don't forget the insect repellent. All sites are available on a first-come, first-served basis, except Ocracoke, where reservations are accepted. For information about private campgrounds, contact the **Dare County Tourist Bureau** (☎ 919/473–2138 or 800/446–6262).

Fishing, whether surf casting or deep-sea fishing, is wonderful here. You can board a charter boat or head your own craft out of **Oregon Inlet Fishing Center** (☎ 919/441–6301 or 800/272–5199) or **Pirates Cove Yacht Club** (☎ 919/473–3906 or 800/367–4728) in Manteo. You don't need a license for saltwater fishing.

With over 600 known shipwrecks off the coast of the Outer Banks, **scuba diving** opportunities are virtually unlimited. The *Monitor* is off-limits, however. The USS *Huron* Historic Shipwreck Preserve, which lies offshore between mile markers 11 and 12, is a popular diving site. Dive shops include **Hatteras Divers** (⊠ NC 12, Hatteras, ☎ 919/986–2557) and **Nags Head Pro Dive Shop** (⊠ U.S. 158, MM 13, ☎ 919/441–7594).

Surfing and **windsurfing** are excellent on the Outer Banks. For lessons and rentals, including windsurfing and kayaking, contact **Kitty Hawk Water Sports** (⊠ U.S. 158 at MM 16 ½, Nags Head, ☎ 919/441–6800 or 800/334–4777) or **Bert's Surf Shop** (⊠ MM 10, Nags Head, ☎ 919/441–1939; ⊠ MM 4, Kitty Hawk, ☎ 919/261–7584).

AM: WGAI 560, adult contemporary; WOBR 1530, vacation information, news. **FM:** WNHW 92, country; WOBR 95.3, adult contemporary; WVOD 99.1, beach, Top 40; WRSF 105.7, country.

VISITOR INFORMATION

Dare County Tourist Bureau (✉ Box 399, Manteo 27954, ☎ 800/ 446–6262) operates the Hatteras Island Welcome Center (no phone) on Bodie Island, just south of the Whalebone Junction intersection of NC 12 near Cape Hatteras National Seashore's northern entrance. The center is open Memorial Day to October 1, daily 9–5, and on weekends in April, May, and November. The bureau can also steer you in the direction of agencies to arrange weekly or monthly housing rentals.

The **National Park Service's Group Headquarters,** at Fort Raleigh National Historic Site in Manteo (✉ Off U.S. 64/264, or write the Superintendent, Rte. 1, Box 675, Manteo 27954), has a 24-hour general information line about Cape Hatteras National Seashore (☎ 919/ 473–2111).

The **National Park Service, Cape Lookout National Seashore** (✉ 3601 Bridges St., Suite F, Morehead City 28557, ☎ 919/728–2250) has information about visiting Cape Lookout.

WILMINGTON AND THE CAPE FEAR COAST

The Wilmington area, between the Cape Fear River and the Atlantic Ocean near the southern end of the North Carolina coast, is simultaneously a beach resort and a shipping and trading center. Artists, golfers, history buffs, naturalists, and shoppers will all find something to appeal to them. The old seaport town of Wilmington has much to celebrate these days, including a once-decayed downtown that has been transformed with new places to shop or dine. On the surrounding Cape Fear Coast, you can tour old plantation houses and azalea gardens, study sea life at the state aquarium, and bask in the sun at nearby beaches.

Wilmington

130 mi south of Raleigh.

The city's long history, including its part in the American Revolution and its role as the main port of the Confederacy, is revealed in a number of sights downtown and in the surrounding area. You can visit Chandler's Wharf, the Cotton Exchange, and Water Street Market, old buildings that are now shopping and entertainment centers. *Henrietta II,* a paddle wheeler similar to those that used to ply the waters of the Cape Fear River, has been put into service as a tourist vessel. Wilmington also has special annual events such as the Azalea Festival, North Carolina Jazz Festival, Christmas candlelight tours, and fishing tournaments.

At the **USS *North Carolina* Battleship Memorial** you can tour a ship that participated in every major naval offensive in the Pacific during World War II. The self-guided tour takes about two hours, and a 10-minute film is shown throughout the day. Narrated tours on cassette can be rented; a 70-minute sound-and-light spectacular, "The Immortal Showboat," is presented nightly at 9 from early June until Labor Day. The ship can be reached by car or by taking the river taxi, mid-June– Labor Day, cost $1, from Riverfront Park. ✉ *Junction of U.S. 74/76 and U.S. 17 and 421, west bank of Cape Fear River,* ☎ 910/251–5797. ☞ *$6; sound-and-light show $3.50.* ☉ *Daily 8 AM–sunset.*

🕭 The **Wilmington Railroad Museum** focuses on railroading from the days of the Wilmington and Weldon Railroad (circa 1840) to the present. Children love climbing on the steam locomotive. ✉ *501 Nutt St.,* ☎ *910/763–2634.* ☞ *$3.* ☉ *Tues.–Sat. 10–5, Sun. 1–5.*

The **Cotton Exchange,** a shopping-dining complex, is housed in eight restored buildings on the Cape Fear River that have flourished as a trading center since pre–Civil War days. ⊠ *321 N. Front St.,* ☎ *910/343–9896.* ⊙ *Mon.–Sat. 10–5:30; some stores open evenings and Sun. 1–6.*

At the **New Hanover County Public Library,** the North Carolina Room attracts researchers and genealogists from all over the country. ⊠ *201 Chestnut St.,* ☎ *910/341–4394.* ◙ *Free.* ⊙ *Mon.–Thurs. 9–9, Fri. 9–6, Sat. 9–5, Sun. 1–5.*

The **Cape Fear Museum** traces the natural, cultural, and social history of the lower Cape Fear region from its beginnings to the present day. ⊠ *814 Market St.,* ☎ *910/341–7413.* ◙ *$4.* ⊙ *Tues.–Sat. 9–5, Sun. 2–5.*

Built in 1770 on the foundations of a jail, the **Burgwin-Wright House** is a fine restoration of a colonial gentleman's town house and includes a period garden. In April 1781 General Cornwallis used the house as his headquarters. ⊠ *224 Market St.,* ☎ *910/762–0570.* ◙ *$5.* ⊙ *Tues.–Sat. 10–3:30.*

St. John's Museum of Art is known for its 13 prints by Mary Cassatt, as well as for its works by North Carolina artists. The museum is housed in three buildings, including the 1804 Masonic Lodge Building, the oldest such lodge in the state. There is also a sculpture garden. ⊠ *114 Orange St.,* ☎ *910/763–0281.* ◙ *$2.* ⊙ *Tues.–Sat. 10–5, Sun. noon–4.*

The **Zebulon Latimer House,** built in 1852 in the Italianate style, is a reminder of opulent antebellum living. ⊠ *126 S. 3rd St.,* ☎ *910/762–0492.* ◙ *$3.* ⊙ *Tues.–Sat. 10–4.*

Chandler's Wharf (⊠ 225 S. Water St.), originally a complex of riverfront warehouses, now contains shops and some good seafood restaurants such as Elijah's. It's a great place to conclude a tour of downtown Wilmington.

Greenfield Lake and Gardens offers picnicking and canoe and paddleboat rentals on a scenic 180-acre lake bordered by cypress trees laden with Spanish moss. ⊠ *S. 3rd St. (U.S. 421), 2½ mi south of downtown,* ☎ *910/763–9371.* ◙ *Free.* ⊙ *Daily.*

At **Poplar Grove Historic Plantation,** an 1850 Greek Revival manor house 9 mi northeast of downtown, you can tour the manor house and outbuildings, see craft demonstrations, shop in the country store, and pet the farm animals. ⊠ *10200 U.S. 17, in Scotts Hill,* ☎ *910/686–9989; 910/686–9503 restaurant.* ◙ *Guided tours $6.* ⊙ *Feb.–Dec., Mon.–Sat. 9–5, Sun. noon–5.*

Airlie Gardens, spectacular in the springtime, are usually open from March through September. The gardens were closed in 1997 because of hurricane damage, however. ⊠ *Airlie Rd. off Rte. 74/76, east of downtown,* ☎ *910/763–4646.* ◙ *$6; $5 May–Oct.* ⊙ *Closed in 1997; call ahead.*

OFF THE
BEATEN PATH

MOORE'S CREEK NATIONAL BATTLEFIELD – Military history buffs will get a bang out of this site where American patriots defeated the Loyalists in 1776. ⊠ *200 Moores Creek Rd., Currie, 20 mi northwest of Wilmington on Rte. 210,* ☎ *910/283-5591.* ◙ *Free.* ⊙ *Daily 8-5.*

TRYON PALACE AT NEW BERN – A visit to this stately residence, about 150 mi from the Outer Banks, 100 mi southeast of Raleigh, and 90 mi from Wilmington, is an ideal overnight trip. The reconstructed Georgian palace, considered the most elegant government building in the country in its time, was the colonial capitol and the home of Royal Governor

William Tryon in the 1770s. It was rebuilt according to architectural drawings of the original palace and furnished in English and American antiques as listed in Governor Tryon's inventory. Costumed interpreters lead tours of the house; tours of the 18th-century formal gardens are self-guided. The John Wright Stanly House (circa 1783), Dixon-Stevenson House (circa 1826), and the New Bern Academy (circa 1809) are part of the Tryon Palace Complex. ⊠ *610 Pollock St., New Bern,* ☎ *919/ 638-1560.* 🎫 *Palace and gardens $8, garden tour $4, combination tour of all buildings and gardens $12.* ⊘ *Mon.–Sat. 9–4, Sun. 1–4.*

Dining and Lodging

$$–$$$ ✕ **Market Street Casual Dining.** This always-busy eatery offers a wide variety of sandwiches and entrées, including seafood and steaks. There's also a bar on the premises. ⊠ *6309 Market St.,* ☎ *910/395–2488. Reservations not accepted. AE, D, MC, V.*

$$–$$$ ✕ **Pilot House.** At this Chandler's Wharf restaurant, known for its seafood, pastas, and fresh vegetables, you can dine outdoors overlooking the Cape Fear River. Sunday brunch, April–October, featuring Lowcountry Southern food, is the most popular in town. ⊠ *2 Ann St.,* ☎ *910/343–0200. AE, D, DC, MC, V.*

$ ✕ **Water Street Restaurant and Sidewalk Café.** A restored two-story brick waterfront warehouse dating from 1835 holds an outdoor café and restaurant that serves up Greek, Mexican, Middle Eastern, and other ethnic cooking. ⊠ *5 Water St.,* ☎ *910/343–0042. AE, MC, V.*

$$$–$$$$ 🏠 **Inn at St. Thomas Court.** You are pampered yet enjoy total privacy at this small, luxurious apartment-type house, which has one- and two-bedroom suites furnished in a traditional style in keeping with the surrounding historic district. A Continental breakfast is included in the rate. ⊠ *101 S. 2nd St., 28401,* ☎ *910/343–1800 or 800/525–0909,* FAX *910/251–1149. 34 suites. Refrigerators, in-room VCRs. AE, D, DC, MC, V.*

$$$ 🏠 **Catherine's Inn.** Built in 1883 in the historic district overlooking the Cape Fear River, this two-story Italianate home, now a B&B, has hardwood floors, a sunken garden, four-poster and canopy beds, and claw-foot tubs. Many items were collected by the innkeepers over the years. ⊠ *410 S. Front St., 28401,* ☎ *910/251–0863 or 800/476–0723. 5 rooms. AE, MC, V.*

$$$ 🏠 **Wilmington Hilton Inn.** Overlooking the Cape Fear River on one side and the city on the other, the spacious Hilton is one of the most convenient places to stay in town. The lobby is plush; guest rooms have an Asian motif and color schemes of blue, green, and gold. ⊠ *301 N. Water St., 28401,* ☎ *910/763–5900 or 800/445–8667,* FAX *910/763– 0038. 168 rooms, 10 suites. Restaurant, lounge, pool, meeting rooms, airport shuttle. AE, D, DC, MC, V.*

$$ 🏠 **Hampton Inn.** This economy chain motel, 3 mi from downtown, is not luxurious but offers such extras as complimentary Continental breakfast, in-room movies, and free local calls. ⊠ *5107 Market St., 28403,* ☎ *910/395–5045 or 800/426–7866,* FAX *910/799–1971. 118 rooms. Pool. AE, D, DC, MC, V.*

Nightlife and the Arts

NIGHTLIFE

Ice House Beer Garden (⊠ 115 S. Water St., ☎ 910/251–1158 or 910/ 763–2084) serves food and beer and showcases a different music group nightly. **Johnny Rockit's** (⊠ 5025 Market St., ☎ 910/791–2001) is known for live rock music on Saturday nights.

The city has its own symphony orchestra, oratorio society, civic ballet, and concert association; and the North Carolina Symphony makes four appearances here each year. For further information, contact the Cape Fear Coast Convention and Visitors Bureau (☞ Visitor Information *in* Wilmington and the Cape Fear Coast A to Z, *below*). **Thalian Hall** (✉ 310 Chestnut St., ☎ 910/343–3664 or 800/523–2820), a magnificent opera house built in 1858, is the site of theater, dance, and musical performances. Theatrical productions are staged by the Thalian Association, Opera House Productions, and Tapestry Players. The annual **Wilmington Jazz Festival,** held in February, and the **Blues Festival,** in August, draw big crowds.

Outdoor Activities and Sports

There are more than a dozen public-access **golf** courses in the Greater Wilmington area. **Beau Rivage Plantation Golf Club** (✉ 6230 Carolina Beach Rd., ☎ 910/395–1300) is an 18-hole course in a natural links setting. The **Cape Golf & Racquet Club** (✉ 535 The Cape Blvd., Wilmington, ☎ 910/799–3110) is an 18-hole resort course with driving range.

South Brunswick County, about 30–40 mi from Wilmington on the coast, is golf heaven, especially the areas around Calabash, Sunset Beach, and Ocean Isle. **Lockwood Folly Golf Links** (✉ 100 Club House Dr., Holden Beach, ☎ 910/842–5666 or 800/443–7891) is a highly rated resort course. **Marsh Harbour Golf Links** (✉ Hwy. 179, Calabash, ☎ 910/579–3161 or 800/552–2660) was rated one of the best 75 public courses in America by *Golf Digest.* **Oyster Bay Golf Links** (✉ Hwy. 179, Sunset Beach, ☎ 910/579–3528 or 800/552–2660) is known for its oyster shell hazards and gator sightings. **Sea Trail Plantation** (✉ 211 Clubhouse Rd., Sunset Beach, ☎ 910/579–4350 or 800/624–6601) has three courses designed by Dan Maples, Rees Jones, and Willard Byrd, respectively.

Shopping

You'll find fun shopping at Chandler's Wharf, the Cotton Exchange, and the Water Street Market, but Wilmington also has many unique shops in the downtown historic district, as well as shopping malls and discount outlets.

Wrightsville Beach

12 mi east of Wilmington.

Wrightsville Beach is a small, quiet island community that's very family-oriented; it has a number of fine restaurants. There's good swimming, boating, and surfing at the beaches here.

Dining and Lodging

$$–$$$ ✕ **Oceanic Restaurant and Grill.** Its Oceanic Pier location gives you the top panoramic view of the Atlantic for miles around—a great backdrop for the fresh seafood, steaks, and chicken served here. ✉ *703 S. Lumina St.,* ☎ *910/256–5551. AE, MC, V.*

$$–$$$ ✕ **Ocean Terrace Restaurant.** Part of the Blockade Runner Resort (☞ *below*), this restaurant attracts large crowds to its Friday lobster night, Saturday seafood buffet, and Sunday brunch. Regular dishes here include grilled New York strip steak with bourbon-shallot butter; sautéed, almond-breaded flounder with shrimp; and sautéed chicken breast with toasted pecans, pears, and apples. ✉ *Blockade Runner Resort Hotel and Conference Center, 275 Waynick Blvd.,* ☎ *910/256–2251 or 800/541–1161. Reservations essential. AE, D, DC, MC, V.*

$$$–$$$$ 🏨 **Blockade Runner Resort Hotel and Conference Center.** This extensive complex is widely known for its food (☞ Ocean Terrace Restaurant, *above*) and summer programs for children. Rooms overlook either the inlet or the ocean. ✉ *275 Waynick Blvd., 28480,* ☎ *910/256–2251 or 800/541–1161,* ℻ *910/256–5502. 150 rooms. Restaurant, pool, health club, boating, bicycles, meeting rooms. AE, D, DC, MC, V.*

Nightlife and the Arts

The **Ocean Terrace Restaurant** in the Blockade Runner Resort (☞ Dining and Lodging, *above*) offers live entertainment Thursday through Sunday, with nationally known acts in the Comedy Zone March–November.

Kure Beach

17 mi south of Wilmington.

Kure Beach is a resort community that's a bit livelier than Wrightsville Beach (☞ *above*); it has amusement parks and a boardwalk with bars. There are historic sites such as Fort Fisher and attractions such as the North Carolina Aquarium. In some places, twisted live oaks still grow behind the dunes. Kure Beach also has miles of beaches; public access points are marked by orange-and-blue signs.

Fort Fisher State Historic Site was the largest and one of the most important earthwork fortifications in the South during the Civil War. There is a reconstructed battery and Civil War relics and artifacts from sunken blockade-runners on site. The fort is part of **Fort Fisher Recreation Area,** with 4 mi of undeveloped beach. ✉ *U.S. 421,* ☎ *910/458–5538.* 🎟 *Free.* ☉ *Apr.–Oct., Mon.–Sat. 9–5, Sun. 1–5; Nov.–Mar., Tues.–Sat. 10–4, Sun. 1–4.*

☜ The **North Carolina Aquarium at Fort Fisher,** one of three state aquariums, has a 20,000-gallon shark tank, a touch pool (where you can handle starfish, sea urchins, and the like), a whale exhibit, and an alligator exhibit. The park is also a natural area where wildflowers, birds, and small animals thrive. You can visit the World War II bunker that stood guard against sea attacks from the Atlantic. ✉ *U.S. 421,* ☎ *910/458–8257.* 🎟 *$3.* ☉ *Mon.–Sat. 9–5, Sun. 1–5.*

Lodging

$$$ 🏨 **Docksider Inn.** In a class of its own, this waterfront hotel in the heart of Kure Beach is nautical both outside and in. Gray with navy shutters, the inn is furnished in light-colored beach-type furniture and enhanced with marine art and artifacts, including a set of 1930s British Admiralty signal flags. An original watercolor adorns each bathroom. ✉ *202 Fort Fisher Blvd. (U.S. 421), 28449,* ☎ *910/458–4200,* ℻ *910/458–6468. 34 rooms. Pool. AE, D, DC, MC, V.*

Southport

30 mi south of Wilmington.

★   From 1792 until 1887, **Southport** was known as Smithville. This small town, which sits quietly at the mouth of the Cape Fear River, changed its name in anticipation of an economic boom that never came—until now. Listed on the National Register of Historic Places, Southport, an increasingly desirable retirement spot, retains its village charm and character. Stately and distinctive homes, antiques stores, gift shops, and restaurants line streets that veer to accommodate ancient oak trees. This town, portrayed in Robert Ruark's novel *The Old Man and the Boy,* is ideal for walking and the movies—*Crimes of the Heart* was filmed here.

If you're approaching the town from Fort Fisher and NC 421, the **Southport–Fort Fisher Ferry** (☎ 910/458–3329), a car ferry, provides an enjoyable river ride between Old Federal Point at the tip of the spit and the mainland. You can see the "Old Baldy" lighthouse on Bald Head Island en route. ☉ *State-operated ferries run every 50 mins, 8:50–6:50; ▣ $3 per car.* ☎ *910/457–5003 for privately owned passenger ferry from Southport to Bald Head Island; ▣ $15 per person; ☉ On the hr (except noon) 8–10.*

At the **Carolina Power and Light Company Visitors Center,** 4 mi north of Southport on NC 87, you can learn about nuclear power through exhibits and movies and then lunch in the picnic area. ✉ *8520 River Rd. SE,* ☎ *910/457–6041.* ▣ *Free.* ☉ *Weekdays 9–4.*

Lodging

$$$$ ☷ **Bald Head Island Resort.** This car-free resort (guests travel the island on foot, by bicycle, or in golf carts) offers privacy in a luxurious, isolated setting. It's accessible only by ferry (☎ 910/457–5003), $15 round-trip from Southport. Activities include golf (a George Cobb course that's also open to the public), tennis, sailing, and fishing. Other favorite pastimes are watching the loggerhead turtles and taking a tour led by a naturalist. Accommodations include rental condos, cottages, and bed-and-breakfast inns; a two-night minimum stay is required. ✉ *Bald Head Island, 28461,* ☎ *910/457–5000 or 800/234–1666,* FAX *910/457–9232. More than 170 rental condos and beach houses. 3 restaurants, pool, 18-hole golf course, 2 tennis courts, boating. AE, DC, MC, V.*

Outdoor Activities and Sports

For golf, the **Gauntlet at St. James Plantation** (✉ NC 211, ☎ 910/253–3008 or 800/247–4806) lives up to its name as a challenging course.

Winnabow

12 mi north of Southport, 18 mi south of Wilmington.

Winnabow is more of a crossroads than a town to visit; the draws here are gardens and a historic site, both off NC 133 near the Cape Fear
★ River. The house at **Orton Plantation Gardens** is not open to the public, but you can walk around 20 acres of beautiful, comprehensive gardens. The former rice plantation holds magnolias, ancient oaks, and all kinds of ornamental plants; the grounds are a refuge for waterfowl. ✉ *9149 Orton Rd. SE, off NC 133,* ☎ *910/371–6851.* ▣ *$8.* ☉ *Mar.–Aug., daily 8–6, Sept.–Nov., daily 10–5.*

At **Brunswick Town State Historic Site,** you can explore the excavations of a colonial town, see Fort Anderson, a Civil War earthworks fort, and have a picnic. ✉ *8884 St. Phillips Rd., off NC 133,* ☎ *910/371–6613.* ▣ *Free.* ☉ *Apr.–Oct., Mon.–Sat. 9–5, Sun. 1–5; Nov.–Mar., Tues.–Sat. 10–4, Sun. 1–4.*

Wilmington and the Cape Fear Coast A to Z

Arriving, Departing, and Getting Around

BY BOAT

Public boat access is offered at Atlantic Marina, Carolina Beach State Park, Masonboro Boat Yard and Marina, Seapath Transient Dock, Wrightsville Gulf Terminal, and Wrightsville Marina. A number of hotels provide docking facilities for their guests. A state-run car ferry connects Fort Fisher with Southport on the coast.

BY BUS
Greyhound Lines serves the Union Bus Terminal (✉ 201 Harnett St., ☎ 910/762–6625 or 800/231–2222). The **Wilmington Transit Authority** (☎ 910/343–0106) provides service every day except Sunday.

BY CAR
Wilmington is served by I–40.

BY PLANE
US Airways and ASA Delta Connection serve the **New Hanover International Airport** (☎ 910/341–4333), ½ mi from downtown Wilmington.

Contacts and Resources

BEACHES

Three beaches—Wrightsville, Carolina, and Kure—are within a short drive from Wilmington, and miles and miles of sand stretch northward to the Outer Banks and southward to South Carolina. The beaches offer activities from fishing to sunbathing to scuba diving, and the towns here have a choice of accommodations. Approximately 100 points of public access along the shoreline are marked by orange-and-blue signs. Some of the smaller beaches have lifeguards on duty, and many are accessible to people with disabilities. Some fishing piers are open to the public. Contact the Cape Fear Coast Convention and Visitors Bureau (☞ Visitor Information, *below*) for more information. Camping, fishing, swimming, and picnicking are permitted at **Carolina Beach State Park** (☎ 910/458–8206; 910/458–7770 marina).

EMERGENCIES

Police (☎ 911). **Ambulance** (☎ 911). **Coast Guard assistance** (☎ 910/343–4881). **Emergency medical attention** is available round the clock at the **Cape Fear Memorial Hospital** (✉ 5301 Wrightsville Ave., ☎ 910/452–8100) and the **New Hanover Regional Medical Center** (✉ 2131 S. 17th St., ☎ 910/343–7000); both hospitals have 24-hour pharmacies as well.

GUIDED TOURS

Cape Fear Riverboats, Inc. offers a variety of cruises aboard a sternwheel riverboat, the *Henrietta II*, that departs from Riverfront Park. ✉ *Docked at the Hilton in downtown Wilmington,* ☎ *910/343–1611 or 800/676–0162.* ⊠ *Sightseeing tours $9, entertainment/dinner cruises $29–$32.50, sunset dinner cruises $22, moonlight cruises $9 (call for boarding times).* ☉ *Sightseeing tours Apr.–Oct., dinner cruises Apr.–Dec, moonlight cruises June–Sept.*

Cape Fear Tours (✉ 8112 Sidbury Rd., Wilmington, ☎ 910/686–7744) offers walking and driving tours of the Wilmington Historic District, mansions, and the beaches for individuals and groups by reservation. Individual tours are $20 per hour.

OUTDOOR ACTIVITIES AND SPORTS

Fishing is very popular in this area. There's surf fishing on the piers that dot the coast, and charter boats are available for off-shore fishing. Four major fishing tournaments, for substantial prize money, are held each year—the Cape Fear Marlin Tournament, the Wrightsville Beach King Mackerel Tournament, the East Coast Open King Mackerel Tournament, and the U.S. Open King Mackerel Tournament. For more information, contact the Cape Fear Coast Convention and Visitors Bureau (☞ Visitor Information, *below*).

Some top **golf** choices are listed in this section, but for more information call the Cape Fear Coast Convention and Visitors Bureau (☞ Visitor Information, *below*) or the South Brunswick Islands Chamber of Commerce (✉ Box 1380, Shalotte 28459, ☎ 910/754–6644).

Wrecks such as the World War II tanker *John D. Gill* make for exciting **scuba diving** off the coast. Aquatic Safaris (✉ 5751–4 Oleander Dr., Wilmington, ☎ 910/392–4386) rents equipment and leads trips.

Surfing and **board sailing** are popular at area beaches, and rentals are available at shops in Wilmington, Wrightsville Beach, and Carolina Beach.

RADIO STATIONS
AM: WAAV 980, news, talk; WBMS 1340, urban contemporary. **FM:** WHQR 91.3, National Public Radio; WGNI 102.7, adult contemporary; WWQQ 101.3, country; WSFM 107.5, classic rock.

VISITOR INFORMATION
Cape Fear Coast Convention and Visitors Bureau (✉ 24 N. 3rd St., Wilmington 28401, ☎ 910/341–4030 or 800/222–4757) has a visitor center that's open weekdays 8:30–5, Saturday 9–4, Sunday 1–4. You can watch a video about the area.

THE MOUNTAINS
Cherokee, Asheville, and the High Country

The majestic peaks, meadows, and valleys of the Appalachian, Blue Ridge, and Smoky mountains characterize the western corner of the state, which is divided into three distinct regions: the southern mountains (home to the Cherokee reservation), the northern mountains, known as the High Country (Blowing Rock, Boone, Banner Elk), and the central mountains, anchored by Asheville, for decades a retreat for the wealthy and famous. National parks, national forests, handmade-crafts centers, and the Blue Ridge Parkway are the area's main attractions, providing prime opportunities for skiing, hiking, bicycling, camping, fishing, canoeing, or just taking in the breathtaking views.

At the southern terminus of the Blue Ridge Parkway and the North Carolina entrance to the Great Smoky Mountains lies the homeland of the Eastern Band of the Cherokee Indians. Through a blending of museums, dramas, assorted outdoor attractions, and everyday living, the Cherokee attempt to explain what's precious in the "Land of the Blue Mist."

The biggest city in the mountains, Asheville has a lovely setting, a choice of hotels and restaurants, and a thriving arts community. The city's revitalized downtown has good shopping, galleries, museums, restaurants, and nightlife.

Picture-book towns such as Boone, Blowing Rock, and Banner Elk have boomed in the 30 years since the introduction of snowmaking equipment. Luxury resorts now dot the valleys and mountaintops. You can take advantage of the many crafts shops, music festivals, theater offerings, and such special events as the Grandfather Mountain Highland Games (☞ Blue Ridge Parkway, *below*). The passing of each season is a visual event here, and autumn is the star.

Cherokee

50 mi west of Asheville.

The 56,000-acre Cherokee Indian Reservation is known as the Qualla Boundary, and the town of Cherokee is its capital. Truth be told, there are two Cherokees. There's the side that offers pop culture, designed to appeal to mass numbers of tourists, many of whom are visiting nearby Great Smoky Mountains National Park; this would include the hard-won Cherokee Tribal Casino. Then there's the Cherokee that explores the richness of the real native culture and the continuing influence of this once-mighty tribe. Though relatively small in number—tribal enrollment is 11,000—these people and their ancestors have been responsible for keeping alive the Cherokee culture. They are the descendants of those who hid in the Great Smoky Mountains to avoid the forced removal of the Cherokee Nation to Oklahoma in the last century, known as the Trail of Tears. They are survivors, extremely attached to the hiking, swimming, trout fishing, and natural beauty of their ancestral homeland.

Everyone interested in understanding the history of the Cherokee should visit the **Museum of the Cherokee Indian,** rated as one of the best native museums in the United States. The displays and artifacts cover 10,000 years. There's an art gallery as well as an outdoor living exhibit of Cherokee life as it was in the 15th century. ⊠ *U.S. 441 at Drama Rd.,* ☎ *704/497–3481.* ☜ *$4.* ⊙ *Mid-June–Aug., Mon.–Sat. 9–8, Sun. 9–5; Sept.–mid-June, daily 9–5.*

The **Qualla Arts and Crafts Mutual,** across the street from the Museum of the Cherokee Indian, is a cooperative that displays and sells items created by 300 Cherokee craftspeople. The store also has a large section of baskets, masks, and wood carvings. ⊠ *U.S. 441 at Drama Rd.,* ☎ *704/497–3103.* ⊙ *June–Aug., daily 8–8; Sept.–Oct., daily 8–6; Nov.–May, daily 8–4:30.*

You can step back more than two centuries when you visit **Oconaluftee Indian Village.** Guides in native costumes will lead you through the village while others demonstrate skills such as weaving, pottery, canoe construction, and hunting techniques. ⊠ *U.S. 441 at Drama Rd.,* ☎ *704/497–2315.* ☜ *$9.* ⊙ *May 15–Oct. 25, daily 9–5:30.*

☺ Every mountain county has significant deposits of gems and minerals, and at the **Smoky Mountain Gold and Ruby Mine,** on the Qualla Boundary, you can search for gems such as aquamarines. Kids love panning precisely because it can be wet and messy. Here they're guaranteed a find. Gem ore can be purchased, too: Gold ore costs $5 per bag. ⊠ *U.S. 441 north,* ☎ *704/497–6574.* ☜ *$4–$10, depending on the ore.* ⊙ *Mar., weekends 9–6; Apr.–Nov., daily 9–9.*

OFF THE
BEATEN PATH

GREAT SMOKY MOUNTAINS RAILWAY – At one of the most popular attractions in western North Carolina, you can choose from five different routes and diesel-electric or steam locomotives. Open-sided cars or cabooses are ideal for picture taking as the spectacular scenery glides by. Dillsboro is about 10 mi south of Cherokee; you can visit a train museum here, too. ⊠ *1 Front St., Dillsboro,* ☎ *704/586–8811 or 800/ 872–4681.* ☜ *Admission varies by route.* ⊙ *No trains Jan.–Mar. and weekdays Apr.–May; call for Nov.–Dec. schedule.*

Dining and Lodging

$–$$ ✕ **Nantahala Village Restaurant.** This roomy restaurant about 10 mi southwest of Cherokee is a favorite of folks in Swain County. The food isn't fancy, but it's good and it's filling. There's trout, chicken, and country ham. Sunday brunch offers a few surprises: huevos rancheros and eggs Benedict, to name a few. ✉ *1900 U.S. 19 west, Bryson City,* ☎ *704/488–9616. D, MC, V. Closed late Nov.–early Mar.*

$$$$ ✕🏨 **Hemlock Inn.** Even if you're not a guest at this inn, which is built on a small mountain that overlooks three valleys, you can make a reservation for dinner Monday through Saturday, and lunch on Sunday. Meals are prepared with native foods, including locally grown fruits and vegetables and mountain honey. Each cozy room is individually decorated with antiques and locally made crafts. ✉ *U.S. 19 west, Bryson City,* ☎ *704/488–2885. 26 rooms. D, MC, V. Closed Dec.–Apr.*

$$–$$$ 🏨 **Holiday Inn Cherokee.** Guest rooms are standard chain fare, but the staff at this well-equipped motel is very friendly. The in-house **Chestnut Tree** restaurant has dinner buffets that are veritable groaning boards, and the on-site native crafts shop, with works by local artists, is a nice touch. ✉ *U.S. 19 S, 28719,* ☎ *704/497–9181 or 800/465–4329,* 📠 *704/497–5973. 150 rooms, 4 suites. Restaurant, 2 pools, sauna, meeting rooms. AE, D, DC, MC, V.*

Nightlife and the Arts

Unto These Hills Outdoor Drama (✉ Mountainside Theater on Drama Rd., just off U.S. 441 N, ☎ 704/497–2111) is a colorful and well-staged history of the Cherokee from the time of Spanish explorer Hernando de Soto's visit in 1540 to the infamous Trail of Tears. It runs from mid-June to mid-August.

Bingo is offered at the 500-seat **Tribal Bingo** (✉ Great Smokies Center on Acquoni Rd., ☎ 704/497–4320 or 800/410–1254). There are early-bird games at 5:30 PM Monday–Thursday and at 5 PM Friday–Sunday. Regular games begin at 7 PM nightly.

The **Cherokee Tribal Casino** (✉ Acquoni Rd. off U.S. 441 N, ☎ 704/497–6835 or 800/659–1115) has plenty of action 24 hours a day, with more than 600 gaming machines, video poker, and video blackjack. At press time, Harrah's was preparing to open the new Cherokee Smoky Moutains casino, which will also be owned by the Eastern Band of the Cherokee. It will replace the existing casino. For information, call 704/497–7777.

Outdoor Activities and Sports

FISHING

There are 30 mi of regularly stocked streams on the **Cherokee Indian Reservation.** To fish in tribal water you need no state license, just a tribal fishing permit, available at nearly two dozen reservation businesses. The permit sells for $5 and is valid for one day. For information, call 704/497–5201 or 800/438–1601.

HIKING

In the downtown area you can cross the Oconaluftee River on a footbridge to **Oconaluftee Islands Park & Trail** (✉ Across from Cherokee Elementary School on U.S. 441) and enjoy a walking trail around the perimeter of the Island Park, which also has picnic facilities. The 1½-mi **Oconaluftee River Trail** begins at the Great Smoky Mountains National Park entrance sign on U.S. 441 (near the entrance to the Blue Ridge Parkway) and ends at the **Mountain Farm Museum/Park Visitor Center.** The trail is flat and well-maintained. A five-minute hike from the Mingo Falls Campground area (⊠ Big Cove Rd. about 4 mi north of Acquoni Rd.) will reward you with a spectacular view of the 200-ft-high **Mingo Falls.**

★ Cherokee is near one of the two main entrances to **Great Smoky Mountains National Park,** where trails abound. For trail maps, contact the Superintendent (⊠ Great Smoky Mountains National Park, Gatlinburg, TN 37738, ☎ 615/436–5615). The park maintains an information bulletin board with basic trail information at the entrance at the junction of mile marker 469.1 and U.S. 441.

Asheville

115 mi west of Charlotte.

The largest and most cosmopolitan city in the mountains, Asheville has been rated, among cities of its size, America's favorite place to live. It has scenic beauty, low levels of pollution, a good airport and road system, a moderate four-season climate, a variety of hotels and restaurants, and a thriving arts community. Banjo pickers are as revered as violinists, mountain folks mix with city slickers, and everyone loves where they live. Particularly noteworthy is the renaissance of the city's downtown, a pedestrian-friendly place with upscale shopping, art galleries, museums, restaurants, and nightlife.

Downtown Asheville is noted for its eclectic architecture. The **Battery Park Hotel,** built in 1924, is neo-Georgian; the **Flatiron Building** (1924) is neoclassical; the **Basilica of St. Lawrence** (1912) is Spanish Baroque; **Pack Place,** formerly known as Old Pack Library (1925), is in Italian Renaissance style; the **S & W Cafeteria** (1929) is Art Deco. In fact, the city has the largest collection of Art Deco buildings in the Southeast outside of Miami.

Pack Place Education, Arts & Science Center houses the Asheville Art Museum, Colburn Gem & Mineral Museum, Health Adventure, YMI Cultural Center (directly across the street), and Diana Wortham Theatre. ⊠ 2 S. Pack Sq., ☎ 704/257–4500. ☜ *Fees vary.* ☼ *June–Oct., Tues.–Sat. 10–5, Sun. 1–5; Nov.–May, Tues.–Sat. 10–5.*

The **Thomas Wolfe Memorial,** built in 1880 in the Queen Anne style, is one of the oldest houses in downtown Asheville. Wolfe's mother ran a boardinghouse here for years, and he used it as the setting for his novel *Look Homeward, Angel.* Family pictures, clothing, and original furnishings fill the house, a state historic site. Guided tours are available. ⊠ 52 Market St., ☎ 704/253–8304. ☜ $1. ☼ *Apr.–Oct., Mon.–Sat. 9–5, Sun. 1–5; Nov.–Mar., Tues.–Sat. 10–4, Sun. 1–4.*

★ The astonishing **Biltmore Estate,** which faces Biltmore Village, was built as the private home of George Vanderbilt. This 250-room French Renaissance château is America's largest private residence (some of Vanderbilt's descendants still live on the grounds, but open the bulk of the home and grounds to visitors). Richard Morris Hunt designed it, and Frederick Law Olmsted landscaped the original 125,000-acre estate (now 8,000 acres). It took 1,000 men five years to complete the gargantuan project. On view are the priceless antiques and art collected by the Vanderbilts, and 75 acres of gardens and formally landscaped grounds. You can also see the state-of-the-art winery and take Christmas candlelight tours of the house. Allow a full day to tour the house and grounds. ⊠ 1 N. Pack Sq. (I–40E from Asheville to U.S. 25 S), ☎ 704/274–6333 or 800/543–2961. ☜ $27.95; *prices for special events vary.* ☼ *Daily 9–5.*

Ten years in the making, the **North Carolina Arboretum** opened major new gardens in 1996 and is already one of the state's jewels. Situated on 426 acres that were part of the original Biltmore Estate, the arboretum completes the vision of Frederick Law Olmsted and showcases Southern Appalachian flora in a stunning number of settings, including the Quilt Garden, whose bedding plants are arranged in patterns reminiscent of Appalachian quilts. A formal Stream Garden capitalizes on the Bent Creek trout stream, which runs through the heart of the grounds. An extensive network of trails is available for walking or mountain biking. ⊠ *Immediately southwest of Asheville, adjacent to Blue Ridge Parkway (near I–26 and I–40)*, ☎ *704/665–2492.* ⛅ *Free; call for group tour fees.* ☉ *Visitor education center Mon.–Sat. 8:30–5; gardens and grounds daylight hrs.*

OFF THE BEATEN PATH

PENLAND SCHOOL OF CRAFTS – This world-famous institution about 45 mi northeast of Asheville on a remote mountaintop is the oldest and largest school for high-quality mixed-media arts and crafts in North America. It has classes in books and paper, glassblowing, ceramics, metalworking, photography, textile arts, and other media. A gallery displays works (some are for sale); call to check hours and winter closing. Classes aren't open to the public, but you can call about a campus tour and also visit the Barns, which houses the studios of artists who live and work at the school. ⊠ *Penland Rd. off NC 19/23, Penland,* ☎ *704/ 765–2359 school, 704/765–6211 gallery and campus tours.*

Dining and Lodging

$$$$ ✕ **Market Place on Wall Street.** Nouvelle cuisine, from seafood to lamb and veal, is served in a relaxed atmosphere. Vegetables and herbs are regionally grown, and bread, pasta, and pastries are made daily on the premises. ⊠ *20 Wall St.,* ☎ *704/252–4162. AE, MC, V. Closed Sun. No lunch.*

$$$ ✕ **Cafe on the Square.** When owners Bill and Shelagh Burns moved to Asheville from San Francisco they brought California-style cuisine with them. Lunch is served, but dinner is where they go all out. The menu, which offers from four to eight specials at each meal, is heavy on fresh seafood and pastas cooked with salsas, chutneys, and simple marinades. Their signature dishes are hickory-smoked chicken in a Marsala-and-shiitake-mushroom sauce and peanut-butter pie. ⊠ *1 Biltmore Ave.,* ☎ *704/251–5565. AE, D, MC, V. Closed Sun.*

$$ ✕ **Mountain Smoke House.** Mountain barbecue and pig-pickin' buffets combined with bluegrass music and clogging make for a lively experience for those who want more than food when they go out. The aroma will lead you to this dinner-only, family-style restaurant, which serves as a showcase for local musicians. ⊠ *20 S. Spruce St.,* ☎ *704/ 253–4871. AE, D, DC, MC, V. No lunch.*

$$ ✕ **West Side Grill.** Have a country-style meal of meat loaf, turkey, roast beef, or baked chicken, with all the trimmings, at this '50s-style diner. Salads and vegetarian fare are also offered. ⊠ *1190 Patton Ave.,* ☎ *704/252–9605. Reservations not accepted. AE, D, MC, V.*

$$ ✕ **Windmill European Grill/Il Pescatore.** As the name implies, the menu is international. This cool, dark, and cozy cellar restaurant specializes in German, Italian, and Indian cuisines. ⊠ *85 Tunnel Rd.,* ☎ *704/253– 5285. AE, D, MC, V. No lunch Tues.–Sat.*

$$$$ ✕🏨 **Grove Park Inn.** Asheville's premier resort, overlooking the Blue
★ Ridge Mountains, is just as beautiful and exciting as it was the day it opened in 1913. Novelist F. Scott Fitzgerald stayed here while his wife, Zelda, was in a nearby sanitarium. Massive lobby fireplaces set the scale, and the hotel is furnished with antique pieces in the rich oak texture

and artistic line of the Arts and Crafts style that was popular in the early 1900s. The restaurants offer plenty of choices: **Horizons** specializes in game dishes, from ostrich to boar; you can also order free-range chicken. ⊠ *290 Macon Ave., 28804,* ☎ *704/252–2711 or 800/438–5800; FAX 704/253–7053 guests, 704/252–6102 reservations. 486 rooms, 24 suites. 4 restaurants, 2 pools, sauna, hot tub, 18-hole golf course, 12 tennis courts, health club, racquetball, children's programs, meeting rooms, airport shuttle. AE, D, DC, MC, V.*

$$$$　✕⊡ **Haywood Park Hotel.** This contemporary downtown hotel was once a department store. **Twenty-Three Page,** the hotel's elegant restaurant, serves seafood and game, and a free Continental breakfast is delivered to your room. A shopping galleria adjoins the property. ⊠ *One Battery Park Ave., 28801,* ☎ *704/252–2522 or 800/228–2522, FAX 704/253–0481. 33 rooms. 2 restaurants, sauna, exercise room. AE, D, DC, MC, V.*

$$$$　✕⊡ **Richmond Hill Inn.** Once a private residence, this elegant Victo-
★　　rian mansion is on the National Register of Historic Places. Rooms in the mansion are furnished with canopy beds, Victorian sofas, and other antiques, while the more modern cottages have contemporary pine poster beds. **Gabrielle's** (reservations essential, and a jacket is required), named for the former mistress of the house—wife of the congressman and ambassador Richmond Pearson—is known for innovative cuisine such as grilled medallions of antelope with wild boar sausage; the restaurant is open to the public only for dinner and Sunday brunch. ⊠ *87 Richmond Hill Dr., 28806,* ☎ *704/252–7313 or 800/545–9238, FAX 704/252–8726. 12 rooms, 9 cottages. Restaurant, croquet, meeting rooms. AE, MC, V.*

$$$　⊡ **Quality Inn Biltmore.** Built on the grounds of the old Biltmore Dairy, this chain hotel is especially convenient for Biltmore Estate visitors. It is attached to the **Biltmore Dairy Bar,** a popular restaurant that offers sandwiches and ice cream, and adjacent to the **Criterion Grill,** a full-service restaurant and lounge. ⊠ *115 Hendersonville Rd., 28803,* ☎ *704/274–1800 or 800/221–2222, FAX 704/274–5960. 160 rooms. Pool, meeting rooms. AE, D, DC, MC, V.*

$$–$$$　⊡ **Cedar Crest Victorian Inn.** This beautiful cottage was constructed by Biltmore craftsmen as a private residence around the turn of the century. Lovingly restored as a bed-and-breakfast inn, it's filled with Victorian antiques. You are treated to afternoon tea, evening coffee or chocolate, and a breakfast of fruit, pastry, and coffee. ⊠ *674 Biltmore Ave., 28803,* ☎ *704/252–1389 or 800/252–0310, FAX 704/252–7667. 13 rooms. Croquet. AE, MC, V.*

$$–$$$　⊡ **Hampton Inn.** You can swim in the enclosed pool and then relax beside the fire in the lobby at this motel off I–26 that's convenient to downtown. Some guest rooms have whirlpool baths. ⊠ *1 Rocky Ridge Rd., 28806,* ☎ *704/667–2022 or 800/426–7866, FAX 704/665–9680. 121 rooms. Indoor pool, sauna, exercise room, airport shuttle. AE, D, DC, MC, V.*

Nightlife and the Arts

One of the best nightspots in Asheville is **Gatsby's** (⊠ 13 W. Walnut St., ☎ 704/254–4248), a cornerstone of the revitalized downtown. World-class acts range from blues to alternative rock and attract college students, professionals, and frequently, celebrities. Next door to the historic Kress building is **31 Patton** (⊠ 31 Patton Ave., ☎ 704/285–0949), where live alternative rock is offered.

Outdoor Activities and Sports

For other activities, *see* The Mountains A to Z, *below.*

GOLF

Colony Lake Lure Golf Resort (✉ 201 Blvd. of the Mountains, Lake Lure, ☎ 704/625–2888), 5 mi from Asheville, has two 18-hole courses known for their beauty. **Etowah Valley Country Club and Golf Lodge** (✉ U.S. 64, Etowah, ☎ 704/891–7141 or 800/451–8174), about 20 mi from Asheville, has three very different nine-hole courses with good package deals. **Grove Park Inn** (✉ 290 Macon Ave., ☎ 704/252–2711 or 800/438–5800) has a beautiful 18-hole course.

HORSEBACK RIDING

Trail rides are offered by several Asheville area stables, including Pisgah View Ranch (✉ Rte. 1, Candler 28715, ☎ 704/667–9100) and Cataloochee Ranch (✉ Rte. 1, Box 500, Maggie Valley 28751, ☎ 704/926–1401 or 800/868–1401).

LLAMA TREKS

You can trek with llamas carrying your pack into the Pisgah National Forest on day and overnight trips with **Windsong Llama Treks, Ltd.** (✉ 120 Ferguson Ridge Rd., Clyde, ☎ 704/627–6111). **Avalon Llama Trek** (✉ 310 Wilson Cove Rd., Swannanoa, ☎ 704/298–5637) leads trips on the lush trails of the Pisgah National Forest.

ROCK CLIMBING

Climbmax (✉ 43 Wall St., ☎ 704/252–9996) is an indoor sport-climbing center for beginners to pros that provides instruction and once-a-month guided trips, known as "Night in the Gym, Day on the Rocks." Things like backpacks and fanny packs are also sold here, but no climbing equipment per se.

SKIING

Ski resorts in the Asheville area include **Cataloochee** (✉ Rte. 1, Box 500, Maggie Valley 28751, ☎ 704/926–0285 or 800/768–0285), **Fairfield–Sapphire Valley** (✉ 4000 U.S. 64W, Sapphire Valley 28774, ☎ 704/743–3441 or 800/533–8268), and **Wolf Laurel** (✉ Rte. 3, Mars Hill 28754, ☎ 704/689–4111).

Shopping

Grovewood Gallery at the Homespun Shops (✉ 111 Grovewood Rd., ☎ 704/253–7651), adjacent to the Grove Park Inn and established by Mrs. George Vanderbilt, sells woven goods, such as blankets, shawls, and baskets, made on the premises. It's closed Sundays from November to May.

Biltmore Village (✉ Hendersonville Rd., ☎ 704/274–5570) on the Biltmore Estate is a cluster of specialty shops, restaurants, galleries, and hotels built along cobblestone sidewalks. Here, where there's a decided turn-of-the-century, English hamlet feel, everything from children's books to music, antiques, one-of-a-kind imports, and wearable art can be found.

Side Trips from Asheville

Within 40 mi of Asheville you can explore a number of towns with attractions from parks to historic sites. Some are resort destinations in themselves.

WEAVERVILLE

18 mi north of Asheville via U.S. 23/19.

This town's state historic site, the **Zebulon B. Vance Birthplace,** is a reconstructed two-story log cabin and several outbuildings. This is where Vance, North Carolina's Confederate governor, grew up. Crafts and chores typical of his period are often demonstrated. Picnic facilities are available. An entrance to the Blue Ridge Parkway is nearby. ✉ *911*

Reems Creek Rd. (Rte. 1103), ☎ *704/645–6706.* ☒ *Free.* ⊙ *Apr.–Oct., Mon.–Sat. 9–5, Sun. 1–5; Nov.–Mar., Tues.–Sat. 10–4, Sun. 1–4.*

HOT SPRINGS
30 mi northwest of Asheville via U.S. 23/19 and 25/70 past Marshall.

This picturesque village is a way station for hikers on the Appalachian Trail. The **Hot Springs Spa**'s mineral springs maintain a natural 100°F temperature year-round and have, since the turn of the century, provided relief for visitors suffering a variety of ailments, including rheumatism and arthritis. ☒ *1 Bridge St.,* ☎ *704/622–7676.* ☒ *$12–$30 per hr, depending on time of day and number of people in tub.* ⊙ *Year-round 9 AM–11 PM.*

BREVARD
40 mi southwest of Asheville on NC 280.

Plenty of nearby waterfalls and the Brevard Music Center (☎ 704/884–2011), which has a seven-week music festival each summer, are draws in this resort town. Nearby Pisgah National Forest has the **Cradle of Forestry in America National Historic Site** (☒ 1001 Pisgah Hwy., ☎ 704/884–5823).

☺ At **Sliding Rock** in summer, you can skid 150 ft on a natural water slide. Wear old jeans and tennis shoes, and bring a towel. ☒ *Pisgah National Forest, north of Brevard, off U.S. 276,* ☎ *704/877–3265.* ☒ *Free.* ⊙ *Daily.*

CHIMNEY ROCK
25 mi southeast of Asheville on U.S. 64/74–A.

You're deep in the Blue Ridge Mountains in Chimney Rock. At **Chimney Rock Park** you can ride an elevator up through a 26-story shaft of rock for a staggering view of Hickory Nut Gorge and the surrounding mountains. Trails, open year-round, lead to 400-ft Hickory Nut Falls, where *The Last of the Mohicans* was filmed. ☒ *U.S. 64/74A,* ☎ *704/625–9611 or 800/277–9611.* ☒ *$6.* ⊙ *Year-round, daily 8:30–4:30.*

FLAT ROCK
21 mi southwest of Chimney Rock, 25 mi south of Asheville via I–26.

Flat Rock has been a summer resort since the mid-19th century. The
★ **Carl Sandburg Home National Historic Site** is the spot to which the poet and Lincoln biographer Carl Sandburg moved with his wife, Lilian, in 1945. Guided tours of their house, Connemara, where Sandburg's papers still lie scattered on his desk, are given by the National Park Service. In summer, *The World of Carl Sandburg* and *Rootabaga Stories* are presented at the amphitheater. ☒ *928 Little River Rd.,* ☎ *704/693–4178.* ☒ *$2.* ⊙ *Daily 9–5.*

The **Flat Rock Playhouse** (☒ Greenville Hwy., ☎ 704/693–0731) has a high reputation for summer stock theater. The season usually runs about late May to mid-October.

SALUDA
7 mi south of Flat Rock via I–26.

At the top of the steepest railroad grade east of the Rockies, this salubrious town along the tracks is strung with antiques and crafts shops in 19th-century brick buildings. The surrounding area offers apple orchards, woods, and waterfalls.

Blue Ridge Parkway

Entrance 2 mi east of Asheville, off I–40.

★ The beautiful **Blue Ridge Parkway** (✉ Superintendent, Blue Ridge Pkwy., 400 BB&T Bldg., 1 Pack Sq., Asheville 28801, ☎ 704/298–0398) gently winds through mountains and meadows and crosses mountain streams for over 450 mi on its way from Cherokee, North Carolina, to Waynesboro, Virginia. This is the most scenic route from Asheville to Boone/Blowing Rock. The parkway is generally open year-round but often closes during inclement weather. Maps and information are available at visitor centers along the highway. Mile markers (MM) identify points of interest and indicate the distance from the parkway's starting point in Virginia.

The **Folk Art Center** sells authentic mountain crafts made by members of the Southern Highland Handicraft Guild. ✉ *MM 382 on Blue Ridge Pkwy.,* ☎ *704/298–7928.* ✪ *Daily.*

☾ Tour an underground mine or dig for gems of your own at **Emerald Village.** ✉ *McKinney Mine Rd. at Blue Ridge Pkwy., MM 334,* ☎ *704/ 765–6463.* ▦ *Museum $3.50, plus cost of gem bucket chosen ($3– $100). A $50 bucket guarantees you a stone, which will be cut free of charge; $100 guarantees two.* ✪ *June–Labor Day, daily 9–6, May and Sept.–Oct., daily 9–5.*

Linville Caverns are the only caverns in the Carolinas. North of Asheville, exit the parkway at mile marker 317.4 and turn left onto U.S. 221. The caverns go 2,000 ft underground and have a year-round temperature of 51°F. ✉ *U.S. 221 between Linville and Marion,* ☎ *704/756– 4171.* ▦ *$4.* ✪ *June–Labor Day, daily 9–6; Apr.–May and Sept.–Oct., daily 9–5; Nov. and Mar., daily 9–4:30; Dec.–Feb., weekends only 9–4:30.*

Linville Falls (MM 316.3) is one of North Carolina's most frequently photographed waterfalls. An easy trail winds through evergreens and rhododendrons to overlooks with views of the series of cascades tumbling into Linville Gorge. There's also a visitor center, a campground, and a picnic area.

Just off the parkway, on U.S. 221, at mile marker 305, is **Grandfather Mountain,** which soars 6,000 ft and is famous for its Mile-High Swinging Bridge. Sweaty-palmed visitors cross the 228-ft-long bridge that sways over a 1,000-ft drop into the Linville Valley. A natural history museum has exhibits on native minerals, flora and fauna, and pioneer life. The annual **Singing on the Mountain** in June is an opportunity to hear old-time gospel music and preaching, and the **Highland Games in July** bring together Scottish clans from all over North America for athletic events and Highland dancing. There's also hiking, picnicking, and an environmental habitat. ✉ *Blue Ridge Pkwy. and U.S. 221, Linville,* ☎ *704/733–4337.* ▦ *$9.* ✪ *Apr.–mid-Nov., daily 8–dusk; mid-Nov.–Mar., daily 8–5, weather permitting.*

Parks along the parkway include **Julian Price Park** (MM 298–295.1), which offers hiking, canoeing on a mountain lake, trout fishing, and camping. The **Moses H. Cone Park** (MM 292.7–295) has a turn-of-the-century manor house (home of a textile magnate) that's now the **Parkway Craft Center.** The center sells fine work by area craftspeople.

Dining and Lodging

$$$$ ✕▦ **Eseeola Lodge and Restaurant.** Built in the 1880s, this rustic lake-
★ side lodge with attractive grounds is the cornerstone of Linville. Rich chestnut paneling and stonework grace the interior rooms. Entrées at

the restaurant may include free-range beef and rainbow trout. ⊠ *U.S. 221, Linville 28646,* ☎ *704/733–4311,* FAX *704/733–3227. 28 rooms. Restaurant, lounge, pool, 18-hole golf course, 8 tennis courts, boating, fishing. MC, V. Closed Labor Day–May.*

$$$-$$$$ ✕🏨 **Switzerland Inn and Chalet Restaurant.** This Swiss-style lodge overlooking the mountains offers lodge rooms, parlor-bedroom suites, and a lovely honeymoon cottage with a fireplace. A full breakfast is included in the room rate. The prime rib and seafood buffet served each Friday night are a big draw, but note that the restaurant doesn't accept reservations. ⊠ *MM 334, off Blue Ridge Pkwy., Box 399, Little Switzerland 28749,* ☎ *704/765–2153 or 800/654–4026,* FAX *704/765–0049. 66 rooms. Restaurant, pool, lounge, 2 tennis courts, shuffleboard. AE, D, MC, V. Closed Nov.–Apr.*

Outdoor Activities and Sports

HIKING

More than 100 trails lead off the Blue Ridge Parkway, from easy strolls to strenuous hikes. For more information on parkway trails, contact the Blue Ridge Parkway (☞ *above*). Another good source is *Walking the Blue Ridge: a Guide to the Trails of the Blue Ridge Parkway* by Leonard Adkins, available at most parkway visitor center gift shops. The **Bluff Mountain Trail** at Doughton Park (MM 238.5) is a moderately strenuous 7½-mi trail winding through forests, pastures, and valleys, and along the mountainside. Moses H. Cone Park's (MM 292.7) **Figure 8 Trail** is an easy and beautiful trail that the Cone family designed specifically for their morning walks. The half-mile loop winds through a tunnel of rhododendron and a hardwood forest. Those who tackle the half-mile, strenuous **Waterrock Knob Trail** (MM 451.2), near the southern end of the parkway, will be rewarded with spectacular views from the 6,400-ft-high Waterrock Knob summit.

ROCK CLIMBING

One of the most challenging climbs in the country is the **Linville Gorge** (MM 317). Permits are available from the District Forest Ranger's Office in Marion (☎ 704/652–2144) or from the Linville Falls Texaco station on U.S. 221.

SKIING

Cross-country skiing is offered at **Moses H. Cone Park** and at **Linville Falls** on the Blue Ridge Parkway (☎ 704/295–7591), and at **Roan Mountain** (☎ 615/772–3303). Tours and equipment are available from **High Country Ski Shop** in Pineola (☎ 704/733–2008).

Blowing Rock

86 mi northeast of Asheville, 93 mi west of Winston-Salem.

Blowing Rock, a tourist mecca since the 1880s, has retained the flavor of a quiet mountain village. Only a few hundred people are permanent residents, but the population swells each summer. To get here from the Blue Ridge Parkway, take U.S. 221/321 just north of the entrance to Moses H. Cone Park. The **Blowing Rock,** considered the state's oldest tourist attraction, looms 4,000 ft over the Johns River Gorge. If you throw your hat over the sheer precipice, it may come back to you, should the wind gods be playful. The story goes that a Cherokee man and a Chickasaw maiden fell in love. Torn between his tribe and his love, he jumped from the cliff, but she prayed to the Great Spirit and he was blown safely back to her. It's a gimmick, but the view from the observation tower is nice, and there's a garden landscaped with mountain laurel, rhododendron, and other native plants. ⊠ *Off U.S. 321,* ☎ *704/295–7111.* 🎫 *$4.* ☺ *Summer 8–8, winter 10–5.*

☺ The **Tweetsie Railroad** is a popular Wild West theme park where you can ride a train beset by train robbers. The park also has a petting zoo, country fair May–October, rides, gold panning, a saloon show, and concessions. ⊠ *U.S. 321/221,* ☎ *704/264–9061 or 800/526–5740.* ☞ *$14.95.* ☼ *Mid-May–Oct., daily 9–6.*

Lodging

$$$–$$$$ ⊞ **Chetola Resort.** This small resort on 70 acres grew out of a turn-of-the-century stone-and-wood lodge that overlooks Chetola Lake. The original building now houses the resort's restaurant and meeting rooms and is adjacent to the 1988 lodge. The best rooms have balconies facing the lake, and the suites are equipped with whirlpool baths. The property adjoins Moses H. Cone Park, with hiking trails and riding facilities. ⊠ *N. Main St., Box 17, 28605,* ☎ *704/295–5500 or 800/243–8652,* FAX *704/295–5529. 37 rooms, 5 suites, 85 condominiums. Restaurant, indoor pool, hot tub, sauna, 6 tennis courts, exercise room, hiking, racquetball, boating, meeting rooms. AE, D, MC, V.*

$$$–$$$$ ⊞ **Maple Lodge Bed & Breakfast.** Just off Main Street, with its shops and restaurants, this 1946 inn has pine paneling in the foyer and twin parlors and pine ceilings and woodwork throughout. Some rooms are small, but most can hold a queen-size bed, antique dresser, table, and chair comfortably. The full breakfast, served in an enclosed porch, includes delicious homemade breads and muffins. ⊠ *15 Sunset Dr., 28605,* ☎ *704/295–3331. 10 rooms, 1 suite. Fans. AE, D, MC, V.*

Outdoor Activities and Sports

HORSEBACK RIDING

In the Blowing Rock area, trail rides are offered by **Blowing Rock Stables** (⊠ U.S. 221, Blowing Rock, ☎ 704/295–7847) and **Elk Creek Stables** (⊠ NC 268, Ferguson, ☎ 910/973–8635).

SKIING

There's downhill skiing at **Appalachian Ski Mountain** (⊠ 940 Ski Mountain Rd., ☎ 704/295–7828 or 800/322–2372).

Shopping

Goodwin Weavers (⊠ Off U.S. 321 Bypass, ☎ 704/295–3394) sells bedspreads, afghans, and other woven goods, as well as home furnishings designed by North Carolina artist Bob Timberlake.

Bolick Pottery (⊠ Off U.S. 321, NC 8, Lenoir, ☎ 704/295–3862), 20 mi southeast of Blowing Rock, sells mountain crafts and pottery, handcrafted on the spot by Glenn and Lula Bolick.

Boone

8 mi north of Blowing Rock.

Boone, named for frontiersman Daniel Boone, is a city of several thousand residents at the convergence of three major highways—U.S. 321, U.S. 421, and NC 105. You'll find mountain crafts in stores and at craft fairs here. **Old Boone Mercantile** (⊠ 104 E. King St., ☎ 704/262–0000) is a classic general store.

Horn in the West, a project of the Southern Highlands Historical Association, is an outdoor drama that traces the story of Daniel Boone's life. ⊠ *Amphitheater off U.S. 321,* ☎ *704/264–2120.* ☞ *$9.* ☼ *Performances nightly at 8:30, except Mon. mid-June–mid-Aug.*

Boone's **Appalachian Cultural Museum** showcases the successes of such mountain residents as stock-car racer Junior Johnson and country singers Lula Belle and Scotty Wiseman, and exhibits a vast collection of antique quilts, fiddles, and handcrafted furniture. ⊠ *University*

Hall near Greene's Motel, U.S. 321, ☎ 704/262–3117. ☜ $2. ☉ Tues.– Sat. 10–5, Sun. 1–5.

Dining and Lodging

$$ ✕ **Mike's Inland Seafood.** Calabash-style (lightly battered and fried) or broiled, the seafood here couldn't taste better if it were served at the ocean. There's a branch in Banner Elk. ⊠ *U.S. 321,* ☎ *704/262– 5605. AE, DC, MC, V. Closed Mon.*

$$$$ ▥ **Hound Ears Club.** This alpine inn, overlooking Grandfather Mountain and a lush golf course, offers comfortable, well-kept rooms dressed in Waverly print fabrics. From April through October, the room rate for special packages includes breakfast and dinner. ⊠ *Off NC 105, 6 mi from Boone; Box 188, 28605,* ☎ *704/963–4321,* FAX *704/963–8030. 29 rooms. Restaurant, pool, 18-hole golf course, tennis court. AE, MC, V.*

$$–$$$ ▥ **Smoketree Lodge.** Grand views of Grandfather Mountain, indoor swimming, and an in-house art gallery showing the work of local artists are highlights of this mountain inn near the ski slopes. Efficiencies are fully equipped. ⊠ *NC 105, Box 3407, 28607,* ☎ *704/963–6505; 800/843–5581 in NC;* FAX *704/963–7815. 46 units. Picnic area, indoor pool, hot tub, sauna, exercise room, recreation room, laundry. AE, D, MC, V.*

$$ ▥ **High Country Inn.** A honeymoon destination that also draws skiers, golfers, and other groups interested in the discount packages, the inn, made of native stone and surrounded by ponds, has accommodations that range from luxurious to comfortable. **Geno's,** a popular sports bar, and **The Waterwheel,** a restaurant specializing in authentic German cuisine, are here. ⊠ *1785 NC 105 S, Box 1339, 28607,* ☎ *704/264–1000 or 800/334–5605,* FAX *704/262–0073. 120 rooms. Restaurant, indoor-outdoor pool, hot tub, sauna, exercise room, meeting rooms. AE, D, MC, V.*

Outdoor Activities and Sports

CANOEING AND WHITEWATER RAFTING

Near Boone, the wild and scenic New River (Class I and II) provides hours of excitement, as do the Nolichucky, Watauga, Wilson Creek, and Toe rivers. One outfitter is **Wahoo's Adventures** (☎ 704/262–5774 or 800/444–7238).

GOLF

Western North Carolina offers many challenging courses. North Carolina High Country Host (☞ Visitor Information *in* the Mountains A to Z, *below*) has information on public courses in Boone, Seven Devils, Newland, and West Jefferson.

Boone Golf Club (⊠ Fairway Dr., ☎ 704/264–8760) is a good 18-hole course for the whole family. **Hound Ears Club** (⊠ NC 105, ☎ 704/963– 4312) has an 18-hole course with great mountain views. **Linville Golf Club** (⊠ Linville, ☎ 704/733–4363), 17 mi from Boone, has a highly rated Donald Ross course.

OFF THE BEATEN PATH

BLUE RIDGE MOUNTAIN FRESCOES – About 45 mi northeast of Boone in Ashe Country, past Blue Ridge Parkway mile marker 258.6, are the Blue Ridge Mountain Frescoes. North Carolina artist Ben Long painted four big-as-life frescoes in two abandoned churches here in the '70s. *The Last Supper* (measuring 17 × 19½ ft) is in the Glendale Springs Holy Trinity Church. The others are in St. Mary's Episcopal Church at Beaver Creek, including *Mary, Great with Child.* Signs from the parkway lead to the churches. ☎ *910/982–3076.* 🎫 *Free.* ☉ *Daily 24 hrs; staffed 10–4. Guide service available by prior arrangement.*

Valle Crucis

5 mi south of Boone.

This tiny mountain town has the state's first rural historic district; vintage stores line the downtown streets. You'll find everything from ribbons and calico to brogans and overalls in the **Mast General Store** (⊠ NC 194, ☎ 704/963–6511). Built in 1882, the store has plank floors worn to a soft sheen and a potbellied stove.

Lodging

$$$$ 🏨 **Mast Farm Inn.** You can turn back the clock and still enjoy modern amenities at this charming pastoral inn. Guests have a choice of rooms in the farmhouse or in the log outbuildings. Breakfast and dinner are included in the rate. ⊠ *Box 704, 28691,* ☎ *704/963–5857,* 𝔽𝔸𝕏 *704/ 963–6404. 13 rooms, 11 with bath. MC, V. Closed early Mar.–late Apr., Dec., and weekdays in Nov.*

Banner Elk

6 mi southwest of Valle Crucis, 11 mi southwest of Boone.

Banner Elk is a popular ski resort town surrounded by the lofty peaks of Grandfather, Hanging Rock, Beech, and Sugar mountains.

Dining and Lodging

$$$ ✕ **Stonewalls.** This contemporary rustic restaurant enjoys one of the best views of Beech Mountain. Fare includes steak, prime rib, fresh seafood, chicken, and homemade desserts. ⊠ *NC 194,* ☎ *704/898– 5550. Reservations not accepted. AE, D, MC, V. No lunch.*

$$$ 🏨 **Beech Alpen Inn.** You have a view of the slopes or the Blue Ridge Mountains at this friendly, rustic country inn, and some rooms have fireplaces and balconies. The restaurant here is open for dinner only. A Continental breakfast is included in the rate. ⊠ *700 Beech Mountain Pkwy., 28604,* ☎ *704/387–2252. 25 rooms. Restaurant. AE, MC, V.*

Outdoor Activities and Sports

CANOEING AND WHITE-WATER RAFTING

The many rivers in the Banner Elk area provide a variety of possibilities. Outfitters include **Edge of the World Outfitters** (⊠ NC 184, Box 1137, Banner Elk 28604, ☎ 704/898–9550 or 800/789–3343).

HORSEBACK RIDING

Trail rides are offered by **Banner Elk Riding Stables** (⊠ NC 184, ☎ 704/898–5424).

SKIING

The Banner Elk area offers downhill skiing at **Ski Beech** (⊠ NC 184, Beech Mountain, ☎ 704/387–2011 or 800/438–2093), **Sugar Mountain** (⊠ Off NC 184, Banner Elk, ☎ 704/898–4521), and **Hawksnest Golf and Ski Resort** (⊠ 1800 Skyland Dr., Seven Devils, ☎ 704/963– 6561 or 800/822–4295). For ski conditions, call 800/962–2322.

The Mountains A to Z

Arriving, Departing, and Getting Around

BY BUS

Greyhound Lines (✉ 2 Tunnel Rd., ☎ 704/253–5353 or 800/231–2222) serves Asheville.

BY CAR

I–40 runs east and west through Asheville. I–26 runs from Charleston, South Carolina, to Asheville. I–240 forms a perimeter around the city. U.S. 23–19A is a major north and west route. The Blue Ridge Parkway runs northeast from Great Smoky Mountains National Park to Shenandoah National Park in Virginia, passing Cherokee, Asheville, and the High Country. U.S. 221 runs north from Little Switzerland to the Virginia border through Blowing Rock and Boone and intersects I–40 at Marion. U.S. 321 intersects I–40 at Hickory and heads to Blowing Rock/Boone.

BY PLANE

Asheville Regional Airport (☎ 704/684–2226) is served by Midway Connections, Atlantic Southeast Airlines, ComAir, and US Airways. US Airways Express (☎ 800/428–4322) serves the **Hickory Airport,** about 40 mi from Blowing Rock.

Contacts and Resources

EMERGENCIES

Dial 911 for **police** and **ambulance** everywhere but the Cherokee Reservation, where the police can be reached at 704/497–4131 and the EMS service at 704/497–6402. Head to **Mission/St. Joseph's Hospital** (✉ 509 Biltmore Ave., Asheville, ☎ 704/255–4000), **Watauga Medical Center** (✉ 336 Deerfield Rd., Boone, ☎ 704/262–4100), **Cannon Memorial Hospital** (✉ 805 Shawneehaw Ave., Banner Elk, ☎ 704/898–5111), or **Blowing Rock Hospital** (✉ 416 Chestnut Dr., Blowing Rock, ☎ 704/295–3136) for emergency medical attention.

GUIDED TOURS

A brochure entitled **"The Asheville Urban Trail"** available at the Downtown Visitor's Center (✉ 151 Hollywood St., ☎ 704/258–6101) provides a self-guided walking tour.

OUTDOOR ACTIVITIES AND SPORTS

For **canoeing** and **whitewater rafting** in the Asheville area, the Chattooga, Nolichucky, French Broad, Nantahala, Ocoee, and Green rivers offer Class I–V rapids. One of the largest outfitters is **Nantahala Outdoor Center** (✉ 13077 U.S. 19W, Bryson City, ☎ 704/488–2175 or 800/232–7238).

Western North Carolina offers many challenging **golf** courses. For a complete listing of public courses in Asheville, Black Mountain, Brevard, Hendersonville, Lake Lure, Old Fort, and Waynesville, contact Asheville's Travel and Tourism Office (☞ Visitor Information, *below*).

If you're into serious **hiking,** you can explore the **Appalachian Trail,** which runs along the crest of the Appalachian Mountains at the North Carolina–Tennessee border. You can pick it up at several points, including at the Newfound Gap Parking Area in Great Smoky Mountains National Park (☎ 615/436–5615) and at Grandfather Mountain (☎ 704/733–4337), where you can get trail maps.

RADIO STATIONS

AM: WSKY 1230, talk; WZQR 1350, country. **FM:** WCQS 88.1, National Public Radio; WSPA 98.9, easy listening; WKSF 99.9, country; WMIT 106.9, Christian.

The **Cherokee Visitor Center** (✉ U.S. 441 Business, ☎ 704/497–9195 or 800/438–1601) provides information on the reservation. In Asheville, the **Visitor Information Center** (✉ 151 Haywood St., 28801, ☎ 704/258–6100), the **Asheville Travel and Tourism Office** (✉ Box 1010, 28802, ☎ 800/257–1300), and the **Downtown Welcome Center** (✉ 14 Battery Park, ☎ 704/255–1093) can answer questions and provide maps. **North Carolina High Country Host** (✉ 1701 Blowing Rock Rd., Boone 28607, ☎ 704/264–1299 or 800/438–7500) is a complete information center for the three High Country counties—Watauga, Ashe, and Avery.

NORTH CAROLINA A TO Z

Arriving and Departing

By Bus

Greyhound Lines (☎ 800/231–2222) links the cities of North Carolina with major cities in the southeastern United States.

By Car

I–40 traverses the state from Asheville in the west to Wilmington in the east. I–85 passes through the Triangle, the Triad, and Charlotte as it crosses from northeast to southwest. I–77 passes through the western part of the state from Virginia through Charlotte to South Carolina, and I–95 carries north-south traffic in the eastern part of the state.

By Plane

Among the major airports in the state are **Charlotte-Douglas International Airport** (☎ 704/359–4013), the **Piedmont Triad International Airport** (☎ 336/665–5666), and the **Raleigh-Durham International Airport** (☎ 919/840–2123).

By Train

Amtrak (☎ 800/872–7245) offers daily service from major cities on the eastern seaboard to the state's main population centers, including Charlotte, Greensboro, Raleigh, Durham, and Southern Pines.

Getting Around

By Bicycle

North Carolina has more than 3,000 mi of mapped and signed bicycle routes, many on scenic country roads. For maps and information, contact the **Office of Bicycle and Pedestrian Information** (✉ Box 25201, Raleigh 27611, ☎ 919/733–2804).

By Bus

Greyhound Trailways System (☎ 800/231–2222) links cities and towns throughout the state.

By Car

The speed limit on interstates varies with location; it's generally 65 or 70 mph. Right turns on red are permitted unless otherwise indicated. The official State Transportation Map may be ordered from the **North Carolina Department of Transportation** (✉ Public Affairs Division, Box 25201, Raleigh 27611, ☎ 919/733–7600; 800/847–4862 outside NC).

By Ferry

Ferries connect coastal communities. Routes and schedules are printed on the official North Carolina Transportation Map (☞ By Car, *above*), or phone 800/293–3779.

By Train
Amtrak (☎ 800/872–7245) offers daily service between many cities and towns.

Contacts and Resources

Emergencies
In almost all cities and towns dial 911 for police or ambulance in an emergency. Most hospital emergency rooms are open 24 hours a day. Smaller ones are often connected by air evacuation systems to major trauma centers.

Fishing
A mandatory state license can be bought at local bait and tackle shops or over the phone (with a credit card) from the **North Carolina Wildlife Commission** (☎ 919/715–4091).

Telephones
At press time several area code changes in North Carolina were announced.

In March 1998, some towns in eastern North Carolina, including Rocky Mount, Wilson, Greenville, Kinston, New Bern, Roanoke Rapids, Elizabeth City, and Manteo, will have a new area code, 252. Calls to the old 919 code will go through until September 1998.

In June 1998, a new 828 area code for part of western North Carolina will be used in Asheville, Cherokee, Hickory, Boone, and points west. Calls to the old 704 code will go through until October 1998.

Visitor Information
The **North Carolina Department of Commerce, Travel and Tourism Division** (✉ 301 N. Wilmington St., Raleigh 27601, ☎ 919/733–4171 or 800/847–4862) offers information packets as well as an information line. Operators can answer questions about everything from beaches to snow conditions.

7 South Carolina

South Carolina's scenic Lowcountry shoreline is punctuated by the lively port city of Charleston, decked out with elegant homes and fine museums, and the recreational resorts of Myrtle Beach and Hilton Head at each end of the coast. Columbia, the state capital, is set in the fertile interior of the state, which stretches toward the Blue Ridge Mountains. Also to the west are the rolling fields of Thoroughbred Country. Upcountry South Carolina, at the northwestern tip of the state, is noted for incredible mountain scenery and white-water rafting.

FROM ITS LOWCOUNTRY SHORELINE, with wide sand
beaches, spacious bays, and forests of palmettos and
moss-draped live oaks, South Carolina extends into
an undulating interior region rich with fertile farmlands, then reaches
toward the Blue Ridge Mountains, whose foothills are studded with
scenic lakes, forests, and wilderness hideaways. What this smallest of
Southern states lacks in land area it makes up for in diversity and enthusiasm. People here like to celebrate. Every month of the year there's
a local festival that turns on regional pride, feting critters like jump-
ing frogs, edibles like peaches and watermelons, or such rarefied delicacies as okra and chitlins.

Updated by
Mary Sue
Lawrence

The historic port city of Charleston, lovingly preserved, links past
with present. Many of its treasured double-galleried antebellum homes
are now authentically furnished house museums. Culturally vibrant,
the city nurtures theater, dance, music, and visual arts, showcased
each spring during the internationally acclaimed Spoleto Festival USA.

Myrtle Beach is the glitzy jewel of the Grand Strand, a 60-mi stretch
of wide white-sand beaches and recreational activities, especially golf,
a top attraction throughout the state. To the south, tasteful, low-key
Hilton Head—a sea island tucked between the Intracoastal Waterway
and the ocean and divided into several sophisticated, self-contained resorts—also offers beautiful beaches and wonderful golf and tennis.
Nearby is the port city of Beaufort, where it's rewarding simply to wander the lovely streets dotted with preserved 18th-century homes.

Columbia, the state capital, is a busy and historic city blessed by three
rushing rivers. Besides museums and a good minor-league baseball team,
the city has one of the country's top zoos and a riverside botanical garden. Nearby lakes and state parks provide abundant outdoor recreation and first-rate fishing, and the Congaree Swamp National
Monument has the oldest and largest trees east of the Mississippi.

Thoroughbred Country, centered around the town of Aiken, is a peaceful area of rolling pastures where top racehorses are trained. Many of
its magnificent mansions were built by wealthy Northerners who win-
tered here at the turn of the century. Upcountry South Carolina, at the
northwestern tip of the state, is less visited than the rest of the state
but well repays time spent here with dramatic mountain scenery, excellent hiking, and challenging white-water rafting.

Since 1670, when the British established at Charleston the first permanent European settlement in the New World, the Palmetto State has
enjoyed periods of great prosperity and endured eras of dismal depression. Its vibrant past is preserved in cherished traditions and an
enduring belief in family, which give resonance to the optimism and
vitality of today's South Carolina.

Pleasures and Pastimes

Beaches

South Carolina's mild climate makes the surf enjoyable from April
through October. The beaches are expanses of white sand—some
serene and secluded, others bustling and lined with high-rises. You can
choose the high-voltage action at busy Myrtle Beach or the more low-
key scene on the resort island of Hilton Head, or just stroll the sands
at Huntington Beach State Park.

Dining

From dishes marinated in tradition to the creatively contemporary, South Carolinians love to cook and share good food. Lowcountry specialties include she-crab soup, stuffed oysters, and infinite variations on pecan pie. Seafood—often the fresh catch of the day—is likely to be traditionally prepared on the Grand Strand and gussied up on Hilton Head. Elsewhere in the state, try barbecue and look for a variety of cuisine, from cosmopolitan to country cookery. And don't write off grits until you've tasted them laced with cheese, topped with *tasso* (spiced ham) gravy, or folded into a veal or quail entrée.

CATEGORY	COST*
$$$$	over $40
$$$	$30–$40
$$	$20–$30
$	under $20

per person for a three-course meal, excluding drinks, service, and 5% tax

Gardens

Gardening devotees can and do build vacations around South Carolina gardens, where camellias, azaleas, other flowering shrubs, and blooming trees abound. Along the coast are some of the nation's most famous, including Middleton Place, with the oldest landscaped garden in America; Cypress Gardens, where cypress trees tower in dark waters with azaleas on the banks; and Brookgreen Gardens, with a superb outdoor sculpture collection set amid giant oaks and colorful flowers. Inland, remarkable gardens planted with roses, iris, or mountain laurel make some small towns a worthwhile side trip. Along the way, in spring, you can see peach orchards in bloom.

Lodging

From predictable, but dependable, chains to luxurious resort hotels and quaint B&Bs, accommodations are available for every budget. Reservations are a must, especially on the coast, and prices do vary with the seasons—in fact, winter rates can be a pleasant surprise. The charms of historic Charleston in particular can be enhanced by a stay at one of its many inns, most in restored structures. Some are reminiscent of European inns; others are tastefully contemporary.

CATEGORY	COST*
$$$$	over $150
$$$	$90–$150
$$	$50–$90
$	under $50

All prices are for a standard double room, excluding 7% tax.

Rivers and Lakes

Rivers and lakes throughout the state afford year-round boating, swimming, fishing, and waterskiing. They are so plentiful in the Upcountry that it is sometimes called South Carolina's Freshwater Coast. Both the Upcountry and the heart of the state have white-water rapids for rafting or kayaking. Canoeing is popular on waters near Columbia. Anglers frequently break records with hauls of largemouth bass, stripers, crappie, and catfish caught in Lakes Marion and Moultrie.

Exploring South Carolina

South Carolina has three basic regions—its 200-mi coastline, its interior heart, and its hilly north country. Charleston and points south are the Lowcountry, distinguished by aristocratic elegance and an accent unlike any other in the South. Because Hilton Head Island in the

South Carolina

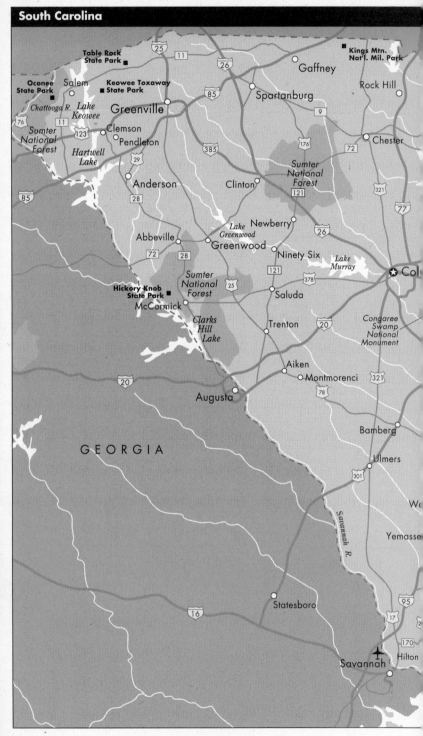

Table Rock
State Park

Kings Mtn.
Nat'l. Mil. Park

25

11

26

Gaffney

Oconee
State Park

Salem

Keowee Toxaway
State Park

85

Spartanburg

Rock Hill

Chattooga R.

Lake
Keowee

Greenville

9

76

11

123

Clemson

Sumter
National
Forest

176

72

Chester

Pendleton

385

321

29

Hartwell
Lake

Sumter
National
Forest

77

85

28

Anderson

Clinton

121

Lake
Greenwood

Newberry

26

Abbeville

Greenwood

72

28

Ninety Six

Lake
Murray

Col

121

Sumter
National
Forest

25

Saluda

378

Congaree
Swamp
National
Monument

Hickory Knob
State Park

McCormick

Clarks
Hill
Lake

Trenton

20

Aiken

Montmorenci

321

20

78

Augusta

Bamberg

GEORGIA

Ulmers

301

Savannah R.

Wo

Yemasse

95

16

Statesboro

17

170

Savannah

Hilton

Charlotte

Monroe

NORTH CAROLINA

Fayetteville

74

601

Pageland

601

Rockingham

95

521

Cheraw

Bennettsville

Lumberton

74

Whiteville

Sandhills State Forest

9

52

701

eree ake

1

Darlington

41

Camden

Florence

Marion

76

20

ia

378

Sumter

Woods Bay State Park

Great Pee Dee R.

95

521

378

Lake City

501

701

9

Calabash

52

Conway

Atlantic Beach

601

Manchester State Forest

Windy Hill Beach

North Myrtle Beach

15

41

Surfside Beach

rangeburg

301

Black R.

521

Murrells Inlet

Myrtle Beach

78

26

Lake Marion

St. Stephen

Andrews

Litchfield Beach

17

Edisto R.

21

Lake Moultrie

45

Santee R.

Pawleys Island

Georgetown

Moncks Corner

17

Hampton Plantation State Park

52

Francis Marion National Forest

McClellanville

oro

ALT 17

Summerville

61

526

Cypress Gardens

41

17/70

ATLANTIC OCEAN

17

Middleton Place

Osborn

Charleston

Mount Pleasant

Isle of Palms

174

James Is.

Johns Is.

Folly Is.

St. Helenas Island

Edisto Island

Kiawah Is.

21

Seabrook Is.

N

fort

170

Hunting Island

Hunting Island State Park

rris and

Bluffton to

Fripp Is.

Daufuskie Is.

0   100 miles

0   150 km

southern part of the state has become world-renowned as a posh resort, it is treated separately here, along with the coastal towns near it. Natives consider the upper coasts part of what they call the Pee Dee (after the Pee Dee River), but the world knows Myrtle Beach and its environs by their more famous other name—the Grand Strand. It refers to the sandy strip of beaches more than 60 mi long.

The Heartland, including the Midlands core of the state, is an eclectic collection of towns and the capital city, Columbia. It also includes Thoroughbred Country, lush pasture for Triple Crown contenders. The Upcountry, noted for mountain scenery, is in the northwest.

Charleston and the Lowcountry appear first here because every traveler to South Carolina should visit that historic city—and most want to. You can travel north from there to the Grand Strand or south to Hilton Head, or west into the Heartland. Thoroughbred Country and the Upcountry follow because they are both easy drives from the center of the state.

Great Itineraries

To enjoy South Carolina to the fullest, you need a week or more to savor the coast and visit briefly inland. But you can have a memorable experience, however brief, by choosing sights that strike your fancy and promising yourself to return another time for more.

IF YOU HAVE 1 DAY

Spend the day in the historic district in ⚁ **Charleston.** Take a carriage ride through the historic district and along the Battery for a look at some of the city's most elegant homes. Next, browse through the shops in the Old City Market area, where most of the carriage tours begin and end. After that, walk south along East Bay Street or any side streets on your way to a couple of the area's museums. You can wander the tree-shaded streets, discovering courtyard gardens and all the little surprises that reveal themselves only to those who seek them out.

IF YOU HAVE 2-3 DAYS

There's plenty to occupy you in and near ⚁ **Charleston.** Expand your itinerary on Day 2 by adding more sights within the historic district (it takes time to tour the many house museums); by browsing in the Shops at Charleston Place or along King Street; by including the Charleston Museum and nearby museums. On the afternoon of Day 2 or Day 3, you could visit Mount Pleasant, with access to Fort Sumter National Monument, nice beaches, and Boone Hall Plantation to the north. Or you can head west of the Ashley River to visit Charles Towne Landing State Park and Magnolia Plantation and Gardens.

IF YOU HAVE 5-6 DAYS

On Day 4, take a leisurely exit from Charleston along SC 61 and see **Drayton Hall** and **Middleton Place** as you make your way inland for a quick visit to ⚁ **Columbia,** with its State House, historic university campus, and zoo and botanical garden. Another choice is to take U.S. 17 north toward the beaches of the **Grand Strand,** where you can stay in busy ⚁ **Myrtle Beach** or more quiet ⚁ **Pawleys Island,** or south toward ⚁ **Beaufort** or ⚁ **Hilton Head Island.** There are beautiful gardens, stately plantations, and fine museums in both directions, or you may choose to go by boat on the ocean or Intracoastal Waterway.

IF YOU HAVE 10 DAYS

Follow the itineraries above and then extend your time in ⚁ **Columbia.** Take a canoe ride on the scenic Saluda River or down the Congaree, and visit Congaree Swamp National Monument. Browse in the South Carolina State Museum and enjoy shopping and dining in the Congaree Vista, a district stretching six blocks from the Congaree River. Take a day trip to historic, horsey **Camden** or **Aiken** to get the flavor of other Heartland towns. On Day 8, head to the Upcountry for magnificent scenery. You can explore ⛰ **Greenville,** perhaps driving north to the Cherokee Foothills Scenic Highway or to Kings Mountain National Military Park, a Revolutionary War site. You might head west and raft on the Chattooga River and spend your last night and day in **Pendleton,** with its historic district and proximity to Clemson and the South Carolina State Botanical Garden.

When to Tour South Carolina

South Carolina is loveliest in spring when azaleas, dogwood, and other flowering trees are in blossom, but flowers brighten every season—even winter, when pansies and camellias thrive. Between mid-March and mid-April, you can catch tours of private mansions in Charleston, and the city is alive with Spoleto events in May and June. Beaufort holds its Water Festival in mid-July. For price breaks on the coast, consider visiting in the off-season, October through February, but remember that some restaurants and a few attractions close around that time, and the water may be cool.

CHARLESTON

At first glimpse, Charleston resembles an 18th-century etching come to life. Its low-profile skyline is punctuated with the spires and steeples of 181 churches, representing 25 denominations—the reason that Charleston, known for religious freedom during its formation, is called the "Holy City." Parts of the city appear frozen in time; block after block of old downtown structures have been preserved and restored for residential and commercial use, and some brick and cobblestone streets remain. Charleston has survived three centuries of epidemics, earthquakes, fires, and hurricanes, and it is today one of the South's loveliest and best-preserved cities. It is not a museum, however: Throughout the year festivals (☞ Festivals *in* Nightlife and the Arts, *below*) add excitement and sophistication.

Besides the historic district, a visit to the city can easily include nearby towns, plantations and outstanding gardens, and historic sites, whether you're exploring Mount Pleasant or the area west of the Ashley River.

The Historic District

In a fairly compact area you'll find churches, museums, and lovely views at every turn. Along the Battery, on the point of a narrow peninsula bounded by the Ashley and Cooper rivers, handsome mansions in the "Charleston style," surrounded by gardens, face the harbor. Their distinctive look is reminiscent of the West Indies. Before coming to the Carolinas in the late 17th century, many early British colonists had first settled on Barbados and other Caribbean islands, where they'd built houses with high ceilings and broad piazzas at each level, to catch the sea breezes. In Charleston, they adapted these designs. One new type—narrow two- to four-story "single houses" built at right angles to the street—emerged partly because buildings were taxed according to frontage length.

Numbers in the text correspond to numbers in the margin and on the Charleston map.

A Good Walk

Before you begin touring, drop by the **Visitor Information Center** ① for an overview of the city and tickets for shuttle services if you want to give your feet a break. Start at the **Charleston Museum** ② across the street, with its large decorative arts collection; then go right on Meeting Street, turning right on Ann Street and walking to Elizabeth Street to the palatial **Aiken–Rhett House** ③. After touring the house, head down Elizabeth Street and turn right on John Street for the **Joseph Manigault Mansion** ④, another impressive house museum dating to the early 1800s. From here, return to Meeting Street, walking south toward Calhoun Street, passing the **Old Citadel Building** ⑤, recently converted into the Embassy Suites. Take a left on Calhoun Street; a half block down is the **Emanuel African Methodist Episcopal Church** ⑥, where Denmark Vesey was a member. From here, you may want to use the shuttle bus DASH to give your feet a rest, or cross the street to Marion Square Mall for a drink and a break.

Retrace your steps on Calhoun Street (passing the Francis Marion Hotel, in the 1920s the highest building in the Carolinas) continuing two blocks west to St. Phillips Street, where you left to end up in the midst of the romantic campus of the **College of Charleston** ⑦, the oldest municipal college in the country. Enter through one of the gated openings on St. Phillips Street for a stroll under the many moss-draped trees. Then head east to King Street, Charleston's main shopping thoroughfare, and turn right; turn left on Hasell Street to see **Congregation Beth Elohim** ⑧, a Greek Revival building. Keep walking down Hasell Street, turning right on Meeting Street and then left down Pinckney Street to the **American Military Museum** ⑨. Two blocks to the south are **Market Hall** ⑩ and the bustling **Old City Market** ⑪. Now is a good time for a carriage ride, many of which leave from here (☞ Contacts and Resources *in* Charleston A to Z, *below*). Across Meeting Street is the classy **Charleston Place** ⑫, with its graceful hotel and cluster of shops. You can browse from one end to the other, exiting on King Street.

Facing you on the opposite corner is the new Saks Fifth Avenue; cross the street and walk a block down Market Street, turning left on quiet Archdale Street to wander through the **St. John's Lutheran Church** ⑬ and the peaceful graveyard of the **Unitarian Church** ⑭. Turn left on Queen Street at the bottom of Archdale and walk two blocks to Meeting Street, where you turn left for the **Gibbes Museum of Art** ⑮, with its spectacular stained-glass dome. Across the street is the **Circular Congregational Church** ⑯. Behind it, on cobblestone Cumberland Street, is the **Old Powder Magazine** ⑰. To the left as you face the building, you'll catch a glimpse of the steeple of **St. Philip's Episcopal Church** ⑱, famous in the city's skyline; it's around the corner on Church Street.

Cross over to picturesque Church Street to the **French Huguenot Church** ⑲ and the **Dock Street Theatre** ⑳ across the street. You might detour here down Queen Street and along Vendue Range to Waterfront Park, to relax in a bench swing overlooking beautiful river views, dramatic fountains, and a fishing pier. Or you can walk south along the park's landscaped garden path to Exchange Street, turning down it to Broad Street and the **Old Exchange Building/Provost Dungeon** ㉑, used to hold prisoners during the American Revolution. Two blocks down Broad Street are the Four Corners of Law, including **City Hall** ㉒, with some historical displays and portraits, and **St. Michael's Episcopal Church** ㉓, the city's oldest surviving church. In the famously affluent neighborhood known as South of Broad are several of the city's lavish house museums: the **Heyward–Washington House** ㉔, a block south of Broad on Church Street; the **Nathaniel Russell House** ㉕ and the **Calhoun Mansion** ㉖, both on Meeting Street; and the **Edmondston–Alston House** ㉗ near the Battery. A park bench in the shade of White Point Gardens, overlooking the Battery, is a splendid, Charleston-style finish.

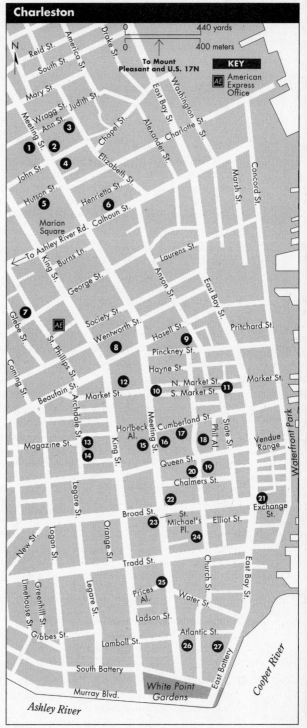

Charleston

TIMING

Plan to spend at least a full day doing the bare bones of this walk. Most of the house museum tours last about 40 minutes, so you might choose two or three that interest you most, or split the walk in half, taking two days to enjoy it fully. If it's high summer, you'll likely be moving with the speed of a Southern drawl, so pace yourself and make use of all those Charleston benches.

Sights to See

❸ Aiken–Rhett House. This stately 1819 mansion, with original wallpaper, paint colors, and some furnishings, was the headquarters of Confederate general P. G. T. Beauregard during his 1864 Civil War defense of Charleston. The house, kitchen, slave quarters, and work yard are maintained much as they were when the original occupants lived here, making this one of the most complete examples of African-American urban life of the period. ⊠ *48 Elizabeth St.,* ☎ *803/723–1159.* ☞ *$6; combination ticket with Nathaniel Russell House (☞ below) $10.* ☉ *Mon.–Sat. 10–5, Sun. 1–5.*

❾ American Military Museum. The museum displays hundreds of uniforms and artifacts from all branches of service, dating from the Revolutionary War. Its collections also include antique toy soldiers, war toys, and miniatures and weaponry. ⊠ *40 Pinckney St.,* ☎ *803/723–9620.* ☞ *$5.* ☉ *Mon.–Sat. 10–6, Sun. 1–6.*

㉖ Calhoun Mansion. Opulent by Charleston standards, this is an interesting example of Victorian taste. Built in 1876, it's notable for ornate plasterwork, fine wood moldings, and a 75-ft domed ceiling. ⊠ *16 Meeting St.,* ☎ *803/722–8205.* ☞ *$10.* ☉ *Feb.–Dec., Wed.–Sun. 10–4.*

★ ❷ Charleston Museum. Housed in a $6 million contemporary complex, this is the oldest city museum in the United States. Founded in 1773, it is especially strong in South Carolina decorative arts. The 500,000 items in the collection—in addition to Charleston silver, fashions, toys, snuff boxes, and the like—include objects relating to natural history, archaeology, and ornithology. The Discover Me Room, designed just for children, has computers and other hands-on exhibits. Two historic homes—the ☞ **Joseph Manigault Mansion** and the ☞ **Heyward–Washington House**—are part of the museum. ⊠ *360 Meeting St.,* ☎ *803/722–2996.* ☞ *$6; combination ticket for museum and houses $15; for 2 sites $10.* ☉ *Mon.–Sat. 9–5, Sun. 1–5.*

⑫ Charleston Place. The city's only world-class hotel, this Orient Express property is flanked by a four-story complex of upscale boutiques and specialty shops (☞ *Shopping, below*). You might peek into the lobby or have cocktails or tea in the intimate Lobby Lounge. The garage and reception area are entered on Hasell Street between Meeting and King streets. ⊠ *130 Market St.,* ☎ *803/722–4900.*

⑯ Circular Congregational Church. The corners of this unusual Romanesque church were rounded off, they say, so the devil would have no place to hide. Simple but pretty, it has a beamed, vaulted ceiling. ⊠ *150 Meeting St.,* ☎ *803/577–6400.* ☉ *Call for tour schedule.*

㉒ City Hall. The intersection of Meeting and Broad streets is known as the Four Corners of Law, representing the laws of nation, state, city, and church. On the northeast corner is graceful City Hall, dating from 1801. The second-floor Council Chamber has interesting historical displays and portraits, including John Trumbull's 1791 satirical portrait of George Washington and Samuel F. B. Morse's likeness of James Monroe. ⊠ *80 Broad St.,* ☎ *803/577–6970 or 803/724–3799.* ☞ *Free.* ☉ *Weekdays 10–5.*

❼ College of Charleston. The lovely, tree-shaded campus of this college, founded in 1770, has a graceful main building, the Randolph House (1828), designed by Philadelphia architect William Strickland. It forms a romantic backdrop for the Cistern, a grassy "stage" where concerts and many activities take place. Within the college, centered at the corner of George and St. Phillips streets, is the **Avery Research Center for African-American History and Culture,** which traces the heritage of Lowcountry African-Americans. ⊠ *Avery Research Center, 125 Bull St.,* ☎ *803/727–2009.* 🖆 *Free.* ☉ *Mon.–Sat. noon–5; mornings by appointment.*

❽ Congregation Beth Elohim. Considered one of the nation's finest examples of Greek Revival architecture, this temple was built in 1840 to replace an earlier one—the birthplace of American Reform Judaism in 1824—that was destroyed by fire. ⊠ *90 Hasell St.,* ☎ *803/723–1090.* ☉ *Weekdays 10–noon.*

NEED A BREAK? On your way to the cluster of sights around Meeting Street, pick up a batch of Charleston's famed benne wafers at **Olde Colony Bakery** (⊠ 280 King St., between Society and Wentworth, ☎ 803/722-2147). *Benne* is an African word that slaves used to describe the sesame seeds on these delicacies.

⓴ Dock Street Theatre. Built on the site of one of the nation's first playhouses, the building combines the reconstructed early Georgian playhouse and the preserved Old Planter's Hotel (circa 1809). The theater, which offers fascinating backstage views, welcomes tours except when technical work for a show is under way. ⊠ *135 Church St.,* ☎ *803/ 720–3968.* 🖆 *Free tours; call ahead for ticket prices and performance times.* ☉ *Weekdays 10–4.*

㉗ Edmondston–Alston House. With commanding views of Charleston Harbor, this imposing home was built in 1825 in the late Federal style and transformed into a Greek Revival structure during the 1840s. It is tastefully furnished with antiques, portraits, Piranesi prints, silver, and fine china. ⊠ *21 E. Battery,* ☎ *803/722–7171.* 🖆 *$7.* ☉ *Tues.–Sat. 10–4:30, Sun.–Mon. 1:30–4:30.*

❻ Emanuel African Methodist Episcopal Church. Home of the South's oldest AME congregation, the church had its beginnings in 1818. It was closed in 1822 when authorities learned that Denmark Vesey had used the sanctuary to plan his slave insurrection, but the church reopened in 1865 at the present site. ⊠ *110 Calhoun St.,* ☎ *803/722– 2561.* ☉ *Daily 9–4; call ahead for tour.*

⓲ French Protestant (Huguenot) Church. This church is the only one in the country still using the original Huguenot liturgy, which can be heard in a special service held each spring. ⊠ *110 Church St.,* ☎ *803/722– 4385.* 🖆 *Donations welcome.* ☉ *Weekdays 10–12:30 and 2–4.*

NEED A BREAK? For a great view of the harbor, the **Vendue Inn** (☞ Lodging, *below*) on Vendue Range, at the end of Queen Street, offers lunch, drinks, and appetizers alfresco on its one-of-a-kind Rooftop Lounge.

⓯ Gibbes Museum of Art. The collections of American art include notable 18th- and 19th-century portraits of Carolinians and an outstanding group of more than 400 miniature portraits. Don't miss the miniature rooms—intricately detailed with fabrics and furnishings and nicely displayed in shadow boxes inset in dark-paneled walls—or the Tiffany-style stained-glass dome in the rotunda. ⊠ *135 Meeting St.,* ☎ *803/ 722–2706.* ☞ *$5.* ⊙ *Tues.–Sat. 10–5, Sun.–Mon. 1–5.*

㉔ Heyward–Washington House. Built in 1772 by rice king Daniel Heyward, this home was the backdrop for Dubose Heyward's book *Porgy,* also beloved as the folk opera *Porgy and Bess.* The neighborhood, known as Cabbage Row, is central to Charleston's African-American history. President George Washington stayed in the house during his 1791 visit. It is full of fine period furnishings by such local craftsmen as Thomas Elfe, and its restored 18th-century kitchen is the only one in Charleston open to visitors. ⊠ *87 Church St.,* ☎ *803/722–0354.* ☞ *$6; for combination ticket,* ☞ *Charleston Museum, above.* ⊙ *Mon.–Sat. 10–5, Sun. 1–5.*

❹ Joseph Manigault Mansion. A National Historic Landmark and an outstanding example of neoclassical architecture, this home was designed by Charleston architect Gabriel Manigault in 1803 and is noted for its carved-wood mantels and elaborate plasterwork. Furnishings are British and French but primarily Charleston antiques, and include rare tricolor Wedgwood pieces. ⊠ *350 Meeting St.,* ☎ *803/723–2926.* ☞ *$6; for combination ticket,* ☞ *Charleston Museum, above.* ⊙ *Mon.– Sat. 10–5, Sun. 1–5.*

❿ Market Hall. Built in 1841 and modeled after the Temple of Nike in Athens, this imposing landmark building includes the **Confederate Museum,** where the Daughters of the Confederacy preserve and display flags, uniforms, swords, and other Civil War memorabilia. The museum, heavily damaged by Hurricane Hugo in 1989, is closed for renovation and may remain so through 1999; however, costumed guides sometimes stand outside and describe the facility for visitors. The collection is temporarily housed at 34 Pitt Street; admission is $2, and it's open Saturday noon–4, Sunday 1–4. ⊠ *88 Meeting St.,* ☎ *803/723–1541.*

★ ㉕ Nathaniel Russell House. One of the nation's finest examples of Adams-style architecture, the Nathaniel Russell House was built in 1808. The interior is notable for its ornate detailing, its lavish period furnishings, and a "flying" circular staircase that spirals three stories with no apparent support. ⊠ *51 Meeting St.,* ☎ *803/724–8481.* ☞ *$6; combination ticket with Aiken–Rhett House (*☞ *above) $10.* ⊙ *Mon.–Sat. 10–5, Sun. 2–5.*

❺ Old Citadel Building/Embassy Suites. Built in 1822 to house state troops and arms, the Old Citadel Building faces Marion Square. This is where the Carolina Military College—The Citadel—had its start. The fortresslike building is now the Embassy Suites Historic Charleston (☞ Lodging, *below*), and The Citadel is now on the Ashley River.

⟳ ⓫ Old City Market. A series of low sheds that once housed produce and fish markets, this area is often called the Slave Market, although Charlestonians dispute that slaves ever were sold there. It now has restaurants, shops, and "gimcracks and gee-gaws" for children, along with vegetable and fruit vendors and local "basket ladies" busy weaving and selling distinctive sweetgrass, pine-straw, and palmetto-leaf baskets— a craft passed through generations from their West African ancestors. ⊠ *Market St. between Meeting and E. Bay Sts.* ⊙ *Daily 9 AM–sunset; hrs may vary.*

NEED A
BREAK?
Indulge the urge to munch on oysters on the half shell, steamed mussels, and clams at **A. W. Shucks** (☎ 803/723–1151) in State Street Market, across from the Market Square Food Court.

🖑 ㉑ **Old Exchange Building/Provost Dungeon.** Originally a customs house, the British used it for prisoners during the Revolutionary War. Today a tableau of lifelike mannequins recalls this era. ⊠ *122 E. Bay St.,* ☎ *803/792–5020.* ⊠ *$4.* ☉ *Daily 9–5.*

⑰ **Old Powder Magazine.** On one of Charleston's few remaining cobblestone thoroughfares, this structure was built in 1713 and used during the Revolutionary War. It is now a museum with costumes, furniture, armor, and other artifacts from 18th-century Charleston. Because the Historic Charleston Foundation is restoring the building, visitors can see the exterior only. Call ahead to see if tours have resumed. ⊠ *79 Cumberland St.,* ☎ *803/723–1623.*

⑬ **St. John's Lutheran Church.** This Greek Revival church was built in 1817 for a congregation that celebrated its 250th anniversary in 1992. Notice the fine craftsmanship in the delicate wrought-iron gates and fence. Musicians may be interested in the 1823 Thomas Hall organ case. ⊠ *5 Clifford St.,* ☎ *803/723–2426.* ☉ *Weekdays 9:30–3.*

㉓ **St. Michael's Episcopal Church.** Modeled after London's St. Martin-in-the-Fields and completed in 1761, this is Charleston's oldest surviving church. Its steeple clock and bells were imported from England in 1764. ⊠ *14 St. Michael's Alley,* ☎ *803/723–0603.* ☉ *Weekdays 9–5, Sat. 9–noon.*

⑱ **St. Philip's Episcopal Church.** The graceful late-Georgian church is the second on its site, built in 1838 and restored in 1994. In the graveyard on the church's side of the street, Charlestonians are buried; in the graveyard on the other side, "foreigners" lie (including John C. Calhoun, who was from Abbeville, South Carolina). ⊠ *146 Church St.,* ☎ *803/722–7734.* ☉ *By appointment.*

⑭ **Unitarian Church.** Completed in 1787, this church was remodeled in the mid-19th century after plans inspired by the Chapel of Henry VII in Westminster Abbey. The Gothic fan-tracery ceiling was added during that renovation. There's an entrance to the church grounds on 161½–163 King Street, amid the antiques shops there. The secluded and romantically overgrown graveyard invites contemplation. ⊠ *8 Archdale St.,* ☎ *803/723–4617 weekdays 8:30–2:30.* ☉ *Call ahead for visiting hrs.*

❶ **Visitor Information Center.** The center gives an introduction to the city and sells tickets for shuttle services (☞ Getting Around *in* Charleston A to Z, *below*). Parking is $1 per hour; the first hour is free if you purchase a shuttle pass. Take time to see *Forever Charleston,* an insightful 20-minute film. ⊠ *375 Meeting St.,* ☎ *803/853–8000 or 800/868–8118.* ⊠ *$2.50 for film.* ☉ *Mar.–Oct., daily 8:30–5:30; Nov.–Feb., daily 8:30–5; shows daily 9–5 on the ½ hr.*

Mount Pleasant and Vicinity

Across the Cooper River bridges, via U.S. 17N, is the town of Mount Pleasant, named not for a mountain or a hill, but for a plantation in England from which some of the area's settlers hailed. In its Old Village neighborhood are antebellum homes and a sleepy, old-time town center with shops and cafés. Along Shem Creek, where the local fishing fleet brings in the daily catch, are good seafood restaurants. Other attractions in the area include museums and plantations.

A Good Tour

There's enough adventure here to stretch over two days, especially if you're a war history buff. On the first day you might drive to **Patriots Point,** veering right off the Cooper River Bridge onto Coleman Boulevard in the direction of Sullivan's Island and the Isle of Palms. Turn right at the signs, then board the museum ships for tours. From here you can catch the ferry for a harbor ride to **Fort Sumter National Monument.** Later, continue along Coleman Boulevard and, just after crossing the boat-lined docks and restaurants at Shem Creek, turn right at Whilden Street for a drive through the Old Village. Returning to Coleman Boulevard, you'll pass The Common, a cluster of shops on your left. Stop here for the **Museum on the Common,** featuring a "Hurricane Hugo Revisited" exhibit: As you make your way across the Ben Sawyer Bridge to Sullivan's Island and the Isle of Palms, you'll see how the area has recovered from Hugo. Follow the signs to **Fort Moultrie.** Spend the rest of the day on the beach or bicycling through Sullivan's Island, a residential community scattered with turn-of-the-century beach houses, or the Isle of Palms, which has a pavilion and more abundant parking.

Another day, you can drive out U.S. 17 North 8 mi to **Boone Hall Plantation** and its famous Avenue of Oaks. Bring a picnic and rent bikes at **Palmetto Islands County Park,** across Boone Hall Creek from the plantation; you'll need a swimsuit for "Splash Island," a mini–water park.

TIMING

You need two days to see all the attractions here; if you have one day or less, choose a few based on your interests.

Sights to See

★ **Boone Hall Plantation.** You approach the plantation along one of the South's most majestic avenues of oaks, which were the model for the grounds of Tara in *Gone With the Wind.* The primary attraction is the grounds, with formal azalea and camellia gardens, as well as the original slave quarters—the only "slave street" still intact in the Southeast—and the cotton-gin house used in the made-for-television movies *North and South* and *Queen.* You may also tour the first floor of the classic columned mansion, which was built in 1935 incorporating woodwork and flooring from the original house. ⊠ *1235 Long Point Rd., off U.S. 17N,* ☎ *803/884–4371.* ⊡ *$10.* ⊙ *Apr.–Labor Day, Mon.–Sat. 8:30–6:30, Sun. 1–5; Labor Day–Mar., Mon.–Sat. 9–5, Sun. 1–4.*

NEED A BREAK?

Driving north of Mount Pleasant along U.S. 17, you can stop and see "**basket ladies**" at roadside stands. If you have the heart to bargain, you *may* be able to purchase the baskets at somewhat lower prices than in Charleston. But remember that you are buying a nearly lost art, and sweetgrass is no longer plentiful in the wild.

☺ **Fort Moultrie.** Here Colonel William Moultrie's South Carolinians repelled a British assault in one of the first Patriot victories of the Revolutionary War. Completed in 1809, this is the third fort on this site at **Sullivan's Island,** which you'll reach on SC 703 off U.S. 17N. The interior has been restored. A 20-minute film tells the history of the fort. ⊠ *W. Middle St., Sullivan's Island,* ☎ *803/883–3123.* ⊡ *Free.* ⊙ *Daily 9–5.*

★ ☺ **Fort Sumter National Monument.** This site, which can be reached from either Charleston's Municipal Marina or Patriot's Point, is on a man-made island in Charleston Harbor. It was here that the first shot of the Civil War was fired on April 12, 1861, by Confederate forces. After a

34-hour bombardment, Union forces surrendered and Confederate troops occupied Sumter, which became a symbol of Southern resistance. The Confederacy held the fort, despite almost continual bombardment, for nearly four years, and when it was finally evacuated it was a heap of rubble. Today National Park Service rangers conduct free guided tours of the restored structure, which includes a free museum (☎ 803/ 883–3123) with historical displays. ☎ *803/722–1691.* ⛴ *Ferry fare $10.50.* ☾ *Tours usually leave from Municipal Marina daily at 9:30, noon, and 2:30, but they vary by season. Tours leave from Patriots Point daily at 10:45 and 1:30; Apr.–Labor Day, additional tour at 4.*

☾ **Museum on The Common.** This small museum has a Hurricane Hugo exhibit prepared by the South Carolina State Museum; it shows the 1989 storm damage through video and photos. ⊠ *217 Lucas St., Shem Creek Village,* ☎ *803/849–9000.* ⛴ *Free.* ☾ *Mon.–Sat. 10–4.*

☾ **Palmetto Islands County Park.** A Big Toy playground, 2-acre pond, paved trails, an observation tower, marsh boardwalks, and a "water island" can be enjoyed in this park across Boone Hall Creek from Boone Hall Plantation. Bicycles and pedal boats can be rented in season. ⊠ *U.S. 17N, ½ mi past Snee Farm, turn left onto Long Point Rd.,* ☎ *803/884– 0832.* ⛴ *$1.* ☾ *Apr., Sept., Oct., daily 9–6; May–Aug., daily 9–7; Nov.–Feb., daily 10–5; Mar., daily 10–6.*

★ ☾ **Patriots Point.** Tours are offered on all vessels here at the world's largest naval and maritime museum, now home to the Medal of Honor Society. Berthed here are the aircraft carrier *Yorktown,* the World War II submarine *Clamagore,* the destroyer *Laffey,* the nuclear merchant ship *Savannah,* and the cutter *Ingham,* responsible for sinking a U-boat during World War II. The film *The Fighting Lady* is shown regularly aboard the *Yorktown,* and there is a Vietnam exhibit. ⊠ *Foot of Cooper River Bridges,* ☎ *803/884–2727.* ⛴ *$9.* ☾ *Labor Day–Mar., daily 9–6:30; Apr.–Labor Day, daily 9–7:30.*

West of the Ashley River

The gardens and houses in this area are highlights of many visits to Charleston.

A Good Tour

Drayton Hall, Magnolia Plantations and Gardens, and Middletown Gardens are each a few miles apart along Ashley River Road, SC 61, about 10 mi northwest of downtown Charleston over the Ashley River Bridge. Still, you'll need time to see them all. One day you could spend a few hours exploring **Charles Towne Landing State Park,** veering off SC 61 onto Old Towne Road (SC 171); then finish your day at **Middleton Gardens.** Another day you might tour the majestic simplicity of **Drayton Hall** before continuing on to **Magnolia Plantations and Gardens** and all their splendor.

TIMING

Nature and garden enthusiasts can easily spend a full day at Magnolia Gardens, Middleton Gardens, or Charles Towne Landing State Park, so budget your time accordingly. Spring is a peak time for the gardens, although they are lovely throughout the year.

Sights to See

★ ☾ **Charles Towne Landing State Park.** Commemorating the site of the original 1670 Charleston settlement, this park on SC 171 North across the Ashley River Bridge has a reconstructed village and fortifications, English park gardens with bicycle trails and walkways, and a replica 17th-century vessel moored in the creek. In the animal park, species native to the region for three centuries roam freely—among them alligators, bison, pumas, bears, and wolves. Bicycle and kayak rentals and cassette and tram tours are available. ⊠ *1500 Old Towne Rd.,* ☎ *803/ 852–4200.* ☒ *$5.* ☉ *Memorial Day–Labor Day, daily 9–6; Labor Day–Memorial Day, daily 9–5.*

★ **Drayton Hall.** Considered the nation's finest example of unspoiled Georgian-Palladian architecture, this mansion is the only plantation house on the Ashley River to have survived the Civil War. A National Historic Landmark built between 1738 and 1742, it serves as an invaluable lesson in history as well as in architecture. Drayton Hall has been left unfurnished to highlight the original plaster moldings, opulent hand-carved woodwork, and other ornamental details. ⊠ *3380 Ashley River Rd.,* ☎ *803/766–0188.* ☒ *$8.* ☉ *Guided tours Mar.– Oct., daily 10–4; Nov.–Feb., daily 10–3.*

☾ **Magnolia Plantation and Gardens.** The 50-acre informal garden, begun in 1685, has a huge collection of azaleas and camellias. You can ride a tram for an overall tour with three stops. Nature lovers may canoe through the 125-acre Waterfowl Refuge, explore the 30-acre **Audubon Swamp Garden** along boardwalks and bridges, or walk or bicycle over 500 acres of wildlife trails. Tours of the manor house, built during Reconstruction, depict plantation life. You can also see the petting zoo and a miniature-horse ranch. ⊠ *Ashley River Rd.,* ☎ *803/571–1266 or 800/367–3517.* ☒ *$9; house tour $5 extra; tram tour $4 extra; swamp tour $10 alone or $4 extra; combination tour available.* ☉ *Daily 8–5:30.*

★ ☾ **Middleton Place.** The nation's oldest landscaped gardens, dating from 1741, are magnificently ablaze with camellias, magnolias, azaleas, roses, and flowers of all seasons planted in floral *allées* and terraced lawns, and around ornamental lakes. Much of the mansion was destroyed during the Civil War, but the south wing has been restored and houses impressive collections of silver, furniture, paintings, and historic documents. In the stable yard craftspeople use authentic tools and equipment to demonstrate spinning, blacksmithing, and other domestic skills from the plantation era. Farm animals, peacocks, and other creatures roam freely. The Middleton Place restaurant serves Lowcountry specialties for lunch daily; a gift shop carries local arts, crafts, and souvenirs. Also on the grounds is a modern, Danish-style inn (access to the gardens is included in the room price) with floor-to-ceiling windows dramatizing views of the Ashley River; here you can sign up for kayaking, canoeing, and biking tours. ⊠ *Ashley River Rd.,* ☎ *803/ 556–6020 or 800/782–3608.* ☒ *$14; house tours $7 extra.* ☉ *Daily 9–5; house tours Tues.–Sun. 10–4:30, Mon. 1:30–4:30.*

Dining

She-crab soup, sautéed shrimp and grits, variations on pecan pie, and other Lowcountry specialties are served all over the Charleston area, but local chefs whip up some creative contemporary dishes as well. Known for outstanding eateries—ranging from fresh seafood houses to elegant French restaurants—Charleston is a mecca for gastronomes. Across the East Cooper Bridge, in trendy Mount Pleasant, there are a number of good restaurants.

American

$$$ ✗ **Anson.** After an afternoon of strolling through the Old City Market, you can walk up Anson Street to one of the better restaurants in town. The softly lit, gilt-trimmed dining room is framed by about a dozen French windows; booths are anchored by marble-top tables.

Anson's serves up dependable American fare—mainly seafood, chicken, and steak—with the occasional international twist in a whimsical special. Desserts are of the rich, Southern variety, so save room. ⊠ *12 Anson St.,* ☎ *803/577–0551. AE, D, DC, MC, V. No lunch.*

$$$ ✕ **Peninsula Grill.** Surrounded by olive green wall coverings, black iron chandeliers, and 18th-century-style portraits, diners at this new hot spot in the Planters Inn (☞ Lodging, *below*) can feast on such delights as lobster citron, wild mushroom grits with oysters, and New Zealand benne-seed-encrusted rack of lamb. For dessert, try the divine lemon tart with lemon sorbet, lemon crisps, and candied lemon. ⊠ *112 N. Market St.,* ☎ *803/723–0700. AE, D, DC, MC, V.*

$$ ✕ **Elliott's on the Square.** This elegant, streamlined restaurant in the newly renovated Francis Marion Hotel (☞ Lodging, *below*) has butter-color walls, black and gold accents, whimsical lighting, and a friendly, cozy bar. Here you can have breakfast or a varied lunch, from cheeseburgers and pasta to pulled duck and fried pot stickers. At dinner, seafood reigns: You might start with the fried oysters with red onion marmalade, or shrimp and basil beignets, and follow with grouper layered with phyllo pastry, spinach, and caramelized onions. ⊠ *387 King St.,* ☎ *803/724–8888. AE, D, DC, MC, V.*

$ ✕ **Mike Calder's Deli & Pub.** Soups, salads, sandwiches, daily home-cooked specials such as Creole seafood casseroles, and 15 different draft beers are offered in an "Old World" setting, once a pharmacy in the historic district. ⊠ *288 King St.,* ☎ *803/577–0123. No reservations. AE, D, MC, V. Closed Sun.*

French

$$$–$$$$ ✕ **Restaurant Million.** This restaurant serves French nouvelle cuisine on Limoges china in a building dating to 1788. The rack of lamb and the five-course ($50) and three-course ($28) prix-fixe meals are outstanding. Downstairs at the casual and less expensive McCrady's (☎ 803/577–0025), inventive appetizers, soups, salads, and grills are served. ⊠ *2 Unity Alley,* ☎ *803/577–3141. Reservations essential in restaurant. Jacket and tie. AE, DC, MC, V. Closed Sun. No lunch in restaurant; no lunch Sat. in McCrady's.*

$–$$ ✕ **Gaulart and Maliclet Cafe Restaurant.** This casual, chic eatery serves Continental dishes—breads and pastries, soups, salads, sandwiches, and specials like seafood Normandy and chicken sesame. ⊠ *98 Broad St.,* ☎ *803/577–9797. AE, D, DC, MC, V. Closed Sun. No dinner Mon.*

Lowcountry

$$ ✕ **Carolina's.** Lively and bustling, Carolina's has long been a favorite. Black, white, and peach decor, terra-cotta tiles, and 1920s French posters create a casual bistro atmosphere. Fans return for the "appeteasers" and the late-night (until 1 AM) offerings, which include everything from smoked baby-back ribs to pasta with crawfish and tasso (spiced ham) in cream sauce. Dinner entrées are selections from the grill: among them, pork tenderloin with Jamaican seasoning and salmon with cilantro, ginger, and lime butter. ⊠ *10 Exchange St.,* ☎ *803/724–3800. Reservations essential. D, MC, V. No lunch.*

$$ ✕ **Slightly North of Broad.** This high-ceiling haunt with brick and
★   stucco walls, and red wooden floors, has several seats looking directly into the exposed kitchen. From here you'll see chef Frank Lee laboring over his inventive—but hardly esoteric—dishes: sautéed quail filled with herbed chicken mousse; pad Thai noodles with shrimp, pork, and an authentic fish sauce; and corn-and-crab soup with spinach ravioli. You can order most items as either an appetizer or an entrée. The extensive wine list is moderately priced. A sister restaurant, Slightly Up the Creek (⊠ 130 Mill St., ☎ 803/884–5005), at Shem Creek in Mount Pleasant, offers similarly fine food plus waterfront views. ⊠

350

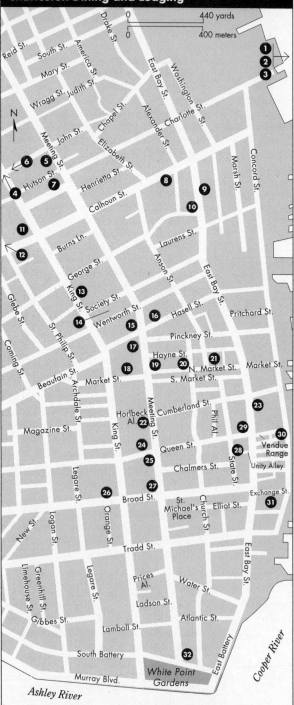

Charleston Dining and Lodging

192 E. Bay St., ☎ *803/723–3424. Reservations not accepted. AE, D, DC, MC, V. Closed Sun. No lunch Sat.*

Lowcountry/Southern

$$–$$$ ✕ **Magnolias.** This popular place, in an 1823 warehouse, is cherished
★ by Charlestonians and visitors alike. The magnolia theme is seen throughout in vivid Rod Goebel paintings, etched glass, wrought iron, and candlesticks. The "uptown/down South" cuisine shines in specialties like the "Down-South" egg roll stuffed with chicken and collard greens with spicy mustard sauce and sweet pepper puree. Equally innovative appetizers include seared yellow grits cakes with tasso gravy and yellow corn relish, and sautéed greens. There's even fried chicken with mashed potatoes and mushroom gravy and, for dessert, a heaping strawberry shortcake biscuit. You may also want to try the **Blossom Cafe** (✉ 171 E. Bay St., ☎ 803/722–9200), owned by the same people. ✉ *185 E. Bay St.,* ☎ *803/577–7771. Reservations essential. AE, DC, MC, V.*

$$ ✕ **Supper at Stacks.** Above the Guilds Inn, formal, prix-fixe, four-course Continental meals ($29) are presented in a grand dining room—the menu changes daily and depends largely on what's fresh. ✉ *101 Pitt St., Mount Pleasant,* ☎ *803/884–7009. Reservations essential for dinner. Jacket and tie. AE, MC, V. Closed Sun.–Mon. No lunch.*

$ ✕ **Alice's Fine Foods.** The food Southerners crave is here in its origi-
★ nal, beloved form: Baked or fried chicken, ribs, fried fish, or other entrées come with a choice of three vegetables, including green beans, collard greens, red rice, macaroni-and-cheese pie, okra and tomatoes, lima beans, rice and gravy, yams, and squash. ✉ *468–470 King St.,* ☎ *803/853–9366. MC, V.*

$ ✕ **Sticky Fingers.** Specializing in ribs six ways (Memphis-style wet and dry, Texas-style wet and dry, Carolina sweet, and Tennessee whiskey) and barbecue, this family-friendly restaurant has locations downtown and in Mount Pleasant and Summerville. Tuesday nights are kids' nights, with supervised games and cartoons in a playroom. ✉ *235 Meeting St.,* ☎ *803/853–7427 or 800/671–5966;* ✉ *U.S. 17 Bypass, Mount Pleasant,* ☎ *803/856–9840;* ✉ *1200 N. Main St., Summerville,* ☎ *803/875–7969. AE, DC, MC, V.*

Seafood

$$ ✕ **Barbadoes Room.** This large, airy plant- and light-filled space has a sophisticated island look and a view out to a cheery courtyard garden, where dinner may be served in warm weather, complete with a big band on Tuesday nights and jazz on Friday evenings. The menu includes she-crab soup; blackened shrimp and scallops; and oyster and crab gratin. The extensive breakfast buffet and Sunday brunch are popular, too. ✉ *115 Meeting St., in the Mills House Hotel,* ☎ *803/577–2400. Reservations essential. D, DC, MC, V.*

$ ✕ **The Wreck.** Dockside and full of wacky character, this spot serves up traditional dishes like boiled peanuts, fried shrimp, shrimp pilaf, deviled crab, and oyster platters in a shabby, candlelit, screened-in porch and small dining area. ✉ *106 Haddrell St., Mount Pleasant,* ☎ *803/ 884–0052. Reservations not accepted. No credit cards.*

Lodging

Rates tend to increase during the Spring Festival of Houses and Spoleto, when reservations are essential. The Charleston Area Convention and Visitors Bureau (✉ Box 975, Charleston 29402, ☎ 803/853–8000 or 800/868–8118) distributes a Visitor Value Days Card entitling the bearer to 10%–50% off at many accommodations between December 1 and March 1.

Hotels and Motels

$$$$ ⊞ **Charleston Place.** Among the city's most luxurious hotels—now an
★   Orient Express property—this graceful, low-rise structure in the historic district is surrounded by upscale boutiques and specialty shops
and ranked world-class. The lobby has a magnificent hand-blown
Venetian-glass chandelier, an Italian marble floor, and antiques from
Sotheby's. Rooms are furnished with period reproductions, linen sheets
and robes, and fax machines. ⊠ *130 Market St., 29401,* ☎ *803/722–
4900 or 800/611–5545,* ℻ *803/724–7215. 400 rooms, 40 suites. 2
restaurants, 2 lounges, minibars, indoor pool, hot tub, sauna, steam
room, exercise room, concierge floors. AE, D, DC, MC, V.*

$$$$ ⊞ **Hawthorn Suites Hotel.** This deluxe hotel across from the City Market includes a restored entrance portico from an 1874 bank, a refurbished 1866 firehouse, and three lush gardens. The spacious suites, all
decorated with 18th-century reproductions and canopied beds, have
full kitchens or wet bars with microwave ovens and refrigerators.
Complimentary full breakfast and afternoon refreshments are included.
⊠ *181 Church St., 29401,* ☎ *803/577–2644 or 800/527–1133,* ℻
*803/577–2697. 162 suites. Restaurant, lounge, hot tub, exercise room,
business services, meeting rooms. AE, D, DC, MC, V.*

$$$$ ⊞ **Mills House Hotel.** Antique furnishings and period decor give great
★   charm to this luxurious Holiday Inn property, a reconstruction of an
old hostelry on its original site in the historic district. Though rooms
are small and a bit standard, there's a lounge with live entertainment
and excellent dining in the **Barbadoes Room** (☞ Dining, *above*). ⊠
115 Meeting St., 29401, ☎ *803/577–2400 or 800/874–9600,* ℻ *803/
722–2712. 214 rooms, 15 suites. Restaurant, 2 lounges, pool. AE, D,
DC, MC, V.*

$$$–$$$$ ⊞ **Embassy Suites Historic Charleston.** The courtyard of the Old Citadel
military school where cadets once marched is now a skylit atrium with
stone flooring, armchairs, palm trees, and a fountain. The restored brick
walls of the breakfast room and some guest rooms in this new hotel
contain original gun ports, reminders that the 1822 building was orig-
inally a fortification. Teak and mahogany furniture, safari motifs, and
sisal carpeting recall the British colonial era. ⊠ *341 Meeting St.,
29403,* ☎ *803/723–6900 or 800/362–2779,* ℻ *803/723–6938. 153
suites. Lounge, pool, exercise room. AE, D, DC, MC, V.*

$$$–$$$$ ⊞ **Francis Marion Hotel.** Built in 1924 as the largest hotel in the Car-
olinas, this recently restored property retains big-band and tea-dance
glamour with its windowed ballrooms, wrought-iron railings, columns,
high ceilings, crown moldings, decorative plasterwork, and scenic
views of Marion Square and the harbor (from some guest rooms you
can see Fort Sumter). A few rooms have their original pedestal sinks
and deep tubs. ⊠ *387 King St., 29403,* ☎ *803/722–0600,* ℻ *803/723–
4633. 160 rooms, 66 suites. Restaurant, lounge, exercise room. AE,
D, DC, MC, V.*

$$–$$$ ⊞ **Best Western King Charles Inn.** Renovated in 1997, this inn in the
historic district is a cut above the typical chain, with a welcoming lobby
and sitting area and spacious rooms furnished with 18th-century pe-
riod reproductions. ⊠ *237 Meeting St., 29401,* ☎ *803/723–7451 or
800/528–1234,* ℻ *803/723–2041. 91 rooms. Dining room, lounge,
pool. AE, D, DC, MC, V.*

$$–$$$ ⊞ **Days Inn Historic District.** Conveniently located, this modest prop-
erty has spacious, quiet rooms and free parking. ⊠ *155 Meeting St.,
29401,* ☎ *803/722–8411 or 800/325–2525,* ℻ *803/733–5361. 124
rooms. Dining room, pool. AE, D, DC, MC, V.*

$$–$$$ 🏨 **Hampton Inn–Historic District.** This downtown chain offering has
★ hardwood floors and a fireplace in the elegant lobby, guest rooms with
period reproductions, a courtyard garden, and complimentary Continental breakfast. This is a front-runner in the economy category. ⊠
345 Meeting St., 29403, ☎ *803/723–4000 or 800/426–7866,* 𝐅𝐀𝐗 *803/
722–3725. 166 rooms, 5 suites. Pool. AE, D, DC, MC, V.*

$$–$$$ 🏨 **Heart of Charleston Quality Inn.** A block from the Gaillard Municipal
Auditorium and Exhibition Hall, the inn is clean and run by a friendly
staff. It draws loyal repeat visitors because of its free parking and a location across from the auditorium that is within walking distance of
many must-see spots. Rooms are motel modern, as you would expect
from this chain. ⊠ *125 Calhoun St., 29401,* ☎ *803/722–3391 or 800/
845–2504,* 𝐅𝐀𝐗 *803/577–0361. 126 rooms. Restaurant, lounge, pool.
AE, D, DC, MC, V.*

$$–$$$ 🏨 **Holiday Inn Charleston/Mount Pleasant.** This hotel just over the
Cooper River Bridge is a 10-minute drive from the downtown historic
district. Everything has been gracefully done: brass lamps, crystal
chandeliers, Queen Anne–style furniture. The "high-tech suites" have
PC cable hookups, large working areas, glossy ultramodern furniture,
and refrigerators. ⊠ *250 U.S. 17, Mount Pleasant 29464,* ☎ *803/884–
6000 or 800/290–4004,* 𝐅𝐀𝐗 *803/881–1786. 158 rooms. Restaurant,
lounge, pool, sauna, exercise room, concierge floor, meeting rooms.
AE, D, DC, MC, V.*

$$–$$$ 🏨 **Sheraton Inn Charleston.** Some rooms in this 13-story hotel outside
the historic district overlook the Ashley River. Spacious rooms and suites
are furnished in Queen Anne style. There's also concierge service, live
entertainment, and free shuttle service to the historic district. ⊠ *170
Lockwood Dr., 29403,* ☎ *803/723–3000 or 800/968–3569,* 𝐅𝐀𝐗 *803/
720–0844. 333 rooms, 5 suites. Coffee shop, dining room, lounge, pool,
exercise room, meeting rooms. AE, D, DC, MC, V.*

Inns and Guest Houses

$$$$ 🏨 **John Rutledge House Inn.** This 1763 house, built by John Rutledge,
★ one of the framers of the U.S. Constitution, is one of Charleston's most
luxurious inns. Ornate ironwork on the facade has a palmetto tree and
eagle motif, signifying Rutledge's service to both his state and his nation. A lavish afternoon tea, plus wine, is served in the ballroom, and
Continental breakfast and newspapers are delivered to your room. Two
charming period carriage houses also accommodate guests. There are
whirlpool tubs in some guest rooms. ⊠ *116 Broad St., 29401,* ☎ *803/
723–7999 or 800/476–9741,* 𝐅𝐀𝐗 *803/720–2615. 11 rooms in mansion, 4 in each of 2 carriage houses. In-room modem lines, business
services. AE, DC, MC, V.*

$$$–$$$$ 🏨 **Cannonboro Inn** and **Ashley Inn.** Two of the most elegant inns in
town, these B&B neighbors on the edge of the historic district have
luxurious rooms, tastefully decorated in period furnishings by owners
Bud and Sally Allen. Guests are treated to a full English breakfast in
piazzas overlooking Charleston gardens. Use of the bicycles, afternoon
sherry, and convenient parking in an off-street lot are all included. *Can-
nonboro:* ⊠ *184 Ashley Ave., 29403,* ☎ *803/723–8572,* 𝐅𝐀𝐗 *803/
723–9080. 6 rooms. Bicycles, business services. MC, V. Ashley:* ⊠ *201
Ashley Ave., 29403,* ☎ *803/723–1848. 6 rooms, 1 suite. Bicycles, busi-
ness services. MC, V.*

$$$–$$$$ 🏨 **Planters Inn.** Rooms and suites are beautifully appointed with op-
ulent furnishings, including mahogany four-poster beds and marble baths.
Each of the 21 rooms in a new addition has a piazza overlooking the
garden courtyard. The inn's Peninsula Grill (☞ Dining, *above*) is very
popular. ⊠ *112 N. Market St., 29401,* ☎ *803/722–2345 or 800/*

845–7082, [FAX] *803/577–2125. 56 rooms, 6 suites. Restaurant, room service, concierge, business services. AE, D, DC, MC, V.*

$$$–$$$$ 🏠 **Two Meeting Street.** As pretty as a wedding cake and just as romantic,
★ this turn-of-the-century inn near the Battery has very private honeymoon suites. There are Tiffany windows, carved English oak paneling, and a chandelier from Czechoslovakia. Guests are treated to afternoon high tea and Continental breakfast. ✉ *2 Meeting St., 29401,* ☎ *803/723–7322. 7 rooms, 2 suites. No credit cards.*

$$$–$$$$ 🏠 **Vendue Inn.** Many rooms of this elegant yet friendly inn look out over the harbor and Waterfront Park. Guest rooms have four-poster beds, cozy seating areas, and large bathrooms. Continental breakfast plus afternoon wine and cheese are complimentary. Climb up to the inn's rooftop terrace bar for sweeping views of the harbor along with drinks and appetizers from the inn's Library Restaurant. ✉ *19 Vendue Range, 29401,* ☎ *803/577–7970 or 800/845–7900. 21 suites. Restaurant, lounge, exercise room, business services, meeting rooms. AE, D, DC, MC, V.*

$$$ 🏠 **Ansonborough Inn.** Formerly a turn-of-the-century stationer's warehouse, this spacious all-suite inn is furnished in period reproductions. It offers hair dryers, irons, a morning newspaper, message service, wine reception, and Continental breakfast, but it's best known for its friendly staff. ✉ *21 Hasell St., 29401,* ☎ *803/723–1655 or 800/522–2073,* [FAX] *803/527–6888. 37 suites. Meeting room. AE, MC, V.*

$$$ 🏠 **Brasington House Bed & Breakfast.** During the afternoon wine-and-cheese get-together or at the family-style breakfast, Dalton and Judy Brasington, educators by profession, will advise you on what to see and do in Charleston. The formal dining room of their restored Greek Revival "single house" in the historic district is filled with antiques and treasures from around the world. ✉ *328 E. Bay St., 29401,* ☎ *803/722–1274 or 800/722–1274,* [FAX] *803/722–6785. 4 rooms. MC, V.*

$$$ 🏠 **Elliott House Inn.** Listen to the chimes of St. Michael's Episcopal Church as you sip wine in the courtyard of this lovely old inn in the heart of the historic district. You can then retreat to a cozy room with period furniture, including canopied four-posters and Oriental carpets. A Continental breakfast is included. ✉ *78 Queen St., 29401,* ☎ *803/723–1855 or 800/729–1855,* [FAX] *803/722–1567. 26 rooms. Hot tub, bicycles. AE, D, MC, V.*

$$$ 🏠 **Maison DuPré.** A quiet retreat off busy East Bay Street, this inn was created out of three restored homes and two carriage houses. It is filled with antiques, and each room contains an original painting by Lucille Mullholland, who operates the inn with her husband, Robert. Enjoy a full Lowcountry tea (with cheeses, finger sandwiches, and cakes) and Continental breakfast, all complimentary. ✉ *317 E. Bay St., 29401,* ☎ *803/723–8691 or 800/844–4667. 12 rooms, 3 suites. MC, V.*

$$–$$$ 🏠 **1837 Bed and Breakfast and Tea Room.** Though not as fancy as some of the B&Bs in town, this inn is long on hospitality; you'll get a sense of what it's really like to live in one of Charleston's beloved homes. Restored and operated by two artists/teachers, the home and carriage house have rooms filled with antiques, including romantic canopied beds. A gourmet breakfast of homemade breads and hot entrées such as sausage pie or ham frittata is included in the rate, as is the afternoon tea (which is also open to the public for a nominal price). ✉ *126 Wentworth St., 29401,* ☎ *803/723–7166. 8 rooms. AE, MC, V.*

Resort Islands

The semitropical islands dotting the South Carolina coast near Charleston are home to several sumptuous resorts that offer a wide variety of packages. Peak season rates (during spring and summer vacations) range from $100 to $250 per day, double occupancy. Costs drop considerably off-season.

$$$$ ✕🏨 **Kiawah Island Resort.** Choose from 150 inn rooms and 500 completely equipped one- to five-bedroom villas and private homes in two luxurious resort villages on 10,000 wooded acres. There are 10 mi of fine broad beaches and an array of recreational opportunities. Dining options are many and varied. At press time the resort was planning to demolish the inn and build a larger hotel, but the rest of the resort will remain open. ✉ *12 Kiawah Beach Dr., Kiawah Island 29455,* ☎ *803/ 768–2121 or 800/654–2924,* FAX *803/768–6099. 150 rooms, 500 villas and private homes. 8 restaurants, 4 18-hole golf courses, 28 tennis courts, boating, fishing, bicycles, shops, children's programs. AE, D, DC, MC, V.*

$$$$ ✕🏨 **Seabrook Island Resort.** A total of 175 completely equipped one- to three-bedroom villas, cottages, and beach houses dot this property. The **Beach Club** and **Island Club,** open to all guests, are centers for dining and leisure activities. **Bohicket Marina Village,** the hub of activity around the island, offers three fine restaurants as well as pizza and sub shops. The marina area includes opportunities for shopping as well as scuba diving, deep sea and inshore fishing charters, and small-boat rentals. ✉ *1002 Landfall Way, Seabrook Island 29455,* ☎ *803/ 768–1000 or 800/845–2475,* FAX *803/768–4946. 175 units. 3 restaurants, 2 pools, 2 18-hole golf courses, 13 tennis courts, horseback riding, boating, parasailing, fishing, bicycles, children's programs. AE, D, DC, MC, V.*

$$$$ ✕🏨 **Wild Dunes.** This serene, 1,600-acre resort on the Isle of Palms has 300 one- to three-bedroom villas for rent, each with a kitchen and washer and dryer. Rooms at the new **Inn at Wild Dunes** are another option. There are two widely acclaimed golf courses, a racquet club, a yacht harbor on the Intracoastal Waterway, and a long list of recreational options. Southern regional specialties are served at **Edgar's,** seafood at the **Tradewinds Restaurant,** and casual fare at the **Dune Deli and Pizzeria.** There's a lounge with live entertainment. ✉ *Box 20575, Charleston 29413,* ☎ *803/886–6000 or 800/845–8880,* FAX *803/886– 2916. 300 units, 93 rooms. 3 restaurants, lounge, 2 18-hole golf courses, 17 tennis courts, health club, water sports, boating, fishing, bicycles, rollerblading, children's programs. AE, MC, DC, D, V.*

Nightlife and the Arts

Concerts

The College of Charleston has a free **Monday Night Recital Series** (☎ 803/953–8228). The **Charleston Symphony Orchestra** (☎ 803/723– 7528) presents MasterWorks Series, Downtown Pops, First Union Family Series, and Annual Holiday Concert at Gaillard Municipal Auditorium (✉ 77 Calhoun St., ☎ 803/577–4500). The orchestra also performs the Sotille Chamber Series at the Sotille Theater (✉ 44 George St., ☎ 803/953–6340), and the Light and Lively Pops at Charleston Southern University (✉ U.S. 78, ☎ 803/953–6340). The **Charleston Concert Association** (☎ 803/722–7667) presents visiting performing arts groups including symphonies, ballets, and operas.

Dance

The **Charleston Ballet Theatre** (✉ 477 King St., ☎ 803/723–7334) performs everything from classical to contemporary dance at locations around the city. The **Robert Ivey Ballet Company** (☎ 803/556–1343), a semiprofessional company that includes several College of Charleston students, gives a fall and spring program of jazz, classical, and modern dance at the Sotille Theater. **Anonymity Dance Company** (☎ 803/

886–6104 or 800/215–6523), a modern dance troupe, performs throughout the city.

Dancing and Music

Lowcountry Legends Music Hall (✉ 30 Cumberland St., ☎ 803/722–1829 or 800/348–7270) is Charleston's Preservation Hall, serving up regional music and folktales. **Serenade** (✉ 37 John St., ☎ 803/973–3333), a 1,000-seat music hall, showcases jazz, blues, calypso, Broadway tunes, and more in the city's only revue. The **Music Farm** (✉ 32 Ann St., ☎ 803/853–3276) features live national and local alternative bands. In the market area, there's the **Jukebox** (✉ 4 Vendue Range, ☎ 803/723–3431), where a disc jockey spins oldies and contemporary rock. The **Chef & Clef Restaurant** (✉ 102 N. Market St., ☎ 803/722–0732) has jazz on one floor and the Red Hot Blues room on another. **Windjammer** (✉ 1000 Ocean Blvd., ☎ 803/886–8596), on the Isle of Palms, is an oceanfront spot with live rock.

Dinner Cruises

For an evening of dining and dancing, climb aboard the luxury yacht, **Spirit of Charleston** (☎ 803/722–2628). Reservations are essential; there are no cruises Sunday and Monday.

Breakfast, brunch, deli and hot luncheons are available and prepared freshly on board the **Charlestowne Princess** (☎ 803/722–1112), which also offers a "Harborlites Dinner" with live entertainment and dancing while cruising the harbor and rivers.

Festivals

The **Fall Candelight Tours of Homes and Gardens** (✉ Box 521, 29402, ☎ 803/722–4630), sponsored by the Preservation Society of Charleston in September and October, offers an inside look at Charleston's private buildings and gardens.

During the **Festival of Houses and Gardens** (✉ Box 1120, 29202, ☎ 803/724–8484), held during March and April each year, more than 100 private homes, gardens, and historic churches are open to the public for tours sponsored by the Historic Charleston Foundation. There are also symphony galas in stately drawing rooms, plantation oyster roasts, and candlelight tours.

MOJA Arts Festival (✉ Office of Cultural Affairs, 133 Church St., 29401, ☎ 803/724–7305), which takes place during the last week of September and first week of October, celebrates the rich heritage of the African continent and Caribbean influences on African-American culture. It includes theater, dance, and music performances, art shows, films, lectures, and tours of the historic district.

Piccolo Spoleto Festival (✉ Office of Cultural Affairs, 133 Church St., 29401, ☎ 803/724–7305) is the spirited companion festival of Spoleto Festival USA, showcasing the best in local and regional talent from every artistic discipline. There are about 300 events—from jazz performances to puppet shows—held at 60 sites in 17 days, from mid-May through early June, and most performances are free.

The **Southeastern Wildlife Exposition** (✉ 211 Meeting St., 29401, ☎ 803/723–1748 or 800/221–5273) in mid-February is one of Charleston's biggest annual events. It features art by renowned wildlife artists.

Spoleto Festival USA (✉ Box 704, 29402, ☎ 803/722–2764), founded by the composer Gian Carlo Menotti in 1977, has become a world-famous celebration of the arts. For two weeks, from late May to early June, opera, dance, theater, symphonic and chamber music performances, jazz, and the visual arts are showcased in concert halls, theaters, parks, churches, streets, and gardens throughout the city.

The reasonably priced **Worldfest Charleston** (⊠ Box 838, 29402, ☎ 803/723–7600 or 800/501–0111), held in mid-November, premieres new films from around the world, offers workshops and seminars, and provides opportunities to meet the producers, directors, and actors.

Film

The **Roxy** (⊠ 245 E. Bay St., ☎ 803/853–7699) offers films from around the world plus wine, beer, coffee drinks, pastries, sandwiches, and pasta. The **American Theater** (⊠ 446 King St., ☎ 803/722–3456), a renovated theater from the 1940s, shows second-run movies in a table-and-chairs setting with pizza, burgers, finger foods, beer, and wine. Upstairs there's a virtual reality game center.

Hotel and Jazz Bars

The **Best Friend Lounge** (⊠ 115 Meeting St., ☎ 803/577–2400), in the Mills House Hotel, has a guitarist playing light tunes Monday–Saturday nights. In the **Lobby Lounge** (⊠ 130 Market St., ☎ 803/722–4900) in Charleston Place, cocktails and appetizers are accompanied by piano. **Charlie's Little Bar,** above the Saracen Restaurant (⊠ 141 E. Bay St., ☎ 803/723–6242), has live jazz or blues most weekends. Live jazz is offered Friday and Saturday evenings at **Henry's Restaurant** (⊠ 54 N. Market St., ☎ 803/723–4363).

Lounges and Bars/Breweries

The bustling **Kiva Han Cafe & Coffee House** (⊠ 235 E. Bay St., ☎ 803/965–5282) has live music plus late-night food and drink. **Southend Brewery** (⊠ 161 E. Bay St., ☎ 803/853–4677) has a lively bar with beer brewed on the premises; the food is good, especially soups. **Zebo** (⊠ 275 King St., ☎ 803/577–7600) brews its beer here and offers tasty meals. **Vickery's Bar & Grill** (⊠ 139 Calhoun St., ☎ 803/723–1558) is a festive night spot with a spacious outdoor patio. You'll find authentic Irish music at **Tommy Condon's Irish Pub & Restaurant** (⊠ 160 Church St., ☎ 803/577–3818). **Club Habana** (⊠ 177 Meeting St., ☎ 803/853–5900) is a fancy, wood-paneled martini bar with a cigar shop downstairs.

Theater

Several groups, including the **Footlight Players** and **Charleston Stage Company,** perform at the Dock Street Theatre (⊠ 135 Church St., ☎ 803/723–5648). Performances by the College of Charleston's theater department and guest theatrical groups are presented during the school year at the **Simons Center for the Arts** (⊠ 54 St. Phillips St., ☎ 803/953–5604). **Pluff Mud Productions** puts on comedies at the Isle of Palms' Windjammer (1000 Ocean Blvd., ☎ 803/886–8596). The **Cavallaro** (⊠ 1478 Savannah Hwy., ☎ 803/763–9222) is the home of several successful dinner theater productions.

Outdoor Activities and Sports

Beaches

The Charleston area's mild climate generally is conducive to swimming from April through October. This is definitely not a "swingles" area; all public and private beaches are family oriented, providing a choice of water sports, sunbathing, shelling, fishing, or quiet moonlight strolls. The **Charleston County Parks and Recreation Commission** (☎ 803/762–2172) operates several public beach facilities.

Beachwalker Park on the west end of Kiawah Island (which is otherwise a private resort) provides 300 ft of beach frontage, seasonal lifeguard service, rest rooms, outdoor showers, a picnic area, snack bar, and a 150-car parking lot. ⊠ *Kiawah Island,* ☏ *803/762–2172.* ☑ *$4 per car (up to 8 passengers).* ☺ *June–Aug., daily 10–7; Apr. and Oct., weekends 10–6; May and Sept., daily 10–6.*

Folly Beach County Park, 12 mi south of Charleston via U.S. 17 and SC 171 (Folly Rd.), has 4,000 ft of ocean frontage and 2,000 ft of river frontage. Lifeguards are on duty seasonally along a 600-ft section of the beach. Facilities include dressing areas, outdoor showers, rest rooms, picnicking areas, beach chairs, raft and shower rentals, and a 300-vehicle parking lot. Pelican Watch shelter is available year-round for group picnics and day or night oyster roasts. ⊠ *Folly Island,* ☏ *803/588–2426.* ☑ *$4 per car (up to 8 passengers).* ☺ *May–Aug., daily 9–7; Apr., Sept., Oct., 10–6; Nov.–Mar., daily 10–5.*

Private resorts with extensive beaches and amenities include **Fairfield Ocean Ridge** (☏ 803/869–2561), on Edisto Island; **Kiawah Island** (☏ 903/768–2121 or 800/654–2924); **Seabrook Island** (☏ 803/768–1000 or 800/845–5531); and **Wild Dunes** (☏ 803/886–6000 or 800/845–8880), on the Isle of Palms.

Participant Sports

BIKING

The historic district is ideal for bicycling, and many city parks have biking trails. Palmetto Islands County Park (☞ Mount Pleasant and Vicinity, *above*) also has trails. Bikes can be rented at the **Bicycle Shoppe** (⊠ 280 Meeting St., ☏ 803/722–8168; ⊠ Kiawah Island, ☏ 803/768–9122). **Sea Island Cycle** (⊠ 4053 Rhett Ave., North Charleston, ☏ 803/747–2453) serves all the local islands. **Island Bike and Surf Shop** (⊠ 3665 Bohicket Rd., Kiawah Island, ☏ 803/768–1158) has bikes, surfboards, and rollerblades for rent.

GOLF

One of the most appealing aspects of golfing the Charleston area is the relaxing pace. With fewer golfers playing the courses than in destinations that are primarily golf-oriented, golfers find choice starting times and an unhurried atmosphere. For a listing of area golf packages, contact the Charleston Area Convention and Visitors Bureau (⊠ Box 975, 29402, ☏ 803/853–8000 or 800/868–8118).

Nonguests may play on a space-available basis at **private island resorts** such as Kiawah Island, Seabrook Island, and Wild Dunes. The prestigious Pete Dye–designed **Ocean Course at Kiawah Island Resort** (☏ 803/768–7272) was the site of the 1991 Ryder Cup. Other championship **Kiawah courses** are the Gary Player–designed **Marsh Point**; Osprey Point, by Tom Fazio; and **Turtle Point,** a Jack Nicklaus layout (☏ 803/768–2121 for all three). **Seabrook Island Resort,** a secluded hideaway on Johns Island, offers two more championship courses: **Crooked Oaks** by Robert Trent Jones Sr., and **Ocean Winds,** designed by William Byrd (☏ 803/768–2529 for both). **Wild Dunes Resort,** on the Isle of Palms, is home to two Tom Fazio designs: the **Links** (☏ 803/886–2180) and **Harbor Course** (☏ 803/886–2301).

Top **public courses** in the area include **Charleston Municipal** (☏ 803/795–6517), **Charleston National Country Club** (☏ 803/884–7799), the **Dunes West Golf Club** (⊠ Mount Pleasant, ☏ 803/856–9000), **Links at Stono Ferry** (⊠ Hollywood, ☏ 803/763–1817), **Oak Point Golf Course** (⊠ Johns Island, ☏ 803/768–7431), **Patriots Point** (⊠ Mount Pleasant, ☏ 803/881–0042), and **Shadowmoss Golf Club** (☏ 803/556–8251).

TENNIS

Courts are open to the public at **Shadowmoss Plantation** (☎ 803/556–8251), **Kiawah Island** (☎ 803/768–2121), and **Wild Dunes** (☎ 803/886–6000).

Spectator Sports

BASEBALL

The minor-league **RiverDogs** (✉ 360 Fishburne St., ☎ 803/723–7241) play at the Joseph P. Riley Jr. Ballpark from April through August.

HOCKEY

The Charleston **Stingrays** (✉ 3107 Firestone Rd., North Charleston, ☎ 803/747–2248), ranked first in the East Coast Hockey League, play at the North Charleston Coliseum to record-breaking crowds from October through March.

Shopping

Shopping Districts

The Market is a complex of specialty shops and restaurants. Don't miss the colorful produce market in the three-block **Old City Market** (✉ E. Bay and Market Sts.) and, adjacent to it, the open-air flea market, with crafts, antiques, and memorabilia. You'll find locally produced sweetgrass and other baskets here. Other such complexes in the historic district are the **Shops at Charleston Place** (✉ 130 Market St.) and **Rainbow Market** (✉ 40 N. Market St.), in two interconnected 150-year-old buildings; **Market Square;** and **State Street Market** (✉ 67 State St.). **King Street** has some of Charleston's oldest and finest shops, along with the new **Saks Fifth Avenue** (✉ 211 King St., ☎ 803/853–9888). From May until September, the festive **Farmer's Market** takes place each Saturday morning in Marion Square.

Antiques

King Street is the center. **Petterson Antiques** (✉ 201 King St., ☎ 803/723–5714) offers curious objets d'art, books, furniture, porcelain, and glass. **Livingston & Sons Antiques,** dealers in 18th- and 19th-century English and Continental furniture, clocks, and bric-a-brac, has a large shop west of the Ashley (✉ 2137 Savannah Hwy., ☎ 803/556–6162) and a smaller one on King (✉ 163 King St., ☎ 803/723–9697). **Birlant & Co.** (✉ 191 King St., ☎ 803/722–3842) presents fine 18th- and 19th-century English antiques, as well as the famous Charleston Battery bench, identical to those on Charleston Green.

Art and Craft Galleries

The **Birds I View Gallery** (✉ 119–A Church St., ☎ 803/723–1276) sells bird paintings and prints by Anne Worsham Richardson. **Birds & Ivy** (✉ 235 King St., ☎ 803/853–8534), which sells garden art and accessories of every type, also has a café in back. **Charleston Crafts** (✉ 38 Queen St., ☎ 803/723–2938) has a fine selection of pottery, quilts, weavings, sculptures, and jewelry fashioned mostly by local artists. The **Elizabeth O'Neill Verner Studio & Museum** (✉ 79 Church St., ☎ 803/722–4246), in a 17th-century house, is open to the public. Prints of Elizabeth O'Neill Verner's pastels and etchings are on sale at the adjacent **Tradd Street Press** (✉ 38 Tradd St., ☎ 803/722–4246). The **Marty Whaley Adams Gallery** (✉ 120 Meeting St., ☎ 803/853–8512) has original vivid watercolors and monotypes, plus prints and posters by this Charleston artist. At **Nina Liu and Friends** (✉ 24 State St., ☎ 803/722–2724), you'll find contemporary art objects including handblown glass, pottery, jewelry, and photographs. The **Virginia Fouché Bolton Art Gallery** (✉ 127 Meeting St., ☎ 803/577–9351) sells original paintings and limited-edition lithographs of Charleston and Low-country scenes.

Books

Chapter Two (⊠ 199 E. Bay St., ☎ 803/722–4238), an independently owned, unique little nook, specializes in local and regional books; there's also a neat section for kids. The **Preservation Society of Charleston** (⊠ Corner of King and Queen Sts., ☎ 803/722–4630) has books and tapes of historic and local interest, sweetgrass baskets, prints, and posters.

Gifts

Charleston Collections (⊠ 233 King St., ☎ 803/722–7267; ⊠ Straw Market, Kiawah Island Resort, ☎ 803/768–7487; ⊠ Quadrangle Center, ☎ 803/556–8911) has Charleston chimes, prints, candies, T-shirts, and more. Charleston's and London's own **Ben Silver** (⊠ 149 King St., ☎ 803/577–4556), premier purveyor of blazer buttons, has over 800 designs, including college and British regimental motifs. He also sells British neckties, embroidered polo shirts, and blazers.

Period Reproductions

Historic Charleston Reproductions (⊠ 105 Broad St., ☎ 803/723–8292) has superb replicas of Charleston furniture and accessories, all authorized by the Historic Charleston Foundation. Royalties from sales contribute to restoration projects. At the **Old Charleston Joggling Board Co.** (⊠ 652 King St., ☎ 803/723–4331), these Lowcountry oddities (on which people bounce) can be purchased.

Side Trips from Charleston

Gardens, parks, and the charming town of Summerville are good reasons to travel a bit farther afield for some day trips.

Moncks Corner

30 mi north of Charleston on U.S. 52.

This town is a gateway to a number of attractions. Here in Santee Cooper Country, named for the two rivers that form a 171,000-acre basin, the area brims with outdoor pleasures centered around the basin and nearby Lakes Marion and Moultrie.

Cypress Gardens, a swamp garden created from what was once the freshwater reserve of the vast Dean Hall rice plantation, is about 24 mi north of Charleston via U.S. 52, between Goose Creek and Moncks Corner. Explore the inky waters by boat, or walk along paths lined with moss-draped cypress trees, azaleas, camellias, daffodils, wisteria, and dogwood. ⊠ *3030 Cypress Gardens Rd.,* ☎ *803/553–0515.* 🖅 *$5 (Mar.–Apr. $6).* 🕙 *Daily 9–5.*

🐣 On the banks of the Old Santee Canal is the **Old Santee Canal State Park,** reached via I–26 and U.S. 52. You can explore on foot or take a canoe. There's also an interpretive center. ⊠ *Rembert C. Dennis Blvd.,* ☎ *803/899–5200.* 🖅 *$3 per car.* 🕙 *Daily 9–6; spring and summer weekends 9–7.*

Francis Marion National Forest consists of 250,000 acres of swamps, vast oaks and pines, and little lakes thought to have been formed by falling meteors. It's a good place for picnicking, camping, boating, and swimming. At the park's **Rembert Dennis Wildlife Center** (⊠ Off U.S. 52 in Bonneau, north of Moncks Corner, ☎ 803/825–3387), deer, wild turkey, and striped bass are reared and studied. ⊠ *35 mi north of Charleston via U.S. 52,* ☎ *803/336–3248.* 🖅 *Free.*

FISHING

Lakes Marion and **Moultrie** are full of bream, striped bass, catfish, and large- and smallmouth bass. For information, contact Santee Cooper Counties Promotion Commission (✉ Drawer 40, Santee 29142, ☎ 803/ 854–2131; 800/227–8510 outside South Carolina).

Summerville

25 mi northwest of Charleston via I–26 (Exit 199), SC 78, or SC 61 and SC 165.

Built by wealthy planters as an escape from hot-weather malaria, this picturesque town is a treasure trove of Victorian buildings, many of which are listed in the National Register of Historic Places. Colorful gardens of camellias, azaleas, and wisteria abound, and many streets curve around tall pines, as a local ordinance prohibits cutting them down. This is a good place for a bit of antiquing in attractive shops. To get oriented, stop by the **Summerville Chamber of Commerce** (✉ 106 E. Doty Ave., Box 670, 29483, ☎ 803/873–2931). It's open weekdays 8:30–12:30 and 1:30–5, Saturday 10–3.

DINING AND LODGING

$$$$
★
╳▦ **Woodlands Inn.** People drive from Charleston for superb meals at this luxury inn's restaurant ($$$–$$$$), which recently joined the prestigious Relais & Châteaux group. There's a three-course ($38) or four-course ($44) menu, plus a more expensive chef's tasting menu. Delicate sauces and subtle touches are key in entrées such as Angus beef with celery root home fries and Barolo wine reduction, and soft-shell crab with doubloon mushrooms, lemon grass, and ginger. Though the inn, built in 1906 as a winter home, backs up to a suburb, it's a first-rate getaway with such niceties as fireplaces and whirlpool or claw-foot tubs. Breakfast is included in the rate, as is a split of champagne at arrival and afternoon tea. ✉ *125 Parsons Rd., 29483, ☎ 803/875– 2600 or 800/774–9999,* ℻ *803/875–2603. 16 rooms, 4 suites. Restaurant, lounge, pool, spa, 2 tennis courts, croquet, bicycles. AE, D, DC, MC, V.*

Charleston A to Z

Arriving and Departing

BY BOAT

Boaters on the Intracoastal Waterway may dock at **City Marina** (✉ Lock-wood Blvd., ☎ 803/724–7357) in Charleston Harbor or **Wild Dunes Yacht Harbor** (☎ 803/886–5100) on the Isle of Palms.

BY BUS

Greyhound (✉ 3610 Dorchester Rd., N. Charleston, ☎ 800/231–2222).

BY CAR

I–26 traverses the state from northwest to southeast and terminates at Charleston. U.S. 17, the coast road, passes through Charleston.

BY PLANE

Charleston International Airport (☎ 803/767–1100) on I–26, 12 mi west of downtown, is served by Air South, Continental, Delta, Midway Connection, United, and US Airways.

Lowcountry Limousine Service (☎ 803/767–7111 or 800/222–4771) charges $15 per person (or $10 per person for two or more) to downtown. If you're traveling from the airport by **car,** take I–26S into the city.

Amtrak (⌧ 4565 Gaynor Ave., N. Charleston, ☎ 803/744–8264 or 800/872–7245).

Getting Around

CHARTS (⌧ 196A Concord, ☎ 803/853–4700) is the only full-service water taxi providing transportation to and from Patriots Point naval and maritime museum. It also offers harbor cruises.

Regular buses run in most of Charleston from 5:35 AM until 10 PM and to North Charleston until 1 AM. The cost is 75¢ exact change (free transfers). DASH (Downtown Area Shuttle) trolley-style buses provide fast service in the main downtown areas. The fare is 75¢; $2 for an all-day pass. For schedule information, call 803/747–0922.

Fares within the city average $2–$3 per trip. Companies include **Yellow Cab** (☎ 803/577–6565), **Safety Cab** (☎ 803/722–4066), and **Lowcountry Limousine Service** (☞ Arriving and Departing, *above*).

Contacts and Resources

Police (☎ 911). **Ambulance** (☎ 911). The **emergency rooms** are open all night at Charleston Memorial Hospital (⌧ 326 Calhoun St., ☎ 803/577–0600) and Roper Hospital (⌧ 316 Calhoun St., ☎ 803/724–2000).

Princess Gray Line Harbor Tours (☎ 803/722–1112 or 800/344–4483) and **Charleston Harbor Tour** (☎ 803/722–1691) ply the harbor. **Fort Sumter Tours** (☎ 803/722–1691) includes a stop at Fort Sumter and also offers Starlight Dinner Cruises aboard a luxury yacht. **Flying High Over Charleston** (☎ 803/569–6148) provides aerial tours. **Adventure Sightseeing** (☎ 803/762–0088 or 800/722–5394) and **Colonial Coach and Trolley Company** (☎ 803/795–3000) offer motor-coach tours of the historic district. **Gray Line** (☎ 803/722–4444) offers tours of the historic district, plus seasonal trips to gardens and plantations.

Charleston Carriage Co. (☎ 803/577–0042), **Old South Carriage Company** (☎ 803/723–9712), and **Palmetto Carriage Works** (☎ 803/723–8145) run approximately one-hour horse- and mule-drawn carriage tours of the historic district, some conducted by guides in Confederate uniforms. **Doin' the Charleston** (☎ 803/763–1233 or 800/647–4487), a van tour, combines its narration with audiovisuals and makes a stop at the Battery.

Chai Y'All (☎ 803/556–0664) shares stories and sites of Jewish interest. **Sweet Grass Tours** (☎ 803/556–0664 for groups) focus on African-American influences on Charleston architecture, history, and culture.

Walking tours are given by **Historic Charleston Walking Tours** (☎ 803/722–6460); **Charleston Strolls** (☎ 803/884–9505); **Architectural Walking Tours of Charleston** (☎ 803/893–2327); and **Charleston Tea Party Walking Tour** (☎ 803/577–5896 or 803/722–1779), which includes tea in a private garden. For a spookier view of the city, take the **Ghosts of Charleston** (☎ 803/723–1670 or 800/854–1670) walking tour. The same guides also celebrate the city in the Story of Charleston walking tour.

Henry's Conway Drug Store (✉ 517 King St., ☎ 803/577–5123). **Tellis Pharmacy** (✉ 125 King St., ☎ 803/723–0682). **Eckerds** (✉ 466 Savannah Hwy., ☎ 803/766–5593).

LODGING ASSISTANCE

Rates tend to increase during the Spring Festival of Houses and Spoleto, when reservations are essential. To find rooms in homes, cottages, and carriage houses, try **Historic Charleston Bed and Breakfast** (✉ 60 Broad St., Charleston 29401, ☎ 803/722–6606). **Southern Hospitality B&B Reservations** (✉ 110 Amelia Dr., Lexington 29072, ☎ 803/356–6238 or 800/374–7422) handles rooms in homes and carriage houses. For historic home rentals in Charleston, contact **Charleston Carriage Houses–Oceanfront Realty** (✉ Box 6151, Hilton Head 29938, ☎ 803/785–8161). For condo and house rentals on the Isle of Palms—some with private pools and tennis courts—try **Island Realty** (✉ Box 157, Isle of Palms 29451, ☎ 803/886–8144).

PERSONAL GUIDES

Contact **Associated Guides of Historic Charleston** (☎ 803/724–6419); **Cary Parker Limousine Service** (☎ 803/723–7601), which offers chauffeur-driven luxury limousine tours; or **Charleston Guide Service** (☎ 803/722–8240), the city's oldest guide service. **Janice Kahn** (☎ 803/556–0664) has done individualized guiding for 25 years.

RADIO STATIONS

AM: WQIZ 810, gospel; WTMA 1250, talk radio; WXTC 1390, sports. **FM:** WBUB 107.5, country; WJZK 96.9, smooth jazz; WSCI 89.3, news, classical, jazz, information line; WWWZ 93.4, urban contemporary; WYBB 98.1, classic rock.

VISITOR INFORMATION

You can pick up the Schedule of Events at the Visitors Center (✉ 375 Meeting St.) or at area hotels, inns, and restaurants. Also see "Tips for Tourists" each Saturday in the *Post & Courier*. **Charleston Area Convention and Visitors Bureau** (✉ Box 975, Charleston 29402, ☎ 803/853–8000 or 800/868–8118) has information on the city and also on Kiawah Island, Seabrook Island, Mount Pleasant, North Charleston, Edisto Island, Summerville, and the Isle of Palms. **Historic Charleston Foundation** (✉ Box 1120, Charleston 29402, ☎ 803/723–1623) and the **Preservation Society of Charleston** (✉ Box 521, 29402, ☎ 803/722–4630) have information on house tours.

MYRTLE BEACH AND THE GRAND STRAND

The lively, family-oriented Grand Strand, a booming resort area along the South Carolina coast, is one of the Eastern Seaboard's megavacation centers. Myrtle Beach alone accounts for about 40% of the state's tourism revenue. The main attraction, of course, is the broad, beckoning beach—60 mi of white sand, stretching from the North Carolina border south to Georgetown, with Myrtle Beach at the hub. All along the Strand you can enjoy shell hunting, fishing, swimming, sunbathing, sailing, surfing, jogging, or just strolling on the beach. But the Strand has something for everyone: more than 80 championship golf courses, designed by Arnold Palmer, Robert Trent Jones, Jack Nicklaus, and Tom and George Fazio, among others; excellent seafood restaurants; giant shopping malls and factory outlets; amusement parks, water slides, and arcades; a dozen shipwrecks for divers to explore; fine fishing; campgrounds, most on the beach; plus antique-car and wax museums, the world's largest outdoor sculpture garden, a half dozen country music shows, an antique pipe organ and merry-go-round, and a museum dedicated entirely to rice.

Myrtle Beach—whose population of 26,000 explodes to about 350,000 in summer—is the center of activity on the Grand Strand. It is here that you find the amusement parks and other children's activities that make the area so popular with families, as well as most of the nightlife that keeps parents and teenagers happy. On the North Strand, there is Little River, with a thriving fishing and charter industry, and the several communities that make up North Myrtle Beach. On the South Strand, the family retreats of Surfside Beach and Garden City offer more summer homes and condominiums. Farther south are towns as alluring to visit as are the myriad sights along the way: Murrells Inlet, once a pirate's haven and now a picturesque fishing village and port; and Pawleys Island, one of the East Coast's oldest resorts, which prides itself on being "arrogantly shabby." Historic Georgetown forms the southern tip.

Myrtle Beach

94 mi northeast of Charleston, 201 mi east of Columbia.

In Myrtle Beach, to capture the flavor and swirl of seaside activity, start at the Myrtle Beach Pavilion Amusement Park and wind your way north on Ocean Boulevard. Here's where you'll find an eclectic assortment of gift and novelty shops—everything from T-shirts to perfect shells—a wax museum and museum of oddities. Turn east when it suits your fancy and make your way back on the beach amid children building sand castles and kids-at-heart flying kites. The sights included here are in Myrtle Beach and north to North Myrtle Beach, with a couple to the south.

Dozens of colorful streetlight displays around major intersections add yet a few more volts of energy to the already pulsating scene, and at Christmas, Myrtle Beach stages one of the largest, most colorful light shows in the South.

☾ **Myrtle Beach Pavilion Amusement Park** has thrill and kiddie rides, the Carolinas' largest flume, video games, a teen nightclub, specialty shops, antique cars, and sidewalk cafés. ⊠ *9th Ave. N and Ocean Blvd.,* ☎ *803/448–6456.* ☞ *Fees for individual attractions; $18.50 1-day pass for unlimited access to most rides.* ☉ *Mid-Mar.–May and mid-Aug.– Oct., weekdays 6 PM–midnight, weekends 1 PM–midnight; June– mid-Aug., daily 1 PM–midnight. Operating hrs can vary, so do call ahead.*

☾ **Ripleys Believe It or Not Museum** is based on the drawings that adults used to see in the newspaper and children enjoy afresh, translated into lively displays of odd facts and figures. Among the more than 750 exhibits is an 8-ft, 11-inch wax replica of the world's tallest man. ⊠ *901 N. Ocean Blvd.,* ☎ *803/448–2331.* ☞ *$6.50.* ☉ *Daily 10–10.*

☾ **Myrtle Beach National Wax Museum** offers drama, sound, and animation in sections highlighting religious, historical, and entertainment people and events. ⊠ *1000 N. Ocean Blvd.,* ☎ *803/448–9921.* ☞ *$5.* ☉ *Late Feb.–mid-Oct., daily 9 AM–11 PM.*

Myrtle Beach is the minigolf capital of the world, featuring courses that
☾ mimic Jurassic Park and Never-Never Land, and **Hawaiian Rumble** is the crown jewel. It features a smoking mountain that erupts fire and rumbles at timed intervals. ⊠ *3210 33rd Ave. S, U.S. 17,* ☎ *803/272– 7812.* ☞ *$4 all day (9–5), $4 per round after 5 PM.* ☉ *Mar.–Dec., daily 9 AM–10 PM.*

★ ☺ **Alligator Adventure** has exciting interactive reptile shows, including an alligator-feeding demonstration. The boardwalks go through marshes and swamps on the 15-acre property, where you'll see wildlife of the wetlands, including the only known collection of rare white albino alligators; the gharial, an exotic crocodilian from Asia; giant Galapagos tortoises; and all manner of reptiles, including boas, pythons, and anacondas. Unusual plants and exotic birds also thrive here. ⊠ *U.S. 17S at Barefoot Landing, North Myrtle Beach,* ☎ *803/361–0789 or 800/ 631–0789,* FAX *803/361–0742.* ☜ *$9.95.* ☻ *Daily 9–9.*

☺ **Myrtle Beach Grand Prix** is auto-mania heaven with Formula 1 race cars, go-carts, bumper boats, mini-go-carts, kiddie cars, and mini-bumper boats for adults and children ages three and up. *Two locations:* ⊠ *3201 Hwy. 17,* ☎ *803/238–2421;* ⊠ *Windy Hill, 3900 U.S. 17S, North Myrtle Beach,* ☎ *803/272–6010.* ☜ *Rides $1.50–$5 each.* ☻ *Mar.–Oct., daily 10 AM–11 PM.*

☺ A new attraction, **Ripley's Aquarium,** has an underwater tunnel exhibit longer than a football field and exotic marine creatures from poisonous lionfish to moray eels and an octopus. Children can examine horseshoe crabs and eels in touch tanks. ⊠ *9th Ave. N and U.S. 17N Bypass,* ☎ *803/916–0888 or 800/734–8888.* ☜ *$12.95.* ☻ *Daily 9 AM–11 PM.*

☺ South of Myrtle Beach, **Wild Water** provides splashy family fun for all ages in 25 rides and activities. ⊠ *910 U.S. 17S, Surfside Beach,* ☎ *803/ 238–9453.* ☜ *$17.99; $11.99 after 3 PM.* ☻ *Memorial Day weekend– Labor Day, Fri.–Mon. 10–7, Tues.–Thurs. 10–8.*

Dining and Lodging

MYRTLE BEACH

$$ ✕ **Collectors Cafe.** A successful restaurant, art gallery, and coffeehouse
★ rolled into one, this unpretentiously arty spot has bright, funky paintings and tile work covering its walls and tabletops. You can shop for a painting while enjoying the veal-stuffed ravioli or barbecued duck over polenta cake with goat cheese cream. ⊠ *7726 N. Kings Hwy.,* ☎ *803/449–9370. AE, D, DC, MC, V. Closed Sun.*

$$ ✕ **Sea Captain's House.** At this picturesque restaurant with nautical decor, the best seats are in the windowed porch room, which overlooks the ocean. The fireplace in the wood-paneled dining room inside is warmly welcoming on cool off-season evenings. Menu highlights include Lowcountry crab casserole and avocado-seafood salad. The breads and desserts are baked here. ⊠ *3000 N. Ocean Blvd.,* ☎ *803/ 448–8082. AE, D, MC, V.*

$–$$ ✕ **Latif's Cafe and Bar.** The lunch crowd loves this light-filled hot spot,
★ with its pastry cases full of homemade breads, cakes, and cookies. The soups are garden fresh, and there are yummy shrimp and black bean cakes, traditional and Asian chicken salads, and homemade salad dressings. ⊠ *503 61st Ave. N,* ☎ *803/449–1716. AE, D, DC, MC, V. No dinner Sun.*

$$$$ ▥ **Kingston Plantation.** The Grand Strand's most luxurious property,
★ the 20-story glass-sheathed tower is part of a complex of shops, restaurants, hotels, and condominiums set amid 145 acres of oceanside woodlands. Guest rooms are highlighted by bleached-wood furnishings and attractive art; all have kitchenettes. ⊠ *9800 Lake Dr., 29572,* ☎ *803/449–0006 or 800/876–0010,* FAX *803/497–1110. 614 suites. 2 restaurants, lounge, 5 outdoor pools, 1 indoor pool, sauna, tennis, aerobics, health club. AE, D, DC, MC, V.*

$$$-$$$$ 🏨 **Breakers Resort Hotel.** The rooms in this oceanfront hotel are airy and spacious, with contemporary decor. Many have balconies and refrigerators. ✉ *2006 N. Ocean Blvd., Box 485, 29578,* ☎ *803/444–4444 or 800/845–0688,* FAX *803/626–5001. 204 rooms, 186 suites. 2 restaurants, lounge, 3 outdoor pools, 1 indoor pool, 4 hot tubs, 3 saunas, exercise room, children's programs, laundry service. AE, D, DC, MC, V.*

$$$-$$$$ 🏨 **Landmark Resort Hotel.** This high-rise oceanfront resort hotel, with a rooftop sundeck and "lazy rivers" (artificial streams) indoors and out, recently added an addition across the street. Rooms are colorfully decorated in a Caribbean motif, and some in the oceanfront building have balconies and refrigerators. ✉ *1501 S. Ocean Blvd., 29577,* ☎ *803/448–9441 or 800/448–6701,* FAX *803/626–1501. 313 rooms, 14 suites in original hotel; 257 suites in addition. Restaurant, lounge, pub, 2 pools, nightclub, recreation room, children's programs. AE, D, DC, MC, V.*

$$$-$$$$ 🏨 **Sheraton Myrtle Beach Resort.** All rooms and suites have a fresh, contemporary look. Oceanfront Lounge, highlighted by tropical colors and rattan furnishings, is a lively evening gathering spot. There's an arcade, too. ✉ *2701 S. Ocean Blvd., 29577,* ☎ *803/448–2518 or 800/992–1055,* FAX *803/449–1879. 211 rooms, 8 suites. Restaurant, indoor pool, outdoor pool, health club. AE, D, DC, MC, V.*

$$$ 🏨 **Chesterfield Inn.** A remnant from the past, this oceanfront brick inn, hidden beneath the towers of Myrtle Beach's glitzier hotels, has been in operation for over a half century. The rooms in the original building are plain and a bit run-down, but many guests prefer them to those in the newer wing. The highlight: Family-style meals are served on white tablecloths in the paneled dining room. ✉ *700 N. Ocean Blvd., 29578,* ☎ *803/448–3177,* FAX *803/626–4736. 57 rooms, 6 kitchenette units. Restaurant, pool, shuffleboard. AE, D, DC, MC, V.*

$$$ 🏨 **Driftwood on the Oceanfront.** Under the same ownership for more than 50 years, the Driftwood is popular with families. Some rooms are oceanfront; all are decorated in sea, sky, or earth tones. ✉ *1600 N. Ocean Blvd., Box 275, 29578,* ☎ *803/448–1544 or 800/942–3456,* FAX *803/448–2917. 90 rooms. 2 pools, exercise room, recreation room. AE, D, DC, MC, V.*

$$$ 🏨 **Holiday Inn Oceanfront.** This oceanfront inn is right at the heart of the action, and rates vary according to the season. The spacious rooms are done in cool sea tones. After beach basking, you can prolong the mood in the inn's spacious, plant-bedecked indoor recreation center, which contains an indoor pool, exercise room, game room, and gift shop. ✉ *415 S. Ocean Blvd., 29577,* ☎ *803/448–4481 or 800/845–0313,* FAX *803/448–0086. 311 rooms. 2 restaurants, 2 lounges, snack bar, 1 indoor pool, 1 outdoor pool, hot tub, sauna, recreation room. AE, D, DC, MC, V.*

$$-$$$ 🏨 **Red Roof Inn.** This chain motel, 400 yards from the ocean, is predictably furnished and well maintained. ✉ *2801 S. Kings Hwy., 29577,* ☎ *803/626–4444 or 800/228–5150,* FAX *803/626–0753. 152 rooms, 14 suites. Restaurant, pool, health club. AE, D, DC, MC, V.*

$$ 🏨 **Days Inn at Waccamaw.** Relax by the pool or in the gazebo after a day of shopping at the nearby Waccamaw Pottery and Outlet Park. The theaters of the Fantasy Harbor complex are also close at hand. Rooms here are clean and functional, filled with contemporary furnishings, and most are equipped with a refrigerator. ✉ *3650 Hwy. 501, 29577,* ☎ *803/236–1950 or 800/325–2525,* FAX *803/236–9415. 160 rooms. Restaurant, lounge, pool, hot tub. AE, D, DC, MC, V.*

NORTH MYRTLE BEACH

Dinner cruises are another dining option here. The cruise ship *Hurricane* and yachts of the Hurricane pleasure fleet (☎ 803/249–3571) depart from Vereen's Marina (✉ U.S. 17N and 11th Ave.). The *Barefoot Princess* (☎ 803/272–7743 or 800/685–6601), a replica of a side-wheel riverboat, offers dinner, sunset, and sightseeing cruises along the Intracoastal Waterway from Barefoot Landing (✉ 4898 U.S. 17S).

$$–$$$ ✕ **Oak Harbor Inn.** Set on a quiet stretch of the beach, this airy, open restaurant overlooks picturesque Vereen's Marina. It's a great local favorite. Specialties include Chicken Annie, a boneless breast of chicken in puff pastry laced with ham and Swiss and blue cheeses, drizzled with Parmesan and Mornay sauce. ✉ *1407 13th Ave. N,* ☎ *803/249–4737. AE, D, MC, V. Closed Sun. No lunch.*

$$ ✕ **Horst Gasthaus.** Dine on knockwurst, bratwurst, sauerbraten, and other traditional German foods at this Bavarian-style restaurant, where there's oompah-pah music every night but Sunday. ✉ *802 37th Ave. S,* ☎ *803/272–3351. AE, D, MC, V.*

Nightlife and the Arts

THE ARTS

Theater productions, concerts, art exhibits, and other cultural events are regularly offered at the **Myrtle Beach Convention Center** (✉ Oak and 21st Ave. N, ☎ 803/448–7166). **Art in the Park,** featuring arts and crafts, is staged in Myrtle Beach's Chapin Park three times during the summer season (☎ 803/626–7444 for details).

CLUBS AND LOUNGES

Clubs offer varying fare, including beach music, the Grand Strand's unique '50s-style sound. During summer, sophisticated live entertainment is featured nightly at some clubs and resorts. Some hotels and resorts also have piano bars or lounges featuring easy-listening music.

South Carolina's only **Hard Rock Cafe, Planet Hollywood,** and **NASCAR Cafe** are just a few of the hot spots in **Broadway at the Beach** (✉ U.S. 17 Bypass between 21st and 29th Aves. N, ☎ 803/444–3200). **Sandals** (✉ 500 Shore Dr., ☎ 803/449–6461) is an intimate lounge with live entertainment. **Coquina Club,** at the Landmark Resort Hotel (✉ 1501 S. Ocean Blvd., ☎ 803/448–9441), features beach-music bands. The shag (the state dance) is popular at **Studebaker's** (✉ 2000 N. Kings Hwy., ☎ 803/448–9747 or 803/626–3855). You can dance the shag at **Duck's** (✉ 229 Main St., North Myrtle Beach, ☎ 803/249–3858). At the **Afterdeck** (✉ Hwy. 17, Restaurant Row, ☎ 803/449–1550) enjoy live bands, dancing, and comedy at an open-air club along the Intracoastal Waterway.

FILM

The **IMAX Discovery Theater** at Broadway at the Beach (✉ U.S. 17 Bypass between 21st and 29th Aves. N., ☎ 803/448–4629) shows educational films, including the beautiful *The Living Sea* with music by Sting, on a six-story-high screen.

MUSIC AND LIVE SHOWS

Country-and-western shows and other live acts have added a new dimension to Grand Strand entertainment. Music lovers have many family-oriented shows to choose from: the 2,250-seat **Alabama Theater** (✉ Barefoot Landing, 4750 U.S. 17, North Myrtle Beach, ☎ 803/272–1111); **Carolina Opry** (✉ 82nd Ave. N, Myrtle Beach, ☎ 803/238–8888 or 800/843–6779); **Dolly Parton's Dixie Stampede** (✉ 8901-B U.S. 17 Business, next door to Carolina Opry, Myrtle Beach, ☎ 803/497–9700); **Legends in Concert** (✉ 301 U.S. 17 Business, Surfside Beach, ☎ 803/238–7827 or 800/843–6779). The elegant **Palace Theater** (✉

Broadway at the Beach, U.S. 17 Bypass between 21st and 29th Aves. N, ☎ 803/448–0588 or 800/905–4228) hosts performances by the likes of Aretha Franklin, Kenny Rogers, and the Radio City Rockettes.

The **Fantasy Harbor** complex (✉ Hwy. 51, across from Waccamaw Outlet Mall) includes five theaters: the 2,000-seat **Gatlin Brothers Theater** (☎ 803/395–6802 or 800/681–7469); **Snoopy's Magic on Ice** (☎ 803/236–8500 or 800/395–6802); **Medieval Times Dinner & Tournament** (☎ 803/236–8080 or 800/436–4386); and the 2,000-seat **All-American Music Theater** (☎ 803/236–8500).

A newcomer to the scene in 1997, the **House of Blues** (✉ 4640 U.S. 17S, North Myrtle Beach, ☎ 803/272–3000 for tickets), adjacent to Barefoot Landing, showcases big names and up-and-coming local talent in blues, rock, jazz, country, and R&B on stages in its Southern-style restaurant and patio as well as in its 2,000-seat concert hall.

Outdoor Activities and Sports

BEACHES

All the region's beaches are family oriented, and most are public. The widest expanses are in **North Myrtle Beach,** where, at low tide, the sand stretches up to ⅛ mi from the dunes to the water. Those who wish to combine their sunning with nightlife and amusement-park attractions can enjoy it all at **Myrtle Beach,** the Strand's longtime hub. Vacationers seeking a quieter day in the sun head for the **South Strand** communities of Surfside Beach and Garden City.

Besides ocean swimming, **Myrtle Beach State Park** has surf fishing, a nature trail, and a pool; there's camping, too, but book in advance. ✉ *U.S. 17, 3 mi south of Myrtle Beach,* ☎ *803/238–5325.* 🎫 *$3 per car.*

FISHING

The Gulf Stream makes fishing usually good from early spring through December. Anglers can fish from 10 piers and jetties for amberjack, sea trout, and king mackerel. Surfcasters may snare bluefish, whiting, flounder, pompano, and channel bass. In the South Strand, salt marshes, inlets, and tidal creeks yield flounder, blues, croakers, spots, shrimp, clams, oysters, and blue crabs. The annual **Grand Strand Fishing Rodeo** (☎ 803/626–7444 Apr.–Oct.) features a "fish of the month" contest, with prizes for the largest catch of a designated species.

GOLF

Many of the Grand Strand's 91 courses are championship layouts; most are public. **Tee Times Central** (☎ 803/347–4653 or 800/344–5590) books tee times for eight courses, including **Myrtle Beach National Golf Club** (☎ 803/448–2308), **Waterway Hills** (☎ 803/449–6488), and **Long Bay** (☎ 803/399–2222). Some popular courses include: in Myrtle Beach, **Arcadian Shores Golf Club** (☎ 803/449–5217); in North Myrtle Beach, **Bay Tree Golf Plantation** (☎ 803/249–1487 or 800/845–6191), **Gator Hole** (☎ 803/249–3543 or 800/447–2668), **Heather Glen Golf Links** (☎ 803/249–9000), and **Robbers Roost Golf Club** (☎ 803/249–1471 or 800/352–2384); near Surfside Beach, **Blackmoor Golf Club** (☎ 803/650–5555); and in Cherry Grove Beach, the much touted **Tidewater** (☎ 803/249–6675).

SCUBA DIVING

In summer, a wide variety of warm-water tropical fish travel to the area from the Gulf Stream. Off the coast of Little River, near the North Carolina border, rock and coral ledges teem with coral, sea fans, sponges, reef fish, anemones, urchins, and crabs. Several outlying shipwrecks are home to schools of spadefish, amberjack, grouper, and barracuda.

Instruction and equipment rentals are available from **Scuba Syndrome** (⊠ 2718 Hwy. 501, ☎ 803/626–6740).

TENNIS

There are more than 200 courts on the Grand Strand. Facilities include hotel and resort courts, as well as free municipal courts in Myrtle Beach, North Myrtle Beach, and Surfside Beach. Among tennis clubs offering court time, rental equipment, and instruction are **Myrtle Beach Racquet Club** (☎ 803/449–4031) and **Myrtle Beach Tennis and Swim Club** (☎ 803/449–4486).

WATER SPORTS

Surfboards, Hobie Cats, Jet Skis, Windsurfers, and sailboats are available for rent at **Downwind Sails** (⊠ Ocean Blvd. at 29th Ave. S, ☎ 803/448–7245) and **Myrtle Beach Yacht Club** (⊠ Coquina Harbor, North Myrtle Beach, ☎ 803/249–5376).

Shopping

DISCOUNT OUTLETS

At **Waccamaw Pottery and Outlet Park** (⊠ U.S. 501 at the Waterway, ☎ 803/236–1100) over 3 mi of shelves in several buildings are stocked with china, glassware, wicker, brass, pewter, and other items, and about 50 factory outlets sell clothing, furniture, books, jewelry, and more. **Hathaway/Olga Warner** (⊠ U.S. 501, ☎ 803/236–5717), in the Factory Shops across from Waccamaw, offers menswear by Chaps, Ralph Lauren, Speedo, and Jack Nicklaus, and women's lingerie. This growing outlet mall has upscale vendors like Royal Doulton.

MALLS

Malls are generally open Monday–Saturday 10–9, Sunday 1–6. **Barefoot Landing** in North Myrtle Beach (⊠ 4898 S. Kings Hwy., ☎ 803/272–8349) is a built over marshland and water, with scores of shops and restaurants. **Briarcliffe Mall** (⊠ 10177 N. Kings Hwy., ☎ 803/272–4040) has 100 specialty shops. **Broadway at the Beach** (⊠ U.S. 17 Bypass, ☎ 803/444–3200 or 800/819–2282) has 75 shops with restaurants and nightlife venues. **Myrtle Square Mall** (⊠ 2501 N. Kings Hwy., ☎ 803/448–2513) has 71 upscale stores and restaurants, and a food court.

Murrells Inlet

15 mi south of Myrtle Beach.

When your family's appetite for more raucous amusement has been sated, head south on U.S. 17 for some of the Grand Strand's quaint and quieter towns. Murrells Inlet, a fishing village with some popular seafood restaurants, is a perfect place to rent a fishing boat or join an excursion. A notable garden and state park provide other diversions from the beach.

★ **Brookgreen Gardens,** begun in 1931 by railroad magnate/philanthropist Archer Huntington and his wife, Anna (herself a sculptor), has more than 500 sculptures by such artists as Frederic Remington and Daniel Chester French. The works are set amid beautifully landscaped grounds, with avenues of live oaks, reflecting pools, and more than 2,000 plant species. Also on the site are a wildlife park, an aviary, a cypress swamp, nature trails, and an education center. ⊠ *West of U.S. 17, 3 mi south of Murrells Inlet,* ☎ *803/237–4218 or 800/849–1931.* ☞ *$7.50.* ☼ *Daily 9:30–4:45.*

Huntington Beach State Park, the 2,500-acre former estate of Archer and Anna Huntington, lies east of U.S. 17, across from the couple's Brookgreen Gardens (☞ *above*). The park's focal point is **Atalaya** (circa

1933), their Moorish-style, 30-room home, open to visitors in season. In addition to the splendid beach, there are nature trails, surf fishing, an interpretive center, a salt-marsh boardwalk, picnic areas, a playground, concessions, and a campground. ⊠ *Off U.S. 17, 3 mi south of Murrells Inlet,* ☎ *803/237–4440.* ☞ *Free; parking fee in peak months.* ☉ *Daily dawn–dusk.*

Dining

$$ ✕ **Planter's Back Porch.** Sip cool drinks in the springhouse of a turn-
★   of-the-century farmhouse, then have dinner in a garden setting. Baskets of greenery decorate white latticework archways between the fireplace-centered main dining room and the airy, glass-enclosed porch. Try baked whole flounder, panned lump crabmeat, or the hearty inlet dinner with several types of fish. ⊠ *U.S. 17 and Wachesaw Rd.,* ☎ *803/651–5263. AE, D, MC, V. Closed Dec.–mid-Mar.*

Nightlife and the Arts

NIGHTLIFE

Drunken Jack's (⊠ U.S. 17 Business, ☎ 803/651–2044 or 803/651–3232) is a popular restaurant with a lounge overlooking the docks.

THE ARTS

In the fall, the **Atalaya Arts Festival** (☎ 803/237–4440) at Huntington Beach State Park is a big draw.

Outdoor Activities and Sports

Capt. Dick's (⊠ U.S. 17 Business, ☎ 803/651–3676) offers half- and full-day fishing and sightseeing trips.

Pawleys Island

10 mi south of Murrells Inlet.

About 4 mi long and ½ mi wide, this island, referred to as "arrogantly shabby" by locals, began as a resort before the Civil War, when wealthy planters and their families summered here. It's mostly made up of weathered old summer cottages nestled in groves of oleander and oak trees. You can watch the famous Pawleys Island hammocks being made, and bicycle around admiring the weathered old beach houses, many dating to the early 1800s. There's golf and tennis nearby, too.

Dining and Lodging

$$ ✕ **Frank's.** Seasonal ingredients make this a local favorite. In a former 1930s grocery store with wood floors, framed French posters, and cozy fireside seating, diners indulge in large portions of fish, seafood, beef, and lamb cooked over an oak-burning grill. The roasted asparagus with prosciutto in phyllo, and pork tenderloin with shiitake mushrooms and a Dijon cream sauce, are just two highlights. Behind Frank's is the more casual Outback at Frank's, specializing in rotisserie chicken and turkey, salads, and lighter fare. ⊠ *10434 Ocean Hwy. (U.S. 17),* ☎ *803/237–3030. Reservations essential. D, MC, V. Closed Sun.*

$ ✕ **Island Country Store.** This little place, though tucked in a not very attractive spot in a shopping center, has terrific crab cakes as well as hickory-smoked barbecue, roasted chicken, and pizza (they deliver, too). ⊠ *The Island Shops, U.S. 17,* ☎ *803/237–8465. AE, MC, V.*

$$$$ ✕🏠 **Litchfield Plantation.** Period furnishings adorn four spacious suites of this impeccably restored 1750 rice-plantation manor-house-turned-country-inn fronted by a majestic avenue of live oaks. You may also stay in retreat cottages on the grounds. A beach-house club a short drive away is part of the package, as is a Continental breakfast. After en-

trées of grouper or steak at the elegant Carriage House Club you can retire to the restaurant's book-lined library. The resort is approximately 2 mi south of Brookgreen Gardens on U.S. 17 (turn right at the Litchfield Country Club entrance and follow the signs). ⊠ *River Rd., Box 290, 29585,* ☎ *803/237–9121 or 800/869–1410,* FAX *803/237–8558. 10 rooms, 7 2- and 3-bedroom cottages. Restaurant, pool, 2 tennis courts, horseback riding, boating, concierge. AE, D, MC, V.*

$$$$ 🏨 **Litchfield Beach and Golf Resort.** The inn's contemporary gray-blue wood suite units, a short walk from the beach, plus diverse rental accommodations, nestle amid the expansive gardenlike grounds, which include three private golf clubs and a racquet club open to guests. Suites are tastefully decorated in pastel tones and light woods, with marble baths, wet bars, refrigerators, and microwave ovens. Similarly furnished one- and two-bedroom units in the five-story Bridgewater complex have private balconies overlooking the pool and the Atlantic Ocean. "Country Club" cottages and marshside villas are ideal for families or couples seeking extra privacy. ⊠ *U.S. 17, 2 mi north of Pawleys Island, Drawer 320, 29585,* ☎ *803/237–3000 or 800/845–1897,* FAX *803/237–4282. 96 hotel suites; 254 condominium, cottage, and villa units. Restaurant, lounge, indoor pool, outdoor pool, hot tub, sauna, 3 18-hole golf courses, 19 tennis courts, exercise room, racquetball, meeting rooms. AE, D, DC, MC, V.*

$$ 🏨 **Ramada Inn Seagull.** This is a well-maintained inn on a golf course (excellent golf packages are available). Outfitted with motel-modern furnishings, the rooms are spacious, bright, and airy. ⊠ *U.S. 17S, Box 2217, 29585,* ☎ *803/237–4261 or 800/272–6232,* FAX *803/237–9703. 99 rooms. Dining room, lounge, pool. AE, D, DC, MC, V.*

Outdoor Activities and Sports

GOLF

Popular courses include **Litchfield Beach and Golf Resort** (☎ 803/237–3000 or 800/849–1897), **Litchfield Plantation** (☎ 803/237–9121 or 800/869–1410), and **Pawleys Plantation Golf & Country Club** (☎ 803/237–8497 or 800/367–9959). **Tee Times Central** (☎ 803/347–4653 or 800/344–5590) books tee times for **Litchfield Country Club** (☎ 803/237–3411), **River Club** (☎ 803/626–9069), and **Willbrook** (☎ 803/247–4900).

TENNIS

Litchfield Country Club (☎ 803/237–3411) offers court time, rental equipment, and instruction.

Shopping

The **Hammock Shops at Pawleys Island** (⊠ 10880 Ocean Hwy., ☎ 803/237–8448) is a complex of two dozen boutiques, gift shops, and restaurants built with old beams, timber, and ballast brick. Outside the Original Hammock Shop, in the Hammock Weavers' Pavilion, craftspeople demonstrate the more than 100-year-old art of weaving the famous cotton-rope Pawleys Island hammocks. Besides hammocks, look for jewelry, toys, antiques, and designer fashions.

Georgetown

10 mi south of Pawleys Island.

Founded on Winyah Bay in 1729, Georgetown became the center of America's Colonial rice empire. A rich plantation culture developed on a scale comparable to Charleston's, and the historic district, which can be walked in a couple of hours, is among the prettiest in the state. Today, oceangoing vessels still come to Georgetown's busy port, and the **Harbor Walk**, the restored waterfront, hums with activity. For information on tours, *see* Contacts and Resources *in* Myrtle Beach and the Grand Stand A to Z, *below.*

The graceful market–meeting building in the heart of Georgetown, topped by an 1842 clock and tower, has been converted into the **Rice Museum** with maps, tools, and dioramas. ⊠ *Front and Screven Sts.,* ☎ *803/546–7423.* ⊒ *$2.* ☉ *Mon.–Sat. 9:30–4:30.*

Prince George Winyah Episcopal Church (named after King George II) still serves the parish established in 1721. It was built in 1737 with bricks brought from England. ⊠ *Broad and Highmarket Sts., Georgetown,* ☎ *803/546–4358.* ⊒ *Donation suggested.* ☉ *Mar.–Oct., weekdays 11:30–4:30.*

Overlooking the Sampit River from a bluff is the **Harold Kaminski House** (circa 1769). It's especially notable for its collections of regional antiques and furnishings, its Chippendale and Duncan Phyfe furniture, Royal Doulton vases, and silver. ⊠ *1003 Front St.,* ☎ *803/546–7706.* ⊒ *$4.* ☉ *Mon.–Sat. 10–5, Sun. 1–4.*

Bellefield Nature Center Museum is at the entrance of Hobcaw Barony, on the vast estate of the late Bernard M. Baruch. Here Franklin D. Roosevelt and Winston Churchill came to confer with him. The museum is used for teaching and research in forestry and marine biology. There are aquariums, touch tanks, and video presentations. ⊠ *On U.S. 17, 2 mi north of Georgetown,* ☎ *803/546–4623.* ⊒ *Museum free; estate $15.* ☉ *Variety of nature tours and estate tours given year-round; call at least 1 month in advance for schedules and fees.*

Hopsewee Plantation, surrounded by moss-draped live oaks, magnolias, and tree-size camellias, overlooks the North Santee River. The circa-1740 mansion has a fine Georgian staircase and hand-carved Adam lighted-candle moldings. ⊠ *U.S. 17, 12 mi south of Georgetown,* ☎ *803/546–7891.* ⊒ *Mansion $5; grounds $2 per car; parking fees apply toward the tour if taken.* ☉ *Mansion Mar.–Nov., Tues.–Fri. 10–4; Dec.–Feb., by chance or appointment. Grounds, including nature trail, year-round, daily dawn–dusk.*

Hampton Plantation State Park preserves the home of Archibald Rutledge, poet laureate of South Carolina for 39 years until his death in 1973. The 18th-century plantation house is a fine example of a Lowcountry mansion. The exterior has been restored; cutaway sections in the finely crafted interior show the changes made through the centuries. The grounds are landscaped, and there are picnic areas. ⊠ *Off U.S. 17, at edge of Francis Marion National Forest, 16 mi south of Georgetown,* ☎ *803/546–9361.* ⊒ *Mansion $2; grounds free.* ☉ *Mansion Thurs.–Mon. 1–4, grounds Thurs.–Mon. 9–6.*

Dining and Lodging

$$–$$$ ✕ **Rice Paddy.** This cozy Lowcountry restaurant can be crowded at lunch,
★   when locals flock in for vegetable soup, garden-fresh salads, and sandwiches. Dinner is more relaxed, and the menu might have broiled seafood, crabmeat casserole, or quail with ham cream grits. ⊠ *Front and Orange Sts.,* ☎ *803/546–2021. AE, D, MC, V. Closed Sun.*

$$ ✕ **River Room.** This restaurant on the Sampit River specializes in char-grilled fish, seafood pastas, and steaks. For lunch you can have shrimp and grits or a variety of sandwiches and salads. The dining room has river views from most tables. It's especially romantic at night when the oil lamps and brass fixtures cast a warm glow on the dark wood and brick interior of the turn-of-the-century building. ⊠ *801 Front St.,* ☎ *803/527–4110. Reservations not accepted. AE, MC, V. Closed Sun.*

$ ✕ **Kudzu Bakery.** Here you can lunch on flavorful soups, sandwiches on homemade breads, and the best desserts in town. ⊠ *714 Front St., ☏ 803/546–1847. MC, V. Closed Wed., Sun. No dinner.*

$$$ 🛏 **Laurel Hill Plantation.** This plantation bed-and-breakfast house, overlooking the marsh near the Intracoastal Waterway, where the Lowcountry meets the Grand Strand, is furnished with country antiques. Guests can read in the hammock, go fishing or crabbing, take a boat ride, or watch the birds. The Morrisons serve a full breakfast and complimentary afternoon refreshments. ⊠ *8913 N. Hwy. 17 (22 mi south of Georgetown), Box 190, McClellanville 29458, ☏ 803/887–3708. 4 rooms. Fishing. No credit cards.*

$$–$$$ 🛏 **1790 House.** Built in the center of town after the Revolution, at the peak of Georgetown's rice culture, this lovely restored white Georgian house with a wraparound porch contains Colonial antique and reproduction furnishings suitable to its age. Guests are treated to gourmet breakfasts, evening refreshments, and the use of bicycles. For a romantic hideaway, request the private carriage house. ⊠ *630 Highmarket St., 29440, ☏ 803/546–4821 or 800/890–7432. 4 rooms, 1 suite, 1 cottage. Bicycles. AE, D, MC, V.*

Myrtle Beach and the Grand Strand A to Z

Arriving and Departing

BY BOAT

Boaters traveling the Intracoastal Waterway may dock at **Hague Marina** (⊠ Myrtle Beach, ☏ 803/293–2141), **Harbor Gate** (⊠ North Myrtle Beach, ☏ 803/249–8888), and **Marlin Quay** (⊠ Murrells Inlet, ☏ 803/651–4444).

BY BUS

Greyhound Bus Lines (☏ 800/231–2222) serves Myrtle Beach.

BY CAR

Midway between New York and Miami, the Grand Strand can be reached from all directions via Interstates 20, 26, 40, 77, 85, and 95, which connect by other routes to U.S. 17, the major north–south coastal route through the Strand.

BY PLANE

The **Myrtle Beach International Airport** (☏ 803/448–1589) is served by US Airways, Air Canada, Air South, American Eagle, Conair, Delta, G. P. Express, Jet Xpress, Midway, and Spirit.

BY TRAIN

Amtrak (☏ 800/872–7245) service for the Grand Strand is available through a terminal in Florence. Buses connect with Amtrak there for the 65-mi drive to Myrtle Beach.

Getting Around

BY TAXI

Service in Myrtle Beach is provided by **Coastal Cab Service** (☏ 803/448–3360 or 803/448–4444) and **Orange Cab** (☏ 803/448–2941).

Contacts and Resources

EMERGENCIES

Dial **911** for emergency assistance. The emergency room is open 24 hours a day at the **Columbia Grand Strand Regional Medical Center** (⊠ Off U.S. 17 at 809 82nd Pkwy., Myrtle Beach, ☏ 803/692–1000) and the **Georgetown Memorial Hospital** (⊠ 606 Black River Rd., Georgetown, ☏ 803/527–7000).

GOLF

Spring and fall, with off-season rates, are the busiest seasons, and there are many packages available in the area; call **Golf Holiday** (☎ 803/448–5942 or 800/845–4653). **Tee Times Central** (☎ 803/347–4653 or 800/344–5590) books tee times at a number of area courses.

GUIDED TOURS

Palmetto Tour & Travel (☎ 803/626–2660) and **Leisure Time Unlimited/Gray Line** (☎ 803/448–9483), both in Myrtle Beach, offer tour packages and guide services. At the **Georgetown County Chamber of Commerce and Information Center** (✉ 1005 Front St., Georgetown, ☎ 803/546–8436 or 800/777–7705), you can arrange to tour historic areas, March–October, by tram, by 1840 horse-drawn carriage, or by boat. You can also pick up free driving- and walking-tour maps. **Georgetown Tour Company** (✉ 627 Front St., Georgetown, ☎ 803/546–6827) offers tram tours of the historic district, a Ghostbusting Tour, and an afternoon Tea 'n Tour.

LATE-NIGHT PHARMACY

The only all-night pharmacy in the area is at the **Columbia Grand Strand Regional Medical Center** (☞ Emergencies, *above*).

LODGING ASSISTANCE

With about 55,000 rooms available along the Grand Strand, it's seldom difficult to find a place to stay, and discounting is rampant. Package deals are offered year-round, the most attractive of them between Labor Day and spring break. You can choose among cottages, villas, condominiums, and hotel-style high-rise units. For the free directories *Grand Hotel and Motel Accommodations* and *Grand Condominium and Cottage Accommodations,* write to the Myrtle Beach Area Convention Bureau (✉ 710 21st Ave. N, Suite J, Myrtle Beach 29577, ☎ 803/448–1629 or 800/356–3016). For Pawleys Island and Litchfield Beach, try Pawleys Island Realty (✉ Box 306, Pawleys Island 29585, ☎ 803/237–4257 or 800/937–7352).

RADIO STATIONS

FM: WDAI 98.5, urban contemporary; WJXY 93.9, country; WJYR 92.1, easy listening; WKZQ 101.7, rock and roll; WNMB 105.9, best of the '60s–'80s; WRNN 94.5, talk; WSYN 106.5, oldies.

VISITOR INFORMATION

Georgetown County Chamber of Commerce and Information Center (☞ Guided Tours, *above*). **Myrtle Beach Area Chamber of Commerce and Information Center** (✉ 1200 N. Oak St., Box 2115, Myrtle Beach 29578, ☎ 803/626–7444; 800/356–3016 for brochures only). **Pawleys Island Chamber of Commerce** (✉ U.S. 17, Box 569, Pawleys Island 29585, ☎ 803/237–1921).

HILTON HEAD AND BEYOND

Anchoring the southern tip of South Carolina's coastline is Hilton Head Island, named after English sea captain William Hilton, who claimed the 42 square mi for England in 1663. It was settled by planters in the 1700s and flourished until the Civil War. Thereafter, the economy declined and the island languished until Charles E. Fraser, a visionary South Carolina attorney, began developing the Sea Pines resort in 1956. Other developments followed, and today Hilton Head's casual pace, broad beaches, myriad activities, and genteel good life make it one of the East Coast's most popular vacation getaways.

Beaufort, some 40 mi north of Hilton Head, is a graceful antebellum town with a compact historic district preserving lavish 18th- and 19th-century homes from an era of immense prosperity, based on silky-textured Sea Island cotton. The "beau" is pronounced as in "beautiful," and Beaufort certainly is. Southeast, on the ocean, lies Fripp Island, a self-contained resort with controlled access. And midway between Beaufort and Charleston is Edisto (pronounced *ed*-is-toh) Island, settled in 1690, also once notable for its Sea Island cotton. Some of its elaborate mansions have been restored; others brood in disrepair.

Hilton Head Island

108 mi southwest of Charleston, 164 mi southeast of Columbia, over bridge on U.S. 278.

Lined by towering pines, palmetto trees, and wind-sculpted live oaks, Hilton Head's 12 mi of beaches are a major attraction, and the semitropical barrier island also has oak and pine woodlands and meandering lagoons. Choice stretches are occupied by various resorts, or "plantations," among them Sea Pines, Shipyard, Palmetto Dunes, Port Royal, and Hilton Head. In these areas, accommodations range from rental villas and lavish private houses to luxury hotels. The resorts are also private residential communities, although many have public restaurants, marinas, shopping areas, and recreational facilities. All are secured, and visitors cannot tour them unless arrangements are made at the visitor office near the main gate of each plantation.

Audubon–Newhall Preserve, in the south of the island, is 50 acres of pristine forest, where you'll find native plant life identified and tagged. There are trails, a self-guided tour, and seasonal plant walks. ⊠ *Palmetto Bay Rd.,* ☎ *803/785–5775.* ☞ *Free.* ☉ *Daily dawn–dusk.*

Sea Pines Forest Preserve is a 605-acre public wilderness tract with walking trails, a well-stocked fishing pond, a waterfowl pond, and a 3,400-year-old Indian shell ring. Both guided and self-guided tours are available. ⊠ *At southwest tip of island, accessible via U.S. 278 (William Hilton Pkwy.),* ☎ *803/842–1449.* ☞ *Sea Pines Plantation $3 per car for nonguests, includes access to preserve.* ☉ *Daily during daylight hrs; closed during Heritage Golf Classic in Apr.*

The **Museum of Hilton Head Island** has a permanent collection depicting Indian life and hosts changing exhibits. Beach walks are conducted on weekdays, and tours of Native American sites, forts, and plantations are given randomly in season. ⊠ *100 William Hilton Pkwy.,* ☎ *803/ 689–6767.* ☞ *Free.* ☉ *Mon.–Sat. 10–5, Sun. noon–4.*

At the **James M. Waddell Jr. Mariculture Research & Development Center,** 3 mi west of Hilton Head Island, visitors may tour the 24 ponds and the research building to see how methods of raising seafood commercially are studied. ⊠ *Sawmill Creek Rd. near intersection of U.S. 278 and SC 46,* ☎ *803/837–3795.* ☞ *Free.* ☉ *Tours weekdays at 10 AM and by appointment.*

OFF THE BEATEN PATH

DAUFUSKIE ISLAND – From Hilton Head, you can go by boat to nearby Daufuskie Island, the setting for Pat Conroy's novel *The Water Is Wide*, which was made into the movie *Conrack*. Most inhabitants, descendants of former slaves, live on small farms among remnants of churches, homes, and schools—reminders of antebellum times. With its unspoiled live oaks, pines, and palmettos, Daufuskie won't remain off the beaten path for long—a plus for employment but a blow to the vestiges of a dying culture. Excursions to the island are run out of Hilton Head by Adventure Cruises (⊠ Shelter Cove Marina, ☎ 803/785–4558), Vagabond Cruises (⊠ Harbour Town Marina, ☎ 803/842–4155), and Calibogue Cruises (⊠ 164-B Palmetto Bay Rd., ☎ 803/785–8242).

You can arrange kayak nature trips at Shelter Cove Marina (☎ 803/384–8125), South Beach Marina (☎ 803/671–2643), and Skull Creek Marina (☎ 803/681–4234).

Dining and Lodging

DINING

$$$ ✕ **Harbourmaster's.** With sweeping views of the harbor, this spacious, multilevel dining room offers such dishes as chateaubriand and New Zealand rack of lamb laced with a brandy demi-glace. Prix-fixe early dinners ($16.95) are offered daily except Sunday. ⌧ *Shelter Cove Marina, off U.S. 278,* ☎ *803/785–3030. Reservations essential. Jacket required at dinner. AE, DC, MC, V. Closed Sun. and Jan. No lunch.*

$$ ✕ **Old Fort Pub.** Tucked away on a quiet site overlooking the marshlands of the Intracoastal Waterway and beside the Civil War ruins of Fort Mitchell, this rustic restaurant specializes in such dishes as oyster pie, corn-crusted pork chops, and mesquite-smoked filet mignon with mushroom cabernet sauce. The ambience is publike casual but the service is not. There's a Sunday brunch. ⌧ *65 Skull Creek Dr.,* ☎ *803/681–2386. AE, D, DC, MC, V.*

$$ ✕ **Sante Fe Café.** Southwestern flavors go hand-in-hand with the deep South at this café, a longtime favorite, in such dishes as cornmeal-crusted oysters, wood-roasted quail, tequila shrimp, and mesquite-grilled lamb chops. ⌧ *U.S. 278 at Plantation Center,* ☎ *803/785–3838. Reservations essential. AE, D, MC, V.*

$$ ✕ **Starfire Contemporary Bistro.** Ultrafresh ingredients are served in a
★   pleasingly unique way at this small bistro with a somewhat formal, yet pleasant, atmosphere. The two owners, who left Denver's Rattlesnake Grill to fill a niche here, have decorated the Starfire with sunshine yellow walls accented with warm touches of wood. Try the wild mushroom soup with roasted rosemary; salmon with spiced seed crust atop a crunchy cucumber salad; and the intense chocolate sorbet with homemade biscotti. ⌧ *37 New Orleans Rd.,* ☎ *803/785–3434. AE, MC, V. No lunch.*

$$ ✕ **Two Eleven Park.** Choose from 75 different wines by the glass and more than 200 by the bottle at this lively wine bar/bistro. Fans come here for the convivial atmosphere and late-night menu (until 11:30), which includes smothered shrimp and beer-batter lobster tail. ⌧ *211 Park,* ☎ *803/686–5212. AE, D, DC, MC, V. No lunch.*

LODGING

Sea Pines, the oldest and best known of Hilton Head's resort developments, or plantations, occupies 4,500 thickly wooded acres with three golf courses, a fine beach, tennis clubs, stables, and shopping plazas. The focus of Sea Pines is **Harbour Town,** built around the charming marina, which has shops, restaurants, some condominiums, and the landmark Hilton Head lighthouse. Accommodations are in luxurious houses and villas facing the ocean or the golf courses.

The Crowne Plaza Resort is the oceanfront centerpiece of **Shipyard Plantation,** which also has villa condominiums, three nine-hole golf courses, a tennis club, and a small beach club. **Palmetto Dunes Resort** has the oceanfront **Hyatt Regency Hilton Head, Hilton Resort,** and other accommodations, along with the renowned **Rod Laver Tennis Center,** a good stretch of beach, three golf courses, and several oceanfront rental villa complexes. At **Port Royal Plantation** there's the posh **Westin Resort,** which is on the beach and has three golf courses and a tennis club.

Hilton Head Central Reservations (⌧ Box 5312, Hilton Head Island 29938, ☎ 803/785–9050 or 800/845–7018, FAX 803/686–3255) represents almost every hotel, motel, and rental agency on the island. Other options are available through the **Hilton Head Condo Hotline** (☎ 803/ 785–2939 or 800/258–5852, ext. 53) and **Hilton Head Reservations and Golf Line** (☎ 803/444–4772).

$$$$ 🏨 **Hyatt Regency Hilton Head Resort.** The island's largest oceanfront resort property has spacious rooms with standard decor and pastel tones; all have balconies. Guests have golf and tennis privileges at the nearby Palmetto Dunes Resort. ⊠ *U.S. 278, Box 6167, 29938,* ☎ *803/785– 1234 or 800/233–1234,* ᴲᴬˣ *803/842–4695. 475 rooms, 31 suites. 3 restaurants, lounge, indoor pool, outdoor pools, spa, health club, beach, boating, concierge floor, convention center. AE, D, DC, MC, V.*

$$$$ 🏨 **Main Street Inn.** Though new, this inn, unlike any other accommo-
★ dation on the island, captures old European opulence. Outside it looks like an Italianate villa or a Charleston Battery home, with gardens, shut-tered French doors, and iron railings. Luxury abounds inside, too, in the antique furnishings and the heart-pine floors covered in Turkish and sisal rugs. Guest rooms have velvet and silk brocade linens, feather duvets, and porcelain and brass sinks. Included in the rate are a Eu-ropean breakfast of imported meats, cheeses, quiche, breads, and pas-tries; traditional British tea with homemade scones and tea sandwiches; and fresh-baked cookies at turndown. ⊠ *2200 Main St., 29926,* ☎ *803/681–3001 or 800/471–3001,* ᴲᴬˣ *803/681–5541. 34 rooms. Bar, breakfast room, pool, hot tub, spa, concierge. AE, MC, V.*

$$$$ 🏨 **Westin Resort, Hilton Head Island.** One of the area's most luxuri-
★ ous properties, the horseshoe-shape Westin sprawls in a lushly land-scaped oceanfront setting. The expansive guest rooms, most with ocean views, have been redecorated with a residential feel: down pil-lows, hunting colors, and comfortable wicker and contemporary fur-niture. All have seating areas and desks. Baths now have marble flooring and distinctive lighting. Public areas display fine Asian porce-lains and paintings. ⊠ *2 Grass Lawn Ave., 29928,* ☎ *803/681–4000 or 800/228–3000,* ᴲᴬˣ *803/681–1087. 412 rooms, 38 suites. 3 restau-rants, 2 lounges, 3 pools, health club, children's programs. AE, D, DC, MC, V.*

$$$–$$$$ 🏨 **Crowne Plaza Resort.** Holiday Inn Worldwide's first property of this caliber in the United States, the oceanfront resort glimmers with brass railings and accents, and shiny wood floors and trim. Decorated in a nautical theme and set in a luxuriant garden, the Crowne Plaza has access to all the amenities of Shipyard Plantation. ⊠ *130 Shipyard Dr., 29928,* ☎ *803/842–2400 or 800/465–4329,* ᴲᴬˣ *803/785–8463. 315 rooms, 25 suites. 2 restaurants, lounge, indoor pool, outdoor pool, spa, 3 18-hole golf courses, health club, racquetball, business services, meeting rooms. AE, D, DC, MC, V.*

$$$–$$$$ 🏨 **Disney's Hilton Head Island Resort.** The island's newest resort op-
★ tion is what you'd expect from Disney—a grand scale with familiar themes. More than 100 villas have fully furnished kitchen, dining, liv-ing, and sleeping areas. The smallest is a studio villa and the largest has three bedrooms and four baths and sleeping accommodations for up to 12; all have marsh or marina views. Decorated in blues, greens, and deep reds, villas have porches with rocking chairs and picnic ta-bles, and suggest the rusticity of Adirondack cabins. The resort offers golf, tennis, and romance packages, beach shuttle service, and access to a fishing pier. A 13,000-square-ft beach house has a fireplace in the living room, a heated pool, and an arcade. ⊠ *22 Harbourside La., 29928,* ☎ *803/341–4100 or 800/453–4911,* ᴲᴬˣ *803/341–4130. 102 units. Restaurant, pool, boating, fishing, bicycles, children's programs. AE, MC, V.*

$$$–$$$$ 🏨 **Hilton Head Island Resort.** There's a Caribbean feel to this five-story resort hotel. The grounds are beautifully landscaped, and the rooms, all oceanside, are spacious and colorfully decorated in a modern style. ⊠ *23 Ocean La., Box 6165, 29938,* ☎ *803/842–8000 or 800/845–8001,* ℻ *803/842–4988. 303 rooms, 20 suites. Restaurant, pool, hot tub, sauna, health club, volleyball, boating, fishing, bicycles. AE, D, DC, MC, V.*

$$$–$$$$ 🏨 **Marriott's Grande Ocean Resort.** Though built as a time-share property, this beautiful oceanfront condo development, within walking distance of shops and restaurants, has a limited number of rentals. The luxurious, fully furnished two-bedroom, two-bath villas come with kitchens, whirlpool tubs, and maid service. ⊠ *51 S. Forest Beach Dr., 29929,* ☎ *803/785–2000 or 800/527–3490,* ℻ *803/842–3413. 140 villas. Deli, lounge, indoor pool, outdoor pool, exercise room. AE, D, DC, MC, V.*

$$–$$$ 🏨 **Holiday Inn Oceanfront Resort.** A handsome high-rise motor hotel, the Holiday Inn is on a broad, quiet stretch of beach. The rooms are spacious and well furnished in a contemporary style. ⊠ *S. Forest Beach Dr., Box 5728, 29938,* ☎ *803/785–5126 or 800/465–4329,* ℻ *803/785–6678. 202 rooms. Restaurant, 2 lounges, pool. AE, D, DC, MC, V.*

$–$$ 🏨 **Red Roof Inn.** This budget-price, two-story inn is popular with families. Clean and functional rooms are just a short drive from the public beaches. ⊠ *5 Regency Pkwy., 29928,* ☎ *803/686–6808 or 800/843–7663,* ℻ *803/842–3352. 112 rooms. Pool. AE, D, DC, MC, V.*

Nightlife and the Arts

NIGHTLIFE

Regatta (⊠ 23 Ocean La., ☎ 803/842–8000), a sophisticated oceanfront nightspot in the Hilton Resort, features live beach and jazz music nightly. **Robber's Row** (⊠ S. Forest Beach Dr., ☎ 803/785–5126), a locally popular lounge in the Holiday Inn Oceanfront Resort, has nightly entertainment. **Signals** (⊠ 130 Shipyard Dr., ☎ 803/842–2400), in the Crowne Plaza Resort, has entertainment every night. **Monkey Business** (⊠ Park Plaza, ☎ 803/686–3545) is a dance nightclub.

Cafe Europa (☎ 803/671–3399), at the Lighthouse in Harbour Town, has nightly piano entertainment. **Hemingway's Lounge** (☎ 803/785–1234) at the Hyatt Regency Hilton Head has live entertainment in a casually elegant setting Tuesday through Saturday. The **Pelican Poolside** (☎ 803/681–4000), an oceanfront lounge at the Westin Resort, has informal entertainment every night but Sunday. **Playful Pelican** (☎ 803/681–4000), the pool bar at the Westin, has a live calypso band Tuesday through Sunday from 1 to 4 PM.

THE ARTS

The **Self Family Arts Center** (⊠ Shelter Cove La., ☎ 803/686–3945) has details on Hilton Head arts events; it includes a theater and art gallery, and features a theater program for youth. In warm weather, free **outdoor concerts** are held at Harbour Town and Shelter Cove. Concerts, plays, films, art shows, theater, sporting events, food fairs, and minitournaments make up Hilton Head's **SpringFest** (☎ 803/686–4944), which runs for the month of March.

Outdoor Activities and Sports

BEACHES

Although the resort beaches are reserved for guests and residents, there are four public entrances to Hilton Head's 12 mi of ocean beach. Two main parking and changing areas are at Coligny Circle, near the Holiday Inn, and on Folly Field Road, off U.S. 278. Signs along U.S.

278 point the way to Bradley and Singleton beaches, where parking space is limited.

BIKING

There are pathways in several areas of Hilton Head (many in the resorts), and pedaling is popular along the firmly packed beach. Bicycles can be rented at most hotels and resorts and at **Harbour Town Bicycles** (⊠ Heritage Plaza, ☎ 803/785–3546), **South Beach Cycles** (⊠ Sea Pines Plantation, ☎ 803/671–2453), and **Hilton Head Bicycle Company** (⊠ 11-B Archer Rd., ☎ 803/686–6888).

CANOEING AND KAYAKING

Outside Hilton Head (⊠ South Beach Marina, ☎ 803/671–2643; ⊠ Shelter Cove Plaza, ☎ 803/686–6996) is an ecologically sensitive company that rents canoes, kayaks, bikes, and rollerblades; it also has nature tours.

FISHING

On Hilton Head, you can pick oysters, dig for clams, or cast for shrimp; supplies are available at **Shelter Cove Marina** at Palmetto Dunes (☎ 803/842–7001). Local marinas offer in-shore and deep-sea fishing charters. Each year a billfishing tournament and two king mackerel tournaments attract anglers.

GOLF

Many of Hilton Head's 29 championship courses are open to the public, including **Palmetto Dunes** (☎ 803/785–1138), **Sea Pines** (☎ 803/842–8484), **Port Royal and Shipyard** (☎ 803/689–5600), **Island West Golf Course** (⊠ U.S. 278, ☎ 803/689–6660), and **Old South Golf Links** (⊠ U.S. 278, ☎ 803/785–5353). **Harbour Town Golf Links at Sea Pines** (☎ 803/671–2448) hosts the MCI Classic every spring.

HORSEBACK RIDING

Many trails wind through woods and nature preserves. Some stables in and near Hilton Head are **Lawton Stables** (⊠ Sea Pines, ☎ 803/671–2586), **Rose Hill Plantation Stables** (⊠ Bluffton, ☎ 803/757–3082), and **Sandy Creek Stables** (⊠ Near Spanish Wells, ☎ 803/689–3423). At **Sea Horse Farms** (☎ 803/681–7749), you can ride on the beach; **Old South** (☎ 803/842–7433) offers landscape riding.

POLO

There are matches every other Sunday during spring and fall at **Rose Hill Plantation** (⊠ Bluffton, ☎ 803/757–4945).

SUMMER CAMP

On Hilton Head Island, all major hotels offer summer youth activities; some have full-scale youth programs. The **Island Recreation Center** runs a summer camp that visiting youngsters can join. ⊠ *Hilton Head Island Recreation Association, Wilborn Rd., Box 22593, Hilton Head Island 29925, ☎ 803/681–7273. ☉ Camp mid-June–late Aug., weekdays.*

TENNIS

There are more than 300 courts on Hilton Head. **Sea Pines Racquet Club** (☎ 803/842–8484), home of the Family Circle Tournament; **Shipyard** (☎ 803/686–8804); and **Port Royal** (☎ 803/686–8803) are highly rated. Clubs that welcome guests include **Palmetto Dunes** (☎ 803/785–1151) and **Van der Meer Tennis Center** (☎ 803/785–8388).

WINDSURFING

Lessons and rentals are available from **Outside Hilton Head** (☞ Canoeing and Kayaking, *above*).

Shopping

MALLS AND OUTLETS

The **Mall at Shelter Cove** (✉ U.S. 278, ½ mi north of Palmetto Dunes Resort, ☎ 803/686–3090) has 55 shops and four restaurants. **Coligny Plaza** (✉ Coligny Plaza, off Coligny Circle, ☎ 803/842–6050) has 60-plus shops, restaurants, a movie theater, and a supermarket. **Shoppes on the Parkway** (✉ U.S. 278, 1 mi south of Palmetto Dunes Resort, ☎ 803/686–6233) comprises 30 outlets, including Dansk, Gorham, and Van Heusen. **Lowcountry Factory Outlet Village** (✉ U.S. 278 at the island gateway, ☎ 803/837–4339) has 45 outlets from Brooks Brothers to Timberland selling clothing and housewares.

ART GALLERIES

The **Red Piano Art Gallery** (✉ 220 Cordillo Pkwy., ☎ 803/785–2318) showcases 19th- and 20th-century works by regional and national contemporary artists.

BOOKS

Authors Bookstore and Cafe (✉ The Village at Wexford, ☎ 803/686–5020) carries a good selection of books focusing on local history and culture.

JEWELRY

The **Bird's Nest** (✉ Coligny Plaza, ☎ 803/785–3737) sells locally made shell and sand-dollar jewelry. The **Goldsmith Shop** (✉ 3 Lagoon Rd., ☎ 803/785–2538) carries classic jewelry and island charms.

NATURE

The **Audubon Nature Store** (✉ The Village at Wexford, ☎ 803/785–4311) has items with a nature theme. The **Hammock Company** (✉ Coligny Plaza, ☎ 803/686–3636 or 800/344–4264) sells gifts and other things with a natural emphasis.

Beaufort

43 mi north of Hilton Head.

Charming homes and churches from Beaufort's prosperous antebellum days as a cotton center grace this historic town on Port Royal Island. Although many private houses in **Old Point,** the historic district, are not usually open to visitors, some may be on the annual Fall House Tour in mid-October, and the Spring Tour of Homes and Gardens, in April or May. The **Greater Beaufort Chamber of Commerce** (☎ 803/524–3163) can provide more information about house-tour schedules.

The **John Mark Verdier House Museum,** built about 1790 in the Federal style, has been restored and furnished as it would have been between 1790 and the visit of Lafayette in 1825. It was the headquarters for Union forces during the Civil War. ✉ *801 Bay St.,* ☎ *803/524–6334.* 🎟 *$4.* ☉ *Mon.–Sat. 10–4:30.*

Built in 1795 and remodeled in 1852, the Gothic-style arsenal that was home of the Beaufort Volunteer Artillery now houses the **Beaufort Museum,** with prehistoric relics, native pottery, and Revolutionary War and Civil War exhibits. ✉ *713 Craven St.,* ☎ *803/525–7077.* 🎟 *$2.* ☉ *Mon.–Tues. and Thurs.–Sat. 10–5.*

St. Helena's Episcopal Church (1724) was turned into a Civil War hospital, and gravestones were brought inside to serve as operating tables. ✉ *501 Church St.,* ☎ *803/522–1712.* ☉ *Mon.–Sat. 10–4.*

Henry C. Chambers Waterfront Park, off Bay Street, is a great place to survey the scene. Barbra Streisand filmed *Prince of Tides* here. Its 7 landscaped acres along the Beaufort River, part of the Intracoastal Waterway, include a seawall promenade, a crafts market, gardens, and a marina. Some events of the popular mid-July Beaufort Water Festival, as well as a seasonal farmers' and crafts market, take place here.

At **Parris Island,** 10 mi south of Beaufort via SC 802, you can observe U.S. Marine Corps recruit training and take a guided tour or drive through in their own vehicles. There's a replica of the Iwo Jima flag-raising monument on the base. The **Parris Island Museum** exhibits uniforms, photographs, and weapons chronicling military history since 1562, when the French Huguenots built a fort on St. Helena. ☎ 803/525–2951. ✉ Free. ☉ Fri.–Wed. 10–4:30, Thurs. 10–7.

St. Helena Island, 9 mi southeast of Beaufort via U.S. 21, is the site of the **Penn Center Historic District** and **York W. Bailey Museum.** Penn Center, established in the middle of the Civil War as the South's first school for freed slaves, today provides community services. The **York W. Bailey Museum** (formerly a clinic) has displays reflecting the heritage of Sea Island blacks. These islands are where Gullah, a musical language that combines English and African languages, developed. ✉ Land's End Rd., St. Helena Island, ☎ 803/838–2432. ✉ Donation suggested. ☉ Tues.–Fri. 11–4 and by appointment.

OFF THE BEATEN PATH
HUNTING ISLAND STATE PARK – This secluded domain of beach, nature trails, and varied fishing has about 3 mi of public beaches. The 1,120-ft fishing pier is among the longest on the East Coast. You can climb the 181 steps of the 140-ft **Hunting Island Lighthouse** (built in 1859 and abandoned in 1933) for sweeping views. The park is 18 mi southeast of Beaufort via U.S. 21; write for cabin and camping reservations. ✉ Hunting Island State Park, 1775 Sea Island Pkwy., St. Helena 29920, ☎ 803/838–2011. ✉ $3 per car Mar.–Oct.; free rest of yr.

Dining and Lodging

$ ✕ **Backstreet Cafe.** Mostly classic Lowcountry dinners are also offered in appetizer portions at this high-ceiling, open café with navy blue walls that open onto the kitchen at the rear. Blackened shrimp and scallops come with homemade apple chutney; other choices are beer-batter catfish with garlic mashed potatoes, fried chicken with red rice, or roast pork with collard greens. ✉ 812 Port Republic St., ☎ 803/521–2100. AE, MC, V. Closed Sun. No lunch Sat.

$ ✕ **Emily's.** Long, narrow, and wood-paneled, Emily's is a lively restaurant and tapas bar that serves until 11. The crowds linger over appetizer-size tapas including chicken spring rolls, lamb chops, and crab wontons. This is definitely not a no-smoking haven. ✉ 906 Port Republic St., ☎ 803/522–1866. AE, MC, V.

$$$$ ✕▣ **Beaufort Inn and Restaurant.** This peach-color 1907 Victorian inn, with its many gables and porches, has a superb restaurant with two small, mahogany-paneled dining rooms and porch dining. Dutch chef Peter de Jong blends Lowcountry elements to create delights such as benne seed shrimp and crab cakes and peanut-crusted chicken in a ginger-cilantro peanut sauce. Guest rooms are decorated with period reproductions, tasteful florals and plaids, and comfortable chairs. All have pine floors; several have fireplaces and four-poster beds. Afternoon tea and a full breakfast (French toast stuffed with brie and sun-dried peaches, cheese omelette with tasso shrimp gravy) are complimentary for guests. ✉ 809 Port Republic St., 29902, ☎ 803/521–9000, FAX 803/521–9500. 15 rooms. Restaurant. AE, MC, V.

$$$$ 🖼 **Rhett House Inn.** A storybook inn (circa 1820) in the heart of the
★ historic district is filled with art and antiques and abounds in such lux-
uries as down pillows and duvets, French linens, CD players in each
room, and fresh flowers. Breakfast, afternoon tea, and evening hors
d'oeuvres are included in the rate. Celebrity visitors have included Barbra Streisand, Jeff Bridges, and Dennis Quaid. ✉ *1009 Craven St., 29902,*
☎ *803/524–9030,* ℻ *803/524–1310. 9 rooms, 1 suite. Bicycles. AE,
MC, V.*

$$$ 🖼 **Two Suns Inn.** This B&B, a restored 1917 neoclassical house over-
looking the Beaufort River, offers large rooms, afternoon tea-and-
toddy hour, and a full breakfast. The inn has extremely down-to-earth
and friendly hosts as well as business facilities. ✉ *1705 Bay St., 29902,*
☎ ℻ *803/522–1122,* ☎ *800/552–4244. 5 rooms. Croquet, horse-
shoes, bicycles, business services. AE, MC, V.*

$$–$$$ 🖼 **Fripp Island Resort.** The resort encompasses the entire island; ac-
cess is limited to guests only. Two- and three-bedroom villas are con-
temporary in decor. The island is 19 mi south of Beaufort via U.S. 21.
✉ *1 Tarpon Blvd., 29920,* ☎ *803/838–3535 or 800/845–4100,* ℻
*803/838–9079. 133 units. 3 restaurants, 6 pools, 18-hole golf course,
10 tennis courts, jogging, boating, bicycles. AE, D, DC, MC, V.*

$$ 🖼 **Best Western Sea Island Inn.** At a well-maintained but standard inn
in the downtown historic district, rooms are pretty basic. Guests re-
ceive free Continental breakfast. ✉ *1015 Bay St., Box 532, 29902,* ☎
803/522–2090 or 800/528–1234, ℻ *803/521–4858. 43 rooms. Pool.
AE, D, DC, MC, V.*

$–$$ 🖼 **Howard Johnson.** This clean and cheerfully staffed hotel sits on the
edge of the marsh a few miles from the historic district. Rooms are spacious and have desks; many have views of the river and marsh. Guests
receive free Continental breakfast. ✉ *3651 Trask Pkwy. (U.S. 21), 29902,*
☎ *803/524–6020 or 800/528–1234,* ℻ *803/521–4858. 43 rooms.
Pool. AE, D, DC, MC, V.*

Nightlife

Bananas (✉ 910 Bay St., ☎ 803/522–0910) has a late-night bar and
live music on weekends. **Plum's** (✉ 904½ Bay St., ☎ 803/525–1946)
is good for a late drink and has live bands during the weekends.

Outdoor Activities and Sports

BIKING

Beaufort is great for bicycling. Rentals are available from **Lowcountry
Bicycles** (✉ 904 Port Republic St., ☎ 803/524–9585).

GOLF

Most golf courses are about a 10- to 20-minute drive from Beaufort.
Try the 27 holes designed by Tom Fazio at **Callawassie Island Club** (☎
800/221–8431); the challenging and beautiful **Cat Island Golf Club** (☎
803/524–0300); or **Dataw Island**'s two courses (☎ 803/838–3838).

Shopping

ANTIQUES

Den of Antiquity (✉ SC 170 W, Beaufort, ☎ 803/521–9990), the
area's largest antiques shop, carries a wide assortment of Lowcountry
and nautical pieces.

ART GALLERIES

On canvas and sculpture as well as on bits of tin roofing, rugs, frames,
and furniture, the colorful, whimsical designs of Suzanne and Eric Longo
decorate their **Longo Gallery** (✉ 407 Carteret St.; 103 Charles St.; ☎
803/522–8933 for both). The **Rhett Gallery** (✉ 901 Bay St., ☎ 803/
524–3339) sells Lowcountry art by members of the Rhett family and
antique maps and prints, including Audubons. On nearby St. Helena

Island, the **Red Piano Too Art Gallery** (⊠ 853 Sea Island Pkwy., ☎ 803/
838–2241), in a huge old wooden building, is filled with quirky folk
and Southern art, beads, and pottery.

JEWELRY

The **Craftseller** (⊠ 818 Bay St., ☎ 803/525–6104) displays jewelry
and other items by Southern craftspeople.

En Route   The ruins of **Sheldon Church,** built in 1753, make an interesting stop
en route from Beaufort to Edisto Island. The church was burned in 1779
and again in 1865. Only the brick walls and columns remain beside
the old cemetery. Get here from Beaufort on U.S. 21 to Gardens Corner, then go west on U.S. 17 and north on SC 21.

Edisto Island

80 mi northeast of Beaufort; take U.S. 17N and then follow SC 174.

On this rural island, magnificent stands of age-old oaks festooned
with Spanish moss border quiet streams and side roads; wild turkeys
may still be spotted on open grasslands and amid palmetto palms. Many
of the island's inhabitants are descendants of former slaves. **Edisto
Beach State Park** has 3 mi of beach with excellent shelling, housekeeping
cabins by the marsh, and campsites by the ocean. Luxury resort development has just begun to encroach around the edges of the park.
For camping reservations, call 803/869–2156 or 803/869–3396.

Dining and Lodging

$$–$$$ ✕ **Old Post Office.** Try the fussed-over pork chop, or the blue-crab-
★   and-asparagus pie, served with the house salad, vegetables, and fresh-
baked bread. The house specialty at this restaurant on Store Creek is
shrimp and grits and, well, anything with grits, rumored to be the best
around these parts. Originally Bailey's General Store and U.S. Post Office, the building contains the original post office boxes. ⊠ *1442 SC
174, 5 mi from Edisto Beach,* ☎ *803/869–2339. MC, V. Closed Sun.
June–Sept., Sun.–Mon. Oct.–May. No lunch.*

$$$ 🏠 **Cassina Point Plantation.** You can live out your fantasies about the
antebellum days at this authentically restored plantation house, now
a B&B surrounded by fields once planted in Sea Island cotton. Fed-
eral troops who occupied the house for three years left their graffiti in
the basement. You may fish in the creek (watch for the playful bot-
tlenose dolphins), go crabbing or shrimping, watch birds, or take a stroll.
A fruit bowl, beverages, and full breakfast come with the room. ⊠ *1642
Clark Rd., Box 535, 29438,* ☎ *803/869–2535. 4 rooms with ½ bath
(2 full hall baths). Croquet, boating. No credit cards.*

$$–$$$ 🏠 **Fairfield Ocean Ridge Resort.** This is a good choice if you want to
combine all the resort amenities with a get-away-from-it-all setting. There
are accommodations in well-furnished two- and three-bedroom villa
units tastefully decorated in contemporary style. ⊠ *1 King Cotton Rd.,
Box 27, 29438,* ☎ *803/869–2561 or 800/845–8500, FAX 803/869–
2384. 100 units. Restaurant, lounge, pool, wading pool, 18-hole golf
course, miniature golf, 4 tennis courts, hiking, beach, boating, fishing.
AE, D, MC, V.*

Hilton Head and Beyond A to Z

Arriving and Departing

BY BOAT

Hilton Head is accessible via the Intracoastal Waterway, with dock-
ing available at **Shelter Cove Marina** (☎ 803/842–7001), **Harbour Town
Marina** (☎ 803/671–2704), and **Schilling Boathouse** (☎ 803/681–2628).

BY CAR

Hilton Head Island is 40 mi east of I–95 (⊠ Exit 28 off I–95S, Exit 5 off I–95N). **Beaufort** is 25 mi east of I–95, on U.S. 21.

BY PLANE

Hilton Head Island Airport (☏ 803/681–6386) is served by US Airways Express and Midway. Most travelers use the **Savannah International Airport** (☏ 912/964–0514), about an hour from Hilton Head, which is served by Delta, US Airways, and Valujet.

Getting Around

BY TAXI

Yellow Taxi (☏ 803/686–6666) and **Lowcountry Taxi and Limousine Service** (☏ 803/681–8294) provide service in Hilton Head; other options include **Low Country Adventure** (☏ 803/681–8212) and **At Your Service** (☏ 803/837–3783). In Beaufort, **A.C. Limousine** (☏ 803/986–8737), **The Point** (☏ 803/522–3576), and **Yellow Cab** (☏ 803/522–1121) provide service.

Contacts and Resources

EMERGENCIES

Dial **911** for police, fire, and ambulance assistance. Emergency medical service is available at the **Hilton Head Medical Center and Clinics** (⊠ Hospital Center Blvd., ☏ 803/681–6122).

GUIDED TOURS

Lowcountry Adventures (☏ 803/681–8212) offers tours of Hilton Head, Beaufort, and Charleston. Hilton Head's **Adventure Cruises** (☏ 803/785–4558) offers dinner, sightseeing, and murder-mystery cruises. Several companies, including **Harbour Town Charters** in Hilton Head (☏ 803/363–2628), run dolphin sightseeing and environmental trips. **Steel Horse Helicopters** (☏ 803/689–6747) offers tours of Hilton Head with a bird's-eye view, starting at $20 for five minutes.

Carolina Buggy Tours (☏ 803/525–1300) can show you Beaufort's historic district. **Carriage Tours of Beaufort** (☏ 803/221–1651) gives tours of the historic district by horse-drawn carriage. **Gullah 'n' Geechie Mahn Tours** (☏ 803/838–7516) has tours of Beaufort and sea islands such as St. Helena that focus on the traditions of African-American culture. Costumed guides sing and act out history during walking tours by the **Spirit of Old Beaufort** (☏ 803/525–0459). Call the **Greater Beaufort Chamber of Commerce** (☏ 803/524–3163) to find out about self-guided walking or driving tours of Beaufort.

LATE-NIGHT PHARMACIES

Revco (⊠ 95 Matthews, Hilton Head, ☏ 803/681–8363) is open until 9.

RADIO STATIONS

AM: WFXH 1130, sports talk. **FM:** WFXH 106.1, classic rock; WAEV 97.3, adult contemporary; WHVZ 99.7, beach, boogie, and blues; WLVH 101.1, soft soul; WJCL 96.5, country; WOCW 92.1, oldies.

VISITOR INFORMATION

Greater Beaufort Chamber of Commerce (⊠ Box 910, 1006 Bay St., Beaufort 29901, ☏ 803/524–3163) has information about Beaufort and the surrounding area. In Hilton Head, your best bet is to stop by the **Welcome Center and Museum of Hilton Head** (⊠ 100 William Hilton Pkwy). You can call the **Hilton Head Island Chamber of Commerce** (⊠ Box 5647, Hilton Head 29938, ☏ 803/785–3673) for information. The two **Hilton Head Welcome Centers,** run by a private real-estate firm, are on U.S. 278 next to the bridge to Hilton Head and at 6 Lagoon Road at the island's south end. The centers provide visitor information and also attempt to entice you into purchasing real estate on Hilton Head.

COLUMBIA AND THE HEARTLAND
Camden, Aiken, Abbeville

South Carolina's Heartland, between the coastal Lowcountry and the mountains, is a varied region of swamps and flowing rivers, fertile farmland, and vast forests of pines and hardwoods. Lakes Murray, Marion, and Moultrie have wonderful fishing, and the many state parks are popular for hiking, swimming, and camping. At the center of the region is the state capital, Columbia, an engaging contemporary city superimposed on cherished historic remnants. It has restored mansions, several museums, a university, a variety of dining, a lively arts scene, and a fine zoo and botanical garden.

In Aiken, the center of South Carolina's Thoroughbred Country, such champions as Sea Hero and Pleasant Colony were trained. The beautiful landscape is studded with the fine mansions of wealthy Northerners such as the Vanderbilts and Whitneys. Throughout the region, towns like Ninety Six, Sumter, and Camden preserve and interpret the past, with historic re-creations, exhibits, and restorations. Several public gardens provide islands of color during most of the year.

Columbia

112 mi northwest of Charleston, 101 mi southeast of Greenville.

In 1786 South Carolina's capital was moved from Charleston to Columbia, in the center of the state along the banks of the Congaree River. One of the nation's first planned cities, Columbia has streets that are among the widest in America—designed this way because it was then thought that stagnant air fostered the spread of malaria. The city soon grew into a center of political, commercial, cultural, and social activity. But in early 1865 General William Tecumseh Sherman invaded South Carolina and incinerated two-thirds of Columbia, though a few homes and public buildings were spared—as was the First Baptist Church, where secession was declared, because a janitor directed Sherman's troops to a Methodist church when asked directions. Today the city is a sprawling blend of modern office blocks, suburban neighborhoods, and the occasional antebellum home. Here, too, is the expansive main campus of the University of South Carolina, including the historic and scenic Horseshoe.

The **Columbia Museum of Art and Gibbes Planetarium** contains the Kress Foundation Collection of Renaissance and Baroque treasures, sculpture, decorative arts, and European and American paintings; there are also changing exhibitions. Children may enjoy the museum's doll collection, and most shows at the planetarium are designed with kids in mind. The museum plans to move to a newly renovated building at the corner of Main and Hampton streets in July 1998. ⊠ *1112 Bull St.,* ☎ *803/799–2810.* ⊠ *$2; planetarium shows 50¢.* ☉ *Tues.–Fri. 10–5, weekends 12:30–5; planetarium shows weekends at 2, 3, and 4.*

Stop by the **Museum Shop** of the Historic Columbia Foundation in the Robert Mills House (⊠ 1616 Blanding St.) in the historic district to get a map and buy tickets to tour four Columbia houses that have been opened to the public. ⊠ *Each house $3; combination ticket to all 4 houses $10.* ☉ *All houses Tues.–Sat. 10:15–3:15, Sun. 1:15–4:15.*

The **Hampton–Preston Mansion** (✉ 1615 Blanding St., ☎ 803/252–1770), dating from 1818, is filled with lavish furnishings collected by three generations of two influential families (☞ Museum Shop, *above*). The classic, columned 1823 **Robert Mills House** (✉ 1616 Blanding St., ☎ 803/252–1770) was named for its architect, who later designed the Washington Monument. It has opulent Regency furniture, marble mantels, and spacious grounds (☞ Museum Shop, *above*). The **Mann–Simons Cottage** (✉ 1403 Richland St., ☎ 803/252–1770) was the home of Celia Mann, one of only 200 free African-Americans in Columbia in the mid-1800s (☞ Museum Shop, *above*). The **Woodrow Wilson Boyhood Home** (✉ 1705 Hampton St., ☎ 803/252–1770) displays the gaslights, arched doorways, and ornate furnishings of the Victorian period (☞ Museum Shop, *above*).

The **Fort Jackson Museum,** on the grounds of the U.S. Army Training Center, displays heavy equipment from the two world wars and exhibits on the life of Andrew Jackson. ✉ *Bldg. 4442, Jackson Blvd.,* ☎ *803/751–7419.* 🎟 *Free.* 🕐 *Tues.–Fri. 10–4, weekends 1–4.*

Ⓒ Exhibits at the **South Carolina State Museum,** in a large, refurbished textile mill, interpret the state's natural history, archaeology, historical development, and technological and artistic accomplishments. One exhibit portrays noted black astronauts (dedicated to South Carolina native Dr. Ronald McNair, who died on the *Challenger*), and another focuses on the cotton industry and slavery. An iron gate made for the museum by Phillip Simmons, the "dean of Charleston blacksmiths," is on display, as is the surfboard that physicist Kary Mullis was riding when he heard he'd won the Nobel Prize. ✉ *301 Gervais St.,* ☎ *803/737–4921.* 🎟 *$4.* 🕐 *Mon.–Sat. 10–5, Sun. 1–5.*

South Carolina's capitol, the **State House,** started in 1855 and completed in 1950, is made of native blue granite in the Italian Renaissance style. Six bronze stars on the outer western wall mark direct hits by Sherman's cannons. The interior is richly appointed with brass, marble, mahogany, and artwork, and a replica of Jean Antoine Houdon's statue of George Washington is on the grounds. The building is closed through 1998 for renovation, but parts of the grounds are open for strolling. ✉ *Main and Gervais Sts.,* ☎ *803/734–2430.* 🎟 *Free.*

A highlight of the sprawling **University of South Carolina,** near the State House, is its original campus—the scenic, tree-lined **Horseshoe**—dating back to 1801 when the school was first established. Researchers explore the special collections on state history and genealogy at the **South Caroliniana Library,** established in 1840. Here, too, is the **McKissick Museum,** with geology and gemstone exhibits and a fine display of silver. *Museum:* ✉ *Sumter St.,* ☎ *803/777–7251.* 🎟 *Free.* 🕐 *Weekdays 9–4, weekends 1–5. Library:* ✉ *Sumter St.,* ☎ *803/777–3131.* 🎟 *Free.* 🕐 *Mon., Wed., Fri. 8:30–5, Tues., Thurs. 8:30–8, Sat. 9–5 (9–1 mid-May–mid-Aug.).*

Ⓒ **Riverfront Park and Historic Columbia Canal,** where the Broad and Saluda rivers meet to form the Congaree, was created around the city's original waterworks and hydroelectric plant. Interpretive markers describe the area's plant and animal life and tell the history of the buildings. ✉ *312 Laurel St.,* ☎ *803/733–8613.* 🎟 *Free.* 🕐 *Daily dawn–dusk.*

★ Ⓒ **Riverbanks Zoological Park and Botanical Garden** contains more than 2,000 animals and birds, some endangered, in natural habitats. Walk along pathways and through landscaped gardens to see polar bears, Siberian tigers, and American bald eagles. The South American primate collection has won international acclaim, and the park is noted for its success in breeding endangered and fragile species. There's also a cage-free aviary, including a tropical rain forest where it really does rain. The aquarium-reptile complex showcases South Carolina, desert, tropical, and marine specimens. A 70-acre botanical garden on the west bank of the Saluda River includes a forested section with trails past historic ruins and spectacular views of the river. ⊠ *I–126 and U.S. 76 at Greystone Riverbanks exit,* ☎ *803/779–8717 or 803/779–8730.* ⊡ *$5.75.* ☉ *Weekdays 9–4, summer weekends 9–5.*

Dining and Lodging

$$–$$$ ✕ **Richard's.** A popular restaurant in the Congaree Vista district toward the river, Richard's serves French-based cooking with a Southern accent—including creamy grits folded into some entrées. Crabmeat hush puppies with summer slaw is just one appetizer that says, "*Oui,* y'all." Try the black truffle mousse paté or Parmesan chips topped with goat cheese. ⊠ *828 Gervais St.,* ☎ *803/799–3071. AE, MC, V.*

$$ ✕ **Blue Marlin.** With polished wood, lines of booths, artsy light fixtures, and an oceanic mural over the bar, this restaurant speaks of bygone years—fitting for an eatery that was once a train station. Start with deviled crab or oyster shooters (raw oysters with jalapeño peppers, each in its own shot glass). Seafood and pasta dishes, always served with steaming collard greens and grits, are the staples here. Fruit cobblers with liqueur-laced whipped cream are popular dessert items. ⊠ *1200 Lincoln St.,* ☎ *803/799–3838. Reservations not accepted. AE, DC, MC, V.*

$$ ✕ **Mangia! Mangia!** Earth tones, hammered copper, and mosaic tiles transform a turn-of-the-century building into an elegant place to dine, and window-side tables have a view of the Columbia skyline across the Congaree River. Try the mussels steamed in wine-garlic sauce, followed by wild mushroom pizza baked in the wood-burning oven. The Tuscan-influenced menu also includes lamb shank roasted in red wine with herbs. The entire restaurant, except for the bar, is no-smoking. ⊠ *100 State St., West Columbia,* ☎ *803/791–3443. AE, MC, V.*

$$ ✕ **Motor Supply Co. Bistro.** Dine on cuisine from around the world at a restaurant in the heart of town. Fresh seafood and homemade desserts are among the many offerings; on Sunday there's a bountiful brunch. A happy hour is celebrated in the bar. ⊠ *920 Gervais St.,* ☎ *803/256–6687. AE, DC, MC, V.*

$–$$ ✕ **California Dreaming.** A splendid example of adaptive reuse, this airy, greenery-bedecked space is the renovated old Union Train Station. The only drawback: an echo that's noticeable when it's crowded. Specialties include prime rib, barbecued baby-back ribs, Mexican dishes, and homemade pasta. The lounge is one of the most popular in town. ⊠ *401 S. Main St.,* ☎ *803/254–6767. AE, MC, V.*

$ ✕ **Maurice Gourmet Barbecue–Piggie Park.** One of the South's best-known barbecue chefs, Maurice Bessinger has a fervent national following for his mustard sauce–based, pit-cooked ham barbecue. He also serves barbecued chicken, ribs, and baked beans, plus hash over rice, onion rings, hush puppies, coleslaw, and home-baked desserts. In addition to scattered drive-through locations, Maurice has grown to three "sit-down" restaurants, all full of country charm. ⊠ *1600 Charleston Hwy.,* ☎ *803/796–0220;* ⊠ *800 Elmwood Ave.,* ☎ *803/256–4377;* ⊠ *1141 Lake Murray Blvd., Irmo,* ☎ *803/732–5555. Reservations not accepted. D, MC, V.*

$$$ ▦ **Adam's Mark.** This upscale downtown hotel is near state offices and the University of South Carolina. Newly renovated, it has leather armchairs, suspended lights, and brass accents in public areas. Guest rooms are contemporary, with armoires and desks. Finlay's Restaurant, in a spectacular atrium with wood-wrapped columns, serves American fare; Players Sports Bar is a new addition. ✉ *1200 Hampton St., 29201,* ☎ *803/771–7000 or 800/444–2326,* ℻ *803/254–2911. 296 rooms, 4 suites. Restaurant, lounge, sports bar, indoor pool, hot tub, health club, business services. AE, D, DC, MC, V.*

$$$ 🏨 **Claussen's Inn.** A small hotel in a converted bakery warehouse in the attractive Five Points neighborhood, the inn is near lively nightlife and specialty shops. A much-needed sprucing-up was completed in mid-1997. Claussen's has an open, airy lobby with a Mexican-tile floor; the rooms, some two-story, are arranged around the lobby. The eight loft suites have downstairs sitting rooms and spiral staircases leading to sleeping areas furnished with period reproductions and four-poster beds. ✉ *2003 Greene St., 29205,* ☎ *803/765–0440 or 800/622–3382,* ℻ *803/799–7924. 21 rooms, 8 suites. Hot tub, meeting rooms. AE, D, MC, V.*

$$$ 🏨 **Richland Street B&B.** Relax on the front porch or in the spacious
★   common area of this no-smoking inn in the heart of Columbia's historic district. Each antiques-furnished room has its own personality; the suite includes a whirlpool tub. The complimentary breakfast includes fresh fruit and Belgian waffles or French toast; there are also afternoon refreshments. ✉ *1425 Richland St., 29201,* ☎ *803/779–700,* ℻ *803/765–0370. 7 rooms, 1 suite. Library. AE, MC, V.*

$$–$$$ 🏨 **Embassy Suites Hotel Columbia.** In the spacious seven-story atrium lobby with skylights, fountains, pools, and live plants, overnight guests have sumptuous complimentary breakfasts and can attend an early-evening manager's cocktail reception. ✉ *200 Stoneridge Dr., 29210,* ☎ *803/252–8700 or 800/362–2779,* ℻ *803/256–8749. 214 housekeeping suites. Indoor pool, health club, billiards, dance club. AE, D, DC, MC, V.*

$–$$ 🏨 **Best Western Riverside Inn.** Close to the University of South Carolina's Williams-Brice Stadium and Coliseum, this newly remodeled inn has comfortable rooms, a complimentary Continental breakfast of breads, fruit, yogurt, grits, and oatmeal, and a cheerful staff. Golf packages are available. ✉ *111 Knox Abbott Dr., 29033,* ☎ *803/939–4688 or 800/528–1234,* ℻ *803/926–5547. 64 rooms. Pool, putting green. AE, D, DC, MC, V.*

$–$$ 🏨 **La Quinta Motor Inn.** At this three-story inn on a quiet street near the zoo, the rooms are spacious and well lit, with large working areas. ✉ *1335 Garner La., 29210,* ☎ *803/798–9590 or 800/531–5900,* ℻ *803/731–5574. 122 rooms. Pool. AE, D, DC, MC, V.*

Nightlife and the Arts

NIGHTLIFE

Cracker Jacks (✉ 1325 Longcreek Dr., ☎ 803/731–5692) features lively beach music (the sound of the Grand Strand) for listening and dancing, and occasionally a lusty floor show. **Nitelites Dance Club** (✉ 200 Stoneridge Dr., ☎ 803/252–8700) at the Embassy Suites Hotel has state-of-the-art lighting and presents a lavish free hors d'oeuvres buffet weekdays 5–7:30. Try **Dance Factory** (✉ 2100 Bush River Rd., ☎ 803/731–0300) at the Sheraton Hotel & Convention Center.

THE ARTS

Call the **South Carolina Philharmonic** (☎ 803/254–7445) for information about scheduled concerts of the Philharmonic, the Chamber Orchestra, and the Youth Orchestra. The **Columbia Music Festival Association** (☎ 803/771–6303) can inform callers about events of the Choral Society, the Opera, Opera Guild, Dance Theatre, Brass Band, Caroliers, and Cabaret Company. The **Koger Center for the Arts** (✉ Assembly St., ☎ 803/777–7500) presents national and international theater, ballet, and musical groups and individual performers.

The **Town Theatre** (⊠ 1012 Sumter St., ☎ 803/799–2510), founded in 1919, stages six plays a year from September to late May, plus a special summer show. The **Workshop Theatre of South Carolina** (⊠ 1136 Bull St., ☎ 803/799–4876) produces a number of plays.

Outdoor Activities and Sports

BASEBALL

The **Columbia Mets** (☎ 803/256–4110), a Class-A affiliate of the New York Mets, play from mid-April through August at Capital City Stadium (⊠ 301 S. Assembly St.) downtown.

CANOEING, KAYAKING, RAFTING

Self-guided canoe trails traverse an alluvial floodplain bordered by high bluffs at the 22,200-acre **Congaree Swamp National Monument** (⊠ 20 mi southeast of Columbia, off SC 48, ☎ 803/776–4396). The water and trees here, including many old-growth bottomland hardwoods, are full of wildlife. **Canoe rentals** are available in Columbia at Adventure Carolina (☎ 803/796–4505) and the River Runner Outdoor Center (☎ 803/771–0353).

Rafting, kayaking, and canoeing on the **Saluda River** near Columbia offer challenging Class III and Class IV rapids. Guided river and swamp excursions can be arranged through Adventure Carolina and River Runner Outdoor Center (☞ *above*).

GOLF

Sedgewood (☎ 803/776–2177) is among the many fine area courses.

HIKING

Congaree Swamp National Monument (☞ Canoeing, *above*) has 22 mi of trails for hikers and nature lovers and a ¾-mi boardwalk for visitors with disabilities. Guided nature walks leave Saturday at 1:30.

Shopping

ANTIQUES AND FLEA MARKETS

Many of Columbia's antiques outlets are in the **Congaree Vista** around Huger and Gervais streets, between the State House and the river. A number of intriguing shops and cafés are in **Five Points,** around the intersection of Blossom and Harden streets. There are antiques shops across the river on Meeting and State streets in **West Columbia.** The **Old Mill Antique Mall** (⊠ 310 State St., W. Columbia, ☎ 803/796–4229) has items from many dealers. The **Thieves Market Antique Flea Mall** (⊠ 502 Gadsden St., Columbia, ☎ 803/254–4997) shows off the wares of dozens of antiques and collectibles dealers.

FARMER'S MARKET

The **State Farmer's Market** (⊠ Bluff Rd., ☎ 803/253–4664) is one of the 10 largest in the country. Fresh vegetables are sold each weekday, along with flowers, plants, seafood, and more, from 6 AM to 9 PM.

Camden

32 mi northeast of Columbia via I–20.

Charming Camden, a town with a horsey history and grand Southern Colonial homes, has never paved its fanciest roads for the sake of the hooves of the horses who regularly trot over them. The Carolina Cup and Colonial Cup are run here; in addition to the races, you'll see champagne tailgate parties with elegant crystal and china.

Camden is South Carolina's oldest inland town, dating from 1732. British General Lord Cornwallis established a garrison here during the Revolutionary War, and burned most of Camden before evacuating it. A center of textile trade from the late 19th century through the 1940s,

Camden attracted Northerners escaping the cold winters; the DuPont family is today one of Camden's major employers. Because General Sherman spared the town during the Civil War, most of its antebellum homes still stand.

☺ The **Historic Camden Revolutionary War Site** re-creates the British occupation of 1780 on the site of the early 19th-century village. Several house restorations display period furnishings, including Cornwallis's headquarters, the **Kershaw–Cornwallis House** (circa 1770). Nature trails, fortifications, a powder magazine, a picnic area, and a crafts shop are also here. ⊠ *U.S. 521, 1½ mi north of I–20,* ☎ *803/432–9841.* ☞ *$4.50.* ☉ *Guided tours Mon.–Sat. 10–4, Sun. 1–4; museum shop daily 10–5.*

Dining and Lodging

$$$ ✕ **Mill Pond Restaurant.** In a historic building overlooking a sprawl-
★   ing mill pond, this restaurant, about a 10-minute drive south of Cam-
den, is one of the state's finest eateries. The creative Southern regional cuisine highlights such starters as grits with andouille sausage, roast peppers, and garlic toast and crab cakes with shrimp tartar sauce. Dinner here is worth the drive. ⊠ *84 Boykin Mill Rd., Rembert,* ☎ *803/424–0261. Jacket and tie. MC, V. Closed Sun. No lunch.*

$–$$ ✕ **Avanti's Restaurant.** Cane-back chairs, fox-hunting prints, and elaborately tiled fireplaces set the tone for an elegant meal in the Victorian Greenleaf Inn (☞ *below*). Avanti's serves wonderful pastas and pork with Italian family-style side dishes, plus great cannoli. ⊠ *1308 Broad St.,* ☎ *803/713–0089. AE, D, MC, V. Closed Sun. No lunch.*

$$ ⌂ **Greenleaf Inn.** Alice Boykin, whose name is to Camden what
★   Carnegie's is to Pittsburgh, opened the Greenleaf in 1993. The inn consists of three buildings: the main inn, with four rooms on the second floor above Avanti's Restaurant (☞ *above*); a nearby carriage house with seven rooms; and a guest cottage, which is particularly good for families. The spacious rooms have classic Victorian furniture and wallpaper; all baths are modern. A complimentary breakfast of pancakes or French toast is delivered to your room. You won't find a nicer or better-value lodging in the region. ⊠ *1308 Broad St., 29020,* ☎ *803/425–1806 or 800/437–5874,* 𝔽𝔸𝕏 *803/425–5853. 8 rooms, 3 suites, 1 cottage. Restaurant. AE, D, MC, V.*

$$ ⌂ **Holiday Inn.** This well-maintained chain offering is 3 mi west of downtown Camden. The restaurant is excellent. ⊠ *U.S. 1/601S, Box 96, Lugoff 29078,* ☎ *803/438–9441 or 800/465–4329,* 𝔽𝔸𝕏 *803/438–9441. 117 rooms. Restaurant, lounge, pool. AE, D, DC, MC, V.*

Nightlife

The **Paddock Restaurant & Pub** (⊠ 514 Rutledge St., ☎ 803/432–3222) has music and dancing.

Outdoor Activities and Sports

EQUESTRIAN EVENTS

Camden puts on two steeplechase events at **Springdale Race Course** (⊠ 200 Knights Hill Rd., ☎ 803/432–6513): the Carolina Cup in late March or early April and the Colonial Cup in November.

GOLF

White Pines Golf Club (☎ 803/432–7442) is an 18-hole, par 72 course.

OFF THE   **CHERAW** – The town's well-preserved, 213-acre historic district holds the
BEATEN PATH   Town Green, part of the original 1768 plan. The district encompasses
more than 50 antebellum public buildings and houses, as well as later structures, including the Market Hall, Town Hall, Lyceum Museum, and

Inglis-McIver Law Office. Stop by the Greater Cheraw Chamber of Commerce (✉ 221 Market St., ☎ 803/537–7681) for a brochure about the area. Cheraw is 55 mi northeast of Camden on U.S. 1; you pass the Carolina Sandhills National Wildlife Refuge en route.

Sumter

30 mi southeast of Camden on U.S. 521; 44 mi east of Columbia on U.S. 378.

Sumter—named for the Revolutionary War hero and statesman General Thomas Sumter—was settled about 1740 as the center of a cultivated plantation district. Today it is home to varied industries, lumbering, agricultural marketing, and nearby Shaw Air Force Base.

The **Sumter County Museum and Archives** (headquarters of the Sumter County Historical Society), in a lovely 1845 Victorian Gothic house, exhibits fine period furnishings, Oriental carpets, vintage carriages, dolls, and various memorabilia. Archival records are valuable for tracing family roots. ✉ *122 N. Washington St.,* ☎ *803/775–0908.* ⊠ *Free.* ☉ *Museum Tues.–Sat. 10–5, Sun. 2–5; archives Tues.–Sat. 10–5.*

Swan Lake Iris Gardens is like Eden when its 6 million irises are in bloom. Royal-white-mute, black-necked, coscoroba, whooper, trumpeter, and black Australian swans paddle leisurely around the 45-acre lake. The 150-acre park also includes walking trails, picnic areas, tennis courts, a playground, and concessions. ✉ *W. Liberty St.,* ☎ *803/775–3304.* ⊠ *Free.* ☉ *Daily 8–sunset.*

Lodging

$$ 🏨 **Holiday Inn.** This well-maintained motor inn is 4 mi west of town, near Shaw Air Force Base. Simple, clean rooms are as you would expect from this chain. ✉ *2390 Broad St. extension, 29150,* ☎ *803/469–9001 or 800/465–4329,* 𝖥𝖠𝖷 *803/469–7001. 124 rooms. Restaurant, pool. AE, D, DC, MC, V.*

$$ 🏨 **Magnolia House.** In Sumter's historic district, this four-columned Greek Revival structure is a nice alternative to the region's generic chain motels. Antiques, many of them French, furnish the rooms; there are also stained-glass windows, inlaid oak floors, and five fireplaces. A full breakfast is included in the rate. ✉ *230 Church St., 29150,* ☎ *803/ 775–6694. 3 rooms, 1 suite. AE, MC, V.*

Nightlife

Plums Restaurant & Lounge (✉ Holiday Inn, 2390 Broad St. Extension, ☎ 803/469–9001) provides pleasant evening unwinding with live entertainment.

Outdoor Activities and Sports

About 30 mi from Sumter, a haunting canoe trail leads into a remote swampy depression at **Woods Bay State Park** (✉ From Sumter, take U.S. 378E to U.S. 301N, ☎ 803/659–44450), where rentals are available for $2 per hour or $10 for a full day.

Aiken

64 mi south of Sumter via U.S. 301/601 and U.S. 78, 56 mi southwest of Columbia via I–20.

Aiken, in Thoroughbred Country, first earned its fame in the 1890s, when wealthy Northerners wintering here built stately mansions and entertained one another with lavish parties, horse shows, and hunts. Many of the mansions—some with up to 90 rooms—remain as a testament to this era of opulence. The town is still a center for all kinds of outdoor activity, including the equestrian events of the Triple Crown, as well as tennis and golf.

The area's horse farms have produced many national champions, which are commemorated at the **Aiken Thoroughbred Hall of Fame** with exhibitions of horse-related decorations, paintings, and sculptures, plus racing silks and trophies. The Hall of Fame is on the grounds of the 14-acre **Hopeland Gardens,** with winding paths, quiet terraces, and reflecting pools. There's a Touch and Scent Trail with Braille plaques. Open-air free concerts and plays are presented on Monday evening mid-July–August. ⊠ *Corner of Dupree Pl. and Whiskey Rd.,* ☎ *803/642–7630.* ⌨ *Free.* ⊙ *Museum fall–spring, Tues.–Sun. 2–5; grounds daily sunrise–sunset.*

The **Aiken County Historical Museum,** in one wing of an 1860 estate, is devoted to early regional culture. It has Native American artifacts, firearms, an authentically furnished 1808 log cabin, and a one-room schoolhouse. ⊠ *433 Newberry St. SW,* ☎ *803/642–2015.* ⌨ *Donations accepted.* ⊙ *Tues.–Fri. 9:30–4:30, weekends 2–5.*

Aiken surrounds the serene and wild **Hitchcock Woods** (⊠ Enter from junction of Clark Rd. and Whitney Dr., Berrie Rd., and Dibble Rd.), 2,000 acres of Southern forest with hiking trails and bridal paths.

If you're looking for something different to do, free tours and wine tastings are offered by **Montmorenci Vineyards** (⊠ U.S. 78, 2 ½ mi east of Aiken, ☎ 803/649–4870); tours by appointment.

OFF THE
BEATEN PATH

HICKORY KNOB STATE RESORT PARK – This park about 64 mi northwest of Aiken has everything for a complete vacation. Take SC 19 and U.S. 25 to U.S. 378, drive west to the town of McCormick, then south until you see signs for the park on the shore of Strom Thurmond Lake. There's fishing, waterskiing, sailing, motor boating, a swimming pool, a tackle shop, nature trails, an 18-hole championship golf course, a pro shop, and tennis courts. A 1770s log cabin, an 80-room lodge, nine duplex lakeside cottages, campgrounds, and a restaurant round out Hickory Knob's offerings. You're also near a stretch of the **Savannah River Scenic Highway,** which follows the Savannah River along the Georgia border, winding 100 mi and past three lakes. ⊠ *Rte. 1, Box 199B, McCormick 29835,* ☎ *864/391–2450 or 800/491–1764.* ⌨ *Free; fees for some activities.* ⊙ *Office daily 7 am–11 pm.*

Dining and Lodging

$$–$$$ ✕ **No. 10 Downing Street.** This stately Southern Colonial dates from
★   1837 and serves some of the best—and most diverse—food in town. The menu changes regularly: One month might focus on such Italian fare as *pollo al prosciutto* (chicken wrapped in prosciutto and fresh herbs with fettucine Alfredo) and baked beef tenderloin with tomatoes, garlic, and oregano; another month may salute country French or regional cuisine. A bakery here is open during all meals. ⊠ *241 Laurens St.,* ☎ *808/642–9062. D, DC, MC, V. Closed Sun.–Mon.*

$ ✕ **Malia's.** At Aiken's new hot lunch and dinner spot, you get international fusion cuisine, including lamb soup with curry; veal with shitake mushrooms and brandy demi-glace; and a baked ham, Brie, and Portobello mushroom sandwich. ⊠ *120 Laurens St.,* ☎ *803/643–3086. D, DC, MC, V. Closed Sun.–Mon.*

$ ✕ **Track Kitchen.** The who's who of Aiken's horsey set can be found here most mornings, feasting on the heavy and hearty cooking of Carol and Pockets Curtis. The small dining room is unpretentious, with walls of mint-green cinder block and simple Formica counters. ⊠ *420 Mead Ave.,* ☎ *803/641–9628. No credit cards. No dinner.*

$$$–$$$$ 🏨 **Willcox Inn.** Winston Churchill, Franklin D. Roosevelt, and the Astors have slept at this elegant inn, built in grand style in the early 1900s. The lobby is graced with massive stone fireplaces, rosewood woodwork, heart-pine floors, and Oriental rugs. Though rooms have fine furnishings such as high four-poster beds, the decor could use a touch-up. ✉ *100 Colleton Ave., 29801,* ☎ *803/649–1377 or 800/368–1047,* ℻ *803/643–0971. 24 rooms, 6 suites. Bar, dining room, croquet. AE, D, DC, MC, V.*

$$ 🏨 **Briar Patch.** You can learn plenty about both the Old and New South from the knowledgeable innkeepers of this terrific B&B, which was formerly tack rooms in Aiken's stable district. Choose either the frilly room with French Provincial furniture or the less dramatic one with pine antiques and a weather vane. Breakfast here is Continental. ✉ *544 Magnolia La. SE, 29801,* ☎ *803/649–2010. 2 rooms. Tennis court. No credit cards.*

Nightlife

There's live entertainment at **Jockey's Lounge** in the Holiday Inn Express (✉ 155 Colony Pkwy., ☎ 803/648–0999).

Outdoor Activities and Sports

EQUESTRIAN EVENTS

In Aiken, **polo matches** are played at Whitney Field (☎ 803/648–7874) on Sunday afternoon September–November and March–July. Three weekends in late March and early April are set aside for the famed **Triple Crown** (☎ 803/641–1111)—thoroughbred trials of promising yearlings, a steeplechase, and harness races by young horses making their debut.

GOLF

The many fine 18-hole courses in the area include **Highland Park Country Club** (☎ 803/649–6029).

Greenwood

55 mi northwest of Aiken via SC 19, U.S. 25, and SC 72; 75 mi west of Columbia via U.S. 378, U.S. 178, and SC 72.

Founded by Irish settlers in 1802, Greenwood received its name from the site's gently rolling landscape and dense forests. Andrew Johnson, the 17th U.S. president, operated a tailor shop at Courthouse Square before migrating to eastern Tennessee. Anglers, swimmers, and boaters head for nearby Lake Greenwood's 200-mi shore. Two sections of Sumter National Forest are nearby, too.

The **Greenwood Museum** has more than 7,000 items in eclectic displays: Native American artifacts, natural history and geology exhibits, and a replicated village street including a one-room school and a general store. ✉ *106 Main St.,* ☎ *864/229–7093.* ⌸ *Free.* ☉ *Tues.–Fri. 9–12:30 and 1:45–5, Sat. 2–5.*

The **Gardens of Park Seed Co.,** one of the nation's largest seed supply houses, maintain colorful experimental gardens and greenhouses 6 mi north on U.S. 178 at Hodges. The flower beds are especially vivid June 15 through July, and seeds and bulbs are for sale in the company's store. The **South Carolina Festival of Flowers**—with a performing-artists contest, a beauty pageant, private house and garden tours, and live entertainment—is held at Park's headquarters annually at the end of June. ✉ *On SC 254, 7 mi north of town,* ☎ *864/941–4213 or 800/845–3369.* ⌸ *Free.* ☉ *Gardens daily; store Mon.–Sat. 9–6.*

Lodging

$$ ⊞ **Inn on the Square.** This inn was fashioned out of a warehouse in the heart of town. Though the rooms suffer from rather unremarkable views, they're bright and spacious with reproduction 18th-century antiques, four-poster beds, writing desks, and such thoughtful touches as turndown service and complimentary morning newspapers. The staff is attuned to the needs of business travelers and vacationers alike. ⊠ *104 Court Sq., 29648,* ☎ *864/223–4488,* FAX *864/223–7067. 48 rooms. Restaurant, lounge, pool. AE, D, DC, MC, V.*

Ninety Six

10 mi east of Greenwood on SC 248.

The town of Ninety Six, on an old Indian trade route, is so named for being 96 mi from the Cherokee village of Keowee in the Blue Ridge Mountains—the distance a young Cherokee maiden, Cateechee, is supposed to have ridden to warn her English lover of a threatened Indian massacre. The **Ninety Six National Historic Site** commemorates two Revolutionary War battles. The visitor center museum has descriptive displays, and there are remnants of the old village, a reconstructed French and Indian War stockade, and Revolutionary-era fortifications. ⊠ *SC 248,* ☎ *864/543–4068.* 🎫 *Free.* ⊙ *Daily 8–5.*

Abbeville

14 mi west of Greenwood on SC 72.

★   **Abbeville** may well be one of inland South Carolina's most satisfying, though lesser-known, small towns. An appealing historic district includes the old business district, early churches, and residential areas. The "Southern cause" was born and died here, where the first organized secession meeting was held and where, on May 2, 1865, Confederate President Jefferson Davis officially disbanded the defeated armies of the South in the last meeting of his war council. The 1830 house where the Confederate council met is the **Burt–Stark House.** ⊠ *306 N. Main St.,* ☎ *864/459–4297 or 864/459–2181.* 🎫 *$3.* ⊙ *Sept.– May, Fri.–Sat. 1–5 or by appointment; June–Aug., Tues.–Sat. 1–5 or by appointment.*

An 1850s jail houses the **Abbeville County Museum,** which contains area memorabilia. It's adjacent to the 1837 log-cabin home of Marie Cromer Siegler, founder of 4-H clubs, and an educational garden. ⊠ *Poplar and Cherry Sts.,* ☎ *864/459–2696.* 🎫 *Free.* ⊙ *Wed., Sun. 3– 5, or by appointment.*

The **Abbeville Opera House** (⊠ Town Sq., ☎ 864/459–2157) faces the historic town square. Built in 1908, it has been renovated to reflect the grandeur of the days when lavish road shows and stellar entertainers came center stage. Current productions range from light, contemporary comedies to Broadway-style musicals. Call to ask about tours.

Dining and Lodging

$ ✕ **Village Grille.** Locals come to this high-ceiling room with pomegranate-
★   color walls and antique mirrors for the herb rotisserie chicken. Other choices are the ribs, homemade pastas, and cordial-laced desserts. The atmosphere is trendy and friendly; the staff bends over backward to please. ⊠ *114 Trinity St.,* ☎ *864/459–2500. AE, MC, V.*

$ ✕ **Yoder's Dutch Kitchen.** Here's authentic Pennsylvania Dutch home cooking in an unassuming redbrick building with a mansard roof. There's a lunch buffet and evening smorgasbord with fried chicken, stuffed cabbage, Dutch meat loaf, breaded veal Parmesan, and plenty of vegetables. Shoofly pie, Dutch bread, and apple butter can be bought to go. ⊠ *U.S. 72,* ☎ *864/459–5556. Reservations not accepted. No credit cards. Closed Sun.–Tues. No dinner Wed.*

$$ 🏠 **Belmont Inn.** Built just after the turn of the century, this restored Spanish-style structure is a popular overnight stop with Opera House visitors. The owners, three local college chums, undertook a major spruce-up in 1996; theater-and-dining package plans are offered. ⊠ *Court Sq., 29620,* ☎ 𝔽𝔸𝕏 *864/459–9625. 24 rooms. Restaurant, lounge, meeting rooms. AE, MC, V.*

The Arts
The **Abbeville Opera House** (⊠ Town Sq., ☎ 864/459–2157) stages high-caliber productions in an early 20th-century setting. Reservations are taken weekdays 10–5.

Shopping
Abbeville's **Town Square** is lined with attractive gift and specialty shops in restored historic buildings dating from the late 1800s.

Columbia and the Heartland A to Z

Arriving and Departing
BY BUS
Greyhound (☎ 800/231–2222) serves all of South Carolina.

BY CAR
I–77 leads into Columbia from the north. I–26, I–20, and U.S. 1 intersect at Columbia.

BY PLANE
Columbia Metro Airport (☎ 803/822–5000) is served by Air South, American Eagle, ComAir/Delta, and US Airways.

BY TRAIN
Amtrak (☎ 800/872–7245) makes stops at Camden, Columbia, Denmark, Dillon, Florence, and Kingstree in the Heartland.

Getting Around
BY BUS
A local utility provides city bus service in and around **Columbia** (☎ 803/748–3019).

BY TAXI
Companies providing service in Columbia include **AAA Airport Shuttle Service** (☎ 803/796–3626), **Blue Ribbon** (☎ 803/754–8163), and **Checker-Yellow** (☎ 803/799–3311). **Gamecock Cab Co.** (☎ 803/796–7700) offers service from Columbia to other cities statewide.

Contacts and Resources
EMERGENCIES
Dial **911** for police, fire, and ambulance assistance. Emergency room services are available at **Richland Memorial Hospital** (⊠ 5 Richland Medical Park, Columbia, ☎ 803/765–7561).

GUIDED TOURS
Richland County Historic Preservation Commission (☎ 803/252–1770) runs guided tours and rents out historic properties. In Sumter, the charismatic former mayor **"Bubba" McElveen** (☎ 803/775–2851) gives walking, bus, and auto tours of the area. The **Aiken Chamber of Commerce** runs a 90-minute tour of the historic district and will customize tours to suit individual interests. Customized tours of Camden are available through either the **Kershaw County Chamber of Commerce**

(☎ 803/432–2525) or from **Greenleaf Tours** (contact Louise Burns, ☎ 803/432–1515).

Eckerd Drugs (✉ 1610 Airport Blvd., W. Columbia, ☎ 803/794–0888), **Kroger Sav-On** (✉ 817 St. Andrews Rd. and 6 other locations, ☎ 803/551–1145), and **REVCO** (✉ 3595 Harden St., ☎ 803/779–1217) are open 24 hours. **Eckerd Drugs** (✉ 818 Harden St., ☎ 803/799–0043) and **REVCO** (✉ 2245 Charleston Hwy., W. Columbia, ☎ 803/796–2586) are open until midnight.

The 41-mi-long **Lake Murray,** just 15 mi west of Columbia via I–26, (Irmo exit), has swimming, boating, picnicking, and superb fishing. There are many marinas and campgrounds in the area. For information, contact the Lake Murray Tourism and Recreation Association (✉ 2184 N. Lake Dr., Irmo 29063, ☎ 803/781–5940).

For **fishing,** Lakes Marion and Moultrie attract anglers after bream, crappie, catfish, and several kinds of bass. Supplies, camps, guides, rentals, and accommodations abound. For information, contact Santee Cooper Counties Promotion Commission (✉ Drawer 40, Santee 29142, ☎ 803/854–2131; 800/227–8510 outside South Carolina).

For information on **hiking** trails in the Francis Marion National Forest and the Sumter National Forest, contact the National Forest Service (✉ 4931 Broad River Rd., Columbia 29210-4021, ☎ 803/561–4000).

In Columbia: **AM:** WCOS 1400, country; WOMG 1320, oldies; WVOC 560, news/talk. **FM:** WLTR 91.3, classical; WMFX 102.3, classic rock; WUSC 90.5, alternative (jazz, blues, folk, reggae).

In Abbeville, contact the **Greater Abbeville Chamber of Commerce** (✉ 104 Pickens St., Abbeville 29620, ☎ 864/459–4600). **Greater Aiken Chamber of Commerce** (✉ 400 Laurens St. NW, Box 892, Aiken 29802, ☎ 803/641–1111) serves the Aiken area. The **Columbia Metropolitan Convention and Visitors Bureau** (✉ Box 15, 29202; Visitors Center, 1012 Gervais St., ☎ 803/254–0479 or 800/264–4884) has brochures, maps, and advice for travelers; the center also presents a short film on area history. **Kershaw County Chamber of Commerce** (✉ 724 S. Broad St., Box 605, Camden 29020, ☎ 803/432–2525) has information and advice on where to go in Camden. **Ninety Six Chamber of Commerce** (✉ Box 8, Ninety Six 29666, ☎ 803/543–2900) provides information on the town and district of Ninety Six.

THE UPCOUNTRY

The Upcountry, in the northwest corner of the state, has long been a favorite for family vacations because of its temperate climate and natural beauty. The abundant lakes and waterfalls and several state parks (including Caesar's Head, Keowee-Toxaway, Oconee, Table Rock, and the Chattooga National Wild and Scenic River) provide all manner of recreational activities. Beautiful anytime, the 130-mi Cherokee Foothills Scenic Highway (SC 11), through the Blue Ridge Mountains, is especially delightful in spring and autumn.

The comfortable communities of Greenville, Spartanburg, Clemson, Pendleton, and Anderson take justifiable pride in their educational institutions, museums, historic preservation, and cultural accomplishments. Any one of them is worth a day's visit.

Greenville

100 mi northwest of Columbia.

Although known for its textile and other manufacturing plants, Greenville has many tree-lined streets and a number of attractions including a zoo and nearby state parks such as Caesar's Head and Table Rock. It's also home to Bob Jones University, which has a gallery of religious art and antiquities.

Housed in an innovative modern building, the **Greenville County Museum of Art** displays American art dating from the Colonial era. Exhibited are works by Paul Jenkins, Jamie Wyeth, Jasper Johns, and noted Southern artists. ⊠ *420 College St., Greenville,* ☎ *864/271–7570.* ☞ *Free.* ☉ *Tues.–Sat. 10–5, Sun. 1–5.*

Dining and Lodging

$$–$$$ ✕ **Seven Oaks.** The seven oaks on the property gave this 1895 home its name. Now an elegant restaurant, it has seven dining rooms with 14-ft curved ceilings, stained glass, and parquet floors. The dinner selections are just as elegant: veal scallopine, mustard-crusted rack of lamb, and sweet-potato bread pudding. ⊠ *104 Broadus Ave.,* ☎ *864/232–1895. AE, D, MC, V. Closed Sun. No lunch.*

$$ ✕ **The 858.** Previously the Elks Lodge #858, this is now one of Greenville's hottest spots. The building's original, funky elevator brings diners to the foyer in style. The artichoke and goat cheese fondue, carpaccio of beef with waffle potatoes, and potato-crusted grouper with roasted shallot cream are almost too pretty to eat. ⊠ *18 E. North St.,* ☎ *864/242–8883. AE, D, MC, V. Closed Sun. No lunch.*

$$ ✕ **Palms Restaurant.** This restaurant, probably Greenville's best, is in the Phoenix—Greenville's Inn (☞ *below*). The modest dining room serves up sophisticated dishes including galantine of duck, sesame-crusted mahimahi, and chocolate truffle cake with espresso sauce. The dark, cozy piano bar with a fireplace and wing chairs is a great place to retire while you wait 20 minutes for a delicious made-to-order hot apple tart with cinnamon ice cream. ⊠ *246 N. Pleasantburg Dr.,* ☎ *864/233–4651. AE, D, DC, MC, V.*

$$ ✕ **Stax Omega Diner.** Here's a contemporary diner with booths and a half-circle counter with stools, where you can order everything from bacon and eggs and burgers to souvlaki, Greek-style chicken, and shrimp and grits. It's all good, and it's open almost around-the-clock. ⊠ *72 Orchard Park Dr.,* ☎ *864/297–6639. AE, D, MC, V.*

$$–$$$ ▤ **Hyatt Regency Hotel.** This standard chain offering's best feature is its central location in the midst of the small, revitalized downtown area of shops and restaurants. Rooms overlooking the atrium are a must. Airport shuttle service is complimentary. ⊠ *220 N. Main St., 29601,* ☎ *864/235–1234,* ℻ *864/232–7584. 327 rooms. Restaurant, lounge, pool, hot tub, health club. AE, D, DC, MC, V.*

$$–$$$ ▤ **Phoenix—Greenville's Inn.** Plantation shutters and four-poster beds adorn this transformed and renovated property, the former Thunderbird Motel. Now guests enjoy the residential feel and hospitality of a Southern inn; the service is excellent. Ask for a room overlooking the courtyard pool area. ⊠ *246 N. Pleasantburg Dr., 29607,* ☎ ℻ *864/233–4651,* ☎ *800/257–3529. 185 rooms. Restaurant, pool. AE, D, DC, MC, V.*

The Arts

The **Peace Center for the Arts** (✉ 101 W. Broad St., ☎ 864/467–3030), which sits along the Reedy River, presents star performers, touring Broadway shows, dance companies, chamber music, and local groups.

Ice-Skating

The **Greenville Pavilion Ice Rink** (☎ 864/322–7529) is the only public indoor rink in the state.

Pendleton

25 mi southwest of Greenville.

Charming Pendleton, a few miles from Clemson University, has a historic district and interesting architecture. The Farmers Hall, built in 1826, was originally a courthouse. The Square, a district of restaurants and shops, faces the Village Green.

The **South Carolina State Botanical Garden,** on the Clemson University campus in nearby Clemson, holds more than 2,000 varieties of plants on over 256 acres, including wildflower, fern, and bog gardens and nature trails. ☎ 864/656–3405. ✑ *Free.*

Lodging

$$ 🏠 **Liberty Hall Inn.** There's great food and lodging at this country inn in the heart of town. The inn, built in the 1840s, caters to business travelers and vacationers. Rooms are furnished in antiques and family heirlooms; a breakfast of waffles, breads, fruit, and yogurt is included. ✉ *621 S. Mechanic St., 29670,* ☎ FAX *864/646–7500,* ☎ *800/643–7944. 10 rooms. Restaurant. AE, D, DC, MC, V.*

Kings Mountain National Military Park

70 mi northeast of Greenville.

This is where the "turning-point" Revolutionary War battle was fought on October 7, 1780. Colonial Tories commanded by British Major Patrick Ferguson were soundly defeated by ragtag patriot forces from the southern Appalachians. Visitor center exhibits, dioramas, and an orientation film describe the action. A paved self-guided trail leads through the battlefield. ✉ *20 mi northeast of Gaffney, SC, off I–85 via a marked side road in North Carolina,* ☎ *864/936–7921.* ✑ *Free.* ☉ *Daily 9–5, until 6 Memorial Day–Labor Day.*

The 6,000-acre **King's Mountain State Park** (☎ 864/222–3209), adjacent to the national military park, has camping, swimming, fishing, boating, and nature and hiking trails.

Upcountry A to Z

Arriving and Departing

BY BUS

Greyhound (☎ 800/231–2222) serves all of South Carolina.

BY CAR

I–85 provides access to Greenville, Spartanburg, Pendleton, and Anderson. I–26 runs from Charleston through Columbia to the Upcountry, connecting with I–385 into Greenville.

BY PLANE

Greenville-Spartanburg Airport (☎ 864/867–7426) is served by US Airways, Delta, Northwest, American Eagle, Continental, Midway, and Air South.

BY TRAIN

Amtrak (☎ 800/872–7245) stops in Greenville.

Contacts and Resources

RAFTING, CANOEING, KAYAKING

The **Chattooga National Wild and Scenic River,** on the border of South Carolina and Georgia, is excellent for guided rafting, canoeing, and kayaking trips. Contact **Wildwater Ltd.** (☎ 864/647–9587 or 800/451–9972) or **Nantahala Outdoor Center** (☎ 864/647–9014 or 800/232–7238).

STATE PARKS

For information about state parks in the area, contact the **South Carolina Division of Tourism** (✉ 1205 Pendleton St., Columbia 29201, ☎ 803/734–0122 or 800/872–3505). **Devils Fork State Park** (✉ 161 Holcombe Circle, Salem 29676, ☎ 864/944–2639), on Lake Jocassee, has luxurious new villas and facilities.

VISITOR INFORMATION

Contact **Discover Upcountry Carolina Association** (✉ Box 3116, Greenville 29602, ☎ 864/233–2690 or 800/849–4766). The **Greater Greenville Convention and Visitors Bureau** (✉ 206 S. Main St., Box 10527, 29603, ☎ 864/421–0000 or 800/717–0023) can provide information.

SOUTH CAROLINA A TO Z

Arriving and Departing

By Boat

Boaters can reach most of South Carolina's coastal cities and towns by the Intracoastal Waterway.

By Bus

Greyhound (☎ 800/231–2222) serves all of South Carolina.

By Car

I–26 traverses the state from northwest to southeast and terminates at Charleston. I–77 leads into Columbia from the north. I–26, I–20, and U.S. 1 intersect at Columbia. I–85 provides access to Greenville, Spartanburg, Pendleton, and Anderson. U.S. 17, a north–south coastal route, runs along the coastal edge of the entire state.

By Plane

Major airports are **Charleston International Airport** (☎ 803/767–1100); **Myrtle Beach International Airport** (☎ 803/448–1589); **Hilton Head Island Airport** (served by US Airways Express); the closest metropolitan airport is **Savannah International Airport** (☎ 912/964–0514), about an hour's drive from Hilton Head; **Columbia Metro Airport** (☎ 803/822–5000); **Greenville-Spartanburg Airport** (☎ 864/867–7426).

By Train

Amtrak (☎ 800/872–7245) stops in Charleston, Camden, Columbia, Denmark, Dillon, Florence, Greenville, Kingstree and Yemassee (near Beaufort).

Getting Around

By Car

The speed limit on interstates is 65 mph. You can turn right during a red light unless otherwise noted by street signs.

Contacts and Resources

B&Bs

For reservation agencies in **Charleston,** *see* Contacts and Resources *in* Charleston A to Z, *above.* For a complete list of B&Bs, write to the **South Carolina Division of Tourism** (✉ 1205 Pendleton St., Columbia 29201, ☎ 803/734–0122 or 800/872–3505) and ask for the pamphlet *Bed & Breakfast of South Carolina.* Write to the **South Carolina Bed and Breakfast Association** (✉ Box 1275, Sumter 29150-1275) for a current state directory of member B&Bs.

Emergencies

Dial 911 for **police, fire,** and **ambulance** assistance.

Guided Tours

Lowcountry Adventures (☎ 803/681–8212) offers tours of Hilton Head, Beaufort, and Charleston. For information about other specific tours, contact the **South Carolina Division of Tourism** (☞ Visitor Information, *below*).

National and State Parks

For information about South Carolina's national park areas, contact the **U.S. Forest Service** (✉ 4931 Broad River Rd., Columbia 29210, ☎ 803/561–4000). Several of South Carolina's 48 state parks operate like resort communities, with everything from deluxe accommodations to golf. For information, contact the **South Carolina Division of Tourism** (☞ Visitor Information, *below*).

Visitor Information

South Carolina Division of Tourism (✉ 1205 Pendleton St., Columbia 29201, ☎ 803/734–0122 or 800/872–3505) has information about the entire state.

Welcome centers: ✉ U.S. 17, near Little River; ✉ I–95, near Dillon, Santee and Lake Marion, and Hardeeville; ✉ I–77, near Fort Mill; ✉ I–85, near Blacksburg and Fair Play; ✉ I–26, near Landrum; ✉ I–20, at North Augusta; and ✉ U.S. 301, near Allendale.

8 Tennessee

Tennessee's dominating characteristics are her music—the blues developed in Memphis; rock came into popularity with the rise of Elvis Presley; country music claims Nashville as its capital— and her scenic geographical borders, the Great Smoky Mountains on the east and the Mississippi River on the west. Here, too, are forests, fields, and streams for the nature lover, outlet malls for the die-hard shopper, and an array of entertainment parks for the whole family.

MOUNTAINS AND MUSIC—these gifts Tennessee was given in abundance and shares generously with millions of guests each year.

Updated by
Charlotte
Durham

Memphis, home of the blues, rises out of the flat, cotton-kissed southwest corner of the state, on the banks of the Mississippi River. Beale Street, in the core of its downtown, nurtured some of the finest talents of the genre, from blues artists W. C. Handy and B. B. King to rockers Elvis Presley and Jerry Lee Lewis. Today, with live music in Handy Park, Beale Street again reverberates with the moody sounds that made it legendary.

Nashville, now Tennessee's largest city, retains its title as the country-music capital of the world. Music City, U.S.A., as it is known, is also the state's capital. Here, in the heart of Tennessee's green, gently rolling hills, country music is king. The recording studios on Music Row are thriving, and the Grand Ole Opry continues to pack its auditorium. The long-running radio-show extravaganza has launched many a singer's and picker's career and is now part of a theme park built around live country music shows.

As for mountains, they don't come any more beautiful than the Great Smokies—site of the nation's most visited national park and part of the Appalachian chain; they're in East Tennessee and are shared by North Carolina. Covered with a dense carpet of wildflowers in spring and ablaze with foliage in autumn, the Smokies—named for the mantle of blue haze that so often blankets them—are a joy to hike or drive through. Spend some time in the little mountain towns and villages dotting the hollows to experience homegrown bluegrass music and traditional cooking, along with the natural warmth of the people.

Pleasures and Pastimes

Dining

If you expect Tennessee dining to be all corn bread, turnip greens, and grits, you're in for a staggering surprise. Here you will find sophisticated restaurants with service as polished as any to be found in the world's greatest cities.

Not so long ago, Memphis offered little more than various neighborhood "home cooking" restaurants, several chop-suey houses, a handful of spaghetti-and-lasagna spots, and numerous establishments serving pork barbecue. Happily, the dining choices have improved dramatically during the past 15 years. In addition to a number of restaurants serving imaginative American cuisine, Memphis now boasts many competent and attractive international dining rooms. Hotel dining in Memphis is being revitalized, and today the city's most inspired dishes are often served in its finer hotels.

Memphis's top culinary attraction, however, remains barbecue, and a visit to one of the 70-odd barbecue restaurants is a must for anyone wanting to savor local color as well as tasty ribs. Memphians debate which is better: wet or dry ribs—a reference to the cooking style, not how moist the meat is. True fanciers should schedule their visit around the International Barbecue Cooking Contest, held during the annual Memphis in May International Festival. This cook-off draws more than 400 teams from around the world (as well as more than 100,000 spectators) for its three-day run on the banks of the Mississippi.

Nashville dining patrons are often casual in dress and prone to linger over meals. The city's mix of politics, country music, conventions, sports,

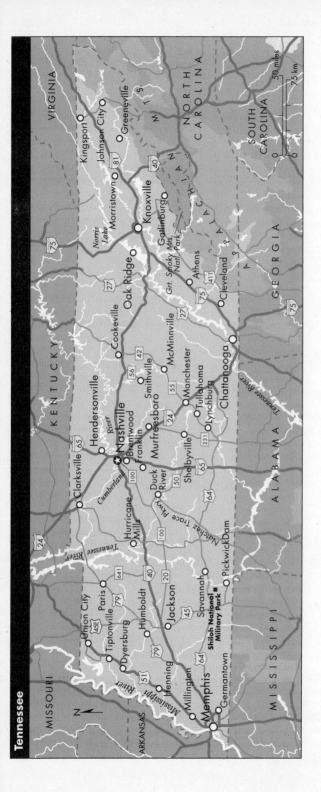

and business means deal making at every meal, lending prosperity and longevity to some of Nashville's best restaurants. Don't be surprised to find waiters, captains, and chefs who have worked in the same place for a decade. Such tenure translates into quality dining. On the other hand, Nashville is notorious for flashes in the pan: restaurants that open with a splash and close with a fizzle—often just a year later.

East Tennessee mountain cooks have long been noted for preparing fresh ingredients many different ways. Corn remains the old standby, used in the making of grits, luscious muffins, corn bread, and savory spoon bread. Barbecued ribs, thick pork chops, and generous slices of country ham with red-eye gravy rank as local favorites. Freshwater fish, such as varieties of trout, walleye, crappie, muskie, and catfish, will also be found in varied and delicious preparations (but remember to save room for home-baked pies and cobblers). Dress is casual unless otherwise noted.

CATEGORY	COST*
$$$$	over $50
$$$	$40–$50
$$	$20–$40
$	under $20

per person for a three-course meal, excluding drinks, service, and 7%–8¾% tax

Lodging

Some restored historic hotels in larger cities offer lodging in settings reminiscent of earlier times. The major resort areas of Gatlinburg and Pigeon Forge have abundant choices.

Memphis hotels are especially busy in the spring, when the Memphis in May International Festival and June's Cotton Carnival Memphis are in progress; in mid-August, when pilgrims observe Elvis Presley's death; between Christmas and New Year's during the St. Jude Liberty Bowl Football Classic; and in early January, when the faithful celebrate Elvis's birth. Be sure to reserve well in advance during those times.

With more than 125 hotels and motels, Nashville offers an impressive selection of accommodations in all price categories and levels of luxury. Although some establishments increase rates slightly during the peak summer travel season, most maintain the same rates year-round. Some downtown luxury hotels offer lower rates on weekends, when the legislators have gone home.

CATEGORY	COST*
$$$$	over $125
$$$	$70–$125
$$	$50–$70
$	under $50

All prices are for a standard double room, excluding 10%–11¾% tax.

Music

Music is everywhere in Tennessee. The blues and rock and roll flood Beale Street in Memphis, while country revels on Nashville's Music Row. If Opryland and Dollywood seem too imposing, the diffusion of top-notch nightspots throughout the state ensures Grammy award–winning talent and rising stars without all the hype.

Outdoor Activities and Sports

Tennesseans take advantage of the state's generally mild climate and spend a lot of time outdoors. Many hunt, fish, hike, or swim at the abundant state parks that dot the landscape. Others prefer to enjoy a picnic or cool off under waterfalls or in caves. And Tennesseans like to cheer for their favorite teams. Professional sports have been slow to reach Tennessee, but fans have been demonstrating their love of football for decades, filling the University of Tennessee's Neyland Stadium in Knoxville to overflowing. Even the latest expansion, boosting seating capacity to over 100,000, isn't likely to sate the appetite.

Exploring Tennessee

Tennessee spans more than 500 mi west to east, but only about 115 mi north to south. The state's three grand divisions are West Tennessee, from the Mississippi River to the Tennessee River near Camden; Middle Tennessee, from the Tennessee River to the Cumberland Plateau at Crossville; and East Tennessee, to the Great Smoky Mountains and the border with North Carolina. All three sections of the state are anchored by major cities with a wealth of cultural and historical attractions, and first-rate lodging establishments.

Great Itineraries

Exploring Tennessee will require some time on the road. Fortunately, hopping on and off I–40 will get you most places you want to go, whether west, middle, or east. Plan to spend at least two days to see the high points of any of Tennessee's major cities: Memphis, Nashville, Knoxville, or Chattanooga. But much of what's interesting about Tennessee is outside the major cities, so if you get to Memphis, for instance, allow some time for side trips to its Western neighbors.

IF YOU HAVE 3 DAYS

Explore ⊞ **Memphis,** home to Elvis Presley's Graceland. Be sure to see the morning or afternoon march of ducks to or from Peabody Hotel's lobby fountain. Listen to the blues on Beale Street, and don't miss the barbecue. Study the history of the great Mississippi River at Mud Island, and the history of music at the Memphis Music Hall of Fame. Take a day to make a side trip from Memphis, perhaps to the Casey Jones Museum in **Jackson** to the northeast, or east to **Shiloh National Military Park** if you're a Civil War buff.

IF YOU HAVE 6 DAYS

Visit ⊞ **Nashville** and its surrounding area. Take in some country music at the Grand Ole Opry, or view the works of Georgia O'Keeffe, Picasso, and Renoir at Fisk University's Van Vechten Art Gallery. Nashville's Music Row has enough museums and halls of fame to pack an entire day. Watch the stars come out at the Hard Rock Cafe in the District or take in a Broadway show at the Tennessee Performing Arts Center. Make time to venture down to **Shelbyville** for the Tennessee Walking Horse National Celebration or to **Lynchburg** to see the home of Jack Daniel's sippin' whiskey. Try to work in a visit to ⊞ **Chattanooga,** a spruced-up, midsize city on the move.

IF YOU HAVE 9 DAYS

Start at one end of the state and head for the other. There's plenty to divert your attention, depending on your interests. If history's your bag, visit the **Hunt-Phelan Home** in ⊞ **Memphis,** where Ulysses S. Grant and Jefferson Davis both broke bread (although not together). Spend a day or two in ⊞ **Nashville,** for some outrageous fun at **Opryland USA,** then head to ⊞ **Pigeon Forge** for more of the same at Dollywood. Tennessee is an outdoors-lover's paradise. There's spectacular scenery and hiking at **Great Smoky National Park,** but those who prefer a less physically challenging outdoor excursion may wish to saunter through ⊞ **Chattanooga**'s most upscale neighborhood at the top of **Lookout Mountain.**

When to Tour Tennessee

Spring and fall are the best times to visit Tennessee. The Smokies and East Tennessee are especially beautiful, but crowded during the fall color change. Be aware that the University of Tennessee home football games draw crowds exceeding 100,000, meaning road congestion. Temperatures stay mild until late June, when humidity begins to pick up. Late July and August heat can make outdoor activities trying.

May brings the W. C. Handy Awards Week to Memphis, when the blues are celebrated with musical performances and other activities centered on Beale Street. The highlight is the W. C. Handy Blues Awards, which is attended by luminaries of the music world. However, the blues emanate from Handy Park most weekends throughout the year. Many people plan their visit to coincide with the monthlong Memphis in May International Festival.

MEMPHIS

Memphis was founded in 1819, but long before that, the Mississippi River on whose banks it was built exerted a powerful influence on the area. Both the river and the people who first appreciated it are celebrated in Memphis today. The Native American river culture that existed here from the 11th through the 15th centuries is documented in archaeological excavations, reconstructions, and exhibits at the Chucalissa Archaeological Museum. The river itself is celebrated with a museum dedicated to its history—part of Mud Island, a unique park occupying an island in the river.

The other significant influence on the city has been the music that has flowed through it. W. C. Handy moved from Alabama to Memphis in 1902–03, drawn by the long-thriving music scene, and it was here that he produced most of the songs that made him famous. The recent history of legendary Beale Street reflects that of all modern Memphis. Economic decline in the mid-20th century brought the city to its knees, and the unrest following the assassination in 1968 of Dr. Martin Luther King Jr. at the Lorraine Motel, just south of Beale, dealt a near-fatal blow. Today, thanks to public improvements and an economy built around such distribution giants as Federal Express, Memphis has been brought back to life, and Beale Street has numerous clubs and restaurants, as it did in its heyday.

When you mention Memphis, one name springs to most minds: Elvis, the undisputed King of Rock and Roll. Although he was actually born across the state line in Tupelo, Mississippi, Elvis put Memphis on the map, recording his first hits here in what came to be known as Sun Studio. His legacy burns bright at Graceland, the estate where he lived, died, and rests in peace. Each year thousands of fans make the pilgrimage to pay homage to the man and his music. Elvis International Tribute Week, held each August at Graceland, has grown to match the myth.

Downtown Memphis

Numbers in the text correspond to numbers in the margin and on the Downtown Memphis map.

Old and new mingle as Memphis progresses on riverfront development and urban renewal. Peabody Place, a collection of offices, shops, restaurants, and apartments, is nearing completion in the area surrounding the Peabody Hotel at 2nd Street and Union Avenue. And for travelers who want to tour the area without parking worries, the downtown trolley system runs a north–south route down Main Street, connecting major attractions.

A Good Walk and Drive

Pick up a map of the city at the **Visitors Information Center** ①, where free parking is available. Walk west on Beale Street to **A. Schwab Dry Goods Store** ②, a most unusual emporium, then sneak a peak at the stately **Orpheum Theatre** ③ at Main Street. Cross to the north side of Beale and walk back east, stopping to visit the **Center for Southern Folklore** ④, where the region's colorful past is chronicled in poignant exhibits. Continue east past **Handy Park** ⑤, where the "Father of the Blues" is immortalized, then learn all about him at **W. C. Handy Memphis Home and Museum** ⑥. Walk farther east on Beale to the **Hunt-Phelan Home** ⑦ for a tour. Head for the south end of downtown to tour the **National Civil Rights Museum** ⑧, on the site where Dr. Martin Luther King Jr. was assassinated in 1968, or north to the **Memphis Music Hall of Fame Museum** ⑨.

Pick up your car and drive north on Front Street to reach the parking lots for **Mud Island** ⑩ and the **Pyramid** ⑪, which are separated by the Wolf River. See them one after the other, then drive east on Adams first to the **Fire Museum of Memphis** ⑫, then on to **Victorian Village** for tours of **Magevney** ⑬, **Mallory Neely** ⑭, and **Woodruff-Fontaine** ⑮ houses. On the way out of downtown, stop at **Sun Studio** ⑯ for a dose of Memphis music history.

TIMING

Spend the morning in the Beale Street Historic District—the Hunt-Phelan Tour alone will take an hour—and work in lunch while you're there. The rest of downtown Memphis will take more than a day to cover, so depending on your schedule, you may want to pick and choose. Most of these attractions are closed Monday; the National Civil Rights Museum is closed Tuesday.

Sights to See

❷ **A. Schwab Dry Goods Store.** Step into the past at this highly eccentric shop where unusual odds and ends like voodoo potions stock the shelves. It's served many a customer since it was founded in 1876, including Elvis. ✉ *163 Beale St.,* ☎ *901/523–9782.*

❹ **Center for Southern Folklore.** Exhibits on the people, music, food, crafts, and traditions of the South, particularly of the Mississippi Delta region, pay tribute to one of America's most flavorful cultural identities. The center will also arrange a walking tour of Beale Street (by reservation only). At the gift shop, you can purchase regional folk art and handiwork, plus cassettes, videos, and books pertaining to the South. ✉ *209 Beale St.,* ☎ *901/525–3655.* ▱ *Free.* ☾ *Mon.–Thurs. 10–8, Fri.–Sat. 10 AM–1 AM, Sun. 11–8.*

❷ **Fire Museum of Memphis.** In Fire Engine House No. 1, a restored 1910 building, curiosity seekers of all ages can learn about the history of firefighting from the 19th century "bucket brigades" to the present in an educational environment designed to increase fire safety awareness. An interactive center comes equipped with video games that teach safety tips and a fire truck that can be climbed, while the Fire Room features the Fire Show, in which hi-tech visual and sound effects simulate an actual fire. Admissions and hours were not available at press time. Call the main office (☎ *901/452–9973*) for details. ✉ *118 Adams Ave.*

❺ **Handy Park.** Pause here to admire the statue of W. C. Handy clutching his famed trumpet. In the core of the Beale Street Historic District, Handy Park is a prime venue for outdoor entertainment, including festivals and impromptu jam sessions. ✉ *Between 3rd and 4th Sts.*

408

A. Schwab Dry Goods Store, **2**

Center for Southern Folkore, **4**

Fire Museum of Memphis, **12**

Handy Park, **5**

Hunt-Phelan Home, **7**

Magevney House, **13**

Mallory Neeley House, **14**

Memphis Music Hall of Fame Museum, **9**

Mud Island, **10**

National Civil Rights Museum, **8**

Orpheum Theatre, **3**

Pyramid, **11**

Sun Studio, **16**

Visitors Information Center, **1**

W. C. Handy Memphis Home and Museum, **6**

Woodruff-Fontaine House, **15**

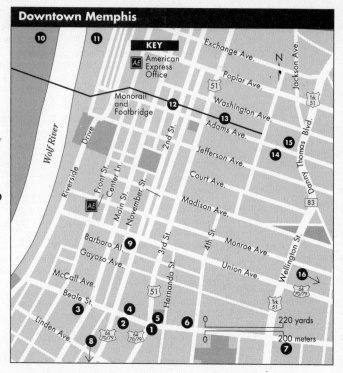

7 Hunt-Phelan Home. Costumed docents transport guests to Memphis in the mid-1800s during tours of this restored antebellum home originally designed by Robert Mills. Ulysses S. Grant began the initial plans for the Battle of Vicksburg in the library, which guards an impressive collection of first-edition books today. A rare 1874 rosewood piano from Steinway and Sons is another house treasure. ⊠ *533 Beale St.,* ☎ *901–344–3166 or 800/350–9009.* 🎫 *$10.* ⊘ *Sept.–Mar., Mon.– Thurs. 10–4, Sun. noon–4; Apr.–May, Mon.–Sat. 10–4, Sun. noon– 4; June–Aug., weekdays 10–4, Sat. 10–5, Sun. noon–5.*

13 Magevney House. This charming little white-clapboard cottage, built in the 1830s, is one of Memphis's oldest dwellings. It's furnished with some of the original possessions of Eugene Magevney, a pioneer schoolteacher and ardent Catholic. The city's first Catholic church service was held in this house, and Magevney later helped build the church next door. ⊠ *198 Adams Ave.,* ☎ *901/526–4464.* 🎫 *Free.* ⊘ *June–Labor Day, Tues.–Sat. 10–4; Labor Day–Dec. and Mar.–May, Tues.–Fri. 10–2 and Sat. 10–4.*

14 Mallory Neely House. Original family furnishings fill this 25-room Italianate Victorian. Note the hand-carved cornices and frescoed ceilings on the first floor, and the stained-glass panels in double front doors. ⊠ *652 Adams Ave.,* ☎ *901/523–1484.* 🎫 *$4.* ⊘ *Mar.–Dec., Tues.– Sat. 10–4, Sun. 1–4, last tour at 3:30.*

★ **9 Memphis Music Hall of Fame Museum.** Exhibits—rare photographs, film footage, audiotapes, and assorted memorabilia—trace the birth and development of blues, country, and rock and roll, particularly Memphis's role in it all. ⊠ *97 S. 2nd St.,* ☎ *901/525–4007.* 🎫 *$7.50.* ⊘ *Mon.–Thurs. 10–6, Fri.–Sat. 10–9, Sun. noon–6.*

⑩ Mud Island. Whether you get there by monorail or pedestrian walkway, Mud Island, a 52-acre park that explores Memphis's intimate relationship with the Mississippi, merits a visit. At the **Mississippi River Museum,** galleries bring the history of the Mississippi to life with exhibits ranging from scale-model boats to life-size, animated river characters (Mark Twain spins his tales anew here) to the Theater of River Disasters. But the most extraordinary exhibit is outside: **River Walk,** a five-block-long scale model of the Mississippi, which replicates its every twist, turn, and sandbar from Cairo, Illinois, to New Orleans, ending in a huge swimming pool bordered by a man-made, sandy beach. Other features include shops, restaurants serving regional foods, and a 5,400-seat amphitheater. The famed World War II B-17 bomber **Memphis Belle,** the first plane of its kind to complete 25 missions without casualties, is housed in an open pavilion topped by a gleaming white dome. The plane has been featured in several films. Though nothing's been set, plans to move the plane off of Mud Island have been discussed, so call ahead if it's of particular interest to you. *Footbridge and monorail:* ✉ *125 Front St.,* ☎ *901/576–7241.* ▨ *$6; grounds only $2; free Thurs. after 4 in summer.* ☽ *Most attractions Apr.–Labor Day, Tues.– Sun., but hrs and days of operation vary so call ahead.*

❽ National Civil Rights Museum. The Lorraine Motel, where Dr. Martin Luther King Jr. was assassinated on April 4, 1968, has been transformed into a museum that documents the struggle of African-Americans and the civil rights movement. A Montgomery, Alabama, bus, like the one in which Rosa Parks refused to give up her seat, sparking an uprising against segregation; scenes of lunch-counter sit-ins; and audiovisual displays are among the exhibits. ✉ *450 Mulberry St.,* ☎ *901/521–9699.* ▨ *$5; free Mon. 3–5.* ☽ *Sept.–May, Mon. and Wed.–Sat. 10–5, Sun. 1–5; June–Aug., Mon. and Wed.–Sat. 10–6, Sun. 1–6.*

Old Daisy Theatre. Inside this Beale Street fixture is the new **Sun Studio Beale Street** museum, with exhibits tracing the history of Beale Street and the creation of the blues. ✉ *329 Beale St.,* ☎ *901/527–6008.* ▨ *$3.* ☽ *Daily noon–8.*

❸ Orpheum Theatre. This former vaudeville palace and movie theater, opened in 1928, has been refurbished as a center for the performing arts. Step inside to admire its crystal chandeliers, gilt decorations, and ornate tapestries. ✉ *203 S. Main St.,* ☎ *901/525–3000.*

⑪ Pyramid. One of Memphis's newer landmarks, the Pyramid, a gleaming, stainless-steel structure and the third-largest pyramid in the world, is at Front and Auction, six blocks north of Adams. This 32-story arena, covering the equivalent of six football fields, opened in 1991 and is home to the University of Memphis Tigers and a venue for concerts and other events. Guided tours are available. ✉ *1 Auction St., at Front,* ☎ *901/526–5177.*

⑯ Sun Studio. Sun Studio is still housed in the original, albeit modest, building into which Elvis himself wandered one day and recorded two songs—one in honor of his beloved mother—for producer Sam Phillips. Pictures of Elvis and other well-loved rockers from B. B. King to Jerry Lee Lewis to Roy Orbison adorn the walls, and their hits play in the background during tours. At night, recording sessions crank up once again, with artists hoping to make it big as their predecessors did. Upstairs there's a small gift shop with well-chosen paraphernalia (guitar picks, drinking glasses) and a hall-of-fame gallery. ✉ *706 Union Ave.,* ☎ *901/521–0664.* ▨ *$7.50.* ☽ *Sept.–May, daily 10–6; June–Aug., daily 9–7.*

At the **Sun Studio Cafe** (⌧ 706 Union Ave., ☎ 901/521–0664), part
of the Sun Studio building, eat like a king (of rock and roll, that is) or
just look at the memorabilia. It was called Taylor's when Elvis ate here,
but in his honor, the menu includes some of his favorite snacks, such as
a fried peanut butter and banana sandwich.

Victorian Village Historic District. This downtown Memphis district comprises some 25 blocks on Adams between Front and Manassas. Here,
18 houses ranging from neoclassical to Gothic Revival have been restored to their appearance in the days when cotton was king. Most are
privately owned, but the ☞ **Magevney House,** ☞ **Mallory Neely
House,** and ☞ **Woodruff-Fontaine House** are open to the public.

❶ Visitors Information Center. Start you tour of downtown Memphis armed
with free maps, brochures, and other literature about Memphis and
the Beale Street Historic District. ⌧ *340 Beale St.,* ☎ *901/543–5333.*

❻ W. C. Handy Memphis Home and Museum. Handy, who wrote some
of his most famous music in this small wood-frame house, is recalled
here through photographs, sheet music, and memorabilia. ⌧ *352
Beale St.,* ☎ *901/527–3427.* ⌧ *$2.* ☉ *Memorial Day–Nov., Mon.–
Sat. 10–5, Sun. 1–5; winter hrs Tues.–Sat. 11–4.*

❶❺ Woodruff-Fontaine House. This exquisite three-story French Victorian
mansion was built in 1870. The grand drawing room is graced with
the original parquet floors and large mirrors. Antique furnishings include Aubusson carpets, marble mantels, and a Venetian crystal chandelier. Browse through the formal garden with its gingerbread playhouse,
now the museum shop. ⌧ *680 Adams Ave.,* ☎ *901/526–1469.* ⌧ *$5.*
☉ *Mon.–Sat. 10–4, Sun. 1–4.*

Greater Memphis

*Numbers in the text correspond to numbers in the margin and on the
Greater Memphis map.*

Graceland is the reason many visitors come to Memphis, but there are
plenty of museums that range in appeal from the simply visual to the
historical.

A Good Drive

Memphis sprawls. The **National Ornamental Metal Museum** ⑰ is tricky
to find (many a visitor has taken an unplanned detour to the first Interstate 55 exit in Arkansas), but worth it. Loop south to **Chucalissa
Archaeological Museum** ⑱, where the mid-South Native American culture is preserved. Continue east to **Graceland** ⑲, the must-see stop. After
Elvis's Jungle Room, a respite at **Dixon Gallery and Gardens** ⑳ in East
Memphis on Park Avenue will restore the soul. Take Park Avenue west
to Goodlett Street, then proceed north to Central Avenue. Turn left (west)
on Central and you'll be headed toward the imposing **Memphis Pink
Palace Museum and Mansion and Sharpe Planetarium** ㉑. From there,
continue west on Central to Airways Boulevard, turn right (north), then
left (west) onto Poplar Avenue where Overton Park is home to **Memphis Brooks Museum of Art** ㉒ and to **Memphis Zoo** ㉓.

TIMING
You could see all this in a day, but it'll be exhausting. Better to narrow down the choices according to your interests. Keep in mind that
Graceland is usually packed and you'll probably have to wait in line
for any of the tours offered there. It's least crowded early in the morning, so try to get there as it opens. Allot about an hour and a half for

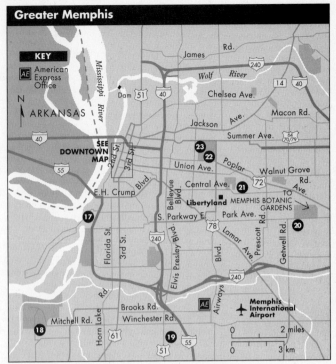

the house tour and at least two more hours for the rest of the Grace-land attractions.

Sights to See

18 Chucalissa Archaeological Museum. At the peaceful, thought-provok-ing Chucalissa Archaeological Museum, about 10 mi southwest of down-town, a simple river culture that existed from AD 1000 to 1500 is immortalized. The 4-acre reconstruction is operated by the University of Memphis, and on-site archaeological excavations are often conducted in summer. In the museum, prehistoric tools, pottery, and weapons and a free 15-minute slide presentation describing Chucalissa life and cul-ture offer clues to the workings of that world. Outside, skilled Choctaw craftsfolk sell jewelry, weapons, and pottery. An annual August pow-wow is a highlight. Budget cuts have forced the museum to consider changes in opening hours so call first. ⊠ *1987 Indian Village Dr.,* ☎ *901/785–3160.* ⊡ *$3.* ☉ *Tues.–Sat. 9–4:30, Sun. 1–4:30.*

20 Dixon Gallery and Gardens. With 17 acres of formal and informal gar-dens and woodlands, Dixon Gallery and Gardens is a welcoming bu-colic enclave near the heart of the city. The estate and its superb art collections once belonged to the late Margaret and Hugo Dixon, phi-lanthropists and cultural leaders. French and American Impressionist paintings, British portraiture and landscapes, and the Stout Collection of 18th-century German porcelain are on display. The gardens are com-posed of regional plants and statuary. ⊠ *4339 Park Ave.,* ☎ *901/761–5250.* ⊡ *$5.* ☉ *Tues.–Sat. 10–5, Sun. 1–5.*

★ **19 Graceland.** The tour of the Colonial-style mansion once owned by Elvis Presley reveals the spoils of stardom—from gold records to glittering show costumes—and a circuit of the grounds (shuttle service is avail-able) leads to Meditation Garden, where Elvis is buried. Separate tours are available for which additional fees are charged. Among them is the

Elvis Presley Automobile Museum, where a continuously run film montage of Elvis on the road is shown drive-in style as viewers sit in seats pulled from 1957 Chevys. Elvis's jet, the *Lisa Marie* (named for his daughter), complete with 24-karat goldplated seat buckles and a queen-size bed covered in light blue ultrasuede, stars in the **Airplanes Tour.** Sincerely Elvis, $3.50 admission, is a small museum with personal items such as home movies, photos, and clothes. There are several restaurants and, of course, shops on the premises along with a post office—few can resist the lure of a Graceland date stamp. ⊠ *3764 Elvis Presley Blvd. (off I–55), 12 mi southeast of downtown,* ☎ *901/332–3322; 800/238–2000 outside TN.* ⊡ *Home tour $9, all attractions $17, parking $2.* ☉ *Memorial Day–Labor Day, daily 8–6; Labor Day–Memorial Day, daily 9–5. Mansion closed Tues. Nov.–Feb.*

㉒ Memphis Brooks Museum of Art. The collections of the Memphis Brooks Museum of Art, in Overton Park, span eight centuries and contain 7,000 pieces, including a notable collection of Italian Renaissance works, plus English portraiture, Impressionist and American modernist paintings, decorative arts, prints, photographs, and one of the nation's largest displays of Doughty bird figurines. ⊠ *1934 Poplar Ave., 38104,* ☎ *901/722–3500.* ⊡ *Permanent collection free; fees vary for major exhibits.* ☉ *Tues., Wed., Fri. 9–4; Thurs. 11–8; Sat. 9–5; Sun. 11:30–5.*

㉑ Memphis Pink Palace Museum and Mansion and Sharpe Planetarium. Clarence Saunders, founder of the Piggly Wiggly self-service stores that are the predecessors of today's supermarkets, built this rambling pink-marble mansion in the 1920s. Exhibits, shown in both the Mansion and an auxiliary museum, are eclectic, including natural and cultural history displays, a hand-carved miniature three-ring circus, and a replica of the original Piggly Wiggly. The Sharpe Planetarium explores the most current cosmic discoveries. The museum also has an IMAX Theater. ⊠ *3050 Central Ave.,* ☎ *901/320–6362.* ⊡ *Planetarium $3.50, museum $5.50, IMAX theater $5.50.* ☉ *Memorial Day–Labor Day, Mon.–Wed. 10–5, Thurs. 10–8, Fri.–Sat. 10–9, Sun. noon–5; Labor Day–Memorial Day, Mon.–Wed. 9–4, Thurs. 9–8, Fri. 9–9, Sat. 10–9, Sun. noon–5.*

㉓ Memphis Zoo. This is one of the South's most notable zoos, home to more than 400 species living on 70 well-kept wooded acres in Overton Park. There's a 12,000-gallon aquarium, Cat Country, Primate Canyon, a natural African veldt setting for larger creatures, a large reptile facility, and an animal-contact area. ⊠ *2000 Galloway St.,* ☎ *901/276–9453.* ⊡ *$6.* ☉ *Mar.–late Oct., daily 9–6 (last admission 5); late Oct.–Feb., daily 9–5 (last admission 4:30).*

⑰ National Ornamental Metal Museum. The nation's only museum preserving the art and the craft of metalworking—from wrought iron to gold—overlooks the Mississippi River. There's also a working blacksmith shop and changing exhibitions and demonstrations. ⊠ *374 W. California Ave. (via I–55N, last exit before bridge),* ☎ *901/774–6380.* ⊡ *$2.* ☉ *Tues.–Sat. 10–5, Sun. noon–5.*

☾ Wild Water and Wheels. A giant wave pool, water slides, raft and inner-tube rides, a man-made river, a kiddie pool, and go-carts, make this 25-acre amusement park a big hit with kids. ⊠ *6880 Whitten Bend Cove (12 mi east of downtown, off I–40),* ☎ *901/382–9283.* ⊡ *$15.* ☉ *Memorial Day–Labor Day, daily 10–8; Apr.–May, weekends only.*

Dining

American

$$$$ ✕ **Folk's Folly Prime Steak House.** Folk's is a Memphis favorite for one simple reason: You can dig into the juiciest sizzling-hot steaks in town. "Steak House" is a bit misleading though—this restaurant resembles a suburban home, with a lounge and five separate dining rooms plus eight private rooms for small parties. The generous vegetable side dishes, such as stuffed baked potatoes and asparagus, are reliably fresh, and heaping portions of seafood and whole lobster are always available. It's in East Memphis, near some of the city's nicest residential areas. ✉ *551 S. Mendenhall St.,* ☎ *901/762–8200. AE, MC, V. No lunch.*

$$$ ✕ **Bistro 122.** This comfortable East Memphis establishment is part neighborhood café, part sophisticated bar. Chef John Colmer works wonders with seafood, matching it with fruity salsas or citrusy sauces. He is known for his Tennessee crab cakes, the best in town. ✉ *5101 Sanderlin,* ☎ *901/761–0663. AE, MC, V.*

$$$ ✕ **Cafe Society.** This sidewalk café in Midtown brings imagination and a fresh range of choices to its lunch and dinner menu. Outdoor tables, across the street from a small park, are popular with the happy-hour crowd. Expect to find treats like coconut-fried shrimp with pineapple chutney, grilled salmon with sesame and poppy-seed crust and shrimp biscayne sauce, and veal and pasta dishes. The best dessert is the Italian cheesecake. ✉ *212 N. Evergreen,* ☎ *901/722–2177. AE, MC, V. No lunch Sat.*

$$ ✕ **Blues City Cafe.** This downtown restaurant specializes in huge steaks and ribs, hamburgers, and hot tamales in a diner setting. ✉ *138 Beale St.,* ☎ *901/526–3637. AE, MC, V. Hrs vary, so call ahead.*

Barbecue

$ ✕ **Charlie Vergos' Rendezvous.** Charlie Vergos has become something
★ of a Memphis ambassador of barbecued ribs: Not only does his downtown basement restaurant draw thousands of tourists each year, but he also ships his ribs by air express all over the country. The walls are filled with memorabilia and bric-a-brac, from old newspaper cartoons to Essolene gas signs. But what really packs in the crowds are the delicious pork loin plate and the barbecued pork ribs. ✉ *52 S. 2nd St.,* ☎ *901/523–2746. Reservations not accepted. AE, MC, V. Closed Sun.–Mon.*

$ ✕ **Corky's.** Expect to wait in line at this no-frills East Memphis barbecue joint, a leader in air-express ribs. One taste of the ribs or pork platter explains why. Letters from customers and articles on Corky's cover the walls. ✉ *5259 Poplar Ave.,* ☎ *901/685–9744. Reservations not accepted. AE, D, DC, MC, V.*

$ ✕ **Interstate Bar-B-Q.** The Neely family has barbecue sauce running through its veins, and it all started here. Jim Neely's nephews have opened their own places around town, but they all learned their secrets here. The long list of barbecue includes barbecue spaghetti, pork sandwiches, beef ribs and links, and Polish and smoked sausage. Save room for the homemade pecan pie. ✉ *2265 S. 3rd St.,* ☎ *901/775–2304. Reservations not accepted. AE, MC, V.*

Continental

$$ ✕ **Paulette's.** This Overton Square restaurant was serving bistro-style cooking before it became popular in Memphis; for more than two decades, Paulette's has retained its vitality. With a crisp, fresh house salad and airy popovers with strawberry butter, Paulette's packs them in at lunch and dinner. Entrées include several crepe dishes, along with grilled salmon, swordfish, and chicken, baked scallops, and brochettes

414

Dining
Automatic Slim's
Tonga Club, **4**
Bistro 122, **14**
Blues City Cafe, **7**
Cafe Olé , **9**
Cafe Society, **10**
Charlie Vergos'
Rendezvous, **3**
Chez Philippe, **5**
Corky's, **16**
Erling Jensen, **18**
Folk's Folly Prime
Steak House, **17**
Fourway Grill, **8**
Interstate Bar-B-Q, **25**
La Tourelle, **13**
Landry's Seafood
House, **6**
Owen Brennan's
Restaurant, **20**
Paulette's, **11**
Restaurant Raji, **15**

Lodging
Adam's Mark Hotel, **19**
Day's Inn
Graceland, **24**
French Quarter Suites
Hotel, **12**
Hampton Inn
Airport, **21**
Holiday Inn Crowne
Plaza, **1**
KOA Kampground, **22**
Peabody Hotel, **5**
Sleep Inn at Court
Square, **2**
Wilson World
Graceland, **23**

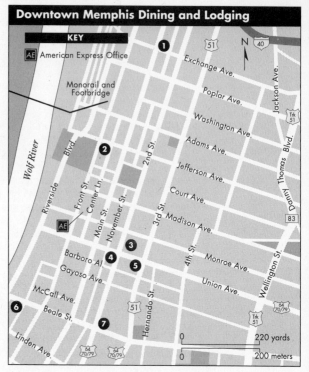

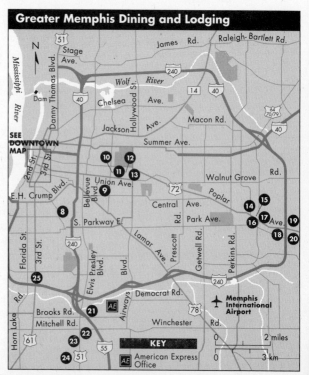

of shrimp or beef. The hot chocolate crepes are sinful. On weekends a pianist plays requests ranging from Gershwin to Beale Street Blues. ⊠ *2110 Madison Ave.,* ☎ *901/726–5128. AE, MC, V.*

French

$$$$ ✕ **Chez Philippe.** The setting is wonderfully lavish—high ceilings, *faux*
★ marble columns, and huge murals depicting a masked ball. The service is impeccable. Most important, the cuisine—Memphis's most innovative and sophisticated—lives up to its regal setting. The menu ranges from delicate terrines to lamb tenderloin in puff pastry to hot soufflés. For 11 years straight *Memphis Magazine's* readers have voted the restaurant Memphis's best. Chez Philippe is located immediately off the Grand Lobby of the Peabody Hotel (☞ Lodging, *below*). ⊠ *Peabody Hotel, 149 Union Ave.,* ☎ *901/529–4188. Reservations essential. AE, DC, MC, V. Closed Sun. No lunch.*

$$$ ✕ **Erling Jensen.** Chef Jensen, formerly of La Tourelle's kitchen, opened this restaurant late in 1996 and has since been packing them in. He characterizes his cuisine as French with global influences, but to put it simply, his rack of lamb is the best in town—the Dover sole and veal tenderloin aren't bad either. ⊠ *1004 S. Yates, off Poplar,* ☎ *901/763–3700. Reservations essential. AE, D, DC, MC, V. No lunch.*

$$$ ✕ **La Tourelle.** This quiet, turn-of-the-century bungalow with fine lace
★ curtains and wood floors is reminiscent of a small country restaurant in France. Specialties include grilled tuna on shrimp couscous and roasted fillet of beef with sweet potato hash. ⊠ *Overton Sq., 2146 Monroe Ave.,* ☎ *901/726–5771. Reservations essential. MC, V. Closed Mon. No lunch Sat.*

$$$ ✕ **Owen Brennan's Restaurant.** This New Orleans–style eatery in an upscale Memphis shopping center specializes in those fine Cajun and Creole dishes that usually require a jaunt to the French Quarter. Favorite dishes include blackened chicken or seafood gumbo. The lavish Sunday brunch is attended religiously, and easy banter, champagne, and jazz flow freely. Best of all, an outdoor patio under towering shade trees offers a cool respite from Memphis's sizzling summer sun. ⊠ *6150 Poplar Ave.,* ☎ *901/761–0990. AE, DC, MC, V.*

Indian

$$$$ ✕ **Restaurant Raji.** Chef-owner Raji Jallepalli blends nouvelle styles and Indian seasonings in creations that range from fragrant Indian consommé with white peppercorns and coriander to grilled scallops and lobster in lentil pastry with a ginger-flavored beurre blanc. There are several dining rooms, all intimate and elegant. ⊠ *712 W. Brookhaven Circle,* ☎ *901/685–8723. Reservations essential. AE, MC, V. Closed Sun.–Mon. No lunch.*

Mexican

$ ✕ **Cafe Olé.** If Mexican with a healthy twist sounds intriguing, this popular midtown hangout is for you. Specialties—sans the animal fats that make most Mexican fare so unappealing—include spinach enchiladas and chili rellenos. The exposed brick walls are decorated with Mexican paintings and ceremonial masks. ⊠ *959 S. Cooper St.,* ☎ *901/274–1504. AE, D, DC, MC, V.*

Seafood

$$ ✕ **Landry's Seafood House.** This remodeled riverfront place is one of Memphis's busiest restaurants. Though it seats more than 300, the wait often exceeds one hour. Patio dining is especially refreshing, if you can get a table. The fare—seafood, steaks, and Cajun—is simple but consistently good. Among the better offerings are shrimp in a brown-butter sauce, flounder stuffed with shrimp and crabmeat, and fried oysters and shrimp. ⊠ *263 Wagner Pl.,* ☎ *901/526–1966. Reservations not accepted. AE, MC, V.*

Southern

$$ ✕ **Automatic Slim's Tonga Club.** This hip restaurant is downtown across from the Peabody Hotel. The split-level dining room is usually crowded. Southwestern and Caribbean fare are served in thick and spicy sauces; signature dishes include deep-fried red snapper with tomato and jalepeño relish and Jamaican jerk duck. ⊠ *83 S. 2nd St.,* ☎ *901/525–7948. AE, MC, V. No lunch Sat.*

$ ✕ **Fourway Grill.** The finest fried chicken in town is served in this tiny establishment near LeMoyne Owen College. Slow-cooked greens will make your mouth water. ⊠ *998 Mississippi Blvd.,* ☎ *901/775–2351. Reservations not accepted. AE, MC, V.*

Lodging

$$$$ ⊞ **Adam's Mark Hotel.** This luxury property, a 27-story circular glass tower, is in the flourishing eastern suburbs of Memphis near I–240. From your glass-walled aerie, you'll have sweeping vistas of Memphis and its outskirts. ⊠ *939 Ridge Lake Blvd., 38120,* ☎ *901/684–6664 or 800/444–2326,* FAX *901/762–7411. 376 rooms, 13 suites. Restaurant, lounge, pool, health club. AE, D, DC, MC, V.*

$$$$ ⊞ **Peabody Hotel.** This 12-story Italianate Renaissance hostelry, a
★   landmark since 1925, was restored impeccably and reopened in 1981 after being closed for a time in the mid-'70s. The lobby preserves its original stained-glass skylights and ornate travertine marble fountain—home to the hotel's famed resident ducks, who waddle down each morning from their penthouse apartment and parade across a red carpet to the stirring sounds of Sousa's "King Cotton March"; the show is repeated each afternoon. ⊠ *149 Union Ave., 38103,* ☎ *901/529–4000 or 800/732–2639,* FAX *901/529–3600. 453 rooms, 15 suites. 4 restaurants, bar, indoor pool, health club. AE, DC, MC, V.*

$$$ ⊞ **French Quarter Suites Hotel.** With its mellow rose-brick exterior and
★   classic architectural lines, this pleasant New Overton Square hostelry is reminiscent of an older, New Orleans–style inn. All the one-bedroom suites have living rooms and whirlpool baths that accommodate two, and some are balconied. ⊠ *2144 Madison Ave., 38104,* ☎ *901/728–4000 or 800/843–0353,* FAX *901/278–1262. 104 suites. Pool, exercise room. AE, DC, MC, V.*

$$$ ⊞ **Holiday Inn Crowne Plaza.** Memphis was the birthplace of Holiday Inns, and this is the flagship of the area's seven-inn fleet. Adjacent to the downtown Convention Center, this sleek high-rise (18 floors) has a concierge floor and sizable meeting facilities, plus ample work space and lighting in the spacious guest rooms and suites. The lobby lounge, a tasteful, greenery-filled retreat, is a pleasant spot to relax and listen to music from the grand piano. ⊠ *250 N. Main St., 38103,* ☎ *901/527–7300 or 800/465–4329,* FAX *901/526–1561. 396 rooms, 7 suites. Restaurant, indoor pool, hot tub, sauna, health club. AE, DC, MC, V.*

$$–$$$ ⊞ **Sleep Inn at Court Square.** This chain hotel is conveniently located near two highways and within walking distance of Mud Island and the Pyramid; Beale Street is a 15-minute walk or a quick trolley ride (there's a stop right out back) away. Extras include a free Continental breakfast, free parking, and free local phone calls. Business rooms have a desk, fax, data port, and VCR. ⊠ *40 N. Front St., 38103,* ☎ *901/522–9700 or 800/627–5337,* FAX *901/522–9710. 124 rooms. Exercise room, laundry service, business facilities. AE, D, MC, V.*

$$ ⚎ **Hampton Inn Airport.** This is a member of the economy-priced sys-
★ tem that was spun off from the Holiday Inn chain. The building has
a pleasing contemporary design. Spacious, well-lighted rooms have Scan-
dinavian-style teakwood furnishings. With a good location for fami-
lies, this is a front-runner in the moderate category. ⊠ *2979 Millbranch
Rd., 38116,* ☎ *901/396–2200 or 800/426–7866,* ℻ *901/396–7034.
128 rooms. Pool. AE, DC, MC, V.*

$$ ⚎ **Wilson World Graceland.** Across the street from Graceland, Wilson
World has caught Memphis's infectious case of Elvismania. Two life-
size portraits of the King grace the lobby. You can take free popcorn
back to your mauve-color room and munch away to free movies on
the Elvis channel. Rooms are equipped with microwaves and refrigerators. ⊠ *3677 Elvis Presley Blvd., 38116,* ☎ *901/332–2107 or
800/945–7667,* ℻ *901/366–6361. 134 rooms. Meeting rooms, airport shuttle. AE, DC, MC, V.*

$ ⚎ **Day's Inn Graceland.** This modest hotel's claim to fame is its prox-
★ imity to Graceland, and it makes the most of that with a guitar-shape
swimming pool and free Elvis Movies 'round the clock. ⊠ *3839 Elvis
Presley Blvd., 38116,* ☎ *901/346–5500,* ℻ *901/345–7452. 61 rooms.
Pool. AE, DC, MC, V.*

$ ⚠ **KOA Kampground.** Stay at this campground with tent and RV sites
as well as cabins and you'll be only a few yards away from Graceland's
entrance. ⊠ *3691 Elvis Presley Blvd., 38116,* ☎ *901/396–7125. 72
camp sites, 4 cabins. Pool, playground, coin laundry. D, MC, V.*

Nightlife and the Arts

For a complete listing of weekly events, check the Playbook section in
the Friday *Memphis Commercial Appeal,* or *The Memphis Flyer,* distributed free at newsstands around the city. The Visitors Information
Center (☞ Memphis A to Z, *below*) will also provide an up-to-date
rundown of events.

Nightlife

At **B. B. King's Blues Club** (⊠ 147 Beale St., ☎ 901/524–5464), live
blues is accompanied by Southern food specialties nightly. At the **New
Daisy Theatre** (⊠ 330 Beale St., ☎ 901/525–8979)—the 900-seat
venue where B. B. King got his start—blues, jazz, and (predominantly)
rock bands perform. The **Rum Boogie Cafe** (⊠ 182 Beale St., ☎ 901/
528–0150) stages live blues nightly. **Alfred's on Beale** (⊠ 197 Beale
St., ☎ 901/525–3711), one of the city's hottest dance clubs, also
serves great food. Rock bands perform Wednesday through Saturday,
and a DJ spins popular dance tunes during the week.

Big-name entertainers and musical groups from the Beach Boys to the
Sex Pistols appear at the **Mud Island Amphitheatre** (☎ 901/576–7241)
from April through October. The **Pyramid** (☞ Sights to See *in* Downtown Memphis, *above*) hosts country and rock artists (among them
Tina Turner and Metallica) who draw large crowds. Year-round, **Mid-
South Coliseum** (⊠ 996 Early Maxwell Blvd., ☎ 901/274–3982)
draws its share of country and rock musicians, plus the occasional trac-
tor pull or wrestling event. Among the offerings at the **Orpheum Theatre** (⊠ 203 S. Main St., ☎ 901/525–3000) are easy-listening and jazz
concerts, traveling Broadway shows, comedians, and a summer film
series. The Orpheum Theatre is also the scene of performances by **Memphis Concert Ballet** (☎ 901/763–0139), which features professional
dancers and celebrity guest artists, and **Opera Memphis** (☎ 901/678–
2706 for tickets).

The Arts

Playhouse on the Square (☎ 901/726–4656), open September–July, has the city's only professional repertory company. **Center Stage,** at the Jewish Community Center (✉ 6560 Poplar Ave., ☎ 901/761–0810), is used for musical performances and visiting authors and lecturers. The city's professional acting group performs at **Circuit Playhouse** (✉ 1705 Poplar Ave., ☎ 901/726–4656), September–June. At **Ewing's Children's Theatre** (✉ 2635 Avery Ave., ☎ 901/452–3968), performances are directed, designed, and acted entirely by children. Community theaters include **Theatre Memphis** (✉ 630 Perkins Extended, ☎ 901/682–8323), which has been acclaimed as one of the best community theaters in the United States. The **Germantown Community Theatre** (✉ 3037 Forest Hill Rd., ☎ 901/754–2680) provides high-caliber performances by amateur thespians. At the University of Memphis, **University Theatre** (✉ 3745 Central Ave., ☎ 901/678–2523) provides a venue for drama students and visiting performers.

Festivals

Memphis in May International Festival (☎ 901/525–4611) began in 1976. Each year the cuisine, crafts, and other cultural offerings of a different country are saluted over four consecutive weekends. Portugal is 1998's honored country.

Outdoor Activities and Sports

Auto Racing

The 600-acre **Memphis Motorsports Park** hosts weekly dirt-track and drag racing. Occasionally, amateurs can race their own cars on the track. ✉ 5500 Taylor Forge Rd., Millington, ☎ 901/358–7223. 🎟 Prices vary. 🕙 Mar.–Nov.

Boating, Biking, and Hiking

Get back to nature at **Meeman-Shelby Forest State Park,** a 12,500-acre tract bordering the Mississippi with boat rental, hiking, and biking. ✉ 10 mi north of Memphis, off U.S. 51, ☎ 901/876–5215. 🎟 Free. 🕙 Daily 7 AM–10 PM.

There are hiking trails at **Shelby Farms Plough Recreation Area** (☎ 901/382–4250), **Lichterman Nature Center** (☎ 901/767–7322), and **T. O. Fuller State Park** (☎ 901/529–7581).

Football

Each December the **St. Jude Liberty Bowl Football Classic** is held at the Liberty Bowl Memorial Stadium (☎ 901/795–7700), which hosts the University of Memphis Tigers and other football teams.

Golf

In June the Tournament Players Club at Southwind Country Club (✉ 3325 Club at Southwind, ☎ 901/748–0534) hosts the **Federal Express–St. Jude Classic,** featuring top pros.

If you prefer playing to watching, the Memphis Park Commission (☎ 901/325–5759) operates two nine-hole and five 18-hole public golf courses, the most accessible of which are **Overton Park** (☎ 901/725–9905), nine holes; **Galloway** (☎ 901/685–7805), 18 holes; and **T. O. Fuller State Park** (☎ 901/543–7581), 18 holes.

Hockey

The **Memphis Riverkings** (☎ 901/278–9009), a minor league club, play November–March at the Mid-South Coliseum, in the Mid-South Fairgrounds complex.

Ice-Skating

The **Ice Capades Chalet,** in the Mall of Memphis (☎ 901/362–8877), is open seven days a week.

Tennis

The **International Indoor Tennis Championship** (☎ 901/765–4400) brings top pros to the Racquet Club in February.

The Memphis Park Commission (☎ 901/325–5759) operates nine facilities that offer tennis lessons, tournaments, and league play. **Leftwich** (☎ 901/685–7907), **Ridgeway** (☎ 901/767–2889), and **Whitehaven** (☎ 901/332–0546) have indoor courts.

Shopping

Deliberate Literate (✉ 1997 Union Ave., ☎ 901/276–0174) has an expansive collection of Random House Publishing Company–only titles which can be browsed in the company of a cappuccino or home-baked good, fresh from the coffee bar.

More than a dozen shopping centers and malls are scattered about Memphis. The **Mid-America Mall** (☎ 901/362–9315), on Main Street between Beale and Poplar, is one of the nation's longest pedestrian malls. **Oak Court Mall** (✉ 4465 Poplar Ave., ☎ 901/682–8928), in the busy Poplar/Perkins area of East Memphis, has 70 specialty stores and two department stores. In Midtown, **Overton Square**'s (✉ 24 S. Cooper St., ☎ 901/272–1495) upscale boutiques and specialty shops coexist with restaurants, artfully restored vintage buildings, and newer structures. **Wolfchase Galleria** (✉ 2760 N. Germantown Pkwy., at Hwy. 64, about 18 mi east of downtown Memphis, ☎ 901/381–2769), opened in 1997, is the county's newest and largest mall.

Belz Factory Outlet Mall (✉ 3536 Canada Rd., Exit 20 off I–40, 20 mi east of downtown Memphis, Lakeland, ☎ 901/386–3180) includes 50 stores from the Boot Factory to Linens 'n Things to Van Heusen.

The **Woman's Exchange** (✉ 88 Racine St., ☎ 901/327–5681) specializes in children's wear and handcrafted items. There's a tearoom for weekday luncheons and a Christmas shop in November and December.

A. Schwab Dry Goods Store (✉ 163 Beale St., ☎ 901/523–9782) is an old-fashioned store whose motto is "If you can't find it at A. Schwab's, you're better off without it!" Elvis shopped here, and you can, too—for top hats, spats, tambourines, bow ties, dresses to size 60, and men's trousers to size 74.

Side Trips from Memphis

The flatness of the northern tip of the Mississippi Delta is a sharp contrast to East Tennessee's mountains. Cotton and soybeans thrive in the rich dirt of West Tennessee, particularly around Henning, the hometown of *Roots* author Alex Haley. Those who love the great outdoors will want to make the two-hour trip north to Tiptonville's Reelfoot Lake, while points east of Memphis, such as Jackson and Shiloh National Military Park, will suit the Civil War buff.

Henning
50 mi north of Memphis.

The quiet, historic byways north of Memphis seem light-years away from this busy river city. Driving northward along U.S. 51 through the fertile Mississippi River bottomlands brings you into the heart of King Cotton's domain. Within an hour, you'll come to Henning, a friendly little town remarkably untouched by its world acclaim as the boyhood home and burial place of Alex Haley, Pulitzer Prize–winning author of *Roots.* At the **Alex Haley House Museum,** the only state-owned historic site in West Tennessee, family portraits, mementos, and furnishings are displayed. ⊠ *200 Church St.,* ☎ *901/738–2240.* ☞ *$2.50.* ☉ *Tues.–Sat. 10–5, Sun. 1–5.*

Tiptonville
105 mi north of Memphis.

Anglers and outdoors lovers of any sort are drawn to Tiptonville, in Tennessee's northwest corner, for its nearby bird and game refuge and spellbinding flora and fauna.

Tiptonville's **Reelfoot Lake** gains a peculiar and mysterious beauty from a romantic scattering of cypress trees and charred stumps. The 13,000-acre lake was formed between 1811 and 1812, when the New Madrid earthquakes caused the Mississippi River to flood into the sinking land where a luxuriant forest once stood. From late November through mid-March the lake is a major sanctuary for American bald eagles. The quiet lake provides good fishing year-round for bass, crappie, trout, bream, and catfish. The Tennessee Department of Conservation conducts eagle-spotting tours at **Reelfoot Lake State Resort Park** (⊠ Rtes. 22 and 78, ☎ 901/253–7756). The **Tiptonville Chamber of Commerce** (⊠ Reelfoot Lake 38079, ☎ 901/253–8144) can answer questions about dining and lodging.

Jackson
85 mi east of Memphis.

Jackson, site of several Civil War battles, also was a major railroad hub. It was home to John Luther "Casey" Jones, who was immortalized in the "Ballad of Casey Jones." The famed engineer became a hero by staying aboard his locomotive in a vain attempt to stop his engine from plowing into another train. For more information on Jackson, call the **Jackson/Madison County Convention & Visitors Bureau** (⊠ 400 S. Highland Ave., Jackson 38301, ☎ 901/425–8333), open weekdays 8:30–4:30.

In **Casey Jones Village,** the Casey Jones Home and Railroad Museum (☎ 901/668–1223) contains a diverse assortment of railroad memorabilia. On the grounds is a replica of Old No. 382, Casey's steam engine. The **Casey Jones Village Old Country Store,** also in the village, has a restaurant, an 1890s-style ice-cream parlor, and gift, souvenir, confectionery, and antiques shops. ⊠ *At U.S. 45 Bypass.* ☞ *Museum $3.50.* ☉ *Jan.–Feb., daily 9–5; Mar.–Dec., daily 8 AM–9 PM.*

Savannah
110 mi east of Memphis on TN 57E.

Scenic Savannah, on the bluff of the Tennessee River, is a small, quiet town that exemplifies the charm and grace of the Southern life. The historic **Cherry Mansion** (⊠ 101 Main St.), built in 1830, served as General Grant's headquarters during the Battle of Shiloh. The house is privately owned, but visitors are allowed to roam the grounds and take pictures.

In the same building as the Chamber of Commerce, the **Tennessee River Museum** has exhibits on the Civil War, the river, and fossils from 65 million years ago, when this area was under water. ⊠ *507 Main St.,* ☎ *901/925–2363.* ☞ *$2.* ☉ *Weekdays 9–5, Sat. 10–5, Sun. 1–5.*

Shiloh National Military Park
100 mi east of Memphis.

Site of one of the Civil War's grimmest and most pivotal battles, Shiloh National Military Park contains almost 4,000 soldiers, many unidentified, in the national cemetery. A self-guided auto tour leads past markers explaining monuments and battle sites. The visitor center runs a film explaining the battle's strategy, complemented by a display of Civil War relics. To get here, head east out of Memphis on U.S. 64, then 10 mi south on TN 22. ☎ *901/689–5275.* ☞ *$2.* ☉ *Visitor center daily 8–5.*

Pickwick Dam
110 mi southeast of Memphis.

Named after a character in Charles Dickens' *Pickwick Papers,* locals have come to call Pickwick Dam the playground of southwest Tennessee's Hardin County.

Pickwick Landing Dam (✉ 14 mi south on TN 128, ☎ 901/925–4342), one of the Tennessee Valley Authority's showcase hydroelectric projects, rises high above the Tennessee River. The **Tennessee River Waterways Museum,** behind Pickwick Dam's locks, displays the archaeological tokens unearthed during the construction of the dam. You're welcome to visit the power plant during daylight hours.

Pickwick Landing State Resort Park (✉ 15 mi south on TN 128, ☎ 901/689–3129) offers a resort inn, a restaurant, playgrounds, swimming beaches, picnic areas, and a par 72, 18-hole golf course.

Memphis A to Z

Arriving and Departing
BY BOAT
The paddle-wheel steamers *Delta Queen, American Queen,* and *Mississippi Queen* (✉ Robin St. Wharf, New Orleans, LA 70130, ☎ 800/543–1949) stop at Memphis and Nashville.

BY BUS
Greyhound Bus Lines (☎ 800/231–2222) offers service throughout the region.

BY CAR
From Memphis, which is encircled by I–240, I–55 leads north to St. Louis and south to Jackson, Mississippi; I–40, east to Nashville and Knoxville.

BY PLANE
Memphis International Airport (☎ 901/544–3495), served by American, Delta, Northwest, and Northwest Airlink, is 9½ mi south of downtown. A Northwest/KLM joint venture provides daily service to Amsterdam. Taxi fare from the airport to downtown Memphis is about $17; try Yellow Cab (☎ 901/577–7700). By car, take I–240 to downtown.

BY TRAIN
Amtrak (✉ 545 S. Main St., ☎ 901/526–0052 or 800/872–7245) operates the *City of New Orleans,* which stops in Memphis on the trip between New Orleans and Chicago.

Getting Around
BY BUS
Memphis Area Transit Authority (☎ 901/274–6282) buses cover the city and immediate suburbs; they run weekdays 4:30 AM–11:15 PM,

Saturday 5 AM–6:15 PM, Sunday 9–6:15. The fare is $1.15, transfers 10¢. There is short-hop service on designated buses between Front, 3rd, and Exchange streets from 9 AM to 3 PM and between downtown and the Medical Center complex from 7 AM to 6 PM. The fare is 35¢.

BY TAXI

The fare in **Memphis** is $2.70 for the first mile, $1.40 for each additional mile. There are stands at the airport and bus station.

BY TROLLEY

The Memphis Area Transit Authority (☞ *above*) operates the 2½-mi Main Street Trolley, 50¢ fare, in downtown Memphis. The Riverfront Loop project, slated for completion in late 1997, will connect the Main Street Trolley at its current end points: the Central Station Intermodal Terminal to the south and the North End Intermodal Terminal to the north. The extension will run adjacent to Riverside Drive.

Contacts and Resources

B&B RESERVATION SERVICES

Bed & Breakfast in Memphis Reservation Service (✉ Box 41621, Memphis 38174, ☎ 901/726–5920 or 800/336–2087, FAX 901/725–0194).

EMERGENCIES

Dial 911 for **police** and **ambulance** in an emergency. Near-downtown hospitals with 24-hour emergency service in Memphis include **Baptist Memorial Hospital Medical Center** (✉ 899 Madison Ave., ☎ 901/227–2727) and **Methodist Hospitals of Memphis** (✉ 1265 Union Ave., ☎ 901/726–7000).

GUIDED TOURS

Memphis Queen Line Riverboats (☎ 901/527–5694 or 800/221–6197) offers 1½-hour sightseeing and two-hour dinner cruises. Sightseeing cruises run daily throughout the year, and dinner cruises run March–November, Wednesday–Sunday. **Blues City Tours** (☎ 901/522–9229) offers riverboat rides.

Carriage Tours of Memphis (☎ 901/527–7542) offers horse-drawn carriage rides.

Blues City Tours (☞ *above*) offers motor-coach tours to Memphis sites including Graceland, Mud Island, and Beale Street, plus nightly tours that include dinner and a show. **Gray Line** (☎ 901/948–8687) operates day and night motor-coach tours to downtown and greater Memphis. **Unique Tours** (☎ 901/527–8876 or 800/235–1984) has three-day, two-night tours of Graceland, the National Civil Rights Museum, Mud Island, and other attractions. The **Center for Southern Folklore** (☞ Sights to See *in* Downtown Memphis, *above*) gives tours of Beale Street, a farm on the Delta, and prominent areas of musical interest. **Heritage Tours** (☎ 901/527–3427) explores the area's rich African-American cultural heritage.

PHARMACY

Walgreen's (✉ 3476 Poplar Plaza, ☎ 901/458–9233).

RADIO STATIONS

AM: WMC 79, news and talk. **FM:** WEGR 103, adult contemporary and easy listening; WHRK 97, rhythm and blues.

VISITOR INFORMATION

Visitors Information Center (✉ 340 Beale St., 38103, ☎ 901/543–5333) is open Monday through Saturday 9–6, Sunday noon–6. **Memphis Convention & Visitors Bureau** (✉ 47 Union Ave., 38103, ☎ 901/543–5300 or 800/873–6282) is open weekdays 8:30–5. The **Tennessee Welcome Center** (✉ 119 N. Riverside Dr. at Jefferson Ave.) opened in 1996. Life-size statues of Elvis Presley and W. C. Handy, and smaller sculptures, murals, and banks of video monitors will supplement the traditional information available. Though the center does not accept phone calls, on-site counselors are available daily during daylight hours to provide assistance.

NASHVILLE

Heralded as Music City, U.S.A., and the country-music capital of the world, Tennessee's fast growing capital city also shines as a leading center of higher education, appropriately known as the Athens of the South. Both labels fit. Nashville has prospered from them both, emerging as one of the South's most vibrant cities in the process. The Nashville Arena, a 20,000-seat facility spanning three blocks at 5th and Broadway, opened in 1996. Connected to the city's convention center by a tunnel, the Arena hosted the **U.S. Figure Skating Championship** in 1997. A successful drive to land a National Football League franchise, coupled with a population gain that has pushed Nashville ahead of Memphis, put Nashville into the major leagues of American cities.

Nashville's "Grand Ole Opry" radio program, which began as station WSM's "Barn Dance" in 1925 and thrived throughout the Great Depression right into today's MTV years, established the town as a music center. The Opry, which has added such popular newcomers as Vince Gill and Emmylou Harris to its cast, now performs in a sleek $15 million Opry House at Opryland. The infusion of talent is attracting a new generation of fans. The Opry is still as gleeful and down-home informal as it was when ticket holders used to jam into the old Ryman Auditorium with handheld fans to combat the sweltering heat. Bolstering Nashville's reputation as a music town are dozens of clubs, performance stages, and television tapings open to the public, as well as memorials to many country-music stars. And, of course, legendary Music Row continues to beckon aspiring singers, musicians, and songwriters with stars in their eyes and lyrics tucked in their back pockets.

Much of Nashville's role as a cultural leader, enhanced by the presence of the Tennessee Performing Arts Center that opened in 1985, is derived from the presence of 16 colleges and universities, two medical schools, two law schools, and six graduate business schools. Several, including Vanderbilt University, have national or international reputations, and many have private art galleries. As ancient Athens was the "School of Hellas," so Nashville, where a full-size replica of the Parthenon graces Centennial Park, fills this role in the contemporary South. The historic sites throughout the city add another dimension.

The Cumberland River horizontally bisects Nashville's central city. Numbered avenues, running north–south, are west of and parallel to the river; numbered streets are east of the river and parallel to it.

Downtown Nashville

Numbers in the text correspond to numbers in the margin and on the Downtown Nashville map.

A Good Walk

Begin at **Bicentennial Mall** ㉔, behind the **State Capitol** ㉕. Then, cross Charlotte Avenue to visit the **War Memorial Building** ㉖, **Tennessee State Museum** ㉗, and **Tennessee Performing Arts Center** ㉘. Walk down 5th Avenue to **Downtown Presbyterian Church** ㉙, then east on cobblestoned, tree-lined Church Street to **The District,** a good spot for lunch, dinner, or dancing. Nearby, toward the river, is **Fort Nashborough** ㉚. South on 1st Avenue is **Riverfront Park** ㉛, a good place for resting before proceeding west to **Ryman Auditorium and Museum** ㉜, on 5th Avenue between Broadway and Commerce Street.

TIMING

Allow most of a day, depending on how long you tend to linger and whether or not you shop for souvenirs. Most of these attractions offer self-guided tours, so you can set your own pace. Keep in mind that the Tennessee State Museum is closed Monday.

Sights to See

㉔ **Bicentennial Mall.** This 19-acre outdoor history park, complete with a 200-ft granite map of Tennessee and a Walk of Counties, was built in 1996 in honor of the state's 200th birthday. The center of attention is a 2,000-seat amphitheater where community bands and children shows are often staged. A welcome center is on premises to greet visitors and answer questions. The adjacent **Farmer's Market** (⊠ 900 8th Ave. N) contains 208 open-air stalls. ⊠ *598 James Robertson Pkwy.,* ☎ *615/ 741–5280.* ☉ *Daily 7 AM–10 PM.*

The District. Thanks to an extensive preservation program begun in the early 1980s, this 16-square-block area between Church Street and Broadway is packed with handsomely restored 19th-century redbrick warehouses and storefronts. On Thursday, June–September, an after-work street party, Dancin' in the District, assembles with live music ranging from jazz to alternative rock. The Wildhorse Saloon, a huge country music dance hall, plus an array of popular chain restaurants and clubs increases the festive atmosphere.

㉙ **Downtown Presbyterian Church.** This Egyptian Revival tabernacle (circa 1851) was designed by noted Philadelphia architect William Strickland. It was recently designated a National Historic Landmark. ⊠ *Corner of 5th and Church St.*

㉚ **Fort Nashborough.** High on limestone bluffs overlooking the river, a crude log fort, built in 1779 to protect and shelter early settlers, overlooks Nashville. It's been painstakingly re-created to serve as a monument to courageous city founders. In five log cabins, costumed interpreters evoke the indomitable spirit of the American age of settlement. ⊠ *170 1st Ave. N,* ☎ *615/862–8400.* ☒ *Free.* ☉ *Daily 9– 5.*

㉛ **Riverfront Park.** Though considerably smaller, the Cumberland River has been as important to Nashville as the Mississippi has been to Memphis. This welcoming green enclave on its banks has an expansive view of the busy barge traffic on the muddy river. The park serves as a popular venue for free summer concerts, block parties, and picnics, as well as a docking spot for riverboat excursions (☞ Contacts and Resources *in* Nashville A to Z, *below*). ⊠ *1st Ave. and Broadway.*

㉜ **Ryman Auditorium and Museum.** A country-music shrine, the Ryman Auditorium and Museum was home to the Grand Ole Opry from 1943 to 1974. The auditorium seats 2,000 for live performances of classical, jazz, pop, gospel, and, of course, country. The museum displays photographs of past Ryman Auditorium performances that guide visitors through the history of both the facility and country music. ⊠ *116 Opry Pl. (5th Ave. N between Broadway and Commerce St.,* ☎ *615/ 254–1445.* ☒ *$5.50.* ☉ *Daily 8:30–4. Call for show schedules and ticket prices.*

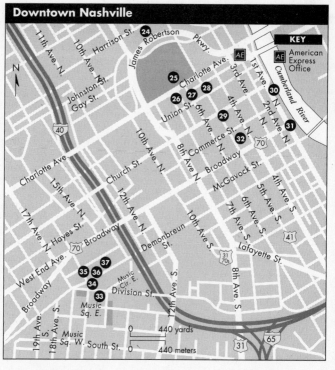

Downtown Nashville

KEY

AE American
Express
Office

25 **State Capitol.** The State Capitol was designed by Philadelphia architect William Strickland, who was so impressed with his Greek Revival
creation that he requested—and received—entombment behind one of
the building's walls. On the grounds—guarded by statues of such Tennessee heroes as Andrew Jackson—the 11th U.S. president, James K.
Polk, and his wife are buried. ⊠ *Charlotte Ave. between 6th and 7th
Aves.,* ☎ *615/741–1621.* ☒ *Free.* ⊘ *Tours weekdays 9–4.*

28 **Tennessee Performing Arts Center.** Part of the State Capitol (☞ *above*)
complex, TPAC, as it's known, comprises Jackson Hall, Johnson Hall,
and Polk Theater—named for the three U.S. presidents Tennessee sent
to Washington. TPAC Friends (☎ 615/298–3877) offers backstage tours
of the center by appointment. ⊠ *505 Deaderick St.,* ☎ *615/741–2692.*
☒ *Free.* ⊘ *Tues.–Sat. 10–5, Sun. 1–5.*

27 **Tennessee State Museum.** More than 6,000 artifacts and rotating art
and history exhibits trace the state's history from the days of Native
American settlement through the Civil War and into the 1900s. ⊠ *505
Deaderick St.,* ☎ *615/741–2692.* ☒ *Free.* ⊘ *Tues.–Sat. 10–5, Sun.
1–5.*

26 **War Memorial Building.** A collection of military memorabilia is housed
here in honor of the state's World War I dead. ⊠ *Corner of 7th and
Union St.,* ☎ *615/726–0518.* ☒ *Free.* ⊘ *Mon.–Sat. 10–5, Sun. 1–5.*

Nashville's Music Row

*Numbers in the text correspond to numbers in the margin and on the
Downtown Nashville map.*

A Good Walk

Music Row is off I–40 (Demonbreun Street exit). The Row itself is
along 16th Avenue, with music publishing offices and recording stu-

dios stretching toward Belmont Boulevard. Park for free at the **Country Music Hall of Fame** ㉝, where a visit includes a trolley ride to Studio B. Later, walk to **Barbara Mandrell Country** ㉞, **Country Music Wax Museum and Mall** ㉟, **Car Collectors Hall of Fame** ㊱, and **Hank Williams Jr. Museum** ㊲. Avoid this area at night.

TIMING

Allow a day to see Music Row attractions.

Sights to See

㉞ **Barbara Mandrell Country.** An intimate look at the career and family life of Barbara Mandrell is facilitated through such details as a replica of the star's bedroom. While there, consider stopping in at the **Recording Studios of America** (☎ 615/254–1282) to record, at a nominal cost, a demo tape of your own. Barbara Mandrell Country also has the Music Row area's best gift shop. ⊠ *1510 Division St.,* ☎ *615/242–7800.* ⌂ *$6.* ◷ *Sept.–May, daily 9–5; June–Aug., daily 9–7.*

㊱ **Car Collectors Hall of Fame.** One of Elvis's Cadillacs, Webb Pierce's "silver dollar car," Marty Robbins's Packard, and 50 other flashy vehicles with country provenances are among the displays. ⊠ *1534 Demonbreun St.,* ☎ *615/255–6804.* ⌂ *$4.95.* ◷ *Sept.–May, daily 9–5; June–Aug., daily 8 AM–9 PM.*

㉝ **Country Music Hall of Fame and Museum.** Costumes, instruments, films, and photos immortalize well-loved country music stars from Roy Acuff to Patsy Cline to Vince Gill. A ticket for the Hall of Fame includes admission to the legendary RCA **Studio B,** two blocks away, and a guided trolley tour of Music Row. Elvis, Dolly Parton, and countless others recorded here; now the studio is a hands-on exhibit area showing how records are produced. ⊠ *4 Music Sq. E,* ☎ *615/256–1639.* ⌂ *$10.75.* ◷ *June–Aug., daily 8–6; Sept.–May, daily 9–5.*

NEED A
BREAK?

At **Jamaica** (⊠ 1901 Broadway, ☎ 615/321–5191), mix and mingle with the lunchtime crowd. You can eat, or just enjoy the 11 saltwater aquariums, hand-painted murals of Jamaican scenery and folks, and live entertainment at the back bar.

㉟ **Country Music Wax Museum and Mall.** More than 60 country stars are lionized here, in wax figures complete with original stage costumes and musical instruments. The two-story mall has restaurants, country wear shops, and more. ⊠ *118 16th Ave. S,* ☎ *615/256–2490.* ⌂ *$5.50.* ◷ *June–Aug., daily 9–9; Sept.–May, daily 9–5.*

㊲ **Hank Williams Jr. Museum.** Family memorabilia include Hank Sr.'s '52 Cadillac and Hank Jr.'s '58 pink Cadillac. ⊠ *1524 Demonbreun St.,* ☎ *615/242–8313.* ⌂ *$4.* ◷ *Mar.–Sept., Mon.–Sat. 8 AM–9:30 PM, Sun. 8–7:30; Oct.–Feb., daily 9–5.*

OFF THE
BEATEN PATH

VAN VECHTEN ART GALLERY – Alfred Stieglitz rewarded Fisk University's progressive arts program with a bequest from his collection of 20th-century paintings and his own superb photographs. Stieglitz's wife, Georgia O'Keeffe, helped install the collection, highlighted by her own paintings, as well as by works by Picasso and Renoir. The gallery also exhibits African sculpture. ⊠ *Fisk University at 18th Ave. N,* ☎ *615/329–8543.* ⌂ *Donation requested.* ◷ *Tues.–Fri. 10–5, weekends 1–4.*

Greater Nashville

Numbers in the text correspond to numbers in the margin and on the Downtown Nashville map.

A Good Drive

Nashville's attractions are like spokes on a wagon wheel, so expect to spend a lot of time in the car. Start with **Opryland USA** ㊳, which will require the bulk of the day's energy. From Opryland, pursue other attractions in a clockwise direction, beginning on Donelson Pike with a visit to the **Hermitage** ㊴, then along Harding Place to **Travellers' Rest** ㊵, **Tennessee Botanical Gardens & Museum** ㊶, and **Belle Meade Mansion** ㊷. **Belmont Mansion** ㊸ is off Hillsboro Road and is near the **Parthenon** ㊹ on West End Avenue. Assuming it opened as scheduled, the **Sankofa-African Heritage Museum** ㊺ at MetroCenter on the I–265 loop is a good place to wind up the tour.

TIMING

Allow at least two days to tour these attractions. Opryland will take a day, and guided tours at the homes can be more time-consuming than self-guided attractions.

Sights to See

㊷ **Belle Meade Mansion.** This stunning Greek Revival house, known as the "Queen of the Tennessee Plantations," is recognized by the Civil War bullet holes that riddle its columns. The mansion is the centerpiece of a 5,300-acre estate that was one of the nation's first and finest Thoroughbred breeding farms. This is also the site of the famous Iroquois, the oldest amateur steeplechase in America, a society event now run each May in nearby Percy Warner Park. A Victorian carriage museum with an impressive collection continues the equine theme. ⊠ *5025 Harding Rd.,* ☎ *615/356–0501.* ⊡ *$7.* ⊙ *Mon.–Sat. 9–5, Sun. 1– 5.*

㊸ **Belmont Mansion.** This 1850s Italianate villa was the home of Adelicia Acklen, Nashville's answer to Scarlett O'Hara, who married "once for money, once for love, and once for the hell of it." On Belmont College's campus, it's a gem right down to its sweeping staircase designed for grand entrances and cast-iron gazebos perfect for romance. ⊠ *1900 Belmont Blvd.,* ☎ *615/386–4459.* ⊡ *$5.* ⊙ *Mon.–Sat. 10–4, Sun. 2–5.*

☾ **Cumberland Museum and Science Center.** Children are invited to look, touch, smell, climb, and listen through interactive exhibits unveiling natural wonders. The planetarium has star and laser shows. ⊠ *800 Ft. Negley Blvd.,* ☎ *615/862–5160.* ⊡ *$6; planetarium $1.* ⊙ *June– Aug., Mon.–Sat. 9:30–5, Sun. 12:30–5:30; Sept.–May, Tues.–Sat. 9:30– 5, Sun. 12:30–5:30.*

☾ **Grassmere Wildlife Park.** This walk-through park, 5 mi south of downtown in suburban Brentwood, contains native Tennessee and North American animals such as cougar, black bear, bison, elk, and river otter. The **Croft Center** has an aviary and an exhibit on fish and reptiles. ⊠ *3777 Nolensville Rd., 5 mi south of Nashville,* ☎ *615/833–1534.* ⊡ *$5.* ⊙ *Daily 9–6.*

㊴ **Hermitage.** About 12 mi east of Nashville (I–40E to Old Hickory Blvd. exit), the life and times of Andrew Jackson, known as "Old Hickory," are reflected with great care. Jackson built the mansion on 600 acres for his wife, Rachel, for whose honor he fought and won a duel. Both are buried in the family graveyard. The **Andrew Jackson Center,** a 28,000-square-ft museum, visitor center, and education center, contains

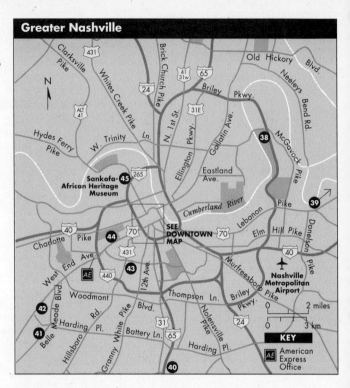

many Jackson artifacts never before exhibited. Knowledgeable guides take you through the mansion, furnished with many original pieces. An 18-minute film, *Old Hickory*, provides further background on the seventh president. Note the guitar-shape driveway. Across the road stands the **Tulip Grove Mansion,** built by Mrs. Jackson's nephew, and the **Hermitage Church,** fondly known as "Rachel's Church." ⊠ *4580 Rachel's La., Hermitage,* ☎ *615/889–2941.* ⛴ *Tulip Grove and church $8.* ☉ *Daily 9–5.*

🖐 **Nashville Toy Museum.** Toy trains, dolls, and models of ships and soldiers complete a collection spanning 150 years. ⊠ *2613 McGavock Pike,* ☎ *615/883–8870.* ⛴ *$3.50.* ☉ *Summer, daily 9–9; rest of yr, daily 9–5.*

🖐 **Nashville Zoo.** Larger than Grassmere (☞ *above*), the Nashville Zoo is home to lions, clouded leopards, white tigers, lemurs, and more than 800 other animals. It's on 50 acres in Joelton, which is about 15 mi north of Nashville. ⊠ *1710 Ridge Rd. Circle,* ☎ *615/370–3333.* ⛴ *$5.50.* ☉ *Memorial Day–Labor Day, daily 9–6; Labor Day–Memorial Day, daily 10–5.*

★ ➌➑ **Opryland USA.** With 120 acres, Opryland rivals Disneyland in entertainment theme park grandeur. Good old-fashioned family entertainment with a heavy dose of country make this Nashville's most popular attraction. There are 70 live shows and almost 30 rides, ranging from Chaos, a $7 million indoor roller coaster with spectacular audiovisual effects, to tame mini–Ferris wheels perfect for tykes. The shows, especially *Country Music USA,* are toe-tapping fun, and music permeates the park. Wanna-bes might test their singing talent at Opryplace Recording Studios.

The theme park was created in part because the enormously popular **Grand Ole Opry** (☎ 615/889–3060)—reserved seats $17, less for

summer matinees—begun in 1925, had
grounds, the Ryman (☞ Sights to See *in* D
Each weekend, top stars perform at the na
show in the world's largest broadcast stud
has overhauled its image as the home o
rent favorites Garth Brooks, Emmylou H
and Marty Stuart, among others. Specia
best chance for last-minute tickets. Otherwise, ...
well in advance.

The **Roy Acuff Museum** (☎ 615/889–6611) contains memorabilia, including many guns and fiddles, belonging to the late "king of country music." Acuff was a fixture at the Grand Ole Opry. **Minnie Pearl's Museum** provides a nostalgic tour of the performer's life. Admission to the museums in Opryland Plaza is included in the general admission to Opryland; hours vary widely, so call first. The *General Jackson,* Opryland's $12 million, four-deck paddle wheeler, offers several two-hour cruises daily; a musical revue is presented in its Victorian Theater (☎ 615/889–6611); lunch cruise is $18.95, dinner $45.95.

Nashville on Stage (☎ 615/889–6611), tickets $18.35–$23.76, books hot-as-a-fresh-biscuit country acts from Tanya Tucker to Marty Stuart; there are three shows a night at three Opryland theaters from May to early October. ⊠ *9 mi northeast of downtown (Exit 11, off Briley Pkwy.), between I–40 and I–65,* ☎ *615/889–6611.* ☎ *$28.99.* ☉ *Grand Old Opry late Mar.–May and Sept.–Oct., weekends 10–9; May–early Oct., daily 10–9.*

44 **Parthenon.** An exact copy of the Athenian original, Nashville's Parthenon was constructed to commemorate Nashville's 1897 centennial. Across the street from Vanderbilt University's campus, in Centennial Park, it's a magnificent sight, perched on a gentle green slope beside a duck pond. Inside is the Cowan Collection, featuring 63 works of art by American artists, traveling exhibits, and such exquisite statuary as the 42-ft *Athena Parthenos,* the tallest indoor sculpture in the Western world. ⊠ *West End and 25th Aves.,* ☎ *615/862–8431.* ☎ *$2.50.* ☉ *Oct.–Mar., Tues.–Sat. 9–4:30; Apr.–Sept., Tues.–Sat. 9–4:30, Sun. 12:30–4:30.*

45 **Sankofa-African Heritage Museum.** Nearly 6,000 square ft at Metro-Center devoted to sculpture artifacts from all parts of Africa is expected to be open to the public in summer 1997. Some pieces date back to 1441. Lectures, musical presentations, and special events are planned. There's free parking and a restaurant on site. Take Exit 265 at Metro-Center, go north four blocks, and turn left. ⊠ *The Winston-Derek Center/MetroCenter, French Broad and Dominion, Box 90883, Nashville 37209,* ☎ *615/321–0535 or 800/826–1888.* ☎ *$2.* ☉ *Weekdays 9–4, Sat. 10–5, Sun. 1–4.*

41 **Tennessee Botanical Gardens & Museum.** Fifty-five acres showcase roses, irises, daffodils, area wildflowers, and herbs. Greenhouses, orchid hothouses, a Japanese garden, streams, and pools make this a delightful spot for a picnic. The art museum, contained in Cheekwood, the 1920s Georgian mansion which was once the private estate of the Leslie Cheek family of Maxwell House coffee fame, maintains a permanent collection of 19th- and 20th-century American art. A traditional Southern lunch is available in the mansion's Pineapple Room, and the gift shop has elegant choices. ⊠ *1200 Forrest Park Dr.,* ☎ *615/356–8000.* ☎ *$6.* ☉ *Mon.–Sat. 9–5, Sun. noon–5.*

40 **Travellers' Rest.** Following the fortunes of pioneer landowner and judge John Overton—the law partner, mentor, campaign manager, and telong friend of Andrew Jackson, whose own home is nearby—this early 19th-century clapboard home metamorphosed from a 1799 four-room cottage to a 12-room mansion with Federal-influenced and Greek Revival additions. Also on the grounds are a restored smoke-house, kitchen house, and formal gardens. Travellers' Rest is off I–65 South at the first of two Harding Place exits. ⊠ *636 Farrell Pkwy.,* ☎ *615/832–2962.* ▣ *$5.* ☉ *Tues.–Sat. 10–5, Sun. 1–5.*

Wave Country. A mile from Opryland, Wave Country has a large wave pool and a three-flume water slide. ⊠ *Two Rivers Pkwy., off Briley Pkwy.,* ☎ *615/885–1052.* ▣ *$5, ½ price after 4.* ☉ *Memorial Day–Labor Day, daily 10–8.*

Dining

American

$$$ ✕ **Belle Meade Brasserie.** Nashville's poshest neighborhood welcomed this comfortable suburban restaurant with open arms in 1988. The menu is a symphony of best-loved recipes from all over the United States—an appetizer of corn fritters and pepper jelly, New York strip steak cowboy-style, San Francisco–style crab cakes, and shrimp and scallops served on a bed of black linguine. Desserts are just as compelling, including a knockout Russian raspberry gratin. ⊠ *101 Page Rd.,* ☎ *615/356–5450. AE, DC, MC, V. Closed Sun. No lunch.*

$$$ ✕ **Merchants.** A $3.2 million renovation of an historic property in downtown Nashville, this former hotel provides three levels of dining and an appealing outdoor patio. Specialties include California-style pizzas, the freshest seafood, and meats grilled over native hardwoods. Lighter fare masters the menu in summer, and all rolls, pastas, and pastries are made fresh daily. Save room for the key lime pie. ⊠ *401 Broadway,* ☎ *615/254–1892. AE, DC, MC, V. No lunch weekends.*

$$ ✕ **F. Scott's.** At this elegant, art deco–inspired café and wine bar patrons enjoy the owners' private collection of impressionist-style art. The emphasis is on nouveau American—dishes such as hickory-smoked venison with fresh corn cakes, seared black pepper–crusted yellow-fin tuna, and roasted rack of lamb with Dijon and herbs. F. Scott's 32-page wine list is one of Nashville's most extensive, with many fine wines available by the glass. ⊠ *2210 Crestmoor,* ☎ *615/269–5861. AE, D, DC, MC, V. No lunch Sat.*

$$ ✕ **Mad Platter.** This local favorite in historic downtown Nashville blends traditional gourmet with California cuisine, using locally available ingredients from the nearby Farmer's Market. The baked salmon with red grapes and feta cheese, rack of lamb, and bananas Foster are favorites here. It's a popular spot for power lunches by day. Jazz music transforms the cozy 18th-century brownstone into a romantic nook at night. ⊠ *1239 6th Ave. N,* ☎ *615/242–2563. Reservations essential for dinner. AE, D, MC, V. No lunch weekends.*

$$ ✕ **106 Club.** A black baby grand and a bar of shiny black enamel and glass brick set the atmosphere in this intimate, art deco–style dining room in suburban Belle Meade. The cuisine is a mix of California nouvelle and international favorites such as Bahamian sailfish. The free-range chicken with pasta primavera is one of the best meals in town. Relax with one of 106's rich desserts and listen to melodies on the baby grand. ⊠ *106 Harding Pl.,* ☎ *615/356–1300. AE, DC, MC, V.*

$$ ✕ **Sunset Grill.** The works of artist Paul Harmon, who divides his time
★   between Nashville and Paris, decorate this hip, postmodern hangout, frequented by country glitterati such as Tanya Tucker. The hickory-smoked Tennessee trout is terrific. The outside courtyard is popular in summer. Tip: Food prices are slashed by 50% after 10 PM (midnight

Dining

Arthur's, **6**

Belle Meade
Brasserie, **11**

Cakewalk
Restaurant, **15**

F. Scott's, **12**

Loveless, **9**

Mad Platter, **18**

Mario's Ristorante
Italiano, **2**

Merchants, **7**

Mère Bulles, the Wine
Bar and Restaurant, **8**

106 Club, **10**

Pancake Pantry, **13**

Sunset Grill, **14**

Wild Boar, **3**

Lodging

Comfort Inn
Hermitage, **22**

Courtyard by
Marriott–Airport, **21**

Hampton Inn
Vanderbilt, **1**

Holiday Inn Crowne
Plaza, **4**

Loew's Vanderbilt
Plaza Hotel, **16**

Opryland Hotel, **20**

Ramada Inn Across
from Opryland, **19**

Shoney's Inn on Music
Row, **17**

Stouffer Nashville
Hotel, **5**

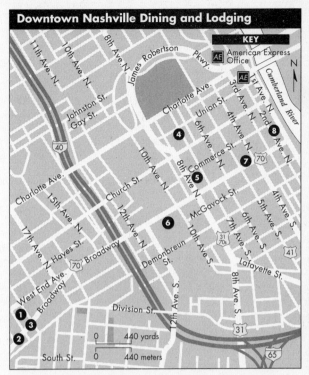

Downtown Nashville Dining and Lodging

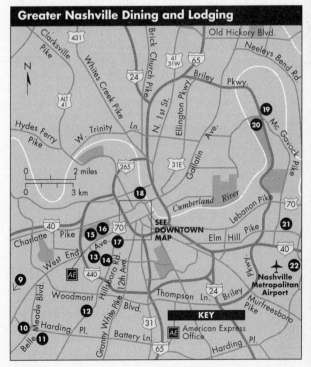

Greater Nashville Dining and Lodging

on weekends). ⊠ *2001A Belcourt Ave.,* ☎ *615/386–3663. AE, D, DC, MC, V. Closed Sun. No lunch Sat.*

Continental

$$$ ✕ **Arthur's.** This restaurant is in the stylishly renovated Union Station, where an upscale hotel has taken the place of the train terminal. The seven-course meals are dazzling (à la carte is also available) and the ambience romantic. The menu changes daily but specialties include rainbow trout, duck, and lamb. Save room for dessert: The bananas Foster is especially filling. The decor is lush, with lace curtains, velveteen-upholstered chairs, white linen, and fine silver service. ⊠ *Union Station, 1001 Broadway,* ☎ *615/255–1494. Jacket and tie. AE, DC, MC, V. No lunch.*

$$$ ✕ **Mère Bulles, the Wine Bar and Restaurant.** Chosen Nashville's most romantic in a *Tennessean Magazine* readers poll, Mère Bulles fits the bill with its brass-trimmed mahogany bar and changing art decorating exposed brick walls. Romantics especially will enjoy tapas and drinks in the cozy lounge, before moving into one of three intimate dining areas, all with views of the river. A specialty is pesto Mère Bulles—shrimp and scallops with walnut-pesto sauce served on a bed of shell pasta. In the heart of The District, the restaurant offers live entertainment downstairs nightly, usually jazz or folk music. ⊠ *152 2nd Ave. N,* ☎ *615/256–1946. Jacket and tie. AE, DC, MC, V.*

$$$ ✕ **Wild Boar.** Decorated like an English hunting lodge with $2.5 mil-
★ lion in original art, this casual restaurant yields culinary treasures for those on the hunt. Rack of venison with seared foie gras is a specialty. The American menu emphasizes game, trout, lobster, duck, and beef dishes, with several that are prepared at the table. The Wild Boar, with 15,000 bottles in its wine cellar, has one of the top wine lists in the world. ⊠ *2014 Broadway,* ☎ *615/329–1313. Reservations essential. AE, D, DC, MC, V. Closed Sun.–Mon. No lunch Sat.*

Mixed Menu

$$ ✕ **Cakewalk Restaurant.** What first catches your eye at this cozy bistro are the intriguing paintings by local artists on the turquoise walls. The eclectic cuisine is equally imaginative, blending the best of nouvelle California, a bit of Southwestern, a dash of Cajun and Creole, and some down-home American specialties thrown in for fun. Desserts are outstanding—especially the Kahlua cake, a four-layer chocolate confection laced with the liqueur. ⊠ *3001 West End Ave.,* ☎ *615/320–7778. DC, MC, V. No lunch Sat.*

Northern Italian

$$$ ✕ **Mario's Ristorante Italiano.** Owner Mario Ferrari is the genius behind this Nashville institution. Country-music stars, visiting celebrities, and local society come here to see and be seen. The atmosphere is elegant but never stuffy, with lots of brass and an impressive wine collection on view. The seafood and veal—such as the *saltimbocca,* veal medallions with mozzarella, prosciutto, mushrooms, and fresh sage—are enormously palate pleasing. ⊠ *2005 Broadway,* ☎ *615/327–3232. Reservations essential, 2–3 days in advance for Fri. and Sat. Jacket and tie. AE, D, DC, MC, V. Closed Sun.*

Southern

$ ✕ **Loveless.** An experience in true down-home Southern cooking. Don't come for the decor—decidedly lax, with red-and-white-checked tablecloths—but rather for the feather-light homemade biscuits and preserves, country ham and red-eye gravy, and fried chicken. ⊠ *8400 Hwy. 100,* ☎ *615/646–9700. MC, V.*

$ ✕ **Pancake Pantry.** A favorite haunt of Garth Brooks and Faith Hill, this crowded diner stylizes pancakes 24 ways and makes its own syrups to boot. Though it's open until 7:30 PM, breakfast is its raison d'être. ⊠ *1796 21st Ave. S,* ☎ *615/383–9333. Reservations not accepted. AE, D, DC, MC, V.*

Lodging

$$$$ 🏨 **Holiday Inn Crowne Plaza.** Downtown, near the State Capitol, this 28-story tower has a vast, skylighted atrium lobby awash with greenery and overseen by glassed-in elevators. Rooms are extra spacious and contemporary with great views of the growing Nashville skyline. The hotel is topped by the Pinnacle, Nashville's only revolving rooftop restaurant. ⊠ *623 Union St., 37219,* ☎ *615/259–2000 or 800/447–9825,* FAX *615/742–6096. 464 rooms, 14 suites. 2 restaurants, coffee shop, lounge, no-smoking rooms. AE, DC, MC, V.*

$$$$ 🏨 **Loew's Vanderbilt Plaza Hotel.** Celebrities and business travelers grav-
★   itate to this quiet European-style luxury hotel known for top-notch service and convenient to Music Row. The pristine white lobby is grand. Musicians play nightly in the piano bar. Gracious guest rooms, some with skyline views, are done with dark cherry furniture. Plaza suites are individually decorated, and the club level rooms have luxurious baths and extra phone and fax lines. ⊠ *2100 West End Ave., 37203,* ☎ *615/ 320–1700 or 800/235–6397,* FAX *615/320–5019. 325 rooms, 13 suites. 3 restaurants, piano bar, health club. AE, DC, MC, V.*

$$$$ 🏨 **Opryland Hotel.** This massive hostelry—one of the 25 largest in the
★   world—is adjacent to Opryland USA. A 1996 addition called the Delta added nearly a thousand rooms, plus an indoor river, a 110-ft-wide waterfall, and an amphitheater under a 4.2-acre glass dome. Harp music is played nightly at the revolving bar at the Cascades, another skylighted interior space with streams, waterfalls, and a half-acre lake. Rooms, which are fairly standard in size, have Victorian floral decor in beige and rose tones; request one overlooking the gardens. The hotel claims to have more meeting space than any other in the nation. The culinary staff is directed by a member of the U.S. Culinary Olympics Team. ⊠ *2800 Opryland Dr., 37214,* ☎ *615/889–1000,* FAX *615/871–5728. 2,870 rooms, 200 suites. 5 restaurants, pool, wading pool. AE, D, DC, MC, V.*

$$$$ 🏨 **Stouffer Nashville Hotel.** This luxurious, ultracontemporary high-rise hotel adjoins the Nashville Convention Center and is also connected to the Church Street Centre Mall. Spacious rooms are furnished with period reproductions. Executive Club concierge floors offer extra privacy and personal services. ⊠ *611 Commerce St., 37203,* ☎ *615/255–8400,* FAX *615/255–8163. 649 rooms, 24 suites. Restaurant, coffee shop, lounge, indoor pool, hot tub, sauna, health club, concierge floors. AE, DC, MC, V.*

$$$ 🏨 **Courtyard by Marriott–Airport.** This handsome, low-rise motor inn with a sunny, gardenlike courtyard offers some amenities you'd expect in higher-priced hotels: spacious rooms, king-size beds, oversize work desks, and hot-water dispensers for in-room coffee. ⊠ *2508 Elm Hill Pike, 37214,* ☎ *615/883–9500 or 800/321–2211,* FAX *615/883–0172. 133 rooms, 12 suites. Restaurant, lounge, no-smoking rooms, hot tub. AE, D, DC, MC, V.*

$$$ 🏨 **Ramada Inn Across from Opryland.** This contemporary-style, well-maintained low-rise motor inn has the closest location to the theme park after the Opryland Hotel. ⊠ *2401 Music Valley Dr., 37214,* ☎ *615/889–0800,* FAX *615/883–1230. 300 rooms, 7 suites. Restaurant, lounge, indoor pool, hot tub, sauna. AE, DC, MC, V.*

$$ 🏨 **Comfort Inn Hermitage.** Near the Hermitage (☞ Sights to See *in Greater Nashville, above*), this inn offers reasonably priced accommodations, some with water beds or whirlpool baths. ⊠ *5768 Old Hickory Blvd., 37076,* ☎ *615/889–5060,* FAX *615/871–4137. 99 rooms, 7 suites. No-smoking rooms, pool. AE, D, DC, MC, V.*

$$ 🏨 **Hampton Inn Vanderbilt.** Near the Vanderbilt University campus and Music Row, this six-story inn is clean and contemporary and especially popular with visiting music executives and musicians. Rooms, done in shades of maroon, green, and cream, are spacious. A multipurpose hospitality suite has a conference table, chairs, and an audiovisual unit for meetings, making this a popular corporate choice. ⊠ *1919 West End Ave., 37203,* ☎ *615/329–1144 or 800/426–7866,* FAX *615/320–7112. 171 rooms. Pool, meeting rooms. AE, D, DC, MC, V.*

$$ 🏨 **Shoney's Inn on Music Row.** On the Trolley Line and a guitar strum away from the Country Music Hall of Fame and other Music Row attractions, this is a typical, clean, chain motel. The inn's namesake restaurant has a good, low-cost, all-you-can-eat breakfast bar. ⊠ *1521 Demonbreun St., 37203,* ☎ *615/255–9977,* FAX *615/242–6127. 134 rooms, 13 suites. Restaurant. AE, DC, MC, V.*

Nightlife and the Arts

For a listing of weekly events, consult the Visitor Information Center or the local newspapers. For information on concerts and special events, call **WSM Radio's entertainment line** (☎ 615/737–9595). **TicketMaster** (☎ 615/737–4849) has information on events at various Nashville venues.

Nightlife

Ace of Clubs (⊠ 114 2nd Ave. S, ☎ 615/254–2237), in the District, is a soulful joint, with a mix of DJs and live bands. **Big River Grille & Brewery Works** (⊠ 111 Broadway, ☎ 615/251–4677) is Nashville's hottest brew-pub.

Grammy Award–winning talent and Music City's up-and-coming stars often try out their latest material at **Bluebird Cafe** (⊠ 4104 Hillsboro Rd., ☎ 615/383–1461) in the posh Green Hills neighborhood. **Cowboys La Cage** (⊠ 4th Ave. and Broadway, ☎ 615/269–2697) features female impersonators in revues of favorite country and pop stars. **Douglas Corner Cafe** (⊠ 2106A 8th Ave. S, ☎ 615/298–1688) is well known for everything from blues to country. **Hard Rock Cafe** (⊠ 100 Broadway, ☎ 615/742–9900) is great for burgers. **Planet Hollywood** (⊠ 322 Broadway, ☎ 615/313–7827) offers pub grub amid the movie artifacts that have made the celebrity-owned chain famous. **Stock Yard Bull Pen Lounge** (⊠ 901 2nd Ave. N and Stock Yard, ☎ 615/255–6464) has nightly live country performers—heavyweights do drop in—and dancing. However, the steak-and-seafood restaurant is unexceptional. Boot scoot over to the **Wildhorse Saloon** (⊠ 120 2nd Ave. N, ☎ 615/251–1000) with its 3,300-ft dance floor and seating for 1,600. The Nashville Network tapes live on the dance floor. For laughs, try **Zanies Comedy Showplace** (⊠ 2025 8th Ave. S, ☎ 615/269–0221).

The Arts

Chaffin's Barn (⊠ 8204 Hwy. 100, ☎ 615/646–9977 or 800/282–2276) offers dinner theater year-round, and stages a live country show daily from Memorial Day to Labor Day. Country music takes center stage at Opryland USA's 4,424-seat **Grand Ole Opry Auditorium** (☎ 615/889–3060). The Nashville Symphony Orchestra's classical and pops series and concerts by visiting performers are staged at **Andrew Jackson Hall** (TicketMaster, ☎ 615/741–2787), part of the Tennessee Performing Arts Center (☞ Sights to See *in* Downtown Nashville, *above*). Chamber concerts, touring Broadway shows, and local theatrical performances take place at the Tennessee Performing Arts Center's (☞ Sights to See *in* Downtown Nashville, *above*) **James K. Polk Theater** (☎ 615/741–7975). Rock and country events are held at the **Nashville Municipal Auditorium** (⊠ 417 4th Ave. N, ☎ 615/862–6395). The **Starwood Amphitheatre** (⊠ 3839 Murfreesboro Rd., ☎ 615/641–5800) is the site of rock, pop, country, and jazz concerts, musicals, and special events; it's also the summer home of the Nashville Symphony. The **Nashville Ballet** (⊠ 2976 Sidco Dr., ☎ 615/244–7233 or 800/333–4849) performs works accompanied by the Nashville Symphony Orchestra. Vanderbilt University stages music, dance, and drama productions (many free) at its **Blair School of Music** (⊠ 2400 Blakemore Ave., ☎ 615/322–7651).

The **Nashville Academy Theatre** (⊠ 724 2nd Ave. S, ☎ 615/254–9103) is home to a professional children's theater troupe that performs September–May.

Festivals

Summer Lights Music City Festival. The first weekend in June, more than a half million visitors attend Nashville's unique music and arts festival, showcasing almost 200 top names from all genres of music on five outdoor stages downtown, at the legislative plaza near Deaderick Street. Artwork by locals is exhibited in warehouses and storefronts along 1st and 2nd avenues. Street vendors sell local fare, while street entertainers fill the Family Arts Arcade. ⊠ *Summer Lights Office, 201 Church Street Centre,* ☎ *615/259–0900.* ✑ *$7.*

International Country Music Fan Fair. Held annually by the Grand Ole Opry and the Country Music Association on the second week in June at the Tennessee State Fairgrounds, Fan Fair is country music's premier event. Many tour companies offer packages, but plan ahead: Tickets sell out months in advance. ⊠ *Fan Fair, 2804 Opryland Dr., 37214,* ☎ *615/889–7503.*

Outdoor Activities and Sports

Auto Racing

Top drivers compete at the **Nashville Motor Raceway** (⊠ State Fairgrounds, ☎ 615/726–1818), from April through October.

Baseball

You can root for Nashville's AAA baseball team from April through mid-September at the **Tim McCarver Stadium** (⊠ 800 Home Run La., ☎ 615/272–1687).

Boating and Fishing

You'll find boat rentals at **J. Percy Priest Lake** (⊠ 11 mi east of Nashville, off I–40, ☎ 615/883–2351) and **Old Hickory Reservoir** (⊠ 15 mi northeast of Nashville via U.S. 31E, ☎ 615/824–7766).

Football

The transplanted Houston Oilers of the **National Football League** are scheduled to begin playing in Nashville in 1999, assuming stadium construction is on schedule. The new stadium is along the Cumberland River near downtown. Until then, their home games will be at the Liberty Bowl Memorial Stadium in Memphis.

Golf

Public courses open year-round are the 18-hole **Harpeth Hills** (⊠ 2424 Old Hickory Blvd., ☎ 615/862–8493) and **Hermitage Golf Course** (⊠ 3939 Old Hickory Blvd., ☎ 615/847–4001) and the nine-hole **Rhodes**

Golf Course (⊠ 1901 Ed Temple Blvd., ☎ 615/862–8463). Hermitage is the site each April of the LPGA Sara Lee Classic.

Hockey

The **Nashville Knights** (☎ 615/255–7825), a farm club of the Atlanta Knights and Tampa Bay Lightning, is the city's minor-league hockey team.

Horseback Riding

You can jog or canter on gentle steeds at **Riverwood Recreation Plantation and Riding Academy** (⊠ Cooper La. off McGavock Pike, 5 mi from Opryland, ☎ 615/262–1794) and **Ramblin' Breeze Ranch** (⊠ 3665 Knight Rd., White's Creek, ☎ 615/876–1029).

Horse Show

For 10 days from late August to early September, Shelbyville, 50 mi southeast of Nashville, holds the **Tennessee Walking Horse National Celebration** (⊠ Box 1010, 37160, ☎ 615/684–5915), the world's greatest walking horse show.

Ice-Skating

Indoor skating is available at **Sportsplex** (⊠ 25th Ave. N at Brandau Ave., ☎ 615/862–8480) in Centennial Park.

Jogging

The 1,700-plus-member running club Nashville Striders (☎ 615/833–4124) can recommend choice spots and will provide information on many summer races. **Centennial Park,** the **Vanderbilt University running track, J. Percy Priest Lake,** and **Percy Warner Park** are great for jogging.

Miniature Golf

Enjoy this uniquely American family sport at **Grand Old Golf** (☎ 615/871–4701), across the street from the Opryland Hotel.

Tennis

Several municipal tennis facilities offer good play. **Centennial Sportsplex Tennis Center** (⊠ 224 25th Ave. N, ☎ 615/862–8490) has outdoor courts plus indoor courts.

Shopping

Shopping Centers

Tri-level **Church Street Centre** (⊠ 625 Church St., ☎ 615/256–6644) is the major downtown shopping area with department stores, smaller chain stores, and numerous boutiques. Present your hotel room key at the service desk and get a coupon book with $200 worth of discounts. **Bellevue Center** (⊠ 7620 Hwy. 70S, off Bellevue exit of I–40W, ☎ 615/646–8690) is Nashville's premier mall, with more than 125 stores, including the Disney Store, Abercrombie & Fitch, Country Road Australia, and the Tennessee Museum Store. The **Mall at Green Hills** (⊠ Hillsboro and Abbott Martin Rd., ☎ 615/298–5478), about 15 minutes from Music Row, has specialty stores such as Brookstone, Williams-Sonoma, Laura Ashley, and Brooks Brothers, plus Dillard's department store. **Factory Outlet Stores of America Outlet Center** (⊠ Briley Pkwy. off I–65, McGavock Pike exit, across from Opryland Hotel, ☎ 500/746–7872) has great bargains. **100 Oaks** (⊠ I–65 South to Exit 79, Armory Drive to Powell, ☎ 615/383–6002) is one of Nashville's more upscale factory outlets.

Antiques

Browse for distinctive 18th- and 19th-century English antiques and objets d'art east of downtown at **Madison Antique Mall** (⊠ 320 Gallatin

Rd. S, ☎ 615/865–4677), close to Music Row at **Nashville Antique Mall** (✉ 657 Wedgewood Ave., ☎ 615/292–3236), or in Andrew Jackson's stomping grounds at **Smorgasbord Antique Mall** (✉ 4144-B Lebanon Rd., Hermitage, ☎ 615/883–5789).

Arts and Crafts
Cumberland Gallery (✉ 4107 Hillsboro Circle, ☎ 615/297–0296) sells the works of major regional artists. For pottery and ceramics, seek out **Forrest Valley Pottery** (✉ 325 Forrest Valley Dr., ☎ 615/356–5136), a working studio, open only by appointment.

Books
Bibliophiles appreciate the three-story **Davis-Kidd Booksellers** (✉ Grace's Plaza in Green Hills, 407 Hillsboro Rd., ☎ 615/385–2645), open late on the weekends. Curl up in a chair with a glass of wine and the latest *New York Times* best-sellers.

Country-and-Western Wear
Nashville Cowboy (✉ 118 16th Ave. S, ☎ 615/242–9497; ✉ 1516 Demonbreun St., ☎ 615/256–2429) carries the latest looks in country clothing. **Boot Country** (✉ 2412 Music Valley Dr., ☎ 615/883–2661) stocks boots of every size and skin as well as accessories and apparel.

Flea Market
From treasures to just plain "junque"—the **Nashville Flea Market** at the Tennessee State Fairgrounds has it all. Usually, 1,000 traders, craftsfolk, and antiques dealers ply their wares the fourth weekend of every month except December. Arrive early for the best finds; stay late for the best deals. ✉ *Wedgewood and Rains Aves.,* ☎ *615/862–5016.* ☺ *Sat. 6–6, Sun. 7–5.*

Music
Country fans can find good selections of compact discs and tapes at **Conway's Twitty Bird Record Shop** (✉ 1530 Demonbreun St., ☎ 615/242–2466). **Ernest Tubb Record Shops** (✉ 2414 Music Valley Dr., ☎ 615/889–2474; ✉ 417 Broadway, ☎ 615/255–7503) carry a full line of classic and new-artist country music on CD, cassette, 45s, and video as well as song books and a variety of souvenirs.

Side Trips from Nashville

The Tennessee Heartland surrounding Nashville is a pocket of gently rolling Cumberland Mountain foothills and bluegrass meadows. It is one of the state's richest farming areas. Such small towns as Lynchburg and Franklin, which historian Shelby Foote calls one of the nation's top Civil War sites, offer wonderful antiques shops and crafts boutiques.

Loretta Lynn's Ranch
65 mi west of Nashville.

Loretta Lynn's Ranch encompasses the entire village of Hurricane Mills. The singer's personal museum is housed in an old restored gristmill. Tours are of the downstairs of the coal miner's daughter's stately antebellum home, a simulated coal mine, and a re-creation of her simple childhood home. Camping, canoeing, paddle boats, trout fishing, and swimming are among the many recreational activities available here. ✉ *North of I–40W to TN 13N (Exit 143),* ☎ *615/296–7700.* ☜ *Tour $10.50, camping $13–$18 per night for 2 people.* ☺ *Mar.–Dec. for tours, Apr.–Oct. for camping.*

Franklin

18 mi south of Nashville.

The town of Franklin rivals Natchez, Mississippi, in charm and Civil War history. A self-guided walking tour begins at the town square and covers several antebellum homes plus the meticulously restored downtown business district, which has more than 50 shops, including several antiques shops and art galleries. Stop at **H. R. H. Dumplin's** (⊠ 428 Main St.) old-fashioned tearoom for a salad or dessert. The **Carnton Plantation,** where some of the Civil War's bloodiest battles were fought, and **Confederate Cemetery** are nearby. So is the entrance to the Natchez Trace Parkway (off I–40), which wends its way through gorgeous scenery in three states. For more information on Franklin and its attractions, call **Williamson County Tourism** (⊠ City Hall, Franklin 37065, ☎ 615/794–1225).

DINING AND LODGING

$$$ ✕⊡ **Lyric Springs Country Inn.** Nestled in the green, rolling hills of nearby
★   Franklin—a renowned Civil War site—the Lyric Springs is a real find. This small bed-and-breakfast inn strikes the right notes with its 1940s Americana and uptown country antiques. Talent agent and owner Patsy Bruce—who penned "Mamas Don't Let Your Babies Grow Up to Be Cowboys"—is the perennial Nashville insider. A full gourmet breakfast is included, and dinner reservations are accepted. ⊠ *7306 S. Harpeth Rd., 37064,* ☎ *615/329–3385 or 800/621–7824,* ⅋ *615/329–3381. 4 rooms. Billiards. MC, V.*

Lynchburg

75 mi southeast of Nashville.

Lynchburg has been depicted worldwide in ads for its best-known product, whiskey. The quaint town is home to the **Jack Daniel Distillery,** the oldest registered distillery in the country, where you can observe every step of the sour-mash-whiskey-making art. ⊠ *On TN 55,* ☎ *615/759–6180.* ⊑ *Free.* ☉ *Guided tours daily 8–4.*

DINING

$ ✕ **Miss Mary Bobo's Boarding House.** This is a Tennessee institution. Diners flock to the two-story 1867 white frame house with a white picket fence to feast family-style at tables groaning with fried chicken, roast beef, fried catfish, stuffed vegetables, and sliced tomatoes fresh from the gardens out back, along with corn on the cob, homemade biscuits, corn bread, pecan pie, lemon icebox pie, fruit cobblers, and strawberry shortcake. ⊠ *½ block from Public Sq.,* ☎ *615/759–7394. Reservations essential, at least 2 wks in advance. One meal served Mon–Sat., promptly at 1 PM. No credit cards.*

Nashville A to Z

Arriving and Departing

BY BOAT

The **Delta Queen Steamboat Co.** (☎ 504/586–0631) offers four-night paddle wheeler cruises on the Mississippi, Ohio, and Cumberland rivers between St. Louis and Nashville, with stops along the way.

BY BUS

Greyhound Bus Lines (⊠ 200 8th Ave. S, and McGavock St., Nashville, ☎ 800/231–2222).

BY CAR

From Nashville, I–65 leads north into Kentucky and south into Alabama, and I–24 leads northwest into Kentucky and Illinois and southeast into Chattanooga and Georgia. I–40 traverses the state east–west, connecting Knoxville with Nashville and Memphis. I–440 connects I–40, I–65, and I–24, and helps circumvent clogged major arteries during Nashville's rush hour. I–840, which will skirt Nashville's north side and connect I–40 with I–24N and I–65N, is under construction.

BY PLANE

Metropolitan Nashville Airport (☎ 615/275–1675), approximately 8 mi from downtown, is served by American, American Eagle, Atlantic Southeast, ComAir, Delta, Northwest, Southwest, TWA, United, US Airways, and US Airways Express.

Shuttle service downtown (☎ 615/275–1180) costs $8–$10 per person. A cab costs about $16. To reach downtown by car, take I–40W.

Getting Around

BY BOAT

Opryland's new, 57-ft **Opryland USA Water Taxis** (☎ 615/889–6611), $10.99 one-way, link the park with Opryland USA, across the river.

BY BUS

Metropolitan Transit Authority (MTA) buses (☎ 615/242–4433) serve the entire county; the fare is $1.35 (exact change), and they run 4 AM–11:15 PM.

BY TAXI

Try **Allied Taxi** (☎ 615/244–7433), **Music City Taxi** (☎ 615/262–0451 or 800/359–9692), or **Madison Rivergate Taxi** (☎ 615/865–4100).

BY TROLLEY

Nashville Trolley Co. (☎ 615/242–4433), fare 90¢ exact change, runs regularly scheduled trolleys through downtown and along Music Row during summer months.

Contacts and Resources

EMERGENCIES

Dial 911 for **police** and **ambulance.** Emergency rooms are open all night at centrally located **Baptist Hospital** (✉ 2000 Church St., ☎ 615/329–5555) and **Vanderbilt University Medical Center** (✉ 1211 22nd Ave. S, ☎ 615/322–7311).

GUIDED TOURS

Belle Carol Riverboat Co. (✉ 106 1st Ave. S, Riverfront Park 37201, ☎ 615/244–3430 or 800/342–2355) offers Cumberland River sightseeing, luncheon, and dinner cruises that depart from the Nashville Old Steamboat Dock at Riverfront Park. From its dock, **Opryland USA** (☎ 615/889–6611) operates 1½-hour daytime cruises with Opryland-style entertainment and two-hour evening dinner cruises aboard its four-deck *General Jackson* showboat.

Gray Line (☎ 615/227–2270 or 800/251–1864) and **Grand Ole Opry Tours** (☎ 615/889–9490) offer tours that include drives past stars' homes and visits to the Grand Ole Opry, Music Row, and The District (historic downtown).

Johnny Walker Tours (☎ 615/834–8585 or 800/722–1524) has three-hour sightseeing tours, Grand Ole Opry, Opryland, and special concert tours.

PHARMACY

Revco (✉ 303 E. Thompson La., ☎ 615/361–3636).

RADIO STATIONS

AM: WLAC 1510, news and talk. **FM:** WPLN 90.3, classical and jazz; WSIX 97.9, country; WSM 95, country.

Nashville Convention & Visitors Bureau (⊠ 161 4th Ave. N, ☎ 615/
259–4700), open weekdays 8–4:30. **Visitor Information Center** (⊠ I–
65 and James Robertson Pkwy., Exit 85, Nashville, ☎ 615/259–
4747), open Labor Day–Memorial Day, daily 9–5 and rest of year,
8–8.

EAST TENNESSEE

East Tennessee combines wholesome vacation ingredients much in the
way a skilled mountain cook creates a sumptuous down-home feast,
with bounty from forests, fields, ice-cold streams, and the family farm.
From the misty heights of the Great Smoky Mountains to the Holston,
French Broad, Nolichucky, and Tennessee rivers, this exquisitely beautiful part of the state beckons with a cornucopia of scenic grandeur
and recreational possibilities from hiking to white-water rafting. The
highest and most rugged elevations are in the Great Smoky Mountains
National Park, a cool and scenic retreat for those seeking relief from
the humidity of summer.

*Numbers in the margin correspond to points of interest on the East
Tennessee map.*

Oak Ridge

162 mi east of Nashville.

The famous "atomic city" was established secretly during World War
II. Some of the original installations here include the **Oak Ridge National Laboratory**, still involved in programs of nuclear fission and mag-
netic fusion energy; the **Graphite Reactor**, 10 mi southwest, now a
National Historic Landmark, with a display area open to the public;
and the **K-25 Visitors Overlook** for views of the **Oak Ridge Gaseous
Diffusion Plant**, where uranium is enriched for use in nuclear reactors.

The **American Museum of Science and Energy** focuses upon uses of nuclear, solar, and geothermal energy, mainly for peaceful purposes. Exhibits include hands-on experiments, demonstrations, and computer
games. A slide show furnishes valuable background on Oak Ridge and
the museum. ⊠ *300 S. Tulane Ave.,* ☎ *423/576–3200.* ▨ *Free.* ☉ *June–
Aug., daily 9–6; Sept.–May, daily 9–5.*

Golf
South Hills Golf Club (⊠ 795 Tuskegee Dr., ☎ 423/483–5747) has an
18-hole golf course open to the public.

Knoxville

46 *25 mi southeast of Oak Ridge.*

In 1786 Patriot General James White and a few pioneer settlers built
a fort beside the Tennessee River. A few years later, territorial Governor William Blount selected White's fort as capital of the newly formed
Territory of the United States South of the River Ohio and renamed
the settlement Knoxville after his long-time friend, Secretary of War
Henry Knox. It flourished from its beginning, and became the state capital when Tennessee was admitted to the Union in 1796.

Throughout the 20th century, Knoxville has been synonymous with
energy: The headquarters of the Tennessee Valley Authority, with its
vast complex of hydroelectric dams and impounded recreational lakes,

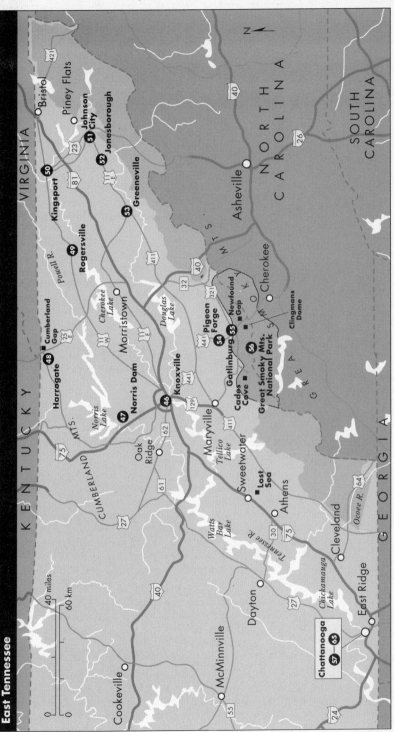

East Tennessee

is here, and during World War II, atomic energy was secretly developed at nearby Oak Ridge (☞ *above*). Today the University of Tennessee adds its own energy—both intellectual and cultural—to this dynamic city, while a new riverfront development, Volunteer Landing, is alive with shops, restaurants, and residential space.

At the **Governor William Blount Mansion,** a modest white-frame structure dating from 1792, the governor and his associates planned the admission of Tennessee as the 16th state in the Union. The home is furnished with original and period antiques, along with memorabilia of Blount's checkered career. A visitor center in the adjacent **Craighead-Jackson House,** built in 1818, presents an introductory slide program, museum exhibits, and a glass collection. ⊠ *200 W. Hill Ave.,* ☎ *423/525–2375.* ☟ *$4.* ☉ *Tues.–Fri. 9:30–4:30, Sun. 1–4:30, Sat. (Mar.–Oct.) 9:30–4:30.*

Different eras of Knoxville history are celebrated at **James White Fort** (⊠ *205 E. Hill Ave.,* ☎ *423/525–6514*), a series of seven log cabins with authentic furnishings and pioneer artifacts. Marble Springs, the summer home of John Sevier, Tennessee's first governor, is preserved at the **John Sevier Historical Site** (⊠ *1220 John Sevier Hwy.,* ☎ *423/573–5508*). The **Armstrong-Lockett House** (⊠ *2728 Kingston Pike,* ☎ *423/637–3163*), an elegant farm mansion dating from 1834, showcases American and British furniture, silver, and ornate appointments, along with terraces and fountains in Italianate gardens.

Mabry-Hazen House served as headquarters for both Confederate and Union forces during the Civil War. It was built by a prominent Knoxvillian, Joseph A. Mabry Jr., in 1858 and is now on the National Historic Register. ⊠ *1711 Dandridge Ave.,* ☎ *423/522–8661.* ☟ *$5.* ☉ *Weekdays 10–5, Sat. 1–5.*

The **McClung Museum,** on the University of Tennessee campus, has diverse collections in anthropology, natural history, geology, science, and fine arts. ⊠ *1327 Circle Park Dr.,* ☎ *423/974–2144.* ☟ *Free.* ☉ *Weekdays 9–5, Sat. 10–3, Sun. 2–5.*

The **Knoxville Museum of Art** is housed in a handsome $10.5 million, 52,000-square-ft structure at World's Fair Park. Designed by renowned museum architect Edward Larrabee Barnes, the four-level concrete-and-steel building is faced in Tennessee pink marble. The museum includes four exhibition galleries, an exploratory gallery for children, a great hall, an auditorium, a museum store, and outdoor sculpture and educational program gardens. ⊠ *World's Fair Park Dr.,* ☎ *423/525–6101.* ☟ *Free, except special exhibits.* ☉ *Tues. 10–9, Wed.–Sat. 10–5, Sun. noon–5.*

☺ The **East Tennessee Discovery Center and Akima Planetarium** contain pioneer tools and clothes, mounted animals, and fresh- and saltwater aquariums. Children love the hands-on and audiovisual exhibits. ⊠ *516 Beaman St., in Chilhowee Park,* ☎ *423/594–1480.* ☟ *$3.* ☉ *Museum weekdays 9–5, Sat. 1–5; planetarium show Sat. at 2:30.*

☺ Plan on a full day at the **Knoxville Zoological Park,** famous for breeding large-cat species and African elephants. Among the 1,100 animals are rare red pandas, wild creatures native to the African plains, polar bears, seals, and penguins. The working miniature steam train, elephant rides, and petting zoo will keep kids occupied for hours. Gorilla Valley, Cheetah Savanna, and Chimpanzee Ridge are among the best exhibits. ⊠ *In Chilhowee Park on Rutledge Pike S, 4½ mi east of I-40*

Exit 392, ☎ *423/637–5331.* 🎫 *$6.50.* ⊘ *Memorial Day–Labor Day, daily 9:30–6; Labor Day–Memorial Day, daily 10–4:30.*

Dining and Lodging

$$–$$$ ✕ **Regas Restaurant.** This cozy Knoxville classic, with fireplaces and
★ original art, has been around for 77 years. The specialty, prime rib, is carefully aged on the premises, baked very slowly all day, then sliced to order and served with creamy horseradish sauce. ⊠ *318 N. Gay St.,* ☎ *423/637–9805. AE, MC, V. No lunch Sat., no dinner Sun.*

$–$$$ ✕ **Copper Cellar/Cumberland Grill.** A favorite of the college crowd and young professionals, the original downstairs Copper Cellar has an intimate atmosphere with friendly service. Upstairs, the Cumberland Grill serves aged Colorado beef, fresh seafood, salads, sandwiches, and award-winning desserts. There's a children's menu and a lavish Sunday brunch. ⊠ *1807 Cumberland Ave., across from University of Tennessee campus,* ☎ *423/673–3411. AE, D, DC, MC, V.*

$ ✕ **Calhoun's.** Delicious barbecued ribs are served in a riverside setting at this sprawling rib-house across the street from the site of one of Knoxville's original hot spots, the long-gone Chisholm's Tavern of pioneer days. Calhoun's barbecued ribs are famous throughout the South, having taken more than one first-place cook-off ribbon. ⊠ *400 Neyland Dr.,* ☎ *423/673–3355. Reservations not accepted. AE, D, DC, MC, V.*

$$$$ 🏨 **Hyatt Regency Knoxville.** This is a handsome, contemporary adap-
★ tation of an Aztec pyramid atop a hill overlooking the Tennessee River, the city, and mountainous hinterlands. The eight-story skylit atrium lobby blends modern furnishings and art in Meso-American motifs with abundant flora and colorful accessories. Rooms, done in light woods and peach and blue pastels, have either windows or balconies that open to fresh breezes. ⊠ *500 Hill Ave. SE, Box 88, 37901,* ☎ *423/637– 1234 or 800/233–1234,* 🖷 *423/522–5911. 361 rooms, 26 suites. Coffee shop, dining room, sports bar, pool, exercise room, volleyball. AE, D, DC, MC, V.*

$$ 🏨 **La Quinta Motor Inn.** The rooms here are spacious and well lighted, with convenient working areas. ⊠ *258 N. Peters Rd., 37923,* ☎ *423/ 690–9777 or 800/531–5900,* 🖷 *423/531–8304. 130 rooms. Pool. AE, D, DC, MC, V.*

Golf

Whittle Springs Municipal Golf Course (⊠ 313 Valley View Dr., ☎ 423/ 525–1022) is an 18-hole golf course open to the public.

Nightlife and the Arts

The Old City, on the north side of downtown, is the site of Knoxville's most varied nightlife, with restaurants and clubs sharing space with the industries that have been in the warehouse district for decades. There is **Patrick Sullivan's** for saloon shenanigans (⊠ 100 N. Central Ave., ☎ 423/637–4255), and **Hooray's** (⊠ 106 S. Central Ave., ☎ 423/546– 6729), and the lounge at the **Orangery Restaurant** (⊠ The Orangery, 5412 Kingston Pike, ☎ 423/588–2964).

The **Knoxville Opera Company** (☎ 423/523–8712) sponsors New York Metropolitan Opera competitions each year, along with two locally produced operatic performances. The **Knoxville Symphony Orchestra** (☎ 423/523–1178) presents seven concerts a year, often with esteemed guest artists. **Lamar House Bijou Theater** in Knoxville (⊠ 803 S. Gay St., ☎ 423/522–0832) stages seasonal ballet, concerts, and plays.

Norris

25 mi northwest of Knoxville.

47 Scenic U.S. 441 leads to Norris, a delightful planned town built in 1933 as a workers' community during construction of the Tennessee Valley Authority's first dam. The **Norris Dam** spans the Clinch River and impounds a 72-mi-long lake and has a visitor lobby and two overlooks. Some of the best views, though, are from **Norris Dam State Park** (⊠ 1261 Norris Fwy., Lake City 37769, ☎ 423/426–7461), which has cabins and campsites. Also in Norris is the **Lenoir Museum,** where Native American, pioneer, Civil War, and regional historical artifacts are displayed. A restored country store and an 18th-century gristmill where you can purchase stone-ground cornmeal are on the grounds.

Norris's prime attraction is the **Museum of Appalachia,** where about 35 log structures—among them a molasses mill powered by mules—have been restored to reflect the hardscrabble life of the early mountaineers. More than 250,000 period furnishings and implements are in the buildings, and there is a working farm. Locals sometimes bring their musical instruments for an old-time hoedown. ⊠ *On TN 61, 1 mi east of I–75 Exit 122,* ☎ *423/494–7680.* ⌑ *$6.* ☉ *Daily 8–5; summer hrs vary.*

Outdoor Activities and Sports

At Norris Lake, there's seasonal angling for striped bass, walleye, white bass, and muskie, as well as boat launch ramps (but no rentals) at **Norris Dam State Resort Park** (⊠ 125 Village Green Circle, Lake City, ☎ 423/426–7461). Largemouth and white bass swim in Cherokee, Douglas, and Fort Loudon Lakes. Trout lovers do best at Tellico-Chilhowee Lakes, especially at night in April and May. Fly-fishing is popular in the Smokies' many streams.

Harrogate

48 *50 mi northeast of Norris.*

Harrogate, by the Virginia border, is home to **Lincoln Memorial University.** Founded in 1896, the school celebrates the Great Emancipator's principles and philosophies. **Lincoln Memorial Museum** contains the world's third-largest collection of Lincolniana. One of the most poignant exhibits is the ebony-and-silver cane Lincoln carried to Ford's Theatre in Washington, D.C., where he was assassinated. ⊠ *On Lincoln Memorial University campus, off U.S. 25E,* ☎ *423/869–6237.* ⌑ *$2.* ☉ *Weekdays 9–4, Sat. 11–4, Sun. 1–4.*

Rogersville

49 *45 mi southeast of Harrogate.*

Along U.S. 25E and 11W, Rogersville is a little hideaway East Tennessee town established in 1786. All of downtown is on the National Register of Historic Places, and it has both the oldest courthouse and inn in the state. A walking tour brochure, available throughout town, guides visitors past the various sites of interest.

Kingsport

50 *30 mi northeast of Rogersville.*

Founded in 1761, Kingsport is along U.S. 11W, surrounded by rolling hills, meadows, and woodlands. At **Exchange Place, Gaines-Preston Farm,** a restored pioneer homestead, craftspeople demonstrate their skills in commodious log houses. Their handmade quilts, baskets, wood carvings, ceramics, and stuffed dolls are sold in nearby shops. ✉ *4812 Orebank Rd.,* ☎ *423/288–6071.* ▢ *Free.* ☉ *Limited hrs; call ahead.*

Golf
Warrior's Path State Park Golf Course (✉ 1687 Fall Creek Rd., ☎ 423/ 323–4990) is open to the public.

Shopping
Iron Mountain Stoneware Plant. Hidden away in the northeastern corner of Tennessee and entirely surrounded by the Cherokee National Forest is the tiny village of Laurel Bloomery, the only place where the high-fired stoneware is made. It is also available through numerous retail outlets in the Appalachian Mountains. ✉ *TN 91, about 8 mi north of junction with U.S. 421,* ☎ *423/727–8888.* ☉ *Daily 8–5.*

Johnson City

51 *22 mi southeast of Kingsport.*

Reached via U.S. 23, Johnson City is an important center for agriculture, manufacturing, and education—it is home to **Washington College,** the oldest institution of higher education in the state, and **East Tennessee State University,** with more than 9,000 students. At **Tipton-Haynes Historic Site,** the 19th-century main house, granary, horse barn, and law office have been authentically restored. ✉ *4 mi south of U.S. 23, Exit 31, via University Pkwy. and S. Roan St.,* ☎ *423/926– 3631.* ▢ *$3.* ☉ *Weekdays 10–4:30.*

OFF THE BEATEN PATH

ROCKY MOUNT – This two-story log mansion, completed in 1772, was Governor William Blount's territorial capitol from 1790 until he moved to Knoxville two years later. Faithful restoration and careful selection of authentic furnishings testify to a simple yet eloquent pioneer lifestyle. Guides decked in period costumes take you through the kitchen, slave quarters, blacksmith shop, and a flax house where weaving is demonstrated. ✉ *4 mi northeast on U.S. 11E at Piney Flats, 200 Hyder Hill Rd.,* ☎ *423/538–7396.* ▢ *$5.* ☉ *Mon.–Sat. 10–5, Sun. 2–6; closed Dec. 21–Jan. 5, weekends Jan.–Feb.*

Jonesborough

52 *10 mi southwest of Johnson City.*

The state's oldest town beckons visitors to admire a trio of antebellum churches, lovely vintage houses, brick and wooden fretwork shops, and the courthouse, all dating from the late 1700s. During October's famous National Storytelling Festival, professional and amateur storytellers from throughout the world come for a weekend to spin their tales. At the **Visitor Center and History Museum** (✉ Just off U.S. 11E on Boone St., ☎ 423/753–1010), a slide show and local art exhibit describe the town's history.

Greenville

53 *25 mi southwest of Jonesborough.*

In 1826 a young Andrew Johnson (later 17th president of the United States) settled in Greenville, a town that had been founded in 1783. After his arduous trek over the mountains from North Carolina, Johnson opened a tailor shop and married. **Andrew Johnson National Historic Site** preserves his primitive tailor shop, the homestead where he lived from 1851 until his death in 1875, and his hilltop grave site, marked by an elaborate monument. Displays in the visitor center include notes he made at his impeachment trial. ⊠ *Depot and College Sts.,* ☎ *423/638–3551.* ▦ *Homestead $2.* ☉ *Daily 9–5.*

Pigeon Forge

⑤④ *25 mi southeast of Knoxville.*

Pigeon Forge, home of mountain native Dolly Parton's namesake theme park, Dollywood, has enough heavy-duty outlet shopping and kids' entertainment to keep families busy for a few days. But the intentionally corn-pone image can become wearing and fails to reflect the quiet folksiness of the Appalachian communities scattered throughout these parts. Pigeon Forge has 200 outlet specialty stores, crafts shops, country hoedown emporiums, and kid-friendly attractions that line the main thoroughfare for several miles.

Among family favorites is **Carbo's Smoky Mountain Police Museum,** housing police memorabilia such as badges, guns, and the car in which legendary West Tennessee sheriff Buford Pusser was killed in a traffic accident. ⊠ *3311 Parkway;* ☎ *423/453–1358.* ▦ *$5.50.* ☉ *Apr., weekends 10–5; May, Fri.–Wed. 10–5; June–Aug., daily 10–5; Sept.–Oct., Fri.–Wed. 10–5.*

The 1830s-era **Old Mill,** beside the Little Pigeon River, still grinds corn, wheat, and rye on water-powered stone wheels. Flour, meal, grits, and buckwheat are for sale. ⊠ *2944 Middle Creek Rd.,* ☎ *423/453–4628.* ☉ *Mon.–Sat. 8:30–6:30.*

★   **Dollywood,** Dolly Parton's popular theme park, embodies the country superstar's own flamboyance—plenty of Hollywood flash mixed with simple country charm that you either love or hate. This endeavor brings to life the folklore, fun, food, and music of the Great Smokies, which inspired many of Parton's early songs. In a re-created 1880 mountain village, scores of talented and friendly craftspeople demonstrate their artistry. Museum exhibits trace Parton's rise to stardom from her backwoods upbringing. There are many amusement rides, but music, of course, is the park's underpinning: Live shows are performed on the park's seven stages, and several times per season, Dolly shows up for a surprise appearance. The gala Harvest Celebration, held from October to early November, features the Smokies' only outdoor crafts festival as well as the Southern Gospel Jubilee. Smoky Mountain Christmas is the star attraction from mid-November through December. When hunger strikes, try Aunt Granny's Restaurant for down-home mountain cookery. ⊠ *1020 Dollywood La.,* ☎ *423/428–9488 or 800/365–5996.* ▦ *$22.10; free next day on tickets purchased after 3.* ☉ *3rd weekend of Apr.–mid-June, daily 9–6; extended hrs mid-June–mid Aug. and most weekends. Closed Thurs. May, Oct.; Tues., Thurs. Sept.; Mon., Tues., Wed. Nov., Dec.*

♻   **Ogle's Water Park.** This family park has a giant wave pool, a kiddie play area, 10 water slides, and miniature golf. ⊠ *2530 Parkway, Pigeon Forge,* ☎ *423/453–8044.* ▦ *$17.95.* ☉ *June–July, daily 10–8; Aug., daily 11–6; May and early Sept., weekends 11–6.*

Dining and Lodging

$ ✕ **Apple Tree Inn Restaurant.** A traditional East Tennessee menu is of-
★   fered here, including fried chicken and spoon bread, a regal soufflé of cornmeal, flour, eggs, buttermilk, and seasonings, served hot from the baking dish. Order family-style or individually in this very relaxed dining room. ⊠ *3215 Parkway,* ☎ *423/453–4961. Reservations not accepted. AE, MC, V. Closed Dec.–Feb.*

$$$ 🏨 **Best Western Plaza Inn.** Convenient to shops, restaurants, and attractions, the Best Western is a best bet for families. Rooms are spacious and well furnished, and some have refrigerators; some overlook mountain scenery, others an indoor swimming pool. ✉ *3755 Parkway, Box 926, 37868,* ☎ *423/453–5538 or 800/232–5656,* FAX *423/453–2619. 198 rooms, 2 suites. 1 indoor and 2 outdoor pools, wading pool, 2 hot tubs, 2 saunas, recreation room. AE, DC, MC, V.*

$$$ 🏨 **Grand Hotel.** This centrally located five-story inn features some ultramodern rooms with water beds and fireplaces. A few rooms even have large whirlpool tubs. ✉ *3171 Parkway, 37863,* ☎ *423/453–1000 or 800/362–1188,* FAX *423/453–0056. 415 rooms, 10 suites. Restaurant, pool, hot tub. AE, DC, MC, V.*

$$$ 🏨 **Holiday Inn.** This inn is in the middle of the action. Its vast Holidome Indoor Recreation Center has something for everyone in the family. Especially pleasant rooms and extra services are available on the concierge floor. ✉ *3230 Parkway, 37863,* ☎ *423/428–2700 or 800/782–3119,* FAX *423/428–2700. 204 rooms, 4 suites. Restaurant, indoor pool, hot tub, sauna, health club. AE, DC, MC, V.*

Nightlife and the Arts

From March through October, hearty chicken-and-ribs dinners are accompanied by a colorful, Western-themed musical show and rodeo at **Dixie Stampede** (✉ 3849 Parkway, ☎ 423/453–4400 or 800/356–1676). The **Music Mansion** (✉ 100 Music Rd., ☎ 423/428–7469) presents an electrifying country music variety show featuring Dollywood's award-winning James Rogers.

Shopping

Three centers offer factory outlet mall shopping in Pigeon Forge: **Belz Factory Outlet Mall** (✉ I–40, Exit 407 [TN66] to Sevierville and follow Hwy. 441 to Pigeon Forge, ☎ 423/453–7317); **Pigeon Forge Factory Outlet Mall** (✉ 2850 Parkway, ☎ 423/428–2828); and **Tanger Factory Outlet Center** (✉ David Rd. and Hwy. 441, ☎ 423/428–7001). **Five Oaks Factory Stores** (✉ Hwy. 66 to 441 South, ☎ 423/453–8401) is in Sevierville, a few miles north of Pigeon Forge.

For mountain crafts, stop in at **Pigeon Forge Pottery** (✉ 2919 Middle Creek Rd., Pigeon Forge, ☎ 423/453–3883), selling internationally esteemed tableware, vases, and bird and animal figurines.

Gatlinburg

55 *8 mi southeast of Pigeon Forge.*

Gateway city to Great Smoky Mountains National Park (☞ *below*), Gatlinburg, popular with honeymooners and families, has steadily expanded from a remote little place with a sprinkling of hotels, chalets, and mountain crafts shops to the sprawling network of minigolf courses and homemade-candy "shoppes" it is today. During the summer, the town is clogged with visitors, complete with the annoyances of traffic jams and packed restaurants. Nevertheless, set in the narrow valley of the Little Pigeon River—actually a turbulent mountain stream—Gatlinburg is Tennessee's premier mountain resort town.

With more than 400 specialty shops, this town is also a browsing mecca. Family attractions include a number of local trout farms, the **Gatlinburg Sky Lift** (☎ 423/436–4307), via which you can reach the top of Crockett Mountain; the **Guinness World Record Museum** (☎ 423/436–9100); and the **Ober Gatlinburg Tramway** (☎ 423/436–5423), which leads to a mountaintop amusement park, ski center, and shopping mall/crafts market. **Arrowmont School of Arts & Crafts** (✉ 556 Parkway St., ☎ 423/436–5860) is a nationally known visual arts complex.

Gatlinburg also hosts numerous festivals, the longest of which is the Smoky Mountain Lights which runs from November through February, when the town is decorated with more than 2 million lights.

Dining and Lodging

$$–$$$ ✗ **Burning Bush Restaurant.** Reproduction antique furnishings and ac-
★   cessories evoke a Colonial atmosphere. Broiled Tennessee quail and beef Rossini—an 8-ounce fillet served on an English muffin with Madeira sauce—are house specialties. Bountiful breakfasts are also offered. ⊠ *1151 Parkway,* ☎ *423/436–4669. AE, D, MC, V.*

$$–$$$ ✗ **Smoky Mountain Trout House.** Of the eight distinctive trout preparations to choose from at this cozy restaurant, an old favorite is trout Eisenhower: panfried, with cornmeal breading and bacon to flavor, and served with bacon-and-butter sauce and a side dish of mushrooms. Prime rib, country ham, and fried chicken are also on the menu. ⊠ *410 N. Parkway,* ☎ *423/436–5416. Reservations not accepted. AE, DC, MC, V. Closed Dec.–Mar. No lunch.*

$ ✗ **Ogle's Restaurant.** Indulge in bountiful feasting, either in the green-
★   and-beige dining room or on the patio, which extends over a turbulent mountain river. The buffet tables offer five choices of country-style meat, such as fried chicken, prime rib, country ham; five vegetables fresh from the farm; and 70 fixin's for your salad. Don't miss the sourwood honey. ⊠ *516 Parkway,* ☎ *423/436–4157. Reservations not accepted. MC, V.*

$ ✗ **Pancake Pantry.** This is a family favorite of repeat guests to the Smokies. Austrian apple-walnut pancakes covered with apple cider compote, black walnuts, apple slices, sweet spices, powdered sugar, and whipped cream are a house specialty. Other selections include waffles, omelets, sandwiches, soups, and fresh salads. Century-old brick, polished-oak paneling, rustic copper accessories, and spacious windows create a delightful ambience. Box lunches are available for mountain picnics. ⊠ *628 Parkway,* ☎ *423/436–4724. Reservations not accepted. No credit cards. No dinner.*

$$$$ 🏨 **Buckhorn Inn.** This small inn run by John and Connie Burns is set
★   on 40 acres of remote woodlands about 6 mi outside Gatlinburg. Guests—including seclusion-seeking diplomats, government officials, and celebrities—have been coming here for more than 40 years. The views of Mt. LeConte and the Great Smokies are spectacular, and the Great Smoky Arts and Crafts Community (☞ Shopping, *below*) is convenient to the inn. Inside, the country-inn atmosphere is reinforced by wicker rockers, paintings by local artists, a huge stone fireplace, and French doors that open onto a large stone porch. All rooms are spacious and some have king-size beds. Outstanding gourmet breakfasts and dinners are included in the rates; savor the home-baked breads, creamed soups, marinated beef tenderloin, and fruit tortes. A four-course dinner is available to guests and nonguests, by reservation. ⊠ *Off U.S. 321, 2140 Tudor Mountain Rd., 37738,* ☎ *423/436–4668. 6 rooms, 4 cottages. Restaurant, hiking, fishing. MC, V.*

$$$ 🏨 **Holiday Inn Resort Complex.** The hotel is near the Convention Cen-
★   ter and the aerial tramway, which in winter whisks ski addicts to the snowy slopes at Ober Gatlinburg. The adjacent Holidome Indoor Recreation Center has a pool and a spacious atrium. ⊠ *520 Airport Rd., 37738,* ☎ *423/436–9201 or 800/465–4329,* ⅧX *423/436–7974. 395 rooms, 7 suites. Coffee shop, dining room, lounge, 2 indoor pools, outdoor pool, hot tub, 2 saunas, putting green, nightclub, meeting rooms. AE, D, DC, MC, V.*

$$–$$$ 🏨 **Best Western Twin Islands Motel.** In the center of Gatlinburg, beside the surging Little Pigeon River, this motel is notable for its low-key contemporary architectural style. All rooms have balconies overlooking the river. Kitchenette units are also available. ⊠ *U.S. 441, Box 648, 37738,* ☎ *423/436–5121 or 800/223–9299,* ⅂⅄ᴷ *423/436–6208. 97 rooms, 10 suites. Restaurant, pool, fishing, playground. AE, DC, MC, V.*

$$–$$$ 🏨 **Park Vista Hotel.** This large hotel on a mountain ledge has modern, lavishly decorated public areas and large, elegantly appointed guest rooms, each with a balcony overlooking colorful gardens, the town of Gatlinburg, the Little Pigeon River, and the mountains beyond. Nonetheless, this white, semicircular contemporary tower, though handsome, is a jarring sight in the Great Smoky Mountains. ⊠ *Airport Rd. at Cherokee Orchard Rd., Box 30, 37738,* ☎ *423/436–9211 or 800/421–7275,* ⅂⅄ᴷ *423/436–5141. 306 rooms, 6 suites. Restaurant, lounge, piano bar, indoor pool, wading pool, hot tub, 2 saunas, meeting rooms. AE, DC, MC, V.*

$$–$$$ 🏨 **Rainbow Motel.** This small, neat, and well-maintained lodging is a pleasant choice for budget-minded vacationers. ⊠ *390 E. Parkway (3 blocks east of U.S. 441), Box 1397, 37738,* ☎ *423/436–5887 or 800/ 422–8922. 41 rooms, 1 efficiency, 2 2-bedroom units. Pool. D, MC, V.*

Golf

Bent Creek Mountain Inn and Country Club (⊠ 3919 E. Parkway, ☎ 423/436–3947) is open to the public.

Nightlife and the Arts

Take the aerial tramway from downtown to Ober Gatlinburg's **Old Heidelberg Restaurant** (☎ 423/430–3094), where there's dancing to DJ-selected rock and roll. Live entertainment and dancing takes place in the lounge at **Sade and Dora's** (⊠ 520 Airport Rd., ☎ 423/436–9201) in the Holiday Inn Resort Complex. Live country can be heard at the Spirits' Lounge in the **Edgewater Hotel** (⊠ 402 River Rd., ☎ 423/436–4151). **Sweet Fanny Adams Theatre and Music Hall** (⊠ 461 Parkway, ☎ 423/436–4038) stages original musical comedies, Gay '90s revues, and old-fashioned sing-alongs.

Shopping

The mountain towns of East Tennessee are known for Appalachian folk crafts, especially wood carvings, corn-husk dolls, pottery, dulcimers, and beautiful handmade quilts. These crafts can be found in shops throughout the state, but a major concentration of them is at the **Great Smoky Arts and Crafts Community,** a collection of 80 shops and craftspersons' studios along 8 mi of rambling country road. Begun in 1937, the community includes workers in leather, pottery, weaving, hand-wrought pewter, stained glass, quilt making, hand carving, marquetry, and more. Everything sold here is made on the premises by the community members. Also here are two restaurants and the popular Wild Plum Tearoom. ⊠ *Off U.S. 321, 3 mi east of Gatlinburg,* ☎ *423/430–5925. For more information:* ⊠ *Box 807, Gatlinburg 37738.*

Great Smoky Mountains National Park

★ 🅰 *45 mi from Knoxville.*

At Great Smoky Mountains National Park, the southern Appalachians reach their ultimate grandeur as 16 peaks soar more than 6,000 ft. Fall brings an unparalleled fiesta of colors to these mountains, and in the early springtime wild azaleas and rhododendron lace the mountainsides with delicate pinks, lavenders, and whites. No wonder hikers, campers, and boaters flock to this park.

From Gatlinburg (☞ *above*), the northern gateway to the park, drive south along the scenic Newfound Gap Road (U.S. 441) to the Sugarlands Visitor Center at park headquarters, where informative films, exhibits, maps, and brochures will fill you in about the park. Driving along on the Newfound Gap Road, stop often at scenic overlooks, perhaps taking time to explore one or more of the nature trails that lead off from many of them. The road ascends to **Newfound Gap** on the Tennessee–North Carolina border, a haunting viewpoint. From here, a 7-mi spur road leads to **Clingmans Dome**—at 6,643 ft, the highest point in Tennessee—where you can walk up a spiral pathway to an observation tower for panoramic views of the Smokies. Autumn is the favorite season for the spectacular foliage.

Cades Cove is at the junction of U.S. 321 and TN 73. This isolated mountain valley, with its 19th-century farmhouses, barns, churches, and an old gristmill still in operation, is one of the region's best attractions. Drive through on the loop road or walk the grounds for a better feel for the area. From spring through autumn, special park ranger programs and demonstrations describe the pioneer agriculture, crafts, and folkways in the Cove. At the old gristmill—open April 5 through October, daily 9:30–5—you can take a tour and purchase stone-ground cornmeal that produces the feather-light corn bread found in country restaurants. For a deep-forest drive, take Parson Branch Road, a quiet, one-way trek out of the park to U.S. 129. The Foothills Parkway will get you back into the park. ⊠ *107 Park Headquarters Rd., Gatlinburg,* ☎ *423/436–1200.* ⊙ *Apr.–May and Sept.–Oct., daily 8–6; June–Aug., daily 8–7; Nov.–Mar., daily 8–4:30.*

Outdoor Activities and Sports

HIKING

An unusually elevated and scenic portion of the **Appalachian Trail** runs along high ridges in the Great Smoky Mountains National Park. The Trail can be easily reached at Newfound Gap from U.S. 441.

HORSEBACK RIDING

McCarter's Riding Stables (☎ 423/436–5354) arranges guided horseback riding in Great Smoky Mountains National Park from March through October.

RAFTING

Rafting in the Smokies (☎ 423/436–5008) offers guided white-water raft trips from April through October.

En Route   Driving between Great Smoky Mountains National Park and Chattanooga along U.S. 321, U.S. 411, or TN 68 will give travelers a chance to visit the **Lost Sea,** outside Sweetwater, where you can explore a 41½-acre underground lake by glass-bottom boat. ☎ *423/337–6616.* ☞ *$9.* ⊙ *Nov.–Feb., daily 9–5; Mar.–Apr., daily 9–6; May–June and Aug., daily 9–7; July, daily 9–8; Sept.–Oct., daily 9–6.*

East Tennessee A to Z

Arriving, Departing, and Getting Around

BY BUS
Greyhound Bus Lines (☎ 800/231–2222) has a station in Knoxville.

BY CAR
I–75 runs north–south from Kentucky through Knoxville, then to Chattanooga, where it enters Georgia. I–81 enters East Tennessee from Virginia at Bristol and continues southwest until it ends at the junction with I–40 northeast of Knoxville. I–40 enters from North Carolina,

traces a northwesterly course to Knoxville, then heads west. U.S. 11 joins Chattanooga with Knoxville.

BY PLANE

Knoxville Airport (☎ 423/970–2773), 12 mi from downtown, is served by American Eagle, ComAir, Delta, Northwest, Trans World Express, United/United Express, and US Airways.

Contacts and Resources

ACCOMMODATIONS

For reservations at hotels, motels, chalets, and condominiums throughout the Great Smoky Mountains area, contact **Smoky Mountain Accommodations Reservation Service** (⊠ 526 E. Parkway, Suite 1, Gatlinburg 37738, ☎ 423/436–9700 or 800/231–2230).

EMERGENCIES

Dial 911 for **police** and **ambulance.** Medical assistance is available in Knoxville at **Baptist Hospital** (⊠ 137 Blount Ave., ☎ 423/632–5011).

GUIDED TOURS

Knoxville Tours, Inc. (☎ 423/688–6232) offers local and area tours, with pickup at Knoxville Quality Inn West (⊠ 7621 Kingston Pike). **Smoky Mountain Tour Connection** (☎ 423/436–2108) in Gatlinburg has native guides for tours in the Smokies. Self-guided-tour maps and brochures are available at many local visitor information centers. In Pigeon Forge, **Smoky Mountain Tours and Pigeon River Bus Line** (☎ 423/453–0864) offer guided tours to Cades Cove, Cherokee (NC), Roaring Fork Motor Nature Trail, and out-of-the-way places in the Great Smoky Mountains.

Step aboard the *Star of Knoxville* (⊠ Neyland Dr., Knoxville, ☎ 423/522–4630) for views of an especially scenic portion of the Tennessee River. One-and-a-half-hour sightseeing excursions as well as lunch and dinner cruises are offered daily April–December.

PHARMACIES

The **Kroger Pharmacy** in Knoxville (⊠ 2217 N. Broadway, ☎ 615/525–4629) is open 24 hours.

RADIO STATIONS

FM: WDEF 92.3, contemporary easy listening; WUSY 101.7, country; WIVK 107.7, country; WMYU 102.1, adult contemporary.

VISITOR INFORMATION

Gatlinburg Convention and Visitors Bureau (⊠ Box 527, Gatlinburg 37738, ☎ 800/822–1998). **Northeast Tennessee Tourism Association** (⊠ Box 415, Jonesborough 37659, ☎ 423/753–4188); open weekdays 8–5. **Knoxville Area Convention and Visitors Bureau** (⊠ 810 Clinch Ave., Box 15012, Knoxville 37901, ☎ 423/523–7263 or 800/727–8045); open daily 8:30–5. **Pigeon Forge Chamber of Commerce** (⊠ Box 1278, Pigeon Forge 37868, ☎ 423/453–5700 or 800/221–9858); open weekdays 8–5, Saturday 8–8. **Rogersville Chamber of Commerce** (⊠ 415 S. Depot, Rogersville 37857, ☎ 423/272–2186); open weekdays 9–4.

CHATTANOOGA

Chattanooga is an up-and-coming river and railroad town with an intriguing past. In less than a decade, Chattanooga has transformed itself from a polluted city struggling to clean up its outmoded industries to a bright, revitalized community that's a model for any small city looking to reinvent itself. Chattanooga's Tennessee Aquarium, the world's largest freshwater aquarium, is a must-see.

Only 12 years ago, Chattanooga ranked among the nation's worst in air pollution. Civic pride and unity (as well as an $850 million downtown revitalization effort) have transformed the ragged downtown area into one of the southeast's most vibrant communities. A rich Civil War history, a verdant mountainous countryside, and the presence of such unabashedly hokey, but popular, tourist attractions as Rock City Gardens and Ruby Falls laid the promising foundation for the city's comeback. City leaders set forth an ambitious program in the mid-1980s to take back Chattanooga: Industry was told to shape up or ship out, and indeed, many factories left—the jobs they took with them were gradually replaced with more service-oriented positions. The 1996 summer Olympics in Atlanta, just two hours away, continued to bolster Chattanooga's progress: The nearby Ocoee River hosted the canoe and kayaking events.

Exploring Chattanooga

Numbers in the text correspond to numbers in the margin and on the Chattanooga map.

A Good Walk and Drive

The **Tennessee Aquarium** ⑤⑦ and the **Creative Discovery Museum** ⑤⑧, both ideal for children, sit on **Ross's Landing Park and Plaza,** a good place from which to start the walking portion of this tour. Nearby is the Bluffview Arts District, home to the **Hunter Museum of Art** ⑤⑨ and **Houston Museum of Decorative Art.** The **Walnut Street Bridge** ⑥⓪ offers pedestrians a chance to sit and rest or to walk and cycle above the Tennessee River. A bit farther away, but within walking distance, is the famed **Chattanooga Choo-Choo** ⑥① and **Warehouse Row,** home to designer outlet stores.

Chattanooga's remaining attractions are clustered near **Lookout Mountain,** where most of the terrain isn't ideal for walking. Drive instead, starting at the **Battles for Chattanooga Museum** ⑥③. From there, it's a short hop to **Incline Railway** and **Point Park,** and not much farther to **Ruby Falls** ⑥②. Cross the Tennessee State line into Georgia for some old-fashioned fun at **Rock City Gardens** ⑥④ and a history lesson at **Chickamauga/Chattanooga National Military Park** ⑥⑤.

TIMING

Allow half a day, longer if you want shop, to complete the walking tour. Expect a long wait at the Tennessee Aquarium during the summer months. You might try going late in the afternoon to avoid the crowds. You won't be able to cover Lookout Mountain in a day, so it's best pick and choose between its sights before you arrive.

Sights to See

⑥③ **Battles for Chattanooga Museum.** A kitschy, dioramic rendering of Chattanooga's Civil War history can be reached by going south on Broad Street and bearing left onto Route 58. ✉ *1110 E. Brow Rd.,* ☎ *423/ 821–2812.* 🖼 *$4.* ☉ *June–Labor Day, daily 8:30–8:30; Labor Day–May, daily 9–5.*

⑥① **Chattanooga Choo-Choo.** Chattanooga's turn-of-the-century Terminal Station, immortalized by Glen Miller, is now a Holiday Inn (☞ Lodging, *below*). Nevertheless it's still one of the area's best-loved attractions. Stop by if only to see the elegant lobby under the original 85-ft freestanding dome which appears much as it did before trains stopped chugging into the terminal in 1973. Though the dining room has a sense of grandeur about it, the food is merely standard. Save your appetite and explore the renovated train cars and a small but fascinating model railroad. ✉ *1400 Market St.,* ☎ *423/266–5000.*

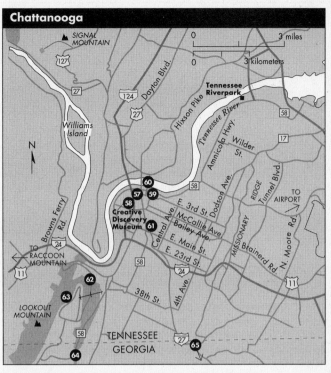

★ ⑥⑤ **Chickamauga/Chattanooga National Military Park.** The 1863 battles
for Chattanooga were some of the most violent ever fought—and they
were a major turning point in the war. At this battlefield, apart from
taking advantage of miles of hiking trails and acres of scenic beauty,
you can explore an extensive gun museum and watch an ingenious audiovisual presentation on the battles. ✉ *U.S. 27, Fort Oglethorpe, GA,*
☎ *706/866–9241.* ✆ *Free.* ☼ *Memorial Day–Labor Day, daily sunrise–sunset; rest of yr, daily 8–4:45.*

⑤⑧ **Creative Discovery Museum.** Hands-on activities, including an artist's
studio, a musician's workshop, and a scientist's lab, have been bringing out the kid in visitors of all ages for three years. ✉ *321 Chestnut
St., 37402,* ☎ *423/756–2738.* ✆ *$7.75.* ☼ *May–Aug., daily 10–5;
Sept.–Apr., Tues.–Sun. 10–5.*

OFF THE
BEATEN PATH

DAYTON – A 36-mi drive north along U.S. 27 from Chattanooga, this
small town was the site of the famous Scopes "Monkey Trial" in 1925.
The room where the trial took place has been preserved at the **Rhea
County Courthouse.** There is also a small museum with displays about
the trial. ✉ *1475 New Market St.,* ☎ *423/775–7801.* ✆ *Free.* ☼
Mon.–Thurs. 8–4, Fri. 8–5:30.

⑤⑨ **Hunter Museum of Art.** In a restored Classical Revival mansion, the
Hunter Museum, part of the Bluffview Arts District, houses an eclectic collection of mostly American painting, photography, and sculpture. ✉ *10 Bluff View,* ☎ *423/267–0968.* ✆ *$5.* ☼ *Tues.–Sat.
10–4:30, Sun. 1–4:30.*

Houston Museum of Decorative Art. This Victorian home, in the
Bluffview Arts District, is packed to the rafters with American decorative arts. The emphasis is on glassware, but of particular note are
the museum's collection of blue Staffordshire and English lusterware

china. ⊠ *201 High St.,* ☎ *423/267–7176.* 🖼 *$4.50.* ⊙ *Mon.–Sat. 9:30–4.*

Incline Railway. The steepest passenger railway in the world, at a grade of 72.7 degrees, Incline Railway seems to defy gravity as its tracks cut a swath straight up Lookout Mountain (☞ *below*). The view is spectacular, but the faint of heart may opt to drive to the top instead. ⊠ *827 E. Brow Rd., Lookout Mountain,* ☎ *423/821–4224.* 🖼 *$6.* ⊙ *Labor Day–Memorial Day, daily 8:30 AM–9:40 PM; trains run every 15–20 mins.*

★ **Lookout Mountain.** Chattanooga's poshest homes sit atop Lookout Mountain. Walk around the neighborhood, being sure to stop by the small museum and bookshop focusing on Lookout Mountain's history. Plan to visit ☞ **Point Park,** and ☞ **Rock City Gardens.** Though Lookout Mountain can be reached by car, ☞ **Incline Railway** is a thrilling alternative.

Point Park. This breezy, wooded promontory, atop Lookout Mountain (☞ *above*), affords sweeping views of the outlying region. Markers remind of the Union soldiers who scrambled up the craggy mountainside in a mad effort to escape the relentless showers of Confederate bullets.

🄓 **Rock City Gardens.** At one time, more than 900 barns throughout the southeastern United States were emblazoned with the words: "See Rock City." Only a few such remain, but visitors still come here year-round. This craggy tribute to fairy tales and geology, just over the Tennessee state line in Georgia, was begun in 1932 as a small network of paths and trails. The project grew through the years, as hand-painted exhibits depicting the tales of Mother Goose and Little Red Riding Hood were gradually added. Walt Disney even consulted with Rock City's founders before designing his own magical kingdom. The garden's position high atop Lookout Mountain (☞ *above*) provides views for hundreds of miles. ⊠ *1400 Patten Rd., Lookout Mountain, GA,* ☎ *706/820–2531.* 🖼 *$7.95.* ⊙ *Daily 8:30–sunset.*

Ross's Landing Park and Plaza. This complex combines the ☞ **Creative Discovery Museum,** the ☞ **Tennessee Aquarium,** and an Imax Theater in a collaborative effort among world-class architects, artists, and landscape designers to provide an open-air retrospective of Chattanooga's long history as the starting point for the infamous Trail of Tears, the site of key Civil War battles, and a major railroad town.

🄑 **Ruby Falls.** There are two elements to these falls: Above ground is a restaurant, souvenir shops, lookout tower, and children's playground, all predictably contained within one castlelike structure. Inside, an elevator whisks groups of visitors several hundred feet below to a natural cave that leads ½ mi to the deepest and highest underground waterfall (145 ft) in America. ⊠ *Lookout Mountain Scenic Hwy.,* ☎ *423/821–2544.* 🖼 *$8.50.* ⊙ *Memorial Day–Labor Day, daily 8 AM–9 PM; Sept.–Oct. and Apr.–May, daily 8–8; Nov.–Mar., daily 8–6.*

★ 🄕 **Tennessee Aquarium.** In 1992 the opening of the largest freshwater facility of its kind capped the city's miraculous recovery, drawing more than a million visitors within its first six months. Chattanooga *is* river country, and this 130,000-square-ft monument to the Tennessee River tells the story. You'll see the 60-pound catfish that prowl the Tennessee and the small, mysterious fish inhabiting Japan's Shimanto River. This world-class aquarium lets visitors view the inhabitants behind glass in a spectacular 60-ft canyon with two living forests and 22 tanks. "Rivers of the World" presents the flora and fauna of six freshwater rivers, from the St. Lawrence to the Zaire. You can also walk inside a replica of a hardwood forest, explore several levels of the Tennessee River, and learn about the formation of the Mississippi River. Designed by the Cambridge Seven Associates, who created Baltimore's National Aquarium, this contemporary riverside structure, crowned with four glass rooftop pyramids, looms oddly above Chattanooga's low, sprawling skyline. ⊠ *1 Broad St.,* ☎ *423/265–0695.* ⊑ *$9.75.* ☉ *Daily 10–6, until 8 on summer weekends.*

☙ **Tennessee Valley Railroad.** Ride the rails of the largest historic railroad still operating in the South aboard a steam locomotive or diesel trains dating from World War II. Children love the train museum on premises. ⊠ *4119 Cromwell Rd., Chattanooga,* ☎ *423/894–8028.* ⊑ *$8.* ☉ *May–Labor Day, Mon.–Sat. 10–5, Sun. noon–5; Apr. and Sept.–Nov., Sat. 10–5.*

⑥⓪ **Walnut Street Bridge.** A promenade connects Ross's Landing Park and Plaza (☞ *above*) to the restored Walnut Street Bridge, the longest pedestrian bridge in the world. In 1978 the bridge was slated for eventual demolition and closed to traffic. But a 15-year struggle to save the bridge by Chattanooga's tenacious preservationists culminated happily with its reopening, as a pedestrian bridge, on May 1, 1993. Thousands gathered to see the completely renovated structure, which, in 1991, had been added to the National Register of Historic Places. Built in 1891, this 2,370-ft truss bridge spans the murky Tennessee River. Architect Garnet Chapin, who hails from Chattanooga and oversaw the restoration of the Statue of Liberty and Ellis Island, managed the project.

Dining

$$$–$$$$ ✗ **Southside Grill.** This downtown neighborhood restaurant reinterprets the food of the region with a gourmet touch. Hardwood floors offset the dark paneled walls which are hung with fine art. Grilled Portobello mushrooms with lobster relish and creamy grits, and grilled rib eye with crawfish cakes and chilled leek soup are just two of the many grilled selections. ⊠ *1400 Cowart St.,* ☎ *423/266–9211. AE, D, DC, MC, V.*

$$–$$$ ✗ **212 Market.** This terrific restaurant near the Tennessee Aquarium
★ (☞ Sights to See, *above*) serves New American cuisine, with an emphasis on healthy fare; the Taylor River enchilada has fresh spinach, black beans, cheeses, and salsa, and the poached salmon is in a tart ginger-lime sauce. For an excellent starter, try the vegetable terrine, served with a sauce *verte* (a green concoction of parsley or basil). The cavernous, contemporary dining room is bright and unpretentious. The food is served on colorful Fiestaware. ⊠ *212 Market St.,* ☎ *423/265–1212. AE, MC, V. No dinner Sun.*

$ ✗ **Big River Grille & Brewing Works.** You can watch the brewing process through a soaring glass wall beside the bar of this restored trolley warehouse, handsomely designed with high ceilings, exposed brick walls, and hardwood floors. Order the sampler for a taste of this microbrewery's four different concoctions. The sandwiches and salads are generous and tasty. ⊠ *222 Broad St.,* ☎ *423/267–2739. Reservations not accepted. AE, D, DC, MC, V.*

Lodging

$$–$$$ ⊞ **Bluff View Inn.** Painstakingly restored and tastefully decorated with
★ 18th-century English antiques and art, this Colonial Revival mansion was built in 1928 on a bluff overlooking the Tennessee River. On the Riverwalk promenade, the River Gallery Outdoor Sculpture Garden is beside the inn, and the Tennessee Aquarium is within easy walking

distance. There are also rooms in two other turn-of-the-century mansions; a complimentary gourmet breakfast is made to order. ⊠ *412 E. 2nd St., 37403,* ☎ *423/265–5033,* FAX *423/265–5944. 13 rooms, 3 suites. Restaurant, café. D, MC, V.*

$$–$$$ 🏨 **Chattanooga Choo-Choo Holiday Inn.** This hotel adjoins the showcase 1905 Southern Railway Terminal, one of the first to be salvaged in the South. It's been renewed with restaurants, lounges, shops, exhibits, well-groomed gardens, and an operating trolley. Children delight in exploring the trains parked on the tracks. Guest rooms are nicely appointed, especially the restored Victorian parlor cars—replete with the heavy brocade and red upholstery ubiquitous in the late 1800s—converted to overnight berths. ⊠ *1400 Market St., 37402,* ☎ *423/266–5000 or 800/465–4329,* FAX *423/265–4635. 303 rooms, 10 suites, 48 railcars. 5 restaurants, lounge, indoor pool, 2 outdoor pools, 2 hot tubs, 3 tennis courts. AE, D, DC, MC, V.*

$$–$$$ 🏨 **Marriott at the Convention Center.** This 16-floor convention hotel, the town's largest, is clean and convenient to such downtown attractions as the Tennessee Aquarium and the tony Warehouse outlet shops. Rooms are spacious, and those on the higher floors have a great view of either the Tennessee River or Lookout Mountain. Adjacent to the city's Convention Center, this hotel is the choice of many business travelers, but families will appreciate its baby-sitting service and well-appointed health club. ⊠ *2 Carter Plaza, 37402,* ☎ *423/756–0002 or 800/841–1674,* FAX *423/266–2254. 327 rooms, 16 suites. 2 restaurants, 2 lounges, indoor pool, outdoor pool, health club, laundry service, airport shuttle. AE, D, DC, MC, V.*

$$–$$$ 🏨 **Radisson Read House—A Plaza Hotel.** The Georgian-style Read House dates from the 1920s and has been restored to the original grandeur that drew heads of state to lodge here in its heyday. The lobby has a large archway, stately columns, and polished walnut panels. Mailboxes from the days when guests stayed for months still neatly line one passageway. Guest rooms in the main hotel continue the Georgian motif; rooms in the annex are more contemporary. ⊠ *827 Broad St., 37402,* ☎ *423/266–4121 or 800/333–3333,* FAX *423/267–6447. 140 rooms, 100 suites. Restaurant, coffee shop, dining room, lounge, pool, sauna, hot tub. AE, DC, MC, V.*

$ 🏨 **Econo Lodge East Ridge.** Rooms are spacious, contemporary in style, clean, and well maintained. ⊠ *1417 St. Thomas St., 37412,* ☎ *423/894–1417 or 800/446–6900. 89 rooms. Restaurant, pool. AE, D, DC, MC, V.*

Nightlife and the Arts

Nightlife

At **Sandbar** (⊠ 1011 Riverside Dr., ☎ 423/622–4432), you'll find Monday's Traveling Riverside Blues Caravan, weekend rock and roll, and special events on Sunday or Wednesday.

The Arts

The **Tivoli Theater** (⊠ 399 McCallie Ave., ☎ 423/757–5042) stages concerts and operas. Throughout the summer free concerts from blues to Celtic play on **Miller Plaza** (⊠ 850 Market St., ☎ 423/265–0771). The **Chattanooga Little Theatre** (⊠ 400 River St., ☎ 423/267–8534) stages 32 productions a year. The **Backstage Playhouse** (⊠ 3264 Branaerd St., ☎ 423/629–1565) is a weekend dinner theater.

Festivals

Chattanooga's mid-June **Riverbend Festival** (☎ 423/265–4112) brings a different slate of entertainers to town for each of nine days and nights. A $15 pin is good for admission to all the 100 or so acts.

Outdoor Activities and Sports

Canoeing and Rafting

The Ocoee River, site of the 1996 Olympic kayaking events, has powerful rapids in the Class III and IV categories. **Cripple Creek Expeditions** (☎ 423/338–8441), open April–October, offers canoe rentals and guided raft trips down the Ocoee's wild waters. The Sequatchie River is a gentler river suitable for year-round floating; try **Canoe the Sequatchie** (☎ 423/949–4400), April–October, for equipment. **Hiwassee Outfitters** (☎ 423/338–8115), open mid-March–early November, in Reliance has canoes, rafts, tubes, and funyaks for beginners and intermediates; the nearby Hiwassee has occasional rapids.

Golf

Brainerd Golf Course (✉ 5203 Old Mission Rd., ☎ 423/855–2692) is open to the public.

Hiking

Tennessee Riverpark (✉ 4301 Amnicola Hwy., ☎ 423/842–0177) is phase one of a 22-mi development.

Shopping

Warehouse Row (✉ 12th and Market Sts., ☎ 423/267–1111) yields some of the best buys in the region (*Woman's Day* named it one of the top five outlet malls in the nation). More than 45 shops, from Ellen Tracy to Perry Ellis to Van Heusen, are ensconced in several restored, redbrick buildings in the heart of the town's historic district.

Chattanooga A to Z

Arriving and Departing

BY BUS

Greyhound Bus Lines (☎ 800/231–2222) has a terminal in Chattanooga.

BY CAR

I–75 runs north–south from Kentucky through Chattanooga and on to Georgia. U.S. 11 joins Chattanooga with Knoxville.

BY PLANE

The **Chattanooga Airport** (☎ 423/855–2200), 8 mi from downtown, is served by American Eagle, Atlantic Southeast, ComAir, Delta, Northwest Airlink, and US Airways.

Getting Around

BY BUS

Carta (☎ 423/629–1473), a free downtown shuttle on quiet and pollution-free electric buses, transports visitors between the Chattanooga Choo-Choo Hotel and the Tennessee Aquarium with stops at all points in between.

Contacts and Resources

EMERGENCIES

Dial 911 for **police** and **ambulance.** Medical assistance is available in Chattanooga at **Erlanger Medical Center** (✉ 975 E. 3rd St., ☎ 423/778–7000).

PHARMACIES

Eckerds (✉ 3532 Brainerd Rd., ☎ 615/629–7323).

VISITOR INFORMATION

Chattanooga Area Convention and Visitors Bureau (✉ 2 Broad St., 37402, ☎ 423/756–8687 or 800/322–3344); open daily 8:30–5:30.

TENNESSEE A TO Z

Arriving and Departing

By Bus
Greyhound (☎ 800/231–2222) links most cities in Tennessee.

By Car
The state's main east–west artery is I–40. I–55 runs north–south in West Tennessee. In Middle Tennessee, I–65 and I–24 cross in Nashville. I–75 links Chattanooga to Knoxville in East Tennessee. I–81 runs from just east of Knoxville through upper east Tennessee.

By Plane
Most visitors use **Memphis International Airport** (☎ 901/544–3495) or **Metropolitan Nashville Airport** (☎ 615/275–1675).

Getting Around

By Car
The speed limit on interstate highways is 65 mph unless otherwise posted. Right turns on red lights are allowed unless a sign indicates otherwise. Scenic highways within Tennessee are marked by a mockingbird sign above the sign giving the route number.

By Train
Amtrak (☎ 800/873–7245) serves most Tennessee communities.

Contacts and Resources

B&B Reservation Services
Tennessee Bed & Breakfast Innkeepers' Association (✉ Box 120428, Nashville 37212, ☎ 423/321–5482 or 800/820–8144); **Bed & Breakfast Adventures** (✉ Box 150586, Nashville, TN 37215, ☎ 615/383–6611 or 800/947–7404); **Bed & Breakfast Host Homes of Tennessee** (✉ Box 110227, Nashville, TN 37222, ☎ 615/331–5244 or 800/458–2421).

Emergencies
In towns and cities, dial 911 for **police** or **ambulance.** Cellular calls to the Highway Patrol are free by dialing *THP (*847).

Visitor Information
To request brochures, call 800/836–6200. Contact the **Tennessee Department of Tourist Development** (✉ 320 6th Ave. N, Nashville, TN 37243, ☎ 615/741–2159).

INDEX

Fodor's Travel Publications

Available at bookstores everywhere, or call 1–800–533–6478, 24 hours a day.

Gold Guides

U.S.

Alaska

Arizona

Boston

California

Cape Cod, Martha's Vineyard, Nantucket

The Carolinas & Georgia

Chicago

Colorado

Florida

Hawai'i

Las Vegas, Reno, Tahoe

Los Angeles

Maine, Vermont, New Hampshire

Maui & Lāna'i

Miami & the Keys

New England

New Orleans

New York City

Pacific North Coast

Philadelphia & the Pennsylvania Dutch Country

The Rockies

San Diego

San Francisco

Santa Fe, Taos, Albuquerque

Seattle & Vancouver

The South

U.S. & British Virgin Islands

USA

Virginia & Maryland

Walt Disney World, Universal Studios and Orlando

Washington, D.C.

Foreign

Australia

Austria

The Bahamas

Belize & Guatemala

Bermuda

Canada

Cancún, Cozumel, Yucatán Peninsula

Caribbean

China

Costa Rica

Cuba

The Czech Republic & Slovakia

Eastern & Central Europe

Europe

Florence, Tuscany & Umbria

France

Germany

Great Britain

Greece

Hong Kong

India

Ireland

Israel

Italy

Japan

London

Madrid & Barcelona

Mexico

Montréal & Québec City

Moscow, St. Petersburg, Kiev

The Netherlands, Belgium & Luxembourg

New Zealand

Norway

Nova Scotia, New Brunswick, Prince Edward Island

Paris

Portugal

Provence & the Riviera

Scandinavia

Scotland

Singapore

South Africa

South America

Southeast Asia

Spain

Sweden

Switzerland

Thailand

Toronto

Turkey

Vienna & the Danube Valley

Special-Interest Guides

Adventures to Imagine

Alaska Ports of Call

Ballpark Vacations

Caribbean Ports of Call

The Complete Guide to America's National Parks

Disney Like a Pro

Europe Ports of Call

Family Adventures

Fodor's Gay Guide to the USA

Fodor's How to Pack

Great American Learning Vacations

Great American Sports & Adventure Vacations

Great American Vacations

Great American Vacations for Travelers with Disabilities

Halliday's New Orleans Food Explorer

Healthy Escapes

Kodak Guide to Shooting Great Travel Pictures

National Parks and Seashores of the East

National Parks of the West

Nights to Imagine

Rock & Roll Traveler Great Britain and Ireland

Rock & Roll Traveler USA

Sunday in San Francisco

Walt Disney World for Adults

Weekends in New York

Wendy Perrin's Secrets Every Smart Traveler Should Know

Worldwide Cruises and Ports of Call

WHEREVER YOU TRAVEL, *H*ELP IS NEVER FAR AWAY.

From planning your trip to providing travel assistance along the way, American Express® Travel Service Offices are always there to help you do more.

The South

Cramer Travel Agency (R)
901 Franklin St. S.E.
Huntsville, AL
205/539-0671

American Express Travel
Service
133 Peachtree Street
Atlanta, GA
404/523-8055

American Express Travel
Service
158 Baronne Street
New Orleans, LA
504/586-8201

Rightway Travel (R)
1425 Jacksonian Plaza
Jackson, MS
601/982-1511

American Express Travel
Service
Southpark Shopping Center
4400 Sharon Road
Charlotte, NC
704/364-3373

Long's Travel Agency, Inc. (R)

33 Office Park Road
Hilton Head Island, SC
803/842-4700

do more ® AMERICAN EXPRESS

Travel

http://www.americanexpress.com/travel
American Express Travel Service Offices
are located throughout the South.
For the office nearest you, call 1-800-AXP-3429.

Fodor's Special Series

Fodor's Best Bed & Breakfasts
America

California

The Mid-Atlantic

New England

The Pacific Northwest

The South

The Southwest

The Upper Great Lakes

Compass American Guides
Alaska

Arizona

Boston

Chicago

Colorado

Hawaii

Idaho

Hollywood

Las Vegas

Maine

Manhattan

Minnesota

Montana

New Mexico

New Orleans

Oregon

Pacific Northwest

San Francisco

Santa Fe

South Carolina

South Dakota

Southwest

Texas

Utah

Virginia

Washington

Wine Country

Wisconsin

Wyoming

Citypacks
Amsterdam

Atlanta

Berlin

Chicago

Florence

Hong Kong

London

Los Angeles

Montréal

New York City

Paris

Prague

Rome

San Francisco

Tokyo

Venice

Washington, D.C.

Exploring Guides
Australia

Boston & New England

Britain

California

Canada

Caribbean

China

Costa Rica

Egypt

Florence & Tuscany

Florida

France

Germany

Greek Islands

Hawaii

Ireland

Israel

Italy

Japan

London

Mexico

Moscow & St. Petersburg

New York City

Paris

Prague

Provence

Rome

San Francisco

Scotland

Singapore & Malaysia

South Africa

Spain

Thailand

Turkey

Venice

Flashmaps
Boston

New York

San Francisco

Washington, D.C.

Fodor's Gay Guides
Los Angeles & Southern California

New York City

Pacific Northwest

San Francisco and the Bay Area

South Florida

USA

Pocket Guides
Acapulco

Aruba

Atlanta

Barbados

Budapest

Jamaica

London

New York City

Paris

Prague

Puerto Rico

Rome

San Francisco

Washington, D.C.

Languages for Travelers (Cassette & Phrasebook)
French

German

Italian

Spanish

Mobil Travel Guides
America's Best Hotels & Restaurants

California and the West

Major Cities

Great Lakes

Mid-Atlantic

Northeast

Northwest and Great Plains

Southeast

Southwest and South Central

Rivages Guides
Bed and Breakfasts of Character and Charm in France

Hotels and Country Inns of Character and Charm in France

Hotels and Country Inns of Character and Charm in Italy

Hotels and Country Inns of Character and Charm in Paris

Hotels and Country Inns of Character and Charm in Portugal

Hotels and Country Inns of Character and Charm in Spain

Short Escapes
Britain

France

New England

Near New York City

Fodor's Sports
Golf Digest's Places to Play

Skiing USA

USA Today The Complete Four Sport Stadium Guide

NOTES